RACE AND RACISM
IN THE UNITED STATES

RACE AND RACISM IN THE UNITED STATES

An Encyclopedia of the American Mosaic

VOLUME 4: U–Documents

Charles A. Gallagher and Cameron D. Lippard,

Editors

 GREENWOOD

AN IMPRINT OF ABC-CLIO, LLC
Santa Barbara, California • Denver, Colorado • Oxford, England

Library of Congress Cataloging-in-Publication Data

Race and racism in the United States : an encyclopedia of the American mosaic / Charles A. Gallagher and Cameron D. Lippard, editors.
    pages   cm
    ISBN 978-1-4408-0345-1 (hardback) — ISBN 978-1-4408-0346-8 (ebook)   1. United States—Race relations—Encyclopedias.
2. United States—Ethnic relations—Encyclopedias.   3. Racism—United States—Encyclopedias.   I. Gallagher, Charles A.
(Charles Andrew), 1962– editor.   II. Lippard, Cameron D., editor.
    E184.A1R254   2014
    305.800973—dc23   2013024041

ISBN: 978-1-4408-0345-1
EISBN: 978-1-4408-0346-8

18 17 16 15 14   1 2 3 4 5

This book is also available on the World Wide Web as an eBook.
Visit www.abc-clio.com for details.

Greenwood
An Imprint of ABC-CLIO, LLC

ABC-CLIO, LLC
130 Cremona Drive, P.O. Box 1911
Santa Barbara, California 93116-1911

This book is printed on acid-free paper ∞
Manufactured in the United States of America

Contents

Alphabetical List of Entries

Topical List of Entries

Civil Rights

Abernathy, David
Affirmative Action
African Blood Brotherhood
Alabama Council on Human Relations (1954–1961)
Albany Civil Rights Movement
American G.I. Forum (AGIF)
American Indian Movement (AIM)
American Indian Religious Freedom Act (1978)
Anti-Lynching Campaign
Anti-Lynching League
Anti-Miscegenation Laws
Arab/Muslim American Advocacy Organizations
Atlanta Compromise, The
Bates, Daisy
Baton Rouge Bus Boycott
Bellecourt, Clyde
Berea College v. Kentucky (1908)
Bethune, Mary McLeod
Black Cabinet
Black Churches
Black Codes
Black Manifesto
Black Nationalism

Black Panther Party (BPP)
Black Power
Black Self-Defense
Black Separatism
Bolling v. Sharpe (1954)
"Bombingham"
Brown, H. Rap
Brown v. Board of Education (1954)
Carmichael, Stokely
Castro, Sal
Chicano Movement
Civil Rights Act of 1875
Civil Rights Act of 1957
Civil Rights Act of 1964
Civil Rights Act of 1968
Civil Rights Movement
Cleaver, Eldridge
Congress of Racial Equality (CORE)
Connor, "Bull"
Conyers, Jr., John
Cooper v. Aaron (1958)
Crusade for Justice (CFJ)
Cumming v. Richmond County Board of Education (1899)

Health and Science

Immigration and Migrations

Popular Culture

List of Primary Documents

U

UC Berkeley Bake Sale

In October 2011, California State Bill 185 awaited Gov. Jerry Brown's signature. This bill, similar to affirmative action, was introduced by Ed Hernandez, D-West Covina, and would allow for California universities to use factors such as race, gender, ethnicity, and national origin when considering an applicant for admission.

This State Bill stirred up a lot of controversy, especially since Californians passed a ballot measure more than 15 years ago that goes against the grain of affirmative action. In 1996, Californians had passed Proposition 209. Proposition 209 prohibited the preferential treatment of minority groups within California. When SB 185 was introduced, lawmakers claimed the bill was a way to undermine Prop. 209, which had been enshrined in California's law system.

The proposed bill stirred up so much controversy that the University of California Berkeley's College Republicans set up a bake sale to mock the new bill. This satirical bake sale, which they named the "Increase Diversity Bake Sale," charged different customers a variety of prices depending on their gender and ethnicity. They also held the bake sale the same day the Associate Students of the University of California (Berkeley's undergraduate student government) organized a phone bank in support of the new legislation.

At the bake sale, white men bought baked goods for $2, while Asian men had to pay $1.50, Latino men paid $1, black men paid 75 cents, and Native Americans paid 25 cents. Women paid 25 cents less according to their race. The college Republicans argued this difference in prices illustrated the injustice of affirmative action. Even Ward Connerly, a multiracial Republican and former member of the University

---

Ward Connerly

One of those who advocated the UC Berkeley bake sale was Ward Connerly, a former member of the University of California Board of Regents. Connerly is a black Republican who believes affirmative action creates injustice.

Connerly believes discrimination does exist in the United States, but affirmative action does not solve the problem. Instead, he sees the solution partly in the quality of education blacks receive. He wants the government to change methods in testing students, reduce the class size, and hire better qualified teachers. According to Connerly, if racism "were to disappear tomorrow, black students would still be getting poor test scores and black families would still be in crisis" (2000: 11).

Connerly also played a major part in the passing of Proposition 209, which prevents any special treatment toward minorities. During the UC Berkeley bake sale, Connerly helped with the sale of cupcakes.

California Board of Regents, who wrote and helped pass Proposition 209, showed up at the event to help with the sale.

This bake sale, a sellout of 300 cupcakes, created a heated debate. Many students deemed the college Republicans to be racist. Before the bake sale took place, student government leaders had also unanimously approved an undergraduate, student-government resolution that condemned any type of satirical discrimination, in response to the bake sale that was to take place later that week. Two vice chancellors also sent out a letter that supported the position of the student government. On October 8, 2011, Governor Brown vetoed the bill.

This is not the first time such a bake sale has taken place. In 2003, similar bake sales were carried out at universities when the nation's highest court was considering two affirmative action cases involving the University of Michigan. Campuses that held such bake sales included the University of Texas at Austin, Texas A&M University, Northwestern University, Indiana University, the University of Michigan, and UC Berkeley.

The court justices voted, with a slim majority of 5 to 4, to uphold the University of Michigan's affirmative action policy for its law school program in *Grutter v. Bollinger* (2003). However, the justices voted 6 to 3 in *Gratz v. Bollinger* (2003) that the university's points system, used in the undergraduate programs, violated the equal protection provisions of the Constitution. This system awarded 20 points to blacks, Hispanics, and Native Americans as a part of the admissions process.

ALAN VINCENT GRISBY AND RASHA ALY

See also

Affirmative Action; *Berea College v. Kentucky* (1908); College Admission, Discrimination in; Ethnic Retention and School Performance

Further Reading:

Asimov, N. "Bake Sale Leaves Bitter Taste; UC Berkeley; Racially Tinged GOP Political Stunt Draws Horde of Counterprotesters." *San Francisco Chronicle*. September 28, 2011.

Associated Press. "College Bake Sales Spark Controversy." *Telegraph Herald*. December 25, 2003.

Connerly, W. *Creating Equal: My Fight Against Race Preferences*. New York City: Encounter Books, 2000.

Spann, G. A. Proposition 209. *Duke Law Journal* 47, no. 2 (1997): 187–325.

Yan, H., and M. Martinez. "A Cupcake Sellout at 'Inherently Racist' Bake Sale by UC Berkeley Republicans." September 27, 2011. http://articles.cnn.com/2011-09-27/us/us_california -racial-bake-sale_1_bake-sale-baked-goods-cupcakes/2?_ s=PM:US (accessed December 1, 2012).

Unauthorized Immigration

Approximately 40 million foreign-born persons lived in the United States in 2011. The vast majority of those were legally present, meaning that the federal government granted them authorization to reside in the country. However, roughly 27 percent of all foreign-born noncitizens (also known as *foreign nationals*) were unauthorized, meaning that they lacked permission to be in the United States. In 2011, the unauthorized population totaled an estimated 11.1 million individuals—including approximately 1 million children under the age of 18—and composed 3.7 percent of the total U.S. population.

Unauthorized immigrants originate from every region of the world, though the vast majority are from Latin America. As of 2010, approximately 58 percent (6.5 million) of unauthorized immigrants in the United States originated from Mexico, while another 23 percent came from other countries in Latin America. Roughly 11 percent of unauthorized immigrants originated from Asia, 4 percent from Europe and Canada, and 3 percent from other countries. Nearly 60 percent entered the United States without inspection, meaning that they lacked valid entry documents and did not enter the United States through a regulated entry point. The remainder entered the United States with legal authorization—such as a temporary visa for work, study, or travel—and overstayed their visa expiration date or otherwise violated the terms of their admission.

Unauthorized immigrants are generally younger than the U.S.-born: whereas the median age of U.S.-born adults is 46.5 years, the median age of unauthorized adults is 36.2 years. This difference primarily accounts for the fact that unauthorized immigrants are more likely than the U.S.-born to be parents of young children: while nearly half of all unauthorized adults are parents of young children, only 29 percent of U.S.-born adults have young children. Nearly

9 million individuals, including 4.5 million children, live in mixed-status families—families in which some members are unauthorized immigrants and other members are either U.S.-born or authorized immigrants. Fifty-three percent of unauthorized immigrants are male.

Nearly two-thirds of the unauthorized adult population has lived in the United States for a decade or longer, with 35 percent living in the United States for more than 15 years. In 2011, 73 percent of unauthorized immigrants lived in just 10 states, with California (2.8 million), Texas (1.8 million), Florida (740,000), New York (630,000), and Illinois (550,000) containing the highest numbers of unauthorized immigrants.

The unauthorized immigrant population has grown steadily over the last three decades, from a low of 2 million in the 1980s to a high of nearly 12 million in 2007. Since 2007, the unauthorized population has steadily declined. Some of this decline is attributed to changes in the flow of unauthorized immigrants from Mexico, the largest source of unauthorized immigration to the United States; since 2007, more Mexican nationals have returned to Mexico than have migrated to the United States, resulting in net zero migration from Mexico.

Additionally, the recent recession and poor economic growth may have impacted the flow of unauthorized immigrants. The vast majority of unauthorized immigrants are economic migrants—individuals who migrate in search of job opportunities. Unauthorized immigration is thus tied to economic opportunity, exhibiting a strong correlation between the prospect of employment in the receiving country (versus a relative absence in the sending country) and the flow of unauthorized immigrants. Though research does not conclusively support the idea that unauthorized immigrants leave during a recession (since the economies of sending countries are generally considered to be worse), the weakened state of the U.S. economy may encourage fewer individuals to migrate without authorization to the United States.

Other factors suggested to influence the size of the unauthorized population include changing economic conditions in sending countries, the proliferation of immigration restrictionist legislation in the United States, and the increasing efficiency of immigration enforcement.

Estimates of the economic impact of unauthorized immigration are varied, though most studies indicate that such

Unauthorized Immigration by Another Name

Unauthorized immigrants are variously referred to as "undocumented immigrants," "undocumented or clandestine workers," "irregular or out-of-status migrants," "illegal immigrants," "illegal aliens," and "illegals," among other terms. In recent years, the Department of Homeland Security, Immigration and Customs Enforcement, practitioners of immigration law, and immigration scholars have routinely used "unauthorized immigrants" to refer to those who lack authorization to be in the United States. This term accurately reflects the active role of the federal government in the authorization or nonauthorization of immigrants. In contrast, terms such as "undocumented immigrants," "undocumented workers," "illegal immigrants," and "illegal aliens" are considered to be imprecise; the first two because some unauthorized immigrants may possess expired or counterfeit documents, the latter two because unauthorized immigration is a violation of civil—rather than criminal—law. In addition, terms that incorporate the word "illegal" have broadly been criticized for their dehumanizing impact on unauthorized immigrants.

immigration has a negligible impact on the U.S. economy. Although unauthorized immigrants increase government expenditures through their use of public services (particularly public education and emergency health care), these immigrants also contribute through taxes. The Congressional Budget Office estimates that the majority of unauthorized immigrants pay federal and state taxes as well as local sales and property taxes. Unauthorized immigrants also contribute to Social Security, although they are prohibited from receiving Social Security benefits. Additionally, unauthorized immigrants are barred from receiving benefits such as Temporary Aid for Needy Families (TANF), Supplemental Security Income (SSI), and Medicaid (excluding emergency Medicaid). At the federal level, the amount that unauthorized immigrants contribute through taxes exceeds the benefits they receive, though immigrant-heavy states such as California and Texas may be disproportionately burdened by the costs of education and health care for such immigrants.

Legal Consequences of Unauthorized Immigration

Unauthorized status is largely treated as a violation of civil immigration law, rather than criminal law. This means that unauthorized immigrants may face civil penalties (in the form of removal and restrictions or exclusion on future lawful entry) for their unauthorized presence in the United States. However, the mere fact of their unauthorized presence in the United States is not in itself a violation of criminal law, and thus it is not subject to criminal penalties. In other words, unauthorized immigrants who are apprehended may be detained and removed (deported), but they do not face criminal penalties as a result of their unauthorized status.

The greatest economic impact of unauthorized immigration is felt by low-wage and low-skill native-born workers, particularly African Americans. Unauthorized immigrants concentrate in low-wage occupations that require little formal education and licensing, such as agricultural work and food processing, domestic labor, and construction. Unauthorized immigrants may thus reduce the wages and job opportunities of low-skill native-born workers who must compete for the same jobs.

In recent years, the issue of unauthorized immigration has gained prominence in the media as policymakers implement restrictionist legislation in states such as Alabama, Arizona, and Georgia. However, most Americans do not identify unauthorized immigration as a top concern. Moreover, Americans have conflicting views on the impact of unauthorized immigration: in 2007, a news poll found that 54 percent of Americans believed that unauthorized immigrants hurt the country more than they helped, while 34 percent believed that they helped more than hurt. In general, Americans favor policies that address unauthorized immigration, but more than 60 percent also favor earned access to legalization for those with unauthorized status.

MEGHAN CONLEY

See also

287g Delegation of Immigration Authority; Anchor Baby; Anti-Immigrant Sentiment; Immigration and Customs Enforcement (ICE); National Origins Act of 1924; Operation Wetback; United States Border Patrol; U.S. Immigration Act of 1965

Further Reading:

Congressional Budget Office. *The Impact of Unauthorized Immigrants on the Budgets of State and Local Governments.* http://www.cbo.gov/publication/41645.

Hoefer, Michael, Nancy Rytina, and Bryan Baker. "Estimates of the Unauthorized Immigrant Population Living in the United States." *Department of Homeland Security Office of Immigration Statistics.* http://www.dhs.gov/xlibrary/assets/statistics/publications/ois_ill_pe_2011.pdf.

Jones-Correa, Michael. *Contested Ground: Immigration in the United States.* Washington, DC: Migration Policy Institute, 2012.

Passel, Jeffrey S., and D'Vera Cohn. *A Portrait of Unauthorized Immigrants in the United States.* Washington, DC: Pew Hispanic Center, 2009.

Suro, Roberto. *America's Views of Immigration: The Evidence from Public Opinion Surveys.* Washington, DC: Migration Policy Institute, 2009.

Underclass, The (Ghetto Poor)

The *underclass* is a term used to describe a specifically urban, very-low-income population characterized by joblessness, geographic concentration, and isolation from the middle class. Gunnar Myrdal coined the term in 1963, to describe people who were extremely economically marginalized as a result of changes in the postindustrial economy. However, the term became used frequently with the release of William Julius Wilson's *The Truly Disadvantaged* (1987). Wilson's work, along with work by Moynihan (1967) and Murray (1984) provided the basis for the widespread use of the term and its impact on U.S. policy dealing with employment, social assistance, housing and criminal justice.

Similar to the Moynihan Report, Charles Murray's *Losing Ground* (1984) argues that welfare dependency is the major source of the underclass's marginalization because it discouraged the nuclear family structure and socialized recipients into dependency and criminality. Murray outlined several metrics for classifying and evaluating the underclass. Rates of dependency, criminality, and births among unmarried women are the main indicators of the underclass in his formulation.

Wilson argued that decline of legal racial discrimination as a result of the Civil Rights Act of 1964 and other societal changes have increased the social isolation of low-income blacks from middle-class role models by allowing upwardly mobile blacks to leave the inner city. He argues that without role models and community institutions provided by these more affluent African Americans, the vicious cycle of poverty grows and pathological behaviors are intensified (1987). Unlike the behavioral focus of Moynihan et al., Wilson focuses on economic disadvantage and isolation, but does include discussion of behavioral patterns. Pathological behaviors Wilson (1987) identifies include teenage pregnancy, promiscuity, drug addiction, and lack of participation in the formal economy. Also, while Moynihan's and Murray's conception of the underclass identifies stigmatized behaviors as the cause of intergenerational poverty, Wilson identifies these behaviors as a result of poverty, rather than the cause.

The 1990s introduced a body of research on the urban "underclass." Wilson (1996) reports that Myrdal's original definition was used by other scholars until the late 1970s when the term came to express acute or persistent poverty rather than joblessness as the defining characteristic. The underclass came to also be defined as people whose poverty is a result of the violation of one or more social norms, categorizing them as members of the undeserving poor. Members of the underclass are feared to threaten mainstream values because they are assumed to reject mainstream values. The undeserving poor has also been defined as people with a low income who violate mainstream norms, are nonwhites, and are seen as individually responsible for their poverty. Wilson later (1996) repudiated the term *underclass*, abandoning it for the term *ghetto poor*, however the term *underclass*, and Wilson's argument, continued to be used extensively in academic and policy circles.

The concept of the underclass has by no means gone uncontested. For example, Jencks (1991) argues that the underclass term mistakenly gives the impression that urban problems are worsening, while Peterson (1991) notes that many of the behavioral aspects of the culture of poverty, like attachment to fancy clothes, episodic romantic attachments, drug addiction, and laziness, are also to be found among the very rich. However, despite detractors, the theory of the underclass pervaded the discourse on race and poverty throughout the 1990's and persists to some degree presently. Geographic segregation is an important consideration in understanding the development and persistence of the

---

William Julius Wilson (1935–)

William Julius Wilson is a distinguished professor of sociology at Harvard University. Wilson's most famous and influential works are *The Declining Significance of Race: Blacks and Changing American Institutions* (1978) and *The Truly Disadvantaged: The Inner City, the Underclass, and Public Policy* (1987). Wilson, disagreeing with both liberal and conservative explanations for racial disparities and the creation of the underclass, argued that global economic changes, especially from manufacturing to a service-based economy, as well as class divisions among African Americans had created a growing underclass. He later chose to use the term *ghetto poor* rather than *underclass*, as the underclass label acquired an expressly pejorative connotation. In *When Work Disappears: The World of the New Urban Poor* (1996), he discussed the detrimental impact of chronic joblessness on people in the inner city, and how joblessness deprived inner city residents of the skills necessary to participate in the formal economy. He continues his study of urban poverty among African Americans in his 2009 book *More Than Just Race: Being Black and Poor in the Inner City*.

---

underclass. Spatial isolation from jobs, the middle class, and other resources is a key component of Wilson's argument, which is bolstered by Massey and Denton's (1993) seminal work, *American Apartheid*.

The term *underclass* has undergone some transformation since the height of its popularity in the 1990s, having been tested empirically, critiqued, and extended. Although scholars are still examining the concept in reference to the urban black poor, it is now frequently being applied to other marginalized groups. The most recent trend in U.S. scholarship is the application of the term to immigrant groups in the United States. Massey and Pren (2012) is an example of such an application to newly immigrated Latinos. The effects of the recent recession have begun to broaden the scope of the underclass to include chronically unemployed formerly working-class people, especially working-class whites. Persistent joblessness and underemployment are much more widespread among nonblack, nonurban populations. Some, like Murray (1984) argue that behavioral aspects of the underclass are increasingly becoming prevalent among jobless whites and other groups.

Renee S. Alston

See also

Racialized Poverty; Welfare Queens

Further Reading:

Auletta, Ken. *The Underclass*. New York: Random House, 1982.

Gans, Herbert. *The War against the Poor: The Underclass and Antipoverty Policy*. New York: Basic Books, 1995.

Jencks, Christopher. "Deadly Neighborhoods." *The New Republic*, (1991) 13 June, pp. 23–32.

Kristof, Nicholas D. "The Decline of White Workers." *New York Times*. February 8, 2012. http://www.nytimes.com/2012/02/09/opinion/kristof-the-decline-of-white-workers.html.

Massey, D., and N. Denton. *American Apartheid: Segregation and the Making of an Underclass*. Cambridge, MA: Harvard University Press, 1993.

Massey, Douglas S., and Karen A. Pren. "Origins of the New Latino Underclass." *Race and Social Problems* (2012): 1–13.

Moynihan, Daniel Patrick, Lee Rainwater, and William L. Yancey. *The Negro Family: The Case for National Action*. Cambridge, MA: MIT Press, 1967.

Murray, Charles. *Losing Ground: American Social Policy, 1950–1980*. New York: Basic Books, 1984.

Myrdal, Gunnar. *Challenge to Affluence*. New York: Random House, 1963.

Peterson, Paul E. "The Urban Underclass and the Poverty Paradox." *Political Science Quarterly*, (1991) 106: 4, pp. 617.637

Wilson, William Julius. *When Work Disappears: The World of the New Urban Poor*. New York: Knopf, 1996.

Underground Railroad

Thousands of fugitive slaves escaped from the South and traveled north to reach freedom in Canada and the northern United States in the years before the Civil War. The network of escape routes, the people who helped the escaping slaves, and the loosely organized system that these people developed became known as the Underground Railroad. It is not certain when the "railroad" began, but as early as 1787, Quakers had organized a system for helping fugitive slaves. By the 1830s, transporting slaves to freedom had become more frequent. Although the exact origin of the name Underground Railroad is unknown, it is thought the name was first used because of the popularity of the new steam-powered railroads or because a slave owner who was unsuccessfully pursuing his runaway slave commented that the slave seemed to have disappeared on an underground road. The word *underground* may also have been used because of the secret nature of the network.

Two Underground Railroad networks existed—the Northern Underground Railroad and the Southern Underground Railroad. Each complemented the other but had different functions. The Southern railroad helped slaves escape and move north. Once the fugitives had crossed the Mason-Dixon Line and the rivers that served as boundaries between slave and free states, the Northern railroad network began its work to keep the fugitives from being captured and returned to their owners in the slave states.

Railroad terms were used in the escape network. "Stations" were the hiding places, places of safety, and stops along the freedom route and were usually spaced between 10 and 30 miles apart. The routes between stations were known as "lines." "Station masters" sheltered the slaves in the stations and provided the fugitives with food, clothing, and protection until they were transported to the next station. Hiding places included homes, barns, churches, and cellars, and well-concealed secret rooms, attics, and crawlspaces within those buildings. Slaves were also hidden in cornfields and wagons, and in one Michigan location, they were hidden in a cave. "Conductors" were primarily white abolitionists or free blacks who traveled to the South to collect the slaves and escort them north. The conductors also arranged transportation for the slaves and were responsible for getting the escapees to the next station. Fugitive slaves usually traveled at night and were hidden by the station masters during the day. Canada was referred to as "Heaven" and "Canaan," and the escaping slaves were referred to as "baggage," "bundles of wood," "loads of potatoes," "parcels," and "cargo."

The Big Dipper and North Star were used as navigation guides for the escapees, and the Big Dipper was referred to as the "drinking gourd." Coded phrases were also used to signify the arrival of slaves, to indicate that fugitive slaves were in the area, to remind escapees that dogs were unable to follow scents through water, and to alert slaves that an escape was being planned. Candles were sometimes placed in windows as codes to indicate "stations" on an escape

Fugitive slaves escape from the eastern shore of Maryland. Engraving from *The Underground Railroad* by William Still, 1872. (Library of Congress)

route because people involved in the Underground Railroad may have known only locations of stations and not the names of the station masters. Church sermons contained coded words to alert railroad participants to the arrival of runaways, and quilt designs informed slaves of routes and available shelter.

Reaching freedom was not an easy task for the fugitives. Some slaves walked to freedom. Others were transported north by boat, train, horse, wagon, and even caskets that were carried by other escapees in "funeral" processions. Black and white abolitionists denounced slavery, and many Quakers and other religious groups that mirrored these attitudes undertook important roles in the Underground Railroad to help escaping slaves on their way to freedom. The names of sympathizers and participants in the railroad network were often not known to each other or to the public. People often worked independently to assist the fugitive slaves because their activity was illegal, and they did not know whom they could trust. Many Quakers served as conductors and station masters. Levi Coffin, a Quaker and former Southerner, had

become active in assisting fugitive runaway slaves in North Carolina before he moved to Indiana. When Coffin moved to Newport, Indiana, near the Ohio border and Ohio River Valley, he continued his efforts and enlisted the assistance of local Quakers. Coffin is said to have been the "president" of the Underground Railroad because of his assistance to more than 2,000 slaves in their attempts to reach freedom.

Harriet Tubman, a Pennsylvania resident and former slave from Maryland, became a famous conductor of the Underground Railroad when she secretly returned to help numerous slaves escape into freedom. Tubman was known as the "Moses of Her People" because of her bravery and dangerous undertakings, and slave owners offered large rewards for her capture because she also was a fugitive slave and was breaking the law in slave states by helping other slaves escape.

The Underground Railroad encompassed 14 Northern states. Most escapees who fled to Canada settled in Ontario, though fugitives' traveling routes through New York and New England reached the province of Quebec. The two most important crossing points into Canada, however, were Niagara Falls and Detroit, Michigan. The Underground Railroad's lines ran thousands of miles and stretched from the Deep South, Virginia, and Kentucky through Ohio, Indiana, and Michigan. From Maryland, lines ran across Pennsylvania, New Jersey, New York, and New England. Routes also ran from Iowa and Missouri to Canada through Illinois, Wisconsin, and Michigan.

Many runaway slaves from the territory west of the Delaware River were taken to Philadelphia before following a route into Canada. One route took the fugitives from Philadelphia to Jersey City, New Jersey, by crossing the Delaware River and then going on to New York. A second route began on the Delaware River approximately 50 miles south of Philadelphia and continued through New Jersey. A third route, which also began on the Delaware River, started near Dover, Delaware, and eventually joined the lines leading from Philadelphia. A fourth line running through New Jersey was a branch of the Philadelphia line that ran through Bucks County, Pennsylvania, and on to New York.

Abolitionists, Quakers, and other progressive religious groups in Boston and other New England cities helped fugitives continue their journey north to Canada. Many of the fugitives reached the New England port cities by ship and then continued their journey by land through New Hampshire and Vermont into Quebec. Other fugitive slaves arrived in New England from Pennsylvania routes that crossed New Jersey and New York before entering New England.

Several escape routes, which began at the Ohio River and continued north through Ohio to Lake Erie or through Indiana and Michigan into Canada, were used by approximately 40,000 fugitive slaves. The Ohio River towns of Marietta and Ripley were important stations. One Ohio route branched out near Washington Court House and continued to Sandusky, Lorian, Ashtabula, or Cleveland before ending at Lake Erie. Another route from the Ohio River took runaways north through Chillicothe or Columbus. The John Rankin home in Ripley, Ohio was an important station on the shores of the Ohio River, and it was at this home where Harriet Beecher Stowe listened to a slave's story from which she later crafted *Uncle Tom's Cabin.*

Indiana's escape routes ran from the Ohio River near Evansville, Jeffersonville, and Madison to the Chicago-Detroit route or to the terminus at Lake Erie near Toledo.

Two main routes led from Evansville—one north to Michigan City close to the Michigan state line and the other through Terre Haute and Lafayette to the Wabash River. Another main line ran through Indianapolis to South Bend and on the Michigan line. The eastern line in Indiana ran north from Fountain City, formerly Newport, to Fort Wayne and beyond, where it either terminated near Toledo or continued into Michigan.

Michigan had at least seven routes, and more than 200 stations harbored slaves before they were transported to Canada and freedom. Some routes ended near Sault Ste. Marie, Port Huron, and Saginaw, but most routes ended in Detroit. Six lines ran through Cass County, one of the state's southern gateways. The county's prairies and rich fertile soil were attractive to Quaker settlers who came to the area in the 1830s, and the townships in which they lived became locations for sheltering and assisting the fugitive slaves as the slaves traveled to freedom. The Illinois line that began near St. Louis and the Quaker line that ran through Cincinnati intersected near Vandalia, a small Cass County community. Nathan Thomas, a Quaker, founding member of the Republican Party, and Kalamazoo County's first physician, was an active conductor for the railroad and helped arrange transportation for more than 1,000 fugitive slaves from his home in Schoolcraft to the next stations in the Battle Creek area.

Slaves escaping through southern Illinois received shelter in Alton and Illinoistown before being transported north. Illinoistown, which is in the modern-day East St. Louis area, presented a potential hazard to the fugitives because of the city's proximity to the slave state of Missouri, but it was a point from which the runaways were led up the Mississippi River to Alton and other stations to the north. Once in Alton, the slaves traveled by tunnel and overland to northern areas. Iowa also had an Underground Railroad network. Towns near the Missouri border such as Salem became important stops for the railroad, as did other Iowa communities such as Tabor and Lewis. Cities across central Iowa also provided shelter for the escaping slaves.

As the exodus of slaves from the South became more pronounced, slave owners began offering rewards for the return of their "property." Some Northerners who were aware of the reward offers pretended to befriend the fugitive slaves but betrayed them to receive the rewards. Slave hunters launched raids into Northern states to gather slaves for return to their owners. Sometimes the raiders were met with resistance, and other times they were able to retrieve the slaves. In 1850, Congress passed the Fugitive Slave Act, which required citizens in free states to assist in the return of slaves to their owners. The federal act made it illegal for anyone to help escaped slaves and fined or imprisoned those who refused to return runaways. The stringent act's purpose was to deter slaves from escaping and to enlist the assistance of those who were aware of the runaways in their region. The act, however, did not deter the efforts or success of the Underground Railroad network.

Before the passage of the Fugitive Slave Act (1850), many runaway slaves did not continue on to Canada but settled in both urban and rural areas where other blacks had settled in Northern states. After the act's passage, it became more dangerous to assist the fugitives and more risky for the fugitives to settle in any area where there was a possibility of being returned to an owner. As a result, many escaping slaves continued on into Canada or fled to the Caribbean or Europe. After the federal act's passage, some states also enacted laws that made it illegal for state and local officials not to assist slave catchers.

The number of slaves who traveled the Underground Railroad to freedom cannot be stated with certainty, but it is estimated that between 70,000 and 100,000 used the routes in attempts to escape to freedom from the 1830s until the 1860s.

NANCY MCCASLIN

See also

Slavery; Slavery in the Antebellum South

Further Reading:

Blockson, Charles L. *The Underground Railroad.* New York: Prentice Hall, 1987.

Bordewich, Fergus M. *Bound for Canaan: The Underground Railroad and the War for the Soul of America.* New York: Amistad Press, 2005.

Burns, Eleanor. *The Underground Railroad Sampler.* San Marcos, CA: Quilt in a Day, 2003.

Hagedorn, Ann. *Beyond the River: A True Story of the Underground Railroad.* New York: Simon & Schuster, 2003.

Mabee, Carleton. *Black Freedom: The Nonviolent Abolitionists from 1830 through the Civil War.* New York: Macmillan, 1970.

Parker, John P. *His Promised Land.* New York: Norton, 1996.

Petry, Ann. *Harriet Tubman: Conductor on the Underground Railroad.* Madison, WI: Turtleback Books/Demco Media, 1971.

United Farm Workers

Founded by Latino labor activist César Chávez in 1962, the California-based United Farm Workers (UFW) is a labor union dedicated to improving the working conditions and lives of agricultural laborers. Over the years, the union has scored victories in labor disputes involving grape, lettuce, strawberry, rose, mushroom, orange, wine, and other agricultural producers. The organization has successfully lobbied for a number of health and labor reforms, including a 2006 California regulation designed to prevent death from overexposure to heat.

The union got its start in late September 1962, when hundreds of delegates attended the National Farm Workers Association (NFWA) in Fresno, California. On September 16, 1965, Chávez and his NFWA colleagues voted to join Filipino workers in a strike against Delano, California, grape growers. The Delano grape strike persisted for five years and would attract nationwide attention. Among those who supported the farm workers were United Auto Workers president Walter Reuther and U.S. senator Robert F. Kennedy. As part of their organizing strategy, the UFW called for a boycott of grape-growing Schenley Industries during the winter of 1965–1966. Later that spring, Chávez and a group of fellow strikers undertook a pilgrimage from Delano to the state capitol in Sacramento to draw attention to the condition of farm labor. In the process of the march to Sacramento, the UFWA and Schenley Industries signed the union's first contract. New challenges soon developed as farm workers called a strike and boycott of the DiGiorgio Fruit Corporation. When DiGiorgio asked Teamsters to combat Chávez and the NFWA, organizers combined forces with the Filipino-American Agricultural Workers Organizing Committee (AWOC). At the time, AWOC was affiliated with the AFL-CIO. The two organizations soon officially became the UFW.

For the next few years, word of the grape boycott spread across the country and world. As the farm workers mission became known, supporters referred to the growing movement as "La Causa." Further endorsing nonviolence as a movement strategy, Chávez went on a 25-day fast in early 1968. Many, including Dr. Martin Luther King, Jr., sent messages of encouragement and solidarity.

Following years of an often-bitter struggle, Delano-area grape growers signed a historic agreement with the union on July 29, 1970. More challenges lay ahead along California's

A United Farm Workers Union of America (UFW) poster urges consumers to boycott lettuce and grapes as part of an effort to pressure growers into improving wages and working conditions for farm workers. (Library of Congress)

central coast, however, as many Salinas Valley lettuce and vegetable growers signed sweetheart deals with the Teamsters to avoid dealing with the UFW. A boycott was called and nearly 10,000 workers walked off the job. In December, Chávez disobeyed a court order to end the boycott. He was jailed in Salinas for two weeks. The following year, boycott and membership efforts continued. By early 1971, the official number of workers affiliated with the UFW stood at more than 70,000. The following year the organization became an independent affiliate of the AFL-CIO and took on the title of the UFW.

Battles with the Gallo winery broke out in the spring of 1973 when the winemaker dealt with the Teamsters rather than with the farm workers' union. Grape workers in Coachella and San Joaquin Valley went on strike and many were arrested for breaking specious antipicketing regulations. Violence, beatings, and two deaths characterized the bitter confrontation before Chávez eventually decided to stop the strike and replace it with a new nationwide grape, lettuce,

and Gallo wine boycott. Soon, nearly 17 million consumers joined the effort. In June 1975, California farm workers gained further support for their cause as Gov. Jerry Brown signed into law the Agricultural Labor Relations Act. This legislation guaranteed agricultural workers the right to organize, vote in monitored secret ballot elections, and bargain with growers. To publicize the new law, Chávez undertook a nearly two-month walk during July and August 1975. The journey began near the Mexican border in San Ysidro and then headed north to Salinas and then to Sacramento. Following this walk, the entourage headed back to the union's headquarters in Keene (near Bakersfield) via California's agriculturally rich Central Valley. The event proved a huge success with thousands showing up to support Chávez and the farm-worker cause.

After continued tension with the UFW, the Teamsters Union decided to leave the fields in 1977. The following year, Chávez called for an end to the grape, lettuce, and Gallo wine boycott as the union continued to make significant gains with growers. Following this effort, the UFW continued to advocate for better wages and safer working conditions as well as a host of other education and community efforts. Important organizing efforts such as the launching of a third grape boycott in 1984 as well as ongoing violence and concerns about health and safety issues characterize the UFW's history into the present era. Along the way, the union made important gains despite continued opposition from growers and politicians.

ANDREW G. WOOD

See also

Chávez, Cesar; Migrant Workers

Further Reading:

Kushner, Sam. *The Long Road to Delano*. New York: International Publishers, 1975.

United Farm Workers. http://www.ufw.org/.

United States Border Patrol

The U.S. Border Patrol, a division of U.S. Customs and Border Protection (CBP), is primarily responsible for monitoring and controlling the flow of goods and people into the United States between official ports of entry. Specifically, the

Border Patrol acts to detect, locate, and apprehend unauthorized entrants, including both migrants and smugglers, who attempt to enter the United States without inspection.

Officially established by Congress through the Labor Appropriation Act of 1924, the U.S. Border Patrol has undergone significant transformations since its creation. Originally, the Border Patrol consisted of a few hundred officers intermittently patrolling select land borders and seaports. As the United States established immigration and border control policies, the size and scope of the Border Patrol has expanded. In the 1990s, the U.S. government responded to increasing numbers of unauthorized immigrants in the interior of the country by focusing on entry prevention; programs such as Operation Hold-the-Line and Operation Gatekeeper were implemented along the U.S.-Mexico border to deter migrants through increased border enforcement.

In 2003, the Border Patrol was incorporated as a division of U.S. Customs and Border Protection (CBP), the largest law enforcement agency within the Department of Homeland Security (DHS). Since then, the size and budget of the Border Patrol has expanded considerably. The number of Border Patrol agents has doubled to approximately 21,000, and the operating budget has increased to more than $3.5 billion annually. Today, Border Patrol agents monitor nearly 6,000 miles of U.S. territory on the Mexican and Canadian borders and more than 2,000 miles of coastal waters. Most of these agents—approximately 18,500—patrol the 2,000-mile U.S.-Mexico border.

The Border Patrol relies on trained agents and specialized technology to detect and locate unauthorized entrants. Agents are trained in specialized tracking skills (known as "signcutting"), which they use to identify signs of human activity and track unauthorized entrants. Signs include footprints, depressions in the soil, clothing fibers, and disturbances in plant and wildlife. In recent decades, the Border Patrol has combined traditional signcutting methods with cutting-edge technology—including infrared night-vision scopes, remotely controlled video cameras and surveillance aircraft, and ground sensors—to detect unauthorized border crossers. The costs to purchase, maintain, and operate such technology is expensive, totaling in the hundreds of millions of dollars to taxpayers.

Simultaneously, the total number of migrant apprehensions on the border has plummeted since the 1990s and

---

Entry Without Inspection (EWI)

With few exceptions, foreign-born noncitizens who travel or immigrate to the United States must apply for a visa to obtain authorization from the U.S. federal government. Upon entering the United States through a regulated port of entry—such as an airport or border checkpoint—visitors and immigrants are required to present their visa and passport for inspection by an officer of U.S. Customs and Border Protection (CBP). During the inspection process, the CBP officer interviews foreign-born entrants regarding their purpose and travel destination and determines whether they are permitted to enter the United States and how long they may stay. Those who enter the United States without engaging in this process have entered "without inspection" and are therefore unauthorized.

---

mid-2000s, when Border Patrol agents apprehended on average more than 1 million unauthorized entrants per year. Since 2007, total apprehensions have decreased steadily, reaching approximately 340,000 apprehensions in 2011, the lowest in four decades. In contrast, the number of interior removals by Immigration and Customs Enforcement (ICE) has increased to a high of nearly 400,000 unauthorized immigrants per year. The decrease in border apprehensions in recent years is largely explained by the fact that fewer migrants are entering the United States without authorization.

The escalation in the number of border patrol agents and the use of surveillance technology, often referred to as *border militarization*, has made it more difficult for migrants to cross the U.S. border without authorization. This has had two primary unintended consequences. First, even as declining numbers of migrants cross the U.S.-Mexico border without authorization, the size of the resident unauthorized population has actually increased in the last few decades. Paradoxically, increased border enforcement has contributed to an increase in the population size and length of stay of unauthorized immigrants in the United States. This is largely explained by the fact that the personal costs and risks of unauthorized entry have increased dramatically, resulting in the need for migrants to remain in the United States for longer periods of time in order to recoup the costs of entry.

Coyote

The Spanish word *coyote*, translated in English as "coyote," refers to those who facilitate the unauthorized migration of people across the U.S.–Mexico border. On the U.S.–Mexico border, *coyotes* are also referred to colloquially as *polleros* (literally, "chicken wranglers"). In years past, migrants relied on local *coyotes* or more experienced family and friends to guide them across the border. As border surveillance and enforcement has intensified, migrants have increasingly employed professional *coyotes* to guide them across the border through remote, and often dangerous, parts of the Arizona Sonoran desert in order to avoid the Border Patrol. Some *coyotes* work independently, though increasingly such guides operate as part of a larger organized crime syndicate. The costs associated with hiring a *coyote* have increased dramatically, often figuring into the thousands of dollars. Additionally, migrants are often at risk from their *coyotes*, who have been known to abandon travelers that are sick or weak or sexually assault unaccompanied migrant women.

Previously, unauthorized migrants from Mexico—the largest source of unauthorized immigration to the United States—engaged in a pattern of circular migration, migrating to the United States to work and returning to Mexico after achieving a specific financial goal; often, migrants crossed the border multiple times in a lifetime. However, as a result of increased border enforcement, both the initial crossing and return migration has become more difficult. Today, migrants must rely on professional *coyotes* to guide them through increasingly isolated and often dangerous terrain in order to avoid the Border Patrol. The costs of hiring a *coyote* have skyrocketed, and migrants must therefore remain in the United States for longer periods of time to recoup the costs of migration; as a result, many establish themselves in communities, making it less likely that they will return willingly to Mexico.

The second unintended consequence of increased border enforcement is an escalation in the number of migrant deaths along the U.S.-Mexico border. Even as unauthorized entry has become less common, it has simultaneously become more dangerous; an average of 350 to 500 migrants die per year while trying to cross the border. As border enforcement has become more efficient, *coyotes* have developed increasingly sophisticated ways to avoid detection. Primarily, this has resulted in migrants traversing the border in remote territories. The isolation of these routes, as well as the difficult terrain, makes the journey longer and much more hazardous. Migrants often experience extreme dehydration and heat exposure, which leads to death in a desert where average daytime temperatures easily exceed 110 degrees in the summer months.

The U.S. Border Patrol has been the target of much criticism from both protectionist and humanitarian groups. Border vigilante militias such as the Minuteman Civil Defense Corps argue that the US government is ineffectual at controlling the border. Thus, such groups voluntarily monitor the border and attempt to apprehend unauthorized entrants.

In contrast, immigrant rights groups such as Amnesty International, the American Civil Liberties Union, and No More Deaths accuse the U.S. Border Patrol of perpetuating a culture of dehumanization against unauthorized entrants. Through interviews with more than 100 migrants, as well as observations of Border Patrol operations, the faith-based

Operation Hold-the-Line and Operation Gatekeeper

Operation Hold-the-Line (formerly known as Operation Blockade) was initiated in 1993 and deployed more than 400 border patrol agents along the border between El Paso and Ciudad Juarez, a highly trafficked corridor for unauthorized entrants. Operation Gatekeeper, initiated in 1994, employed a similar strategy along the San Diego corridor. These operations reflected a shift in the Border Patrol's procedures toward a strategy of "prevention through deterrence" and "targeted enforcement." It was thought that the presence of a concentrated and visible population of agents along these heavily trafficked migrant corridors would largely deter entry by unauthorized immigrants and better enable agents to apprehend those who did attempt to cross the border in these areas. However, critics find that this strategy has contributed to an increased number of migrant deaths, as unauthorized entrants subsequently began crossing the U.S.–Mexico border in increasingly remote and dangerous areas to avoid apprehension by U.S. Border Patrol agents.

humanitarian group No More Deaths has documented the Border Patrol's verbal and physical abuse of migrants as well as their failure to provide adequate food, water, and medical treatment to migrants in their custody.

Border Patrol agents are also criticized for their use of lethal force along the border. A recent example is the October 2012 death of 16-year-old José Antonio Elena Rodriguez, a Mexican national who was shot multiple times and killed by a Border Patrol agent. Rodriquez, who at the time was throwing rocks at the agent, is one of a number of Mexican youth who have been killed after throwing rocks across the border. A second prominent example involves the case of Anastasio Hernandez Rojas, a Mexican national who was hog-tied, Tasered, and beaten by Border Patrol agents until he suffered a heart attack. Recently released eyewitness video of the beating, including audio of Hernandez Rojas pleading for his life, has raised renewed criticism for the Border Patrol's use of lethal force.

MEGHAN CONLEY

See also

287g Delegation of Immigration Authority; Anchor Baby; Anti-Immigrant Sentiment; Immigration Act of 1965; Immigration and Customs Enforcement (ICE); National Origins Act of 1924; Operation Wetback; Unauthorized Immigration; Vigilantism

Further Reading:

Cornelius, Wayne. "Death at the Border: Efficacy and Unintended Consequences of US Immigration Control Policy." *Population and Development Review* 27, no. 4 (2001).

Koslowski, Rey. *The Evolution of Border Controls as a Mechanism to Prevent Illegal Immigration.* Washington, DC: Migration Policy Institute, 2011.

Massey, Douglas S., Jorge Durand, and Nolan J. Malone. *Beyond Smoke and Mirrors: Mexican Immigration in an Era of Economic Integration.* New York: Russell Sage, 2002.

No More Deaths. *Humanitarian Aid is Never a Crime.* http://www.nomoredeaths.org.

U.S. Customs and Border Protection. *Overview.* http://www.cbp.gov/xp/cgov/about/mission/.

Universal Negro Improvement Association (UNIA)

The Universal Negro Improvement Association (UNIA) was founded and led by Marcus Garvey, a Pan-African nationalist, and it became the largest black organization in American history, with millions of followers and tens of thousand of members across the United States. The UNIA enabled Garvey to become one of the most important black leaders of the 1920s. Indeed, one cannot understand the significance of the UNIA without understanding Garvey. Garvey's passion and charisma, along with his message that blacks should help themselves, unite with one another, and reject integration, caused many other black leaders, such as W.E.B. Du Bois, to revile Garvey, while Garvey's supporters admired him and worked tirelessly for the UNIA.

Marcus Garvey was born on August 17, 1887, in St. Ann's Bay, Jamaica, a British colony at that time. He worked as an apprentice printer and witnessed the terrible living and working conditions on the island as well as the nature of colonial rule and racism. In 1911, he moved to England, where he met African intellectuals and read widely about African history and culture. This motivated Garvey to work for the advancement of all people of African descent, in Africa and the Americas. When he returned to Jamaica in 1914, he founded the Universal Negro Improvement and Conservation Association and African Communities League. Garvey admired the work of Booker T. Washington, particularly Washington's focus on building up the wealth and skills of the black community, and therefore he hoped to develop a trade school along the lines of Tuskegee. However, he found limited opportunities in Jamaica.

With problems mounting in Jamaica, Garvey left for the United States in 1916, as part of an influx of Caribbean immigrants to urban areas, in particular New York City. Garvey decided to tour the United States to speak on black pride and how to restore black greatness—on this tour, he became an amazing orator who captivated all who listened. His message found a receptive audience in black communities facing economic dislocation, racism, segregation and disfranchisement at the height of Jim Crow. He organized the first U.S. branch of the UNIA in 1917, and began to publish the *Negro World*, which articulated his Black Nationalist ideas and informed readers about the activities of the UNIA. Garvey set up his UNIA headquarters in Harlem, New York City, the home to a new and emerging black disaffected and urban working class.

From his office in New York, Garvey pushed for a back-to-Africa movement, and an Africa free from European colonial rule; a cause he passionately pursued all his life. As a result,

Marcus Garvey founded the Universal Negro Improvement Association in Jamaica in 1914. It sought to develop racial pride among Africans in America and throughout the world to create a homeland in Liberia. (Library of Congress)

he became the most popular black leader in the United States, and the UNIA mushroomed in size, with scores of local chapters throughout the nation. The pageantry and titles of the UNIA also attracted followers in droves. For example, the African Legionaries and Black Cross Nurses in splendid garb marched through the streets of Harlem in a show of black pride—the like of which had never been seen before. But the UNIA was more than just image; it had a real message and agenda. The UNIA focused on the goals of economic advancement and the uniting of all people of African descent. The UNIA funded many black businesses and provided loans and insurances to developing a community. The UNIA certainly invested their money in their mission. For example, evidence survives of dozens of UNIA-funded grocery stores, restaurants, laundries, printing presses, factories, and the like. These businesses served as symbols of black progress but also provided jobs, incomes, and opportunities. The

center of UNIA activity was in Harlem, but in cities across the United States, the UNIA owned similar facilities. Thus the UNIA uplifted many African Americans, men and women, and it gave African Americans the belief in their own abilities, which led to self-help.

The UNIA was so successful in part because of Garvey, but there was more to it than that. Timing was a major contributor to the success of the UNIA. The prophet of self-help for African Americans, Booker T. Washington, had died in 1915, and the recently formed National Association for the Advancement of Colored People (NAACP) and the Urban League could not fill the void at that time. The UNIA preached self-help and provided a practical agenda for everyday black men and women to succeed. In addition, after World War I, African Americans wanted a new type of country and better conditions; millions had recently moved North in the Great Migration, and they needed a leader and an organization that represented them and their aspirations. The UNIA would provide this and much more.

Scholars have debated who joined the UNIA in the United States. From the evidence, it is clear that the membership fell into two categories. There was a cadre of leaders with experience and a history of organizing. Perhaps the most famous was Thomas Fortune, an editor, activist, and ally of Booker T. Washington. Other black leaders from the intelligentsia also became leaders, such as Henrietta Vinton Davies. In addition, many black religious leaders also joined and held prominent positions in the UNIA. Not surprisingly, perhaps, a vast number of local leaders were from the Caribbean. The rank and file of the UNIA is also fascinating. All the members (and leaders) were black; there were no white members (as in the case of the NAACP). Most were Americans, and it seems that most were determined to improve their lives. In fact, many were small businessmen, hard-working laborers, and young people who wanted to do well and had determination and belief in self-help and black power. One scholar successfully argues that many of the members or followers of the UNIA were first-generation, Southern-born African Americans living in the urban North. Men and women joined in huge numbers. It is true that the UNIA was rather masculine and somewhat sexist, though for its time, this was not that unusual. However, many women held local leadership positions and played key roles in campaigns, organizing, and recruitment. Women joined in large numbers and worked hard to make the UNIA a success.

In the past, historians have suggested that the UNIA was more dominant in the North than the South of the United States. However, a recent study of black political struggle plausibly argues that in fact the majority the UNIA was located in the South in rural areas and small towns. Over half of the local UNIA divisions were in the South, with Louisiana having the most divisions in the South. Although major cities such as New Orleans, Atlanta, and Raleigh had significant UNIA activity, the small towns of the South witnessed the most activity. The UNIA's *The Negro World* was widely circulated in the South, and local organizers became radicalized. Many of the organizers and followers of the UNIA in the South would become activists in the modern civil rights movement of the 1950s and 1960s.

Garvey was a charismatic leader, but a poor businessman. Although the UNIA provided thousands of jobs to poor blacks and set up many businesses (black owned and operated) several of the UNIA's ambitious programs failed. For example, in 1919, Garvey purchased three ships and developed the Black Star Steamship Line, selling stock to African Americans, as a symbol of black power. The line failed due to high costs and mismanagement. In the early 1920s, Garvey sought to work with the Liberian government to settle African Americans there, but this also ultimately failed. Garvey also hoped to get the League of Nations to grant the UNIA possession of the former German colony of Tangaruka. This failed too, not least because the European colonial powers could not allow an independent black nation in Africa. As a result the Pan-Africanist agenda of the UNIA did not succeed in a material sense. Through it all, however, Garvey's adherence to Black Nationalism, Pan-Africanism, and pro–working class aspirations made him a hero to his followers.

The UNIA's relationship with other black organizations at the time was very tense. Garvey and other leaders of the UNIA dismissed the work of the NAACP as too narrow and controlled by whites, and Garvey believed that integration was a fool's errand. Indeed, the UNIA did not build alliances with other black organizations and black leaders. The philosophy and political approach of the UNIA was too different to the NAACP and the Urban League, for example. W.E.B. Du Bois despised Garvey and opposed the UNIA (though late in his life, Du Bois adopted many of the tenets of Black Nationalism). A. Philip Randolph, a key black leader in Harlem, saw Garvey as a fool. Garvey and the UNIA responded in kind, and the divisions within the black leadership did not help the plight of everyday African Americans, but it does illustrate the gamut of opinion on how to solve the problems of Jim Crow, racism, and political powerlessness.

As Garvey's power and prestige increased and the number of the UNIA's adherents swelled, the U.S. government worried about Garvey's influence and the radicalism of the UNIA as it empowered a restless black urban population, along with disgruntled black intellectuals. Thus, the federal government sought to discredit Garvey and smash the UNIA. A young J. Edgar Hoover masterminded the campaign to destroy Garvey and the UNIA. Garvey was arrested on mail fraud charges, convicted, and sentenced to five years in jail in 1925. Without their magnetic leader, the UNIA declined rapidly into a shell of its former self. For example, the businesses owned by the UNIA closed, and much of its property was sold. There was no leader to take over from Garvey; he *was* the UNIA. Although President Calvin Coolidge commuted Garvey's sentence in 1927, he was deported back to Jamaica (he was never a U.S. citizen). He left a hero to many African Americans. In Jamaica, Garvey tried to continue the work of the UNIA, but the old magic was lost. In 1935, he left for Great Britain, where he died in 1940 a broken man.

In his lifetime, Garvey worked tirelessly for the equal rights of people of African descent, and he dismissed the idea of integration. He saw the struggle for equality in the United States as only part of the problem facing people of color. The UNIA made a huge difference in the lives of African Americans, particularly the poor. The UNIA empowered blacks, helped the poor with various social programs, and rejected racism and integration. The UNIA was radical, with a far-reaching and transformative agenda. In Pan-Africanism, Garvey and the UNIA hoped to unite a mass world movement to liberate Africans from European and white control. In this endeavor, the UNIA failed. However, the legacy of the UNIA and Garvey is crucial. He provided hope and inspiration to a more militant group of younger blacks. In the 1960s, he became an icon to Malcolm X, the black power movement, and the independence movements in the Caribbean and Africa.

JAMES M. BEEBY

See also
Garvey, Marcus

Further Reading:
Burkett, Randall. *Garveyism as a Religious Movement: The Institutionalization of a Black Civil Religion.* Metuchen, NJ: Scarecrow Press, 1978.
Cronon, E. David. *Black Moses: The Story of Marcus Garvey and the Universal Negro Improvement Association.* Madison: University of Wisconsin Press, 1955.
Garvey, Marcus. *Philosophy and Opinions of Marcus Garvey.* New York: Atheneum, 1969.
Hahn, Steven. *A Nation Under Our Feet: Black Political Struggles in the Rural South from Slavery to the Great Migration.* Cambridge, MA: Harvard University Press, 2003.
Stein, Judith. *The World of Marcus Garvey: Race and Class in a Modern Society.* Baton Rouge: Louisiana State University Press, 1991.

Urban Renewal

The term *urban renewal* is used to signify government-facilitated urban-planning projects during the middle of the 20th century. These projects attempted to redevelop large portions of American inner cities that had fallen into decay. When the term is used in the proper historical sense, it refers to the clearance of huge tracts of land for construction of new buildings (rather than the refurbishment of existing buildings that is common today). Urban renewal became common practice in the 1960s, but most of today's urban planners and historians consider it a failed social experiment that isolated poor minorities and resulted in the proliferation of social ills that continue to challenge cities throughout the United States.

As a result of shifting demographics in most of the older cities throughout the country between 1920 and 1950, inner cities were largely abandoned to lower-class minority populations. This shift occurred for several social and economic reasons. First, with the decrease of agricultural jobs and the increase of industrialization, African Americans were moving from rural to urban areas and migrating north. Real and perceived economic opportunity and a desire to escape Southern racist practices fueled this movement. As African Americans moved into the cities, the bulk of available and affordable housing was older housing stock located within the inner city, and much of it was beginning to decline. This housing stock fell into disrepair as a result of middle-class whites leaving the city for new, modern suburbs.

This exodus of whites, often referred to as white flight, was partly due to racist attitudes but was also fueled by the economic prosperity that followed World War II. During the 1950s family incomes rose along with the affordability of private transportation. This allowed much of the middle class to purchase an automobile, resulting in decreased demand on public transportation and for shorter travel distances. New housing sprang up as World War II veterans took advantage of government housing loans, and many whites achieved the American Dream. As their old homes emptied, African Americans moving into the city took occupancy.

Most families who wished to stay in their original neighborhoods ultimately left as African Americans took over housing in larger and larger numbers, desegregation was forced upon public facilities and schools, and declining property values threatened their financial security. Housing discrimination exacerbated the problem because African Americans who migrated to the cities were forced to live in the older portions of inner cities that were increasingly neglected by absentee white landlords who were unable to sell their property. Much of the housing stock in these areas quickly became uninhabitable according to modern health and safety standards; however, many poor minority families had little choice to live elsewhere or power over the condition if they were renting the property.

Because of the pattern of disrepair, deterioration, vacancy, and abandonment, financial institutions refused loans, stemming the flow of capital to those geographic areas (this practice is called redlining and is illegal, although housing loan studies indicate that it still exists). The needs of the poor, black, inner-city population placed additional burdens on city governments for services, particularly social services, and resulted in tax increases. This increased financial strain on the middle class helped push nearly all middle-class whites to the suburbs, where they were insulated from the poor.

Regardless of the housing conditions and slum status, many of these impoverished areas were vibrant communities. However, as city leaders watched their tax base erode, the need to draw jobs and people back into the city and to protect existing economic institutions from the spread of urban blight became apparent. Many of the slum areas were targeted for renewal because of their proximity to these institutions and the threat they posed to established white business districts and some remaining white elite residential areas.

Some scholars view these decisions as racial displacement ("black removal" rather than "urban renewal"); others view the target areas as simply being the most obvious places for necessary action because of the condition of the area and need. Additionally, much has been written on the political aspects of these decisions, yet few analysts have presented alternatives for successful renewal without negatively impacting any citizens.

To move forward with urban renewal projects, the government used eminent domain to seize and raze these areas. Urban renewal projects were undertaken in many cities, including Newark, Detroit, New Orleans, Cincinnati, and Chicago. Huge tracts of land were cleared to make way for new medical complexes, university development and expansion, new industry, and other economic hubs that would help draw money back into the city. In addition to developing the former slum land into new forms, highways needed to be built to accommodate the increase in the use of the private automobile and to provide better transportation arteries for people who continued to work and shop in the city. This was essential to maintain economic viability because many people no longer wished to use or no longer had the option of public transit because of housing location.

As a result of these urban renewal projects, whole communities were uprooted as the housing was demolished. The poor African American community carried the burden of these decisions but had little political or economic power to challenge authorities and the power elite. Nor did community members have many options once their housing stock was destroyed. These actions and their subsequent results were legalized in the form of the housing acts of 1949 and 1954. These acts provided federal funds to local municipalities to acquire large parcels of property and clear them of existing structures to prepare them for redevelopment. Because of the scale of these urban projects and the resulting displacement of whole communities, the Federal Housing Administration mandated replacement housing. Compliance with this provision for an adequate supply of housing (with rents set at levels within the economic means of the displaced) was mandatory if local governments wanted to use federal funds for these projects. Modern public housing was the solution.

Those who could afford to move into other private housing did, but a significant portion of displaced families moved into the public housing. Because of the social and political climate of the times, ghetto areas were targeted for these housing structures. This required clearing more land occupied by poor, minority populations. The result was the demolition of low-density housing, which was replaced by high-density towers of poor families. The most extreme example is the infamous Cabrini Green in Chicago, which quickly became known for gangs, drugs, and murder. At one point it housed approximately 15,000 residents in 3,500 units. Today, fewer than 5,000 people remain as the Chicago Housing Authority replaces these buildings with low-density, mixed-income units, largely because of what was learned from the urban renewal social experiment of the 1950s and 1960s. Those methods of physical and social planning led to increased segregation of poor minorities and isolation from educational, social, and economic opportunity.

Not all African American inner-city neighborhoods were demolished. However, these did not escape the negative effects of urban renewal. Those that were not completely cleared were often bisected by highway projects. The resulting noise and air pollution led to further decline of the area, and often the areas of highway construction were public lands that had previously served as parks and community areas. Examples of highway construction projects that bisected and caused decay are Interstate 10 through the North Claiborne area in New Orleans and the expressway built through the West End of Cincinnati.

DENESE M. NEU

See also

Fair Housing Act of 1968; Fair Housing Amendment of 1988; Fair Housing Audits; U.S. Department of Housing and Urban Development

Further Reading:

Davis, J. E. *Contested Ground: Collective Action and the Urban Neighborhood*. Ithaca, NY: Cornell University Press, 1991.

Hirsch, Arnold. *Making the Second Ghetto: Race and Housing in Chicago, 1940–1960*. New York: Cambridge University Press, 1983.

Jencks, Christopher. *Rethinking Social Policy: Race, Poverty, and the Underclass*. Cambridge, MA: Harvard University Press, 1992.

Massey, Douglas S., and Nancy A. Denton. *American Apartheid: Segregation and the Making of the Underclass*. Cambridge, MA: Harvard University Press, 1993.

Seligman, Amanda I. *Block by Block: Neighborhoods and Public Policy on Chicago's West Side*. Chicago: University of Chicago Press, 2005.

U.S. Commission on Civil Rights (USCCR)

The U.S. Commission on Civil Rights (USCCR) was founded in 1957 as part of the Civil Rights Act of 1957 as an independent, fact-finding arm of the federal government. Its mission consists of investigating complaints about, collecting information related to, appraising federal laws and policies with regard to, making reports on, and issuing public-service announcements about discrimination based on race, color, religion, sex, age, disability, national origin and in the administration of justice. The USCCR can hold hearings, issue advisories, and consult with both governmental officials and private organizations, but it does not have any enforcement powers. In 1983, the legislation establishing it was renewed.

The major aim of the civil rights legislation founding the USCCR was to increase the number of African Americans who were registered to vote (other provisions of the law made it a crime to interfere with a citizen's right to vote, though enforcement was weak); thus, much of its early work focused on voting rights. Other early issues included school desegregation, employment opportunities, and property rights. It held hearings on these issues and issued reports aimed at both government policymakers and the general public. In the 1970s, it began to investigate issues of concern to Asian Americans, Native Americans, and Latino/a migrant workers and issued its first Spanish-language report (on the Equal Rights Amendment). Other issues addressed throughout the 1980s and 1990s include domestic violence, housing equality, immigration, Hawaiian homelands, girls' sports, and the

---

American Civil Liberties Union (ACLU)

The American Civil Liberties Union (ACLU) was established in 1920 by a group of people concerned about violations of the Bill of Rights (the first 10 amendments to the U.S. Constitution). The civil liberties movement, which culminated in the creation of the ACLU, was a reaction to the censorship, draft, and espionage laws enacted during World War I. From its inception, the ACLU has had a reputation for being radical, mainly because it mostly has defended radicals. The cases the ACLU has championed have been in line with the organization's credo of free speech, press, and assembly. The mission of the ACLU is to work through the courts and the legislature to defend the rights and liberties of individuals as granted by the laws and the U.S. Constitution, regardless of the politics, race, or religion of the individual. To this end, the ACLU has appeared before the Supreme Court and other federal courts on numerous occasions, both as direct counsel and by filing amicus briefs. Roger Baldwin, one of the founders of the organization, served as executive director of the ACLU from 1920 to 1950.

The ACLU boasts almost half a million members and has offices in most states. The main sources of funding for this nonprofit organization are annual membership dues and contributions from private foundations, but not the government. The ACLU has, historically, defended the civil liberties of all people, even during times of national crisis. Since the events of September 11, 2001, the ACLU, under new leadership, has expanded its outreach to the Arab and Muslim American communities across the United States, and has even hired a staff member to advocate on their behalf. The ACLU has been in the forefront of the legal and public relations battles, defending the civil rights of Arab and Muslim men who have been most affected by the passage of the Patriot Act. The ACLU published a report on civil liberties after September 11 that provides a historical perspective in times of crisis.

MEHDI BOZORGMEHR AND ANNY BAKALIAN

economic status of various ethnic groups. The USCCR also issued reports on discrimination and governmental relations in particular states and localities. Some of the most recent reports have addressed police brutality, voting irregularities in the 2000 U.S. presidential election, bioterrorism, health care, the Americans with Disabilities Act, Affirmative Action, and asylum seekers.

The USCCR also advises individuals on filing civil rights complaints, particularly in cases where citizenship rights might be limited (as in the case of prison inmates, military personnel, and Native Americans living on reservations). Regional offices and state advisory committees deal with issues in specific localities. The USCCR meets monthly at a time and place announced in advance. Additionally, the USCCR maintains the Robert S. Rankin Civil Rights Library in Washington, D.C. This library is accessible to the general public and maintains a collection of the USCCR's own publications, along with books, journals, magazines, and electronic resources addressing such subjects as campus tension, disabilities, discrimination, education, the elderly, housing, racism, and women's issues.

Since the USCCR has no enforcement power, its ability to have a significant impact on the civil rights of Americans has been somewhat limited, though not nonexistent. It has played an important role in educating Americans about their civil rights and helping individuals learn how to file complaints of civil rights violations. The fact that it is required by law to contain an equal number of Republicans and Democrats has helped it serve as a nonpartisan force that brings agreement on important issues. The reports issued by the USCCR have been extremely useful for nongovernmental civil rights organizations in their struggles for legislative, judicial, and policy changes, especially because an authoritative governmental body has prepared them.

MIKAILA MARIEL LEMONIK ARTHUR

See also

Civil Rights Movement; Hate Crimes in America; Hate Groups in America

Further Reading:

Thurgood Marshall Law Library of the University of Maryland. "Historical Publications of the United States Commission on Civil Rights." http://www.law.umaryland.edu/ edocs/USCCR/ html%20files/usccrhp.asp.

U.S. Department of Housing and Urban Development (HUD)

The Department of Housing and Urban Development (HUD) is the federal agency created in 1965 with the mission of handling housing issues and community-supportive services. HUD evolved from the Federal Housing Administration (FHA), which was established in 1934. It served as a review committee for banks and other loan institutions to make loans available to low-income families as a part of President Lyndon B. Johnson's War on Poverty in 1964.

One of the essential missions of HUD since its creation has been to use all of its programs and the direct authority given by civil rights legislation to eliminate racial discrimination in housing and to promote integration of the races.

Robert C. Weaver became the first African American ever appointed to the Cabinet when President Lyndon B. Johnson asked him to head the Department of Housing and Urban Development in 1966. (Yoichi R. Okamoto/Lyndon B. Johnson Library)

HUD's responsibilities and authority derive from a series of executive orders and laws that have become progressively broader in scope. The first was President John F. Kennedy's Executive Order of 1962, which prohibited racial discrimination in housing financed by FHA- or Veterans Affairs (VA)- insured mortgages and in federally assisted public housing. The Kennedy action was, therefore, limited; the great bulk of housing was conventionally financed; that is, non-FHA or non-VA. Moreover, FHA and VA housing was affected only if it was financed after the executive order was initiated.

Two years later, the Civil Rights Act of 1964 was passed. Title VI of this law prohibited racial discrimination in housing or in any other construction receiving federal financial assistance. The law extended to housing constructed in urban renewal areas and to all public housing, no matter when it was initiated. However, most financing of housing in the country remained unaffected.

Finally, the Fair Housing Act of 1968 (Title VIII of the Civil Rights Act) prohibited racial discrimination based on race, color, religion, sex, national origin, handicap, or familial status in the sale, rental, and use of nearly all housing (about 80 percent), as well as in mortgage lending, sales, and advertising practices. The act provided the secretary of HUD with investigation and enforcement responsibility for curbing discriminatory practices. The Housing and Community Development Act of 1974 added more responsibility for reducing the isolation of income groups and promoting diversity within neighborhoods. In this respect, HUD played a leading role in administering the Fair Housing Act to eliminate racial discrimination in housing.

HUD's efforts, however, encountered three limitations. First, HUD's power to control various forms of housing discrimination rested on its authority to investigate complaints from persons who claimed they had been discriminated against on racial grounds. It could not initiate a court action itself. Many cases that did not lack merit remained unresolved and were frequently transferred to the U.S. Commission on Civil Rights (USCCR). This recognition led to 1988 amendments that greatly increased the department's enforcement role by allowing it to investigate, conciliate, and prosecute complaints.

Second, HUD was far from an effectual organization. For example, according to the USCCR, which studied nearly 2,000 complaints received by HUD during 1972 and 1973,

HUD had not effectively pursued many of the complaints it had received. More than 20 percent of these complaints reached the conciliation stage, and 80 percent were dropped without any relief to the complainants. Furthermore, many of the unpursued complaints were simply neglected. About 25 years later, the 2000 HUD fact sheet reported that HUD handled over 12,000 inquires and about 6,300 complaints (53 percent) were filed in 1999. Of those, 39 percent were settled, and in 5 percent of the cases, findings of discrimination were issued.

Third, it has been noted that HUD's efforts have had minimal impact on preventing or eliminating housing discrimination not only because of legal limitations in its enforcement power and administration, but also because of de facto racial discrimination, which is subtle, hard to discover, and harder to monitor. For example, suburban zoning commissions, to increase tax revenues, often zone residential land in such a way that all but the most expensive homes are barred. This zoning can effectively restrict most blacks.

In the purchase and sale of new and existing homes, real estate agents and mortgage lending institutions also practice subtle forms of discrimination by dealing personally with both buyers and sellers. Redlining around certain run-down city neighborhoods is another form of racial discrimination practiced by lenders. Even if its motive seems economic, the effect is to make it hard or impossible for even reliable individual residents of the redlined communities to get a loan to sell or improve their houses. For these and other reasons, the enforcement of antidiscrimination laws by HUD in housing is much more challenging than in public transportation, education, and jobs.

SOOKHEE OH

See also
American Apartheid; Predatory Lending; Urban Renewal

Further Reading:
HUD. *Fair Housing Laws and Presidential Executive Orders.* http://www.hud.gov/ offices/fheo/FHLaws/index.cfm.
Mayer, Neil. "HUD's First 30 years: Big Steps Down a Longer Road." *Cityscape: A Journal of Policy Development and Research* 1, no. 3 (1995): 1–29.
McFarland, Carter. *Federal Government and Urban Problems: HUD: Successes, Failures, and the Fate of Our Cities.* Denver, CO: Westview Press, 1978.

U.S. Immigration Acts

Intended or not, the Immigration and Naturalization Act of 1965 brought a momentous change in the country-of-origin composition of immigrants to the United States. In that sense, the act truly represents a historical shift in U.S. immigration policies. To understand its significance, the history of U.S. immigration laws prior to the passage of the act must be reviewed.

Immigration before 1924

With the opening of the western frontier, the U.S. economy demanded a large influx of workers. This pull factor in America that began in the 17th century and remained until the Civil War brought a huge surge in European immigration. Most of these immigrants came from the British Isles and other Western European countries and were Protestants. These white Protestant immigrants and their descendants emerged as the dominant group in the United States. Their dominance generated the image of America as a white, Protestant society.

As expected, there was a lull in immigration during the Civil War. Immediately afterward, though, the industrialization of the U.S. economy again required large numbers of workers. Once again, America obtained the needed labor force from immigrants. But the immigrants of this period came mostly from Eastern and Southern European countries. A great majority of these new immigrants were not only illiterate but also brought religious traditions—Catholicism, Judaism, and Eastern Orthodoxy—different from those of the dominant group. They suffered prejudice, discrimination, and even physical violence by the dominant white Protestant group. For a long time, these immigrants and their children were treated as second-class citizens at best. World War I eventually halted immigration from Eastern and Southern European countries. Then, as blacks began migrating to the North in significant numbers, these white immigrants and their descendants were gradually assimilated into mainstream America.

Several groups of non-Europeans began arriving in the United States in the middle of the 19th century. For example, as the United States acquired Texas and what would become California, New Mexico, and other western states from Mexico through an annexation or war between 1845 and 1848, a large number of Mexicans became members of U.S. society,

but they were treated as immigrants. In the early part of the 20th century, many Mexican migrant workers moved to the United States as well. As a whole, though, Mexican Americans were relatively small in number and concentrated in the former Mexican territory.

Beginning in the mid-19th century, a limited number of Chinese immigrants arrived in Hawaii and California. When the Chinese Exclusion Act of 1882 prohibited the Chinese from immigrating to the United States, the immigration of the Japanese to Hawaii started. A small number of Korean immigrants also arrived to the United States between 1903 and 1905. Then, Japanese labor migration was stopped by the Gentlemen's Agreement in 1908 and Filipino workers immigrated in substantial numbers. But most of these Asian immigrants and their descendants, numbering about a half million, were confined to the Hawaiian Island and the West Coast. As expected, these non-European immigrants were too small in number to dent the image of the United States as the land of white men.

This short review of American immigration history bespeaks the racial stratification in the United States that existed in the 19th century and in the early part of the 20th century. The native-born whites, the descendants of Western European immigrants, enjoyed a highly respected racial position and were regarded as the dominant group. Although the immigrants from Eastern or Southern European countries and their descendants were eventually accepted as white Americans, they were not socially well respected. Nonwhite and non-European immigrants were in the worst situation, at the bottom. They were brought to meet the need for cheap labor, but the United States did not want to accept them as a part of America. Even their U.S.-born descendants were not allowed U.S. citizenship for a long period of time.

National Origins Act of 1924

The U.S. government began a sweeping regulation of the immigration flow in the early part of the 20th century. The immigration law that faithfully reflected this regulation was passed in 1924. The 1924 National Origins Act spelled out the national origins of immigrants the United States would like to accept. As reflected in its name, it stipulated that the number of immigrations allowed from European countries should be based on the race/ethnic composition of the U.S. population. This law heavily favored immigration from the British Isles and other Western European countries, as Western European Americans maintained a numeric dominance among the U.S. population.

The 1924 immigration law did allow for immigration from Eastern and Southern European countries. But their number was limited because of a small proportion of the native-born population of Eastern and Southern European ancestry. The number of immigrants from these parts of Europe was further reduced when the calculation of the ethnic composition of the population was made on the basis of the 1880 census, instead of the 1920 census, as originally conceived. The 1924 immigration law virtually prohibited immigration from non-European countries, with the exception of Mexicans. It also had a special provision that completely banned immigration from Asian countries. With the enforcement of the 1924 National Origins Act, no Asian country, with the exception of the Philippines, a U.S. colony at that time, was able to send immigrants.

Immigration Reform in 1965

The 1924 immigration law was enforced until the end of World War II in 1945. Afterward, the United States was forced to critically review the immigration laws for several reasons. First, the experience of World War II made Americans more tolerant of racial and religious differences. Second, the civil rights movement in the 1950s and 1960s sensitized the issue of racial equality. Viewed with this perspective, U.S. immigration laws clearly violated the principle of racial equality. Third, in the early 1960s, the heart of the Cold War period, the United States had to abolish its racist immigration policy for the diplomatic purpose of gaining more support from Third World countries at the United Nations. Fourth, the escalation of Cold War tensions rendered the racist U.S. immigration policy problematic. Along with the escalation of the Cold War, U.S. military involvement in various parts of the world greatly expanded the numbers of refugees. Fifth, the growing globalization of mass media spread the American way of life throughout the world and increased the number of people in the other parts of the world eager to move to the United States. Sixth, there was a growing need for foreign professional workers, especially foreign medial professionals, in the 1960s, which could not have been met by the native workforce alone.

Even though a couple of small-scale changes had already been made to the 1924 National Origins Act, the McCarran-Walter Act of 1952 was the first attempt to address to these issues. Nevertheless, it was a reluctant transitional response at best. This law reaffirmed the national origins system of the 1924 law but eased some restrictions, such as the ban on non-European immigrants and their descendants acquiring U.S. citizenship. It also legally accepted some non-European immigrants and refugees. Since this law had maintained the main tenet of the 1924 National Origins Act, however, U.S. immigration policies remained racially restrictive until 1965.

President John F. Kennedy sent his immigration reform law to Congress in July 1963; it was intended to eliminate the racially biased national-origins system. This bill called for an abolition of the national-origins system over a five-year period but retained the nonquota system for the Western Hemisphere. It also specified that the total number of immigrants outside the Western Hemisphere be only 165,000 annually, with no one country permitted to have more than 10 percent of the total. Visas were expected to be granted on the basis of preference categories in which one-half of immigrant visas would be granted to persons with special skills, training, or education advantageous to the U.S. economy and the rest to close relatives of U.S. citizens.

The Johnson administration also stressed admitting persons with skills, education, and desirable occupations and wanted to grant half of the visas to such people. Preferences to those with close family ties in the United States came second. Congressman Edward Feighan won his battle with the Johnson administration and reversed these preferences, though. Congressman Feighan's preferences heavily favored immigration based on family reunion. As a result, the final proposal contained only two preference categories—the Third and Sixth Preferences—and allowed 20 percent maximum of total immigrant visas to be granted for those with professions, skills, occupations, and special talents needed in the United States.

The act phased out the national-origin quotas over a three-year period. Effective July 1, 1968, the act provided 170,000 visas for persons from the Eastern Hemisphere and 120,000 from the Western Hemisphere per year. No one country in the Eastern Hemisphere was to have more than 20,000 visas. However, immediate family members, such as spouses, minor children (under 21), and parents of

American citizens, and a few others such as ministers were exempt from the numerical limits. In 1978, the U.S. Congress passed a law providing for a worldwide immigration cap of 290,000 without differentiating Eastern and Western Hemispheres.

Post-1965 Immigrants from Non-European Countries

After the Second World War, the United States experienced rapid suburbanization and high rates of interethnic marriages among descendants of various white immigrants. Eventually, various white ethnic groups merged into one single group: white Americans, or European Americans. As the U.S. Congress amended immigration laws to abolish discrimination based on national origin and to open the door for immigration to non-European countries, many legislators nonetheless preferred to have more European immigrants. As a way to facilitate European immigration, they supported the legal device that stressed family reunion. Legislators thought that heavy emphasis on family reunion would definitely favor immigration from European countries, because a great majority of Americans were descendants of past European immigrants.

However, contrary to policymakers' expectations, emphasis on family reunification has instead facilitated immigration in large numbers from Asian, Latin American, and Caribbean countries. Right after the passage of the act, Greece, Italy, Portugal, and some other Southern European countries sent more people than before to the United States, while fewer immigrants came from Northern and Western European countries. By the mid-1970s, however, immigration from Southern European countries, except Portugal, also decreased. While European immigration declined, immigration from Asian countries, Mexico, the Caribbean Basin, and Latin American countries increased. These non-European Third World countries accounted for three quarters of the 4 million immigrants of the 1970s. Since then, the immigration flow in the United States has consisted dominantly of immigrants from two areas of the world: Mexico and other Latin American countries, and Asian countries.

To explain the dominance of non-European immigrants in the post-1965 era, the following factors need to be considered. First, immediately after the full enforcement of the 1965 Immigration Act, many Asian and Middle Eastern professionals, especially medical professionals, immigrated as beneficiaries of occupational immigration preferences. But Western European professionals were not motivated to come here because they were paid well in their native countries. Soon, these occupational immigrants from Asian and Middle Eastern countries became naturalized citizens and brought their parents and married brothers and sisters. Since there were few Latino and Asian naturalized citizens in 1965, policymakers did not realize the "multiplier effects" of family-based immigration.

Second, the U.S. military and political involvement in Asian, Latin American, and Caribbean countries has brought in huge numbers of refugees and women who are married to U.S. soldiers. After the fall of South Vietnam, more than 1 million Southeast Asian refugees have come to the United States. Large numbers of refugees have also originated from Cuba, El Salvador, Ecuador, Haiti, and even China, and the presence of the U.S. forces in the Philippines, South Korea, and Vietnam has brought many Asians married to U.S. service men and women. These refugees and U.S. soldiers' spouses have brought many more married brothers and sisters and their own family members, using family-union preferences that grant eligibility for naturalization after only three years. Many Jews from the former Soviet Union and many people from other Eastern European countries have entered the Unites States as refugees since the early 1990s, but no significant number of refugees has originated from the politically stable northwestern European countries.

Third, the 1965 Immigration Act has gone through some revisions, and two revisions have affected the dominance of non-European immigrants as significantly as the original law did. The 1986 Immigration Reform and Control Act provided for an amnesty program for illegal residents. As a result, about 3 million illegal residents became permanent residents at the end of the 1980s and the early 1990s. Two-thirds were Mexicans, and the vast majority originated from non-European countries. They have brought their immediate family members and many of them have invited their brothers and sisters and parents through naturalization.

The Immigration Act of 1990 further revised the 1965 Immigration Act, which has had a strong effect on the increase in the number of Asian professional immigrants as well as in the total number of annual immigrants. It increased the total number of immigrants per year by about 40 percent, to 700,000 through 1994 and thereafter to 675,000. It also increased employment-based visas (heavily professionals) by three times, to 140,000, to meet the shortage of professionals, especially in the information technology (IT) field. So many Asian professionals, especially those in the IT industry, have come as beneficiaries of the occupational immigration since the early 1990s. Many of these professional Asian immigrants have become naturalized citizens and brought their family members. Computer specialists and other professionals from India, China, and the Philippines are strongly motivated to immigrate to the United States because of a big gap in their earnings potential, but professionals from northwestern European countries have little motivation because they do well in their own countries.

Effects of the 1965 Immigration Act

There were several intended and unintended effects of the act. First, the overall number of immigration increased dramatically. In fact, the United States would have experienced a population decrease without the increased immigration. According to U.S. censuses, the major population growth in the last several decades was coming from either immigration itself or children of immigrants. In that sense, without substantial increases in immigration, the U.S. economy could not have maintained its robustness. Second, the racial/ethnic composition of the U.S. population has altered drastically due to a large influx of non-European immigration. In 1970, Hispanics (4.5 percent) and Asian Americans (.07 percent) composed only tiny fractions of the population. The 2000 census reports a huge increase in both minority groups, with Hispanics accounting for 13 percent of the U.S. population and Asian Americans 3.5 percent. The proportion of white Americans decreased from 87 percent in 1970 to 70 percent in 2000, and it will continue to decline to the extent that white Americans will turn into a numerical minority. Most experts predict that whites will account for a little more than a half of the U.S. population by the mid-21st century. The vast influx of non-European immigrants since the mid-1960s has changed the United States from a black-white, biracial society to a multiracial society. Third, a large proportion of the post-1965 immigrants from non-European countries, particularly Asian countries, brought human capital in the form of high

education and professional skills, as well as vast amounts of money to the United States. Although these middle- and upper-middle-class immigrants struggle to adjust to life in the United States, a great majority of their children are likely to receive a college education and will work as professionals. They will be highly visible and active in the mainstream American society. This is seen today, and, in the future, their visibility will only increase. One consequence of this is the high out-marriage among children of immigrants. It will only accelerate the race/ethnic multiplicity of the U.S. population.

By contrast, the 1990 Immigration Act has brought a heavy influx of Latino and Caribbean immigrants from lower socioeconomic groups, which is very different than the post-1965 immigrants. Compared with Asian immigrants, immigrants from Mexico, other Latin countries, and the Caribbean Islands include more political refugees, many low-skilled workers, and many undocumented workers. Researchers have indicated that because many of their families are poor and have settled in minority neighborhoods, the children of Caribbean black and many Latino immigrants generally have poor performance in school, and many have failed to complete high school. Given racial discrimination and a lack of blue-collar jobs owing to deindustrialization, these children have bleak prospects for jobs without a high school diploma. Researchers cautiously predict that they may fill the low layers of the racial hierarchy in the United States in the future.

Fourth, the influx of Third World immigrants in the post-1965 era has contributed to cultural and religious diversity. Because of transnational ties, the children of post-1965 immigrants have advantages over European immigrants from the early 20th century and before in preserving their ethnic cultural traditions and language. The children of Latino immigrants have a huge advantage in retaining their mother tongue because many Latinos speak the same common language. According to one analysis of data from the 1989 Current Population Survey that provides monthly labor force data, the majority of second-generation Latinos aged 24 to 44 are perfectly bilingual (Lopez 1996: 200). The mass migration of Third World immigrants has also contributed to religious pluralism in the United States. The influx of immigrants from Asia and the Middle East has brought several non-Judeo-Christian religions—Islam, Buddhism,

Hinduism, and Sikhism—into the mix of American culture. Also, the mass migration of Catholics from Latin America, the Caribbean Islands, and Asia has contributed to the diversification of American Catholics as well as the substantial increase in the Catholic population.

SHIN KIM AND KWANG CHUNG KIM

See also

287g Delegation of Immigration Authority; Anchor Baby; Anti-Immigrant Sentiment; Immigration and Customs Enforcement (ICE); National Origins Act of 1924; Operation Wetback; Unauthorized Immigration; United States Border Patrol

Further Reading:

Bryce-Laporte, Roy S. *Sourcebook on the New Immigration*. New Brunswick, NJ: Transaction Books, 1980.

Hing, Bill Ong. *Making and Remaking Asian America through Immigration Policy, 1850–1990*. Stanford, CA: Stanford University Press, 1993.

Keely, Charles B. *The Immigration Act of 1965: A Study of the Relationship of Social Science Theory to Group Interest and Legislation*. New York: Keely Publishers, 1978.

King, Desmond S. *Making Americans: Immigration, Race, and the Origins of the Diverse Democracy*. Cambridge, MA: Harvard University Press, 2000.

Min, Pyong Gap, ed. *Mass Migration to the United States: Classical and Contemporary Periods*. Walnut Creek, CA: AltaMira, 2002.

Reimers, David M. *Still the Golden Door: The Third World Comes to America*. New York: Columbia University Press, 1986.

U.S. v. Cruikshank (1875)

U.S. v. Cruikshank (92 U.S. 542) was a U.S. Supreme Court case involving a conspiracy to deny the voting rights of a large group of black men in Louisiana. The Supreme Court, in its ruling, set forth the principle that although the federal government was supreme over state governments, it could not "grant nor secure rights to citizens" not expressed nor implied under its protection, and that "[s]overeignty, for the protection of the rights of life and personal liberty within the respective States, rests alone with the states." The ruling became a cornerstone in the abrogation of any federal responsibility in ensuring that state governments respect the civil rights of African Americans. In deciding *Cruikshank*, the Court opted for a narrow interpretation of the Fourteenth Amendment to the Constitution and refused to expand federal jurisdiction, even though the outcome clearly denied justice.

The case began with an incident on Easter Sunday, April 13, 1873, during Reconstruction, when a mob of white Democrats attacked and killed about 280 black Republicans in Colfax, Louisiana, during a contested local election. The blacks had sought protection inside the courthouse, which was guarded by a small contingent of so-called Negro Militia. The white mob also purported to be a militia, but it acted under its own authority, and contained many members of the White League and the Ku Klux Klan. After the attack, federal officials arrested and tried three white men for leading the mob. The three were convicted under the federal Enforcement Act of 1870, which made it a crime to interfere with any citizen's constitutional rights, in this case the right to vote. The defendants then appealed their convictions. Eventually the case worked its way to the U.S. Supreme Court.

The Supreme Court at the time was anxious to reassert its authority, particularly over matters pertaining to the South, where the legislative branch of government had exercised almost unlimited authority since the end of the Civil War. The Court's ruling in the case was unanimously in favor of the accused. Because the original indictment against the three white men did not allege that their actions were based upon race, their interference with the victims' right to vote was not a federal crime. The Court ruled that the Bill of Rights applied only to the relationship between citizens and the federal government, not the relationship between citizens and their state government. The First Amendment right to assembly "was not intended to limit the powers of the State governments in respect to their own citizens" and that the Second Amendment "has no other effect than to restrict the powers of the national government."

The ruling set forth that the Due Process and Equal Protection clauses of the Fourteenth Amendment protected citizens only from government action, not from the actions of other citizens. Thus, the federal government had no authority to protect blacks, or in theory, any citizen who attempted to vote, from mobs. Such protections would have to come from the state governments. With Southern state governments increasingly in the hands of Redeemers—white Democrats who firmly believed in white superiority and the exclusion of blacks from all aspects of the political process—such protection would not be forthcoming.

The *Cruikshank* ruling seriously hampered federal efforts at Reconstruction. The ruling sent a message to blacks and whites across the South that the federal government would do nothing to ensure the safety of blacks attempting to vote. Instead, ensuring the safety of voters was a state responsibility, and the states ignored that responsibility. More than any other court ruling, *U.S. v. Cruikshank* nullified the Fifteenth Amendment to the Constitution, and eliminated blacks from voting booths across the South. With Southern state governments under the control of white Democrats who were committed to white supremacy, and the federal government abdicating any responsibility to ensure the rights of black men to vote, the adoption of Jim Crow legislation was all but inevitable. Not until the passing of the Civil Rights Acts of 1957 and 1964 would the federal government again take a direct role in ensuring that blacks were able to exercise their right to vote.

Barry M. Stentiford

See also:

Voting and Race

Further Reading:

Goldman, Robert M. *Reconstruction and Black Suffrage: Losing the Vote in Reese and Cruikshank*. Lawrence: University Press of Kansas, 2001.

Kahn, Ronald, and Ken I. Kersch. *The Supreme Court and American Political Development*. Lawrence: University Press of Kansas, 2006.

Kersch, Ken I. *Constructing Civil Liberties: Discontinuities in the Development of American Constitutional Law*. New York: Cambridge University Press, 2004.

U.S. v. Reese (1876)

In *U.S. v. Reese* (92 U.S. 214), the U.S. Supreme Court ruled, with two dissentions, that the Fifteenth Amendment the Constitution did not guarantee the right of citizens to vote, but instead only prevented states and the federal government from using race, color, or previous condition of servitude specifically as a reason for denying the vote. The case was the first test of the meaning of the Fifteenth Amendment, and in its ruling, the Court interpreted the amendment in the narrowest terms possible.

The case began when two inspectors of a municipal election in Kentucky refused to register the vote of a black man, William Garner, in a local election. The election officials were indicted in federal court under Sections 2 and 3 of the Enforcement Act of 1870. Section 2 required that administrative preliminaries to elections be conducted without regard to race, color, or previous condition of servitude, while Section 3 forbade wrongful refusal to register votes where a prerequisite step "required as aforesaid" had been omitted. The ruling held that Section 3 was unenforceable because it did not specifically use the terms "race," "color," or "previous condition of servitude." The Fifteenth Amendment stated that the right to vote would "not be denied or abridged by the United States or any State," but made no mention about protecting that right from individuals who denied others the right to vote. The Court ruled that the Enforcement Act was still valid at the federal level, but had no authority as far as state or local elections.

The ruling held that all the Fifteenth Amendment did was prevent exclusion from voting specifically on racial grounds. The result of the decision was that states were free to develop literacy tests, grandfather clauses, poll taxes, and other means to disenfranchise blacks as long as they did not specifically list race as a reason for denying the vote. The *Reese* decision, along with *U.S. v. Cruikshank*, effectively ended any remaining chance that Reconstruction would result in a biracial society, or at least one where blacks would be able to participate in the political process. Following *Reese*, Mississippi led the South in developing a host of requirements for voting, which while they did not specifically mention skin color, had the intended result of disenfranchising most blacks and very few whites.

Barry M. Stentiford

See also

Racial Gerrymandering; Voter ID Requirements; Voting and Race

Further Reading:

Goldman, Robert M. *Reconstruction and Black Suffrage: Losing the Vote in Reese and Cruikshank*. Lawrence: University Press of Kansas, 2001.

Kahn, Ronald, and Ken I. Kersch. *The Supreme Court and American Political Development*. Lawrence: University Press of Kansas, 2006.

Kersch, Ken I. *Constructing Civil Liberties: Discontinuities in the Development of American Constitutional Law*. New York: Cambridge University Press, 2004.

Excerpt from *U.S. v. Reese* (1875)

The Fifteenth Amendment does not confer the right of suffrage upon any one. It prevents the States, or the United States, however, from giving preference, in this particular, to one citizen of the United States over another on account of race, color, or previous condition of servitude. Before its adoption, this could be done. It was as much within the power of a State to exclude citizens of the United States from voting on account of race, &c., as it was on account of age, property, or education. Now it is not. If citizens of one race having certain qualifications are permitted by law to vote, those of another having the same qualifications must be. Previous to this amendment, there was no constitutional guaranty against this discrimination: now there is. It follows that the amendment has invested the citizens of the United States with a new constitutional right which is within the protecting power of Congress. That right is exemption from discrimination in the exercise of the elective franchise on account of race, color, or previous condition of servitude. This, under the express provisions of the second section of the amendment, Congress may enforce by "appropriate legislation."

It remains now to consider whether a statute, so general as this in its provisions, can be made available for the punishment of those who may be guilty of unlawful discrimination against citizens of the United States, while exercising the elective franchise, on account of their race, &c.

It would certainly be dangerous if the legislature could set a net large enough to catch all possible offenders, and leave it to the courts to step inside and say who could be rightfully detained, and who should be set at large. This would, to some extent, substitute the judicial for the legislative department of the government. The courts enforce the legislative will when ascertained, if within the constitutional grant of power. Within its legitimate sphere, Congress is supreme, and beyond the control of the courts; but if it steps outside of its constitutional limitations, and attempts that which is beyond its reach, the courts are authorized to, and when called upon in due course of legal proceedings, must, annul its encroachments upon the reserved power of the States and the people.

To limit this statute in the manner now asked for would be be make a new law, not to enforce an old one. This is no part of our duty.

We must, therefore, decide that Congress has not as yet provided by "appropriate legislation" for the punishment of the offence charged in the indictment; and that the Circuit Court properly sustained the demurrers, and gave judgment for the defendants....

MR. JUSTICE CLIFFORD and MR. JUSTICE HUNT dissenting.

MR. JUSTICE CLIFFORD [excerpt]:

I concur that the indictment is bad, but for reasons widely different from those assigned by the court.

States, as well as the United States, are prohibited by the Fifteenth Amendment of the Constitution from denying or abridging the right of citizens of the United States to vote on account of race, color, or previous condition of servitude; and power is vested in Congress, by the second article of that amendment, to enforce that prohibition "by appropriate legislation."

Since the adoption of that amendment, Congress has legislated upon the subject; and, by the first section of the Enforcement Act, it is provided that citizens of the United States, without distinction of race, color, or previous condition of servitude, shall, if otherwise qualified to vote in state, territorial, or municipal elections, be entitled and allowed to vote at all such elections, any constitution, law, custom, usage, or regulation of any State or Territory, or by or under its authority, to the contrary notwithstanding.

Beyond doubt, that section forbids all discrimination between white citizens and citizens of color in respect to their right to vote; but the section does not provide that the person or officer making such discrimination shall be guilty of any offence, nor does it prescribe that the person or officer guilty of making such discrimination shall be subject to any fine, penalty, or punishment whatever.

V

Valdez, Luis (b. 1940)

Luis Valdez is considered to be the father of Chicano theater, the instigator of the contemporary Chicano theatrical movement, and its most outstanding playwright. Valdez has distinguished himself as an actor, director, playwright, and filmmaker; however, it was in his role as the founding director of El Teatro Campesino, a theater of farm workers in California, that his efforts inspired young Chicano activists across the country to use theater as a means of organizing students, communities, and labor unions.

Valdez was born on June 26, 1940, into a family of migrant farm workers in Delano, California. The second of 10 children, he began to work the fields at the age of six and to follow the crops. Although Valdez's education was constantly interrupted, he nevertheless finished high school and went on to San Jose State College, where he majored in English and pursued his interest in theater. While there, he won a playwriting contest with his one-act play *The Theft* (1961), and in 1963 the Drama Department produced his play *The Shrunken Head of Pancho Villa*. After graduating from college in 1964, Valdez joined the San Francisco Mime Troupe and learned the techniques of agitprop (agitation and propaganda) theater and Italian *commedia dell'arte* ("comedy of art"), both of which influenced Valdez's development of the basic format of Chicano theater: the one-act presentational *acto* or "act." In 1965 Valdez enlisted in César Chávez's mission to organize farm workers in Delano into a union. It was there that Valdez brought together farm workers and students into El Teatro Campesino to dramatize the plight of the farm workers. The publicity and success gained by the troupe led to the spontaneous appearance of a national Chicano theater movement.

In 1967, Valdez and El Teatro Campesino left the unionizing effort to expand their theater beyond agitprop and farm worker concerns. From then on Valdez and the theater have explored most of the theatrical genres that have been important to Mexicans in the United States, including religious pageants; vaudeville with the down-and-out *pelado*, or underdog figure; and dramatized *corridos*, or ballads. The new type of socially engaged theater that El Teatro Campesino pioneered led to the creation of a full-blown theatrical movement in fields and barrios across the country. For more than three decades, El Teatro Campesino and Valdez have dramatized the political and cultural concerns of Latinos, initially among workers and their supporters, but later among students in universities and among the general public through the legitimate stage, television, and film media.

During the late 1960s and the 1970s, El Teatro Campesino produced many of Valdez's plays, including *Los Vendidos* (1967, *The Sell-Outs*), *The Shrunken Head of Pancho Villa* (1968), *Bernabé* (1970), *Dark Root of a Scream* (1971), *La Gran Carpa de la Familia Rascuachi* (1974), and *El Fin del*

Teatro Campesino founder Luis Valdez stands in solidarity with the United Farm Workers Union, 1966. (Gerald French/Corbis)

Mundo (1976). In 1978, Valdez broke into mainstream theater in Los Angeles with the Mark Taper Forum's production of his *Zoot Suit* and in 1979 with the Broadway production of the same play. In 1986, he had a successful run of his play *I Don't Have to Show You No Stinking Badges* at the Los Angeles Theater Center. In *Bernabé*, one of Valdez's most poetic plays, a young village idiot is transformed into a natural man by his marriage to La Tierra ("The Earth") and his subsequent death. Employing Aztec mythology and symbols in a tale about contemporary barrio characters, the play explores the pre-Colombian heritage of Chicano society. The Maya theme of death-is-life and life-is-death was developed here and continued to appear in Valdez's later works. The writing of *Bernabé* marked the beginning of Valdez's search for the meaning of Aztec and Maya legends, history, and philosophy, but also revealed the influence of Spanish playwright Federico García Lorca, who also strove

to elevate the country folk to heroic and mythic stature. Valdez's play *Mummified Deer* (2004) is perhaps his most psychologically intimate and revealing work, exploring the Yaqui heritage of his grandmother. In a mature blending of all that Valdez has accomplished in structure and style, *Mummified Deer* revisits dramatic space as interpreted by tent theater and the fluid transition from exterior political themes, such as enslavement and genocide against the Yaqui by the Porfirio Díaz government, to the more interior exploration of motherhood, family shame, and indigenous identity.

Valdez's screenwriting career began with early film and television versions of Corky González's poem, *I Am Joaquín* (1969), and with his own *Los Vendidos*, and later with a film version of *Zoot Suit* (1982). But his real incursion into major Hollywood productions and success came with his writing and directing of *La Bamba* (1987), the screen biography of

Chicano rock and roll star Ritchie Valens. Other screen plays include *Corridos* (1987) and the successful television movies *La Pastorela* (1991) and *The Cisco Kid* (1993). Valdez's plays, essays, and poems have been widely anthologized. He has published three collections of plays: *Luis Valdez—The Early Works* (1990), *Zoot Suit and Other Plays* (1992), and *Mummified Deer and Other Plays* (2005). Valdez's awards include an Obie (1968), three Los Angeles Drama Critics Awards (1969, 1972, and 1978), a special Emmy Award (1973), the San Francisco Bay Critics Circle for Best Musical (1983), and honorary doctorates from San Jose Sate University, Columbia College, and the California Institute of the Arts.

NICOLÁS KANELLOS

Further Reading:

Huerta, Jorge. *Chicano Drama: Performance, Society, and Myth.* New York: Cambridge University Press, 2000.

Veterans Groups

Veterans groups are voluntary fraternal organizations whose members shared a common experience of serving in the U.S. armed forces, usually, but not always, during wartime. Until the latter half of the 20th century, most veterans groups were segregated, although in some areas outside of the South where blacks were relatively few, black veterans were often allowed to join, either officially or unofficially. In areas with larger black populations, black veterans formed their own groups, although such black groups were usually chapters of larger white-dominated organizations.

During the Jim Crow era, the very existence of the black veteran had often been denied, in that the image of the American soldier during wartime shown in movies and books was of a white man. Black participation was usually mildly celebrated during wartime, but forgotten and denied after the fighting ended. As serving in the military has historically been tied to the concept of the citizen, and thus the obligation to serve was often linked to the right to vote, the denial or denigration of black military service was a cornerstone in upholding Jim Crow. In general, veterans groups followed the practice of the U.S. military in that they allowed blacks to join, but segregated them into separate chapters or posts, reserving all state and national leadership positions to white men. Only when the military itself began integrating, albeit slowly, did veterans organizations begin integrating.

American military veterans have formed formal and informal groups since colonial times, but the latter half of the 19th century saw the rise of large politically active veterans groups, notably the Grand Army of the Republic (GAR), composed of Union veterans from the Civil War. The GAR remained a conservative political voice in the North until age thinned its ranks into oblivion around the end of World War I. As the Union army was by the last year of the Civil War almost 10 percent black, and the Union navy in general had black sailors as part of the crews on warships, the potential for black membership in the GAR was high. However, many blacks who served in Union forces in the Civil War came from the South, and many returned to the South following the war, where GAR chapters did not exist. Additionally, in some areas, white veterans did not allow blacks to join the local GAR post. The very low membership of black veterans in the GAR worked against the development of separate GAR chapters for black members. Some chapters, particularly in areas that had been strongholds of abolitionist sentiment before and during the war, occasionally had one or two black members.

Conversely, Confederate veterans groups by the turn of the century increasingly sought to publicize black participation in the Confederate armies, in order to support the post-Reconstruction reinterpretation that slavery had played a minuscule part in causing the war. Some Confederate veterans groups thus maintained an ambivalent stance toward black Confederate veterans, publicizing their existence to the North to refute Northern claims that the South fought to defend slavery, yet at the same time Southern whites denied that blacks had earned the right to exercise their political rights through their service in the Civil War. However, as black participation in the Confederate armies had been minuscule, the black veterans who did exist were more of a novelty to most of the South.

The mass participation in the military during the wars of the 20th century led to a new flowering of veterans organizations. Prior to World War I, veterans organizations were normally for veterans of a particular war. However, the 20th century saw the creation of large veterans organizations,

American G.I. Forum (AGIF)

The American G.I. Forum (AGIF) is a civil rights organization devoted to securing equal rights for Hispanic American veterans. The AGIF was founded on March 26, 1948, by Hector P. Garcia, a young army veteran and a physician from Corpus Christi, Texas. He was also a member of the League of United Latin American Citizens. When World War II was over in 1945, millions of veterans returned home looking to the G.I. Bill, which guaranteed educational, medical, housing, and other benefits. But a significant proportion of Mexican American and other Hispanic veterans throughout the United States were denied those benefits. Garcia called for an organized struggle with more than 700 other Hispanic veterans to address problems of discrimination and inequalities they have endured.

The AGIF demanded that the G.I. Bill of Rights of 1944 apply equally to Hispanic veterans. It also fought to ensure adequate hospital care for the wounded. The organization successfully put Mexican American representation on draft boards. In 1949, AGIF launched a widespread protest movement against racial discrimination by the director of the Rice Funeral Home in Three Rivers, Texas, who refused the use of the chapel for the funeral of Private Felix Longoria. The protest stirred the nation and finally forced political leaders, including Lyndon B. Johnson, then a senator from Texas, to intervene and have him interred at Arlington National Cemetery with a full military funeral. In 1954, the AGIF was involved with other organizations in a landmark civil rights legal case, *Hernandez v. The State of Texas*. Today, the AGIF focuses on employment training and counseling for veterans through its two programs, the Veteran Outreach Program, which provides employment training and counseling in the Southwest, and SER—Jobs for Progress, which operates employment training centers and provides residential and other services in the continental United States and Puerto Rico.

Dong-Ho Cho

reflecting the mass involvement in war that characterized much of the century. The new veterans organizations created in the 20th century varied in requirements for membership. The American Legion was the broadest, accepting veterans from any branch of the military, regardless of whether the veteran served in war or peace, or if the veteran had volunteered for military service or been drafted. The Veterans of Foreign Wars (VFW) was more selective, requiring members to have served in combat. Black chapters of these larger organizations began within a few years of their formation. The American Legion began granting charters to black posts in the 1920s. Part of the justification for granting charters to black posts came from the self-images of the American Legion, that it spoke for all veterans and was thus the main voice to lobby Congress regarding veterans' issues. Since all veterans, black or white, benefitted from the activities of the American Legion, then black veterans should share part of the financial burden of supporting the Legion's efforts through their dues.

Veterans organizations played several roles in society. Foremost, they gave veterans an opportunity to gather with others who had shared a similar life experience. At the same, their collective voice gave veterans more power in society than they had since the decades after the Civil War. However, veterans organizations tended to follow the Jim Crow practices that existed in the military, and thus most major veterans organizations such as the American Legion and the VFW had separate chapters for black veterans. Only during the 1960s and 1970s would individual chapters drop the color bar.

Barry M. Stentiford

See also
World War II

Further Reading:
Edgerton, Robert B., *Hidden Heroism: Black Soldiers in America's Wars*. Boulder, CO: Westview Press, 2001.
Mason, Herbert Malloy, Jr. *VFW: Our First Century*. Lenexa, KS: Addax Publishing Group, 1999.
Rumer, Thomas. *The American Legion: An Official History, 1919–1989*. New York: M. Evans and Co., 1990.
Severo, Richard, and Lewis Milfords. *The Wages of War: When America's Soldiers Came Home: From Valley Forge to Vietnam*. New York: Simon & Schuster, 1989.

Vietnam War and Race Riots

As the Vietnam War progressed, its connection to the civil rights movement became more pronounced. Race riots in the United States in the 1960s often reflected combined resentments—a perceived inequality of the impact of the war in Vietnam on African Americans and growing frustrations with discrimination and racism at home. Thus, riots and violence ensued among African Americans, both in the army in Vietnam and in the United States (*see* Long Hot Summer Riots, 1965–1967).

The home front saw riots both directly and indirectly connected to Vietnam. One of the more famous domestic episodes was the Jackson State University Incident (1970). In the wake of the invasion of Cambodia and the violence at Kent State University, riots erupted at Jackson State University in Mississippi. The conflict at Jackson State was sparked by racial tensions in town and was brought to a head by antiwar protests. Two dead and 12 wounded signaled the volatile mix of race, frustration over civil rights, and antiwar agitation.

Racial tensions enveloped not only life at home, but within the armed services itself as the war expanded and became more unpopular in the late 1960s. The interracial violence coupled with Black Power that marked the home front also scarred the military. Discrimination was not alien to the military, and the same polarization that marked many breakdowns in American society was reflected in the rank and file of the armed services as many black soldiers sought to embrace their culture.

War showed strains in the system of military justice as the services tried to weed out what they noted as undesirables; a large number of these were black militants who challenged the system and the war. Because so many blacks served in the military, and were—especially in beginning of war—at a disproportionate number to whites, tensions increased. In addition, those normal stresses seen in society at large were heightened because of the military situation and the war. Punishment often fell more heavily on those categorized as black militants.

As the war expanded after 1965, opposition became an important issue among African American activists. For example, Martin Luther King, Jr., especially in the last year of his life, broke with President Lyndon Johnson over the war. The riots that coursed through the Watts district of Los Angeles in 1965 and in Harlem in 1964 had negative effects on the military, but the widespread violent reaction to the 1968 assassination of King brought the greatest racial turmoil to the armed forces. Growing numbers of blacks were frustrated. Increased impatience with the war and the delays in racial progress in the United States led to race riots on a number of ships and military bases.

On August 30, 1968, the American prisoners in the Long Binh military stockade rioted. Blacks made up nearly 90 percent of the population. The prisoners voluntarily segregated themselves. The prison was incredibly dangerous with inhumane conditions and severe overcrowding that only worsened racial tensions. Prisoners often taunted the mostly white guards with Black Power signs. Racial tensions, combined with allegations of rampant drug use, were the primary causes of the uprising. In the end, one inmate was killed and 58 inmates and five military policemen were injured before the military police used tear gas to break up the riot. Following a quick U.S. Army investigation, the U.S. command announced that racial tensions caused the riot. The command also claimed that most of the inmate injuries were caused by inmates fighting among themselves. Nearly a month later, 12 black inmates were still holding out in a section of the stockade. Eventually, six of the black inmates accused of starting the riot were charged with the murder or conspiracy to commit the murder of the white inmates.

Earlier in August, American prisoners in the Marine Corps brig at Danang rioted and set fire to cell blocks. Military police had to use tear gas to quell the riot. Two months later, in response to a weekend of incidents with racial overtones and tension between blacks and whites, the U.S. Navy imposed restrictions on movement in the Danang region.

At the Navy base at Cam Ranh Bay, white sailors donned Ku Klux Klan–style outfits, burned crosses, and raised the Confederate flag. In February 1969, riots at Fort Benning, Georgia, followed when a black soldier awaiting discharge vented frustration over being assigned to menial labor and attacked white troops. That same summer in Camp Lejeune, North Carolina, 43 men were charged when blacks and Puerto Ricans beat up white U.S. Marines. In March 1970, in Goose Bay, Labrador, Canada, white airmen, apparently angered because local white women danced with blacks, stabbed a black man, thereby triggering random beatings of whites in retaliation.

The services dealt with issues by trying to grant concessions—both real and symbolic. For example, military brass accepted a modified afro, tolerated the Black Power salute, and cracked down on the use of racial epithets and offensive words. But these efforts did not resolve the problems. In October 1972, on the aircraft carrier *Kitty Hawk*, a series of incidents occurred that underscored the thin barrier that held back racial tensions. The *Kitty Hawk*, a mostly white ship, experienced trouble on board after a brawl in an enlisted man's club in Subic Bay. The first confrontation, involving a group of black sailors and a detachment of Marines, was defused by the executive officer, an African American. However, this did not end the situation, and small groups of up to 25 blacks raged through the ship, attacking whites and pulling many sleeping sailors from their berths to beat them with their fists, chains, metal pipes, fire extinguisher nozzles, and broom handles. About 150 armed sailors moved through the ship spreading the hostility. The executive officer followed them and finally managed to end the threat of violence.

Although some men were charged, the *Kitty Hawk* incident, along with the other outbreaks of violence in the armed services, all reflected the fact the military was not immune from the stresses of society. The racial confrontations that raged across the United States were carried to the armed forces and did not subside until the war ended and changes were made. The military repeatedly provided a microcosm of the war's growing effect on race relations at home and how those tensions helped to exacerbate racial antagonism, at times culminating in violence.

GARY GERSHMAN

See also
Civil Rights Movement; Long Hot Summer Riots (1965–1967)

Further Reading:
Buckley, Gail. *Strength for the Fight: A History of Black Americans in the Military*. New York: Random House, 2001.
Glines, C. V. "Black vs. White—Trouble in the Ranks." *Armed Forces Management* 16 (June 1970): 20–27.
Rivera, Oswald. *Fire and Rain*. New York: Four Walls Eight Windows, 1990.
Shields, Patrick M. "The Burden of the Draft: The Vietnam Years." *Journal of Political and Military Sociology* 9 (Fall 1982): 215–28.
Terry, Wallace. *Bloods: An Oral History of the Vietnam War by Black Veterans*. New York: Random House, 1984.
Tucker, Spencer C., ed. *Encyclopedia of the Vietnam War: A Political, Social, and Military History*. Santa Barbara, CA: ABC-CLIO, 1998.

Vigilantism

The Merriam-Webster dictionary defines a vigilante as "a member of a volunteer committee organized to suppress and punish crime summarily (as when the processes of law are viewed as inadequate)." Rosenbaum (1974) describes vigilantism as "acts or threats of coercion in violation of the formal boundaries of an established sociopolitical order which, however, are intended by the violators to defend that order from forms of subversion." Simply stated, vigilantism is an effort by an individual or individuals to maintain the status quo and to preserve the values of the society when those values are threatened by a perceived danger. Vigilantism may also develop as a reaction to a feeling of relative deprivation that entails a sense of possible goal attainment or access to resources to which individuals believe that they are entitled. Violence is often a fundamental part of the process. When individuals have high value expectations but diminishing capacity to obtain those values, the propensity for violence is greater and the target of violence will be the individual or individuals who are perceived as blocking access to just rewards. The maintenance of the status quo will allow individuals access to their goals. Therefore, vigilantism is viewed as a conservative phenomenon.

Rosenbaum types vigilantism in three categories: crime control, social group control, and regime control. Crime control vigilantes react to increasing crime that must be brought under control. Social group vigilantes view a different group of individuals as trying to change or redistribute values within the society. Regime control vigilantes tend to view the regime as ineffective in maintaining the status quo, and violence is directed toward the regime itself. The collective violence of vigilantes may be viewed as an attempt to keep social inferiors and marginal groups in the proper place of the societal hierarchy. The degree of violence used is related to "relational distance" and "cultural distance." Violence increases as relational distance or the degree in which individuals' lives intersect decreases. Individuals are harsher on unknown offenders. The degree of cultural differences such as language, dress, and religion also increases the degree of violence. Therefore, racial and ethnic groups represented by immigrants can often be the target of vigilantism and have been historically.

American vigilantism generally seeks to return to a certain level of status quo and tends to be both local in nature and extralegal. The movements are seen as a response to a failure of the law or government to remedy perceived threats and problems. Typically, vigilante groups display a three-tiered arrangement where the upper level supplies leadership, the middle level provides actors, and a lower level is filled with marginalized individuals who may end up as targets. Vigilante groups share an "Ideology of Vigilantism" that consists of the doctrine of vigilance, a philosophy of vigilantism, and an economic rationale. The doctrine of vigilance insists that individuals need to be aware of threats that might change the status quo, while the economic rationale suggests that it is cheaper for individuals to remedy problems than the government. The "philosophy of vigilantism" relies on deeply ingrained American values such as self-preservation, the right of revolution, and popular sovereignty that states that individuals have a right to self-preservation. Three hundred and twenty-six known vigilante movements have occurred in the United States.

The first known movement occurred in 1767 as the South Carolina Back Country Regulators. The victims are often a different ethnicity and socioeconomic class than the perpetrator, especially when the violence is defined as social group control. Immigrants have historically and are currently a continuous target of vigilantes. The Southern Poverty Law Center (SPLC) examined violence perpetrated against immigrants in many parts of the country and found that harassment, beatings, and racial profiling were common. In some cases, immigrants were killed. A number of efforts to control border crossings between Mexico and the United States have resulted in the formation of vigilante groups. In the early 21st century, the southwestern area of the United States has experienced new vigilante-type movements. The Anti-Defamation League (ADL) suggests that groups such as the Rescue Ranch, which formed in 2000, are vigilante efforts

The Back Legion

The Ku Klux Klan (KKK) experienced a decline in membership during the 1930s, and as an effort to keep the local chapter alive, Dr. William Jacob Shepherd founded the Black Legion. The organization would revolutionize the idea of authoritarian leadership in the KKK, create a disciplined and cruel vigilante group, and grow as high as 100,000 members in four Midwestern states. The white robes of the KKK were replaced with red-trimmed black robes sporting a white skull and crossbones. Members had to be white, native-born, Protestant, and American citizens. Members were required to buy a firearm and participate in an initiation rite where they stated the opposition to all the perceived threats to white Americans. Leaders believed that the white race was surrounded by Catholics, Jewish moneylenders, communists, and African Americans who intended to destroy their way of life. Members were pressured to recruit new members, and often new members were conscripted from the workplace. In 1932, an electrician named Virgil H. Effinger took over leadership of the strictly urban organization. Effinger reorganized the structure to reflect a military hierarchy and moved the organization into a new era of violence and cruelty as members tried to enforce sexual and racial order. In 1936, Warner Brothers produced *The Black Legion* starring Humphrey Bogart, which depicted the organization's activities.

to control illegal border crossings. The group has taken the law into their own hands in an effort to curtail an immigrant invasion and assist the government's failure to control the arrival of immigrants. Such groups as these are often found in association with white supremacist groups and express a fear of "loss of Anglo cultural dominance."

The United States has a long history of vigilante efforts to restore law and order to society. Many early efforts of vigilantism were designed to reduce criminal activity but later changed to restoring status quo values and norms as different racial and ethnic groups were viewed as threatening dominant groups. Ethnocentrism, the idea that one's culture is the best, along with relative deprivation has often served as a motivator for these actions. In the later 20th century and the early 21st century, these vigilante efforts have been focused in the immigration issues that face the nation.

R. Randall Adams

Further Reading:

Amann, Peter H. "The Black Legion as an American Hybrid." *Comparative Studies in Society and History* (1983) 25: 490–524.

Anti-Defamation League. "Border Disputes: Armed Vigilantes in Arizona." http://www.adl.org (accessed December 2, 2012).

Brown, Richard Maxwell. *Strain of Violence: Historical Studies of American Violence and Vigilantism.* New York: Oxford University Press, 1975.

Buechler, Steven M. *Social Movements in Advanced Capitalism.* New York: Oxford University Press, 2000.

De la Roche, Roberta Senechal. "Collective Violence as Social Control." *Sociological Forum* (1996) 11: 97–128.

Gurr, Ted Robert. *Why Men Rebel.* Princeton, NJ: Princeton University Press, 1970.

Jacobs, David, Jason T. Carmichael, and Stephanie l. Kent. "Vigilantism, Current Racial Threat, and Death Sentences." *American Sociological Review* (2005) 70: 656–77.

Merriam-Webster Dictionary. http://www.merriam-webster.com/dictionary/vigilante (accessed December 17, 2012).

Rosenbaum, H. John, and Peter C. Sederberg. "Vigilantism: An Analysis of Established Violence." *Comparative Politics* (1974) 6: 541–70.

Southern Poverty Law Center. "Climate of Fear: Latino Immigrants in Suffolk County, N.Y." http://www.splcenter.org (accessed December 12, 2012).

Southern Poverty Law Center. "Under Siege: Life for Low-Income Latinos in the South." http://www.splcenter.org (accessed December 12, 2012)

Vincent Chin Case (1982)

In June 1982, Chinese American Vincent Chin, age 27, was murdered in Detroit, Michigan, by two white automobile-factory workers, who mistook him for being Japanese and blamed him for the loss of American automotive jobs. The ensuing court cases and community activism became symbolic of the ongoing fight of Asian Americans against anti-Asian violence as well as their quest for the protection of their civil rights and equal protection under the law. On June 19, Chin was out with friends at a Detroit bar, celebrating his upcoming wedding, when Ronald Ebens and his stepson, Michael Nitz, taunted them and a fight broke out. Both groups were kicked out of the bar, but Ebens and Nitz went to their car, retrieved a baseball bat, and again accosted Chin and his friends in the parking lot. Ebens and Nitz chased them for 20 minutes, finally catching Chin outside a McDonald's restaurant. While Nitz held Chin, Ebens brutally beat him with the baseball bat, shattering his skull. Chin died four days later from his injuries.

Both men were charged with second-degree murder, but in a plea bargain, Ebens agreed to a lesser charge of manslaughter. In a much-criticized decision, Judge Charles Kaufman sentenced each of the men to three years of probation and fines of $3,870. Asian Americans in Detroit and eventually across the United States were outraged by the decision to issue such a light sentence for such a brutal murder. Chinese Americans joined with Korean, Japanese, and Filipino Americans to form Citizens for Justice to work for a just response to Chin's case. Chin's mother, Lily, overcame her limited English to become a prominent spokesperson for the cause. Her great-grandfather had immigrated to the United States in the 19th century to work in railroad construction. Chin's father, Hing, had immigrated to the United States in 1922 and served in the U.S. Army in World War II. The parents had worked in a Chinese laundry until Hing's death, when Lily began working in an automobile factory. But following her son's murder and the disappointing trial results, Chin's mother, feeling deprived of hope for a decent life in the United States, returned to China.

In response to the intense criticism of his decision, Judge Kaufman explained that the sentences were predicated on both men being citizens of the community; they were either employed (Ebens was an auto-factory foreman) or in school (Nitz had been laid off and was a part-time student); they had no prior record; and, in the judge's opinion, they were unlikely to repeat their offense. Newspaper editorials in Michigan decried the implication that if one was employed or in school one essentially could get a license to kill for only $3,800. After an investigation, the U.S. Justice Department found evidence of a civil rights violation, and in 1983 a federal grand jury indicted both men on charges of violating Chin's right to enjoy a public space. In 1984, a federal jury in the U.S. District Court found Ebens guilty but acquitted Nitz. Ebens was sentenced to 25 years in prison but was let go after posting a $20,000 bond. His conviction was later overturned on a technicality in a 1986 retrial. Neither man served jail time for the murder of Chin.

A documentary film, *Who Killed Vincent Chin?*, produced by Christine Choy and Renee Tajima in 1988, explored the case and the ensuing community activism. The film included recollections of those who knew Chin, those who had witnessed the events, the heroic appeals of Chin's mother, and, perhaps most striking, footage of Ronald Ebens. The film has become a classic in the continuing struggle to stop anti-Asian violence and protect the civil rights of Asian Americans. Chin's case played a significant role in mobilizing a new generation of Asian Americans to resist the stereotyping, discrimination, and violence that had been directed against their community for more than a century.

KENNETH J. GUEST

Further Reading:

Chan, Sucheng. *Asian Americans: An Interpretive History.* New York: Twayne Publishers, 1991.

Wu, Frank H. *Yellow: Race in America beyond Black and White.* New York: Basic Books, 2003.

Vocational Education

Vocational education, also known as industrial education or curriculum, has, for hundreds of years, provided black Americans with technical and ideological training to replicate and accept their low-wage and servant-class status. Courses in schools at every educational level throughout the nation trained the sons and daughters of slavery as manual laborers, janitors, chauffeurs, laundresses, servants, cooks, maids, porters, and bellmen. To "civilize" and control, rather than allow for upward mobility, schools, in both the North and South before and after the Civil War, subjected blacks to vocational education. Institutionalized by Booker T. Washington and like-minded white philanthropists, vocational education became the predominant method of educating blacks through the civil rights period in America with a legacy that continues into present-day segregated schools.

Schools employing vocational education trained blacks for "Negro jobs," those that working-class whites eschewed to move up the socioeconomic ladder. Manual labor, rather than scholarship, defined educational excellence as

As the founder of the Hampton Institute, American Civil War veteran Samuel Chapman Armstrong made an important contribution to the education of both African Americans and Native Americans. His school served as a model for others, including the Tuskegee Institute, started by his most famous pupil, African American leader Booker T. Washington. (Library of Congress)

administrators self-consciously and intentionally provided blacks with very different educational courses than those experienced by whites in America's newly developing public education system. This curriculum has resulted in generations of blacks trained to constitute a docile industrial caste of semi- and low-skilled workers.

Throughout the South, in all forms of education, from elementary and secondary to college, the primary form of education that most blacks received was vocational education. Promoted by Gen. Samuel Chapman Armstrong, founder of Hampton Institute, Booker T. Washington, his mentee, carried on the tradition at Tuskegee Institute. Perceived as the black community's spokesman and voice of authority on educational issues, Washington preached to educational experts nationally to ensure that the burgeoning education being made available to blacks would be vocational.

Guiding this philosophy was Washington's 1895 proclamation, known as the Atlanta Compromise. In this highly publicized speech at the World's Fair, Washington advised the sons and daughters of slaves to be as separate as the fingers on the hand and to cast down their buckets where they stood to "dignify and glorify common labor." Washington believed that blacks should be trained to excel in the jobs to which they were allotted by whites prior to moving up the social, political, and economic ladder. In these low-skill jobs reminiscent of slavery, Washington advised African Americans to be patient, thrifty, and industrious so that whites would see their diligence and allow them to move up. Industrial education, according to Washington, would promote blacks' achievement within a strict Jim Crow system rather than challenge a system that forbid blacks from many occupations, particularly the professions. As such, vocational curriculum promoted the values of Jim Crow laws and perpetuated black citizens' second-class status by training them not only to fulfill but also to accept and validate their menial roles within society.

In the post-Reconstruction South through the civil rights era, most black children received only the most rudimentary education. School boards and local governments refused to fund public education for black children, instead using blacks' taxes to build schools for white children. Many black parents worked hard to educate their children by contributing funds from their minimal incomes to build schools and hire teachers, but their efforts were often thwarted by the Ku Klux Klan and other vigilantes by destroying schools and scaring away teachers. While many children and parents believed in the transformative value of education for social and economic improvement, few children attended school for longer than three or four months a year (so that they could aid their parents in sharecropping) or for more than four years. The schools they attended were often located miles away from home, with no transportation besides their poorly shod feet, in one-room, drafty buildings with dozens of other children of all ages, and a teacher often with little more education than the oldest in the room. As a result, blacks in the South were disastrously uneducated compared with their Northern counterparts, both black and white.

Two historical forces combined to generate thousands of schools in the South for those who clearly needed them, but which also institutionalized vocational education throughout the land. First, nearly abandoned by the defunct Freedmen's Bureau, Southern blacks were desperate for education. Second, a generation of wealth built through America's industrial revolution that saw the rise in a variety of industries, from oil and steel to retail and railroads, found largely Northern white men with philanthropic ideologies seeking worthwhile causes. Believing in the need of training blacks for their own industries and enterprises (though at the lowest level) while simultaneously using their finances for a philanthropic cause, many Northern white philanthropists were attracted to possibilities of building schools and financing teachers, provided that they subscribed to their philosophies.

After Reconstruction, philanthropists stepped into the void created by the Freedman's Bureau's departure and changed the educational landscape for Southern blacks. Many of these men viewed black education as misguided missionary work and set out to train millions of black youth to fulfill their role as menial laborers in the growing industrial economy. The largest donor to these schools was Julius Rosenwald (founder of Sears) who served on the Board of Directors of Tuskegee. Consulting with Washington, Rosenwald donated funds to build nearly 5,000 schools. Although providing schools to many children who otherwise would have been without education, the ideology employed in many of these schools largely replicated the racial hierarchy by ensuring that students attending them would be unable to pursue higher education. Indeed, many philanthropists forbid headmasters from employing a liberal arts curriculum in common schools.

In these schools, vocational education taught black students to be productive and obedient servants, rather than productive citizens. Children learned basic writing and math skills with limited vocabularies. Insufficient desks, pencils, papers, and books were supplemented with a wide variety of tools, such as cooking utensils, gardening tools, and cleaning supplies, necessary for children preparing to enter the servant class. A notable absence in the curriculum of the larger schools is the lack of required academic core curriculum. Many floor plans find not a single room devoted to academic endeavors, but sufficient space for barbering, janitoring, hairdressing, laundries, and rooms for learning how to be a maid. For many children attending these schools, the highest profession to which they could aspire was teaching nonacademic curriculum in the same low-quality schools to which they were subject.

Both children and their parents critiqued this curricular emphasis given their desire to improve their opportunities through education. Students, in particular, sought education that would transcend their parents' daily lives of oppression through menial jobs and transform them into students prepared for higher education and white-collar professions. Therefore, parents counseled their children against enrollment in industrial courses, especially avoiding majoring in this curriculum, and instead encouraged them to take "elective" academic courses.

Although designed for widespread Southern implementation, local black leaders, teachers, and a small number of progressive whites believing in the value of academic education for the black community subverted the emphasis on vocational education. W.E.B. Du Bois was a particularly vocal critic of vocational education who recognized the insidious effects that this curriculum would have on generations of black youth and their potential to develop their intellects to the best of their abilities, move out of the segregated caste system in which they were embedded, and integrate into America's social and economic community. Though often required to submit reports to the funding sources, teachers and black leaders nevertheless worked hard to instill their schools with a liberal arts curriculum, hire teachers well trained for this curriculum, and produce students who could compete with their white counterparts. Particularly in large cities with large populations of black students, educators created academically rigorous learning environments for their students that nurtured both their minds and their spirits by instilling in them a knowledge of black history and culture. These schools, though they received considerably less funding than those of whites, succeeded in fostering a sense of community, as teachers nurtured African American children and provided them with safe spaces to learn, express their ideas, and develop the tools necessary to survive in a white world.

Vocational education was not just reserved for blacks in Southern schools. In Northern schools, as in the South, black students in segregated schools and in segregated classes within integrated schools were trained to be servants, washerwomen, cooks, bellhops, and elevator operators in white-owned homes and businesses. In cities such as Newark, Philadelphia, Boston, and New York City, African American children received separate and inferior education similar to that of their Southern counterparts. Interestingly, this vocational training in the North was similar to that received by racialized European immigrants in many urban centers as well. In larger cities, boys and girls often attended sex-segregated junior and senior high schools were young women were taught to cook, sew, and clean while boys were taught to polish shoes, to work an elevator, and the most efficient ways to carry luggage. For example, in New York City during the 1950s, the Board of Education assigned white children to academic high schools where they learned subjects necessary for a college entrance diploma, but sent blacks to vocational high schools where they learned to be servants and earned a high school certificate. This was little more than an attendance certificate and did not meet college admission requirements, thereby producing the same underclass of workers prepared only for the lowest-skilled jobs in urban areas.

Therefore, in both the rural South and urban North, blacks attended segregated, underfunded, and academically lacking schools for nearly 80 years prior to efforts to change schools and their curriculum through integration following the landmark 1954 *Brown v. Board of Education* decision. As schools for Southern white students improved, those for blacks remained in the same impoverished conditions as they had been in the years immediately following slavery. Drafty and rundown, these schools served only to reproduce the social hierarchy in the South by failing to upgrade curriculum during and after the World Wars and continuing to employ industrial education or teach students only the most basic skills. The differences between black and white students widened as high schools were built for white students in areas far from where the (mostly rural) black population lived.

At the college level, black education, with few exceptions (such as Morehouse, Howard, and Fisk) was similarly abysmal to that found in lower grades. Many colleges could not support or maintain sufficient professors, laboratory equipment, or libraries to provide students with an academically rigorous curriculum beyond the high school level. To improve their colleges financially, administrators collaborated with white philanthropists or state governments dedicated to blacks' political disenfranchisement and economic subordination. Colleges, particularly those including the words "agricultural," "technical," and "mechanical," were often the only ones available to blacks. Indeed, many were developed by states required to provide black students with "separate but equal" education due to lawsuits challenging the lack of higher education for blacks and their unwillingness to desegregate more prestigious state schools due to the ruling racial ideology of the era.

Blacks attending these colleges learned rudimentary math and reading skills while engaging in trades to pay for their tuition, oftentimes constructing the very buildings in which they were to live and learn. Particularly problematic was that many trades students learned were outdated and of no practical use to these young students. For example, in some schools, black men learned how to make bricks by hand and then bake them out in the sun. However, mechanized brickmaking had already been invented as a more efficient way to make uniformly sized bricks, thereby making this training irrelevant. Others plowed fields with horses and oxen even as tractors and mechanized plows became commonplace. Teachers at these schools were also required to construct school buildings and work in the fields to provide role models of a hard work ethic and the value of hard labor for students.

Students were not taught the most technically skilled careers, such as training that would prepare them to become plumbers, electricians, or printers. Instead, they were trained to be apprentices. For example, in carpentry classes, rather than learning to build an entire house, students learned to make window sashes and frames but little else. These were intentional efforts by the schools to ensure that blacks were not trained to compete with whites for high-skill jobs and to maintain and justify a segregated labor force given the differences in skills. These efforts worked, as many graduates of Hampton in the late 1800s could be found working as porters and waiters.

Many attending schools such as Hampton protested the mediocre commitment to academic subjects and simultaneous exaltations to perform hard labor throughout much of the school year. Those in academic courses found themselves simply reviewing what they had learned in grade school, particularly those in the program of study to become teachers in Southern schools. Students demanded practical and technical training as to all, rather than just the most basic aspects,

of the trades to ensure their ability to compete and acquire for jobs in local labor markets.

MELISSA F. WEINER

See also
Educational Achievement Gap

Further Reading:
Anderson, James D. *The Education of Blacks in the South, 1860–1935.* Chapel Hill: University of North Carolina Press, 1988.
Kozol, Jonathan. *Shame of the Nation: The Restoration of Apartheid Schooling in America.* New York: Three Rivers Press, 2006.
Tyack, David. *The One Best System: A History of American Urban Education.* Cambridge, MA: Harvard University Press, 1974.
Watkins, William H. *The White Architects of Black Education: Ideology and Power in America, 1865–1954.* New York: Teachers College Press, 2001.

Voter ID Requirements

Voter ID requirement calls for voters to show a valid identification at the polls before they cast a ballot. Thirty-three states have passed such laws, and others are likely to join them in near future. These laws have two key distinctions: (1) In states that passed "strict" laws, voters cannot cast ballots without first presenting a valid photo ID. Those who are unable to show ID are given a provisional ballot, which is kept separate from regular ballots. Should these provisional ballot voters return to election officials within a prescribed time and show an acceptable ID, their provisional ballot is counted; otherwise, it is excluded. The states that passed strict photo ID amendment but covered under section 5 of the Voting Rights Act (e.g., Mississippi and Alabama) require preclearance from the federal government prior to their implementation. (2) In states that have "nonstrict" laws, voters who are unable to show an acceptable ID may be permitted to sign an affidavit of identity, or poll workers may be permitted to vouch for them, if they have a personal knowledge of who they are. Sixteen states fall under this category.

The proponents of voter ID laws base their argument on two premises: first, there is a need to prevent voter fraud at any cost to have a fair election; and second, it is a matter of "common sense" to show a valid ID at the polls, just like we do it when boarding airplanes, buying alcohol, and engaging in other activities. In George Weigel's (William E. Simon Chair in Catholic Studies at the Ethics and Public Policy Center) words:

> If you can't buy beer at the ballpark without valid ID, or withdraw money from your savings account without valid ID, or get on a plane without valid ID, or pick up a medical prescription without a valid ID, you shouldn't be admitted to a voting booth without valid ID. Enough Chicago-graveyard-voting jokes are enough.

They are concerned that ineligible voters, including former felons, noncitizens, nonresidents, and those who had already voted may engage in illegally casting ballots without voter ID requirement. They claim that the National Voter Registration Act of 1993 had worsened these problems to the extent that officials could purge deadwood from the registration polls. For all these reasons, they believe, a photo identification or a valid identification should be needed to curb such corrupt activities. To them, the need to preserve public confidence in election provides adequate justification for the voter ID laws.

Critics of the voter ID laws maintain they are expensive, time consuming, and unnecessary, not only for individuals but also for the states with such laws. In large part, it is viewed as Republicans' way of blocking minority voters, whose support they seldom get because of their increasingly conservative political ideology. Richard L. Hasen (a professor of law and political science at the University of California, Irvine) is confident that "many Republican legislators and political operatives support voter ID laws for two purposes: first, to depress Democratic turnout, and second to gin up the Republican base." Critics also point out that the United States has been trying to increase access and improve voter participation for minorities through amendments and section 5 of the 1965 Voting Rights Act, and now the voter ID laws are reversing the trend. Their memories trace back to the 1960 presidential contest, when Democratic candidate John F. Kennedy defeated his Republican opponent Richard Nixon by a narrow 0.2 percent of the popular vote because of the Republicans' "Operation Eagle Eye," which deterred legitimate voter participation and intimidated voters of color. Similar claims of voter suppression on the part of critics and voter fraud on the part of advocates of voter ID laws, specifically picture ID laws, continued in subsequent elections. This

controversy especially takes central place whenever closely contested elections take place, like in the recent example of 2000 presidential election between Republican Bush and Democrat Gore.

Empirical data show that the number of bona fide voters who would fail to carry IDs to voting booths is significantly higher than that of fraudulent ones. For example, the Ohio statewide survey found only four instances of ineligible persons voting or attempting to vote in 2002 out of over 9 million votes cast (0.00004%). In Georgia, Secretary of State Cathy Cox has stated that she could not recall one documented case of voter fraud relating to the impersonation of a registered voter at the polls during the 10-year period that she was in the office. South Carolina state attorney general David Wilson attempted to justify the new ID law by claiming that over 900 "dead voters" might have voted in recent elections, but managed to identify only six individuals to support his exaggerated claim. On the other hand, nearly 10 percent of eligible voters do not have driver's licenses or state-issued photo ID because their moving patterns may hinder them from having a photo ID showing their current address or they may have to pay substantial fees for ID cards and required backup documents (e.g., about $100 for a driver's license, $45 for a birth certificate, $97 for a passport, or over $200 for naturalization papers). Conceivably, the burden of these fees and other difficulties in obtaining photo ID could keep eligible voters from voting. Some studies estimated that the "strict" voter ID laws would disfranchise nearly 20 million Americans, but deter negligible voter fraud. The U.S. Department of Justice itself came up with an estimated disfranchisement of 80,000 African Americans when Section 5 is applied to challenge the voter identification law in South Carolina, where 25 percent of African American citizens, compared to only 8 percent of their white counterparts, do not have valid IDs.

The nonparticipation of such a large number of voters resulting from the stricter voter ID laws generates political outcomes that are unlikely to reflect accurately on the electorate at large. As Charlie Crist, former Republican governor of Florida, wrote in the *Washington Post*:

> Cynical efforts at voter suppression are driven by an un-American desire to exclude as many people and silence as many voices as possible. Our country has never solved anything with less democracy, and

we're far better off when more citizens can access the polls—no matter which party mobilizes the most voters to them.

Moreover, the Help America Vote Act (HAVA) provides for asking for documentary proof of identity at the polls from a limited range of voters. The range includes citizens registering for the first time in a jurisdiction, by mail, whose application information had not already been verified against other state or federal databases. The HAVA also has a list of acceptable documents of proof—current utility bills, bank statements, paychecks, and other government documents. Election officials can also verify the eligibility by comparing signatures on the ballot envelope against the one on the registration form. Therefore, policy-makers should redirect their efforts to secure reliable data on the nature and extent of voter fraud by region instead of weighing on their political ideologies (conservative vs. liberal) or subjective fears and opinions. Additionally, they should consider alternative and effective ways of preventing it while ensuring the voter turnout is unaffected. The one-size-fits-all policy of voter ID laws does not seem to be the right measure.

KOMANDURI MURTY AND JIMMY D. MCCAMEY

See also

Racial Gerrymandering; Voting and Race; Voting Rights Act of 1965

Further Reading:

Ansolabehere, Stephen, and Nathaniel Persily. "Vote Fraud in the Eye of the Beholder: The Role of Public Opinion in the Challenge to Voter Identification Requirements." *Harvard Law Review* 121 (2008): 1737–74.

Brennan Center for Justice at New York University School of Law. "Policy Brief on Voter Identification." http://www .brennancenter.org/content/resource (accessed November 21, 2012).

Overton, Spencer. "Voter Identification." *Michigan Law Review* 105 (2007): 631–81.

Voting and Race

The history of voting rights in the United States is intricately related to the history of race relations. The right to vote is rooted in the Bill of Rights, which plays a vital role in American law and government. The original U.S. Bill of Rights came into effect via the first 10 constitutional amendments on December 15, 1791. This original Bill of Rights legally excluded racial and gender minorities (American Indians, African Americans, and women) and protected only white men. African American males were given the vote by the Fifteenth Amendment, which was the third of the Reconstruction amendments and was ratified on February 3,1870. Thomas Mundy Peterson was the first African American to vote after the adoption of the amendment when he cast his vote at City Hall in Perth Amboy, New Jersey, on March 31, 1870.

Even though blacks gained suffrage in 1870, social practices of discrimination and prejudice prevented many black citizens in the United States from being able to exercise their voting rights for some time. After the passage of the Fifteenth Amendment, the Southern states vowed to maintain their white supremacy and worked to keep African Americans away from the polls. These states employed several tactics such as literacy tests and poll taxes to block the black vote, also adding "grandfather clauses" to voting rights that excluded all whose ancestors had not voted in the 1860s. Additionally, the Supreme Court decision in *Plessy v. Ferguson* in 1896 facilitated social and economic segregation by legalizing "separate but equal" facilities for the races. This meant that separate voting facilities just for African Americans could be designed in such a way and with discriminatory voting policies so as to discourage blacks from voting. In subsequent years, African Americans were reduced to second-class citizenship under the Jim Crow segregation system and were subjected to mob lynchings, a convict lease system, chain gangs, and hate crimes perpetrated by racist groups such as the Ku Klux Klan. During that time, African Americans continued their struggle for equal rights and fair treatment as citizenry, including their right to the vote. Several organizations were formed to fight for these equal rights, including the National Association for the Advancement of Colored People and the National Urban League, which gained the support of educated and intelligent African American leaders like Booker T. Washington, W.E.B. DuBois, and A. Philip Randolph.

Nevertheless, these racial discriminatory practices in the American political landscape, especially among the former Confederate states, continued throughout the late 19th and

Literacy Test

The literacy test was one of the techniques used by Southern states to keep blacks from voting during the Jim Crow period. After President Abraham Lincoln signed the Emancipation Proclamation in 1863, the federal government guaranteed, through the support of its troops, the right of blacks to vote in the South. However, when the federal government decided to withdraw its troops from the South in 1896, the white supremacist governments in the Southern states slowly took away most of the civil rights of black residents. One of the first rights taken was voting. Since the Fifteenth Amendment gave blacks the right to vote in 1869, the Southern states could not legally prevent blacks from voting. Therefore, they instituted a literacy test and other measures. The literacy test required that a citizen be able to read to be eligible for voting. Blacks had a much lower literacy rate than whites at that time, so it systematically eliminated them from voting. Moreover, the test was usually arbitrary and depended on the whim of the white registrar. For example, in Florida, one of the questions included in the test was "How many windows are in the White House?"

Although the law required every voter to take the literacy test, African Americans who were brave enough to face all the intimidations and humiliations would often take the test. When they passed it, they were still denied the right to vote. With the passage of the Civil Rights Act in 1964, the federal government abolished the literacy test as a condition for voting. This decision enabled Southern blacks to exercise their right to vote and to elect their own representatives to local and national offices.

FRANCOIS PIERRE-LOUIS

early 20th centuries. During this time, African Americans were systematically excluded from the vote despite the Fifteenth Amendment that guaranteed them suffrage. This discrimination continued until President Lyndon Johnson issued a call to Congress on March 15, 1965, to "pass legislation which will make it impossible to thwart the 15th Amendment." As a result, the Voting Rights Act of 1965 was passed, which prohibits discrimination in voting. Section Five of this act requires that certain states with a history of voter discrimination must clear any change to their election laws with federal officials in Washington. This Voting Rights Act is considered a landmark piece of national legislation in the history of the Civil Rights movement in the United States and it has done much to prevent racial discrimination in voting. The act was reauthorized in 2006 when President George W. Bush extended its provisions for 25 more years.

Historically, black citizens have also been underrepresented in the American political system. The 2008 presidential election of Barack Obama marked a historically significant moment in American politics as Obama became the first African American to hold the office. Furthermore, the election also signaled an increase in the amount of minorities participating in the vote: 66 percent of non-Hispanic

whites, 65 percent of African Americans, and nearly 49 percent of Asians and Hispanics voted in this election. Many media pundits and political analysts regarded the voter turnout of whites and blacks in this election to be the highest. Also, compared to the 2004 presidential election, the 2008 election marked an increase of 5 million votes (4 percent) in the voting rates for each of the minority groups: 2 million African American, 2 million Hispanic, and 600,000 Asian votes were cast in this election. On the other hand, non-Hispanic white votes decreased by one percentage point in 2008. Furthermore, 74 percent of non-Hispanic whites and 70 percent of African Americans registered for voting in the 2008 presidential election, setting their respective new records, whereas these rates were not as high either for Hispanics (59 percent) or for Asians (55 percent). Regionally speaking, the South experienced the highest African American voting rate, while the Northeast and West experienced a higher non-Hispanic white voting rate than that of African Americans. Between Democratic candidate Obama and his Republican opponent McCain, the racial differences among voters were very pronounced: McCain won whites 55–43 percent, while Obama won blacks 95–4 percent, Hispanics 67–31 percent, and Asians 62–35 percent. This election showed that not only are more minorities in the United States voting than

---

Race Card in Political Campaigns

The "race card," in political campaigns, is the use of coded words, racial stereotypes, and issues by white candidates against blacks and other minority candidates. The most typical example of using the race card in a political campaign to appeal to white voters was seen in 1988. Michael Dukakis was nominated as the Democratic Party candidate to challenge Vice President George Bush for the presidency. Bush attacked Dukakis for being too soft on crime and used as an example of his liberal view the parole of Willie Horton, an African American who was convicted of rape in the state of Massachusetts. While he was released on a furlough program, Horton traveled to Maryland, where he robbed a house and raped a white woman. Capitalizing on whites' fear of crime and of African Americans, Bush's campaign mounted several advertising programs in which a black man was shown going through a revolving door and accusing Dukakis of being too soft on crime, particularly crime committed by blacks. As white America is afraid of black crimes associated with assault, robbery, and rape, the publicity around the release of Horton further alienated voters from Dukakis.

Politicians do not explicitly mention it, but it is a common understanding that even when speaking of combating crime, they are specifically appealing to white voters who think that blacks are the cause of this problem. Since the passage of the Civil Rights Act of 1964, politicians, the media, and those who harbor the white supremacist viewpoint have found different ways to make race a salient issue in American politics without ever mentioning it.

FRANCOIS PIERRE-LOUIS

---

ever before, but that the minority vote can be a powerful deciding factor in election outcomes.

Historically, many election candidates relied heavily on the nation's mainstream white population support. However, changing demographics in the United States over the last 50 years have begun to prove the importance of racial minorities including blacks, Asian Americans, and Hispanics to election outcomes. Similar to the 2008 presidential election, in the 2012 presidential election, Republican candidate Mitt Romney received 59 percent of white votes, and still lost the election to Obama because of his failure to reach out the minority groups in swing states like Nevada, Colorado, Virginia, and Florida. These states, which were once considered to be strong Republican states, have shifted in recent years as minority populations there have grown. On the other hand, Obama carried the minority votes in the United States by a margin of approximately 80 percent, with many crediting this minority vote as the strongest deciding factor in the election.

In conclusion, Republicans are clearly paying the price for relying largely on white population support and ignoring minority interests in shaping their vision and policies. Although Democrats are gaining minority support, they cannot win with minority support alone (that is, without a sizable white population support) because much of the racially

diverse population is not old enough to vote. Thus, both parties have begun to compete much more strongly for the votes of Hispanics, blacks, and Asians rather than relying solely on the traditional mainstream support of whites.

KOMANDURI MURTY AND JIMMY D. MCCAMEY

Further Reading:

File, Thom, and Sarah Crissey. *Current Population Reports: Voting and Registration in Election of November 2008, P20–562RV*. Washington, DC: U.S. Government Printing Office, July 2012. www.census.gov/prod/2010pubs/p20–562.pdf

Milestone Documents. Washington, DC: National Archives and Records Administration, 1995. http://www.ourdocuments.gov/doc.php?flash=true&doc=44.

Novkov, Julie. "Rethinking Race in American Politics." *Political Research Quarterly* 61 (2008): 649–59.

Voting Rights Act of 1965

Despite the Fifteenth and Nineteenth amendments to the U.S. Constitution, which enfranchised black men and women, Southern voter registration boards used poll taxes, literacy tests, and other bureaucratic impediments to deny African Americans their legal right to vote. Southern blacks also risked harassment, intimidation, economic reprisals,

Redistricting

When new census data becomes available every 10 years, the redrawing of voting districts is required under the equal protection clause of the Constitution to assure equal representation of voters living in the districts. The Voting Rights Act of 1965 sought to eliminate discriminatory election processes by declaring in Section 2 that "no voting qualification or prerequisite to voting or standard practice or procedure shall be imposed or applied . . . in a manner which results in a denial or abridgement of the right of any citizen of the United States to vote on account of race or color." This meant that the old tradition of racial gerrymandering, prevalent in the South, could be illegal. No longer could black voters be packed into a particular district or split among districts to dilute their votes. The act also placed districts with a history of voting discrimination under federal supervision for redistricting or any other changes in voting law.

The 1982 amendments to the Voting Rights Act allowed so-called minority-majority districts to be created, which gave concentrated minorities in those districts the power to elect their own candidates. Congress specifically stated, however, that these amendments did not imply proportional representation: that is, there was no intention to legislate a mandate that a minority with 10 percent of the total population should elect 10 percent of the representatives. With these new rules, minority representation in Congress increased dramatically in the 1992 elections.

The laws affecting redistricting remains in flux as cases make their way through the courts. The U.S. Supreme Court has made it clear, however, that drawing districts on the basis of race, any race, is illegal. Yet communities of interest are to be left intact. The Court has also found that drawing district boundaries for purely political reasons, including the reelection of incumbents, is legal.

Benjamin F. Shearer

and physical violence when they tried to register or vote. As a result, until the early 1960s African Americans had little, if any, political power, either locally or nationally. Participants and activists in the civil rights movement, under the guidance of the Rev. Dr. Martin Luther King, Jr. and the Southern Christian Leadership Conference, staged nonviolent demonstrations in Albany, Georgia, and Birmingham, Alabama, partly to protest the systematic disenfranchisement of African Americans.

Adopted on August 6, 1965, the Voting Rights Act was extended in 1970, 1975, and 1982, and is considered the most successful piece of civil rights legislation adopted by the U.S. Congress. The act codified the Fifteenth Amendment's permanent guarantee that no person shall be denied the right to vote on account of race or color. The act contains several special provisions that impose even more stringent requirements on "covered" jurisdictions in certain areas of the country, meaning that no voting changes were legally enforceable until approved by a three-judge court in the District of Columbia or by the attorney general of the United States. The requirement that certain state and local governments obtain federal approval prior to implementing any

changes to their voting procedures is known as "preclearance." This far-reaching statute was a response to the compelling evidence of continuing interference with attempts by African American citizens to exercise their right to vote. The following states (or parts of the state) that are subject to preclearance are Alabama, Mississippi, Alaska, New Hampshire, Arizona, New York, California, North Carolina, South Carolina, Florida, Georgia, South Dakota, Louisiana, Texas, Michigan, and Virginia.

At the time the act was first adopted, only one-third of all African Americans of voting age were on the registration rolls in the specially covered states, while two-thirds of eligible whites were registered. Now black voter registration rates are approaching parity with those of whites in many areas, and Hispanic voters in jurisdictions added in 1975 to the list of those specially covered by the act are not far behind. Enforcement of the act has also increased the opportunity of black and Latino voters to elect representatives of their choice by providing a vehicle for challenging discriminatory election methods, such as racially gerrymandered districting plans or at-large elections that may dilute minority groups' voting strength. Virtually excluded from all public offices in

President Lyndon B. Johnson moves to shake hands with Dr. Martin Luther King, Jr. in the capitol rotunda following the signing of the Voting Rights Act on August 6, 1965. The law was the first national legislation to guarantee all Americans the right to vote. (Yoichi R. Okamoto/Lyndon B. Johnson Library)

Voting Rights Amendments of 1975

In 1975 the U.S. Congress amended the Voting Rights Act of 1965 (sections 4 and 203) to protect the voting rights of citizens of certain ethnic groups whose language is other than English. The amendment was partly the result of the Mexican American Legal Defense and Educational Fund's argument before Congress that English-only elections in Texas had the same effects as the literacy requirements, which were abolished by the 1965 Voting Rights Act. The language provision of the 1975 act was therefore intended to enable members of linguistic minorities—Spanish-speaking groups, American Indians, Asian Americans, and Alaskan Natives—to participate effectively in the electoral process. It required states and political subdivisions to conduct elections in the language of the named minority groups when more than 5 percent (a minimum of 10,000 voters) of the voting-age citizens of a given jurisdiction are members of a single linguistic-minority group, and either the English literacy rate was below the national average or the voter turnout in the last English-only election was less than 50 percent of the voting-age population of that jurisdiction. The act required that written election materials in the language of the minority groups be offered, and for American Indians and Alaskan Natives, whose languages are oral languages only, verbal assistance and publicity. Implementation of the act was left to the state legislatures.

Carmenza Gallo

the South in 1965, black and Hispanic voters are now substantially represented in the state legislatures and local governing bodies throughout the region.

The 1965 Voting Rights Act serves as a cornerstone piece of legislation that ensures all racial minorities have fair access to casting a ballot and fair opportunities for their votes to be meaningful. This law also protects the voting rights of many people who have limited English-language proficiency. Section 203 of the Voting Rights Act protects the voting rights of linguistic-minority groups by requiring that particular jurisdictions print ballots and other election materials in the minority language as well as in English and provide oral translation at the polls.

TARRY HUM

See also

Voter ID Requirements; Voting and Race

Further Reading:

Asian American Legal Defense and Education Fund. "Asian American Access to Democracy in the 2002 Elections in New York City." 2003.

W

Wages of Whiteness, The

For whiteness studies, David R. Roediger's *The Wages of Whiteness: Race and the Making of the American Working Class* serves as a canonical text for the critical interrogation of white supremacy. Roediger (2007) details how white workers of antebellum America psychologically, culturally, and discursively negotiated the "fear of dependency on wage labor," the discipline required of wage laborers in a burgeoning capitalistic economy, and the republican ideologies of masculine independence and freedom by constructing identities based on their whiteness. Previous Marxist scholarship discussing the intersections of race and class presented oversimplified conceptualizations of racial identity and privilege by describing them as an effect of economic conditions. Privileging class, traditional Marxist analyses failed not only to account for the dynamic interrelation of class and race but also to acknowledge the agency of laborers in constructing racial identities and sustaining racism.

Roediger (2007) works against traditional Marxist analyses by blending neo-Marxism, psychoanalytic theory, and social-constructionist theories of language to describe the development of whiteness as a racial identity in 19th-century America. Such work disciplined white laborers, demanding great physical and psychological sacrifice. Wage dependence and labor discipline, though, acutely contradicted the ideals of republican independence and freedom that had permeated American consciousness since the American Revolution, a dependence that engendered uncomfortable comparisons to the supposedly morally degenerate lives of slaves and freed African Americans. To reconcile the reality of wage dependence with their republican ideals, lessen their anxiety, and reject comparisons to slaves and freed African Americans, white laborers engaged in a parasitic relationship, projecting onto slaves and freed African Americans white anxieties that defined them "as embodying the preindustrial, erotic, careless style of life [that] white worker[s] hated and longed for" and developing a white racial identity in contradistinction to a degraded, darker "other" (Roediger 2007: 14). White laborers could rest assured that although they may work for wages and internalize industrial discipline, at least "they belonged to the ranks of 'free white labor'" (Roediger 2007: 47).

To demonstrate his argument, Roediger (2007) presents Irish-American laborers as a paradigmatic case of white racial formation. Initially, Irish emigrants, popularly described as sordid and simian, were considered a racial corollary to African Americans. Many particularly nationalistic 19th-century whites conflated the Irish with African Americans, believing that an "Irishman was a 'nigger,' inside out" (133). The similarities between the two groups made comparisons inevitable. Both groups experienced commensurate economic privation and social alienation, living contiguously in the squalor of the slums. Instead of nurturing solidarity

Reviews of *Wages of Whiteness*

Wages of Whiteness has earned overwhelmingly positive reviews from reviewers, winning the Merle Curti Award from the Organization of American Historians for the best book discussing American social history. Nevertheless, some reviewers note that the text needs a more comprehensive discussion of the conflation of race and slavery and their relation to the formation of whiteness; accepts too willingly the dichotomy between preindustrial and industrial work; requires discussion of the white working class of the antebellum South; and fails to account for the formation of working-class blackness. Other scholars critique *Wages of Whiteness* for insufficiently discussing the influence of gender and sexuality in the formation of white racial formation. Two particularly insightful critiques permeating several reviews are that Roediger fails to provide a solution for challenging white supremacy and leaves no opportunities for labor to serve as a driving force in contesting inequitable racial relations and facilitating social change. As a result, some reviewers consider the book unduly pessimistic and depressing.

with African Americans, however, the Irish working class conceptualized their struggles with emigration, poverty, and the anxiety wrought by industrial capitalism against them, developing a particularly virulent form of racism. The vast number of Irish emigrants afforded them political capital, especially with pro-slavery Democrats, which they leveraged to define themselves as white and marshal whiteness for economic and political gain. Seeking to gain political power, Democrats courted Irish Catholics by offering them protection from anti-Irish movements, political participation, and acceptance of their nascent whiteness in exchange for their votes, a partnership that "gave birth to new ideologies stressing the importance of whiteness" (Roediger 2007: 141).

Roediger (2007) also diligently describes the cultural and ideological components of white racial formation, analyzing racially coded entertainment, like minstrel shows, and popular discourse. For instance, Roediger details the emergence of semantically loaded words used to distinguish between the supposed "free labor" of white workers and that of slaves and to construct whiteness and simultaneously differentiate it from blackness. For Roediger, the semantic shifts of words, like "coon," "boss," "help," "hired man," "freeman," to take on racially coded meanings demonstrates the discursive construction of whiteness in the language of labor. Moreover, Roediger's insightful analysis of the psychological and cultural import and purpose of blackface festivals and minstrel shows details how white laborers negotiated the anxiety wrought by the ascetic routines and abstemious life demanded by industrial capitalism. Blackface festivals and minstrel shows provided an opportunity for white laborers to act black, projecting onto African Americans the preindustrial gratifications that an industrial morality rejected while simultaneously experiencing those gratifications. Donning blackface, white laborers could parody industrial morality, attribute the dissipation of preindustrial gratifications to African Americans, and construct whiteness based on the new, racially coded industrial conventions. The proliferation and popularity of blackface minstrel shows speaks to their essential role in the cultural, ideological, and psychological formation of working-class whiteness against the touchtone of a fabricated blackness. Undoubtedly, in its third edition, Roediger's text remains a must-read for anyone studying the formation of white racial identities.

NICHOLAS N. BEHM

See also

Third Wave Whiteness; Whiteness Studies; White Privilege

Further Reading:

Allen, Theodore W. "On Roediger's *Wages of Whiteness*." 2002. http://clogic.eserver.org/4–2/allen.html#note14 (accessed December 5, 2012).

Bernstein, Iver. "*The Wages of Whiteness*: Race and the Making of the American Working Class by David Roediger." *Journal of American History* 79, no. 2 (1992): 1120–21.

Brody, David. "*The Wages of Whiteness: Race and the Making of the American Working Class* by David Roediger." *Journal of Interdisciplinary History* 24, no. 2 (1993): 378–80.

Glickman, Lawrence B. "I'm All White, Jack." *The Nation*, February 17, 1992, 207–9.

Holt, Thomas C. "*The Wages of Whiteness: Race and the Making of the American Working Class* by David Roediger; *The Rise and Fall of the White Republic: Class Politics and Mass Culture in Nineteenth-Century America* by Alexander Saxton." *International Labor and Working-Class History* 45 (1994): 86–95.

Ignatiev, Noel. "*The Rise and Fall of the White Republic: Class Politics and Mass Culture in Nineteenth-Century America* by Alexander Saxton; *The Wages of Whiteness: Race and the Making of the American Working Class* by David Roediger." *Labour/Le Travail* 30 (1992): 233–40.

Roediger, David R. *The Wages of Whiteness: Race and the Making of the American Working Class.* London: Verso, 2007.

Wallace, George (1919–1998)

George Corley Wallace was an Alabama governor who fought desegregation efforts during the 1960s. Wallace was born in Clio, Alabama, on August 25, 1919. As a child, Wallace expressed a great desire to involve himself in politics, seeing it as a way to help him, and others, out of poverty. After receiving an undergraduate degree from the University of Alabama, he enrolled in law school. Shortly after graduation, he was called to serve his country in the Army Air Corps during World War II. Almost immediately upon his return from the Pacific theater, he began a long career of public service. He served as a circuit judge, and later, he served in the Alabama House of Representatives. Wallace initially took a progressive stand on issues of civil rights and integration in particular. This changed dramatically after he lost a gubernatorial election in 1958 to a candidate who took a stronger stand against integration. Wallace blamed his loss on his moderate stand on civil rights issues.

Wallace first gained national attention when he physically stood in the doorway of the building where students at the University of Alabama registered for classes. His intention was to fulfill a campaign promise to physically prevent African American students from registering for classes at an all-white school. While the stand was largely symbolic and completely ineffective in preventing his goal of preserving segregation, this scene was displayed to a national audience by way of network television. This event propelled his political career that would span two decades as an elected official.

During this time in office, he campaigned against the expansion of integration. He regularly spoke against integration and used his position as governor to slow the progress of integration and impede the spread of civil rights for African Americans. He served as Alabama governor for four terms, 1963 to 1967, 1971 to 1975, 1975 to 1979, and 1983 to 1987.

He was a presidential candidate for the Democratic Party in 1964, 1972, and 1976. He also ran as an independent in 1968. During Wallace's first term as governor, an Alabama governor could not succeed himself. After a failed attempt to eliminate this restriction, he convinced his wife, Lurleen, to run for governor. She succeeded and was governor from 1967 until her death in May 1968. Having his wife in office enabled him to continue to influence Alabama's state government and provided a base of support for his campaign for president through his American Independent Party. Although he won the electoral votes of several Southern states, he came up short in his presidential bid. After his reelection to the Alabama governorship in 1970, he began his third attempt to run for the presidency. This time, he ran for president as a Democrat. After a respectable showing in early primaries, he was shot by a gunman while campaigning at a shopping mall in Maryland. One of the bullets lodged near his spinal cord and left him paralyzed from the waist down. This injury effectively ended his presidential campaign and any future hopes of becoming president. After an easy reelection as Alabama's governor in 1974, he attempted his fourth and final run for the presidency. After weak showings in early primaries, he withdrew from the race. He mounted his final gubernatorial campaign in 1982. Once again, he was successful. He decided not to run for reelection in 1986, citing complications from injuries stemming from the gunshot wounds, which took a toll on his health.

After his retirement from public service, Wallace spent a great amount of time apologizing for his actions and words that caused so much harm to so many people. He visited with many of the leaders of the civil rights era and other elected African Americans for the purpose of asking their forgiveness.

Many of his former adversaries publicly forgave Wallace for his actions and stated he had a changed heart. Wallace died of heart failure on September 13, 1998.

JAMES NEWMAN

See also
Segregation

Further Reading:
Carter, Dan T. *The Politics of Rage.* New York: Simon and Schuster, 1995.

Lesher, Stephan. *George Wallace: American Populist.* Reading, MA: Addison-Wesley, 1994.

McMillen, Neil R. *The Citizens' Council: Organized Resistance to the Second Reconstruction, 1954–64.* Urbana: University of Illinois Press, 1971.

Rohler, Lloyd. *George Wallace: Conservative Populist.* Westport, CT: Greenwood Press, 2004.

War and Racial Inequality

Minorities have fought in all the wars of the United States. During the Revolutionary War, about 5,000 African Americans fought for American independence. During the War of 1812, blacks served in the U.S. Navy as well as in both mixed and segregated regiments in the U.S. Army. During the Mexican-American War, numerous free blacks answered the call of Congress for 50,000 volunteers. After Congress permitted black recruits into the military in 1862 and the Emancipation Proclamation took effect on January 1, 1863, the War Department created the Bureau of Colored Troops. The bureau developed 149 segregated units commanded by white officers, many of whom were unenthusiastic about leading armed blacks into battle. About 186,000 blacks served in the army, and another 30,000 in the navy, during the Civil War. When the war ended, Congress institutionalized segregated military units when it authorized the all-black 9th and 10th Cavalry, which became known as the Buffalo Soldiers, and the 24th and 25th Infantry.

Maintaining a standing army was a long-held American fear stemming from Revolutionary War days. Thus, when war came on the horizon, the government scurried to put military forces together, and the issue of race became secondary to recruitment. That remained so after the Civil War. A total of 10,000 blacks volunteered in army service during the Spanish-American War, and 404,000 blacks served in the army during World War I, almost 11 percent of the total force and separately recruited from whites. Curiously, however, the navy remained an integrated force up until 1900. The prevailing belief among military leaders was that with white direction, all-black units could work effectively, even though many blacks were assigned to menial tasks.

The Selective Service Act of 1940 took the factor of race out of military recruitment in law, but not in practice. President Franklin D. Roosevelt resisted the entreaties of civil rights leaders to integrate the military, although some progress was made in improving the assignments of black soldiers. During World War II, 1 million blacks served in the military, mostly in the army, but 145,000 served in the U.S. Air Force and another 150,000 in the navy. In 1942, the U.S. Marines permitted its first black recruit. The military forces remained segregated until President Harry S. Truman required their integration on July 26, 1948, in Executive Order 9981. By the end of 1954, 300 all-black units had been integrated into the services, and the legacy of a physically segregated military ended.

Integration came to be seen as a military imperative that would assure combat readiness and efficiency. During the Korean War, military planners discovered that integrated forces resulted in significant efficiencies because the race element was eliminated from the tasks of procurement, assignment, and training. Race came to be seen as another factor in every equation that simply produced more work rather than better work. Training, for example, could be more effective if based on individual talent rather than race. Yet in the time up to and including the Vietnam War, the military services found themselves embroiled in racial problems that nearly brought them to a standstill. Racial violence among military personnel became commonplace. White officers were for the most part unaware of black issues and tended to perceive dissatisfaction as disrespect.

Among the many hard-learned lessons of Vietnam was that racism was so powerful as to render a fighting force useless. If commanders could not communicate with their troops and vice versa, if respect on both sides was completely lacking, the enemy was within. Indeed, it became very clear that racism remained in the integrated military. In the early days of the Vietnam War, black combat deaths had mounted to more than 20 percent of all casualties, nearly twice the percentage of black youths in the total U.S. population. This prompted President Lyndon B. Johnson, at the behest of civil rights leaders, to decrease the number of blacks in combat. Yet by the end of the war, the casualties of black enlisted men were still over 14 percent of all casualties. Data on Latinos was not maintained.

The full integration of the military forces would never be possible until all the vestiges of racism in the form of white supremacy were removed. Excessive minority casualties could not be avoided, and battle-ready, effective fighting forces achieved, without opening up the officer ranks to minorities. When the all-volunteer force came into being in 1973, only 2.8 percent of all military officers were black. Twenty years later, about 19 percent of active military officers were minorities: 8.8 percent black, 4 percent Hispanic, 3.2 percent Asian-American, and 0.6 percent Native-American. Yet the minorities made up nearly 40 percent of all enlisted personnel: 21.7 percent black, 9.6 percent Hispanic, 4 percent Asian American, and 1.2 percent Native American.

Beliefs in racial inequality formed American experience in war. Who would lead, who would follow, who would die: all were determined in part by beliefs tainted with racism. Abolitionist Frederick Douglass urged blacks to enter into military service during the Civil War because he thought that fighting for the Union would bring all the benefits of full citizenship to them. He could not have imagined that he spoke more than a hundred years too soon.

BENJAMIN F. SHEARER

See also
Cold War; Mexican American War; World War I; World War II

Further Reading:
Buckley, Gail Lumet. *American Patriots: The Story of Blacks in the Military from the Revolution to Desert Storm*. New York: Random House, 2001.
Moskos, Charles C., and John Sibley Butler. *All That We Can Be: Black Leadership and Racial Integration the Army Way*. New York: Basic Books, 1996.

War on Poverty and the Great Society

In the early 1960s, President John F. Kennedy brought new attention and energy to America's social problems, particularly poverty. In 1962, Michael Harrington's influential book *The Other America*, which detailed the prevalence of poverty in affluent America, was published and caught the attention of President Kennedy and other politicians. Harrington's accessible and persuasive book helped to popularize the movement to end poverty in the United States. Kennedy initially looked toward improved social work as the best

method for eliminating poverty. He hoped that strong social services could help poor families make better choices and improve their lives. But Kennedy quickly changed his views on the causes of poverty and began to understand poverty as a social and structural problem rather than a problem of individual pathology.

After President Kennedy was assassinated, Lyndon B. Johnson increased the policy emphasis on structural opportunities in the War on Poverty and Great Society programs. On March 16, 1964, Johnson proposed to begin a "war on poverty." One of the hallmarks of the War on Poverty was its ambitious attempt to end poverty by creating a more just society. The central legislation of this proposal was the Economic Opportunity Act of 1964. The antipoverty programs of the 1960s were far more complex than those of the New Deal. They aimed, in President Johnson's words, "at the causes, not just the consequences of poverty." Johnson wanted to create new opportunities for whole groups of people who had formerly been left out of many mainstream social and economic opportunities. The Great Society programs were extremely ambitious. They attempted to increase job opportunities and education for the young and to empower the disenfranchised.

Social-science research had played a significant role in motivating the War on Poverty. In addition to Harrington, economist Robert Lampman provided evidence that economic growth was no longer affecting poverty as it once had. This seemed to suggest that the poor were becoming detached from the larger American society. Sociologist Leonard Cottrell brought his research on the ecology of neighborhoods to the discussions of community development as a solution to poverty. Sociologists Lloyd Ohlin and Richard Cloward developed sophisticated structural models to explain poverty and delinquency and to identify target areas for government reform. Before this awakening of interest in poverty, there had been remarkably little government or academic research on the subject. In the early 1960s, a comprehensive bibliography on poverty did not fill two typewritten pages. The first official statistics on poverty in the United States were not released until 1965.

What happened to the war on poverty and the ambitions of the great society is controversial. One argument is that the war in Vietnam took attention and resources away from the war on poverty. Undoubtedly, there is truth in this argument. The war and the social changes of the late 1960s changed the political context. In the early 1960s, Harrington's argument that poverty was pulling people away from an otherwise cohesive society had resonance. The United States seemed affluent and stable. It did not seem unreasonably ambitious to think that it could solve the problem of poverty. By the late 1960s, the Vietnam War, race riots, and social unrest drained away the focus and ambition of the War on Poverty.

Other factors have also been noted for the failure of the War on Poverty. Many of the ambitious programs were never fully funded or permitted to develop. It was also hard to measure the successes of the programs. Since the programs aimed not only to reduce poverty but also to create a more just and equitable society, it was difficult to produce evidence of their success. Arguably, racial tensions also undermined support for the programs among white Americans. The themes of empowerment and community participation were perhaps more threatening in the volatile context of racial politics in the late 1960s. Some conservative critics have argued that the premise of the War on Poverty was misguided. The state, they argue, cannot reduce poverty by creating government programs.

Since the 1960s, Americans have become skeptical about the positive impact that government can have on poverty. Welfare reform in 1996 was largely premised on the idea that the less involved government was in poor families' lives, the better off they would be. Nonetheless, there have been some clear successes in reducing poverty in the United States. Most notably, before the Social Security system was established, the elderly were among the poorest Americans. Now they are among the most affluent. The War on Poverty and the Great Society programs represent a brief moment of optimism that researchers and government could create a partnership to improve society and eliminate, or at least reduce, poverty. Whether those ambitions could have been achieved with a greater social commitment remains an open question.

ROBIN ROGER-DILLON

Further Reading:
Aaron, Henry J. *Politics and the Professors*. Washington, DC: Brookings Institution Press, 1978.
Harrington, Michael. *The Other America*. Baltimore: Penguin, 1981.

Patterson, James. *America's Struggle against Poverty*. Cambridge, MA: Harvard University Press, 1986.

Waring, J. Waties (1880–1968)

Julius Waties Waring was a federal judge appointed to the Eastern District of South Carolina on January 26, 1942. Nominated by U.S. senator Ellison DuRant ("Cotton Ed") Smith, a white supremacist, Waring was the son of a Confederate war veteran, and for most of his long life he moved in the exclusive circles of the Charleston Club, the St. Cecilia Society, and the Charleston Light Dragoons.

Waring graduated with honors from the College of Charleston in 1900, and passed the bar two years later. In 1913, he married socialite Annie Gammell, and they had one daughter, Anne. In 1920, he established the Waring and Brockinton law firm, became active in South Carolina's white Democratic Party politics, and in 1931 was appointed city attorney for Mayor Burnett Maybank's administration. Maybank later became governor (1939–1941) and ultimately a U.S. senator (1941–1954). By 1938, Waring had advanced in the Democratic Party to Charleston's point man for Cotton Ed Smith's senatorial campaign.

During his first two years on the federal bench, Waring functioned as a traditional and rather unremarkable jurist, but in 1945, he began to question Southern mores. That year, Viola Duvall filed a class action suit on behalf of Charleston's black teachers, who earned substantially less than the city's white teachers. National Association for the Advancement of Colored People (NAACP) attorney Thurgood Marshall presented the case, and Waring ruled that if black teachers could offer educational credentials comparable to white teachers, they were entitled to receive comparable pay.

In 1946, Waring divorced his wife of 32 years and married Elizabeth Avery Mills Hoffman, a Northern divorcée and outspoken critic of segregation. When the judge subsequently demanded that black men and women be addressed as Mr., Miss, or Mrs. in his court, abolished segregated jury seating, and appointed a black bailiff, many of his old friends blamed Elizabeth Waring for turning him against the Southern way of life. He insisted, however, that "when you're practicing law you're representing a particular interest [but] . . .

when you're on the bench you're not interested in who wins the case. You're interested in seeing the case handled justly and right."

Gradually, the Warings became almost completely ostracized by Charleston's white society, and the judge was no longer welcome at St. Cecelia Society Balls or in the private clubs that he had frequented for over 40 years. Former friends insisted that they had abandoned him because of his scandalous divorce rather than for his new ideas about racial justice.

In the summer of 1946, Waring presided in a suit brought against a white South Carolina police officer by black army veteran Isaac Woodward. After his discharge from the army at Fort Benning, Georgia, Woodward had boarded a bus for North Carolina. At the first rest stop, he and the driver argued about how much time the soldier had taken. The police were called and Woodward was charged with drunk and disorderly conduct. When he denied being drunk, the arresting officer beat him so severely that both his corneas were destroyed and he was permanently blinded. The officer's defense was that he believed Woodward had tried to take his gun. Since there were no witnesses, the jury refused to convict. Waring described both the U.S. attorney's defense of Woodward and the jury's verdict as "disgraceful."

That October, George Elmore, black manager of the Waverly Five and Dime in Columbia, South Carolina, was denied a ballot for the Democratic primary at Richland County's Ward Ninth Precinct. Again, the NAACP brought suit, this time to challenge the constitutionality of the white primary. As the Democratic Party was the only party in the state, voting in the primary was more important than voting in the general election, since whoever won the primary won the election. Denying blacks access to the primary effectively denied them voting rights. Thurgood Marshall argued *Elmore v. Rice* before Judge Waring on February 21, 1947, and on July 12, Waring ruled that South Carolina's Democratic Party could not legally exclude qualified blacks from voting in primary elections, a decision that was upheld on appeal by the U.S. Supreme Court. When Democratic Party officials attempted to evade his ruling by requiring that all registered voters swear allegiance to separation of the races, Waring threatened to hold the county chairs in contempt and either fine or imprison them. They backed down, and the votes of 35,000 South Carolina blacks counted that year.

Waring became one of the most hated men in the white South. Several attempts were made to impeach him, since federal judgeships are lifetime appointments, but he was never removed.

Waties and Elizabeth Waring scandalized their neighbors by entertaining blacks in their Charleston home, and she outraged the community when, in a 1949 presentation at the city's black YWCA, she referred to segregationists as "sick, confused, and decadent people." Her address was widely reported in the national press. Both Warings believed that Southern white moderates were more destructive to the cause of black civil rights than virulent segregationists, since moderates maintained that segregation and reform could coexist. Waring knew that was impossible. Southern moderates, and even those who considered themselves liberals, subscribed to what he called "the false god of gradualism." Waring knew that voluntary desegregation was a Southern pipe dream, and he became a strong advocate of federal intervention to abolish legal segregation.

Early in 1950, Joseph Armstrong DeLaine, the black principal of Silver School in Summerton, South Carolina, sued the Clarendon County School District to provide bus transportation for black pupils as it did for whites. Once again, Thurgood Marshall presented the case before Judge Waring, who assured the NAACP attorney that he was wasting the NAACP Legal Defense Fund's time and money in suing to force school districts to fund dual education systems. Waring suggested that Marshall withdraw the suit and refile a class action challenging the constitutionality of segregated schools. Marshall took his advice and, on May 28, 1951, argued *Briggs v. Elliott* before a panel of three federal judges, including George Bell Timmerman, a segregationist; John Parker, a moderate; and Waring. As expected, the NAACP lost the decision, but in a scathing dissent, Waring declared that the 1896 *Plessy v. Ferguson* decision that established the principle of "separate but equal" accommodations based on race was unconstitutional. Anticipating the Warren Court's historic 1954 decision, Waring argued that separate educational facilities were inherently unequal. Appealed all the way to the U.S. Supreme Court, *Briggs v. Elliott* became one of the four cases heard in *Brown v. Board of Education*, and although the Warren Court never cited his dissent, *Briggs* is perhaps Judge Waring's greatest contribution to American judicial history.

Waring retired in 1952, and he and his wife moved to New York City, where they were active in a variety of civil rights organizations. To the end of his life, the judge supported the use of aggressive federal intervention to break the back of racial segregation. He died on January 20, 1968, and Elizabeth Waring died a few months later. Both are buried in Charleston's Magnolia Cemetery.

Mary Stanton

See also

National Association for the Advancement of Colored People (NAACP)

Further Reading:

Brown, Cynthia Stokes. *Refusing Racism: White Allies in the Struggle for Civil Rights.* New York: Teachers College Press, 2002.

Southern, David W. "Beyond Jim Crow Liberalism, Judge Waring's Fight against Segregation in South Carolina 1942–52." *Journal of Negro History* 66 (Autumn 1981): 209–27.

Yarbrough, Tinsley E. *A Passion for Justice: J. Waties Waring and Civil Rights.* New York: Oxford University Press, 1987.

Washington, Booker T. (1858–1915)

African American leader Booker Taliaferro Washington was born into slavery in a slave cabin on a Virginia tobacco plantation to a white father who he did not know and a slave mother who could not read or write. His mother taught him lessons in thrift and virtue. These lessons, in addition to the slave code of ethics, in which it was acceptable to steal from those who enslaved you, would prove useful to Washington throughout his life. After the Emancipation Proclamation was signed, he and his family moved to West Virginia. As a young man, he learned of the Hampton Institute and, on October 1, 1872, began his journey to Hampton, Virginia. He completed this journey, by foot and by railroad. Part of Washington's entrance requirements to Hampton Institute included sweeping the auditorium. He cleaned the auditorium more than once, which is a testament to Washington's diligence, hard work, and personal development.

While Washington had his challengers, he also served as an inspiration to many around the world. His approach has been criticized and dismissed for more overt displays of racial protest and petition for social change. Washington was called "the great accommodator" by W.E.B. Du Bois and has even been called an "Uncle Tom" for being too compromising with whites and for going so far as telling jokes in black dialect to white audiences. Washington's accommodating stance and compromise with whites can be understood within the context of the Jim Crow South, his Tuskegee project, and his demands for blacks' individual and economic development.

Washington wanted blacks to be self-sufficient but to understand the collective struggle. He pushed for advancement despite oppression and was very devoted and committed to his efforts, despite the overt and more covert obstacles that he faced. Washington believed that both blacks and whites were responsible for making blacks productive and valuable to America's industrial growth. This great compromise was achieved through soliciting the support of whites while urging blacks not to agitate whites or challenge the status quo in demand of civil rights. Washington also called for blacks to forego social parity with whites in favor of greater economic development, and he felt it was possible to be segregated from whites but for there to still be economic ties to whites. He accomplished this by gaining middle- and upper-class whites' economic support for the Tuskegee Institute.

Washington wanted to change black America from all angles and did not believe that blacks would forever be second-class citizens. He believed that there were contexts in which blacks would be advanced and have educational and economic opportunities. Washington, therefore, asked blacks to reflect on the accomplishments since the Emancipation Proclamation and how much more can be accomplished if blacks work together and form an economic base for self-sufficiency. This self-sufficiency would also make blacks and whites economically interdependent, rather than blacks being solely dependent on whites, and allow blacks to be prepared for their full citizenship rights and integration in American society.

With integration and assimilation in American society, Washington pushed for blacks to advance but not to isolate themselves socially by servicing blacks only or only supporting businesses because they were black-owned. Washington's challenge to blacks was to maintain an individual will through which the collective will can be mobilized and realized. Individual will included skill attainment, higher education when attainable, sobriety, and devoutness.

Booker T. Washington on African American Citizenship

On December 20, 1901, Booker T. Washington appealed to a predominantly white audience at the Outlook Club in Montclair, New Jersey, to focus on the economic security of African Americans, not deportation.

Booker T. Washington addressed the Outlook Club here to-night, and pleased a big audience, who applauded heartily his remarks. His subject was "The Citizenship of the American Negro."

Among other things he said, that there were over 9,000,000 colored people in the United States, and that the way to solve the negro problem is not by deporting the negroes.

"When 600 started for Liberia some time ago some people thought the question had been solved, but 600 black babies were born the next day. Deportation won't work.

"You can't set apart land for the Negroes and wall them in. One wall would not keep the Negroes in, and five walls would not keep the white men out. You can't absorb them, for the minute you get 1 percent of black blood in a white man, he becomes a negro. Nor are there any signs or indications of decay in the race."

The speaker said that with the different colored persons included in our new possessions, altogether over 18,000,000, he thought that the white man had a big problem before him. The speaker recommended as one solution of the problem that the white man make the negro more useful, and help him to secure an education. The negro candidly responds to stimulating influences. The speaker compared two parts of Alabama, one where instruction had been given the negroes and another where dense ignorance prevailed—and showed that intelligence and education had brought in their track land ownership, prosperity, and higher morality.

"The material or industrial betterment of a people," he said, "always improves their morality. Dependence upon law alone will not accomplish everything. Through sympathy, active help, and financial assistance the white people can do much for the negro. The problem will not [go] down till settled in justice and righteousness."

Source: "Citizenship of the Negro: B. T. Washington Tells Montclair People that Education and Kindness Will Solve the Problem," *New York Times*, December 21, 1901.

Washington was greatly inspired by abolitionist Frederick Douglass because Douglass was also born into slavery and learned and understood the virtues of being self-made and focusing on individual development. Douglass argued that blacks failed to attain a skill base and this failure is the foundation for the "Negro problem." Douglass, therefore, was an advocate of blacks learning a trade so that they can gain parity with whites and have greater opportunities. In agreement with this sentiment, Washington thought that earning a dollar through a trade was worth more than the opportunity to spend a dollar in white establishments. Industrial education was deemed a necessity by Washington, whereas higher education was an option, not a priority. Washington knew that the majority of blacks would not have access to higher education, although Washington's own children did.

Washington and Douglass both believed that the South was the best place for blacks, that blacks should not move to the North, and that blacks should accumulate wealth in order to be more self-sufficient and have greater opportunities. Both Washington and Douglass also compared the potential for the development and advancement of blacks with the realized development and advancement of Jews. The Jews were admired for their pride, their unity, and their success upon assimilation, despite obstacles. Instead of complaining, blacks should have individual motivation and advancement so that they can advance as a people and actually contribute to society. The importance of learning a trade and the belief that blacks were to blame for the "Negro problem" was deemed simplistic in its logic by the critics of both Douglass and Washington because economic development was not *the* solution to the "Negro problem."

Washington and Douglass differed in that Washington placed greater emphasis on the individual accountability, self-sufficiency, and self-reliance components of Douglass's message whereas Douglass's overall message was more militant. In his militancy, Douglass maintained an assimilation stance without mocking blacks and making jokes about black dialect in front of white audiences. Douglass was often critical of whites' acts of oppression and partially attributed the conditions of blacks to this oppression. Unlike Washington, Douglass did not make jokes about blacks in front of whites or appear to go too far in his attempts at assimilating. Washington criticized this militancy because it had generally lost its effectiveness. Political and social agitation did not have a substantial grounding in economic development. However, Douglass did not live in the South and, despite the obstacles that Northern blacks faced, could afford to take a more militant approach.

Washington and Du Bois are often presented as adversaries with contrasting and conflicting views; however, they shared the ultimate objective, but differed mostly in strategy. Washington was similar to Du Bois in that he was committed to social change and social action and used various institutions to bring about such change, including the Tuskegee Institute and the National Negro Business League. He did not openly discuss all of his affiliations and strategies for change but rather covertly fought for change. Washington knew that change was a process.

Among Du Bois's criticisms of Washington was that his advice was sought by presidents, politicians, philanthropists, and scholars, and that he was made into the Negro representative. Washington's appointment as the Negro representative was seen as a contradiction to the funding and support whites provided to Washington's Tuskegee Institute. This created the image that Washington's interests and efforts were not purely in the interests of Negroes but were, instead, greatly influenced by whites. Whites supported Tuskegee and upheld him as the only valued black leader as long as he advocated segregation. Washington solicited this support of middle- and upper-class whites to back Tuskegee financially and to keep lower-class whites from interfering with Washington's efforts.

To understand Washington's stance, he must be placed within the context of the Jim Crow South, just as to understand Du Bois's and Douglass's approaches, they must be placed in the more Northern contexts in which they lived. Northern blacks faced inequality but in a different type of an environment, and were more educated, economically independent, and critical. Washington's approach of entrepreneurship and thriftiness appealed to Northern blacks.

However Northern blacks did not support Washington's belief that there can and should be protest without the appearance of protest and that fights for civil and political rights should be abandoned in favor of individual and economic development. He felt as though Du Bois and others were showing whites "their hands" rather than focusing on silent protest that would result in the development and true advancement of the Negro. The Tuskegee Institute was one example of slow change and long-term investment for a larger goal. In the Jim Crow South, revolt and overt protest would have resulted in Washington being lynched and the struggle being lost.

Washington's efforts had been overshadowed and largely overlooked while Du Bois's and his counterparts' efforts of desegregation and social justice were advanced. Washington's platform appealed to blacks' needs and urged blacks to forego their more immediate wants. As a result of the increased unpopularity of Washington's approach in favor of the approach of Du Bois and his counterparts, there continued to be a shortage of black entrepreneurs, and blacks' consumerism and dependency on whites increased with desegregation and an increase in voting and civil rights. Therefore, the efforts of Du Bois and his counterparts were successful in the short term, but blacks failed to become more self-sufficient as Washington envisioned. Washington's message is not completely lost because he continues to serve as a motivation and challenge to black entrepreneurs and blacks who are concerned with individual and collective moral and economic development.

RUTLEDGE M. DENNIS

See also

Du Bois, W.E.B.; Jim Crow Laws

Further Reading:

Adegbalola, Gaye Todd. "Interviews: Garvey, Du Bois, and Booker T." *Black Books Bulletin* 3 (Spring 1975).

Brock, Randall E. "Cast Down Your Buckets Where You Are." *Crisis* 99 (1992): 2.

Burns, Haywood. *Afro American Studies: An Interdisciplinary Journal* 1, no. 1 (May 1970).

Champion, Danny. "Booker T. Washington versus W.E.B. Du Bois: A Study in Rhetorical Contrasts." In *Oratory in the New South*, edited by Waldo W. Braden. Baton Rouge: Louisiana State University Press, 1979.

Cunnigen, Donald, Rutledge M. Dennis, and Myrtle Gonza Glascoe, eds. *Research in Race and Ethnic Relations*, vol. 13,

The Racial Politics of Booker T. Washington, 105–31. Oxford: JAI Press, 2006.

Flynn, John P. "Booker T. Washington: Uncle Tom or Wooden House." *Journal of Negro History* 54 (July 1969).

Hancock, Gordon B. "Booker T. Washington: His Defense and Vindication." *Negro Digest* 13, no. 7 (May 1964).

Harlan, Louis R. "Booker T. Washington in Biographical Perspective." *American Historical Review* 75 (1970): 1581–99.

Washington, Booker T. *Up from Slavery*. Garden City, NY: Doubleday, 1900.

Washington (D.C.) Riot of 1919

The five-day rioting in Washington, D.C., started on July 19, 1919, when a mob of several hundred off-duty white soldiers, sailors, and marines entered a black residential area to avenge the jostling of a white woman by two black men the night before. The jostled woman was described in some accounts as a sailor's wife, but was identified in the *New York Times* as Mrs. Elsie Stephnick, wife of an employee of the U.S. Naval Aviation Department, who had been on her way home from the Bureau of Printing and Engraving. The white mob assaulted several black people and vandalized the home of a black family. The next night, white mobs again rampaged, doing even more damage. Several black people were attacked by soldiers at 15th Street and New York Avenue, NW. The third night, July 21, the tide turned, and blacks attacked whites and police. Black men in automobiles drove around the city shooting.

Key officials serving at the time were Chief of Police Major Pullman; Secretary of War Baker; Chief of Staff General March; Marine Corps Commandant Major General Barnett; and Navy Secretary Josephus Daniels. Maj. Gen. William G. Haan commanded 1,000 soldiers, marines, and cavalrymen to bring order. Although it was confirmed that uniformed troops had participated in the riots, General Haan attributed that to the large number of recently discharged soldiers in the area, and he was sure that no active-duty soldiers participated. With the perpetrators and the peacemakers wearing the same uniforms, stopping the riots was a complicated endeavor.

The rioting ended after four people had been killed, as many as 30 people were hospitalized, and finally, a powerful thunderstorm broke over the city, sending the rioters indoors. Dead were Detective Sergeant Harry Wilson and Kenneth Crall, both white, and Randall Neal and Thomas Armstrong, black. Some of the worst fighting had been at Seventh and T Streets in the black neighborhood, where police and soldiers confronted a large group of black rioters. During the fighting, black women stationed at windows and on rooftops threw bottles and other projectiles at the authorities.

Shortly after the turn of the century, social attitudes in Washington, D.C., had begun to change toward black residents. The city essentially became more Southern, adopting Jim Crow policies and gradually eliminating black employees and members from the government and organizations. This strengthening of the racial divide flourished under the Wilson administration. Washington, D.C.'s black leadership reacted with a militant stance, achieving a first step in January 1919, when District Commissioner Brownlow established an all-black platoon in the fire department, ensuring promotions for the department's black veterans. This act, and the activism behind it, may have been a factor in the riots.

George E. Haynes, sociologist and founder of the Urban League, was the director of the Division of Negro Economics in the U.S. Department of Labor at the time. Haynes's article "Race Riots in Relation to Democracy" (1919) named four factors at work behind the rioting. Two factors were the new black militancy and the growing separation and antagonism between the races. A third was that the United States had become a world power, so U.S. race relations would now reflect on international relations, particularly regarding nations of color. Finally, the sensational journalism preceding the violence promoted and stoked the fear of black crime, providing the primary motivating undercurrent.

James Weldon Johnson agreed, and met with the city editor of the *Washington Post* to explain to him how the *Post* and the other daily newspapers were responsible. The city editor "stood as one struck dumb" (Johnson 1919). The D.C. branch of the National Association for the Advancement of Colored People had been active regarding the situation as far back as July 9, when it sent letters to the Washington, D.C., daily papers, telling them that their inflammatory headlines and articles had the potential to provoke a race riot. An article in the socialist black journal *The Messenger* said that the Washington newspapers incited the D.C. riot, U.S. soldiers and sailors started it, and the black people of D.C., determined to resist, finished it, demonstrating that they were not afraid to kill or die for liberty and home.

James Weldon Johnson also met with U.S. senators, including Sen. Charles Curtis from Kansas, asking for a congressional investigation of the riots. Johnson believed that black people had saved Washington by their determination not to run and to defend their lives and their homes. He felt that the Chicago and D.C. riots marked a turning point in the nation's attitude toward race relations. Senator Curtis did sponsor a resolution requesting an investigation.

JAN VOOGD

See also

Race Riots in America; Red Summer Race Riots of 1919; Washington (D.C.) Riots of 1968. Documents: The Report on the Memphis Riots of May 1866 (July 25, 1866); Account of the Riots in East St. Louis, Illinois (July 1917); The Cook County Coroner's Report Regarding the 1919 Chicago Race Riots (1919); A Southern Black Woman's Letter Regarding the Recent Riots in Chicago and Washington (November 1919); The Final Report of the Grand Jury on the Tulsa Race Riot (June 25, 1921); Testimony from *Laney v. United States* Describing Events during the Washington, D.C., Riot of July 1919 (December 3, 1923); The Governor's Commission Report on the Watts Riots (December 1965); Cyrus R. Vance's Report on the Riots in Detroit (July–August 1967); The Reports of the Oklahoma Commission to Study the Tulsa Race Riot of 1921 (2000–2001); The Draft Report of the 1898 Wilmington Race Riot Commission (December 2005)

Further Reading:

Green, Constance McLaughlin. *The Secret City: A History of Race Relations in the Nation's Capital.* Princeton, NJ: Princeton University Press, 1967.

Hawkins, W. E. "When Negroes Shot a Lynching Bee into Perdition." *The Messenger* 2, no. 9 (September 1919): 28–29.

Haynes, George E. "Race Riots in Relation to Democracy." *Survey* 42 (1919): 697–99.

Johnson, James Weldon. "The Riots: An N.A.A.C.P. Investigation." *The Crisis* 18, no. 5 (September 1919): 241–43.

Kitchens, John W., ed. *Tuskegee Institute News Clippings File Microfilm.* Sanford, NC: Microfilming Corporation of America, 1981. Reel 10, Frame 986.

"Race Riot at Capital: Soldiers and Sailors Make Raid on Negro Quarter." *New York Times*, July 20, 1919, 4.

Seligmann, Herbert. "Race War?" *New Republic* 20, August 13, 1919, 49.

"Service Men Beat Negroes in Race Riot at Capital." *New York Times*, July 21, 1919, 1.

Washington (D.C.) Riots of 1968

Following the assassination of Dr. Martin Luther King, Jr. in Memphis, Tennessee, on April 4, 1968, civil disorder broke out in nearly 110 U.S. cities. By far, the riot that occurred in Washington, D.C., between April 4 and 8 was the worst, bringing the city to a standstill. Schools closed, 1,000 buildings burned, 1,097 people were injured, 6,100 were arrested, and 12 people lost their lives. Damages exceeded $27 million.

The first place the rioting occurred was at 14th and U Streets, in the northwest quadrant of the city. This area was at the heart of one of the black neighborhoods. It was a busy hub of activity, serving as a bus transfer point and the home of stores, businesses, theaters, and offices for such civil rights organizations as the National Association for the Advancement of Colored People, the Student Nonviolent Coordinating Committee (SNCC), and the Southern Christian Leadership Conference.

When the news of the assassination was first broadcast over the airways, it was received in stunned silence and utter disbelief. Then it was announced that businesses were asked to close in respect for Dr. King. On 14th and U Streets, a small band of young people, mostly black males, were gathering. They decided that they would go from business to business telling them that they should close. Soon the group was joined by Stokely Carmichael, who appeared on the scene. He was the West Indian–born former leader of the SNCC who was known as a black activist. When he joined the crowd, it began to grow larger. The mood of the crowd changed. The crowd became angry and menacing. No longer were they asking the business owners to close—they were demanding that they do so. Carmichael left the area when anger turned to violence. Carmichael was well aware that he was being watched closely by local and federal authorities since he was viewed by them as a volatile agitator. But the violence escalated into breaking windows and wide-scale looting. Rioters threw rocks at motorists. The windshield of the first police car on the scene was broken in the melee. Eventually, local police quelled the rioters. As they secured the area around 14th and U Streets, trouble erupted in other parts of the city. On the following morning, Walter Washington, the first black mayor of the city, had workers cleaning up the damage. For many in the city, this was presumed to be the end of the trouble. But it was not.

The aftermath of a riot in Washington, D.C., following the assassination of Martin Luther King, Jr. in 1968. (Library of Congress)

That day, Stokely Carmichael resurfaced and held a news conference in which he boldly declared that "America killed Dr. Martin Luther King, Jr. last night." He continued, "We have gone full swing into the revolution" (Judge 2005). After the news conference, he went onto the campus of Howard University, which he had formerly attended. There were two activities in progress to commemorate Dr. King. There was a commemoration service in Cramton Auditorium and a rally a few steps away in front of Douglass Hall. At the rally, several speeches were given, including remarks by Carmichael. He drew a pistol, waved it over his head, and predicted that retaliatory action would occur to avenge the King assassination. Someone lowered the American flag and raised a flag of Ujamma. It symbolized a black nationalist student group. A reporter from the *Washington Post* newspaper interpreted the tone of the rally as "vehemently anti-white" (Judge 2005). When the attendees at the rally left and proceeded south on Georgia Avenue, the main street near the university, the crowd clashed with local police. A violent confrontation ensued.

By the afternoon, rioting, looting, and violence again erupted in other parts of the city. This happened mostly in black neighborhoods. In the areas where there was trouble, upwards of thousands of people roamed around with impunity. Stores, businesses, and a few homes were burned. When some storekeepers were forced to leave their stores for their own safety, many made signs that read *Soul Brother* or *I am a Brother*. These signs were displayed prominently in the windows and on doors of businesses owned by all races. They hoped that this would serve as a deterrent to having their businesses looted or burned. Sometimes it worked, and sometimes it did not. Children and adults could be seen running up and down the street with clothes, shoes, food, furniture, appliances, liquor, and any other items that were easy to grab and carry away. Some stores had all of their merchandise taken and were then torched. Some rioters were seen using carts and suitcases to carry away their loot. On April 5, the rioters reached within a few blocks of the White House. A mob mentality reigned for nearly three days and nights in some parts of the city. In other parts of the city, where the rioters had not reached, many citizens huddled in their homes in fear that they and their neighborhood might fall victim to what was happening in the troubled neighborhoods. An eerie, smoldering silence fell over the city as the news media described the devastation that continued to mount.

In 1968, the full complement of the Washington, D.C., Metropolitan Police Department was 3,100. Clearly, they were outnumbered and not fully prepared to deal with the rioters. They had never before faced a similar situation. Also, it was a sensitive matter of race, because the majority of police officers were white and the majority of rioters were black. Again, Mayor Walter Washington and other community leaders walked the streets and spoke through the media, pleading for calm. A curfew was imposed in the city. It began at 5:30 P.M. and ended at 6:30 A.M. President Lyndon B. Johnson issued an executive order to bring in 13,600 federal troops, including national guardsmen. They were immediately deployed to protect the U.S. Capitol, the White House, and various locations around the city. The federal military presence in Washington during the 1968 riots was the largest of any since the Civil War. President Johnson declared Sunday, April 8, 1968, a day of national mourning. Thirty-five years later, many of the areas struck by the riot had not been fully rebuilt. While some movement for rebuilding has begun, there remain scars and blight that can be traced directly to the riot of 1968.

BETTY NYANGONI

See also

Carmichael, Stokely; King, Martin Luther, Jr.; Race Riots in America; Washington (D.C.) Riots of 1919. Documents: The Report on the Memphis Riots of May 1866 (July 25, 1866); Account of the Riots in East St. Louis, Illinois (July 1917); The Cook County Coroner's Report Regarding the 1919 Chicago Race Riots (1919); A Southern Black Woman's Letter Regarding the Recent Riots in Chicago and Washington (November 1919); The Final Report of the Grand Jury on the Tulsa Race Riot (June 25, 1921); Testimony from *Laney v. United States* Describing Events during the Washington, D.C., Riot of July 1919 (December 3, 1923); The Governor's Commission Report on the Watts Riots (December 1965); Cyrus R. Vance's Report on the Riots in Detroit (July–August 1967); The Reports of the Oklahoma Commission to Study the Tulsa Race Riot of 1921 (2000–2001); The Draft Report of the 1898 Wilmington Race Riot Commission (December 2005)

Further Reading:

Gilbert, Ben W., and the *Washington Post* Staff. *Ten Blocks from the White House: Anatomy of the Washington Riots of 1968*. Washington, DC: Praeger, 1968.

Judge, Mark Gauvreau. "Quiet Riots." *American Spectator*, October 28, 2005. http://www.spectator.org/dsp_article.asp?art_id=8940.

Melder, Keith. *Magnificent Obsession*, 2nd ed. Washington, DC: Intac, 1997.

"Nation's Capital Still Recovering from 1968 Riots." *CNN*, April 4, 1998. http://www.cnn.com/Us/9804/04/mlk.dc.riots.

Smith, Sam. *Multitudes: An Unauthorized Memoir*. 1997. http://prorev.com/mmfire.htm.

Watson, Thomas E. (1856–1922)

Thomas E. Watson was a Georgia attorney, publisher, and politician who served as a Democrat in the Georgia State House of Representatives (1882–1883), a Populist in the U.S. House of Representatives (1890–1892), and a Democrat in the U.S. Senate (1920–1922). The Populist Party convention nominated him as its vice-presidential candidate in 1896 to run with William Jennings Bryan and as its presidential candidate in 1904 and 1908. Watson also ran unsuccessfully to keep his seat in Congress in 1892 and 1894. Although Watson served no more than a total of five years in public office, he exerted a tremendous influence on Southern and national politics with his flamboyant political oratory and his support for other candidates. Watson is best known for his controversial political career and sudden about-face. In the early years he advocated a more egalitarian creed and championed the political and economic rights of poor white and black farmers. In the later years he gained notoriety for his virulent antiblack, anti-Semitic, and anti-Catholic views.

Watson was born in McDuffie County, Georgia, to a slaveholding family and spent most his childhood on his grandfather's plantation. After attending Mercer University, Watson practiced law but maintained a strong connection to agrarian life. He entered politics at the age of 23 in support of the small farmers who had revolted against the state's leading industrial capitalists. In the 1880s, Watson supported the economic platform of the National Farmers' Alliance, and in the 1890s, he became a prominent leader in the Populist

Party. Both the Alliance and the Populist Party challenged the entrenched power of the Democratic Party in the South. Aggrieved farmers called for such reforms as the dissolution of corporate monopolies, government regulation of railroads, a graduated income tax, the establishment of cooperative buying plans, and relief from high-interest credit. Watson discovered that the key to political success lay in soliciting not just the votes of white farmers but also the votes of African Americans. Both the Democrats and the Populists recognized that if the white vote splintered, then the black vote could decide an election. The two parties battled with each other for the political loyalties of black voters and engaged in a variety of tactics, including persuasion, fraud, bribery, and violence.

Poor white and black farmers in the South often struggled with the same economic difficulties, and Populists tried to draw attention to the farmers' common grievances and enemies. In Watson's early career, he labored to build a new political alliance that united the races economically. He pointed out how racial antagonism had been used by white elites to oppress the farming class. When Watson campaigned for his seat in the Georgia Assembly in 1882, he received a substantial number of black votes. In the 1890s, he denounced laws that limited black suffrage and called for the right of African American men to cast a ballot without coercion or fear of intimidation. The Populist leader also spoke out against lynching and, at one point, provided refuge to a black minister who was an ardent party member being sought by a mob. Many of Watson's contemporaries considered him to be somewhat radical in his stance. Yet there were limits to biracial cooperation. Watson never promoted the right of African Americans to hold public office. He made it very clear that he did not want "social equality" of the races. For most white Southerners, this phrase conjured up images of intermarriage between the races, blacks socializing with whites, equal access to public accommodations, and interracial schools. Whether Watson genuinely believed in a limited kind of equality or acted out of political expediency is still debated.

After failing a second time to regain his seat in Congress in 1894, Watson retreated from public life and politics for eight years. When he reentered the political fray, he had changed his mind about the merits of black suffrage. In 1906, Watson supported the Democratic candidacy for governorship of Hoke Smith, who championed black disfranchisement and was a vocal advocate of white supremacy. Watson and Smith argued that black political equality would undoubtedly lead to "social equality." During the course of the campaign, white newspapers inflamed racial tensions by detailing alleged sexual assaults on white women by black men and other supposed black criminal atrocities. These lurid reports provoked a riot in which whites attacked and killed dozens of blacks as well as destroyed many black-owned businesses. Shortly after, Smith won the election in an overwhelming victory. Two years later the Georgia legislature rewrote the state constitution to severely curtail, if not abolish, black suffrage.

Watson's alliance with Smith marked the beginning of a significant shift in the tenor of his political rhetoric. He unleashed a fury of vitriolic attacks on Catholics, Jews, and African Americans and earned a reputation as one of the South's most notorious orators. The year Smith won the election, Watson founded a newspaper, the *Jeffersonian,* and a magazine, *Watson's Jeffersonian Magazine,* which he used as mouthpieces for racial and religious bigotry. He warned about black domination, the sexual threats priests posed to white Protestant women, and the danger of the Jewish aristocracy. Watson's frenzied tirades were so outrageous that he provoked the U.S. Post Office to ban the *Jeffersonian* from the mail and the U.S. Justice Department to try him for obscenity. The former Populist leader continued to rail against industrial capitalists and the oppression of the farming class, but his racial and religious obsessions occupied most of his attention from 1910 onward. Watson's reactionary political style was emblematic of a new breed of politicians known as demagogues, who appealed to the prejudices and baser emotions of the people. Until the last day of his life, Watson persisted in lashing out at his perceived enemies. He died in 1922 of a cerebral hemorrhage following a lengthy struggle with illness.

NATALIE J. RING

See also

Anti-Semitism; Racism

Further Reading:

Crowe, Charles. "Tom Watson, Populists, and Blacks Reconsidered." *Journal of Negro History* 55 (April 1970): 99–116.

Fingerhut, Eugene R. "Tom Watson, Blacks, and Southern Reform." *Georgia Historical Quarterly* 60 (Winter 1976): 324–43.

Historic Home of Thomas E. Watson, Hickory Hill. Watson-
    Brown Foundation. http://www.hickory-hill.org/index.html
    (accessed June 1, 2008).
Shaw, Barton. *The Wool Hat Boys: Georgia's Populist Party*. Baton
    Rouge: Louisiana State University Press, 1984.
Woodward, C. Vann. *Tom Watson: Agrarian Rebel*. New York:
    Oxford University Press, 1938.

Welfare Queens

Welfare queen is an expressly derogatory term for a woman fraudulently collecting and/or using public assistance benefits. A common stereotype of welfare recipients is that they are mainly African American, uneducated, and lazy single mothers. What distinguishes the image of the welfare queen from the general stereotype is the idea that these women are using the benefits inappropriately and fraudulently to live lavish, irresponsible lifestyles.

The term welfare queen was cemented in the public imagination by a story former President Ronald Reagan told repeatedly while was campaigning for the Republican presidential nomination for the 1976 election. It featured a woman from the South side of Chicago, who had been arrested for welfare fraud, having 80 names, 30 addresses, 12 Social Security cards, and four non-existent deceased husbands for whom she was collecting veterans' benefits, in addition to Medicaid, food stamps, and welfare benefits under each of the 80 names for a grand total of 150 thousand dollars annually. The individual was never identified and such a case was never verified. It was likely an exaggerated amalgamation of several people accused of welfare fraud. The purpose of the story and the character of the welfare queen was to draw attention to what many right-leaning conservatives believed were pervasive problems with the expansion of welfare programs. Since the welfare queen character built on already existing notions about welfare recipients in general, it was useful in eroding support for public assistance.

The character of the welfare queen is associated with what is referred to as the "welfare crisis," which references the rising number of people, especially single mothers, receiving public assistance, allegedly leading to a variety of social problems, especially long-term dependency. This crisis is generally thought to have begun in the 1960s and,

Undeserving Poor

The undeserving poor is a concept that has existed in European and, subsequently, American society for centuries. Dividing the poor into deserving and undeserving allowed those with resources to determine which people are worthy of assistance. A key feature of the undeserving poor is some sort of causal responsibility for their poverty. Alcoholism, gambling, criminality, promiscuity, and laziness are some of the attributes qualifying an individual as undeserving of assistance. The label *underclass* began to become synonymous with the undeserving poor in many instances, even though it was originally used to describe the results of specific economic conditions leading to persistent, extreme poverty. Assumptions about the poor related to the distinction between deserving and undeserving were central to the development of social policy related to poverty, and continue to have an impact on current debates about public assistance.

according to some, continues today. By the 1960s, after decades of migration by African Americans from the South to cities in the North that were both unprepared and unwilling to accommodate black migrants, unemployment rates were high, while poverty and a serious lack of decent affordable housing plagued the urban black population. Single mothers and children born to unwed mothers increased and, despite the clear need for assistance, states did not extend Aid to Dependent Children (ADC) to people deemed unworthy of the assistance, like unmarried mothers.

The characteristics associated with the welfare queen are a combination of stereotypical characteristics of African Americans, the undeserving poor, and the underclass: aversion to work, teenage pregnancy, addiction to drugs, criminality, dishonesty, and taking advantage of the system. Despite the fact that the fertility rate of women receiving assistance is lower than that for all women in the same age categories, recipients are perceived as being promiscuous and dishonest, relying on government assistance to bear and support children out of wedlock or even bearing children for the express purpose of receiving more benefits.

The character of the welfare queen can be understood using sociologist Patricia Hill Collins' (2009 [1990]) concept of "controlling images." Controlling images are designed to make social injustices like racism, sexism, and poverty appear to be natural and inevitable parts of everyday life. One of several controlling images that Collins identifies is that of the "welfare mother." She argues that the welfare mother image allows blacks to be racially stereotyped as lazy by blaming welfare mothers for passing on poor work ethic, to reinforce the dominant idea that value and financial security should only be acquired through heterosexual marriage, and that expensive policies are failures and can be eliminated for a cost savings. Collins argues that the welfare mother controlling image was not necessary until black women were able to access assistance they were previously denied.

Another framework for understanding the welfare queen is as a "narrative script," a sequence of events that set up predictable roles and actions that offer clear indicators of what is most likely to follow. Journalist Franklin Gilliam Jr. argues that the narrative script for the welfare queen tells observers that most welfare recipients are women, and that most of those women are African American. In a study on reactions to images of black mothers who were welfare recipients, Gilliam (1999) found that, among white respondents, exposure to the welfare queen image reduced support for various welfare programs, increased stereotyping of African Americans, and increased support for maintaining traditional gender roles.

The term welfare queen is not as common as it was in the 1980s and 1990s, but the concept and public perceptions about the prevalence of fraud and irresponsibility is still quite widespread. Reincarnations of the welfare queen character can be seen in public discourse about taxes, on neighborhood association website message boards, and heard in political discussions about entitlement programs. Though the term "welfare queen" may not be used explicitly, the repercussions of this stereotype continue to permeate throughout society.

RENEE S. ALSTON

See also

Racialized Poverty; Temporary Assistance to Needy Families (TANF); The Underclass (Ghetto Poor)

Further Reading:

Blake, John. "Return of the 'Welfare Queen'". CNN.com. Monday, January 23, 2012. 2012. http://www.cnn.com/2012/01/23/politics/weflare-queen/index.html

Collins, Patricia Hill. *Black Feminist Thought: Knowledge, consciousness, and the politics of empowerment.* New York: Routledge, 2009 [1990].

Gans, Herbert J. 1990. "Deconstructing the Underclass." *Journal of the American Planning Association.* Vol. 56, No. 3.

Gilens, Martin. *Why Americans Hate Welfare: Race, Media, and the Politics of Antipoverty Policy.* Chicago: University of Chicago Press, 1999.

Gilliam, Franklin D., Jr. "The 'Welfare Queen' Experiment: How Viewers React to Images of African-American Mothers on Welfare." *Journalist Trade.* Summer (1999): 49-52, 1999.

Handler, Joel F., and Yeheskel Hasenfeld. *Blame Welfare, Ignore Poverty and Inequality.* New York: Cambridge University Press, 2007.

Katz, Michael B. *The Undeserving Poor: From the War on Poverty to the War on Welfare.* New York: Pantheon, 1989.

Zucchino, David. *Myth of the welfare queen: A Pulitzer Prize-winning journalist's portrait of women on the line.* New York: Scribner, 1997.

Wells-Barnett, Ida B. (1862–1931)

Ida Bell Wells-Barnett was born July 16, 1862, in Holly Springs, Mississippi, to James Wells, a carpenter, and Elizabeth Warrenton Wells, a cook. She was the eldest of eight children, four girls and four boys, two of whom died in early childhood. Her father was respected as a community leader and was known locally as a "race man" because of his commitment to civil rights, community development, and educational opportunity. Both of her parents offered strong role models for hard work, responsible citizenship, and positive living, and they instilled into their children a keen sense of duty to God, family, and community.

Wells-Barnett attended elementary and high school at Shaw University, later renamed Rust College. She was well on her way to laying a solid foundation for life when both her parents and her youngest brother died suddenly in the yellow fever epidemic that struck her area in 1878. To keep her siblings together and sustain their family, she left school and secured a teaching position in the public schools of rural Mississippi. This career path took her to Shelby County, Tennessee, and to the city of Memphis.

As a teacher in the Memphis area, she interacted with African American people who were centrally involved in creating a brighter day for African Americans, just as her parents had worked to do in Holly Springs. The community took pride generally in being forward-looking and culturally and intellectually vibrant. They worked aggressively to take advantage of opportunities and to function as productive and responsible citizens. Wells-Barnett also continued to be active in the African Methodist Episcopal (AME) Church, as well as in others, and she was able to hear and meet many nationally renowned people, including Frederick Douglass, Blanche K. Bruce, Henry McNeal Turner, and Frances Ellen Watkins Harper.

Wells-Barnett also became active in the local literary clubs. Through these activities, she became a contributor and later editor of the *Evening Star* and columnist for the *Living Way*, both periodicals in Memphis. In 1884, she brought a lawsuit against the Chesapeake, Ohio, and Southwestern Railroad Company for Jim Crow practices that resulted in her being physically thrown off a train. She won, but the ruling was overturned by the Tennessee Supreme Court. Her first editorial was an invitation from the *Living Way* to write about her ordeal. The editorial was well received by the African American community, and Wells-Barnett was invited to write a column.

Using the pen name "Iola," Wells-Barnett was fiercely dedicated to justice and social reform. Her popularity as a journalist grew, and her column was syndicated in several papers across the nation. By 1889, she had left her teaching job and become co-owner of a newspaper, *Free Speech and Headlight*, with Rev. F. Nightingale and J. L. Fleming. In 1891, she and Fleming bought out Nightingale and shortened the name of the paper to *Free Speech*. By this point, Wells-Barnett was firmly established as a successful businesswoman and a highly respected journalist with a well-deserved reputation as a sharp-tongued political observer.

From this springboard, Wells-Barnett fashioned a remarkable career as a political activist and as an investigative journalist, especially with regard to the lynching of African American men, women, and children. Her list of accomplishments is long. She made two speaking tours of England, Scotland, and Wales, in 1893 and 1894. She was active over the next decades in several political organizations and movements, including the National Afro-American League, Afro-American Council, National Association of Colored Women (NACW), National Equal Rights League, Ida B.

Wells Woman's Club, National American Woman's Suffrage Association, the Niagara movement, the woman's suffrage movement, and the international peace movement. She was a cofounder of the National Association for the Advancement of Colored People in 1910, and founder of the Negro Fellowship League in 1910 and the Alpha Suffrage Club in 1913. She ran for Illinois state senate in 1930 and lost. She worked arduously until her death as a self-determined crusader for justice and died of uremic poisoning on March 25, 1931, in Chicago.

Thomas Moss, Calvin McDowell, and Henry Stewart, three enterprising and well-respected African American men in Memphis, owned and operated a grocery store, the People's Grocery Company, in a suburban area of the city that was popularly called the Curve because the streetcar line curved sharply at that point (Wells-Barnett 1970: 47–76). Moss, a mail carrier, was the president of the company and worked in the store at night, while his partners operated the business during the day. In this mostly African American neighborhood, their store was able to compete successfully for business with a store that was white owned and operated. Before the People's Grocery, the white-owned store had held a monopoly, and the owner was much agitated by the success of his competition. He became openly hostile.

According to Wells-Barnett in *Crusade for Justice*, one incident that became violent was a quarrel between white boys and African American boys over a game of marbles. A fight ensued between the two groups that escalated into a fight between the fathers of the boys. The African American father won the fight, but the white father, the grocery store owner, swore out a warrant for the arrest of the African Americans. The People's Grocery owners were drawn into the tense dispute. The case was dismissed with nominal fines, but the victory for the African Americans was met by a threat that the People's Grocery would be forcibly closed by the white contenders on the next Saturday night.

In the face of such direct threats, Moss, McDowell, and Stewart sought legal counsel and found that, because the Curve was outside of the city limits of Memphis, they would be justified in protecting themselves. They did. They armed several men and stationed them at the rear of the store in preparation for repelling any attack that might occur. As threatened, that Saturday night, armed whites came to the rear of the store. The guards fired on them and wounded three. Others of the attacking group fled. The next morning, Moss, McDowell, and Stewart were dragged from their homes, and they and over 100 other African American men were arrested and jailed.

According to Wells-Barnett, the next morning the white newspaper reported that on the evening before, white law enforcement officers had been wounded while discharging their duty to hunt down criminals who were being harbored in the People's Grocery. Instead of being described as a successful grocery, the store was presented as an unsavory hangout for thieves and thugs who engaged in drinking and gambling. This account and others sensationalized the incident and enflamed racism. Groups of white men were permitted throughout the day on Sunday to view the imprisoned African American men, and white men gathered on the streets and in other meeting places to discuss the insurrection and its remedies. Although Memphis had not been a site of lynchings since the Civil War, the African American community became alarmed. Several African American men volunteered to stand guard at the jail to ensure the safety of those incarcerated. By the third night, they thought that the situation had calmed down and that the crisis had ended. They went home.

That night, March 9, 1892, a white mob was admitted to the jail. They took Moss, McDowell, and Stewart from their cells, loaded them on a train car that ran in back of the jail, carried the men a mile north of the city limits, and shot them to death. Wells-Barnett explained that the white newspaper reported the following details:

> "It is said that Tom Moss begged for his life for the sake of his wife and child and his unborn baby"; that when asked if he had anything to say, told them "tell my people to go West—there is no justice for them here"; that Calvin McDowell got hold of one of the guns of the lynchers and because they could not loosen his grip a shot was fired into his closed fist. When the three bodies were found, the fingers of McDowell's right hand had been shot to pieces and his eyes were gouged out. This proved that the one who wrote that news report was either an eyewitness or got the facts from someone who was. (Wells-Barnett 1970: 50–51)

The deaths of the three men were reported as "by hands unknown," with no attempt by law enforcement to actually

As an anti-lynching crusader and the founder of the African American women's club movement and other civil rights organizations, Ida Wells-Barnett was one of the most influential African American women of the late 19th and early 20th centuries. (Getty Images)

find the killers. The African American community was outraged by both the lynchings and the fact that the men who were lynched were clearly upstanding citizens rather than criminals of any kind. Their agitation fed rumors that spread through the white community indicating that African Americans were congregating at the Curve. A judge of the criminal court issued an order to the sheriff to "take a hundred men, go out to the Curve at once, and shoot down on sight any Negro who appears to be making trouble" (Wells-Barnett 1970: 51). The white male community responded accordingly. They gathered, obtained weapons, went to the Curve, fired arbitrarily into groups of African Americans, and achieved their objective. They took possession of the People's Grocery Company and consumed and destroyed its contents at will. In the days that followed, creditors sold the remaining stock at auction, and the rivalry of the People's Grocery with the white-owned store was summarily ended.

When these incidents occurred, Ida B. Wells-Barnett was in Natchez, Mississippi, on a marketing development trip for her newspaper. By the time she returned home, Moss had already been buried. The death of Moss and his two business partners was quite a blow to Wells-Barnett. Moss and his wife Betty were personal friends, and she was godmother to their daughter Maurine. Wells-Barnett was incensed by the injustice. She wrote editorials against the conditions for African Americans in Memphis and urged African Americans, as Moss had recommended, to "save our money and leave a town which will neither protect our lives and property, nor give us a fair trial in the courts, but takes us out and murders us in cold blood when accused by white persons" (Wells-Barnett 1970: 52). African Americans started leaving Memphis in large numbers, especially with the opening of Oklahoma (Indian Territory) for settlement. When the white backlash to this migration sought to discourage the departures with stories of danger and distress, Wells-Barnett went to Oklahoma to investigate and discover the truth. She sent letters to the *Free Speech* reporting her findings, and the migration continued, drawing people, not only from Memphis, but also Arkansas, Mississippi, and other parts of Tennessee.

In addition to migration as a political strategy, Wells-Barnett also understood the power of economic leverage. She made speeches in local churches and wrote editorials that encouraged a boycott of the streetcar system, a business that benefited greatly from African American patronage. This campaign stands historically as an important precursor of the more contemporary Montgomery bus boycott.

Friends warned Wells-Barnett that such activities were dangerous. Wells-Barnett, however, was unrelenting in her campaign for justice. Instead of modifying her approach, shortly after the three lynchings, she bought a gun. In *Crusade for Justice*, she stated the following:

I expected some cowardly retaliation from the lynchers. I felt that one had better die fighting against injustice than to die like a dog or a rat in a trap. I had already determined to sell my life as dearly as possible if attacked. I felt if I could take one lyncher with me, this would even up the score a little bit. But fate decided that the blow should fall when I was away. (Wells-Barnett 1970: 62)

Wells-Barnett continued to write editorials and to conduct investigations, not only on African American settlement in Indian Territory and on the streetcar boycott, but also on lynchings. She paid particular attention to the fact that lynchings were typically not a reaction of whites to the criminal behavior of African Americans. Instead, she documented that they were acts of terrorism designed to intimidate and oppress African American victims (men, women, and children) who were making political or economic progress. Most provocatively, however, Wells-Barnett also found that lynchings were used not just for political and economic control, but also for social control. She discovered that several lynchings were the violent reaction of whites to the voluntary romantic liaisons between white women and African American men. Wells-Barnett felt compelled to speak the truth.

Three months after the lynchings of her friends, on May 21, 1892, Wells-Barnett quickly wrote a short editorial before departing for travel to the East. She wrote the following:

Eight Negroes lynched since last issue of the *Free Speech*: one at Little Rock, Ark., last Saturday morning where the citizens broke into the penitentiary and got their man; three near Anniston, Ala.; one near New Orleans; and three at Clarksville, Ga., the last three for killing a white man, and five on the same old racket—the new alarm about raping white women. The same programme of hanging, then shooting bullets into the lifeless bodies was carried out to the letter. Nobody in this section believes the old threadbare lie that Negro men assault white women. If southern white men are not careful, they will over-reach themselves and public sentiment will have a reaction; a conclusion will then be reached which will be very damaging to the moral reputation of their women.

With this editorial, Wells-Barnett set off a dramatic response from the white community in Memphis that would have significant consequences for her personal safety. However, there was a simultaneous effect. She also set herself on a rising trajectory of public activism that would propel her through the remainder of her life as a local, national, and international leader against lynching and mob violence and in support of general social justice.

Two days after the editorial appeared, the *Commercial Appeal*, a white newspaper in Memphis, reproduced it and, according to Wells-Barnett, published its own editorial, calling on the chivalrous white men of Memphis to do something to avenge this insult to the honor of their women. It said, "The Black wretch who had written that foul lie should be tied to a stake at the corner of Main and Madison Streets, a pair of tailor's shears used on him and he should then be burned at a stake" (Wells-Barnett 1970: 66).

In other words, Mr. Carmack, whom Wells-Barnett names as the author of the editorial, called for yet another lynching. The white community of Memphis responded accordingly. An extralegal committee was formed and mob violence was again unleashed. On May 27, 1892, the committee ransacked the offices of the *Free Speech* and destroyed all of the equipment, and they had every intention of torturing and killing the owners. They were foiled in this latter pursuit, however. Wells-Barnett's business partner, J. L. Fleming, received a timely warning from a sympathetic white citizen that he should leave the city. Having been in a similar crisis with an earlier paper, the *Marion Headlight* in Marion, Arkansas, Fleming left immediately, barely escaping before the committee reached the *Free Press* offices.

As indicated above, as the female writer of the editorial rather than the male writer that Carmack presumed her to be, Wells-Barnett was not in Memphis when the attack occurred. She had written the editorial before leaving for her trip East. Her itinerary was in support of multiple interests. Her first stop was Philadelphia, where she attended the annual meeting of the AME Church. At the end of the conference, she went on to New York at the invitation of T. Thomas Fortune, editor of the *New York Age*, a paper in which her newspaper column was syndicated. Her Memphis editorial was published during the first leg of her trip.

When Wells-Barnett reached New York, Fortune informed her of the details of the mob violence and the threats of more violence that were occurring in Memphis. He impressed on her that it was not safe for her to return to her home and that the threat was quite specific. After the white leaders of Memphis discovered that Wells-Barnett, not her male partner, was actually the author of the editorial, they let it be known that if she ever set foot in Tennessee again, she would be tortured and killed on sight. In effect, the clear and present danger to Wells-Barnett expressed openly by the white citizens of Memphis forced her into an exile from the South that lasted 30 years.

This exile, however, was not the end of the story. It was the beginning of a provocative new page in Wells-Barnett's career as a journalist, political activist, and community leader. She became a reporter for the *New York Age*, where she told her story of exile in a feature article on June 25, 1892. As she stated in her autobiography,

> Having lost my paper, had a price put on my life, and been made an exile from home for hinting at the truth, I felt that I owed it to myself and to my race to tell the whole truth now that I was where I could do so freely. (Wells-Barnett 1970: 69)

After the publication of this article, two African American women, Maritcha Lyon of Brooklyn and Victoria Earle Matthews of New York, hosted a testimonial dinner for Wells-Barnett. Lyon, an educator and writer, was one of the first African American women to be named assistant principal in a Brooklyn public school. Matthews was a fellow journalist who wrote for several newspapers, including the *New York Age*. She was also well known as the founding director of the White Rose Mission, a shelter for the increasing number of African American women and girls who were migrating to Northern cities from the South in search of better opportunities. In New York, the White Rose Mission functioned as a community center for women and children, offering educational opportunities focused on self-improvement and Christian living. New and inexperienced in an urban environment filled with danger, especially to women alone, the women were particularly vulnerable to sexual assault and exploitation and to what was perceived to be lifestyles that were inappropriate for pious and respectable women. The mission helped to keep these Southern migrants off the streets, involved with more positive activities, and focused on developing skills that helped them to secure adequate employment.

As women leaders who were active in social reform and experienced in community development activities, both Lyon and Matthews were very much attuned to the need to support Wells-Barnett and to bring attention to the ongoing need across the nation for social justice. On October 5, 1892, at Lyric Hall in New York, they brought together 250 African American women from the New York area, Philadelphia, and Boston. The group included some of the most recognizable and notable African American women leaders of the day.

Among them, for example, were Josephine St. Pierre Ruffin, Gertrude Bustill Mossell, Susan Smith McKinney Steward, and Sarah Smith Garnet.

Josephine St. Pierre Ruffin and her husband George were prominent citizens of Boston. He was a lawyer and politician who served as a city councilman, a state legislator, and a municipal judge. Ruffin was noted for her work across racial lines through numerous organizations in Massachusetts, including the Associated Charities of Boston, the Massachusetts State Federation of Women's Clubs, and the Boston Kansas Relief Association, an organization that supported African American migrants. She was also a journalist and a member of the New England Women's Press Association, composed largely of white women.

Gertrude Bustill Mossell developed a national reputation as a writer and journalist, with her articles and columns appearing in newspapers across the nation. Ultimately, she became particularly well known for the publication of *The Work of the Afro-American Woman* (1894). Her family was among the free-black elite of 19th-century Philadelphia. For many generations, the female members of the Bustill family had built a remarkable record of social and political activism, as noted by their work as pioneering educators and as leaders of the Female Anti-Slavery Society. Mossell continued this tradition as an educator, activist, and journalist, a career choice that was facilitated by her ongoing affluence in being the wife of physician Nathan F. Mossell.

Susan Smith McKinney Steward and Sarah Smith Garnet were sisters who were also present at the testimonial. They were the daughters of Sylvanus and Ann S. Smith, both active in social and political reform and members of the African American elite of Brooklyn. Steward was a physician, the first African American woman to practice medicine in New York State and the third in the nation. Her highly successful practice was with the Brooklyn Woman's Homeopathic Hospital and Dispensary and with the Brooklyn Home for Aged Colored People. In addition, she served as president of the Women's Christian Temperance Union Number 6 in Brooklyn and was active in various social causes. The widow of clergyman William S. McKinney and later the wife of Theophilus Gould Steward, chaplain of the 25th U.S. Colored Infantry, Steward was also a prolific writer across a range of her professional interests as well as her religious and spiritual interests.

Her sister, Sarah Smith Tompkins Garnet, was a prominent educator, the first African American woman to be appointed principal of a public school in the borough of Manhattan. She was the widow of James Tompkins, an Episcopal minister, and later married Henry Highland Garnet, a Presbyterian minister, abolitionist, and diplomat. Garnet was an impassioned opponent of discrimination in education and a civil rights advocate. She was a member of many charitable and reform organizations, and she and her sister often served as delegates to national and international meetings.

Many such women of high energy and commitment across three states attended the testimonial for Wells-Barnett and heard her story. They presented her with $500 to enable her work and a gold, pen-shaped brooch to commemorate the occasion. From this gathering, Wells-Barnett went on two anti-lynching tours in England, Scotland, and Wales; published three pamphlets against lynching (*Southern Horrors: Lynch Law in All Its Phases*, 1892; *A Red Record*, 1895; *Mob Rule in New Orleans*, 1900), and came to be acknowledged as a steadfast champion of justice. Settling in Chicago, she married Ferdinand L. Barnett, an attorney, and raised a family, but her activism did not end. Wells-Barnett founded a suffrage club for women and a community development organization, ran for public office, and continued to speak and write in support of social justice.

Simultaneously, the New York gathering also firmly planted the seeds of organized political reform at a national, rather than just the local level for African American women in general. The leaders who attended, Wells-Barnett included, went on with like-minded women from across the nation to form the NACW in 1896, an organization through which they were able to engage actively in the social and political discourses that surrounded them, nationally and internationally, and to accomplish the vital work of social and political reform. This organized, socially conscious, politically active moment constituted the inception of what has since been named the Black Clubwomen's movement. The point to be emphasized is that the Black Clubwomen's movement was well connected to all of the major social movements of the time: civil rights, women's rights, labor rights, settlement, international peace, and more, and Wells-Barnett was very active in all of them.

The turn of the 20th century, in fact, was a time in which trials and challenges for the African American community were great, which, in effect, provided even more inspiration for African American women to use their talents and abilities well at every occasion that presented itself for remedy and reform. Wells-Barnett, therefore, was not alone in the energy that she brought to the cause of social justice, but she was, nevertheless, distinctive. In the 1890s, after her Memphis press was destroyed, she rose to national and international fame as the most visible and outspoken African American woman in the world and as the person who sustained the most active of the anti-lynching campaigns of her era, directing attention against lynching and other causes for the next four decades.

Despite her record of achievements as a journalist and highly visible community activist, historical accounts about this era for most of the 20th century were not particularly inclusive of Wells-Barnett's accomplishments. In effect, she almost literally disappeared from the public record and from public consciousness within her own lifetime. Her achievements did not go down in either national lore or in history books. She was not celebrated as the darling of the black press, a central investigator and spokesperson against lynching, or as a courageous crusader across the United States and Great Britain for truth and justice. By the second decade of the 20th century, her involvement in the public sphere seemed a faint shadow of her earlier prominence.

While Wells-Barnett retained public regard in the city of Chicago and in the state of Illinois, as indicated by the fact that the city of Chicago named a housing project in her honor, her national presence waned, not to be rejuvenated until decades after her death when the research and scholarship of the late 20th century in women's studies and African American studies reclaimed and reinstated her contributions. Today, she is recognized as a tireless champion against lynching and a stellar exemplar of socially and politically conscious activism despite the racist and sexist conditions that surrounded her. Moreover, her life and work as a community activist and journalist have been instrumental in raising provocative questions about the impact of race, sex, and class on achievement and on how such achievements are publicly acknowledged and valued or not. The effect of this renewal of interest is that justice prevails. Wells-Barnett's contributions in several areas of achievement have been documented, and she is indeed celebrated as an astute businesswoman, a provocative investigative journalist, a passionate proponent of civil and women's rights, a champion of truth and justice, and a national and international leader.

JACQUELINE J. ROYSTER

See also
Anti-Lynching Legislation; Civil Rights Movement; Lynching; National Advancement of Colored Women (NACW)

Further Reading:
The American Experience: Ida B. Wells—A Passion for Justice. Directed by William Greaves. PBS, 1989.
Aptheker, Bettina, ed. Lynching and Rape: An Exchange of Views. New York: American Institute for Marxist Studies, 1977.
DeCosta-Willis, Miriam. Ida B. Wells: The Memphis Diaries. Boston: Beacon Press, 1994.
Diggs-Brown, Barbara. "Ida B. Wells-Barnett: About the Business of Agitation." In A Living of Words: American Women in Print Culture, edited by Susan Albertine. Knoxville: University of Tennessee Press, 1995.
Duster, Alfreda M. Crusade for Justice: The Autobiography of Ida B. Wells. Chicago: University of Chicago Press, 1970.
Harris, Trudier, compiler. Selected Works of Ida B. Wells-Barnett. New York: Oxford University Press, 1991.
Hendricks, Wanda. "Ida B. Wells-Barnett and the Alpha Suffrage Club of Chicago." In One Woman, One Vote: Rediscovering the Woman Suffrage Movement, edited by Marjorie Spruill Wheeler. Troutdale, OR: New Sage Press, 1995.
Humrich, Shauna Lea. "Ida B. Wells-Barnett: The Making of a Reputation." Master's thesis, University of Colorado, 1989.
Hutton, Mary M. B. "The Rhetoric of Ida B. Wells: The Genesis of the Anti-Lynch Movement." Ph.D. dissertation, University of Indiana, 1975.
Logan, Shirley W., ed. With Pen and Voice: A Critical Anthology of Nineteenth-Century African American Women. Carbondale: Southern Illinois Press, 1995.
McMurry, Linda O. To Keep the Waters Troubled: The Life of Ida B. Wells. New York: Oxford University Press, 1998.
Newkirk, Pamela. "Ida B. Wells-Barnett." In Profiles in Journalistic Courage, edited by Robert Giles and Robert Snyder. New Brunswick, NJ: Transaction Publishers, 2001.
Royster, Jacqueline Jones. "To Call a Thing by Its True Name: The Rhetoric of Ida B. Wells." In Reclaiming Rhetorica, edited by Andrea Lunsford, 167–84. Pittsburgh: University of Pittsburgh Press, 1995.
Royster, Jacqueline Jones. Southern Horrors and Other Writings: The Anti-Lynching Campaign of Ida B. Wells, 1892–1900. Boston: Bedford Books, 1997.
Royster, Jacqueline Jones. "Ida B. Wells-Barnett." In Encyclopedia of the Harlem Renaissance, 2 vols, edited by Cary D. Wintz and Paul Finkelman, 98–101. New York: Routledge, 2004.

Rydell, Robert W., ed. *The Reason Why the Colored American Is Not in the World's Columbian Exposition*. Urbana: University of Illinois Press, 1999.

Schechter, Patricia. "Unsettled Business: Ida B. Wells against Lynching, or How Antilynching Got Its Gender." In *Under Sentence of Death: Lynching in the South*, edited by Fitzhugh Brundage. Chapel Hill: University of North Carolina Press, 1997.

Thompson, Mildred I. "Ida B. Wells-Barnett: An Exploratory Study of an American Black Woman, 1893–1930." In *Black Women in United States History*, vol. 15, edited by Darlene Clark Hine. New York: Carlson Publishing, 1990.

Tucker, David M. "Miss Ida B. Wells and Memphis Lynching." In *Black Women in American History: From Colonial Times Through the Nineteenth Century*, vol. 4, edited by Darlene Clark Hine, 1085–95. New York: Carlson Publishing, 1990.

Wells-Barnett, Ida. *Crusade for Justice: The Autobiography of Ida B. Wells*. Edited by Alfreda M. Duster. Chicago: University of Chicago Press, 1970.

When Affirmative Action Was White

When Affirmative Action Was White is a book written by professor of political science and history Ira Katznelson. In this text, Katznelson presents a critical historic overview of affirmative action policies (*see also* Affirmative Action entry). The main thesis of this book explores the "untold history" of this enduringly contentious legislation. This untold history includes several sociopolitical mechanisms used to exclude blacks from federal policy provisions. Katznelson's book reframes the genesis of affirmative action by reminding readers that social welfare is not working "reversely" to the detriment of whites, but has in fact worked to the benefit of whites and to the exclusion of racial minorities for decades prior to the 1960s historical reference point.

The Civil Rights Act of 1964 is typically cited as one of the first official pieces of legislations on affirmative action. However, Katznelson argues that both lay and scholarly discourse on affirmative action misses the entire era of race-based federal policies that gave preferential treatment to whites. Katznelson mainly focuses on President Franklin's New Deal and President Truman's Fair Deal acts as the two federal policies that worked to the benefit of white Americans at the exclusion of racial minorities. These two policies are often noted as the pivotal federal legislation responsible for creating middle-class America by facilitating suburbanization, mass consumption, and obtainment of wealth among many other entitlements. Katznelson concedes that the quality of life increased overall in America, but the gains were not shared equally across racial lines.

The consequences of these federal policies led to drastic inequalities between whites and blacks in the areas of housing, employment, wealth, health care, and education that carry into the present day. Katznelson identifies several mechanisms used to discriminate against blacks in an ostensibly nonracist way. These mechanisms include: outright omitting African Americans from legislation, relying on the discretion of Southern bureaucrats to withhold provisions, and omitting antidiscriminatory provisions. Katznelson specifically devotes some time to discuss the role of the Selective Service Readjustment Act (1944), or the G.I. Bill.

The G.I. Bill was an initiative to secure education, employment, housing, and many other provisions for returning war veterans. However, Katznelson argues that the G.I. bill exacerbated rather than narrowed the economic and educational differences between blacks and whites. Blacks were denied admission to the best colleges and were often relegated to Historically Black Colleges and Universities, or HBCUs, which were often unaccredited, understaffed, and had limited majors. There were similar limitations in job training. Black veterans were denied admission to white vocational schools, which had the best equipment and facilities. There were also disparities in job placement. Black veterans would go from skilled military assignments as truck drivers to dishwashers, from communications experts to porters. Banks also routinely denied access to loans that the G.I. Bill promised.

According to Katznelson, if we were to reconsider social welfare policies from the early 20th century, our entire conception of affirmative action will have to change. Specifically, Katznelson calls for the expansion of the current affirmative action programs to include restitution in the form of tax breaks and housing and education vouchers for racial minorities. Whether or not this ideological shift has the potential to come into fruition, especially given the current sociopolitical climate in the United States, remains in question as affirmative action continues to be one of the most contentious policies of our time.

Alan Vincent Grigsby and Rasha Aly

Further Reading:
Katznelson, Ira. *When Affirmative Action Was White: An Untold History of Racial Inequality in Twentieth Century America.* New York: W.W. Norton, 2005.
Katznelson, Ira. "When Is Affirmative Action Fair? On Grievous Harms and Public Remedies." *Social Research* 73, no. 2 (2006): 541–68.
Lipson, Daniel. "Where's the Justice? Affirmative Action's Severed Civil Rights Roots in the Age of Diversity." *Perspectives of Politics* 6, no. 4 (2008): 691–706.
Lipson, Daniel. "The Resilience of Affirmative Action in the 1980s: Innovation, Isomorphism, and Institutionalization in University Admissions." *Political Research Quarterly* 64, no. 1 (2011): 132–44.

White, Walter (1893–1955)

Walter Francis White, a civil rights leader, authority on American race riots and lynchings, and writer who published his first works during the Harlem Renaissance, was born on July 1, 1893, in Atlanta, Georgia.

White was one of seven children born to George White, a postman, and his wife, Madeline (née Harrison) White, a schoolteacher. The family lived on the border between the African American and white neighborhoods. After graduating from the high school located on the Atlanta University campus, White matriculated at Atlanta University and graduated in 1916. In the summer of 1915, White began working at Standard Life Insurance Company, where he accepted full-time employment after earning his college degree.

In 1916, White became secretary of the newly formed Atlanta branch of the National Association for the Advancement of Colored People (NAACP), which was founded in response to the Atlanta school board's recent decisions to eliminate the seventh and eighth grades in African American schools to provide more funding for white schools. The first president of the Atlanta NAACP was Harry Pace, who was an officer at Standard Life. In 1918, White accepted James Weldon Johnson's offer to become assistant secretary of the NAACP's New York office, and, in 1929, White succeeded Johnson as the NAACP's executive secretary.

Walter White served the cause of African Americans as assistant and executive secretary of the National Association for the Advancement of Colored People (NAACP) from the 1920s until the 1950s. He came to be the most devoted fighter in the effort to stamp out lynching in the United States after World War I. (Library of Congress)

In addition to White's work as a preeminent civil rights leader, he was a prolific author. White wrote two novels—*Fire in the Flint* (1924) and *Flight* (1926)—which focus on lynching and "passing" for white, respectively, and a nonfiction work about lynching, *Rope and Faggot: The Biography of Judge Lynch* (1929). White also helped promote the work of other Harlem Renaissance writers such as poets Countee Cullen and Claude McKay as well as of such novelists as Rudolph Fisher, Nella Larsen, and Dorothy West. After the Harlem Renaissance, White wrote three additional book-length works: *A Rising Wind: A Report on the Negro Soldier in the European Theatre of War* (1945); *A Man Called White: The Autobiography of Walter White* (1948); and *How Far the Promised Land?* (1955), which was published posthumously and chronicles African American achievement. White, who contributed articles to such publications as *The Crisis, American Mercury, Saturday Evening Post*, and *Reader's Digest*, was a war correspondent for the *New York Post* from 1943 to 1945, and a columnist for the *Chicago Defender*. White continued his work as executive secretary of the NAACP and as a writer until he suffered a heart attack and died at his New York home on March 21, 1955. At his funeral four days later, 1,500 individuals filled St. Martin's Protestant Episcopal Church to capacity, and an additional crowd of 1,500 people listened to the service on loudspeakers outside the church.

White, who was arguably the leading expert on American race riots and lynchings during the first half of the 20th century, retained boyhood memories of the 1906 Atlanta riot. When he was 13, White rode with his father as he performed his postal duties. They reached Peachtree Street where one of the establishments was the Crystal Palace, a barbershop that catered to a nonblack clientele and was owned by Alonzo Herndon, a prominent African American. White and his father saw a lame African American employee from the Crystal Palace try in vain to outrun a mob of white men. After the mob caught the man, he was beaten with clubs and fists and left dead on the street in a pool of blood.

As White and his father continued riding through the streets of Atlanta, the mail cart and their light skin protected them; the mob was not bold enough to attack the cart, which was government property, and the rioters assumed that the cart's driver and passenger were white. The mail cart then collided with a carriage from which clung three African Americans, while the white driver lashed both the horses and the rioters who pursued the carriage. After White and his father kept their cart from turning over, they rescued an elderly African American woman who was being chased by the mob; White's father handed the reins to him as he lifted the lady into the cart, and White lashed the horse to run faster.

The next day, friends of White's father warned him that the rioters were going to march from Peachtree Street to Houston Street, where the Whites lived. That night, the rioters stood outside White's home with torches. The son of the Whites' grocer identified their residence as the home of "that nigger mail carrier" and urged the mob to burn the house down because it was "too nice for a nigger to live in!" (White 1948: 11). White and his father, possessing firearms, waited for the men to step onto their lawn. As the rioters moved to the front of the lawn, White, with his light skin, blonde hair, and blue eyes, claimed his identity as an African American. White writes, "In that instant there opened up within me a great awareness; I knew then who I was. I was a Negro, a human being with an invisible pigmentation" (White 1948: 11). Friends of White's father, who were barricaded in a nearby building, fired shots at the mob, causing the rioters to retreat.

Twelve years after the Atlanta riot, White moved to New York to become the NAACP's assistant secretary, and 12 days after he began working at the civil rights organization where he performed clerical and office tasks, a racial crime diverted his attention away from his office work. Jim McIlherron, an African American sharecropper, who defended himself when his employer physically attacked him, was slowly burned to death by a mob in Estill Springs, Tennessee. White and the other NAACP officials realized that if they sent a telegram protesting the lynching to the governor of Tennessee, it would have minimal effect. White then volunteered to travel to Tennessee to investigate the incident. According to David Levering Lewis, "With his eyes and hair, refined accent, and nervous energy, he looked and behaved far more the Wall Street broker than a man destined to be director of the nation's principal civil rights organization" (1981: 131). Posing as a white man interested in buying farmland, White gained the trust of the Estill Springs residents who admitted that McIlherron's employer was not justified in beating him, yet they asserted that McIlherron had to be murdered because he hit a white man, and they had to keep other African Americans from getting out of hand. White returned to New York and published his findings.

The Estill Springs lynching marked the first of more than 40 lynchings as well as eight race riots that White personally investigated between 1918 and 1929, and it established a pattern that he followed in subsequent investigations. White traveled to the troubled areas; passed as a white reporter, land speculator, etc.; gained the confidence of white individuals who spoke candidly about the horrific racial events; and then returned to New York to publish his findings. White, who took a pay cut when he gave up his job at Standard Life Insurance to work with the NAACP, sacrificed his comfortable lifestyle to put himself in harm's way during his undercover investigations. After three members of the Lowman family were murdered near Aiken, South Carolina, White's investigation revealed that the Ku Klux Klan was responsible for the lynchings of the young woman and two men. When several local newspapers criticized the lynchers, the sheriff's response was to announce his intention to request that the grand jury indict White for "bribery and passing for white" (White 1948: 59). On other occasions, White received death threats from the Klan.

In 1919, race riots occurred in such places as Washington, D.C.; Chicago, Illinois; Omaha, Nebraska; Philadelphia, Pennsylvania; and Elaine, Arkansas. The Chicago riot taught White that when a white mob is out of control, a Northern city could be as dangerous as a Southern town such as Estill Springs. The Chicago violence also taught him not to assume that he was well known by other African Americans. Although appearing white proved to be an advantage for him when he was among whites, his light complexion nearly ended his life when an African American, assuming he was white, shot at him.

In October 1919, White traveled to Phillips County, Arkansas, after a meeting held by African American sharecroppers at a local church erupted into chaos as an armed mob and some of the sharecroppers exchanged gunfire. After more than 200 African Americans were killed, many black men, women, and children fled the county. The rest were placed in stockades and awaited their appearance before a kangaroo court. White arrived in Phillips County and introduced himself to the governor of Arkansas as a reporter for the *Chicago Daily News* who had little knowledge of African Americans. The governor, assuming White was white, welcomed him; the politician, who described White as brilliant, gave him a letter of recommendation to use in case he ran into trouble in Phillips County. As White was conducting his investigation, an African American man warned him that white men were after him. White quickly boarded a train. As the conductor collected White's fare, he told him that he was leaving "just when the fun is going to start" (White 1948: 51) because the lynching of a man who was passing for white was imminent. When White's train arrived in Memphis later that evening, he heard that he had been lynched in Arkansas that afternoon. Among the tributes to White's work as an investigator are the Spingarn Medal, which he received in 1937, and the *Ballad of Walter White*, a poem by Langston Hughes.

Although White became too well known to continue conducting his undercover investigations, he continued to seek justice for the victims of lynchings and riots. White also attempted to help restore law and order to the troubled areas. When local and state officials did not halt the rioting

in Detroit in 1943, White asked the governor of Michigan to request federal troops. Noticing Gov. Harry Kelly's reluctance, White contacted the War Department in Washington and was told that a Michigan official would have to contact the commanding general of the area, who was stationed in Chicago. After White shared that information with Kelly, the governor finally requested the federal troops, and order was restored after 30 hours of rioting. During that period, 34 people were killed, and more than 600 were injured.

White was a peacemaker during the Harlem Riot in August 1943 (*see* New York City Riot of 1943 entry). The riot was the result of a rumor that an African American soldier died after he had been shot in the back by a white police officer. White rode with Mayor Fiorello LaGuardia through the streets of Harlem before he convinced the mayor to allow well-known African Americans to ride through Harlem in sound trucks. As objects were thrown at them, White and at least two other prominent black men rode through Harlem proclaiming that the soldier was only slightly injured and urging the residents to return to their homes; eventually the crowd dispersed.

During Walter White's tenure with the NAACP, he worked diligently to end racial discrimination in education, employment, and voting, as well as in the arts and military. Armed with courage and tenacity, White sought justice for the victims of hate crimes and equal rights for African Americans. His deeds as assistant secretary and executive secretary of the NAACP during the first half of the 20th century helped pave the way for subsequent victories in the civil rights movement.

LINDA M. CARTER

See also
Civil Rights Movement; Harlem Renaissance; Lynching

Further Reading:
Janken, Kenneth R. *White: The Biography of Walter White, Mr. NAACP.* New York: New Press, 2003.
Janken, Kenneth R. "Walter Francis White." In *African American Lives*, edited by Henry Louis Gates, Jr., and Evelyn Brooks Higginbotham, 879–81. New York: Oxford University Press, 2004.
Johns, Robert L. "Walter White." In *Notable Black American Men*, edited by Jessie Carney Smith, 1209–12. Detroit: Gale Research, 1998.
Lewis, David Levering. *When Harlem Was in Vogue.* New York: Knopf, 1981.

Meier, August, and Elliott Rudwick. "Walter White." In
    Dictionary of American Negro Biography, edited by Rayford
    W. Logan and Michael R. Winston, 646–50. New York: W.W.
    Norton, 1982.
"Walter White, 61, Dies in Home Here." *New York Times*, March
    22, 1955.
White, Walter. *A Man Called White: The Autobiography of Walter
    White*. New York: Viking Press, 1948.

White Citizens' Council

Formed in 1954 in Indianola, Mississippi, the White Citizens' Council was an organization that developed in reaction to desegregation efforts mandated by the U.S. Supreme Court's decision in *Brown vs. Board of Education*. According to various accounts, many local white businessmen, lawyers, politicians, and other prominent members of the community were inspired by a speech (or a transcript of this speech that was circulated among white segregationists) given by Tom P. Brady, a circuit judge from 1950–1963 who later became a Mississippi Supreme Court justice in 1963. In this speech, titled "Black Monday," Brady condemned the Supreme Court's desegregation decree and argued that racial integration was a threat to the white race and the "Southern way of life." Taking Brady's warnings seriously, Robert B. "Tut" Patterson, a World War II veteran who managed a local 1,500-acre cotton planation and is widely identified as the "founder" of the White Citizens' Council, called for a gathering of concerned whites to discuss ways to challenge racial integration. This first meeting was soon followed by a second, well-attended gathering at the local town hall in Indianola, in July 11, 1954. At this second meeting, the White Citizens' Council was born. By 1955, approximately 60,000 people were listed in Patterson's membership list and comprised 253 councils. A year later, the White Citizens' Council became known as the Citizens' Councils of America and were active in 30 states (Anti-Defamation League). By 1957, there were approximately 250,000 members of these Citizens' Councils.

What presumably distinguished the Citizens' Councils of America from other segregationist and white supremacist organizations such as the Ku Klux Klan was that the former presumably rejected violence, openly listed prominent

Robert Patterson founded the White Citizens' Councils in Mississippi in 1954 in response to the U.S. Supreme Court decision in *Brown v. Board of Education* that overturned the doctrine of separate but equal and declared racial segregation in public schools unconstitutional. The White Citizens' Councils actively opposed integration in the 1950s and 1960s and were succeeded by the Council of Conservative Citizens, founded in 1988. (Library of Congress)

members of the community as its members, and sought to accomplish their objectives through political and economic pressure. For example, in a well-known incident that occurred in Yazoo City, Mississippi, on August 5, 1955, a local chapter of the NAACP submitted a petition of 53 signatures to the local school board demanding that they obey the Supreme Court's ruling to desegregate. In response, the local Citizens' Council publicly denounced these 53 signers—most of whom were black businessmen and professionals—as "agitators" and encouraged the local white community to take action against them. Referring to this specific case, James Cobb (2010) writes: "one by one those who signed the petition lost their jobs or whatever 'business' or 'trade' they had with whites. Some blacks moved quickly to remove their names from the list. Others held out but eventually followed suit. Many of those who removed their names found it impossible to get their jobs back, nor could they find new employment." Although avoiding physical violence, Citizens' Councils nonetheless used racist rhetoric and warned local white communities that desegregation would result in, among other outcomes, "racial mongrelization" as well as an increase in black-on-white rape and other forms of violence.

According to several writers, the Citizens' Councils of America also embraced anti-Semitism. Daniel Levitas (2002), for example, notes that on August 31, 1954, one month after the Council's founding meeting, Robert Patterson circulated a reading list for Council members and potential members, and many items on this list included anti-Semitic literature. Some of this literature associated Judaism with communism and warned whites that Jews were the architects and "driving force" behind the civil rights movement. Jewish communists and liberals, in effect, had plans to undermine white America. By the 1960s, however, the victories of the civil rights movement pushed "Southern states and their elected officials to gradually liberalize." Thus, the Citizens' Councils of America lost much of its momentum and became "moribund by the 1970s" (Anti-Defamation League).

Yet by the 1980s there was a rebirth of this organization. Tapping into largely unfounded concerns about, among other things, preferential treatment for blacks and other racial minorities, an alleged black-on-white crime epidemic, and government handouts to parasitical racial minorities who refuse to work, 30 men (among them founder Robert Patterson; former segregationist governor of Georgia, Lester Maddox; and former Louisiana congressman, John Rarick) met to renovate the Council movement in Atlanta, Georgia, in 1985. This effort entailed using old Citizens' Council mailing lists to garner support. What resulted from these efforts was the establishment of a new organization called the Council of Conservative Citizens (CCC).

According to the Southern Poverty Law Center (SPLC), the CCC rapidly gained (or regained) supporters, including prominent individuals such as U.S. senator Trent Lott and Georgia congressman Bob Barr, as well as well-known white supremacist/separatists such as Jared Taylor. Since the early 1990s, the CCC has also used the criticism directed against the symbolism of the Confederate battle flag by the NAACP and other groups as a "powerful rallying point" to convince

Southern whites of the alleged ongoing attack against "Southern heritage" (Anti-Defamation League). In more recent years, the CCC has continued attracting prominent white politicians. In fact, the SPLC reports that from 2000 to 2004, at least 38 federal, state, and local elected officials have attended and/or spoken CCC events. Today, the CCC has chapters in 20 states and continues to have links to various elected officials. A review of the main CCC Web site reveals that they continue fighting for white nationalist/separatist causes including, among other issues, the confederate flag as a symbol of Southern pride, anti-nonwhite immigration, reverse discrimination against whites, black-on-white crime, affirmative action, and Obama's "big government" that presumably favors undeserving racial minorities.

LUIGI ESPOSITO

See also

Nazism; Whiteness Studies; White Nationalism; White Supremacy

Further Reading:

Anti-Defamation League, "Council of Conservative Citizens." http://www.adl.org/learn/ext_us/CCCitizens.asp (accessed September 22, 2012).

Brady, Tom P. *Black Monday: Segregation and Amalgamation—America Has Its Choice.* Winona, MS: Association of Citizens' Councils, 1955.

Cobb, James C. "The Real Story of the White Citizens' Council." http://www.hnn.us/articles/134814.html (accessed September 23, 2012).

Levitas, Daniel. "The White Nationalist Movement." http://www.splcenter.org/get-informed/intelligence-files/ideology/white-nationalist/the-white-nationalist-movement (accessed September 21, 2012).

Levitas, Daniel. *The Terrorist Next Door.* New York: St. Martin's Press, 2002.

White Flight

White flight originally denoted the post–World War II movement of Caucasian Americans out of inner cities that were predominantly African American and into the homogeneity of white suburbs. The term is synonymous with *white flux.* Although the mobility pattern is commonly believed to be racially based, arguments have been made (Bickford) that issues of wealth and class (not race and ethnicity) may be at the root of this social phenomenon. Other studies (Farley 1976) find substantial segregation patterns after adjusting for both educational achievement and income, confirming the hypothesis that suburban segregation cannot be explained by socioeconomic status alone, and may well be based on racial bias.

This massive emigration of whites also had a grave snowball effect on the economy of the inner city. As wealthier residents moved out of the inner city, higher tax dollars and property taxes followed the mobile Caucasian. When this happens on a broad scale, inner cities are eventually left devoid of essential financial resources. Inner-city schools suffer, crime rises, and buildings deteriorate, making it even less desirable for middle- and upper-class residents to remain in the city's core.

As minority affluence rises, the African American family becomes much more economically mobile and is able to migrate from urban, inner-city residential settings into the more lucrative suburbs of the United States. Middle- and upper-class African Americans are able to buy homes in previously all-white neighborhoods.

Closely tied to the term *white flight* are the phrases *racial steering* and *redlining*. Racial steering is a practice used by realtors to direct clients only to homes and neighborhoods of their own perceived racial category. Whites are shown homes in white neighborhoods, blacks are shown homes in all-black neighborhoods, Latinos are shown homes in Hispanic neighborhoods. Redlining occurs when realtors circle in red pen the areas of the city that are considered too risky to provide mortgages for homes, most likely homes of minority populations.

White flight also has an opposing trend surfacing throughout American cities today. Gentrification denotes the process by which many cities have put forth extreme efforts and money to revitalize their inner cities and downtown areas. Old buildings are refurbished into elegant apartments. Abandoned storefronts become occupied by high-end stores. A portion of the affluent white population returns to the inner city. Although this process brings higher revenue to the city and improves the aesthetics of the urban area, there are social consequences. Cheap housing is razed and eliminated, driving thousands of economically fragile people into the state of homelessness. Single-room occupancy hotels that once provided substandard, yet financially affordable

housing for the poor are either refurbished into luxury condominiums or leveled to provide space for new high-end residential structures.

SHEILA BLUHM MORLEY

See also

American Apartheid; Blockbusting; Hypersegreation; Racial Steering; Residential Segregation; Surburban Segregation

Further Reading:

Bickford, Eric. "White Flight: The Effect of Minority Presence on Post World War II Suburbanization." http://www.eh.net/Clio/Publications/flight.shtml.

Farley, Reynolds. "Components of Suburban Population Growth." In *The Changing Face of the Suburbs*, edited by Barry Schwartz. Chicago: University of Chicago Press, 1976.

White League

The White League was an all-white paramilitary group that formed during Reconstruction in the 19th century to remove Republicans from office and restore Democrats to power in states across the South. The league is best known for its role in the political ferment that followed the contentious election of 1872 in Louisiana. It played a significant role in three major disturbances in Colfax, Coushatta, and Liberty Place.

The conditions that gave rise to the formation of the White League were manifold. Soon after the Civil War, white Southerners formed militias, ostensibly to protect whites from the threat of black violence and crime. This gave whites opportunity to unlawfully seize property and weapons from blacks and mutilate and murder them. It is out of this tradition that the White League formed, but it directed violence against the black population as a whole, as well as against Republican officials.

In the election of 1872, Louisiana Democrats attempted to usurp power by running John D. McEnery for governor and claiming victory. However, the Republicans claimed that William Pitt Kellogg had won the election, and President Ulysses S. Grant recognized Kellogg as Louisiana's new governor. Trouble followed when, in 1873, Kellogg appointed one white Republican and one black to fill positions previously assigned to white conservatives at the Colfax courthouse. A black militia, sanctioned by Kellogg, formed to protect the Republican officials. A group of whites, including some members of the White League, attacked the courthouse, killing more than 69 people. Participants of the massacre at Colfax were charged with violating the civil rights of those they had murdered and of infringing on the Enforcement Acts. Their case went to the U.S. Supreme Court, where it was decided that the states were responsible for the enforcement of civil rights. Conservative whites interpreted this ruling to mean they were free to terrorize blacks and Republicans at will, as long as they were careful not to provoke the federal government into sending in troops.

In 1874, many conservatives joined the White League. These new members used the local press to recruit members and to brandish threats to the Republicans. They held regular rallies inciting men, women, and even children to participate in acts against the Republicans and blacks. Adding fuel to the sweltering hostility were rumors, instigated by the local press, of black schemes to attack whites.

The league threatened to lynch Republicans in Natchitoches, St. Martin, Avoylles, Winn, and elsewhere, effectively vacating seats for the Democrats. In the summer of 1874, violence erupted in Coushatta when league members murdered several blacks who had attacked whites. It was assumed that the league was behind the brutal murders of six white Republicans who had been acquitted of accusations that they had masterminded the black uprisings. In September, federal troops arrived in Shreveport, Louisiana.

On September 14, 1974, 3,500 armed members of the White League faced off against 3,600 police officers and black militia troops in what is known as the Battle of Liberty Place. A one-hour fight ensued, resulting in 38 men killed and 79 wounded. The triumphant White League overran the city hall, the statehouse, and the arsenal, and installed John McEnery as governor. After three days, federal troops arrived in New Orleans and restored Kellogg to power. The league surrendered and dispersed, but not before they had inspired other Southern states to engage in similar tactics. In the election of 1876, political violence, intimidation, and fraud secured the Democratic victory and, consequently, brought an end to Reconstruction in Louisiana.

GLADYS L. KNIGHT

See also

Ku Klux Klan (KKK); Reconstruction Era; White Supremacy

Further Reading:

Taylor, Joe Gray. "Louisiana: An Impossible Task." In *Reconstruction and Redemption in the South*, edited by Otto H. Olsen, 202–30. Baton Rouge: Louisiana State University Press, 1980.

White Mobs

White mobs were disorderly crowds that ruthlessly terrorized and victimized blacks and their supporters, particularly between the 1800s and 1960s. Unlike racist organizations, white mobs were loosely organized, spontaneous, and ephemeral. Nevertheless, they exhibited similar motives, activities, and characteristics, and were equally frightful. James Weldon Johnson, author and activist, aptly described his confrontation with a mob when he said, "On the other side of the fence, Death was standing. Death turned and looked at me and I looked at Death" (Dray 84).

The motives of white mobs varied throughout history. During the period of growing opposition to the antislavery movement, white mobs formed to riot and, if necessary, even kill sympathetic whites and free blacks in the North. After the Civil War, white mobs sporadically formed to attack newly freed blacks and anyone else committed to advancing their cause. White mobs worked independently of, and concurrently with, vigilante organizations like the Ku Klux Klan to destroy the Freedmen's Bureau's schools, to beat black and white teachers, and to intimidate and kill Republican politicians during Reconstruction in the South.

Between the 1880s and 1930s, numerous blacks were lynched. White mobs were largely responsible for these lynchings, as well as for the antiblack riots that occurred. Violence was to the mob a tool to enforce the racist and discriminatory Jim Crow laws, to maintain white supremacy and black oppression, and to thwart black resistance. White mobs attacked any black person who violated Jim Crow or racial etiquette or threatened the status quo. White mobs, feeding off their fear that black men were a threat to white women, lynched numerous black men on hearing accusations of gazing at, speaking to, touching, and assaulting white women. Sometimes they created rumors of rape to create an opportunity to destroy prosperous black communities.

An African American home in flames, the work of a white mob during the burning of Rosewood in 1923. The town was burned by a racist mob who also murdered at least eight other African American residents. (UPI-Bettmann/Corbis)

Many, if not most, of the rape accusations were unfounded and untried in a court of law. Due to rampant racism in the judicial court system and biased all-white juries, just trials were an anomaly.

In the 1940s, white mobs rioted in black communities as a result of competition for housing and employment opportunities. In the 1950s and 1960s, white mobs were responsible for the violent opposition to the forced integration of formerly all-white schools and to the demonstrations of the civil rights movement. The motives of the white mobs often stemmed from a deep and unsatiated racial animosity toward blacks. This racial hatred was what unified and solidified the white mobs.

White mobs employed an assortment of violent methods, which frequently resulted in death. Specific targets rarely survived to tell their tales. Hence Johnson's fear as he faced a white mob, though he was one of the few who escaped unharmed. When a white mob was on the rampage, it targeted any available black men, women, and children. White mobs were known to lynch the elderly as well as pregnant women. When the black community at large was the target, homes and property were seized or destroyed, and more than a few lives were lost. The common methods of violence between the 1860s and 1930s were beating, shooting, burning, and lynching. Sometimes the lynchings involved all the above. During the civil rights movement, white mobs were notorious for pelting objects at demonstrators and bombing.

White mobs had common characteristics. They were generally male dominated (with more female involvement during the mid-20th century) and were not necessarily affiliated with a racist organization. The size of the mob ranged from a dozen to several thousand and comprised a mixture of economic backgrounds. Most of the participants lived next door to the black community they targeted and brazenly pursued their victims without disguises. Sometimes, men from outside the community were enlisted or willingly participated without invitation. Although many mobs formed spontaneously, others were organized several days, weeks, or months prior to the culminating activity. Furthermore, most mob activities were not isolated, self-sustaining affairs.

Although formal racist organizations and white mobs sometimes worked privately and in disguise, a number of mobs relied heavily on outside sources and unabashedly acted out their crimes. On several occasions, mob activities were not random, spontaneous events, but deliberate plots devised by whites with economic, social, or political power. During Reconstruction, conservative Democrats often masterminded white mob activities. In the Memphis (Tennessee) Riot of 1866, the affluent whites of the neighborhood manipulated and controlled the middle-class white rioters. State and local officials rarely challenged white mob violence. By neglecting to act, they allowed the mob to carry out its will without fear of penalty. Some officials even encouraged antiblack violence, just as police and elected officials would later warn white mobs of impending black demonstrations and permitted their violent attacks during the civil rights movement in the 1960s. In this atmosphere of tolerance and approval, white mobs assaulted blacks openly and shamelessly.

The press also helped fuel the activities of white mobs by providing an effective means of communicating imminent lynchings to the local community and beyond. Whites traveled from afar on trains and set up camps in anticipation of the event. As many as several thousand people were known to attend a single lynching. Food was served; children played; photos were taken, and the press stood ready with pen and paper to report the events. The audience, usually (but not necessarily) all white, often participated in the chilling torture and death of the victim. Men, women, and

children were known to stab or beat the victims. After the death of the victim, the community sometimes rushed on the body and severed fingers, toes, organs, or any other part of the body for a keepsake. Afterward, the mob, and sometimes members of the community, small children included, posed proudly beside the ravaged body for the camera.

GLADYS L. KNIGHT

See also

Lynching; Race Riots in America

Further Reading:

Dray, Philip. *At the Hands of Persons Unknown: The Lynching of Black America*. New York: Random House, 2002.
Pfeifer, Michael J. *Rough Justice: Lynching and American Society, 1874–1947*. Urbana: University of Illinois Press, 2004.

White Nationalism

White Nationalism can be described as both an ideology and a movement that seeks to advance the cause of white supremacy and/or white separatism. The primary objective among most White Nationalists in the United States is to restore white rule and/or reestablish a "sovereign white nation" within the United States. As an ideology, White Nationalism in the United States is rooted in the belief that this country's greatness "derives from its racial character as an all-White nation" (Levitas). The idea that the United States is, or was meant to be, a white nation can be traced to the very inception of this country. As discussed by Joe Feagin (2010), in 1787, "fifty-five men met in Philadelphia to write a constitution for the first 'democratic' nation, yet one for *Whites only*." Indeed, shortly after the Constitution was ratified, the U.S. Congress passed the Naturalization Act of 1790, which mandated that only whites can be citizens of the United States. Whites continued to have exclusive rights and privileges over other groups well after the abolition of slavery, as exemplified by the famous Dred Scott case. In short, these racial privileges have always been predicated on the idea that whites—and whites only—are the rightful citizens of this nation.

As a movement, White Nationalism first developed in reaction to efforts taken by the federal government to enforce the equal rights of blacks during the Reconstruction era. With the passing of the Thirteenth, Fourteenth, and Fifteenth Amendments, Southern whites feared the dominant position they considered rightfully theirs was under attack. Groups such as the Ku Klux Klan used intimidation and violence to challenge what they considered to be a threat against white supremacy. By 1896, the implied racial backlash provided the social context on which the U.S. Supreme Court ruled on the doctrine of "separate but equal" in the *Plessy vs. Ferguson* case. Particularly in the South, racial segregation laws were passed in virtually every state to keep blacks "in their place." These laws were often enforced through the use of lynchings and other acts of racial brutality. Although Jim Crow laws were largely absent in the Northern states, racial violence, as well as policies such as "restrictive covenants" were nonetheless widely used during the first half of the 20th century to keep people of color from white communities (e.g., Massey and Denton 1993). All these efforts reflected a broader ideology of white supremacy and the belief that non-whites—particularly blacks—are "outsiders" that should be kept out of white society.

In 1948, President Harry Truman's initiative to end racial segregation in the armed forces caused another uproar among large segments of the white population. A bit later, white fear and resentment reached new heights with the civil rights movement. Demands by the federal government to desegregate schools and other institutions were seen as an outright attack on white America. As discussed by Daniel Levitas, the 1964 Civil Rights Act and the 1965 Voting Rights Act, combined with Lyndon Johnson's War on Poverty, "sealed the fate of Southern segregationist and Northern bigots alike." Much like during the Reconstruction era, large segments of the white population saw the federal government as antithetical to the interests of decent, hardworking white people. Throughout the 1980s and 1990s, this general sentiment generated a wave of racial fears and politicized prejudices rooted in the assumption that whites are increasingly victims of a government that prioritizes the interests of undeserving racial minorities. This narrative of reverse discrimination inspired the creation of various White Nationalist organizations, such as the Council of Conservative Citizens, an offshoot of the Whites Citizens' Council, which was founded in 1985 in Atlanta, Georgia. This organization aims to align itself with elected officials to oppose, among other issues, affirmative action programs and progressive immigration policies.

Especially since the late 1990s, the White Nationalist movement has (with a few exceptions) largely abandoned open calls for racial violence and instead uses the idea of white victimhood as its raison d'être. As discussed by Carol M. Swain, beginning in the 1990s the White Nationalist movement in the United States has sought to persuade white Americans to join its cause by emphasizing, among other things, the dangers of multiculturalism, racial quotas in hiring and school admissions, high black-on-white crimes rates, and lax immigration policies. Many White Nationalist groups also emphasize the threat of sharia law being instituted in the United States because of this country's presumably blind tolerance for diversity. There is also a clear anti-Semitic/anti-Zionist bent among many White Nationalist organizations that claim the U.S. government has, for the past several decades, been hijacked by Zionist Jews who prioritize the interests of Israel over those of white Americans.

In the last four years, the election of an African American president, an economic crisis, a perceived "invasion" of Mexicans and other foreigners entering the country illegally, and projected demographic shifts whereby whites will no longer be the numerical majority in the United States within the next few decades have further reinforced the appeal of White Nationalism among many white Americans. Many in the white community argue that Obama's "big government" is designed to uplift the lives of undeserving racial minorities at the expense of hard-working white people. In fact, according to *Stormfront*, a popular White Nationalist internet forum established in the 1990s, the site got over 2,000 new members the day after Barack Obama was elected as president in 2008. As of 2012, the Southern Poverty Law Center listed 147 active White Nationalist groups in the United States. Among the most prominent organizations include the Council of Conservative Citizens, American Third Position, and American Renaissance. In recent years, White Nationalists have used the internet, as well as music, to spread their message to increasing numbers of people.

LUIGI ESPOSITO

See also

Ku Klux Klan (KKK); Nazism; White Citizens' Council; White Supremacy

Further Reading:

Feagin, Joe. *The White Racial Frame.* New York: Routledge, 2010.

Levitas, Daniel. "The White Nationalist Movement." http://www.splcenter.org/get-informed/intelligence-files/ideology/white-nationalist/the-white-nationalist-movement (accessed September 25, 2012).

Massey, Douglas, and Nancy Denton. *American Apartheid: Segregation and the Making of the Underclass.* Cambridge, MA: Harvard University Press, 1993.

Swain, Carol M. *The New White Nationalism in America: Its Challenge to Integration.* Cambridge: Cambridge University Press, 2002.

White Privilege

Central to the theoretical project of whiteness studies is not only conceptualizing whiteness as an historically constituted and contested racial formation, but also defining it as a pervasive system of racial privileges that materially, socially, and politically advantage many white people at the expense of people of aggrieved racial formations.

The project of identifying and defining racial privileges originated in the pivotal scholarship of W.E.B. Du Bois (1956 [1935]), a prominent 20th-century scholar and activist. Du Bois (1956 [1935]) noted that 19th-century poor white laborers exchanged class consciousness for race privilege, choosing the "public and psychological wage[s]" of whiteness instead of establishing coalitions based on economic marginalization with freed slaves and other disenfranchised African Americans. As a result, poor white laborers, especially ethnic immigrants—like the Irish—whose racial heritage was deemed dubious by the white aristocracy, gained social advantages and psychological benefits in recompense for their complicity with white supremacy, leveraging these advantages for material and political gain.

Building on the work of Du Bois, the literature of whiteness studies attempts to define, identify, and intervene in the exercise of white privilege: the collective unearned material, political, and social advantages, psychological benefits, and positive life chances granted to persons who perform and reinforce whiteness. The myriad privileges of whiteness are both the products and constitutive elements of structural white supremacy. For example, a privilege that is instrumental to masking whiteness as the universal, invisible racial touchstone is white racial unconsciousness. Whereas people of color remain constantly cognizant of their race as they negotiate a society inherently structured by racial inequality, many white people possess the privilege of going through life without ever having to think about, reflect on, and question their own racialization and their possible complicity in sustaining inequitable racial relations. White racial unconsciousness reproduces whiteness as the human norm in contradistinction to racial "others." Indeed, white racial consciousness emerges only when whiteness and white privilege are contested, as when a white person is temporarily a racial minority in a social setting. In such situations, whiteness is marshaled or an ethnic identity is resuscitated to cloak whites in minority status, claim victim-status (as in claims of reverse discrimination), and/or rationalize the unearned advantages from which many whites have benefited.

Equally critical to the maintenance of structural white supremacy, many white people possess the privilege of invoking color-blind ideology to dismiss the existence of racial inequality and explain away racial social disparities, like disproportionate rates of incarceration, broadening social segregation, and incommensurate proportions of wealth between whites and other racial formations. Bolstered by the ostensibly incontrovertible assumption of equality and protected by the invisibility of whiteness, color-blind ideology enables claims of a postracial America, one in which racism no longer matters in determining the life chances, material reality, and political capital of people of color. The racial privilege of invoking color-blind ideology also has the effect of conferring individuality onto many white people, allowing them to think of themselves and to expect to be treated as individuals whose material success rests on hard work and determination rather than the advantages of enduring racial stratification. This encourages many whites to develop a worldview that emphasizes individualism, masking the group-based advantages from which they may benefit, rendering group-based claims of racial inequality as illegitimate, and perpetuating the myth of meritocracy.

Moreover, white privilege permeates seemingly disinterested social situations and interpersonal interactions. For instance, many white people never have to worry about racial profiling, never have to question whether their skin color disadvantages them when applying for financial products, and never have to consider whether interpersonal conflicts are the result of racial prejudice. White people can generally rest assured that other people in power will look like them and that they will learn from historical material that lionizes their descendants' contributions to the construction of civilization.

Although the conferral and exercise of white privilege does not occur uniformly, many white people benefit from the existence of the privileges of whiteness and can generally rely on them as assets that they can leverage for material and political gain. The privileges of whiteness constitute and are constituted by the social and political power of whiteness as a racial formation, existing in a reciprocal relationship that reinforces and perpetuates each other and that work in concert to condition many white people to strategically evade, deny, or fail to see racial stratification.

NICHOLAS N. BEHM

See also

Third Wave Whiteness; Whiteness Studies

Further Reading:

Andersen, Margaret L. "Whitewashing Race: A Critical Perspective on Whiteness." In *White Out: The Continuing Significance of Racism*, edited by Ashley W. Doane and Eduardo Bonilla-Silva, 21–34. New York: Routledge, 2003.

Bonilla-Silva, Eduardo. *Racism Without Racists: Color-Blind Racism and the Persistence of Racial Inequality in the United States*. Lanham, MD: Rowman & Littlefield, 2006.

Delgado, Richard, and Jean Stefancic, eds. *Critical White Studies: Looking Behind the Mirror*. Philadelphia: Temple University Press, 1997.

Doane, Woody. "Rethinking Whiteness Studies." In *White Out: The Continuing Significance of Racism*, edited by Ashley W. Doane and Eduardo Bonilla-Silva, 3–18. New York: Routledge, 2003.

Du Bois, W. E. B. *Black Reconstruction in America*. New York: Russell, 1956 [1935].

Frankenberg, Ruth. *The Social Construction of Whiteness: White Women, Race Matters*. Minneapolis: University of Minnesota Press, 1993.

Gallagher, Charles A. "Playing the White Ethnic Card: Using Ethnic Identity to Deny Contemporary Racism." In *White Out: The Continuing Significance of Racism*, edited by Ashley W. Doane and Eduardo Bonilla-Silva, 145–58. New York: Routledge, 2003.

Lipsitz, George. *The Possessive Investment of Whiteness: How White People Profit from Identity Politics*. Philadelphia: Temple University Press, 2006.

McIntosh, Peggy. "White Privilege: Unpacking the Invisible Knapsack." In *White Privilege: Essential Readings on the Other Side of Racism*, edited by Paula S. Rothenberg, 109–13. New York: Worth Press, 2005.

Rothenberg, Paula S. "Introduction." In *White Privilege: Essential Readings on the Other Side of Racism*, edited by Paula S. Rothenberg, 1–5. New York: Worth Press, 2005.

White Savior Films

White savior films are a genre in the cinematic arts that present a low-class, minority group (generally Latino or black) or person of color that struggles through the social order, particularly that of the educational and judicial systems, and is saved and redeemed by the actions and counsel of a white character. The "white savior" manifests in the figure of a teacher, lawyer, or other position of power over nonwhites, and uses that power or their personal skills to save or assist the characters of color. Some examples of these movies are *Glory* (1989), *Dangerous Minds* (1996), *Amistad* (1997), *Finding Forester* (2000), *The Last Samurai* (2003), *Freedom Writers* (2008), *The Blind Side* (2009), *The Help* (2011), and *Django Unchained* (2013).

The white savior film has ideological roots in the late 19th-century racial and cultural paradigms of "manifest destiny" and the "white man's burden." In both cases, beliefs in the inherent superiority of whites over nonwhites rationalized support for white paternalistic policies and laws that structured both U.S. westward expansion and the U.S. foreign policy. These movements came to represent an increasingly taken-for-granted zeitgeist; a world populated by people of color thought unredeemable without righteous white paternalism. By the early 1900s, the trope of white paternalism soon morphed into the "Great White Hope," as white boxers attempted to dethrone the first black heavyweight-boxing champion, Jack Johnson (1908–1915). Throughout the remained of the century, a moribund white supremacist order required a racial savior that promised to sediment a social order premised on white benefactors and nonwhite recipients. By the 1980s the United States bore

Film still from *Django Unchained*, starring Christoph Waltz (left), and Jamie Foxx (right). (Sony Pictures/AP Photo)

witness to the first cadre of white savior films like *Cry Freedom* (1987), *Mississippi Burning* (1988), *A Dry White Season* (1989), *Glory* (1989), and the Indiana Jones trilogy (1981, 1984, 1989).

The white savior film is an important cultural device and artifact of the supposed "postracial" and "color-blind" era of the new millennium. These films help to repair the myth of white supremacy and natural paternalism by showcasing whites who go the extra mile to help people of color who cannot or will not help themselves, thus establishing social order, teaching nonwhites right from wrong, and framing the white savior as the only character able to recognize these moral distinctions and act upon them.

In these films, the white messiah is sometimes portrayed as a misfit within the white mainstream society because of his involvement with the nonwhite "othered" group. However, he is often portrayed as a hero, or even idolized, by the characters of color. As a consequence, the nonwhite groups and people portrayed in these films are followers and only exist in relationship to the white savior; they are framed as incapable of overcoming their own marginalization or oppression.

In a climate in which many whites believe they are unfairly victimized by a antiwhite, politically correct society, white fatigue with hearing of racial matters, and the valorizing of diversity and multiculturalism qua interracial reconciliation and amity, white savior films deliver a message that resonates with desires for a postracial era. These interracial depictions of friendly and cooperative race relations eschew any blatant message of white supremacy while they rely on an implicit message of white paternalism and antiblack stereotypes of contented servitude, obedience, and acquiescence.

BIANCA GONZALEZ SOBRINO AND MATTHEW W. HUGHEY

Further Reading:

Cammarota, Julio. "Blinsided by the Avatar: White Saviors and Allies Out of Hollywood and in Education." *Review of Education, Pedagogy, and Cultural Studies* 33, no. 3 (2011): 242–59.

Hughey, Matthew W. "The White Savior Film and Reviewers' Reception." *Symbolic Interaction* 33, no. 3 (2010): 475–96.

Hughey, Matthew W. "Racializing Redemption, Reproducing Racism: The Odyssey of Magical Negroes and White Saviors." *Sociology Compass* 6 no. 9 (2012): 751–67.

Moore, Wendy Leo, and Jennifer Pierce. "Still Killing Mockingbirds: Narratives of Race and Innocence in Hollywood's Depiction of the White Messiah Lawyer." *Qualitative Sociology Review* 3 no. 2 (2007): 171–87.

Vera, Hernán, and Andrew M. Gordon. *Screen Saviors: Hollywood Fictions of Whiteness*. Lanham, MD: Rowman & Littlefield, 2003.

White Supremacy

This concept refers to both a racial ideology about the superiority of people socially defined as white, as well as a series of social structures and institutional practices that both reflect and support (either deliberately or unintentionally) this ideology. Although terms such as *white* and *black* were not commonly used prior to the 17th century, these terms, particularly in the United States, became increasingly popular with the advent of racial slavery. That is, these racial terms were invented to legitimize a system of racial supremacy that benefitted whites and normalized the subordination and presumed inferiority of non-European groups, especially blacks. On the basis of these racial beliefs, the first U.S. Congress declared that U.S. citizenship was limited to white persons only in 1790. The same racial logic legitimized the famous Dred Scott decision, in which the U.S. Supreme Court ruled that blacks are not U.S. citizens and therefore not entitled to constitutional rights.

As a racial ideology or belief system, white supremacy has taken various forms throughout U.S. history. During the 1700s and early 1800s, debates and discussions about the roots of white supremacy often revolved around the issue of divine creation. Theories of polygenesis were often employed to explain why whites were a unique and superior race. These theories questioned whether God created only one species of humanity and legitimized a distinction between whites (i.e., "Children of God," full-fledged human beings, etc.), and "others." Accordingly, defining blacks and other nonwhites as beings who were not fully human legitimized policies and practices that deprived these people of their "human rights" (Omi and Winant 1994).

By the late 19th and early 20th centuries, white supremacy and the idea of racial hierarchies took on a scientific turn. The popularity of social Darwinism during this time, coupled with the belief in race as a "biological fact," led to a series of beliefs that further legitimized white supremacy and the subordination of nonwhites. An emphasis on racial biology, for example, gave credence to the idea that different races have unique behavioral tendencies. Prominent social scientists of this time, such as Lester Ward, argued that black men had a biological drive to want to rape white women as an attempt to improve their "racial stock." The notion of racial biology was also linked to the presumed intellectual deficiencies or low IQs that were allegedly typical among nonwhites, as well as the belief that nonwhites, particularly blacks, were naturally prone to violence. All these beliefs—illustrated in films such as *The Birth of a Nation*—encouraged racial fears, emboldened efforts to retain the "purity" of the white race, and reinforced white support for racist laws and practices (e.g., Jim Crow Laws, antimiscegenation laws, eugenics, etc.) that were designed to sustain white supremacy. Indeed, from the late 1890s to the first half of the 1950s, white supremacy, particularly in the South, was legally sustained through the so-called separate but equal doctrine that was mandated by the U.S. Supreme Court in *Plessy vs. Ferguson*. In actuality, critics argue that this decision legitimized a racially divided society that was separate and unequal.

By the mid-1950s and especially by the 1960s, the civil rights movement succeeded in eradicating racial segregation laws and challenging overt racial bigotry. However, far from vanquished, white supremacy in the United States took on a more subtle and unobtrusive character. Indeed, various writers have argued that white supremacy during the post–civil rights era is not typically overt but rather hides behind liberal values associated with free competition, meritocracy, and equality of opportunity. Among sociologists who endorse this position, perhaps one of the best known is Eduardo Bonilla-Silva, who argues that the aforementioned liberal values currently form part of a color-blind ideology

American Nazi Party (ANP)

Founded by George Lincoln Rockwell (1918–1967) in the 1960s, the American Nazi Party was dedicated to the preservation of white power. Rockwell, claiming to be inspired by reading Adolph Hitler's *Mein Kampf*, vowed to exterminate homosexuals, Jews, blacks, and other groups. In the 1960s, the American Nazi Party had only a small membership but gained notoriety nonetheless, particularly as a result of Rockwell's famous 1966 interview with *Roots* author Alex Haley for *Playboy* magazine and his public call for "White Power" in response to the Black Power movement. In the 1960s, Rockwell organized the harassment of civil rights workers in the South. In the 1970s, the ANP organized confrontations against integrationists and eventually spawned another organization, the National Socialist White People's Party. The American Nazi Party, now based in Michigan and run by Rocky Suhayda, uses the Internet to attract membership. The official symbol of the American Nazi party is a red flag bearing a black swastika, a variation of Hitler's Third Reich flag.

VICTORIA PITTS

that encourages a denial of racial differences while emphasizing the notion of treating everyone the same. By encouraging this sort of color-blind liberal logic, all meaningful challenges to the enduring system of white supremacy (e.g., affirmative action programs) in the United States are discredited as acts of "reverse discrimination" (Bonilla-Silva 2001). As a result, patterns of racial/ethnic discrimination and inequality that persist in health care, criminal justice, employment, housing, and education are deracialized and treated as innocent by-products of competition and/or personal or cultural deficiencies. Solutions to these problems, therefore, involve encouraging racial minorities to make the necessary personal/cultural adjustments to deal with these problems in a propitious manner (e.g., work harder, take school more seriously, speak proper English, etc.). Yet by personalizing these problems, the prevailing system of white supremacy is left intact behind a liberal façade.

Furthermore, current research points to a system of white supremacy being legitimized and reproduced through common-sense assumptions that frame a white view of reality, as in Joe Feagin's (2010b) notion of the "white racial frame," or through a "racial grammar" that subtly (and often inadvertently) supports white supremacy through the usage of white norms and standards that are taken be universal and ahistorical. Considering these more recent developments, it appears that, with the exception of white supremacist groups that continue to push for an openly racist agenda, the current system of white supremacy in the United States appears far less blatant (or even deliberate) but nonetheless just as effective in sustaining white privilege.

LUIGI ESPOSITO

See also

Ku Klux Klan (KKK); Nazism; Whiteness Studies

Further Reading:

Bonilla-Silva, Eduardo. *White Supremacy and Racism in the Post–Civil Rights Era*. Boulder, CO: Lynne Rienner, 2001.

Bonilla-Silva, Eduardo. "The Invisible Weight of Whiteness: The Racial Grammar of Everyday Life in Contemporary America." *Ethnic and Racial Studies* 35 (2012): 173–94.

Feagin, Joe. *Racist America*, 2nd ed. New York: Routledge, 2010a.

Feagin, Joe. *The White Racial Frame*. New York: Routledge, 2010b.

Graves, Joseph. *The Emperor's New Clothes: Biological Theories of Race at the Millennium*. New Brunswick, NJ: Rutgers University Press, 2001.

Omi, Michael, and Howard Winant. *Racial Formations in the United States*, 2nd ed. New York: Routledge, 1994.

Whiteness Studies

In the 1990s, whiteness studies emerged as a body of scholarship charged with examining and documenting the historical and contemporary formation of whiteness as a racial identity and the distribution and exercise of white privilege. Whiteness studies has emerged and proliferated within a historical context where a multitude of sociopolitical factors agitate, like the evisceration of race-conscious civil rights policies; the changing racial demographics of the United States and concomitant white anxiety; the acceleration of global capitalism; and the growth of intellectual movements such as feminism, poststructuralism, critical race theory, and postcolonial theory.

Scholarship on Whiteness Studies

Scholars insightfully criticize whiteness studies for advancing reductive discussions of whiteness by conceptualizing it as an omnipotent, monolithic category that imperially determines the social and political relations within Western countries, a conceptualization that serves only to reify whiteness and white people as the primary social actors constructing human history. Some scholarship in whiteness studies essentializes whiteness by conceptualizing it only in relation to other racial formations, disregarding the constitutive influence of gender, class, sexual orientation, and other social constructions. Furthermore, in the literature of whiteness studies, whiteness is a cryptic concept, seemingly meaning all things to all people, possibly making it theoretically and conceptually meaningless. If whiteness is inherently nebulous, it becomes impossible to observe and document empirically in order to trace how it functions and circulates to maintain white supremacy within racialized social systems. However, more theoretically informed third wave whiteness scholarship addresses these criticisms by marshaling empirical, interdisciplinary, and innovate methodologies that comprehensively analyze how whiteness and white identities are locally deployed, discursively constructed, and extemporaneously reinvented to maintain structural white supremacy.

Whiteness studies has experienced wide diffusion in popular media and academic disciplines, becoming the subject of innumerable articles and books. Although the disciplinary orientation of the scholarship of whiteness studies may vary, the interrelated theoretical principles of that scholarship remain largely consistent, emphasizing the normalization and invisibility of whiteness, the systemic influence of white privilege, and the social construction of race.

Fundamental to whiteness studies is the recognition that whiteness—the historically and socially constructed dispositions, ideologies, and identities that generally white persons perform and embody—exists as the invisible, unacknowledged social and racial norm. Critical, then, to the progressive racial politics of whiteness studies is to make whiteness visible as a historically contested and constructed racial identity and to identify the ways in which whiteness functions as the taken-for-granted norm against which all other racial categories are constituted and defined. The invisibility of whiteness and its canonization as the universal racial touchstone exist in a mutually reinforcing relationship: the unintelligibility of whiteness inhibits the ability of many white people to think critically about their own racialization; conversely, white racial unconsciousness precludes an understanding of how whiteness sustains systemic racial inequality. Many white people simply think of themselves as natural and normal without acknowledging how this self-conceptualization is racially coded. Whiteness, then, is always operative, permeating all social relations and spaces

and enabling many white people to pejoratively mark and race "others" while denying difference and defining itself by what it is not—not black, not Latino, not Chicano, etc.

Additionally, whiteness studies conceptualizes whiteness as a pervasive system of racial privileges, building on W.E.B. Du Bois's (1956 [1935]) notion of the "public and psychological wage[s]" of whiteness. The macro and micro racial privileges of whiteness are myriad, constructing racial stratification, sustaining white structural supremacy, and advantaging many white people politically, socially, and economically—albeit not in uniform ways. White privilege, then, is the collective unearned material, political, and social advantages, psychological benefits, and positive life chances granted to persons who perform and reinforce whiteness. For instance, since whiteness serves as the universal norm, many white people never have to think of themselves as racial subjects, conveniently exteriorizing racism as someone else's problem. Many white people never have to consider how they materially benefit from the structural white supremacy that pervades school funding, curriculum, and instruction; motivates racist lending and realty practices that maintain de facto segregation; and influences the accumulation of wealth.

A third central component of whiteness studies is the theorizing of race as a social construct, a fluid category that is the product of the interaction of unequal relations of power, political capital, and wealth. For much of U.S. history, race was widely considered a biological attribute, enabling many white people—particularly segregationists—to rationalize racial stratification and segregation with inherently racist claims of intellectual, racial, and moral superiority. Conceiving race as a social construct, however, reveals how persons identifying with aggrieved racial groups are differently racialized by the ideologies and discourses underpinning whiteness to maintain racial inequality. Many of the germinal texts of whiteness studies trace the historical formation and contemporary reinvention of whiteness, emphasizing the complex interrelations of whiteness with class, nation, gender, and other social constructs, and highlighting the ideological and discursive ways in which whiteness comes into being by "othering" historically aggrieved racial formations.

Given the 21st-century realities of exponentially expanding global capitalism and rapidly changing demographics, whiteness studies will likely remain socially and academically relevant as it continues its imperative work of persistently interrogating constructions of whiteness, documenting deployments of white privilege, and contesting inequitable racial relations nationally and globally.

NICHOLAS N. BEHM

See also

Third Wave Whiteness; *Wages of Whiteness, The*; White Privilege

Further Reading:

Andersen, Margaret L. "Whitewashing Race: A Critical Perspective on Whiteness." In *White Out: The Continuing Significance of Racism*, edited by Ashley W. Doane and Eduardo Bonilla-Silva, 21–34. New York: Routledge, 2003.

Crenshaw, Kimberlé Williams, Neil Gotanda, Gary Peller, and Kendall Thomas, eds. *Critical Race Theory: The Key Writings that Formed the Movement.* New York: New Press, 1995.

Delgado, Richard, and Jean Stefancic, eds. *Critical White Studies: Looking Behind the Mirror.* Philadelphia: Temple University Press, 1997.

Doane, Woody. "Rethinking Whiteness Studies." In *White Out: The Continuing Significance of Racism*, edited by Ashley W. Doane and Eduardo Bonilla-Silva, 3–18. New York: Routledge, 2003.

Du Bois, W. E. B. *Black Reconstruction in America.* New York: Russell, 1956 [1935].

Frankenberg, Ruth. *The Social Construction of Whiteness: White Women, Race Matter.* Minneapolis: University of Minnesota Press, 1993.

Gallagher, Charles A. "White Like Me? Methods, Meaning, and Manipulation in the Field of White Studies." In *Racing Research, Researching Race: Methodological Dilemmas in Critical Race Studies*, edited by France Widdance Twine and Jonathan W. Warren, 67–92. New York: New York University Press, 2000.

Harris, Cheryl I. "Whiteness as Property." *Harvard Law Review* 106, no. 8 (1993): 1709–37.

Lipsitz, George. *The Possessive Investment of Whiteness: How White People Profit from Identity Politics.* Philadelphia: Temple University Press, 2006.

Rothenberg, Paula S. "Introduction." In *White Privilege: Essential Readings on the Other Side of Racism*, edited by Paula S. Rothenberg, 1–5. New York: Worth Press, 2005.

Twine, France Winddance, and Charles Gallagher. "Introduction: The Future of Whiteness: A Map of the 'Third Wave.'" *Ethnic and Racial Studies* 31, no. 1 (2008): 4–24.

Wilkins, Roy (1901–1981)

Roy Wilkins was a prominent leader in the civil rights movement. He remained a staunch supporter of nonviolence in the face of white retaliatory violence and the rise of black militancy during the 1960s. His reaction to the uprisings that were endemic to the urban black communities of the time illustrate the magnitude of his sympathy toward oppressed blacks and his unwavering resolve to attack injustice through peaceable means.

Wilkins was born on August 30, 1901, in St. Louis, Missouri. He obtained a degree in sociology and worked as a journalist at the *Minnesota Daily* and as the editor of *St. Paul Appeal* and *Kansas City Hall*. In 1929, he married a social worker named Amanda "Minnie" Badeau. In 1963, he served as the executive secretary of the National Association for the Advancement of Colored People (NAACP) and replaced W.E.B. Du Bois as the editor of *The Crisis*, the official magazine of the NAACP, when the latter left the organization. Wilkins was more conservative than his predecessor, who eventually migrated to Ghana, West Africa, so disillusioned was he with the United States.

Among Wilkins's numerous accomplishments were his testimonials at congressional hearings, his influence with U.S. presidents, such as John F. Kennedy, Lyndon B. Johnson, and Richard Nixon, and his prominent role in such civil rights triumphs as *Brown v. Board of Education* and the Civil Rights Act of 1964. As a result of these victories, Wilkins strongly believed that "if you pushed the government long

ROY WILKINS, EXEC. SEC'Y, DISPLAYS HANGMAN'S
NOOSE SENT TO ASSOCIATION'S HEADQUARTERS FROM
PERRY, FLORIDA.

Roy Wilkins was a lifelong activist in the civil rights movement and a leader of the National Association for the Advancement of Colored People (NAACP) for nearly 50 years. (Library of Congress)

enough, hard enough, and in enough of the right places, change could be accomplished" (Wilkins 1982: 127). Wilkins picketed on several occasions and did not limit himself to behind-the-scenes activism.

Wilkins was not only concerned with ending segregation; he also tackled the issue of white violence against blacks. In the 1930s, he and other NAACP members attempted unsuccessfully to encourage Franklin D. Roosevelt to support anti-lynching legislation. Although he supported the Freedom Rides, because of the dangers they would inevitably meet in the Deep South, he called the riders' strategy "desperately brave" and "reckless" (Wilkins 1982: 283). While the freedom riders indeed met with violence at the hands of the Ku Klux Klan and white mobs, Wilkins convinced President John F. Kennedy and his brother, Attorney General Robert F. Kennedy, to provide federal protection for the riders. Wilkins realized that the whites who attacked the activists afforded him an opportunity to press for greater involvement from the Kennedy administration, which had previously believed that there was no immediate need for civil rights.

But the brutality against blacks continued: at the University of Mississippi, where whites opposed the registration of James Meredith; in Birmingham, Alabama, where demonstrators were met with vicious dogs and police brutality; and in Jackson, Mississippi, where protestors encountered truculent whites. Following these events, when Kennedy gave a televised speech announcing his support for immediate social change, Wilkins finally received the affirmation he had so longed to hear. On the following day, Wilkins received a phone call telling him that Medgar Evers, whom Wilkins described as "one of the bravest, most selfless men ever to throw in his lot with the N.A.A.C.P." had been murdered (Wilkins 1982: 290). A week later, Kennedy informed the nation of his impending civil rights legislation.

But the violence continued and manifested in unexpected ways. On November 22, 1963, Kennedy was assassinated. President Johnson, Kennedy's former vice president, signed the Civil Rights Act of 1964. The youthful members of the Student Nonviolent Coordinating Committee and the Congress of Racial Equality, with whom Wilkins had collaborated, became increasingly disheartened after each episode of violence and with the plodding or nonexistent response from the local and federal government. They eventually succumbed to the militant and separatist ideologies of Black Power. To Wilkins's horror, the erstwhile nonviolent civil rights organizations began to advocate violence. He believed this ideology was detrimental to the cause of civil rights and further widened the gulf between blacks and whites.

Early in 1967, a bomb exploded in the car of Wharlest Jackson, the former treasurer of the NAACP. Wilkins asserted that "through the murder, God had offered the United States Senate a second chance to enact a civil rights bill allowing the federal government to punish such assassins," but Congress continued to hold up essential legislation (Wilkins 1982: 324). In the summer of 1967, the New York Police Department told Wilkins that the Revolutionary Action Movement (RAM) was plotting to assassinate him and other civil rights leaders who promoted passive resistance and cooperation with whites and their institutions. The militants planned to blame whites for the murders to incite violence in the black ghettos. Guards were immediately assigned to Wilkins, who was accustomed to being intimidated by whites, but was bewildered that members of his own race would threaten his life. Soon after, RAM members were incarcerated for planning the assassinations.

Throughout that summer and after, black ghettos throughout the nation went up in flames as a result of riots triggered largely by incidences of police brutality and injustice (*see* Long Hot Summer Riots, 1965–1967). But the origins of the violence were far more deeply rooted and included such issues as racism, unemployment, poverty, lack of opportunities, and alienation. Although Wilkins (1982) strongly opposed violence as a means of protest, he sympathized with the black rioters, as illustrated in the following excerpt from his autobiography:

> The change of the early sixties had come perilously late. In those months after the Harlem and Watts ghettos went up in flames, the ordinary ghetto dweller elsewhere could see little improvement in his daily life. The new laws passed by Congress applied mostly to the South and meant very little to him. It was easy for him to feel that he had been abandoned by his government and his country, that he was isolated, of no importance in the United States. Nobody could stand those feelings. So he leaned over, picked up a rock, and heaved it at the biggest plate-glass window he could see. (326)

Wilkins died in New York on September 8, 1981.

GLADYS L. KNIGHT

See also
Civil Rights Movement; National Association for the Advancement of Colored People (NAACP)

Further Reading:
Wilkins, Roy, with Tom Matthews. *The Autobiography of Roy Wilkins: Standing Fast.* New York: Penguin Books, 1982.

Williams, Bert (1874–1922)

A century ago, the most famous African American, aside from Booker T. Washington, was entertainer Egbert Austin "Bert" Williams. Born on November 12, 1874, in Nassau, Bahamas, Williams immigrated with his family at the age of two years, living first in New York City. The family returned to the Bahamas, but again migrated to the United States,

living in Florida and in San Pedro, California. The family's finances made it impossible for Williams to pursue a college degree, so he began his career as an entertainer with Martin and Selig's Mastodon Minstrels in 1893. He was joined in the company by George Walker, with whom he would form a successful partnership that would last for over a decade. Beginning in 1896, the two, billed as "The Two Real Coons," found considerable success in vaudeville and in all-black musical reviews.

As minstrel performers, Walker and Williams were remarkable not just as black men in blackface. They also managed to undermine the stereotype "coon" characters as they worked within the conventions of minstrelsy. Despite their reliance on black stage dialect and stereotyped behaviors, the performers often played characters who were as clever and ambitious as the men behind the burnt cork masks.

In 1903, the pair starred in *In Dahomey*, the first all-black musical produced on Broadway. The show toured in England and played for a birthday celebration for the Prince of Wales. The "Cakewalk," a dance featured in the show, became a sensation on both sides of the Atlantic. Other successes followed, but Walker's failing health forced his retirement in 1909. In 1910, Williams joined Flo Ziegfield's Follies as the company's first black headliner, a move that outraged many of the show's white cast members. He returned to the Follies regularly through 1919. He also appeared in a number of Biograph shorts and recorded dozens of disks for Columbia Records.

Williams called the character he reprised on stage and in recordings the "Jonah Man," a hard-luck everyman whose misfortune provides the occasion for an audience's laughter. His signature song, "Nobody," exemplified the gentle humor and pathos of that character. And while Williams retained the blackface makeup and the speech of the minstrel coon, his dignified stage persona, subtle humor, and precise execution defied the stereotype. Many of his comic monologues obliquely challenged the racial order.

Offstage, Williams found less humor in Jim Crow America. A great celebrity, he still was refused lodging and service while on tour. He confided to his colleague and friend Eddie Cantor that having to ride the service elevator at the back of a hotel would not be so bad had he not still recalled the applause from the evening's show. His frequent European tours provided a contrast to the burdensome limitations of

American life. Williams died on March 4, 1922, a few days after collapsing during a show in Detroit.

Williams insisted that there was nothing "disgraceful in being a colored man" but that he "often found it inconvenient—in America." Throughout his career, he artfully made clear that distinction.

JAMES IVY

See also

Williams v. Mississippi (1898)

Further Reading:

Chude-Sokei, Louis. *The Last "Darky": Bert Williams, Black-on-Black Minstrelsy, and the African Diaspora.* Durham, NC: Duke University Press, 2006.

Debus, Allen G. "Bert Williams on Stage: Ziegfeld and Beyond." Liner notes to *Bert Williams: The Middle Years, 1910–1918.* Archeophone Records, 2002–2005.

Debus, Allen G., and Richard Martin. Liner notes to *Bert Williams: The Early Years, 1901–1909.* Archeophone Records, 2004.

Forbes, Camille F. "Dancing with 'Racial Feet': Bert Williams and the Performance of Blackness." *Theatre Journal* 56 (2004): 603–25.

Martin, Richard, and Meagan Hennessey. Liner notes to *Bert Williams: His Final Releases, 1919–1922.* Archeophone Records, 2001–2004.

Smith, Eric Ledell. *Bert Williams: A Biography of the Pioneer Black Comedian.* Jefferson, NC: McFarland, 1992.

Williams, Bert. "The Comic Side of Trouble." *American Magazine* 85 (January 1918): 33–35.

Williams, Robert F. (1925–1996)

Robert Franklin Williams was born on February 26, 1925, in Monroe, North Carolina. One of his early memories was witnessing the violent beating and arrest of a black woman by "Big" Jesse Alexander Helms, a white policeman and father of U.S. senator Jesse Helms. Five years later, Williams and a friend enrolled in a National Youth Administration job training program near Monroe, where he organized a protest of unequal training curriculum and segregationist camp policies that activated a Federal Bureau of Investigation file in his name. The next year, he witnessed the Northern face of race violence when, while living in Detroit with his brother Edward and working briefly for the Ford Motor Company, he was caught up with his brother and sister-in-law in a racial fight at Belle Isle during the Detroit race riot (*see* Detroit [Michigan] Riot of 1943 entry).

Returning to Monroe, Williams graduated from Winchester Street High School in 1944 and served 18 months as an Army draftee at the end of World War II, where his exposure to the fears and weaknesses of his fellow white soldiers disabused him of any notion that whites had any well-organized or powerful superiority to blacks. Williams received weapons training and took a creative writing course that developed the two major icons—the gun and the pen—that became his signature weapons. He spent much of his army time in the brig for a variety of acts of defiance, including failure to obey orders, disrespect toward officers, and being AWOL several times.

His political career began in 1956 when he was elected president of the Monroe branch of the National Association for the Advancement of Colored People (NAACP), a group that at the time had only six members. Williams recruited furiously from the working and poor classes of Monroe's African American community, swelling the branch membership to over 250. That same year, he organized the Black Militia, an armed self-defense group, in response to threats he had received as a consequence of efforts to integrate local recreational facilities and in defense of Dr. Albert E. Perry, a local physician and leader.

In 1958, Williams advocated on behalf of eight-year-old David Exell "Fuzzy" Simmons and 10-year-old James Hanover Grissom Thompson, who had been found guilty and sent to reform school for playing a kissing game with white girls. Williams's work clearing the boys' names and bringing national and international attention to what became known as the Kissing Case embarrassed the U.S. government and was followed by the branch's protest of the acquittal of Louis Medlin, a white Monroe resident charged in 1959 with assaulting and intending to rape a black woman who was eight months' pregnant.

Williams argued that African American women and men would defend themselves with arms if necessary in the wake of the acquittal, saying, "If it's necessary to stop lynching with lynching, then we must be willing to resort to that method" (Mayfield 1961). This led to his suspension and subsequent expulsion from the national NAACP, but endeared him to many in the radical left as well as to those drawn to the more confrontational politics of voices such as Malcolm X. He was reelected to his position as president of the Monroe NAACP branch.

In 1961, the Freedom Riders came to Monroe, and Williams assisted them, although he refused to accept the philosophy of nonviolence that they observed (*see* Freedom Rides entry). When a white mob began to attack them, African Americans—some armed—rose to their defense. In the resulting conflict and turmoil, a white couple was given refuge in the Williams home. As a result, local law enforcement charged Williams with kidnapping and used the incident to raid the homes of other African Americans, disarming them as a consequence. To escape the trumped-up charge, Williams, his wife Mabel, and their two sons (John and Franklin) fled Monroe, then the country.

The Williams family took up residence in Cuba, where, over the course of the next five years, they broadcast *Radio Free Dixie*, a music, news, and commentary show advocating armed self-defense and black self-determination; published *The Crusader* (a newsletter Williams had started in 1959); and networked with an international coterie of revolutionaries, theoreticians, and activists. During their first year there, Williams published his signature manifesto, *Negroes with Guns*, which detailed the Monroe movement and the philosophy that had grown out of it. Black Panther Party cofounder Huey P. Newton credited the book with having a great influence on his political philosophy. After his ongoing differences with Fidel Castro caused him to move his family to Mao Tse Tung's China in 1966, Williams spent three years touring Asia and Africa from his base there. Considering himself a "militant revolutionary nationalist" ("In Memory" 1996), Williams was made chairman of Max Stanford's Revolutionary Action Movement (RAM) and president-in-exile of Milton and Richard Henry's Republic of New Africa (RNA). His legacy lies in the impact his philosophy of self-determination and self-defense had on groups such as RAM, the RNA, the Deacons for Defense and Justice, and the Black Panthers, among others.

In 1969, after negotiations with the U.S. government, Williams returned from exile, settling in Baldwin, Michigan. Seven years later, after a protracted struggle to avoid extradition to North Carolina, the kidnapping charges against him were dropped. He spent the last decade and a half of his life as an elder statesman, college and community lecturer, and

local activist with groups such as Baldwin's People's Association for Human Rights. Williams died of Hodgkin's Disease on October 15, 1996. His papers are housed at the University of North Carolina.

GREGORY E. CARR

See also

Civil Rights Movement; *Negroes with Guns*; *Radio Free Dixie*

Further Reading:

Freedom Archives, ed., and Robert F. Williams. *Robert F. Williams: Self Respect, Self Defense and Self Determination (An Audio Documentary as Told by Mabel Williams)*. Edinburgh, Scotland: AK Press, 2005.

"In Memory of Robert F. Williams: A Voice for Armed Self-Defense and Black Liberation." *Revolutionary Worker* 882, November 17, 1996. http://rwor.org/a/firstvol/882/willms.htm.

Mayfield, Julian. "Challenge to Negro Leadership." *Commentary* 31, no. 4 (April 1961).

Tyson, Timothy. *Radio Free Dixie: Robert F. Williams and the Roots of Black Power*. Chapel Hill: University of North Carolina Press, 1999.

Williams, Robert F. *Negroes with Guns*. Detroit, MI: Wayne State University Press, 1998 [1962].

Williams v. Mississippi (1898)

Williams v. Mississippi, 170 U.S. 213 (1898), limited the power of constitutional amendments and affected Reconstruction in the South. In *Williams*, the U.S. Supreme Court unanimously ruled that disenfranchisement clauses, literacy tests, and the grandfather clause used in Mississippi did not discriminate against African Americans by violation of the Fifteenth Amendment. The Fifteenth Amendment in 1870 made it unconstitutional to affect the right to vote because of race or previous condition of servitude. As a result of the ruling in *Williams*, many other Southern states adopted qualifications for black voters and effectively limited the numbers of eligible black voters and potential jurors.

In *Williams v. Mississippi*, an all-white jury indicted Henry Williams, an African American man from Mississippi, for murder in 1898. He was sentenced by another all-white jury to be hanged, but Williams challenged the indictment and trial. He argued that he did not receive a fair trial because blacks were excluded from serving on the jury, which constituted a violation of the equal protection clause of the Fourteenth Amendment. Since only qualified voters could be eligible for jury duty and Mississippi had literacy and poll tax qualifications for voting, the number of registered black voters was severely limited.

The low number of qualified black voters was in large part due to the implementation of the Mississippi Plan by the Mississippi Democrats in 1890. The plan included laws to prevent blacks from voting without disenfranchising poor whites and making explicit reference to race. One law included high literacy and property requirements for African American voters. Another law, the poll tax regulation, enforced an annual tax that a person had to pay in order to vote. Legislators also used a "grandfather clause" to secure the votes of poor whites, since this rule exempted anyone from these tests who had voted or whose grandfathers had voted before 1867. If an African American met all of the requirements to vote, then an "understanding" clause blocked his eligibility. This clause allowed registrars to ask potential voters any questions about the state constitution before registering to vote.

Even though African American voters faced several prerequisites to vote in Mississippi, the Supreme Court decided on April 25, 1898, that the possibility of discrimination did not invalidate the Mississippi provisions. It stated that Williams had not proved that the administration of Mississippi suffrage provisions were discriminatory because these mechanisms did not directly mention race and there was no evidence that these provisions were given in a discriminatory manner to exclude voters based on race. Hence, literary tests, poll taxes, and other voting requirements tests did not violate the Fifteenth Amendment, provided they were applied to all applicants. The *Williams* decision provided a legal basis for blocking Africans Americans from voting and serving on juries and ensuring white political supremacy in the South. The ruling also essentially marked the lack of protection of African Americans' civil rights by the federal judiciary. The Civil Rights Act of 1964 and the Voting Rights Act of 1965 later superseded *Williams*, since they prohibited exclusionary tests and devices in states and areas of disproportionate minority voters.

DORSIA SMITH SILVA

See also

Disenfranchisement; Jim Crow Laws; Voting Rights Act of 1965

Further Reading:

Ayers, Edward L. *The Promise of the New South: Life after Reconstruction.* New York: Oxford University Press, 1992.

McMillen, Neil R. *Dark Journey: Black Mississippians in the Age of Jim Crow.* Urbana: University of Illinois Press, 1990.

Wilmington (North Carolina) Riot of 1898

The Wilmington (North Carolina) Riot of 1898 was a violent coup d'état engineered by the North Carolina Democratic Party, resulting in the death of hundreds of African American residents of Wilmington, the forceful expulsion of thousands of others, and the removal of a democratically elected government of black and white Republicans and Fusionists. The ultimate goal of this white supremacy rebellion was to reverse the political and economic progress African Americans had made since Reconstruction (1865–1877).

The broad context of the riot is to be found in the post-Reconstruction period that started in 1877 when the federal army pulled out of the South, giving Southern legislatures the opportunity to start a steady course of disenfranchising the newly freed black population. During Reconstruction, a number of legal tools had given hope to African Americans, notably the Thirteenth, Fourteenth, and Fifteenth Amendments to the U.S. Constitution that respectively abolished slavery, gave citizenship and equal protection of the law to African Americans, and extended the right to vote to black men. In addition, the Civil Rights Act of 1866, the Force Acts of 1870 and 1871, and the Civil Rights Act of 1875, among other laudable efforts, sought to protect African Americans against the increasing violence of white supremacist groups in the South and the general discrimination and segregation that followed the end of the Civil War. Reconstruction had seen a number African Americans occupying positions of power in elected office. On the other hand, post-Reconstruction was characterized by a relentless effort on the part of Southern legislatures to disenfranchise the black population, especially the elected officials and professionals. The grandfather clause, literary tests, poll taxes, sharecropping (a reconfiguration of the plantation system), and violence were some of the strategies used by white vigilante organizations to defraud the promises of the three amendments and prevent African Americans from enjoying the rights and privileges conferred by citizenship, including the right to vote and hold office. In a revealing decision, in 1883 the U.S. Supreme Court pronounced the Civil Rights Act of 1875 unconstitutional, thus legalizing discrimination and segregation against blacks in transportation and public facilities. The 1896 Supreme Court decision known as *Plessy v. Ferguson* further consolidated the Jim Crow laws of the South and thus sanctioned the segregationist and discriminatory principle of separate but equal. The lynching of African Americans in the last two decades of the 19th century reached the thousands. It is in this context of violence, white supremacy rule, and political disenfranchisement of blacks that the Wilmington, North Carolina, race riot has to be understood.

The immediate cause of the riot is found in the result of the 1894, 1896, and 1898 elections in Wilmington, which white democrats lost to Republicans and Fusionists, a relatively large number of whom were black. As a result of these democratic elections, blacks were appointed to various positions in the administration of the city, leading white Democrats to cry foul over what they called Negro domination. If a number of African Americans had achieved real economic and political power, this constituted a threat to white supremacists, who could not tolerate such a rise to power. This was a tradition inherited from a long period of slavery, in which the only suitable position for the supposedly inferior blacks was to serve the superior white man. Thus, the idea of a black man in power summoning a white man, giving orders to a white man, or inspecting a white man's home, or simply questioning a white man, was an affront to the ideology of white supremacy. A contemporary novelist, Charles Chesnutt, dramatized the coup d'état of 1898 in Wilmington, in his 1901 novel *The Marrow of Tradition*.

The North Carolina newspapers played a critical role in the campaign to disenfranchise African Americans in Wilmington. For example, the *Raleigh News and Observer* and the *Wilmington Messenger* ran a ruthless campaign demeaning African Americans in general but reserving the most severe disparagement for black civil servants and professionals. In the months leading to the 1898 elections, newspapers were saturated with articles that depicted lawlessness, black self-assertion and takeover, and sexual crimes by blacks, a favorite pretext for white supremacists to start mass violence against blacks in the post-Reconstruction South. In the days leading to the 1898 election, Alex Manly, the mixed-race editor of a local black-owned newspaper, the *Wilmington Daily Record*, claimed that "poor white men [were being] careless in the matter of protecting their women," further claiming that "our experience among poor white people in the country teaches us that women of that race are not any more particular in the matter of clandestine meetings with colored men than the white men with the colored women" (August 18, 1898). Manly's editorial was a reaction to a speech delivered the previous year by Rebecca Latimer Felton, the first woman ever to become a U.S. senator, in which she forcefully sanctioned the lynching of black men to protect white women from black men, whom she referred to as "ravening human beasts" (quoted in Sundquist 1993: xvii). In reality, Manly's editorial condemned lynching and the ideology of white supremacy and its deceptive and violent ways bent on galvanizing racial strife. Manly also condemned the hypocrisy of white supremacists, who did not hesitate to ruin the morality of black women but cried foul at the idea of a black man being intimate with a white woman. The Democratic newspapers seized on what they fanatically characterized as an attack against white womanhood to mount a campaign aimed at provoking race tensions. In doing so, they deliberately focused on one aspect of Manly's editorial, namely, the fact that white women were attracted to black men whose own fathers were white. For white supremacists, it was inconceivable to condone the sin of amalgamation. The irony was that many blacks in the Wilmington population were descendants or sons and daughters of such relationships through rape (in the period of slavery) or even love. Instead of lynching Manly for his editorial, the white supremacists calculated to use it for political purpose: to forcibly remove the interracial coalition of black and white Republicans and Fusionists from power.

On November 9, 1898, the day after the election that the Democrats had lost to Republicans and Fusionists, the Secret Nine at the forefront of the violence presented what they called the "White Declaration of Independence," rejecting the black man's right to vote and hold office and calling for the government to be given to the white population paying most of the taxes. For the Secret Nine, only whites had the right to a job in the city. They also reiterated their earlier condemnation of Manly's editorial for its affront on white womanhood and they demanded his expulsion from the city. Alfred Moore Waddell, a former Confederate officer and congressman, along with a committee he headed, brought the declaration to 32 black leaders in Wilmington and requested a reply the next day, with the expectation of submission to total white control. Mailed, instead of being carried in person, the reply missed the November 10 deadline.

When a mob of armed white men from Wilmington and surrounding towns and farms gathered on November 10 at 8:00 A.M., Waddell led them to offices of the *Daily Record*. From 500 white men, the group quickly grew to 2,000 men as the mob progressed through town. The office was ransacked and fire broke out, burning the office down. In an act that speaks of the spectacle-like nature of race riots, the mob had a picture taken in front of the building.

The riot spread within hours, and because of superior weapons, ample supply of guns and ammunition, and the help of the state militia, the white supremacy mobs defeated the blacks who had resolved to defend themselves. The rioters quickly spread their criminality throughout the city. The white Republican mayor of the city, Dr. Silas P. Wright, and the city council members of both races were forced to resign. Waddell, with the support of the prominent members of the city, proclaimed himself mayor. Alexander Manly and other blacks, who were expecting violence to erupt, had already left town. The white mob was intent on driving the blacks in general, but specifically black jobholders and professionals, out of town.

The white Democrats, who took over the reigns of government after overthrowing the democratically elected Republicans and Fusionists, put the death toll at 12 or 14, but more objective estimates put the death toll in the hundreds. Another result of this mass violence against blacks led to many leaving the city, and to property being illegally seized. The Wilmington race riot of 1898 made national headlines, but neither Congress nor the president intervened to protect the black population of Wilmington, North Carolina, as indeed both branches of government generally did little or nothing against the violence that accompanied the Jim Crow laws, in spite of the Fourteenth Amendment's promise of "equal protection of the laws."

The Wilmington, North Carolina, race riot was dramatized in a number of fictional works, including Celia Bland's *The Conspiracy of the Secret Nine*, Philip Gerard's *Cape Fear Rising*, and Charles W. Chesnutt's *The Marrow of Tradition*. Chesnutt's 1901 novel is a complex commentary on white violence, the undying galvanizing power of race, and the virulent segregation and discrimination that characterized the post-Reconstruction South, all of which produced tense racial relations that contemporaries of Chesnutt, such as W.E.B. Du Bois in his *Souls of Black Folk* (1903), also chastised in their own works.

In a way of commenting on Manly's editorial, Chesnutt complicates the situation by exploring the entangled family history of the leading white supremacist in the novel, the white newspaper editor General Carteret. His wife Olivia learns that she is the sister of Janet Miller, wife of a prominent black doctor in the city (named Wellington in the novel). Olivia's father fathered Janet with a black woman. Through this substory, Chesnutt's work avoids the easy taxonomy of race by showing the complexity of race relations in the South as complicated by white-black sexual relations, including the rape of black women by white slave owners, but also free love affairs between the two races, thus reaffirming the truthfulness of Manly's editorial. As the story of Olivia Carteret and Janet Miller shows in *The Marrow of Tradition*, this was a reality that the white supremacists were not ready to accept when they overthrew the government of the interracial political coalition of black and white Republicans and Fusionists. Chesnutt's novel also highlights the class issue that the mob mentality of the 1898 race riot obfuscates. While the riot was the work of a white mob that resulted in the triumph of white supremacy and the disenfranchisement of African Americans in both the real riot and the novel, in both cases the class issue is an important part of the process. In the real riot, it is the political elite of the North Carolina Democratic Party that engineered the riot, while in the novel, Carteret and Belmont are the brains of the riot; McBane, whom the two aristocrats despise because of his low class, follows in the name of white supremacy.

All in all, the Wilmington, North Carolina, race riot of 1898 was the culmination of the ideology of white supremacy. It disenfranchised the black population of the city, thus betraying the promises of both the Fourteenth and Fifteenth Amendments to the U.S. Constitution. The riot definitely established the Jim Crow tenets of racism, separation, and discrimination in North Carolina, and these would prevail until the civil and voting rights acts were enacted by Congress in the 1960s.

AIMABLE TWAGILIMANA

See also

Race Riots in America; Reconstruction Era; White Mobs; White Supremacy. Documents: The Report on the Memphis Riots of May 1866 (July 25, 1866); Account of the Riots in East St. Louis, Illinois (July 1917); The Cook County Coroner's Report Regarding the 1919 Chicago Race Riots (1919); A Southern Black Woman's Letter Regarding the Recent Riots in Chicago and Washington (November 1919); The Final Report of the Grand Jury on the Tulsa Race Riot (June 25, 1921); Testimony from *Laney v. United States* Describing Events during the Washington, D.C., Riot of July 1919 (December 3, 1923); The Governor's Commission Report on the Watts Riots (December 1965); Cyrus R. Vance's Report on the Riots in Detroit (July–August 1967); The Reports of the Oklahoma Commission to Study the Tulsa Race Riot of 1921 (2000–2001); The Draft Report of the 1898 Wilmington Race Riot Commission (December 2005); Regarding the Recent Riots in Chicago and Washington, November 1919

Further Reading:

Cecelski, David S., and Timothy B. Tyson, eds. *Democracy Betrayed: The Wilmington Race Riot of 1898 and Its Legacy*. Chapel Hill: University of North Carolina Press, 1998.

Hossfeld, Leslie H. *Narrative, Political Unconscious and Radical Violence in Wilmington, North Carolina*. New York: Routledge, 2005.

Sundquist, Eric J. "Introduction." In Charles W. Chesnutt, *The Marrow of Tradition*. New York: Penguin Books, 1993 [1901], vii–xliv.

Women of All Red Nations (WARN)

Women of All Red Nations (WARN) was formed in the middle 1970s "to address issues directly facing Indian women and their families." WARN has some notable alumnae. For example, Winona LaDuke, who ran for vice president of the United States on the Green Party ticket with Ralph Nader in 1996 and 2000, was a WARN founding member.

When the American Indian Movement (AIM) began in the 1960s, women members found themselves playing supporting (and, some asserted, subservient) roles. In 1974, at Rapid City, South Dakota, Native women from more than 30 nations met and decided, among other things, that "truth

and communication are among our most valuable tools in the liberation of our lands, people, and four-legged and winged creations." The formation of WARN enabled politically active Native American women to speak with a collective voice on issues that affected them intensely. At the same time, WARN members, with chapters throughout the United States, worked to support a large number of Native American men in prisons.

Members of WARN also form liaisons with non-Native feminist groups, such as the National Organization of Women, to advocate policies of concern to minority women. The group's main priorities include the improvement of educational opportunities, health and medical care (including reproductive rights), resistance to violence against women, an end to stereotyping, support for treaties, and protection of the environment, including campaigns against uranium mining and milling, a long-time threat to Lakota and Navajo women as well as men.

One critical issue raised by WARN is the widespread sterilization of Native American women in government-run hospitals, an extension of a eugenics movement aimed at impeding the population increase of groups believed by some in government to be poor and/or mentally defective. These programs had ended for most of non-Indian groups after World War II (Germany's Nazis having given eugenics an extremely bad reputation), but they continued on Indian reservations through the 1970s. Wherever Indian activists gathered during the Red Power years of the 1970s, conversation inevitably turned to the number of women who had had their tubes tied or their ovaries removed by the Indian Health Service. Communication spurred by activism provoked a growing number of Native American women to piece together and name what amounted to a national eugenics policy carried out with copious federal funding.

WARN and other women's organizations publicized the sterilizations, which were performed after pro forma "consent" of the women being sterilized. The "consent" sometimes was not offered in the women's language, and often followed threats that they would die or lose their welfare benefits if they had more children. At least two 15-year-old girls were told they were having their tonsils out before their ovaries were removed. The enormity of government-funded sterilization, as well as its eugenics context, has been documented by Sally Torpy in her thesis, "Endangered Species:

Native American Women's Struggle for Their Reproductive Rights and Racial Identity, 1970s–1990s," written at the University of Nebraska at Omaha.

No one even today knows exactly how many Native American women were sterilized during the 1970s. One basis for calculation is provided by the General Accounting Office, whose study covered only four of 12 IHS regions over four years (1973–1976). Within those limits, the study documented the sterilization of 3,406 Indian women. Another estimate was provided by Lehman Brightman (Lakota), who devoted much of his life to the issue. His educated guess (without exact calculations to back it up) is that 40 percent of Native women and 10 percent of Native men were sterilized during the decade. Brightman estimates that the total number of Indian women sterilized during the decade was between 60,000 and 70,000. The women of WARN played a central role in bringing involuntary sterilization of Native American women to an end.

BRUCE JOHANSEN

See also

American Indian Movement (AIM); Red Power Movement

Further Reading:

American Indian Movement: http://www.aimovement.org.

Johansen, Bruce E. "Reprise/Forced Sterilizations." *Native Americas* 15 (Winter 1998): 4, 44–47.

Torpy, Sally J. "Endangered Species: Native American Women's Struggle for Their Reproductive Rights and Racial Identity: 1970s–1990s." Master's thesis, University of Nebraska, 1998.

Works Progress Administration (WPA)

On May 6, 1935, President Franklin D. Roosevelt issued Executive Order 7034, which created the Works Progress Administration (WPA). Authorized by the Emergency Relief Appropriation Act, the WPA was established to alleviate unemployment caused by the Great Depression. Between 1935 and 1943, the WPA employed 8.5 million Americans in the completion of 1.5 million publicly financed projects, which ranged from the building of bridges and schools to the writing of travel guidebooks, the painting of murals in public buildings, and the production of theatrical performances.

A Works Projects Administration (WPA) poster promotes consumption of healthy foods including dairy products, eggs, fruit, vegetables, bread, cereal, and meat. The WPA was a New Deal agency that created jobs for unemployed Americans during the Great Depression. When World War II began to offer more jobs, President Franklin D. Roosevelt shut down the WPA on December 4, 1943. (Library of Congress)

The federal government expressly forbade discrimination in the hiring of workers for WPA projects, but unemployed African Americans soon found that this directive was ignored by relief administrators in the South. In most instances, it was more difficult for African Americans to qualify for WPA jobs, and they were paid less than their white co-workers. This was especially true in Atlanta, where white workers were paid $32.66 per month while their black counterparts received a mere $19.29. In addition, blacks were restricted to manual and unskilled positions regardless of education, experience, or ability. Only 100 African Americans out of 4,000 WPA workers in St. Louis worked in white-collar positions. In Memphis, administrators removed blacks from the relief rolls in order to force them to pick cotton on nearby farms. On the whole, fewer African Americans were able to qualify for relief work, with only 350,000 employed annually.

As a result of these restrictive measures, there were only 11 African American supervisors in the whole of the Southern states five years after the program began.

Many Southern whites, in spite of their success in restricting African Americans from fully benefiting from the WPA, deeply resented the fact that black WPA workers labored outside their traditional work roles, and did all they could to discourage participation. For example, armed guards monitored the labor of female construction workers in Jackson, Mississippi. White Southern Democrats also opposed the program because it was perceived to strengthen the power of the federal government over that of the states. Nor were they sanguine in 1936 when President Roosevelt received 76 percent of black votes, which resulted in African Americans becoming a powerful voting bloc within the Democratic Party. Consequently, the WPA was frequently used as a weapon by conservative Democrats to castigate Roosevelt's New Deal reforms.

Arguably, the Works Progress Administration was the most efficient public works program in the history of American government. It averaged a payroll of $2,112,000 per month between the years 1935 and 1941, which provided significant assistance to destitute Americans. For African Americans in particular, the WPA provided much needed employment despite the fact that it condoned segregation and discrimination. At its height, the WPA was the greatest source of income for African Americans living in the Southern United States, while a quarter of a million black citizens were taught to read as a result of their involvement in the program. Perhaps more importantly, in giving African Americans employment outside of agriculture and domestic service, the Works Progress Administration strengthened their resolve in the struggle to dismantle legalized segregation.

WAYNE DOWDY

See also

Great Depression; New Deal; Roosevelt, Franklin D.

Further Reading:

Biles, Roger. *Memphis in the Great Depression*. Knoxville: University of Tennessee Press, 1986.

Biles, Roger. *A New Deal for the American People*. DeKalb: Northern Illinois University Press, 1991.

Cobb, James C., and Michael V. Namorato, eds. *The New Deal and the South*. Jackson: University Press of Mississippi, 1984.

World War I

World War I involved the United States directly for only about a year and a half. The war occurred during one of the worst periods of oppression of black people in the United States since the end of slavery. Yet, the war also began to unleash forces that would, in the long run, begin the dismantling of Jim Crow. About 400,000 black men, and some black women, served in the American military during the war, which subjected them to the military's version of Jim Crow, while at the same time exposing many of them to a world beyond Jim Crow in Europe. Additionally, the economic mobilization of the war years brought new economic possibilities, and began the Great Migration of blacks from the rural South to the urban South, and eventually to the urban North. However, in the two years following the end of the war, blacks were victims of the worst racial violence since Reconstruction.

Jim Crow was justified in part by the idea that black men were naturally cowards, or that they would not fight for the United States. Most history of black participation in previous wars had been largely purged from historical memory. Men who would not fight were not fit to vote. Thus, many in the military and government, especially Southern whites, were hesitant over the idea of using blacks in combat. While most racists had little problem with using blacks in the military in support or transportation units, the idea of arming blacks and training them to kill Germans threatened to undermine the whole Jim Crow system. Black leaders put pressure on the federal government to allow black men to serve in the infantry, hoping that a strong showing of black men defending the United States would give a moral argument for allowing black men to vote. Under pressure from blacks and their white liberal allies, the government adopted a policy whereby Selective Service was instructed to induct blacks as well as whites, and for the Army to create new infantry regiments and even divisions of black men.

When the United States declared war on the Central Powers in April 1917, the regular army contained two infantry and two cavalry regiments of African Americans, for a total of almost 10,000 black men. This number included an influx of 4,000 men who joined during a recruiting drive in 1916. Of these four black regiments, three remained in the United States throughout the war, while one served in the Philippines. The National Guard contained another 10,000 black

Returning Soldiers

Having fought for democracy abroad, black soldiers returning from service in World War I hoped that their participation in the war effort would mean better treatment and more respect for African American rights at home. Black soldiers thus became a metaphor for these rising expectations and helped spur within the African American community the civic engagement, political militancy, and sociocultural activities that marked the New Negro renaissance between 1918 and the Great Depression. Northern migrants and Southern debt peons alike contributed 2.3 million African American men who registered for the draft. About 370,000 eventually served in all military branches, 200,000 overseas, mostly as stevedores and laborers, and 42,000 in combat duty.

W.E.B. Du Bois urged African Americans to "close ranks" (1918) in supporting the U.S. war effort while simultaneously pushing for the establishment of a training camp for black officers at Fort Des Moines, Iowa. Domestically, the racist film *The Birth of a Nation* (1915), the presidency of segregationist Woodrow Wilson, and the mistreatment of black military enlistees was partially offset when some white American soldiers praised black military bravery and the French celebrated African American heroism by awarding one of the four black regiments, New York's 369th (the "Harlem Hellfighters," the longest-serving U.S. regiment), the Croix de Guerre.

Soldiers returned, in the words of Du Bois in the May 1918 issue of *Crisis* magazine, "fighting," demanding that the United States "Make way for Democracy! We saved it in France, and by the Great Jehovah, we will save it in the United States of America, or know the reason why." They were instead greeted by escalating race violence. Some soldiers were lynched for wearing their uniforms. Ku Klux Klan membership soared. African Americans—including many combat-trained veterans—fought back, literally and figuratively. The flood of northward migration momentarily slowed, then exploded. A decade-long explosion of activism included demands for Southern voting rights and antisegregation legislation, Pan-Africanism, anti-lynching campaigns, and the birth of the "Jazz Age," led by the 369th Regiment's band and its leader, James Reese Europe.

GREGORY E. CARR

men, almost all of whom were from Northern states. However, most black men who served in the military during the First World War, like their white counterparts, entered the military through Selective Service. Thirty-four percent of black registrants were later drafted, compared to 24 percent for whites. A total of 13 percent of draftees were black, although blacks constituted only around 10 percent of the total population. However, in the spring and early summer of 1917, whites were actively sought for voluntary enlistment into the military, whereas most blacks were denied enlistment, so that the eventual wartime army roughly reflected the ratio of blacks to whites in the nation. W.E.B. Du Bois, among other black intellectuals, urged blacks to support the war effort fully, believing that black opposition would be used to justify further oppression, whereas faithful support of the nation during wartime would bring recognition of the rights of blacks as Americans. In September 1917, Emmett J. Scott, former secretary to Booker T. Washington, was appointed special assistant to the U.S. secretary of war.

Scott's mission was to assure that Selective Service did not discriminate.

With the war coming at the height of the Progressive Era, the Army attempted to use "scientific" intelligence testing to place drafted men into the most suitable position. Two professors, Walter D. Scott and Robert Yerkes, developed a series of questions that they believed measured innate intelligence, but actually tested familiarity with upper middle-class white culture. With 90 percent of blacks from the rural South illiterate, their knowledge of, for example, characters in the works of Charles Dickens was limited. According to the tests, almost half of all white and 89 percent of black draftees rated as "morons." While white supremacists tried to use the tests as "proof" that blacks were inferior to whites, the tests also showed that, on average, black Northerners outscored rural white Southerners. Such reports angered white Southerners, and the Army disregarded the tests.

Most blacks who served in the military during the war served in the Army. The Marine Corps admitted no blacks, while the navy took in about 1 percent. Of 400,000 blacks who served in the war, some 42,000 served in combat, a ratio slightly lower than for whites. Before the war, the black regular army regiments were stationed in the West or at overseas posts, as with most white regiments. However, the needs of the rapid mobilization for the war made necessary the construction of large mobilization and training camps, the majority of which were in the South, where land was cheaper and the warmer climate would allow more training over the winter of 1917–1918. Many blacks in the Army assumed that their status as soldiers of the United States would protect them from Jim Crow, and for many Northern blacks, their time at training camps in the South would be their first experience with Jim Crow.

However, the Army was sensitive to the opposition it faced from Southern political leaders over the very idea of arming and training black men, and bringing large numbers of them together. Southern political leaders often protested to the federal government when they found a black unit was to be stationed nearby. Among Southern whites, the use of black men by the federal government during the Civil War and Reconstruction was seen as an act of barbarity. The Army feared the backlash from any incident that might occur. As a result, the Army imposed strict Jim Crow–style regulations over its black soldiers, and in general sought to ship black units to Europe quickly, often before they had been properly trained or equipped. However much the Army attempted to mollify Southern whites by keeping the black soldiers under tight control, incidents were bound to occur.

The worst incident came on August 23, 1917, at Camp Logan, near Houston, Texas, involving soldiers from the 24th Infantry regiment, one of the four black regular army regiments. Many members of the 24th were relatively new soldiers, and the regiment had only recently been transferred to the South, where it was providing protection for a new training facility while it was under construction. However, the 24th, as with many regular regiments, had recently lost many of its long-term noncommissioned officers who had been assigned to the newly forming regiments in the national army. Additionally, many of the soldiers in the 24th had little firsthand experience with Jim Crow, and assumed their status as soldiers of the United States would shield them. Instead, the soldiers found themselves constantly harassed

by civilians and police. When one of their own was arrested by local police, about 100 soldiers from two battalions used their army weapons in an attempt to free him. In the resulting melee, 16 white people died, including five policemen, and about a dozen others wounded. In the aftermath, the Army tried by courts-martial 155 men in all. Nineteen of the men were hanged by the Army, with no advanced public notice. The incident shocked blacks, who saw it as a lynching. Throughout the South, white communities interpreted the violence in Houston as an example of what happens when Northern blacks come to the South, and whites in the South became even more vigilant in ensuring Northern blacks respect the color line. The secretary of war, Newton D. Baker, a liberal, told President Woodrow Wilson that Jim Crow was the cause of the problems with the black units.

Racial violence between white civilians and black soldiers, such as in Houston, was used to justify keeping black soldiers in labor battalions and not issuing them weapons. As labor units, the African Americans performed superbly. One regiment, working as stevedores at a French port, was expected to unload 6,000 tons a month, based on French estimates. In September 1918 alone, they unloaded 800,000 tons. But many blacks, both soldiers and civilians, resented their serving only as laborers and clamored for black combat units. The Army relented and reluctantly agreed to create more infantry units. Since segregation was the rule of the day in the Army, black units were not comingled with white units. Instead, the Army took the various black National Guard regiments and battalions and mixed them with newly formed regiments of black draftees, to create two new divisions, the 92nd and the 93rd.

Blacks also wanted to see black officers, not just black enlisted men. The Army had, at the start of the war, very few black officers. Indeed almost all of the officers in the four black regular army regiments were white, although almost all of the officers in the black National Guard units were black. The highest ranking black officer at the start of the war was Lt. Col. Charles A. Young, a West Point graduate who served with the 10th Cavalry in Arizona. The Army received complaints from Southern congressmen when white Southern junior officers were assigned to the 10th, which would mean serving under Colonel Young. Despite a flawless record, including combat in Cuba and Mexico, Young was forcibly retired, allegedly on medical grounds, but in reality

Excerpt from "Negro Troops in France," 1919

Robert Russa Moton (1867–1940) was an African American author and educator. He was appointed principal of Tuskegee Institute in 1915, following the death of Booker T. Washington, and served in that position until he retired in 1935. This letter written by Moton, who visited France after the war, urged black soldiers to rise above Jim Crow upon their return to the United States:

A letter that I saw written by a lady overseas to another lady in the United States, stated that the writer had been told by the Colonel of a certain unit, whose guest she was, that he would not feel it safe for her to walk, even with him, through this camp of Negro soldiers.

Another letter from a high official in a very important position with the overseas Negro troops, written unofficially to a very prominent official on this side, stated, that, in the 92nd Division alone, there had been at least thirty cases of the unmentionable crime.

Another rumor, equally malignant and damaging, was to the effect that the fighting units commanded by Negro officers had been a failure. On other words, "the whispering gallery," which was most active in France on phases of life overseas, said that the 92nd Division, in which Negroes in American took special pride, and with good reason, had failed utterly; that, wherever they had been engaged, the Negro officers had gone to pieces; and that in some cases the men had to pull themselves together after their officer had shown the "white feather" [shown cowardice].

Moton's remarks to black soldiers later in his trip:

The record you have made in this war, of faithfulness, bravery, and loyalty, has deepened my faith in you as men and as soldiers, as well as in my race and country. You have suffered hardships and many privations. You have been called upon to make many sacrifices. Your record has sent a thrill of joy and satisfaction to the hearts of millions of white and black Americans, rich and poor, high and low. Black mothers and wives, sweethearts, fathers, and friends have rejoiced with you and with our country in your record.

You will go back to America as heroes, as you really are. You will go back as you have carried yourselves over here—in a straightforward, manly, and modest way. If I were you, I would find a job as soon as possible, and get to work. To those who have not already done so, I would suggest that you get hold of a piece of land and home as soon as possible, and marry and settle down. Save your money, and put it into something tangible. I hope no one will do anything in peace to spoil the magnificent record of your troops have made in the war.

Source: Southern Workman, May 5, 1919, 219–24.

to placate Southern congressmen. Colonel Young appealed his retirement, but was not returned to active service until just before the war ended. Southern congressmen insisted that in no situation would white men be commanded by a black man. They dropped their opposition to the Army creating a black Officers Candidate School only when the Army assured them that black officers would never command white troops. At Fort Des Moines in Iowa, some 639 black men received commissions—106 as captains and the rest as lieutenants—out of 1,250 candidates. Almost all of these black officers were then assigned to the new black infantry regiments in the army. However, even as officers, these men soon found that the Army treated them as inferiors and subjected them to the same Jim Crow as enlisted black soldiers.

Prejudice against black soldiers within the Army created the self-fulfilling prophecy of failure of black soldiers in battle. The most notorious example was the 92nd Division. The division suffered from poor training, lack of equipment, no artillery, and uneven officer quality. While some of the officers, especially the lower-ranking officers, were black, most officers, including all the higher-ranking officers, were white. Many of the white officers assigned to black units were either the castoffs from other divisions or self-identified racists in the belief that they "knew how to handle blacks." Thrown into battle on unfamiliar terrain two days after arrival in the Argonne, two battalions from the 368th Regiment failed in combat, while others performed well. The failure of some elements of the 92nd was projected to the entire division, and then to all black soldiers. The failure of the 92nd was cited as "proof" that blacks were naturally unfit for combat. As a result, most black combat soldiers had their weapons taken away and were employed in manual labor, especially as stevedores. This stigma would last through World War II.

In sharp contrast to the experience of the 92nd Division was that of the 93rd. The 93rd Division was "loaned" to the French Army, in part to ward off pressure from the French to take control of the entire American Expeditionary Force. While the French Army was segregated by colonial or metropolitan origins of each regiment, it was not technically segregated on the color line. More importantly, the French had no stereotype of Africans or blacks being cowards or unfit to serve as soldiers. The French separated the four regiments of the 93rd and attached them to French divisions. Black American officers were shocked to find that French officers treated them as equals, as brother officers, something that never occurred in the U.S. Army. With French equipment, proper training, and capable leadership, the African American regiments performed well, earning 550 French decorations, including 180 of the Croix de Guerre, while suffering 35 percent casualties. They held their front for 191 days without losing territory, while capturing many Germans. The French government was so pleased with the performance of the black American soldiers that it heaped honors and praise on the fighting ability of the black Americans, which in turned led to the U.S. government requesting that the French cease its high praise, lest the black Americans come home demanding that they be treated as equals.

The worst period of violence against blacks came in the two years after the war, when postwar economic readjustment put many strains on American society. While labor violence erupted in Washington State and Oregon, and in Boston the police strike took the occupation of the city by the State Guard to restore order, the worst violence in the nation was racial. Mississippi had the worst violence since the end of Reconstruction. Some whites bemoaned that they would have to lynch thousands of black men in order to restore the status quo as it had been before the war. Whites feared black men who had fought Germans—a white people—in Europe,

and who had been "spoiled by French whores," would forget their place in America. While black Americans would celebrate units such as the 369th Regiment, the "Harlem Hellfighters," which saw heroic service with the French Army, white America soon forgot all about black service and loyalty during the war, and instead subjected blacks to increased racism and savage violence, lest blacks think the war might change race relations in the nation. The experience would be a bitter lesson for black Americans.

BARRY M. STENTIFORD

See also
Du Bois, W.E.B.; Veterans Groups; World War II

Further Reading:
Buckley, Gail L. *American Patriots: The Story of Blacks in the Military from the Revolution to Desert Storm*. New York: Random House, 2002.

Donaldson, Gary A. *The History of African-Americans in the Military*. Malabar, FL: Krieger Publishing Company, 1991.

Du Bois, W.E.B. "Returning Soldiers." *The Crisis*. May 1918.

Du Bois, W.E.B. "Close Ranks." *The Crisis*. July 1918.

Edgerton, Robert B. *Hidden Heroism: Black Soldiers in America's Wars*. Boulder, CO: Westview Press, 2001.

Robinson, Cedric J. *Black Movements in America*. New York: Routledge, 1997.

Schneider, Mark Robert. *"We Return Fighting": The Civil Rights Movement in the Jazz Age*. Boston: Northeastern University Press, 2002.

Slotkin, Richard. *Lost Battalions: The Great War and the Crisis of American Nationality*. New York: Henry Holt, 2005.

World War II

World War II was a pivotal event in history as it marked the emergence of modern America. The country came out of the war as a world economic and military power. Thousands of war veterans moved to the middle-class thanks to housing and education loans through the federal GI Bill (officially known as the Serviceman's Readjustment Act). The role of government changed as did the place of African Americans and women in society. During the war, factories increased production to provide war goods to the armed services. The creation of this defense industry allowed African Americans and women to attain better-paying factory jobs that were never open to them before. After working in factories during the war, American women began to permanently move out of the home and into the workforce, changing gender and family dynamics. Many African American workers left the rural South to take advantage of job opportunities in the cities of the North and West. New types of jobs were open to black women, as many moved out of domestic positions and into the service sector. Most African Americans were eager to contribute to the war effort. Many black men, in an attempt to show their patriotism, joined the armed forces. Segregation in the military and the treatment of blacks as second-class citizens at home angered many blacks and prompted them to advocate for equality in America as the country was fighting for freedom and against fascism in Europe.

During the war, the nation's factories increased production to make goods for the war, providing much-needed jobs in the wake of the Great Depression. Since many white men had gone to war, women and African Americans took their places in factories. The availability of better-paying factory jobs attracted rural blacks to industrial centers all over the country. African Americans living in rural areas of the South migrated to Southern cities, which were industrializing for war production. Hundreds of thousands of Southern blacks who wanted to escape violence and Jim Crow chose to leave the South completely, migrating to cities in the North and West. This migration, often referred to as the Second Great Migration, caused various effects in the places from which migrants left and those to which they traveled. Many blacks found better-paying positions during the war in factories producing goods for the military. This notwithstanding, they also faced discrimination in their new homes. Moreover, overcrowding of black communities and subsequent expansion of black residence into other communities, competition over war industry employment, unequal access to skilled employment, and race antagonisms were all effects of the World War II migration.

Blacks moved en masse to cities in the West such as Oakland and Los Angeles, where huge shipyards and new aerospace industries were located. African Americans also moved to cities with heavy industry—for example, steel and automobile factories, which could be easily converted to produce war goods. The black populations of Detroit and Chicago skyrocketed during the war. Black migrants also continued to settle in New York City even though the city's factories converted to wartime production much later than other cities because of the lack of heavy industry.

The influx of blacks in Northern and Western cities caused changes to the population of these cities, which often led to racial tension and competition over jobs and resources. As more and more blacks moved into Western cities in areas where they had never lived, African Americans faced increased discrimination from white residents. In these new areas of black settlement like Los Angeles and Richmond, California, black residence was restricted to declining neighborhoods.

More and more blacks moved to Detroit and Chicago, cities with a large black population, settling in the existing black neighborhoods and straining the community resources available. Because the number of blacks skyrocketed in these cities and the areas where they could reside did not, the migration resulted in overcrowding of black neighborhoods, higher mortality rates, and increased crime. The standard of living in many of these urban black communities declined.

Though the industries of the North and West attracted Southern blacks, there were other factors pushing them to leave the South. Technological innovations displaced agricultural black laborers in the South, prompting many to look for employment in urban factories. The mechanical cotton picker made the sharecropper system obsolete. Mechanization of farming through the adoption of tractors, harvesters, and sprayers made the need for black farm workers decline. Therefore, World War II provided industrial opportunities for blacks looking to leave a Southern economy that had less and less of a place for them. As the migration continued, the black community in Southern rural areas was gradually erased.

Many black migrants were not initially able to take advantage of the labor shortages in the early years of the war, especially in construction, heavy industry, and the aircraft industry. Employers hired white workers, ending white unemployment, while blacks remained without jobs, without training, and deprived of income because of reductions in Depression-era federal relief programs. Many companies, especially aviation factories that produced planes for the military, refused to employ black workers, a policy supported by the trade unions representing white workers. The United States Employment Service (USES), a federal agency, continued to fill "white-only" requests from factory employers.

The Employment Service's general policy was to operate according to the pattern of the local community; therefore, if industries in a community did not hire black workers, their office would not, either. The policy of the USES reinforced discriminatory hiring practices of employers. For these reasons, during the early war years, African Americans often had trouble finding any position other than custodian in war industries.

In the South, where much defense industry was located, the National Youth Administration could not enroll blacks in training programs. There were no technical schools for blacks in the South, and because of Jim Crow laws, blacks could not enroll in white schools to learn these skills. In their efforts to exert greater control in government worker recruitment, Southern governors increasingly relied on closed shop agreements with trade unions of the American Federation of Labor (AFL). This collusion between local governments and the AFL would restrict who received the expanding employment benefits, a fact that had large implications for African Americans since they were often excluded from AFL membership. Southern employers preferred to use white women instead of blacks to fill labor vacancies in order to preserve the racial configuration and power relations of Southern society. In this way, federal mobilization agencies became the battleground over labor control in the South.

In 1943, circumstances in the labor market changed, which prompted factories nationwide to open their doors to black workers. Increased demand for war production and a manpower shortage forced factories to hire black workers. With labor shortages becoming more acute each day and the government considering plans for manpower allocation, employers began to relax the bars to hiring, and unions found it more difficult to maintain restrictive policies. African Americans began to find skilled and semiskilled positions in the nation's factories, earning more money than they had before. Black women in particular moved out of domestic jobs and into jobs in factories and service industries.

In the South, employment of blacks in factories unsettled race relations. Whites in the rural South who were anxious about miscegenation openly resented wage increases for African Americans. These advances made Negroes too independent in their eyes, which was a dangerous development because it would foster African Americans' quest for social equality. Many blacks received war jobs, and some even managed to obtain skilled positions in plants. In general, however, the most menial and work-intensive jobs were given to black workers. White workers largely rose in status and income, but black workers entering the labor market took over the worst positions. Moreover, the traditional labor system of the South was being disrupted. To ensure adequate and efficient war production, the War Manpower Commission recruited Southern black workers to move to the Midwest and West Coast. This further undermined the low-wage labor system of Southern industries and large-scale agriculture.

The migration affected social and racial patterns in Northern and Western cities also. In Western cities, where few blacks had lived before the war, the migration had enormous employment and social effects. The massive wartime influx of black migrants to Los Angeles and San Francisco changed the racial and regional composition of the population. The arrival of unskilled migrants who would work for less pay prompted a restructuring of production methods from craftsmanship to mass production. In response, unions tightened their control on membership, excluding black workers. The Brotherhood of Boilermakers, the AFL craft union for shipyard workers, was the most vocal opponent of the new labor process.

In reaction to black migration, white residents often placed more stringent social controls on African Americans. Between 1940 and 1945, over 340,000 black people migrated to California to take advantage of employment opportunities in the new war industries. After the passage of Executive Order 8802 banning race discrimination in defense industries, black workers accelerated their movement into the state. As black newcomers flooded the cities, whites abandoned them, confining African Americans to isolated neighborhoods. Increased racial segregation, changing economic and social relations, forging of bonds between black old-timers and newcomers, and expansion of the black industrial workforce were all results of the migration. Municipalities from Los Angeles to San Francisco responded to the influx of black migrants by establishing more stringent social, political, and economic restrictions on all black residents, newcomers and longtime residents alike. Local newspapers and police departments began to characterize crime in racial terms, giving a distorted picture of black criminal activity and stigmatizing the entire community.

The new migration also had political effects. The influx of new black working-class voters and the corporatist nature of municipal politics during the war enabled a coalition of labor, blacks, and other progressive groups to mount an attack on conservative rule. Under the leadership of a united labor movement, this coalition grew to become major contenders in postwar urban politics, especially in Oakland.

Variations of the patterns and processes in California were at work in Detroit, Chicago, and New York City as well. Centers of production provided blacks with greater economic and social opportunities, and facilitated the rise of the black middle. However, due in part to migration, the cities' blacks faced pervasive discrimination and competition from whites, which caused blacks to have to endure inferior employment opportunities, substandard housing, inadequate health facilities, inferior education, and problems with drugs, crime, and insecurity. The migration of blacks to urban areas during World War II indelibly affected the social, political, and economic landscape of American cities.

African Americans had been treated as second-class citizens for more than a century in the United States. Many blacks believed that white Americans would more likely see blacks in this country as full citizens if they proved their love for and dedication to the country. As in World War I, black men volunteered as soldiers fighting to defend the nation and its democratic principles in an effort to demonstrate their bravery and their status as American citizens. Most black soldiers, however, were never accepted as equals. When blacks enlisted in the military, many were placed in segregated combat units, training schools, and camp facilities. Moreover many black soldiers, though trained, never saw actual combat. Instead they made up the service and supply units, often acting as porters and messmen, the same positions to which many black men had been relegated as civilians.

African American organizations like the National Association for the Advancement of Colored People (NAACP), the National Urban League (NUL), and the Brotherhood of Sleeping Car Porters (BSCP) pressured the government to end segregation in the armed forces. Walter White, executive secretary of the NAACP, and A. Philip Randolph, president of the BSCP, met with President Franklin D. Roosevelt and other military officials to express their views. These leaders advocated for integration of the military and asked the federal government to denounce discriminatory practices, goals that were not fully reached until President Harry S. Truman's executive order in 1948.

Black soldiers were also targets of racial violence in American cities. Mobs of whites attacked black soldiers, many of whom were in uniform. During the war, incidents of racial violence increased as they had in previous American wars. Racial violence took place involving white and black soldiers in several American cities including Alexandria, Louisiana (1942); Florence, South Carolina (1942); Phoenix, Arizona (1942); Flagstaff, Arizona (1943); and Vallejo, California (1943). Violence broke out between black soldiers and white soldiers, police, and civilians in these incidents.

The challenges to equality that African Americans faced during the war exploded in 1943. More than 240 racial incidents occurred in 47 different towns and cities during that year. Full-scale race riots broke out in Detroit, Harlem, and Los Angeles, and numerous lynchings occurred in a number of different states. Tensions between whites and blacks in many cities were exacerbated by migration, overcrowding in defense centers, competition for jobs, and conflict over housing. These tensions erupted in violence and in some cases escalated to race riots.

The Detroit Race Riot of 1943 was the most infamous and destructive race riot that year. A dispute between black youths and whites over access to the Belle Isle amusement park started the riot. The violence moved to the black section of the city, and African Americans began to stone white-owned stores and cars driven by whites. Many blacks rioted out of frustration about limited economic opportunities, police brutality, substandard housing, segregation, and inadequate recreational facilities. White rioters were acting out racial prejudice, and many were angry about having to compete with blacks for jobs, housing, and recreational facilities. The two days of racial violence ended with nine whites and 25 blacks dead. Nearly 700 people were injured. The riot resulted in nearly $2 million worth of property stolen or damaged before state and federal troops regained order.

Similar dynamics set off a riot in Harlem less than two months later. The frustration blacks felt at employers' continued refusals to employ them in higher-paying war industries contributed to an explosion of discontent in the summer of 1943. On the night of August 2, a riot began in response to a white police officer shooting an off-duty black soldier. The police charged the soldier with interfering in the arrest of a black woman in the lobby of a Harlem hotel. False rumors circulated accusing the officer of having killed the soldier who was trying to defend his mother. In response to the rumors, black rioters broke store windows, looted, damaged property, and attacked policemen. By the morning of August 3, five persons had been killed, 400 injured, and hundreds of stores had been looted. Property damage was estimated at $5 million. Many African American leaders believed this burst of violent action was an outgrowth of the lack of economic opportunities for New York City's African Americans.

The underlying causes of the racial violence in Detroit and New York City illustrate how African Americans felt in other centers of defense production during the war. Police violence and competition over limited resources and jobs contributed to a rash of racial conflicts between whites and blacks during the war. Though violence was one manifestation of black frustration, black leaders and black organizations sought other methods to alleviate some of the problems blacks in cities faced.

Increasingly, scholars have identified World War II as a catalyst for black activism and a more militant African American consciousness. African Americans linked the issues of victory over fascism abroad with victory over racism at home and began a campaign for racial equality. The "Double V Campaign" was the term used for the myriad of activities undertaken by black leaders and organizations to achieve full citizenship for African Americans. "Double V," a term initially used in a newspaper article appearing in the *Pittsburgh Courier*, stood for "Victory at Home and Abroad."

Black workers used the mobilization process and federal programs to gain economic and social mobility. Labor activism was especially important to African Americans because legislation was passed in 1941 prohibiting discriminatory hiring practices in war industries. During the war African American demands for civil rights were focused on the workplace. Black workers and activists, following in the footsteps of A. Philip Randolph, emerged as leaders in local and national struggles for black rights. African Americans used the need for factory workers and fair employment to force the federal government into acting for the equality of black workers. Southern black activists in trade unions and civic organizations, local offices of the NUL and NAACP, and

other locally based grassroots groups comprised a national effort to get African Americans jobs in war projects.

Black organizations took action to resist discrimination in 1941. In April Lester Granger, Executive Secretary of the NUL; Walter White, leader of the NAACP; Channing Tobias of the YMCA; Mary McLeod Bethune of the National Youth Administration; and A. Philip Randolph of the Brotherhood of Sleeping Car Porters asked President Roosevelt to forbid discrimination in the armed forces and defense industries. Secretary of War Henry Stimson and Secretary of the Navy Frank Knox refused to desegregate the armed forces, and Roosevelt did not insist. Afraid of angering employers and Southern Democrats, the president merely issued a statement condemning discrimination. The black delegation felt that this was not enough and proposed a march on Washington, D.C., at a meeting in Chicago. Randolph agreed to lead the March on Washington Movement and publicly announced plans for such a march to demand an executive order to end racial discrimination in defense industries.

This outpouring of black discontent and the threat of a mass protest forced the federal government to relent. On June 25, 1941, the pressure from the March on Washington Movement pushed President Roosevelt to issue an executive order banning discriminatory hiring practices in industries with government war contracts. Not only did Executive Order 8802 prohibit discrimination in hiring practices, but also prohibited government training programs from discriminating against black workers as well. Finally, the executive order established the Fair Employment Practices Commission in the Office of Production Management. The committee was to receive and investigate complaints of discrimination in violation of the executive order, and take appropriate steps to redress grievances which it found to be valid.

The March on Washington Movement was the beginning of a newer, more militant, outright demand for civil rights; a demand spurred by economic hardships. Black organizations pressured government agencies to enforce fair employment legislation. In 1945, a breakthrough in fair employment legislation came in New York with the passage of the Ives-Quinn Law, which outlawed discriminatory hiring practices in the state. Black newspapers continuously ran stories on discrimination against black soldiers and workers, informing black readers of the prejudice and rallying support for the activities of black organizations to alleviate these problems.

There is also evidence that black servicemen after fighting in the war refused to accept prewar racial practices. Black veterans, many of whom had lived in the South, were more likely to reenlist, and twice as likely to relocate to a different region after the war.

Many historians believe that World War II was a catalyst for processes that ended in the ghettoization of urban black communities. Moreover, many use the end of the war as the marker of the beginning of urban decline. They argue that racism prevented blacks from moving into the middle class, and restrictive covenants, redlining, and denial of federal housing loans kept blacks out of the growing suburbs. Consequently, many African Americans were trapped in decaying cities. Moreover, racist implementation of the federal GI Bill also gave unfair economic advantage to white war veterans who could use government loans for housing to buy homes in the suburbs and tuition loans to go to college. Using the GI Bill, white veterans and their families entered the middle class, while black veterans were not afforded those opportunities. Some link the more militant protests it engendered to the beginning of the civil rights movement.

No matter the arguments about the long-term effects of the war, the Second World War was very significant for African Americans. The availability of factory jobs to African Americans, which prompted migration, changed the face of American cities. Black men and women were able to find better-paying jobs in factories, and black women moved out of domestic occupations and into clerical and service positions after the war. For the first time, the majority of blacks no longer resided in rural Southern areas. In fact, after the 1940s, the African American population was no longer concentrated in the South, but spread more evenly throughout the country. World War II created not only modern America, but modern black America as it was known for the rest of the 20th century.

CARLA J. DuBose

See also

Civil Rights Movement; Japanese Americans, Redress Movement for; Japanese Internment; Veterans Groups; World War I; Zoot Suit Riots

Further Reading:

Blum, John M. *V Was for Victory: Politics and American Culture during World War II*. San Diego, CA: Harcourt Brace Jovanovich, 1976.

Capeci, Dominic J. Jr., and Martha Wilkerson. *Layered Violence: The Detroit Rioters of 1943*. Jackson: University of Mississippi, 1991.

Chamberlain, Charles D. *Victory at Home: Manpower and Race in the American South during World War II*. Athens: University of Georgia Press, 2003.

Dalfiume, Richard M. "The 'Forgotten Years' of the Negro Revolution." *Journal of American History* 55, no. 1 (June 1968): 90–106.

Johnson, Marilynn S. *The Second Gold Rush: Oakland and the East Bay during World War II*. Berkeley: University of California Press, 1993.

Lemann, Nicholas. *The Promised Land: The Great Black Migration and How It Changed America*. New York: Albert A. Knopf, 1991.

Lynch, Hollis R. *The Black Urban Condition: A Documentary History, 1866–1971*. New York: Crowell, 1973.

McGuire, Phillip. "Desegregation of the Armed Forces: Black Leadership Protest and World War II." *Journal of Negro History* 68, no. 2. (Spring 1983): 147–58.

Polenberg, Richard. *War and Society: The United States, 1941–1945*. Philadelphia: J. B. Lippincott, 1972.

Wynn, Neil. *The Afro-American and the Second World War*. New York: Holmes and Meier, 1976.

Wynn, Neil. "The 'Good War': The Second World War and Postwar American Society." *Journal of Contemporary History* 31, no. 3 (July 1996): 463–82.

Wounded Knee Massacre

Since the bitter cold day it happened in 1890, there has been controversy over whether Wounded Knee was a battle or a massacre. It has also been called the last battle of the Indian Wars.

Twenty-two years had passed since the 1868 Treaty at Fort Laramie established the Great Sioux Reservation. It was a desperate time for the Sioux. Their reservation that had once sprawled across portions of what are now several states now consisted of small islands of land surrounded by white homesteaders. Their rich culture was disappearing and being replaced by something both alien and unsatisfying. Their young children were being educated in special schools that taught them to reject their own culture and to replace it with the values and morals of the dominant white culture.

The Sioux were ripe for the coming of the latest Indian messiah, Wovoka, and his message of a return to the old ways. Wovoka was a Paiute, living in Nevada close to Lake Tahoe. On New Year's Day in 1889 there was a solar eclipse in Nevada. The Paiutes called it "the day the sun died." According to historian Rex Alan Smith, on that same day, Wovoka had a vision that he was taken to heaven. He was told the old world was to be destroyed and replaced by a fresh one. The dead would live again and everyone would be young and happy. The buffalo would return and the white man would disappear. All the Indians had to do was to perform the dance of the souls departed—the Ghost Dance.

Wovoka's vision was peaceful, but as it radiated out to other Indians it was imbued with the flavor of individual tribes. The Sioux added a strain of militarism. Adding volatility to the mix was the Sioux leader Sitting Bull, who had returned with his people to the United States from Canada in July 1881. Life on the reservation did not suit him and he longed for the old ways. Among his own people, he became a symbol of resistance and a hindrance to the plans of men such as James McLaughlin, agent at Standing Rock Reservation.

With the spread of the new religion, increasing numbers of Indians professed a belief in a Christian God. In addition, Wovoka told his adherents to farm and send all of their children to school. These were all things that should have been desirable to the white man. In fact, one of the primary duties of an Indian agent was to replace Native religious beliefs with Christian dogma. It would seem that the new Indian religion was doing just that. However, Standing Rock Indian Agent James McLaughlin called it an "absurd craze" and described the dance as "demoralizing, indecent and disgusting." He found no reason to change his opinion when he finally witnessed a dance a month after submitting his original assessment.

Shortly before 6 A.M. on December 15, 1890, Lt. Bull Head and 43 other Indian policemen arrived at Sitting Bull's cabin to arrest him. According to historian Robert M. Utley, Sitting Bull initially agreed to go peacefully, but as he was leaving his cabin a crowd began to gather. They jostled the policemen and shouted at them to release Sitting Bull, who began to struggle with his captors. Catch the Bear, one of Sitting Bull's followers, shot Lt. Bull Head in the leg. As he fell, Bull Head fired a shot into Sitting Bull's chest, and Red Tomahawk, another policeman, fired a shot into the back of the unarmed

chief's skull, killing him instantly. A fierce, brutal skirmish erupted, and, when it was all over, Sitting Bull, his young son Crow Foot, and six other tribesmen lay dead. In addition, four Indian policemen were dead and three were wounded, two of them mortally.

Frightened that the killing of Sitting Bull might be the first action in an all-out war, a mixed band of Sioux, under the leadership of Minneconjou Chief Big Foot, fled the Cheyenne River reservation. Several fugitives fleeing Sitting Bull's camp joined him en route. Big Foot was headed for the safety of Pine Ridge, hoping that the influential Chief Red Cloud could protect his people. However, some feared he was leading his band into the Badlands to join the hostile Ghost Dancers who were already gathered there. Major Samuel Whitside, with four troops of the Seventh Cavalry, was ordered to intercept and capture him.

Three days after Christmas of 1890, Whitside and the Seventh Calvary caught up with Big Foot and his band of 120 men and 230 women and children. During the night, Whitside's commander, Colonel James W. Forsyth, assumed command. He told Whitside that the Sioux were to be disarmed and shipped to a military prison in Omaha, Nebraska. The Indians were clothed in rags, and the children were hungry and cold. Big Foot had developed pneumonia during the flight across the Badlands in subzero weather. He was so weak he could barely sit up.

A council was called and Forsyth told the assembled warriors they would be asked to give up their guns. With the recent slaughter at Sitting Bull's camp fresh in their minds, the Sioux were fearful of being unarmed and vulnerable. They decided to give up their broken and useless guns and keep their working guns handy. Forsyth soon surrounded the camp. He had 470 soldiers and a platoon of Indian scouts under his command. Four Hotchkiss artillery pieces ringed the encampment.

The next day the Indians provided only an assortment of broken and outdated weapons. Forsyth knew there were more guns, so he ordered a search of the camp to gather up all the remaining weapons. Forsyth knew it was a delicate process that could easily lead to a violent reaction. As a precaution, only officers were allowed to enter teepees and search the women.

The tension rapidly increased with the Sioux warriors angrily objecting to the searches of their women. Historian Rex

Alan Smith writes that, as the search continued, Yellow Bird, a Minneconjou medicine man, began to dance and chant and throw handfuls of dirt into the air. He called upon the young men to have brave hearts and told them their "ghost shirts" would protect them from the soldier's bullets. One young man leapt to his feet angrily brandishing his gun saying he had paid good money for it and would not give it up. Some said it was a man named Black Coyote while other witnesses claimed it was a man named Hosi Yanka, which means "deaf." Two soldiers came behind the young man and tried to seize his weapon. In the ensuing scuffle, it went off. At that point, several young warriors threw off their blankets and fired a brief and ragged volley into the ranks of the soldiers. Lieutenant James Mann remembered thinking, "The pity of it! What can they be thinking of?" Almost simultaneously the soldiers lines erupted with gunfire. Big Foot was one of the first to die.

After that initial volley, the Sioux began to flee in all directions. Many fled to a nearby ravine that soon became the target of the Army's Hotchkiss guns on the hills above Wounded Knee. Most who fled to the ravine did not survive. Others were chased down and killed, some more than three miles from the scene of the massacre. In the end, nearly 300 Indians were killed, mostly women and children. Sixty soldiers, many who were victims of "friendly fire," were also killed.

In a story headlined "Horrors of War," the *Omaha World-Herald*'s correspondent told of wounded Indian mothers with their babies and the agonies endured bravely by the injured:

> There was a woman sitting on the floor with a wounded baby on her lap and four or five children around her, all her grandchildren. Their father and mother were killed. There was a young woman shot through both thighs and her wrist broken. Mr. Tibbles had to get a pair of pliers to get her rings off. There was a little boy with his throat apparently shot to pieces.
>
> They were all hungry and when we fed this little boy we found he could swallow. We gave him some gruel and he grabbed with both his little hands a dipper of water. When I saw him yesterday afternoon, he looked worse than the day before, and when they feed him now, the food and water come out the side of his neck.

Col. Forsyth was court-martialed, accused of mistakenly placing his men so that they fired into their own ranks, but he was found innocent. In a possible attempt to justify the events at Wounded Knee, the Army awarded 19 Medals of Honor to participants in the engagement. Five additional Medals of Honor were awarded for skirmishes along nearby White Clay Creek. This represented the largest number of Medal of Honor winners for any single engagement in U.S. history.

BARRY M. PRITZKER

See also

Indian Removal and the Creation of Indian Territory; Native American, Forced Relocation of; Native Americans, Conquest of

Further Reading:

Jensen, Richard, Eli Paul, and John E. Carter. *Eyewitness to Wounded Knee*. Lincoln: University of Nebraska Press, 1991.

Pritzker, Barry M. *Native Americans: An Encyclopedia of History, Culture and Peoples*, 2 vols. Santa Barbara, CA: ABC-CLIO, 1998.

Tibbles, Thomas Henry. *Buckskin and Blanket Days: Memoirs of a Friend of the Indians*. New York: Doubleday, 1988.

Utley, Robert M. *The Lance and the Shield: The Life and Times of Sitting Bull*. New York: Henry Holt, 1993.

X

Xenophobia

The Merriam-Webster Dictionary defines xenophobia as "fear and hatred of strangers or foreigners or of anything that is strange or foreign." Yakusho describes xenophobia as "a form of attitudinal, affective, and behavioral prejudice toward immigrants and those perceived as foreign" (Yakusho 2009: 43). Simply stated, xenophobia is a fear or dislike of anyone that an individual might find different from their normative expectations. The criteria for being different might include but not be limited to ethnic background, racial designations, religion, or the culturally different. Xenophobia is often based on stereotypes, and immigrants are perceived to be a threat. Stephan and Stephan pose an "integrated theory of prejudice" that defines four types of threats that immigrants may pose. *Realistic threats* represent a political and economic challenge to in-groups and those in power. *Symbolic threats* challenge values, beliefs, morals, and attitudes thus threatening the host culture's worldview. *Intergroup anxiety* and *negative stereotypes* provide motivation for immigrant avoidance in that interaction may be frustrating or unpleasant. In the framework of these threats, immigrants are associated with declining economies, overpopulation, pollution, violence, criminality, and erosion of culture. Stereotyping immigrants as poor, uneducated, and prone to violence reinforces the sentiments of fear and hostility. The results are the increased nativism seen in the 21st century.

Friedman describes nativism as "a deep-seated American antipathy for internal 'foreign' groups of various kinds (national, cultural, religious) which has erupted periodically into intensive efforts to safeguard America from such perceived threats." (Friedman 1967: 408) Nativism as xenophobia has reoccurred periodically in American history and has often used immigrants as a scapegoat for national problems. Historically three traditions of nativism or xenophobia have been recorded as the anti-Catholic tradition, the antiradicalism tradition that opposed socialism and communism, and the radical nationalism tradition that paints America as an Anglo-Saxon nation. Modern nativism, however, is characterized by an antipathy for non-English speakers, a belief that immigrants take advantage of American generosity, and a belief that immigrant serve to drain social services. Throughout American history, these xenophobic beliefs have been codified and institutionalized through state, local, and federal laws.

Prior to 1875, there was no direct federal legislation restricting the admission of the foreign-born to the United States. However, some federal and state regulations, designed not to limit the number of entrants but the type of immigrant, were enacted and thus began a long history of institutionalized xenophobia. Restrictions applied to the destitute, the physically handicapped, certain races, and those engaged in immoral activities. From 1788 until 1921, the United States imposed no annual restrictions on the number of individuals allowed to enter the country. Many of the immigrants arrived from Germany, Ireland, and French Canada, and as development began in the West, a large number of Chinese immigrants arrived in the 1840s.

The destruction of the agrarian South during the Civil War of 1861–1865 was accompanied by an accelerated growth of business in the North. Advances in mechanization of industry and a growth in infrastructure brought 10 million immigrants to the United States from 1861 until 1890. Austria and Scandinavia joined the United Kingdom, Germany, and Canada as place of origin for new immigrants, while the Central Pacific Railroad continued to recruit Chinese workers for the West. Many of these immigrants were unskilled workers who could be trained for growing industrialization. In 1864, Congress passed the Act to Encourage Immigration (Contract Labor Act) at the behest of business's need for a larger labor force. The act allowed private business to recruit foreign workers and pay for their transportation to the United States and in return, immigrants pledged up to 12 months of their wages as repayment. Transportation repayment, combined with "maintenance" fees, created an immigrant worker status similar to indentured servitude. Resistance to the rising number of Chinese immigrants recruited by the railroads and fleeing China's internal turmoil led to the congressional passage of the 1882 Chinese Exclusion Act, which represented the first significant effort by the government to restrict levels of immigration. The 1882 act was followed in 1885 by the Allen Contract Act, which prohibited businesses from providing financial assistance to immigrant workers. The Immigration Act of 1882 assigned the responsibility of examining new immigrants to the Secretary of the Treasury. This was followed by the Immigration Act of 1891, which ended all state involvement in immigration issues and created the Bureau of Immigration (BI) within the Treasury Department. However, the BI was moved in 1903 to the Department of Commerce and Labor. The role of immigration enforcement was assumed with the 1904 creation of a set of inspectors to patrol the Mexican border to stop illegal immigration. In 1906, the BI became the Bureau of Immigration and Naturalization and in 1913 was assigned to the Department of Labor. In an effort to understand immigration impact, the 1907 United States Immigration Commission was created as an ambitious social science project designed to establish a formal immigration policy. The Dillingham Commission, named for Sen. William Dillingham, was composed of three members of the House of Representatives, three members of the Senate, and three outside experts, and produced a final report in 1911. The report suggested the definition of "superior" and "inferior" races, rules governing selectivity and restrictions on immigration, and pointed to economically adverse effects of unlimited immigration. A series of immigration acts followed the submission of the report that represented efforts to control immigration through screening, numerical quotas, and banning of selected categories. The restrictions and quotas created by the Immigration Acts of 1917, 1921, and 1924 remained in effect until 1965.

The end of World War II brought about a series of global changes, and the United States became one of the most influential nations due to its military, political, and economic power. Presidents Truman, Eisenhower, and Kennedy viewed immigration reform as a national imperative, but Congress refused to change the overall policies until the Johnson administration. Overt racial bans could no longer be tolerated, and in 1965, the Immigration Act lifted national quotas, centered immigration policy on family reunification, and established a seven-category visa program.

America has a long history of xenophobic attitudes and behaviors. The fear and hostility demonstrated toward immigrants has been institutionalized and continued into the 21st century. However, several efforts have sought to promote a more positive atmosphere for immigrants and to reform the xenophobic approach. The 1986 Immigration Reform and Control Act (IRCA) allowed approximately 3 million "illegal" migrants to engage on a path to citizenship. At the beginning of the 21st century, attention has once again turned to questions of immigration and citizenship.

A series of immigration articles appeared in the *Wall Street Journal* from late January 2013 until early February. American lawmakers are seeking to reform immigration guidelines and address new as well as "illegal" immigrants who arrive in the country. Central to the arguments are how to provide a timely process for gaining citizenship and encourage much-needed workers. However, many individuals oppose reform using old arguments. Some suggest that "illegals" are being rewarded for criminal activity, while others argue that new immigrants depress wages and limit opportunities for the native born. Thus as attempts to reform immigration laws continue, xenophobia also continues to be a deterrent.

R. Randall Adams

Further Reading:

Briggs, Vernon M., Jr. *Mass Immigration and the National Interest.* New York: M. E. Sharpe, 2003.

Friedman, Norman L. "Nativism." *Phylon* (1967) 28: 408–15.

Merriam–Webster Dictionary. http://www.merriam-webster .com/dictionary/xenophobia (accessed December 16, 2012)

Mikulich, Alex. "U.S. Xenophobia and Racism—The Presence of the Past." Jesuit Social Research Institute JustSouth Quarterly. http:/www. Loyno.edu/

us-xenophobia-and-racism-presence-past-o (accessed December 19, 2012)

Sanchez, George J. "Face the Nation: Race, Immigration, and the Rise of Nativism in the Late Twentieth Century America." *International Migration Review* (1997) 31: 1009–30.

Smith, James P., and Barry Edmonston, eds. *The New Americans: Economics, Demographic, and Fiscal Effects of Immigration.* Washington, D.C.: National Academy Press, 1997.

Stephan, W. G., and C. W. Stephan. "An Integrated Threat Theory of Prejudice." In *Claremont Symposium on Applied Social Psychology*, edited by S. Oskamp. Hillsdale, NJ: Lawrence Erlbaum, 2000.

Yakusho, Oksama. "Exenophobia: Understanding the Roots and Consequences of Negative Attitudes toward Immigrants." *Counseling Psychologist* (2009) 37: 36–66.

Z

Zoot Suit Riots

The Zoot Suit Riots, the most important 20th-century example of white violence against Mexican Americans, occurred in 1943 in Los Angeles, the city with the largest Mexican population in the United States. The riots were so named because their victims, young Mexican American males, followed the fad of wearing long, loose-fitting jackets with wide shoulders, baggy trousers, and flat-topped hats.

On June 3, 1943, two incidents precipitated the riots. Some Mexican boys, on their way home from a police-sponsored club meeting, were attacked by a group of white hoodlums in a Los Angeles neighborhood. Second, the same evening, 11 white sailors on leave were attacked, and one of them hurt badly, by assailants whom the victims identified as Mexican youths. When the police found no one to arrest as suspects, in retaliation, about 200 white marines, soldiers, and sailors drove through the Mexican area in taxis and randomly attacked Mexican young men on the streets. Cars passing on the streets were stopped, and Filipino and black riders as well as Mexicans were pushed out and punched at random. Some Mexican men were stripped of their clothes, left cowering on the pavements and bleeding, surrounded by mobs of men. But the police did nothing to stop it. Instead, they arrested the Mexican victims. The media incited the riots by emphasizing a mass retaliation by Mexican zoot-suiters. As a result, the bloody attacks lasted four days.

Although an incident involving white sailors and Mexican young men triggered the riots, Anglos' deep-seated prejudice against Mexicans contributed to the racial aggressions. Also, the Los Angeles media's sensational accounts of Mexican young gangs in the previous years contributed to the riots.

PYONG GAP MIN

See also

Race Riots in America. Documents: The Report on the Memphis Riots of May 1866 (July 25, 1866); Account of the Riots in East St. Louis, Illinois (July 1917); The Cook County Coroner's Report Regarding the 1919 Chicago Race Riots (1919); A Southern Black Woman's Letter Regarding the Recent Riots in Chicago and Washington (November 1919); The Final Report of the Grand Jury on the Tulsa Race Riot (June 25, 1921); Testimony from *Laney v. United States* Describing Events during the Washington, D.C., Riot of July 1919 (December 3, 1923); The Governor's Commission Report on the Watts Riots (December 1965); Cyrus R. Vance's Report on the Riots in Detroit (July–August 1967); The Reports of the Oklahoma Commission to Study the Tulsa Race Riot of 1921 (2000–2001); The Draft Report of the 1898 Wilmington Race Riot Commission (December 2005)

Further Reading:

Garcia, F. Chris, and Rudolph P. de la Garza. *The Chicano Political Experiences: Three Perspectives*. North Scituate, MA: Duxbury, 1977.

McWilliams, Carey. *North from Mexico: Spanish-Speaking People in the United States*. Westport, CT: Greenwood Press, 1968.

Mexican Americans lined up outside a Los Angeles jail en route to court after the Zoot Suit Riots, June 9, 1943. (Library of Congress)

Primary Documents

Massachusetts Slaves' Petition (1777)

Introduction

The Declaration of Independence and other declarations and constitutions of the revolutionary period variously asserted equality and liberty. When the Revolutionaries declared that "all men were created equal," did they not mean all men? Slaves heard, and some read, the ringing arguments for freedom and equality that whites used to justify the American Revolution. It should come as no surprise that, given these principles, some would challenge slavery. This 1777 petition from Massachusetts slaves to the General Court was one such challenge.

Primary Source

To the Honorable Counsel & House of Representatives for the State of Massachusetts Bay in General Court Assembled, January 13, 1777

The petition of A Great Number of Blacks detained in a State of slavery in the Bowels of a free & Christian Country Humbly shows that your Petitioners apprehend that they have in Common with all other men a Natural and Unalienable Right to that freedom which the Great Parent of the Universe hath Bestowed equally on all mankind and which they have Never forfeited by any Compact or agreement whatever—but that

were Unjustly Dragged by the hand of cruel Power from their Dearest friends and some of them Even torn from the Embraces of their tender Parents—from A populous Pleasant and plentiful country and in violation of Laws of Nature and of Nations and in defiance of all the tender feelings of humanity Brought here Either to Be sold Like Beasts of Burden & Like them Condemned to Slavery for Life—Among A People Professing the mild Religion of Jesus; A people Not Insensible of the Secrets of Rational Being, Nor without spirit to Resent the unjust endeavors of others to Reduce them to a state of Bondage and Subjection. Your honor Need not to be informed that A Life of Slavery Like that of your petitioners Deprived of Every social privilege of Every thing Requisit to Render Life Tolerable is far worse than Nonexistence.

In imitation of the Laudable Example of the Good People of these States, your petitioners have Long and Patiently waited the Event of petition after petition By them presented to the Legislative Body of this state and cannot but with Grief Reflect that their Sucess hath been but too similar; they Cannot but express their Astonishment that It has Never Been Considered that Every Principle from which America has Acted in the Course of their unhappy Difficulties with Great Britain Pleads Stronger than A thousand arguments in favor of your petitioners. They therefore humbly Beseech your honors to give this petition its due weight & consideration

& cause an act of the Legislature to be passed Whereby they may be Restored to the Enjoyments of that which is the Natural Right of all men—and their Children who were Born in this Land of Liberty may not be heard as Slaves after they arrive at the age of twenty one years. So may the Inhabitants of this State, No longer chargeable with the inconsistency of acting themselves the part which they condemn and oppose in others, Be prospered in their present Glorious struggle for Liberty and have those Blessings to themselves.

Source: *Massachusetts Slaves' Petition.* Collections of the Massachusetts Historical Society, 5th Series, III. Boston, 1877, 436–37.

See also: Abolitionist Movement; Slave Codes; Slave Families; Slave Revolts and White Attacks on Black Slaves; Slave Trade; Slavery; Slavery in the Antebellum South. Documents: Pennsylvania Act for the Gradual Abolition of Slavery (1788); Olaudah Equiano (1789); Fugitive Slave Act (1793); Act to Prohibit the Importation of Slaves (1807); Emancipation Proclamation (June 1866); Ida B. Wells' Expose on Lynching (1895)

Pennsylvania Act for the Gradual Abolition of Slavery (1780)

Introduction

In April 1775, the first abolitionist society in the world was established in Philadelphia, Pennsylvania. By the time of the American Revolution, Pennsylvania Quakers had emancipated their slaves, and the number of slaves remaining in the colony was relatively small. Nevertheless, it was thought that the new Revolutionary government of Pennsylvania, dominated by Scotch-Irish settlers, was not interested in abolition. However, under the leadership of Revolutionary president George Bryan, the Pennsylvania Assembly on March 1, 1780, passed the Act for the Gradual Abolition of Slavery. The Pennsylvania action was copied by other Northern states over the next several years.

Primary Source

An Act for the gradual Abolition of Slavery.

Section I. When we contemplate our abhorrence of that condition, to which the arms and tyranny of Great Britain were exerted to reduce us—when we look back on the variety of dangers to which we have been exposed, and how miraculously our wants in many instances have been supplied, and our deliverances wrought, when even hope and human fortitude have become unequal to the conflict—we are unavoidably led to a serious and grateful sense of the manifold blessings which we have undeservedly received from the hand of that Being, from whom every good and perfect gift cometh. Impressed with these ideas, we conceive that it is our duty, and we rejoice that it is in our power, to extend a portion of that freedom to others. . . . It is not for us to enquire why, in the creation of mankind, the inhabitants of the several parts of the earth were distinguished by a difference in feature or complexion. It is sufficient to know that all are the work of an Almighty Hand. We find, in the distribution of the human species, that the most fertile as well as the most barren parts of the earth are inhabited by men of complexions different from ours, and from each other; from whence we may reasonably, as well as religiously, infer, that he who placed them in their various situations, hath extended equally his care and protection to all, and that it becometh not us to counteract his mercies. We esteem it a peculiar blessing granted to us, that we are enabled this day to add one more step to universal civilization, by removing, as much as possible, the sorrows of those who have lived in undeserved bondage. . . .

Sect. II. And whereas the condition of those persons who have heretofore been denominated Negro and Mulatto slaves, has been attended with circumstances which not only deprived them of the common blessings that they were by nature entitled to, but has cast them into the deepest afflictions by an unnatural separation and sale of husband and wife from each other and from their children—an injury, the greatness of which can only be conceived by supposing that we were in the same unhappy case. In justice, therefore, to persons so unhappily circumstanced, and who, having no prospect before them whereon they may rest their sorrows and their hopes, have no reasonable inducement to render their service to society, which otherwise they might. . . .

Sect. III. Be it enacted, and it is hereby enacted, by the representatives of the freemen of the commonwealth of Pennsylvania, in general assembly met, and by the authority of the same, That all persons, as well Negroes and Mulattoes and others, who shall be born within this state from and after the passing of this act, shall not be deemed and considered as servants for life, or slaves; and that all servitude for life, or slavery of children, in consequence of the slavery of their mothers, in the case of all children born within this state, from and after the passing of this act as aforesaid, shall be, and hereby is utterly taken away, extinguished and forever abolished.

Sect. IV. Provided always, and be it further enacted, by the authority aforesaid, That every Negro and Mulatto child born within this state after the passing of this act as aforesaid (who would, in case this act had not been made, have been born a servant for years, or life, or a slave) shall be deemed to be, and shall be, by virtue of this act, the servant of such person, or his or her assigns, who would, in such case, have been entitled to the service of such child, until such child shall attain unto the age of twenty-eight years. . . .

Sect. V. And be it further enacted by the authority aforesaid, That every person, who is or shall be the owner of any Negro or Mulatto slave or servant for life, or till the age of thirty-one years, now within this state, or his lawful attorney, shall, on or before the said first day of November next, deliver or cause to be delivered in writing to the clerk of the peace of the county, or to the clerk of the court of record of the city of Philadelphia . . . the name, and surname, and occupation or profession of such owner . . . and also the name and names of any such slave and slaves, and servant and servants for life or till the age of thirty-one years, together with their ages and sexes severally and respectively set forth and annexed . . . in order to ascertain and distinguish the slaves and servants for life and till the age of thirty-one years, within this state, who shall be such, on the said first day of November next, from all other persons. . . .

Sect. VII. And be it further enacted by the authority aforesaid, That the offences and crimes of Negroes and Mulattoes, as well slaves and servants as freemen, shall be enquired of, adjudged, corrected and punished in like manner as the offences and crimes of the other inhabitants of this state . . . except that a slave shall not be admitted to bear witness against a freeman. . . .

Sect. IX. And be it further enacted by the authority aforesaid, That the reward for taking up runaway and absconding Negro and Mulatto slaves and servants, and the penalties for enticing away, dealing with, or harbouring, concealing or employing Negro and Mulatto slaves and servants, shall be the same, and shall be recovered in like manner as in the case of servants bound for four years.

Sect. X. And be it further enacted by the authority aforesaid, That no man or woman of any nation or colony, except the Negroes or Mulattoes who shall be registered as aforesaid, shall at any time hereafter be deemed, adjudged or holden within the territories of this commonwealth as slaves or servants for life, but as free-men and free-women; except the domestic slaves attending upon delegates in Congress from the other American states, foreign ministers and consuls, and persons passing through or sojourning in this state and not becoming resident therein, and seamen employed in ships not belonging to any inhabitant of this state, nor employed in any ship owned by any such inhabitant. Provided such domestic slaves be not aliened or sold to any inhabitant, nor (except in the case of members of Congress, foreign ministers and consuls) retained in this state longer than six months.

Sect. XI. Provided always, and be it further enacted by the authority aforesaid, That this act or any thing in it contained, shall not give any relief or shelter to any absconding or runaway Negro or Mulatto slave or servant. . . .

Sect. XII. And whereas attempts may be made to evade this act, by introducing into this state Negroes and Mulattoes bound by covenant, to serve for long and unreasonable terms of years, if the same be not prevented:

Sect. XIII. Be it therefore enacted by the authority aforesaid, That no covenant of personal servitude or apprenticeship whatsoever, shall be valid or binding on a Negro or Mulatto, for a longer time than seven years, unless such servant or apprentice were, at the commencement of such servitude or apprenticeship, under the age of twenty-one years; in which case such Negro or Mulatto may be holden as a servant or apprentice respectively, according to the covenant, as the case shall be, until he or she shall attain the age of twenty-eight years. . . .

John Bayard, Speaker.

Enacted into a Law at Philadelphia, on Wednesday, the first day of March, Anno Domini, 1790.

Thomas Paine, Clerk of the General Assembly.

Source: An Act for the Gradual Abolition of Slavery, Supreme Executive Council of Pennsylvania, March 1, 1780. Pennsylvania State Archives.

See also: Abolitionist Movement; Slave Codes; Slave Families; Slave Revolts and White Attacks on Black Slaves; Slave Trade; Slavery; Slavery in the Antebellum South. Documents: Massachusetts Slaves' Petition (1777); Olaudah Equiano (1789); Fugitive Slave Act (1793); Act to Prohibit the Importation of Slaves (1807); Emancipation Proclamation (June 1866); Ida B. Wells' Expose on Lynching (1895)

Alexander Falconbridge: Describing the African Slave Trade (1788)

Introduction

The African slave trade was the most condemned aspect of slavery in the early republic. The middle passage—the journey between West Africa and the Americas—was criticized even as the institution of slavery was defended. In the following excerpt, Alexander Falconbridge describes many of the horrors that he witnessed aboard a slave ship. Falconbridge, who was employed as a surgeon aboard the ship, later served as the governor of a British colony for freed slaves in Sierra Leone. The conditions on board the ships convinced enough Americans, even slave owners, to prohibit future slave imports. As a result, the United States ended its participation in the transatlantic slave trade in 1808. This predated the abolition of slavery by five and a half decades.

Primary Source

The men Negroes, on being brought aboard the ship, are immediately fastened together, two and two, by handcuffs on their wrists and by irons rivetted on their legs. They are then sent down between the decks and placed in an apartment partitioned off for that purpose. The women also are placed in a separate apartment between decks, but without being ironed. An adjoining room on the same deck is appointed for the boys. Thus they are all placed in different apartments.

But at the same time, however, they are frequently stowed so close, as to admit of no other position than lying on their sides. Nor will the height between decks, unless directly under the grating, permit the indulgence of an erect posture; especially where there are platforms, which is generally the case. These platforms are a kind of shelf, about eight or nine feet in breadth, extending from the side of the ship toward the centre. They are placed nearly midway between the decks, at the distance of two or three feet from each deck, Upon these the Negroes are stowed in the same manner as they are on the deck underneath.

In each of the apartments are placed three or four large buckets, of a conical form, nearly two feet in diameter at the bottom and only one foot at the top and in depth of about twenty-eight inches, to which, when necessary, the Negroes have recourse. It often happens that those who are placed at a distance from the buckets, in endeavoring to get to them, rumble over their companions, in consequence of their being shackled. These accidents, although unavoidable, are productive of continual quarrels in which some of them are always bruised. In this distressed situation, unable to proceed and prevented from getting to the tubs, they desist from the attempt; and as the necessities of nature are not to be resisted, ease themselves as they lie. This becomes a fresh source of boils and disturbances and tends to render the condition of the poor captive wretches still more uncomfortable. The nuisance arising from these circumstances is not infrequently increased by the tubs being much too small for the purpose intended and their being usually emptied but once every day. The rule for doing so, however, varies in different ships according to the attention paid to the health and convenience of the slaves by the captain. . . .

Upon the Negroes refusing to take sustenance, I have seen coals of fire, glowing hot, put on a shovel and placed so near their lips as to scorch and burn them. And this has been accompanied with threats of forcing them to swallow the coals if they any longer persisted in refusing to eat. These means have generally had the desired effect. I have also been credibly informed that a certain captain in the slave-trade, poured melted lead on such of his Negroes as obstinately refused their food. . . .

The hardships and inconveniences suffered by the Negroes during the passage are scarcely to be enumerated or conceived. They are far more violently affected by seasickness than Europeans. It frequently terminates in death, especially among the women. But the exclusion of fresh air is among the most intolerable. For the purpose of admitting this needful refreshment, most of the ships in the slave trade are provided, between the decks, with five or six air-ports on each side of the ship, of about five inches in length and four in breadth. In addition, some ships, but not one in twenty, have what they denominate wind-sails. But whenever the sea is rough, and the rain heavy it becomes necessary to shut these and every other conveyance by which the air is admitted. The fresh air being thus excluded, the Negroes' rooms soon grow intolerable hot. The confined air, rendered noxious by the effluvia exhaled from their bodies and being repeatedly breathed, soon produces fevers and fluxes which generally carries off great numbers of them.

During the voyages I made, I was frequently witness to the fatal effects of this exclusion of fresh air. I will give one instance, as it serves to convey some idea, though a very faint one, of their terrible sufferings. . . . Some wet and blowing weather having occasioned the port-holes to be shut and the grating to be covered, fluxes and fevers among the Negroes ensued. While they were in this situation, I frequently went down among them till at length their room became so extremely hot as to be only bearable for a very short time. But the excessive heat was not the only thing that rendered their situation intolerable. The deck, that is the floor of their rooms, was so covered with the blood and mucus which had proceeded from them in consequence of the flux, that it resembled a slaughter-house. It is not in the power of the human imagination to picture a situation more dreadful or disgusting. Numbers of the slaves having fainted, they were carried upon deck where several of them died and the rest with great difficulty were restored. It had nearly proved fatal to me also. The climate was too warm to admit the wearing of any clothing but a shirt and that I had pulled off before I

went down. . . . In a quarter of an hour I was so overcome with the heat, stench and foul air that I nearly fainted, and it was only with assistance I could get back on deck. The consequence was that I soon after fell sick of the same disorder from which I did not recover for several months. . . .

Source: Falconbridge, Alexander. *An Account of the Slave Trade on the Coast of Africa.* London: J. Phillips, 1788.

See also: Abolitionist Movement; Slave Codes; Slave Families; Slave Revolts and White Attacks on Black Slaves; Slave Trade; Slavery; Slavery in the Antebellum South. Documents: Massachusetts Slaves' Petition (1777); Pennsylvania Act for the Gradual Abolition of Slavery (1780); Olaudah Equiano (1789); Fugitive Slave Act (1793); Fear of Slave Revolt in New Orleans (1804); Emancipation Proclamation (1863); Fourteenth Amendment (June 1866); Ida B. Wells' Expose on Lynching (*The Red Record*, 1895)

Olaudah Equiano: Horrors of the Middle Passage (1789)

Introduction

Olaudah Equiano (also known as Gustavus Vassa), the 18th century's most prominent African author in the English-speaking world, had been taken near his African village and sold into slavery in the Caribbean region when he was 11 years old. Ten years later, he purchased his freedom and eventually settled in England. Equiano published The Interesting Narrative of the Life of Olaudah Equiano, *the first substantial slave narrative, in 1789. The excerpt below recounts the horrors of the Middle Passage across the Atlantic Ocean from Africa to the Americas in the bowels of a slave ship. Equiano's autobiography encouraged antislavery sentiment in the northern United States and profoundly influenced the 19th-century African American slave narratives that would follow.*

Primary Source

The first object which saluted my eyes when I arrived on the coast, was the sea, and a slave ship, which was then riding at anchor, and waiting for its cargo. These filled me with astonishment, which was soon converted into terror, when I was carried on board. I was immediately handled, and tossed up to see if I were sound, by some of the crew; and I was now persuaded that I had gotten into a world of bad spirits, and that they were going to kill me. Their complexions, too, differing so much from ours, their long hair, and the language they spoke (which was very different from any I had ever heard), united to confirm me in this belief. Indeed, such were the horrors of my views and fears at the moment, that, if ten thousand worlds had been my own, I would have freely parted with them all to have exchanged my condition with that of the meanest slave in my own country.

When I looked round the ship too, and saw a large furnace of copper boiling, and a multitude of black people of every description chained together, every one of their countenances expressing dejection and sorrow, I no longer doubted of my fate; and, quite overpowered with horror and anguish, I fell motionless on the deck and fainted. When I recovered a little, I found some black people about me, who I believed were some of those who had brought me on board, and had been receiving their pay; they talked to me in order to cheer me, but all in vain. I asked them if we were not to be eaten by those white men with horrible looks, red faces, and long hair. They told me I was not, and one of the crew brought me a small portion of spirituous liquor in a wine glass; but being afraid of him, I would not take it out of his hand. One of the blacks therefore took it from him and gave it to me, and I took a little down my palate, which, instead of reviving me, as they thought it would, threw me into the greatest consternation at the strange feeling it produced, having never tasted any such liquor before. Soon after this, the blacks who brought me on board went off, and left me abandoned to despair.

I now saw myself deprived of all chance of returning to my native country, or even the least glimpse of hope of gaining the shore, which I now considered as friendly; and I even wished for my former slavery in preference to my present situation, which was filled with horrors of every kind, still heightened by my ignorance of what I was to undergo. I was not long suffered to indulge my grief; I was soon put down under the decks, and there I received such a salutation in my nostrils as I had never experienced in my life: so that, with the loathsomeness of the stench, and crying together, I became so sick and low that I was not able to eat, nor had

I the least desire to taste anything. I now wished for the last friend, death, to relieve me; but soon, to my grief, two of the white men offered me eatables; and, on my refusing to eat, one of them held me fast by the hands, and laid me across, I think, the windlass, and tied my feet, while the other flogged me severely. I had never experienced anything of this kind before, and, although not being used to the water, I naturally feared that element the first time I saw it, yet, nevertheless, could I have got over the nettings, I would have jumped over the side, but I could not; and besides, the crew used to watch us very closely who were not chained down to the decks, lest we should leap into the water; and I have seen some of these poor African prisoners most severely cut, for attempting to do so, and hourly whipped for not eating. This indeed was often the case with myself.

In a little time after, amongst the poor chained men, I found some of my own nation, which in a small degree gave ease to my mind. I inquired of these what was to be done with us? They gave me to understand, we were to be carried to these white people's country to work for them. I then was a little revived, and thought, if it were no worse than working, my situation was not so desperate; but still I feared I should be put to death, the white people looked and acted, as I thought, in so savage a manner; for I had never seen among any people such instances of brutal cruelty; and this not only shown towards us blacks, but also to some of the whites themselves. One white man in particular I saw, when we were permitted to be on deck, flogged so unmercifully with a large rope near the foremast, that he died in consequence of it; and they tossed him over the side as they would have done a brute. This made me fear these people the more; and I expected nothing less than to be treated in the same manner. I could not help expressing my fears and apprehensions to some of my countrymen; I asked them if these people had no country, but lived in this hollow place (the ship)? They told me they did not, but came from a distant one. "Then," said I, "how comes it in all our country we never heard of them?" They told me because they lived so very far off. I then asked where were their women? had they any like themselves? I was told they had. "And why," said I, "do we not see them?" They answered, because they were left behind. I asked how the vessel could go? They told me they could not tell; but that there was cloth put upon the masts by the help of the ropes I saw, and then the vessel went on; and the white men had some spell or magic they put in the water when they liked, in order to stop the vessel. I was exceedingly amazed at this account, and really thought they were spirits. I therefore wished much to be from amongst them, for I expected they would sacrifice me; but my wishes were vain—for we were so quartered that it was impossible for any of us to make our escape.

While we stayed on the coast I was mostly on deck; and one day, to my great astonishment, I saw one of these vessels coming in with the sails up. As soon as the whites saw it, they gave a great shout, at which we were amazed; and the more so, as the vessel appeared larger by approaching nearer. At last, she came to an anchor in my sight, and when the anchor was let go, I and my countrymen who saw it, were lost in astonishment to observe the vessel stop—and were now convinced it was done by magic. Soon after this the other ship got her boats out, and they came on board of us, and the people of both ships seemed very glad to see each other. Several of the strangers also shook hands with us black people, and made motions with their hands, signifying I suppose, we were to go to their country, but we did not understand them.

At last, when the ship we were in, had got in all her cargo, they made ready with many fearful noises, and we were all put under deck, so that we could not see how they managed the vessel. But this disappointment was the least of my sorrow. The stench of the hold while we were on the coast was so intolerably loathsome, that it was dangerous to remain there for any time, and some of us had been permitted to stay on the deck for the fresh air; but now that the whole ship's cargo were confined together, it became absolutely pestilential. The closeness of the place, and the heat of the climate, added to the number in the ship, which was so crowded that each had scarcely room to turn himself, almost suffocated us.

This produced copious perspirations, so that the air soon became unfit for respiration, from a variety of loathsome smells, and brought on a sickness among the slaves, of which many died—thus falling victims to the improvident avarice, as I may call it, of their purchasers. This wretched situation was again aggravated by the gaffing of the chains,

now became insupportable, and the filth of the necessary tubs, into which the children often fell, and were almost suffocated. The shrieks of the women, and the groans of the dying, rendered the whole a scene of horror almost inconceivable. Happily perhaps, for myself, I was soon reduced so low here that it was thought necessary to keep me almost always on deck; and from my extreme youth I was not put in fetters. In this situation I expected every hour to share the fate of my companions, some of whom were almost daily brought upon deck at the point of death, which I began to hope would soon put an end to my miseries. Often did I think many of the inhabitants of the deep much more happy than myself. I envied them the freedom they enjoyed, and as often wished I could change my condition for theirs. Every circumstance I met with, served only to render my state more painful, and heightened my apprehensions, and my opinion of the cruelty of the whites.

One day they had taken a number of fishes; and when they had killed and satisfied themselves with as many as they thought fit, to our astonishment who were on deck, rather than give any of them to us to eat, as we expected, they tossed the remaining fish into the sea again, although we begged and prayed for some as well as we could, but in vain; and some of my countrymen, being pressed by hunger, took an opportunity, when they thought no one saw them, of trying to get a little privately; but they were discovered, and the attempt procured them some very severe floggings.

One day, when we had a smooth sea and moderate wind, two of my wearied countrymen who were chained together (I was near them at the time), preferring death to such a life of misery, somehow made through the nettings and jumped into the sea; immediately, another quite dejected fellow, who, on account of his illness, was suffered to be out of irons, also followed their example; and I believe many more would very soon have done the same, if they had not been prevented by the ship's crew, who were instantly alarmed. Those of us that were the most active, were in a moment put down under the deck; and there was such a noise and confusion amongst the people of the ship as I never heard before, to stop her, and get the boat out to go after the slaves. However, two of the wretches were drowned, but they got the other, and afterwards flogged him unmercifully, for thus attempting to prefer death to slavery. In this manner we continued to undergo more hardships than I can now relate, hardships which are inseparable from this accursed trade. Many a time we were near suffocation from the want of fresh air, which we were often without for whole days together. This, and the stench of the necessary tubs, carried off many.

During our passage, I first saw flying fishes, which surprised me very much; they used frequently to fly across the ship, and many of them fell on the deck. I also now first saw the use of the quadrant; I had often with astonishment seen the mariners make observations with it, and I could not think what it meant. They at last took notice of my surprise; and one of them, willing to increase it, as well as to gratify my curiosity, made me one day look through it. The clouds appeared to me to be land, which disappeared as they passed along. This heightened my wonder; and I was now more persuaded than ever, that I was in another world, and that every thing about me was magic.

At last we came in sight of the island of Barbadoes, at which the whites on board gave a great shout, and made many signs of joy to us. We did not know what to think of this; but as the vessel drew nearer, we plainly saw the harbor, and other ships of different kinds and sizes, and we soon anchored amongst them, off Bridgetown. Many merchants and planters now came on board, though it was in the evening. They put us in separate parcels, and examined us attentively. They also made us jump, and pointed to the land, signifying we were to go there. We thought by this, we should be eaten by these ugly men, as they appeared to us; and, when soon after we were all put down under the deck again, there was much dread and trembling among us, and nothing but bitter cries to be heard all the night from these apprehensions, insomuch, that at last the white people got some old slaves from the land to pacify us. They told us we were not to be eaten, but to work, and were soon to go on land, where we should see many of our country people. This report eased us much. And sure enough, soon after we were landed, there came to us Africans of all languages.

We were conducted immediately to the merchant's yard, where we were all pent up together, like so many sheep in a fold, without regard to sex or age. As every object was new to me, everything I saw filled me with surprise. What struck me first, was, that the houses were built with bricks and stories, and in every other respect different from those I had seen in Africa; but I was still more astonished on seeing people on horseback. I did not know what this could mean; and, indeed, I thought these people were full of nothing but magical arts. While I was in this astonishment, one of my fellow prisoners spoke to a countryman of his, about the horses, who said they were the same kind they had in their country. I understood them, though they were from a distant part of Africa; and I thought it odd I had not seen any horses there; but afterwards, when I came to converse with different Africans, I found they had many horses amongst them, and much larger than those I then saw.

We were not many days in the merchant's custody, before we were sold after their usual manner, which is this: On a signal given (as the beat of a drum), the buyers rush at once into the yard where the slaves are confined, and make choice of that parcel they like best. The noise and clamor with which this is attended, and the eagerness visible in the countenances of the buyers, serve not a little to increase the apprehension of terrified Africans, who may well be supposed to consider them as the ministers of that destruction to which they think themselves devoted. In this manner, without scruple, are relations and friends separated, most of them never to see each other again.

I remember, in the vessel in which I was brought over, in the men's apartment, there were several brothers, who, in the sale, were sold in different lots; and it was very moving on this occasion, to see and hear their cries at parting. O, ye nominal Christians! might not an African ask you—Learned you this from your God, who says unto you, Do unto all men as you would men should do unto you? Is it not enough that we are torn from our country and friends, to toil for your luxury and lust of gain? Must every tender feeling be likewise sacrificed to your avarice? Are the dearest friends and relations, now rendered more dear by their separation from their kindred, still to be parted from each other, and thus prevented from cheering the gloom of slavery, with the small comfort of being together, and mingling their sufferings and sorrows? Why are parents to lose their children, brothers their sisters, or husbands their wives? Surely, this is a new refinement in cruelty, which, while it has no advantage to atone for it, thus aggravates distress, and adds fresh horrors even to the wretchedness of slavery.

Source: Equuiano, Olaudah. *The Interesting Narrative of the Life of Olaudah Equiano, or Gustavus Vassa, the African, Written by Himself.* New York: W. Durell, 1791, 47–50.

See also: Abolitionist Movement; Slave Codes; Slave Families; Slave Revolts and White Attacks on Black Slaves; Slave Trade; Slavery; Slavery in the Antebellum South. Documents: Massachusetts Slaves' Petition (1777); Pennsylvania Act for the Gradual Abolition of Slavery (1788); Fugitive Slave Act (1793); Act to Prohibit the Importation of Slaves (1807); Emancipation Proclamation (June 1866); Ida B. Wells' Expose on Lynching (1895)

Fugitive Slave Act (1793)

Introduction

Enacted on February 12, 1793, the Fugitive Slave Act implemented Article IV, Section 2 of the Constitution, which prohibited states from freeing persons "held to Service or Labour" and required states to return fugitives to the state from which they had fled. The Fugitive Slave Act specifically recognized the role of agents in securing escaped slaves, and it authorized judges and magistrates to approve the transfer of slaves. Fines were also adopted to punish those who attempted to rescue runaways.

Primary Source

An act respecting fugitives from justice, and persons escaping from the service of their masters.

Section 1. Be it enacted by the Senate and House of Representatives of the United States of America in Congress assembled, That whenever the executive authority of any state in the Union, or of either of the territories northwest or south of the river Ohio, shall demand any person as a fugitive from justice, of the executive authority of any such state or territory to which such person shall have fled, and shall moreover produce the copy of an indictment found, or an affidavit made before a magistrate of any state or territory as aforesaid, charging the person so demanded, with

having committed treason, felony or other crime, certified as authentic by the governor or chief magistrate of the state or territory from whence the person so charged fled, it shall be the duty of the executive authority of the state or territory to which such person shall have fled, to cause him or her to be arrested and secured, and notice of the arrest to be given to the executive authority making such demand, or to the agent of such authority appointed to receive the fugitive, and to cause the fugitive to be delivered to such agent when he shall appear: But if no such agent shall appear within six months from the time of the arrest, the prisoner may be discharged. And all costs or expenses incurred in the apprehending, securing, and transmitting such fugitive to the state or territory making such demand, shall be paid by such state or territory.

Section 2. And be it further enacted, That any agent, appointed as aforesaid, who shall receive the fugitive into his custody, shall be empowered to transport him or her to the state or territory from which he or she shall have fled. And if any person or persons shall by force set at liberty, or rescue the fugitive from such agent while transporting, as aforesaid, the person or persons so offending shall, on conviction, be fined not exceeding five hundred dollars, and be imprisoned not exceeding one year.

Section 3. And be it also enacted, That when a person held to labour in any of the United States, or in either of the territories on the northwest or south of the river Ohio, under the laws thereof, shall escape into any other of the said states or territory, the person to whom such labour or service may be due, his agent or attorney, is hereby empowered to seize or arrest such fugitive from labour, and to take him or her before any judge of the circuit or district courts of the United States, residing or being within the state, or before any magistrate of a county, city or town corporate, wherein such seizure or arrest shall be made, and upon proof to the satisfaction of such judge or magistrate, either by oral testimony or affidavit taken before and certified by a magistrate of any such state or territory, that the person so seized or arrested, doth, under the laws of the state or territory from which he or she fled, owe service or labour to the person claiming him or her, it shall be the duty of such judge or magistrate to give a certificate thereof to such claimant, his agent or attorney, which shall be sufficient warrant for removing the said fugitive from labour, to the state or territory from which he or she fled.

Section 4. And be it further enacted, That any person who shall knowingly and willingly obstruct or hinder such claimant, his agent or attorney in so seizing or arresting such fugitive from labour, or shall rescue such fugitive from such claimant, his agent or attorney when so arrested pursuant to the authority herein given or declared; or shall harbor or conceal such person after notice that he or she was a fugitive from labour, as aforesaid, shall, for either of the said offences, forfeit and pay the sum of five hundred dollars. Which penalty may be recovered by and for the benefit of such claimant, by action of debt, in any court proper to try the same; saving moreover to the person claiming such labour or service, his right of action for or on account of the said injuries or either of them.

Source: The Fugitive Slave Clause of the U.S. Constitution, Article 4, Section 2, Clause 3. *Proceedings and Debates of the House of Representatives of the United States at the Second Session of the Second Congress, Begun at the City of Philadelphia, November 5, 1792*, Annals of Congress, 2nd Congress, 2nd Session (November 5, 1792, to March 2, 1793), 1414–15.

See also: Abolitionist Movement; Slave Codes; Slave Families; Slave Revolts and White Attacks on Black Slaves; Slave Trade; Slavery; Slavery in the Antebellum South. Documents: Massachusetts Slaves' Petition (1777); Pennsylvania Act for the Gradual Abolition of Slavery (1780); Olaudah Equiano (1789); Fear of Slave Revolt in New Orleans (1804); Act to Prohibit the Importation of Slaves (1807); The Emancipation Proclamation (1863); Fourteenth Amendment (June 1866)

Fear of Slave Revolt in New Orleans (1804)

Introduction

The fear of slave rebellions ran rampant throughout the South during the early 19th century, and several did indeed occur. In the wake of the 1803 Louisiana Purchase as well as the 1804 Haitian Revolution, many new residents—including French
refugees from Haiti and white U.S. slave owners, with their slaves—settled in the territory of Louisiana and the city of New Orleans, eventually outnumbering the city's free blacks. The new residents opposed Congress's ban on the importation of slaves from other countries, and Southern landowners continued to smuggle slaves into Louisiana. This tense atmosphere led to the 1804 letter below from William C. C. Claiborne of New Orleans, the first governor of Louisiana, to U.S. secretary of state James Madison. Claiborne had managed the transfer of the Louisiana territory from France to the United States following the Louisiana Purchase one year earlier, and he was now concerned about an imminent slave rebellion, which never occurred. However, one of the largest U.S. slave revolts—the German Coast Uprising—did erupt in New Orleans in January 1811, seven years after Claiborne's letter to Madison.*

Primary Source

To James Madison.
New Orleans Sept. 20th 1804

Sir,

I enclose you a Petition addressed to me, and signed by a number of respectable Inhabitants of this City. You will discover there is Some apprehension of an insurrection among the Negroes and that much alarm exists, altho I am not myself of opinion that we are in as imminent danger, as the Memorialists seem to think, I have nevertheless taken every means of precaution in my power. The Patrols at night have been strengthened and are well armed. The Orleans Battalion Of Volunteers and the City Grenadiers are furnished with Public Muskets and Ammunition, ordered to lay upon their arms, and be ready for Action at a moments warning. The City Militia in case of alarm either by day or night are also directed to rendezvous in Front of the Government House and await my orders; The Guard of Regular Troops now in this City are furnished with twenty four rounds of Cartridge, and their pieces are kept constantly charged, and that part of the Army which is now encamped a few Miles from the City is placed in a Situation to move the instant the occasion may require.

I again repeat, I do not myself think there is good cause for the alarm; but if danger should arise I am prepared to meet it, and I pledge myself for the security of the Lives and property of my fellow Citizens.

I am Sir with great Respect
Your most obdt. St.
(Signed) William C. C. Claiborne.

The Honble.
James Madison
Secty. of State

> **Source:** Claiborne, William Charles Cole. *Official Letter Books of W.C.C. Claiborne, Volume 2: 1801–1816.* Jackson, MS: State Department of Archives and History, 1917.
>
> **See also:** Abolitionist Movement; Fourteenth Amendment; Fugitive Slave Act; Slave Codes; Slave Families; Slave Revolts and White Attacks on Black Slaves; Slave Trade; Slavery; Slavery in the Antebellum South. Documents: Massachusetts Slaves' Petition (1777); Pennsylvania Act for the Gradual Abolition of Slavery (1780); Olaudah Equiano (1789); Act to Prohibit the Importation of Slaves (1807); Emancipation Proclamation (1863); Excerpts from Ida B. Wells's Exposé on Lynching (1895)

Act to Prohibit the Importation of Slaves (1807)

Introduction

The U.S. Congress passed this piece of landmark legislation to end the profitable international slave trade on March 2, 1807, and President Thomas Jefferson promptly signed the act, making it law. The act went into effect on January 1, 1808, prohibiting from that time on the importation of African slaves to the United States.

Primary Source

An Act to Prohibit the Importation of Slaves into any Port or Place Within the Jurisdiction of the United States, From and After the First Day of January, in the Year of our Lord One Thousand Eight Hundred and Eight.

Be it enacted by the Senate and House of Representatives of the United States of America in Congress assembled, That

from and after the first day of January, one thousand eight hundred and eight, it shall not be lawful to import or bring into the United States or the territories thereof from any foreign kingdom, place, or country, any negro, mulatto, or person of colour, with intent to hold, sell, or dispose of such negro, mulatto, or person of colour, as a slave, or to be held to service or labour.

SECTION 2. And be it further enacted, That no citizen or citizens of the United States, or any other person, shall, from arid after the first day of January, in the year of our Lord one thousand eight hundred and eight, for himself, or themselves, or any other person whatsoever, either as master, factor, or owner, build, fit, equip, load or otherwise prepare any ship or vessel, in any port or place within the jurisdiction of the United States, nor shall cause any ship or vessel to sail from any port or place within the same, for the purpose of procuring any negro, mulatto, or person of colour, from any foreign kingdom, place, or country, to be transported to any port or place whatsoever, within the jurisdiction of the United States, to be held, sold, or disposed of as slaves, or to be held to service or labour: and if any ship or vessel shall be so fitted out for the purpose aforesaid, or shall be caused to sail so as aforesaid, every such ship or vessel, her tackle, apparel, and furniture, shall be forfeited to the United States, and shall be liable to be seized, prosecuted, and condemned in any of the circuit courts or district courts, for the district where the said ship or vessel may be found or seized.

SECTION 3. And be it further enacted, That all and every person so building, fitting out, equipping, loading, or otherwise preparing or sending away, any ship or vessel, knowing or intending that the same shall be employed in such trade or business, from and after the first day of January, one thousand eight hundred and eight, contrary to the true intent and meaning of this act, or any ways aiding or abetting therein, shall severally forfeit and pay twenty thousand dollars, one moiety thereof to the use of the United States, and the other moiety to the use of any person or persons who shall sue for and prosecute the same to effect.

SECTION 4. And be it further enacted, If any citizen or citizens of the United States, or any person resident within the jurisdiction of the same, shall, from and after the first day of January, one thousand eight hundred and eight, take on board, receive or transport from any of the coasts or kingdoms of Africa, or from any other foreign kingdom, place, or country, any negro, mulatto, or person of colour, in any ship or vessel, for the purpose of selling them in any port or place within the jurisdiction of the United States as slaves, or to be held to service or labour, or shall be in any ways aiding or abetting therein, such citizen or citizens, or person, shall severally forfeit and pay five thousand dollars, one moiety thereof to the use of any person or persons who shall sue for and prosecute the same to effect; and every such ship or vessel in which such negro, mulatto, or person of colour, shall have been taken on board, received, or transported as aforesaid, her tackle, apparel, and furniture, and the goods and effects which shall be found on board the same, shall be forfeited to the United States, and shall be liable to be seized, prosecuted, and condemned in any of the circuit courts or district courts in the district where the said ship or vessel may be found or seized. And neither the importer, nor any person or persons claiming from or under him, shall hold any right or title whatsoever to any negro, mulatto, or person of colour, nor to the service or labour thereof, who may be imported or brought within the United States, or territories thereof, in violation of this law, but the same shall remain subject to any regulations not contravening the provisions of this act, which the legislatures of the several states or territories at any time hereafter may make, for disposing of any such negro, mulatto, or person of colour.

SECTION 5. And be it further enacted, That if any citizen or citizens of the United States, or any other person resident within the jurisdiction of the same, shall, from and after the first day of January, one thousand eight hundred and eight, contrary to the true intent and meaning of this act, take on board any ship or vessel from any of the coasts or kingdoms of Africa, or from any other foreign kingdom, place, or country, any negro, mulatto, or person of colour, with intent to sell him, her, or them, for a slave, or slaves, or to be held to service or labour, and shall transport the same to any port or place within the jurisdiction of the United States, and there sell such negro, mulatto, or person of colour, so transported as aforesaid, for a slave, or to be held to service or labour, every such offender shall be deemed guilty of a high

misdemeanor, and being thereof convicted before any court having competent jurisdiction, shall suffer imprisonment for not more than ten years nor less than five years, and be fined not exceeding ten thousand dollars, nor less than one thousand dollars.

SECTION 6. And be it further enacted, That if any person or persons whatsoever, shall, from and after the first day of January, one thousand eight hundred and eight, purchase or sell any negro, mulatto, or person of colour, for a slave, or to be held to service or labour, who shall have been imported, or brought from any foreign kingdom, place, or country, or from the dominions of any foreign state, immediately adjoining to the United States, into any port or place within the jurisdiction of the United States, after the last day of December, one thousand eight hundred and seven, knowing at the time of such purchase or sale, such negro, mulatto or person of colour, was so brought within the jurisdiction of the Unified States, as aforesaid, such purchaser and seller shall severally forfeit and pay for every negro, mulatto, or person of colour, so purchased or sold as aforesaid, eight hundred dollars; one moiety thereof to the United States, and the other moiety to the use of any person or persons who shall sue for and prosecute the same to effect: Provided, that the aforesaid forfeiture shall not extend to the seller or purchaser of any negro, mulatto, or person of colour, who may be sold or disposed of in virtue of any regulation which may hereafter be made by any of the legislatures of the several states in that respect, in pursuance of this act, and the constitution of the United States.

SECTION 7. And be it further enacted, That if any ship or vessel shall be found, from and after the first day of January, one thousand eight hundred and eight, in any river, port, bay, or harbor, or on the high seas, within the jurisdictional limits of the United States, or hovering on the coast thereof, having on board any negro, mulatto, or person of colour, for the purpose of selling them as slaves, or with intent to land the same, in any port or place within the jurisdiction of the United States, contrary to the prohibition of this act, every such ship or vessel, together with her tackle, apparel, and furniture, and the goods or effects which shall be found on board the same, shall be forfeited to the use of the United States, and may be seized, prosecuted, and condemned, in any court of the United States, having jurisdiction thereof And it shall be lawful for the President of the United States, and he is hereby authorized, should he deem it expedient, to cause any of the armed vessels of the United States to be manned and employed to cruise on any part of the coast of the United States, or territories thereof, where he may judge attempts will be made to violate the provisions of this act, and to instruct and direct the commanders of armed vessels of the United States, to seize, take, and bring into any port of the United States all such ships or vessels, and moreover to seize, take, and bring into any port of the United States all ships or vessels of the United States, wheresoever found on the high seas, contravening the provisions of this act, to be proceeded against according to law, and the captain, master, or commander of every such ship or vessel, so found and seized as aforesaid, shall be deemed guilty of a high misdemeanor, and shall be liable to be prosecuted before any court of the United States, having jurisdiction thereof; and being thereof convicted, shall be fined not exceeding ten thousand dollars, and be imprisoned not less than two years, and not exceeding four years. And the proceeds of all ships and vessels, their tackle, apparel, and furniture, and the goods and effects on board of them, which shall be so seized, prosecuted and condemned, shall be divided equally between the United States and the officers and men who shall make such seizure, take, or bring the same into port for condemnation, whether such seizure be made by an armed vessel of the United States, or revenue cutters hereof, and the same shall be distributed in like manner, as is provided by law, for the distribution of prizes taken from an enemy: Provided, that the officers and men, to be entitled to one half of the proceeds aforesaid, shall safe keep every negro, mulatto, or person of colour, found on board of any ship or vessel so by them seized, taken, or brought into port for condemnation, and shall deliver every such negro, mulatto, or person of colour, to such person or persons as shall be appointed by the respective states, to receive the same, and if no such person or persons shall be appointed by the respective states, they shall deliver every such negro, mulatto, or person of colour, to the overseers of the poor of the port or place where such ship or vessel may be brought or found, and shall immediately transmit to the governor or chief magistrate of the state, an account of their proceedings, together with the number of such Negroes, mulattoes,

or persons of colour, and a descriptive list of the same, that he may give directions respecting such Negroes, mulattoes, or persons of colour.

SECTION 8. And be it further enacted, That no captain, master or commander of any ship or vessel, of less burthen than forty tons, shall, from and after the first day of January, one thousand eight hundred and eight, take on board and transport any negro, mulatto, or person of colour, to any port or place whatsoever, for the purpose of selling or disposing of the same as a slave, or with intent that the same may be sold or disposed of to be held to service or labour, on penalty of forfeiting for every such negro, mulatto, or person of colour, so taken on board and transported, as aforesaid, the sum of eight hundred dollars; one moiety thereof to the use of the United States, and the other moiety to any person or persons who shall sue for, and prosecute the same to effect: Provided however, That nothing in this section shall extend to prohibit the taking on board or transporting on any river, or inland bay of the sea, within the jurisdiction of the United States, any negro, mulatto, or person of colour, (not imported contrary to the provisions of this act) in any vessel or species of craft whatever.

SECTION 9. And be it further enacted, That the captain, master, or commander of any ship or vessel of the burthen of forty tons or more, from and after the first day of January, one thousand eight hundred and eight, sailing coastwise, from any port in the United States, to any port or place within the jurisdiction of the same, having on board any negro, mulatto, or person of colour, for the purpose of transporting them to be sold or disposed of as slaves, or to be held to service or labour, shall, previous to the departure of such ship or vessel, make out and subscribe duplicate manifests of every such negro, mulatto, or person of colour, on board such ship or vessel, therein specifying the name and sex of each person, their age and stature, as near as may be, and the class to which they respectively belong, whether negro, mulatto, or person of colour, with the name and place of residence of every owner or shipper of the same, and shall deliver such manifests to the collector of the port, if there be one, otherwise to the surveyor, before whom the captain, master, or commander, together with the owner or shipper, shall severally swear or affirm to the best of their knowledge and belief, that the persons therein specified were not imported or brought into the United States, from and after the first day of January, one thousand eight hundred and eight, and that under the laws of the state, they are held to service or labour; whereupon the said collector or surveyor shall certify the same on the said manifests, one of which he shall return to the said captain, master, or commander, with a permit, specifying thereon the number, names, and general description of such persons, and authorizing him to proceed to the port of his destination. And if any ship or vessel, being laden and destined as aforesaid, shall depart from the port where she may then be, without the captain, master, or commander having first made out and subscribed duplicate manifests, of every negro, mulatto, and person of colour, on board such ship or vessel, as aforesaid, and without having previously delivered the same to the said collector or surveyor, and obtained a permit, in manner as herein required, or shall, previous to her arrival at the port of her destination, take on board any negro, mulatto, or person of colour, other than those specified in the manifests, as aforesaid, every such ship or vessel, together with her tackle, apparel and furniture, shall be forfeited to the use of the United States, and may be seized, prosecuted and condemned in any court of the United States having jurisdiction thereof; and the captain, master, or commander of every such ship or vessel, shall moreover forfeit, for every such negro, mulatto, or person of colour, so transported, or taken on board, contrary to the provisions of this act, the sum of one thousand dollars, one moiety thereof to the United States, and the other moiety to the use of any person or persons who shall sue for and prosecute the same to effect.

SECTION 10. And be it further enacted, That the captain, master, or commander of every ship or vessel, of the burthen of forty tons or more, from and after the first day of January, one thousand eight hundred and eight, sailing coastwise, and having on board any negro, mulatto, or person of colour, to sell or dispose of as slaves, or to be held to service or labour, and arriving in any port within the jurisdiction of the United States, from any other port within the same, shall, previous to the unlading or putting on shore any of the persons aforesaid, or suffering them to go on shore, deliver to the collector, if there be one, or if not, to the surveyor residing at the port of her arrival, the manifest certified by the collector or surveyor of the port from whence she sailed, as

is herein before directed, to the truth of which, before such officer, he shall swear or affirm, and if the collector or surveyor shall be satisfied therewith, he shall thereupon grant a permit for unlading or suffering such negro, mulatto, or person of colour, to be put on shore, and if the captain, master, or commander of any such ship or vessel being laden as aforesaid, shall neglect or refuse to deliver the manifest at the time and in the manner herein directed, or shall land or put on shore any negro, mulatto, or person of colour, for the purpose aforesaid, before he shall have delivered his manifest as aforesaid, and obtained a permit for that purpose, every such captain, master, or commander, shall forfeit and pay ten thousand dollars, one moiety thereof to the United States, the other moiety to the use of any person or persons who shall sue for and prosecute the same to effect.

Source: An Act Prohibiting Importation of Slaves of 1807, Ch.22, 2 Stat. 426.

See also: Abolitionist Movement; Fourteenth Amendment; Fugitive Slave Act; Slave Codes; Slave Families; Slave Revolts and White Attacks on Black Slaves; Slave Trade; Slavery; Slavery in the Antebellum South. Documents: Massachusetts Slaves' Petition (1777); Pennsylvania Act for the Gradual Abolition of Slavery (1780); Olaudah Equiano (1789); Act to Prohibit the Importation of Slaves (1807); Emancipation Proclamation (1863); Excerpts from Ida B. Wells's Exposé on Lynching (1895)

Andrew Jackson: Indian Removal Message to Congress (1829)

Introduction

President Andrew Jackson's message on the removal of Southern American Indians, part of his first annual message to the U.S. Congress of December 1829, precipitated government removal of Native Americans from their lands in the Eastern United States and exiled them to reservations in the West. Despite some public sympathy for the Native Americans, especially the Cherokee in Georgia, Jackson argued that if the American Indians remained within existing states, they would constitute a foreign people, contradicting the prohibition of states within other states found in Article IV, Section 3 of the Constitution. Congress subsequently adopted the

Indian Removal Act of 1830, approving Jackson's proposed policy. The Supreme Court decisions in Cherokee Nation v. Georgia *(1831) and* Worcester v. Georgia *(1832) proved inadequate to protect Native American interests in the face of state, presidential, and congressional opposition, and they were ultimately forced off their land, culminating in the devastating and dramatic removal of the Cherokees in 1838 on the Trail of Tears.*

Primary Source

It gives me pleasure to announce to Congress that the benevolent policy of the government, steadily pursued for nearly thirty years, in relation to the removal of the Indians beyond the white settlements is approaching to a happy consummation. Two important tribes have accepted the provision made for their removal at the last session of Congress, and it is believed that their example will induce the remaining tribes also to seek the same obvious advantages.

The consequences of a speedy removal will be important to the United States, to individual states, and to the Indians themselves. The pecuniary advantages which it promises to the government are the least of its recommendations. It puts an end to all possible danger of collision between the authorities of the general and state governments on account of the Indians. It will place a dense and civilized population in large tracts of country now occupied by a few savage hunters. By opening the whole territory between Tennessee on the north and Louisiana on the south to the settlement of the whites it will incalculably strengthen the southwestern frontier and render the adjacent states strong enough to repel future invasions without remote aid. It will relieve the whole state of Mississippi and the western part of Alabama of Indian occupancy, and enable those states to advance rapidly in population, wealth, and power.

It will separate the Indians from immediate contact with settlements of whites; free them from the power of the states; enable them to pursue happiness in their own way and under their own rude institutions; will retard the progress of decay, which is lessening their numbers, and perhaps cause them gradually, under the protection of the government and through the influence of good counsels, to cast off their savage habits and become an interesting, civilized, and

Christian community. These consequences, some of them so certain and the rest so probable, make the complete execution of the plan sanctioned by Congress at their last session an object of much solicitude.

Toward the aborigines of the country no one can indulge a more friendly feeling than myself, or would go further in attempting to reclaim them from their wandering habits and make them a happy, prosperous people. I have endeavored to impress upon them my own solemn convictions of the duties and powers of the general government in relation to the state authorities. For the justice of the laws passed by the states within the scope of their reserved powers they are not responsible to this government. As individuals we may entertain and express our opinions of their acts, but as a government we have as little right to control them as we have to prescribe laws for other nations.

With a full understanding of the subject, the Choctaw and the Chickasaw tribes have with great unanimity determined to avail themselves of the liberal offers presented by the act of Congress, and have agreed to remove beyond the Mississippi River. Treaties have been made with them, which in due season will be submitted for consideration. In negotiating these treaties, they were made to understand their true condition, and they have preferred maintaining their independence in the Western forests to submitting to the laws of the states in which they now reside. These treaties, being probably the last which will ever be made with them, are characterized by great liberality on the part of the government. They give the Indians a liberal sum in consideration of their removal, and comfortable subsistence on their arrival at their new homes. If it be their real interest to maintain a separate existence, they will there be at liberty to do so without the inconveniences and vexations to which they would unavoidably have been subject in Alabama and Mississippi.

Humanity has often wept over the fate of the aborigines of this country, and philanthropy has been long busily employed in devising means to avert it, but its progress has never for a moment been arrested, and one by one have many powerful tribes disappeared from the earth. To follow to the tomb the last of his race and to tread on the graves of extinct nations excite melancholy reflections. But true philanthropy reconciles the mind to these vicissitudes as it does to the extinction of one generation to make room for another. In the monuments and fortresses of an unknown people, spread over the extensive regions of the West, we behold the memorials of a once powerful race, which was exterminated or has disappeared to make room for the existing savage tribes. Nor is there anything in this which, upon a comprehensive view of the general interests of the human race, is to be regretted. Philanthropy could not wish to see this continent restored to the condition in which it was found by our forefathers. What good man would prefer a country covered with forests and ranged by a few thousand savages to our extensive republic, studded with cities, towns, and prosperous farms, embellished with all the improvements which art can devise or industry execute, occupied by more than 12 million happy people, and filled with all the blessings of liberty, civilization, and religion?

The present policy of the government is but a continuation of the same progressive change by a milder process. The tribes which occupied the countries now constituting the Eastern states were annihilated or have melted away to make room for the whites. The waves of population and civilization are rolling to the westward, and we now propose to acquire the countries occupied by the red men of the South and West by a fair exchange, and, at the expense of the United States, to send them to a land where their existence may be prolonged and perhaps made perpetual.

Doubtless it will be painful to leave the graves of their fathers; but what do they more than our ancestors did or than our children are now doing? To better their condition in an unknown land our forefathers left all that was dear in earthly objects. Our children by thousands yearly leave the land of their birth to seek new homes in distant regions. Does humanity weep at these painful separations from everything, animate and inanimate, with which the young heart has become entwined? Far from it. It is rather a source of joy that our country affords scope where our young population may range unconstrained in body or in mind, developing the power and faculties of man in their highest perfection. These remove hundreds and almost thousands of miles at their own expense, purchase the lands they occupy, and support

themselves at their new homes from the moment of their arrival. Can it be cruel in this government when, by events which it cannot control, the Indian is made discontented in his ancient home to purchase his lands, to give him a new and extensive territory, to pay the expense of his removal, and support him a year in his new abode? How many thousands of our own people would gladly embrace the opportunity of removing to the West on such conditions? If the offers made to the Indians were extended to them, they would be hailed with gratitude and joy.

And is it supposed that the wandering savage has a stronger attachment to his home than the settled, civilized Christian? Is it more afflicting to him to leave the graves of his fathers than it is to our brothers and children? Rightly considered, the policy of the general government toward the red man is not only liberal but generous. He is unwilling to submit to the laws of the states and mingle with their population. To save him from this alternative, or perhaps utter annihilation, the general government kindly offers him a new home, and proposes to pay the whole expense of his removal and settlement.

In the consummation of a policy originating at an early period, and steadily pursued by every administration within the present century—so just to the states and so generous to the Indians—the executive feels it has a right to expect the cooperation of Congress and of all good and disinterested men. The states, moreover, have a right to demand it. It was substantially a part of the compact which made them members of our Confederacy. With Georgia there is an express contract; with the new states an implied one of equal obligation. Why, in authorizing Ohio, Indiana, Illinois, Missouri, Mississippi, and Alabama to form constitutions and become separate states, did Congress include within their limits extensive tracts of Indian lands, and, in some instances, powerful Indian tribes? Was it not understood by both parties that the power of the states was to be coextensive with their limits, and that, with all convenient dispatch, the general government should extinguish the Indian title and remove every obstruction to the complete jurisdiction of the state governments over the soil? Probably not one of those states would have accepted a separate existence—certainly it would never have been granted by Congress—had it been understood that they were to be confined forever to those small portions of their nominal territory the Indian title to which had at the time been extinguished.

It is, therefore, a duty which this government owes to the new states to extinguish as soon as possible the Indian title to all lands which Congress themselves have included within their limits. When this is done the duties of the general government in relation to the states and the Indians within their limits are at an end. The Indians may leave the state or not, as they choose. The purchase of their lands does not alter in the least their personal relations with the state government. No act of the general government has ever been deemed necessary to give the states jurisdiction over the persons of the Indians. That they possess by virtue of their sovereign power within their own limits in as full a manner before as after the purchase of the Indian lands; nor can this government add to or diminish it.

May we not hope, therefore, that all good citizens, and none more zealously than those who think the Indians oppressed by subjection to the laws of the states, will unite in attempting to open the eyes of those children of the forest to their true condition, and by a speedy removal to relieve them from all the evils, real or imaginary, present or prospective, with which they may be supposed to be threatened.

> **Source:** *A Compilation of the Messages and Papers of the Presidents 1789–1897, vol. 2*, James D. Richardson, ed., 1920, 500–29.

> **See also:** Dawes Act (1887); Indian Claims Commissions; Indian Reorganization Act (1934); Indian Reservations

Indian Removal Act (1830)

Introduction

Enacted on May 28, 1830, after one of the most contentious and bitter debates in Congress with the exception of the arguments over slavery, the Indian Removal Act proceeded to shift most of the nations of Indian tribes in the eastern United States to what was deemed "Indian country" in present-day Oklahoma. In the most notorious of the Indian removal efforts,

President Andrew Jackson ordered the Cherokee nation off its land in Georgia in 1833. Although the tribe fought against the order in the U.S. court system, it was eventually forced to comply. As the Cherokee made their arduous journey to Oklahoma, starvation, illness, cold, and despair resulted in thousands of deaths, so that the journey is now remembered as the Trail of Tears.

Primary Source

An Act to provide for an exchange of lands with the Indians residing in any of the states or territories, and for their removal west of the river Mississippi.

Be it enacted by the Senate and House of Representatives of the United States of America, in Congress assembled, That it shall and may be lawful for the President of the United States to cause so much of any territory belonging to the United States, west of the river Mississippi, not included in any state or organized territory, and to which the Indian title has been extinguished, as he may judge necessary, to be divided into a suitable number of districts, for the reception of such tribes or nations of Indians as may choose to exchange the lands where they now reside, and remove there; and to cause each of said districts to be so described by natural or artificial marks, as to be easily distinguished from every other.

And be it further enacted, That it shall and may be lawful for the President to exchange any or all of such districts, so to be laid off and described, with any tribe or nation of Indians now residing within the limits of any of the states or territories, and with which the United States have existing treaties, for the whole or any part or portion of the territory claimed and occupied by such tribe or nation, within the bounds of any one or more of the states or territories, where the land claimed and occupied by the Indians, is owned by the United States, or the United States are bound to the state within which it lies to extinguish the Indian claim thereto.

And be it further enacted, That in the making of any such exchange or exchanges, it shall and may be lawful for the President solemnly to assure the tribe or nation with which the exchange is made, that the United States will forever secure and guaranty to them, and their heirs or successors, the country so exchanged with them; and if they prefer it, that the United States will cause a patent or grant to be made and executed to them for the same: Provided always, That such lands shall revert to the United States, if the Indians become extinct, or abandon the same.

And be it further enacted, That if, upon any of the lands now occupied by the Indians, and to be exchanged for, there should be such improvements as add value to the land claimed by any individual or individuals of such tribes or nations, it shall and may be lawful for the President to cause such value to be ascertained by appraisement or otherwise, and to cause such ascertained value to be paid to the person or persons rightfully claiming such improvements. And upon the payment of such valuation, the improvements so valued and paid for, shall pass to the United States, and possession shall not afterwards be permitted to any of the same tribe.

And be it further enacted, That upon the making of any such exchange as is contemplated by this act, it shall and may be lawful for the President to cause such aid and assistance to be furnished to the emigrants as may be necessary and proper to enable them to remove to, and settle in, the country for which they may have exchanged; and also, to give them such aid and assistance as may be necessary for their support and subsistence for the first year after their removal.

And be it further enacted, That it shall and may be lawful for the President to cause such tribe or nation to be protected, at their new residence, against all interruption or disturbance from any other tribe or nation of Indians, or from any other person or persons whatever.

And be it further enacted, That it shall and may be lawful for the President to have the same superintendence and care over any tribe or nation in the country to which they may remove, as contemplated by this act, that he is now authorized to have over them at their present places of residence: Provided, That nothing in this act contained shall be construed as authorizing or directing the violation of any existing treaty between the United States and any of the Indian tribes.

And be it further enacted, That for the purpose of giving effect to the Provisions of this act, the sum of five hundred thousand dollars is hereby appropriated, to be paid out of any money in the treasury, not otherwise appropriated.

Source: Indian Removal Act. U.S. Statutes at Large 148 (1830): 411.

See also: Dawes Act (1887); Indian Claims Commissions; Indian Reorganization Act (1934); Indian Reservations

Cherokee Nation v. Georgia (1831)

Introduction

Cherokee Nation v. Georgia *was among the most important cases to come before the U.S. Supreme Court in its first half century. Together with* Worcester v. Georgia *(1832), which involved many of the same issues,* Cherokee Nation *established the legal underpinnings for the relationship between government and Indian nations. At issue was the state of Georgia's attempts to take control of Cherokee land protected by treaties between the federal government and the Cherokees. In a 4–2 decision, the Court recognized the Cherokees' status as a sovereign nation but not a foreign nation, a fine distinction that denied them the right to bring their case before the Court.*

Primary Source

MR. CHIEF JUSTICE MARSHALL delivered the opinion of the Court.

This bill is brought by the Cherokee Nation, praying an injunction to restrain the State of Georgia from the execution of certain laws of that State which, as is alleged, go directly to annihilate the Cherokees as a political society and to seize, for the use of Georgia, the lands of the Nation which have been assured to them by the United States in solemn treaties repeatedly made and still in force.

If Courts were permitted to indulge their sympathies, a case better calculated to excite them can scarcely be imagined. A people once numerous, powerful, and truly independent, found by our ancestors in the quiet and uncontrolled possession of an ample domain, gradually sinking beneath our superior policy, our arts and our arms, have yielded their lands by successive treaties, each of which contains a solemn guarantee of the residue, until they retain no more of their formerly extensive territory than is deemed necessary to their comfortable subsistence. To preserve this remnant, the present application is made.

Before we can look into the merits of the case, a preliminary inquiry presents itself. Has this Court jurisdiction of the cause?

The third article of the Constitution describes the extent of the judicial power. The second section closes an enumeration of the cases to which it is extended, with "controversies" "between a State or the citizens thereof, and foreign states, citizens, or subjects." A subsequent clause of the same section gives the supreme Court original jurisdiction in all cases in which a State shall be a party. The party defendant may then unquestionably be sued in this Court. May the plaintiff sue in it? Is the Cherokee Nation a foreign state in the sense in which that term is used in the Constitution?

The counsel for the plaintiffs have maintained the affirmative of this proposition with great earnestness and ability. So much of the argument as was intended to prove the character of the Cherokees as a State as a distinct political society, separated from others, capable of managing its own affairs and governing itself, has, in the opinion of a majority of the judges, been completely successful. They have been uniformly treated as a State from the settlement of our country. The numerous treaties made with them by the United States recognize them as a people capable of maintaining the relations of peace and war, of being responsible in their political character for any violation of their engagements, or for any aggression committed on the citizens of the United States by any individual of their community. Laws have been enacted in the spirit of these treaties. The acts of our Government plainly recognize the Cherokee Nation as a State, and the Courts are bound by those acts.

A question of much more difficulty remains. Do the Cherokees constitute a foreign state in the sense of the Constitution?

The counsel have shown conclusively that they are not a State of the union, and have insisted that, individually, they are aliens, not owing allegiance to the United States. An aggregate of aliens composing a State must, they say, be a foreign state. Each individual being foreign, the whole must be foreign.

This argument is imposing, but we must examine it more closely before we yield to it. The condition of the Indians in relation to the United States is perhaps unlike that of any other two people in existence. In the general, nations not owing a common allegiance are foreign to each other. The term *foreign nation* is, with strict propriety, applicable by either to the other. But the relation of the Indians to the United States is marked by peculiar and cardinal distinctions which exist nowhere else.

The Indian Territory is admitted to compose a part of the United States. In all our maps, geographical treatises, histories, and laws, it is so considered. In all our intercourse with foreign nations, in our commercial regulations, in any attempt at intercourse between Indians and foreign nations, they are considered as within the jurisdictional limits of the United States, subject to many of those restraints which are imposed upon our own citizens. They acknowledge themselves in their treaties to be under the protection of the United States; they admit that the United States shall have the sole and exclusive right of regulating the trade with them, and managing all their affairs as they think proper; and the Cherokees, in particular, were allowed by the treaty of Hopewell, which preceded the Constitution, "to send a deputy of their choice, whenever they think fit, to Congress." . . .

They may, more correctly, perhaps, be denominated domestic dependent nations. They occupy a territory to which we assert a title independent of their will, which must take effect in point of possession when their right of possession ceases. Meanwhile they are in a state of pupilage. Their relation to the United States resembles that of a ward to his guardian. . . .

The Court has bestowed its best attention on this question, and, after mature deliberation, the majority is of opinion that an Indian tribe or Nation within the United States is not a foreign state in the sense of the Constitution, and cannot maintain an action in the Courts of the United States....

But the Court is asked to do more than decide on the title. The bill requires us to control the Legislature of Georgia, and to restrain the exertion of its physical force. The propriety of such an interposition by the Court may be well questioned. It savours too much of the exercise of political power to be within the proper province of the judicial department. But the opinion on the point respecting parties makes it unnecessary to decide this question.

If it be true that the Cherokee Nation have rights, this is not the tribunal in which those rights are to be asserted. If it be true that wrongs have been inflicted, and that still greater are to be apprehended, this is not the tribunal which can redress the past or prevent the future....

Source: *Cherokee Nation v. Georgia*, 30 U.S. 1 (1831).

See also: Dawes Act (1887); Indian Claims Commission; Indian Reorganization Act (1934); Indian Reservations

Slave Codes of the State of Georgia (1848)

Introduction

Africans were brought to North America from the early 16th century as indentured servants or "bondservants." In the middle of the 17th century, Southern colonies began to develop a hereditary system of slavery based on race, to tie African workers to permanent bondage. By the middle of the 18th century, all Southern colonies had established this new race-based slavery system. They further developed increasingly restrictive statues, known as slave codes, that limited the rights of slaves.

Primary Source

SEC. I. Capital Offences
1. Capital crimes when punished with death.
The following shall be considered as capital offences, when committed by a slave or free person of color: insurrection, or an attempt to excite it; committing a rape, or attempting it on a free white female; murder of a free white person, or murder of a slave or free person of color, or poisoning of a human being; every and each of these offences shall, on conviction, be punished with death.

2. When punished by death, or at discretion of the court.
And the following, also, shall be considered as capital offences, when committed by a slave or free person of color: assaulting a free white person with intent to murder, or with a weapon likely to produce death; maiming a free white person; burglary, or arson of any description; also, any attempt to poison a human being; every and each of these offences shall, on conviction, be punished with death, or such other punishment as the court in their judgement shall think most proportionate to the offence, and best promote the object of the law, and operate as a preventive for like offences in future.

3. Punishment for manslaughter.
And in case a verdict of manslaughter shall be found by the jury, the punishment shall be by whipping, at the discretion of the court, and branded on the cheek with the letter M.

4. Punishment of slaves for striking white persons.
If any slave shall presume to strike any white person, such slave upon trial and conviction before the justice or justices, according to the direction of this act, shall for the first offence suffer such punishment as the said justice or justices shall in his or their discretion think fit, not extending to life or limb; and for the second offence, suffer death: but in case any such slave shall grievously wound, maim, or bruise any white person, though it shall be only the first offence, such slave shall suffer death.

5. When the striking a white person justifiable.
Provided always, that such striking, wounding, maiming, or bruising, be not done by the command, and in defense of the person or property of the owner or other person have the care and government of such slave, in which case the slave shall be wholly excused, and the owner or other person having the care and government of such slave, shall be answerable, as if the act has been committed by himself.

6. Punishment for burning or attempting to burn houses in a town.

The willful and malicious burning or setting fire to, or attempting to burn a house in a city, town, or village, when committed by a slave or free person of color, shall be punished with death.

7. Punishment for burning or attempting to burden houses in the country.

The willful and malicious burning a dwelling house on a farm or plantation, or elsewhere, (not in a city, town or village) or the setting fire thereto, in the nighttime, when the said house is actually occupied by a person or persons, with the intent to burn the same, when committed by a slave or free person of color, shall be punished by death.

8. Trials of offenders for arson.

The trial of offenders against the provisions of this act, shall be had in the same courts, and conducted in the same manner, and under the same rules and regulations as are provided by the several acts now in force in this state for the trial of capital offences, when committed by a slave or free person of color.

9. Punishment of free persons of color for inveigling slaves.

If any free person of color commits the offence of inveigling or enticing away any slave or slaves, for the purpose of, and with the intention to aid and assist such slave or slaves leaving the service of his or their owner or owners, or in going to another state, such person so offending shall, for each and every such offence, on conviction, be confined in the penitentiary at hard labor for one.

10. Punishment for circulating incendiary documents.

If any slave, Negro, mustizoe, or free person of color, or any other person, shall circulate, bring, or cause to be circulated or brought into this state, or aid or assist in any manner, or be instrumental in aiding or assisting in the circulation or bringing into this state, or in any manner concerned in any written or printed pamphlet, paper, or circular, for the purpose of exciting to insurrection, conspiracy, or resistance among the slaves, Negroes, or free persons of color of this state, against their owners or the citizens of this state, the said person or persons offending against this section of this act, shall be punished with death.

SEC. II. Minor Offences.

11. Punishment for teaching slaves or free persons of color to read.

If any slave, Negro, or free person of color, or any white person, shall teach any other slave, Negro, or free person of color, to read or write either written or printed characters, the said free person of color or slave shall be punished by fine and whipping, or fine or whipping, at the discretion of the court.

12. Punishment of free persons of color for trading with slaves.

If any slave or slaves, or free persons of color shall purchase or buy any of the aforesaid commodities from any slave or slaves, he, she, or they, on conviction thereof, before any justice of the peace, contrary to the true intent and meaning of this act, shall receive on his, her, or their bare back or backs, thirty-nine lashes, to be well laid on by a constable of said county, or other person appointed by the justice of the peace for that purpose: Provided, that nothing herein contained shall prevent any slave or slaves from selling poultry at any time without a ticket, in the counties of Liberty, McIntosh, Camden, Glynn, and Wayne.

13. Punishment of slaves for harboring slaves.

If any free person or any slave shall harbor, conceal, or entertain any slave that shall run away, or shall be charged or accused of any criminal matter, every free Negro, mulatto, and mustizoe, and every slave that shall harbor, conceal, or entertain any such slave, being duly convicted thereof according to the direction of this act, if a slave, shall suffer such corporeal punishment, not extending to life or limb, as the justice or justices who shall try such slave shall in his or their discretion think fit; and if a free person, shall forfeit the sum of thirty shillings for the first day, and three shillings for every day such slave shall have been absent from his or her owner or employer, to be recovered and applied as in this act hereafter directed.

14. Punishment of free persons of color for harboring slaves.

All free persons of color within this state, who shall harbor, conceal, or entertain a slave or slaves who shall be charged or accused or any criminal matter, or shall be a runaway, shall, upon conviction (in addition to the penalty already provided for in said section), be subject to the same punishment as slaves are under said section of the above recited act.

15. Constables authorized to search suspected premises for fugitive slaves.

Any lawful constable having reason to suspect that runaway slaves, or such Negroes who may be charged or accused of any criminal offence, are harbored, concealed, or entertained in the house or houses of such slaves or free persons of color, they or any of them are authorized to enter such houses, and make search for the said runaway or runaways, or accused criminal or criminals.

16. Persons of color not allowed to preach or exhort without written license.

No person of color, whether free or slave, shall be allowed to preach to, exhort, or join in any religious exercise with any persons of color, either free or slave, there being more that seven persons of color present. They shall first obtain a written certificate from three ordained ministers of the gospel of their own order, in which certificate shall be set forth the good moral character of the applicant, his pious deportment, and his ability to teach the gospel; having a due respect to the character of those persons to whom he is to be licensed to preach, said ministers to be members of the conference, presbytery, synod, or association to which the churches belong in which said colored preachers may be licensed to preach, and also the written permission of the justices of the inferior court of the county, and in counties in which the county town is incorporated, in addition thereto the permission of the mayor, or chief officer, or commissioners of such incorporation; such license not to be for a longer term than six months, and to be revocable at any time by the person granting it.

17. Punishment for preaching or exhorting without license.

Any free person of color offending against this provision, to be liable on conviction, for the first offence, to imprisonment at the discretion of the court, and to a penalty not exceeding five hundred dollars, to be levied on the property of the person of color; if this is insufficient, he shall be sentenced to be whipped and imprisoned at the discretion of the court: Provided, such imprisonment shall not exceed six months, and no whipping shall exceed thirty-nine lashes.

18. Prosecution by indictment.

Each offence under this act may be prosecuted by indictment in the superior court of the county in which the same shall have been committed, and the penalties shall be recoverable by qui tam action in the superior or inferior court, one half to the use of the informer, and the other to the use of the county academy.

19. Slaves giving information of design to poison, how rewarded.

Every Negro, mulatto, or mustizoe, who shall hereafter give information of the intention of any other slave to poison any person, or of any slave that hath furnished, procured or conveyed any poison to be administered to any persons, shall, upon conviction of the offender or offenders, be entitled to and receive from the public of this province, a reward of twenty shillings, to be paid him or her by the treasurer yearly and every year, during the abode of such Negro, mulatto, mustizoe in this province, on the day that such discovery was made, and shall also be exempted from the labor of his or her master on that day; and every justice before whom such information and conviction is made, is hereby required to give a certificate of every such information, which certificate shall entitle the informant to the reward aforesaid: Provide always, nevertheless, that no slave be convicted upon the bare information of any other slave, unless some circumstances or overt act appear, by which such information shall be corroborated to the satisfaction of the said justices and jury.

20. Punishment for giving false information.

In cases any slaves shall be convicted of having given false information, whereby any other slave may have suffered wrongfully, every such false informer shall be liable to, and suffer the same punishment as was inflicted upon the party accused.

21. Punishment of slaves for teaching other to poison.

In case any slave shall teach and instruct another slave in the knowledge of any poisonous root, plant, herb, or other sort of a poison whatever, he or she offending shall, upon conviction thereof, suffer death as a felon; and the slave or slaves so taught or instructed, shall suffer such punishment, not extending to life or limb, as shall be adjudged and determined by the justices and jury before whom such slave or slaves shall be tried.

22. Punishment of slaves for killing, marking, or branding cattle.

In case any slave or slaves shall be found killing, marking, branding, or driving any horse or neat cattle, contrary to the directions of this act, every such slave or slaves, being convicted thereof by the evidence of a white person, or of a slave, shall be punished by whipping on the bare back, not exceeding thirty-nine lashes, by order or warrant of any justice of the peace before whom the fact shall be proved.

23. Offences not defined, how punished.

All other offences committed by a slave or free person of color, either against persons or property, or against another slave or person of color, shall be punished at the discretion of the court before whom such slave or person of color shall be tried, such court having in view the principles of humanity in passing sentence, and in no case shall the same extend to life or limb.

ART. II. Prosecution of Offences
SEC. I. Commencement of Prosecution.
24. Tribunal for the trial of free persons of color.

An act passed at Milledgeville on the sixteenth day of December, eighteen hundred and eleven, entitled an act to establish a tribunal for the trial of slaves within this state; the court therein established is hereby made a tribunal for offences committed by free persons of color, to all intents and purposes, as if the words free persons of color had been inserted in the caption, and every section of the said act to establish a tribunal for the trial of slaves within this state.

25. Arrests and trial of slaves and free persons of color.

Every slave or free person of color, charged with any offence contained in this act, shall be arrested and tried, pursuant to an act entitled, "An act to establish a tribunal for the trial of slaves within this state," passed the sixteenth day of December, eighteen hundred and eleven, and the seventh, eighth and ninth sections of this act, and shall receive sentence agreeably to the requisitions contained in this act.

26. Offences, how prosecuted.

Upon complaint being made to, or information received upon oath, by any justice of the peace, of any crime having been committed by any slave or slaves within the county where such justice is empowered to act, such justice shall, by warrant from under his hand, cause such slave or slaves to be brought before him, and give notice thereof, in writing, to any two or more of the nearest justices of the peace of said county, to associate with him on a particular day, in said notice to be specified, not exceeding three days from the date of said notice, for the trial of such slave or slaves; and the justices so assembled, shall forthwith proceed to the examination of a witness or witnesses, and other evidence, and in case the offender or offenders shall be convicted of any crime not capital, the said justices, or a majority of them, shall give judgement for the inflicting any corporeal punishment, not extending to the taking away life or member, as in their discretion may seem reasonable and just, and shall award and cause execution to be done accordingly; and in case it should appear to them, after investigation, that the crime or crimes wherewith such slave or slaves stand or stands charged, is a crime or crimes for which he, she, or they ought to suffer death, such slave or slaves shall immediately be committed to the public jail of said county, if any, provided it should be sufficient, or to the custody of the sheriff or said county, or to the nearest sufficient jail thereto.

27. Inferior court to be notified.

The said justices shall, within three days next thereafter, give notice, in writing, to one of the justices of the inferior court of said county, of such commitment, with the names of the witness or witnesses, and such justice of the inferior court shall, within three days after the receipt thereof, direct the sheriff of said county, whose duty it shall be to summon a jury of twelve free white persons of said county, to be drawn in the manner hereinafter pointed out, to attend in like manner.

28. Duty of justice notified.

When any justice of the inferior court shall have received notice of the commitment of any slave or slaves, or free person or persons of color, (under the description of a free Negro or Negroes, mulatto, or mustizoe), to jail, in pursuance of the second section of an act entitled, "An act to establish a tribunal for the trial of slaves in this state," passed the sixteenth day of December, eighteen hundred and eleven, it shall be the duty of the said justice of the inferior court, within three days after the receipt thereof, to give notice, in writing, of such commitment, to the justices of the inferior court, or a majority of them, together with the clerk of said court, requiring their attendance at the court house of said county, where such slave or slaves, or person or persons of color, as aforesaid, may have been committed, on a particular day, in said notice to be specified in writing, not exceeding ten days from the date of said notice.

29. Continuance may be granted for cause.

The said court, so constituted as a aforesaid, shall immediately proceed to such trial, unless it should appear necessary for the said court, either for the want of sufficient proof, or any other sufficient reason, to delay the same, as in their judgement may seem for the furtherance of justice.

30. Clerk of inferior court to act as prosecuting officer.

In all prosecutions for a capital offence against any slave or free person of color, the clerk of the inferior court shall act as the prosecuting officer in behalf of the sate.

31. Accusation to be preferred by clerk in writing.

It shall be the duty of such justices, clerk, and jurors, to attend accordingly, and the said court, when so assembled, shall cause the clerk of said court to commit the charge or accusation alleged against such slave or slaves in writing, therein particularly setting forth the time and place of the offence, and the nature thereof.

32. Record of proceedings, subpoenas for witnesses, rules of evidence.

It shall be the duty of the clerk to make a record of the proceedings against such slave or slaves, separated and distinct from other records of his office, and he shall also issue subpoenas and other writs necessary to procure the attendance of a witness or witnesses, at the instance of either party, and that in all cases respecting the admission of evidence against people of color, the rules shall be the same as heretofore practiced in this state.

SEC. II. Trial.

33. Jurors, how drawn and summoned.

The justices of the inferior court, at their regular terms, shall draw, in the manner pointed out by law, not more than thirty-six, nor less than twenty-six jurors, twenty-four of whom shall be directed by such justices of the court to be summoned as aforesaid, to attend at the day and place pointed out for the trial of such slave or slaves, in manner aforesaid; and in case a sufficient number of those summoned should not attend, the said court shall direct the panel to be made up by talesmen, and all defaulting jurors so summoned in the manner pointed out by this act, shall be fined as in other cases pointed out by law.

34. At what time jurors to be drawn.

So much of the eighth section of the before recited act, as requires, the justices of the inferior courts in this state to draw a jury of thirty-six, at their regular terms, for the trial of such slave or slaves, person or persons of color, as aforesaid, shall be, and the same is hereby repealed; and in lieu of such regular drawing of jurors, it shall be the duty of such justices, or a majority of the, forthwith after being notified of such commitment as aforesaid, to cause to be drawn fairly and impartially from the jury box the names of persons subject to serve as jurors, not less than twenty-six nor more than thirty-six jurors, who shall be summoned according to the requisitions of the before-recited act, to attend at the time and place pointed out for the trial of such slave or slaves, or person or persons of color, by the said justices of the inferior court.

35. Challenging jurors; number allowed state and defendant.

The owner or manager of such slave or slaves, shall have the right of challenging seven of the said number summoned, and the said court five on the part of the sate, and the remaining twelve shall proceed to the trial of such slave or slaves.

36. Oath of jurors.

As soon as the justices and jury shall be assembled, as aforesaid, in pursuance of the direction of this act, the said jury shall take the following oath: "I, A. B., do solemnly swear, in the presence of Almighty God, that I will truly and impartially try the prisoner or prisoners, brought upon his, her, or their trial, and a true verdict give according to evidence, to the best of my knowledge; so help me God."

37. Trial by jury.

The said court shall cause twelve persons of those summoned, to be empaneled and sworn (the usual oath on such occasions made and provided) as jurors, to whom the said charge or accusation, in writing, and the evidence, shall be submitted.

38. Jury failing to render verdict, proceedings.

If [in] any court held hereafter, within this state, for the trial of a slave or slaves, or free person or persons of color, the jury empaneled and sworn for such trial, shall, from any cause, fail to render a verdict, it shall and may be lawful for said court to adjourn to a succeeding day, not exceeding thirty days from the day of adjournment; and at the time of its adjournment, and before is shall adjourn, said court shall draw, agreeable to the provisions of the before-recited act, not less than twenty-six, and not more than thirty-six jurors, who shall be summoned to attend said adjournment, in the mode prescribed in the acts aforesaid; and the proceedings of said adjournment shall be in all respects the same as those pointed out in the before-recited acts.

39. Jury may be completed by talesman.

In all cases where a sufficient number of the jurors summoned shall fail to attend, it shall be lawful for the court to complete the requisite number by summoning talesmen.

SEC. III. Evidence.
40. Persons considered competent witnesses.

On the trial of a slave or free person of color, any witness shall be sworn who believes in God and a future state of rewards and punishments.

41. Slaves, when competent witnesses.

The evidence of any free Indians, mulattoes, mustizoes, Negroes, or slaves, shall be allowed and admitted in all cases whatsoever, for or against another slave, accused of any crime or offence whatsoever, the weight of which evidence, being seriously considered and compared with all other circumstances attending the case, shall be left to the justices and jury.

42. Justices may compel the appearance and answer of witnesses.

The said justices, or any of them, are hereby authorized, empowered, and required, to summon and compel all persons whatsoever, to appear and give evidence upon the trial of any slave, and if any person shall neglect or refuse to appear, or appearing shall refuse to give evidence, or if any master or other person, who has the care and government of any slave, shall prevent and hinder any slave under his charge and government, from appearing and giving evidence in any matter depending before the justices and jury aforesaid, the said justices may, and they are hereby fully empowered and required, upon due proof made of such summons being served, to bind every such person offending as aforesaid, by recognizance, with one or more sufficient sureties, to appear at the next general court, to answer such their offence, and contempt, and for default of finding sureties to commit such offenders to prison, for any term not exceeding the space of two months.

SEC. IV. Verdict, Judgement, and Sentence.
43. Verdict and judgement.

The said jurors by their verdict shall say whether such slave or slaves are guilty or not guilty, and if a verdict of guilty should be returned by such jury, the court shall immediately pronounce the sentence of death by hanging, or some other punishment not amounting to death.

44. Sentence of death.

Whenever a slave or free person of color is brought before the inferior court to be tried for an offence deemed capital, it shall be the duty of said court to pass such sentence as may be pointed out by law for the offence of which slave or free person of color may be guilty.

45. Punishment to be proportionate to the offence.

In all cases where the jury, on the trial of any slave or free person of color, shall return a verdict of guilty, the court shall pass the sentence of death on such slave or free person of color, agreeably to the requisitions and subject to the same restrictions as are required by the before-recited act, or proceed to inflict such other punishment as in their judgement will be most proportionate to the offence, and best promote the object of the law, and operate as a preventive for [of] like offences in future.

46. Suspension of sentence in minor offences.

Where any jury shall find a verdict of guilty against any such slave or slaves, or person or persons of color as aforesaid, in pursuance of the fifth section of the act referred to in the preceding section, it shall and may be lawful for the said court to suspend the passing sentence against such slave or slaves, or person or persons of color as aforesaid, for any term of time not exceeding two day.

ART III. Correction of Errors, Pardon, Executions, and Costs.
SEC. I. Correction of Errors.
47. Exceptions may be taken; proceedings.

In all trials and proceedings before justices of the peace and justices of the interior courts, under any by virtue of the act passed on the sixteenth day of December, eighteen hundred and eleven, and of the act passed on the nineteenth day of December, eighteen hundred and sixteen, in relation to slaves and free persons of color, and of any acts amendatory thereof, when either party shall be dissatisfied with any decision of the court before whom such trial and proceedings may be had, affecting the real merits thereof, such party shall and may offer exceptions in writing to such decisions, which shall be signed by such party, or his or her attorney; and if the same shall be overruled by said court, the party making the exceptions may or twenty days' notice to the opposite party, or his or her attorney, apply to one of the judges of the superior court, and if such judge shall deem the exceptions sufficient, he shall forthwith issue a writ of certiorari to said justices, or to the clerk of the inferior court, as the case may be, requiring the proceedings in said matter to be certified and sent to the superior court next to be held in and for the county in which said proceedings or trial may have been had; and at the term of the court to which such proceedings shall be certified, said superior court shall determine thereon, and make such order, judgement and decisions, as shall be agreeable to law and justice.

48. When execution may be suspended.

When exceptions shall be offered in manner aforesaid, the said justices before whom said trials or proceedings may be, shall suspend the execution of their judgement and sentence for forty days; and when a certiorari shall be sanctioned in manner aforesaid, the judge issuing the same shall order the said judgement and sentence to be suspended until the final order and decision of said superior court shall be had in the cause.

49. When judge of superior court may fix day of execution.

Whenever a certiorari shall be granted agreeable to the provisions of the before-mentioned act, passed on the twenty-second day of December, eighteen hundred and twenty-nine, if sentence shall have been passed and a day fixed when the same shall be carried into effect by the inferior court before whom the slave or slaves, or free person or persons of color, were had and convicted; and if, after considering said certiorari, the judge of the superior court before whom the same may be, shall be of the opinion that the sentence of the inferior court should not be altered or disturbed, he is hereby authorized and directed to order the execution of said sentence on some other day than that fixed by said inferior court shall have passed before the final hearing and discussion of said certiorari.

50. When new trial may be granted; proceedings.

If the judge of the superior court before whom any *certiorari*, as contemplated by the before-recited act, passed on the twenty-second of December, eighteen hundred and twenty-nine, shall be argued and considered, shall, after considering the same, be of opinion that error has been committed in the court before, and that a new trial should be had, he shall pass such order as may be necessary to effect this object; and the inferior court to whom said order may be directed shall obey the same; and whenever a new trial shall be ordered, said inferior court shall assemble on the day to be specified in said order, shall draw a jury, have them summoned in the manner prescribed by the before-recited acts, and in all cases of a new trial, the presenting shall in all cases be the same as those presented in the before-mentioned acts.

51. Pardon of capital offences.

In every case of conviction, for a capital felony, the owner of the slave, or guardian of the free person of color convicted, may apply to the court before which the conviction shall have taken place, and obtain a suspension of the execution of the sentence, for the purpose of applying to the governor for a pardon, and it shall be in the power of the governor to grant said pardon.

52. Offences not capital, court may grant time to obtain pardon.

On a conviction for any other offence not punishable by death, the court may, at its discretion, grant a suspension of the execution of the sentence for the purpose of enabling the owner of a slave, or guardian of a free person of color, to apply to the governor for a pardon, or commutation of the punishment in such manner, and upon such terms and conditions as he may think proper to direct.

SEC. III. Executions and Costs.
53. Execution of sentence.

All and every the constable and constables in the several parishes within this province, where any slave shall be sentenced to suffer death, or other punishment, shall cause execution to be done of all the orders, warrants, precepts, and judgements of the justices hereby appointed to try such slaves, for the charge and trouble of which the said constable or constables respectively shall be paid by the public, unless in such cases as shall appear to the said justice or justices to be malicious or groundless prosecutions, in which cases the said charges shall be paid by the prosecutors.

54. Officer may press slaves to aid in executing sentence.

And that no delay may happen in causing execution to be done upon such offending slave or slaves, the constable who shall be directed to cause execution to be done, shall be, and he is hereby empowered to press one or more slave or slaves in or near the place where such whipping or other corporeal punishment shall be inflicted, to whip or inflict such other corporeal punishment upon the offender or offenders; and such slave or slaves so pressed shall be obedient to, and observe all the orders and directions of the constable in and about the premises, upon pain of being punished by the said constable by whipping on the bare back not exceeding twenty lashes, which punishment the said constable is hereby authorized and empowered to inflict; and the constable shall, if he presses a Negro, pay the owner of the said Negro two shillings out of his fee for doing the said execution: and in cases capital, shall pay to the Negro doing the said execution the sum of two shillings, over and above the said fee to his owner.

55. State not liable to owner for slave executed.

The state shall in no instance be answerable for, or liable to pay the owner whatever for any Negro slave or slaves who may laws of this state.

56. Expenses of prosecution, when paid by master.

All expenses and fees chargeable by any of the public officers, for prosecuting any Negro slave or slaves, convicted of any crime, not capital, against the laws of this state, shall be paid by the owner or owners of such slave or slaves.

57. When paid by the count.

But in all cases where any slave shall be convicted of any crime whereby he, she, or they may suffer death, the expenses attending the trial and execution of such slave or slaves shall be paid by the county where they shall be executed.

58. Fee of officer executing sentence.

For whipping or other corporeal punishments not extending to life, the sum of five shillings; and for any punishment extending to life, the sum of fifteen shillings; and such other charges for keeping and maintaining such slaves, as are by the act for erecting the workhouse appointed; for levying of which charges against the prosecutor, the justices are hereby empowered to issue their warrant.

59. Clerk and sheriff's fees.

The following shall be the fees of the clerk in such cases, to wit:

Clerk's Fees.

For attending the court to draw jury $1.25
For drawing up specifications of the charge 2.00
For attending each trial 1.25
For recording the proceedings of trial 87 1/2

For copying order, or sentence, and delivering the same to the sheriff 50

And the following shall be the fees of sheriffs in such cases, to wit:

Sheriff's Fees.

For summoning jury 4.00
For attending each trial 1.25

For executing order of sentence of the court the same as contained in the general fee bill.

Source: *Codification of the Statue Law of Georgia*, 2nd ed. William A. Hotchkiss, comp. Augusta: Charles E. Grenville, 1848.

See also: Abolitionist Movement; Slave Codes; Slave Families; Slave Revolts and White Attacks on Black Slaves; Slave Trade; Slavery; Slavery in the Antebellum South. Documents: Massachusetts Slaves' Petition (1777); Pennsylvania Act for the Gradual Abolition of Slavery (1788); Olaudah Equiano (1789); Fugitive Slave Act (1793); Act to Prohibit the Importation of Slaves (1807); Emancipation Proclamation (June 1866); Ida B. Wells' Expose on Lynching (1895)

Excerpts from Treaty of Guadalupe Hidalgo (1848)

Introduction

The settlement of Anglos in Texas, Mexico, led to the independence of Texas from Mexico and then its annexation by the United States in 1845. The U.S. annexation of Texas led to the breakout of the Mexican-American War in May 1846. The war was closed by the Treaty of Guadalupe Hidalgo, by which the United States gained not only Texas but New Mexico and upper California.

Treaty of Peace, Friendship, Limits, and Settlement between the United States of America and the United Mexican States Concluded at Guadalupe Hidalgo, February 2, 1848; Ratification Advised by senate, with Amendments, March 10, 1848; Ratified by President, March 16, 1848; Ratifications Exchanged at Queretaro, May 30, 1848; Proclaimed, July 4, 1848.

Primary Source

In the Name of Almighty God:

The United States of America and the United Mexican States, animated by a sincere desire to put an end to the calamities of the war which unhappily exists between the two republics and to establish upon a solid basis relations of peace and friendship, which shall confer reciprocal benefits upon the citizens of both, and assure the concord, harmony, and mutual confidence wherein the two people should live, as good neighbors have for that purpose appointed their respective plenipotentiaries—that is to say, The President of the United States has appointed Nicholas P Trist, a citizen of the United States, and the President of the Mexican Republic has appointed Don Luis Gonzaga Cuevas, Don Bernardo Couto, and Don Miguel Atristain, citizens of the said republic, who, after a reciprocal communication of their respective full powers, have, under the protection of Almighty God, the author of peace, arranged, agreed upon, and signed the following:

Treaty of Peace, Friendship, Limits, and Settlement between the United States of America and the Mexican Republic. . . .

Article VIII

Mexicans now established in territories previously belonging to Mexico, and which remain for the future within the limits of the United States, as defined by the present treaty, shall be free to continue where they now reside, or to remove at any time to the Mexican republic, retaining the property which they possess in the said territories, or disposing thereof, and removing the proceeds wherever they please, without their being subjected, on this account, to any contribution, tax, or charge whatever.

Those who shall prefer to remain in the said territories, may either retain the title and rights of Mexican citizens, or acquire those of citizens of the United States. But they shall be under the obligation to make their election within one year from the date of the exchange of ratifications of this treaty; and those who shall remain in the said territories after the expiration of that year, without having declared their intention to retain the character of Mexicans, shall be considered to have elected to become citizens of the United States.

In the said territories, property of every kind, now belonging to Mexicans not established there, shall be inviolably respected. The present owners, the heirs of these, and all Mexicans who may hereafter acquire said property by contract, shall enjoy with respect to it guarantees equally ample as if the same belonged to citizens of the United States.

Article IX

The Mexicans who, in the territories aforesaid, shall not preserve the character of citizens of the Mexican republic, conformably with what is stipulated in the preceding article, shall be incorporated into the Union of the United States, and be admitted at the proper time (to be judged of by the Congress of the United States) to the enjoyment of all the rights of citizens of the United States, according to the principles of the Constitution; and in the mean time shall be maintained and protected in the free enjoyment of their liberty and property, and secured in the free exercise of their religion without restriction.

Article X

[Stricken out by the U.S. Amendments]

Article XI

Considering that a great part of the territories which, by the present treaty, are to be comprehended for the future within the limits of the United States, is now occupied by savage tribes, who will hereafter be under the exclusive control of the government of the United States, and whose incursions within the territory of Mexico would be prejudicial in the extreme, it is solemnly agreed that all such incursions shall be forcibly restrained by the government of the United States whensoever this may be necessary; and that when they cannot be prevented, they shall be punished by the said government, and satisfaction for the same shall be exacted—all in the same way, and with equal diligence and energy, as if the same incursions were meditated or committed within its own territory, against its own citizens.

It shall not be lawful, under any pretext whatever, for any inhabitant of the United States to purchase or acquire any Mexican, or any foreigner residing in Mexico, who may have been captured by Indians inhabiting the territory of either of the two republics, nor to purchase or acquire horses, mules, cattle, or property of any kind, stolen within Mexican territory by such Indians.

And in the event of any person or persons, captured within Mexican territory by Indians, being carried into the territory of the United States, the government of the latter engages and binds itself, in the most solemn manner, so soon as it shall know of such captives being within its territory, and shall be able so to do, through the faithful exercise of its influence and power, to rescue them and return them to their country. or deliver them to the agent or representative of the Mexican government. The Mexican authorities will, as far as practicable, give to the government of the United States notice of such captures; and its agents shall pay the expenses incurred in the maintenance and transmission of the rescued captives; who, in the mean time, shall be treated with the utmost hospitality by the American authorities at the place where they may be. But if the government of the United States, before receiving such notice from Mexico, should obtain intelligence, through any other channel, of the existence of Mexican captives within its territory, it will proceed forthwith to effect their release and delivery to the Mexican agent, as above stipulated.

For the purpose of giving to these stipulations the fullest possible efficacy, thereby affording the security and redress demanded by their true spirit and intent, the government of the United States will now and hereafter pass, without unnecessary delay, and always vigilantly enforce, such laws as the nature of the subject may require. And, finally, the sacredness of this obligation shall never be lost sight of by the said government, when providing for the removal of the Indians from any portion of the said territories, or for its being settled by citizens of the United States; but, on the contrary, special care shall then be taken not to place its Indian occupants under the necessity of seeking new homes, by committing those invasions which the United States have solemnly obliged themselves to restrain.

Article XII

In consideration of the extension acquired by the boundaries of the United States, as defined in the fifth article of the present treaty, the government of the United States engages to pay to that of the Mexican Republic the sum of fifteen millions of dollars.

Immediately after the treaty shall have been duly ratified by the government of the Mexican republic, the sum of three millions of dollars shall be paid to the said government by that of the United States, at the city of Mexico, in the gold or silver coin of Mexico. The remaining twelve millions of dollars shall be paid at the same place, and in the same coin, in annual installments of three millions of dollars each, together with interest on the same at the rate of six per centum per annum. This interest shall begin to run upon the whole sum of twelve millions from the day of the ratification of the present treaty by the Mexican government, and the first of the installments shall be paid at the expiration of one year from the same day. Together with each annual installment, as it falls due, the whole interest accruing on such installment from the beginning shall also be paid. . . .

A. H. Sevier
Nathan Clifford
Luis de la Rosa

> **Source:** Treaty of Guadalupe Hidalgo, February 2, 1848; Perfected Treaties, 1778–1945; Record Group 11; General Records of the United States Government, 1778–1992; National Archives.

> **See also:** Guadalupe Hidalgo, Treaty of; Mexican American War; Spanish-American War

The Emancipation Proclamation (1863)

Introduction

In September 1862, President Abraham Lincoln issued the Emancipation Proclamation, according to which, all slaves within states or parts of states in rebellion against the United States would be free effective on January 1, 1863. Black slaves in other states were not influenced by the Emancipation Proclamation. Moreover, it did not set free even those slaves within Confederate-controlled areas, as those state governments did not heed it. But it led many black slaves in Confederate states to flee to Northern states, with nearly 200,000 freed slaves joining the Union army to fight against Confederate states. Giving black slaves the motive to fight for the Union army was important to President Lincoln's timing in proclaiming their emancipation. It was the Thirteenth Amendment, passed in December 1865, that abolished slavery in the entire United States.

Primary Source

By the President of the United States of America: A Proclamation

Whereas, on the twenty-second day of September, in the year of our Lord one thousand eight hundred and sixty-two, a proclamation was issued by the President of the United States, containing, among other things, the following, to wit: "That on the first day of January, in the year of our Lord one thousand eight hundred and sixty-three, all persons held as slaves within any State or designated part of a State, the people whereof shall then be in rebellion against the United States, shall be then, thenceforward, and forever free; and the Executive Government of the United States, including the military and naval authority thereof, will recognize and maintain the freedom of such persons and will do no act or acts to repress such persons, or any of them, in any efforts they may make for their actual freedom.

"That the Executive will on the first day of January aforesaid, by proclamation, designate the States and parts of States, if any, in which the people thereof, respectively, shall then be in rebellion against the United States; and the fact that any State or the people thereof shall on that day be, in good faith, represented in the Congress of the United States by members chosen thereto at elections wherein a majority of the qualified voters of such States shall have participated, shall, in the absence of strong countervailing testimony, be deemed conclusive evidence that such State and the people thereof are not then in rebellion against the United States."

Now, therefore, I, Abraham Lincoln, President of the United States, by virtue of the power in me vested as Commander-In-Chief, of the Army and Navy of the United States in time of actual armed rebellion against the authority and government of the United States, and as a fit and necessary war measure for suppressing said rebellion, do, on this first day of January, in the year of our Lord one thousand eight hundred and sixty-three, and in accordance with my purpose so to do publicly proclaimed for the full period of one hundred days from the day first above mentioned, order and designate as the States and parts of States wherein the people thereof, respectively, are this day in rebellion against the United States the following, to wit:

Arkansas, Texas, Louisiana (except the Parishes of St. Bernard, Plaquemines, Jefferson, St. John, St. Charles, St. James, Ascension, Assumption, Terrebone, Lafourche, St. Mary, St. Martin, and Orleans, including the city of New Orleans), Mississippi, Alabama, Florida, Georgia, South Carolina, North Carolina, and Virginia (except the forty-eight counties designated as West Virginia, and also the counties of Berkely, Accomac, Northhampton, Elizabeth City, York, Princess Ann, and Norfolk, including the cities of Norfolk and Portsmouth), and which excepted parts, are for the present, left precisely as if this proclamation were not issued.

And by virtue of the power and for the purpose aforesaid, I do order and declare that all persons held as slaves within said designated States, and parts of States, are, and henceforward shall be free; and that the Executive Government of the United States, including the military and naval authorities thereof, will recognize and maintain the freedom of said persons.

And I hereby enjoin upon the people so declared to be free to abstain from all violence, unless in necessary self-defence; and I recommend to them that, in all case when allowed, they labor faithfully for reasonable wages.

And I further declare and make known that such persons of suitable condition, will be received into the armed service of the United States to garrison forts, positions, stations, and other places, and to man vessels of all sorts in said service.

And upon this act, sincerely believed to be an act of justice, warranted by the Constitution upon military necessity, I invoke the considerate judgment of mankind, and the gracious favor of Almighty God.

In witness whereof, I have hereunto set my hand and caused the seal of the United States to be affixed.

Done at the City of Washington, this first day of January, in the year of our Lord one thousand eight hundred and sixty three, and of the Independence of the United States of America the eighty-seventh.

By the President: ABRAHAM LINCOLN
WILLIAM H. SEWARD, Secretary of State.

> **Source:** Emancipation Proclamation, January 1, 1863; Presidential Proclamations, 1791–1991; Record Group 11; General Records of the United States Government; National Archives.

> **See also:** Abolitionist Movement; Slave Codes; Slave Families; Slave Revolts and White Attacks on Black Slaves; Slave Trade; Slavery; Slavery in the Antebellum South. Documents: Massachusetts Slaves' Petition (1777); Pennsylvania Act for the Gradual Abolition of Slavery (1780); Olaudah Equiano (1789); Fugitive Slave Act (1793); Fear of Slave Revolt in New Orleans (1804); Emancipation Proclamation (1863); Fourteenth Amendment (June 1866); Ida B. Wells' Expose on Lynching (*The Red Record*, 1895)

Fourteenth Amendment (June 1866)

Introduction

The Thirteenth Amendment, passed by Congress in December 1865, liberated all black slaves. But Southern states began to pass black codes to control ex-slaves. The Fourteenth Amendment was passed by Congress in June 1866 to ensure that all blacks, including ex-slaves, were granted U.S. citizenship and that they would have all the rights and privileges any other citizen had.

Primary Source
14th. Amendment to the U.S. Constitution

Section 1. All persons born or naturalized in the United States, and subject to the jurisdiction thereof, are citizens of the United States and of the State wherein they reside. No State shall make or enforce any law which shall abridge the privileges or immunities of citizens of the United States; nor shall any State deprive any person of life, liberty, or property, without due process of law; nor deny to any person within its jurisdiction the equal protection of the laws.

Section 2. Representatives shall be apportioned among the several States according to their respective numbers, counting the whole number of persons in each State, excluding Indians not taxed. But when the right to vote at any election for the choice of electors for President and Vice President of the United States, Representatives in Congress, the Executive and Judicial officers of a State, or the members of the Legislature thereof, is denied to any of the male inhabitants of such State, being twenty-one years of age,* and citizens of the United States, or in any way abridged, except for participation in rebellion, or other crime, the basis of representation therein shall be reduced in the proportion which the number of such male citizens shall bear to the whole number of male citizens twenty-one years of age in such State.

Section 3. No person shall be a Senator or Representative in Congress, or elector of President and Vice President, or hold any office, civil or military, under the United States, or under any State, who, having previously taken an oath, as a member of Congress, or as an officer of the United States, or as a member of any State legislature, or as an executive or judicial officer of any State, to support the Constitution of the United States, shall have engaged in insurrection or rebellion against the same, or given aid or comfort to the enemies thereof. But Congress may by a vote of two-thirds of each House, remove such disability.

Section 4. The validity of the public debt of the United States, authorized by law, including debts incurred for payment of pensions and bounties for services in suppressing insurrection or rebellion, shall not be questioned. But neither the United States nor any State shall assume or pay any debt or obligation incurred in aid of insurrection or rebellion against the United States, or any claim for the loss or emancipation of any slave; but all such debts, obligations and claims shall be held illegal and void.

Section 5. The Congress shall have power to enforce, by appropriate legislation, the provisions of this article.

* Changed by section 1 of the 26th amendment.

> **Source:** Fourteenth Amendment to the Constitution, June 1866; The Charters of Freedom; National Archives.

> **See also:** Abolitionist Movement; Slave Codes; Slave Families; Slave Revolts and White Attacks on Black Slaves; Slave Trade; Slavery; Slavery in the Antebellum South. Documents: Massachusetts Slaves' Petition (1777); Pennsylvania Act for the Gradual Abolition of Slavery (1788); Olaudah Equiano (1789); Fugitive Slave Act (1793); Act to Prohibit the Importation of Slaves (1807); Emancipation Proclamation (June 1866); Ida B. Wells' Expose on Lynching (1895)

Excerpts from the Report of the Select House Committee on the Memphis Riots of May 1866 (July 25, 1866)

Introduction

Reproduced below are excerpts from the report of the House Select Committee charged with investigating the Memphis, Tennessee, race riots of 1866. The passages contain eyewitness testimony regarding the atrocities committed during the Memphis violence.

Primary Source
RAPE

The crowning acts of atrocity and diabolism committed during these terrible nights were the ravishing of five different colored women by these fiends in human shape, independent of other attempts at rape. The details of these outrages are of too shocking and disgusting a character to be given at length in this report, and reference must be had to the testimony of the parties. It is a singular fact, that while this mob was breathing vengeance against the Negroes and shooting them down like dogs, yet when they found unprotected colored women they at once "conquered their prejudices," and proceeded to violate them under circumstances of the most licentious brutality.

FRANCES THOMPSON

The rape of Frances Thompson, who had been a slave and was a cripple, using crutches, having a cancer on her foot, is one to which reference is here made. On Tuesday night, seven men, two of whom were policemen, came to her house. She knew the two to be policemen by their stars. They were all Irishmen. They first demanded that she should get supper for them, which she did. After supper the wretches threw all the provisions that were in the house which had not been consumed out into the bayou. They then laid hold of Frances, hitting her on the side of the face and kicking her. A girl by the name of

LUCY SMITH

about sixteen years old, living with her, attempted to go out the window. One of the brutes knocked her down and choked her. They then drew their pistols, and said they would shoot them and fire the house if they did not let them have their way. The woman, Frances Thompson, was then violated by four of the men, and so beaten and bruised that she lay in bed for three days. They then took all the clothes out of the trunk, one hundred dollars in greenbacks belonging to herself, and two hundred dollars belonging to another colored woman, which had been left to take care of her child, besides silk dresses, bed-clothing, &c. They were in the house nearly four hours, and when they left they said they intended "to burn up the last God damned nigger, and drive all the Yankees out of town, and then there would be only some rebel niggers and butternuts left." The colored girl, Lucy Smith, who was before the committee, said to be sixteen or seventeen years old, but who seemed, from her appearance, to be two or three years younger, was a girl of modest demeanor and highly respectable in appearance. She corroborated the testimony of Frances Thompson as to the number of men who broke into the house and as to the policemen who were with them. They seized her (Lucy) by

the neck and choked her to such an extent that she could not talk for two weeks to anyone. She was then violated by one of the men, and the reason given by another for not repeating the act of nameless atrocity was, that she was so *near dead he would not have anything to do with her*. He thereupon struck her a severe blow upon the side of the head. The violence of these wretches seemed to be aggravated by the fact that the women had in their room some bed-covering or quilting with red, white, and blue, and also some picture of Union officers. They said, "You niggers have a mighty liking for the damned Yankees, but we will kill you, and you will have no liking for anyone then." This young girl was so badly injured that she was unable to leave her bed for two weeks.

Another case is that of

REBECCA ANN BLOOM

who was ravished on the night of the 2nd of May. She was in bed with her husband, when five men broke open her door and came into her house. They professed to have authority to arrest Mr. Bloom, and threatened to take him to the station house unless he should pay them a forfeit of twenty-five dollars. Not having the money, he went out to raise it, and while absent one of the men assaulted the wife and threatened to kill her if she did not do as he wished. Brandishing his knife, and swearing she must submit to his wishes, he accomplished his brutal purpose. This is from the testimony of Mrs. Bloom, taken before the Freedmen's Bureau commission, and is corroborated by the testimony of Elvira Walker, taken before the committee, and also by Mrs. Bloom's husband, Peter Bloom.

Another case is that of

LUCY TIBBS

A party of seven men broke into her house on Tuesday night and demanded to know where her husband was. She had with her two little children of the ages of five and two years, respectively. She implored them not to do anything to her, as she was just there with her "two little children." While the others of the party were plundering the house, one man threatened to kill her if she did not submit to his wishes; and although another man, discovering her situation, interfered, and told him to let that woman alone—that she was not in a situation for doing that, the brute did not desist, but succeeded in violating her person in the presence of the other six men. She was obliged to submit, as the house was full of men, and she thought they would kill her, as they had stabbed a woman the previous night in her neighborhood.

WHAT LUCY TIBBS SAW

This woman lived in the immediate neighborhood, and was in the situation to see, and did see, a great deal that transpired during the riotous proceedings. This witness was intelligent and well-appearing, and the committee was strongly impressed with the truth and fairness of her testimony. She saw two colored soldiers shot down on Tuesday night, not ten rods apart. One of the men, she states, was killed by John Pendergrast, who keeps a grocery in her neighborhood. She was looking right at him when he shot the man. After being shot, the soldier made an effort to get up the bayou, and Pendergrast went to a policeman, got another pistol and shot him in his mouth. This man had no sooner been killed by Pendergrast—the witness being within a few feet at the time—than another colored man came in sight. *They beat him and kept him down until they loaded their pistols then they shot him three times, burst his head open and killed him.* She knew of four colored people being killed, their bodies lying within two hundred yards of her house for two days and nights, beside the body of Rachel Hatcher, to whom allusion is made in another part of this report. She testifies to other matters, and particularly to the conduct of Policeman Roach, one of the most murderous of them all, and who is understood still to be in Memphis. She testifies also to the shooting of a colored man by a white man of the name of Galloway, and of another colored man by the name of Charley Wallace, being shot by a Mr. Cash. Her brother, Robert Taylor, a member of the 59th Regiment, was killed on Tuesday afternoon. He had $300 in possession of his sister, the witness, of which she was robbed. She states further, in regard to a man who lives in the next house to her, that he was called outside of his house and shot down. They shot him three times and then said, "Damn you, that will learn you how to leave your old master and mistress," and took $25 from his pocket. His name was Fayette Dickerson. The white men she knew in this crowd of murderers and robbers were the old man Pendergrast and

his two sons, Mr. Cash, a boy called Charley Toller, and also a wretch by the name of

Charley Smith, who professed to have belonged to the Union army, and who had been teaching a school of colored people, but who had now joined these other men in their robberies and murders. Another case of rape is that of

HARRIET ARMOR

On Wednesday morning, in open day, two men came into her room. One of them, by the name of Dunn, living on South street, under the pretext of hunting for arms, entered and barred the door, and both of them violated her. This outrage was attended with circumstances of too disgusting and shocking a character to be mentioned except by the most distant allusion. The testimony of this witness is substantially corroborated by other witnesses.

SHOOTING AND BURNING OF RACHEL HATCHER

The shooting and burning of a colored girl by the name of Rachel Hatcher was one of the most cruel and bloody acts of the mob. This girl Rachel was about sixteen years of age. She was represented by all to be a girl of remarkable intelligence, and of pure and excellent character. She attended school, and such had been her proficiency that she herself had become a teacher of the smaller scholars. Her mother, Jane Sneed, testified before the committee that on Tuesday night the mob came to her house, took a man out, took him down to the bridge and shot him. They then set fire to the house of an old colored man by the name of Adam Lock, right by the house of the witness. Her daughter, Rachel, seeing the house of a neighbor on fire, proposed to go and help get the things out. While in the house, enraged in an act of benevolent heroism, the savages surrounded the burning building, and with loaded revolvers threatened to shoot her. In piteous tones she implored them to let her come out; but one of the crowd—the wretched Pendergrast—said, "No; if you don't go back I will blow your damned brains out." As the flames gathered about her, she emerged from the burning house, when the whole crowd "fired at her as fast as they could." She was deliberately shot and fell dead between the two houses. Her clothes soon took fire and her body was partially consumed, presenting a spectacle horrible to behold. The mother of Rachel was, in the meantime, inside her own house trying to get out a man who was wounded that night, and who she was afraid would be burnt up. When she came back, she saw the dead body of her daughter, the blood running out of her mouth. There was an Irishman about her house at this time by the name of Callahan, with the largest pistol in his hand she had ever seen. He demanded that her husband should come out until he could shoot him. But his life was saved at that moment by the appearance of two regulars, who told them to go to the fort.

CALLAHAN AND M'GINN

Among the parties who robbed the houses of Sneed and Adam Lock were Callahan, one George McGinn, and a young man whose name witness did not know. Callahan was seen to go off with a feather-bed on one arm and a pistol in the other hand, and the young man was seen to have the hoop skirt and the Balmoral skirt of the girl Rachel who was killed the night before.

These facts are testified to by a German woman of the name Garey, whose husband was a confectioner. At the time these things were carried off, a large crowd ran into Callahan's store, and he came out with bottles and things and treated them. The crowd was very noisy, and made a great many threats. They said the next night they wanted to kill there "d—d Yankee niggers"—calling such people as this German witness "Yankee niggers."

OTHER BURNINGS AND SHOOTINGS

Witnesses testified as to the circumstances of other burnings and shootings. A house containing women and little children was set on fire, and was then surrounded by armed men. Scorched by the extending flames the terrified inmates rushed out, but only to be fired upon when fleeing from their burning dwelling. It was reported that the arm of a little child was shot off. A woman and her little son were in a house which was fired. She begged to be permitted to come out, but the murderer (Pendergrast) shot at her. She got down on her knees and prayed him to let her out. She had her little son in there with her. They told her that if she did not go back they would kill her. McGinn was in this crowd, and the scene moved even his adamantine heart to mercy. He said, "This is a very good woman; it is a pity to burn her up. Let her come out." She came out with her boy; but it happened he had on

blue clothes. That seemed to madden them still more. They pushed him back and said, "Go back, you d—n son of a b—h." Then the poor heart-broken mother fell on her knees and prayed them to let her child out; *it was the only child she had*; and the boy was finally permitted to escape from the flames. Pendergrast went into a grocery and gave ammunition to a policeman to load his pistol. They then started up a Negro man who ran up the bayou, and told him to come to them. He was coming up to them, when they put a pistol to his mouth, shot his tongue off, killing him instantly. This man's name was Lewis Robertson.

ATTEMPT TO BURN LUCY HUNT

One Chris. Pigeon, an Irishman, went with others to the house of Lucy Hunt, a colored woman, and threatened if they could not get in they would burn them all up. They did set fire to the house in which Lucy lived, and when she attempted to come out they pushed her back into the fire three or four times. One of them caught her by the throat and said he was going to burn her up. One of the gang put his pistol to her head and said, "G—d d—n you, if you leave I will shoot you." She thinks she owes her life to the appearance of some soldiers. They broke open her trunk and robbed her of $25, the proceeds of sixteen months' work at the fort, where she had been cooking for a company of soldiers. And they not only robbed her of her money, but of all her clothes, and everything she had, leaving her nearly naked and penniless.

MARY BLACK AND MARIA SCOTT

They also broke into the house of Mary Black on Wednesday night. This same Pigeon was in the crowd. They poured turpentine on the bed and set the house on fire. There was in the house opposite Mary Black, at the time, a little girl twelve years old, and an old colored woman by the name of Maria Scott. After they had set fire to the house, they attempted to keep them in, and when asked to let them out they replied, they intended to burn them up. Witness had no doubt they would have done so had it not been for the appearance of the regulars.

SHOOTING OF JOSEPH WALKER

Among the instances of shooting and killing was that of Joseph Walker, a colored man who was returning home from his work during the riotous proceedings, and going round by way of the Tennessee and Mississippi railroad depot. The depot agent, a man by the name of Palmer, ordered him to halt, while Palmer's brother, from the top of a car called out, "Shoot the d—n son of a b—h." He thereupon pulled out his pistol and shot at him three times, but hit him only once. The ball was in the body of witness at the time he was before the committee, the doctor having been unable to extract it. He was so badly injured that he has been unable to work since. He has a wife, sister, mother, brother and child, all of whom are dependent on him for support. The ruffians who shot this man hold responsible positions under the Tennessee and Mississippi Railroad Company, and the attention of the others of that company is called to that fact, so that if the laws cannot be vindicated in bringing them to punishment, it may be seen whether they will be employed by a railroad company that seeks support from the public. The testimony is, that after Joseph Walker had escaped from these men they went after another black man whom they saw dodging round the bayou.

THE KILLING OF BEN. DENNIS

Perhaps there is nothing that can more fully illustrate the feeling in the city of Memphis than the impunity with which the most brutal and dastardly crimes were committed upon white persons also, and upon those not even remotely connected with the riotous proceedings than the murder of Dennis on Thursday, after the riots were substantially at an end. It seems that Dennis was a man of respectable connections, and of a good disposition, who had served a year in the rebel army; that he went into a saloon to take a drink, and while there met a colored barber, who was an old acquaintance, and spoke to him in a kind and friendly manner. At this time an Irishman was sitting behind a screen, eating his dinner, and when he heard the kind words of Dennis to the Negro he rushed out and demanded to know how Dennis dared to talk that way to a Negro. Dennis made some reply, then the Irishman deliberately shot him. He fell on the floor and died in ten minutes. The murderer was escorted to the station-house, and according to the testimony of the station-keeper was retained there for a term of *five or ten minutes*, and no one appearing against him, he was set at liberty. The statement is, though not in proof, that while at the station-house, someone made the remark

that he had "only shot a nigger," and that was no cause for his detention. No further effort has been made to bring this murderer to justice.

ATTEMPT TO BURN MARY JORDAN AND HER CHILDREN

There are but few acts of the mob which equal in barbarism that of the outrage committed upon Mary Jordan. She had just lost her husband, and was in her house with her three children, the youngest of which being seven months old and very sick. They had been shooting down colored people in her neighborhood, and she was very much frightened, expecting that she would herself be shot down. While she and her three children, the oldest of which being only sixteen years, were in her house, the mob set fire to a house adjoining, and the flames communicated to her dwelling. They refused to allow her or her children to come out. She started out, and told her children to follow her. Her eldest daughter said, "Mother, you will be shot." She replied she had rather be shot than burned. While she was escaping from the flames into the streets it was raining, and she could get no shelter. Her child got wet, and afterwards died. She states there were policemen in that crowd, as she knew them by the stars they wore. She lost everything she had. When, however, the house was all in flames, she ran out with her little children, with her baby in her arms. They fired at her, the bullets coming all around her, and she would have been hit had she not ran around the corner of the house and got out of the way. While running away with her baby in her arms a man put a pistol to her breast and asked her what she was doing. She told him she was trying to save her baby.

THE MURDER OF LONG

Scarcely a more brutal murder was committed than that of Shade Long. He with his wife and two children were in their house while a mob of twenty or thirty men came to it and demanded admittance. Long was very sick, and had been in bed for two weeks. They broke into the house, and told him to get up and come out, that they were going to shoot him. He told them he was very sick. They replied that they did not "care a d—n." They took him out of doors, and told him that if he had anything to say, to "say it very quick;" that they were going to kill him. They asked him if he had been a soldier. He replied that he had not, but had been in the employ of the government. Then one of them stepped back and shot him, putting a pistol to his head and firing three times. He scuffled about a little and looked as if he was trying to get back to the house, when they told him that if he did "not make haste and die" they would shoot him again. Then one of them kicked him, and another shot him after he was down. They shot him through the head every time. They then robbed the poor woman of fifty-five dollars in paper money and fifteen dollars in silver, and went away.

THE SHOOTING OF WOMEN AND CHILDREN

The shooting of Rachel Hatcher and the subsequent burning of her body has already been alluded to in detail. Adeline Miller, a colored girl, about twenty years old, on the first evening of the mob was standing at the door of a family grocery kept by an Italian named Oicalla. She seems to have been discovered by some person in the mob at a distance, who deliberately fired at her, the ball taking effect and killing her instantly.

Rhoda Jacobs, a young girl twenty years old, lived with her mother, who had three other young children living with her. On one night during the riots a gang of five or six men came to the door and demanded admittance. They pretended to be looking for some man. One of the ruffians pulled out his pistol and told the mother that if she did not light the candle quick he would shoot her brains out. The light disclosed that there was somebody in a bed behind the door, and it turned out to be this girl Rhonda, with her little sister, who was eight years old. Seeing the man with the pistol she screamed out, "O! I am a woman! I am a woman! Don't shoot!" But that did not stay the hand of the assassin, who deliberately fired into the bed. The witness was before the committee, and in answer to the question, "Where did he shoot you?" says, "The ball came into my arm, grazed two of my fingers, went through between the lips of my little sister lying in bed with me, entered my breast, *and the bullet is right there now.*"

This girl could not identify any of the parties. She looked at the pistol in the hands of a man and said she was so afraid they would shoot her mother that she did not think of herself at all; that he had his pistol at her mother's head, and had it cocked. The little girl was not much hurt, the ball only grazing

her lips. After accomplishing this brilliant feat they left the house. The mother then describes the scene as follows:

I looked at my daughter and thought that death was upon her. The ball had gone through her arm, had hit her fingers, and shot into her breast, and, what I did not see till afterwards, the ball had glanced the child's lips. I fixed up my daughter's wounds by the *light of the burning house* on the other side of the street, and put them all to bed. I put out my lamps for fear they would come back again. It was a fuss all the time, and I dared not put my head out. . . .

A gang consisting, among others, of Mike Cotton, S. D. Young, and Billy Barber, together with a policeman, went to the house of Richard Lane, colored man, in which he kept a salon. They demanded a light, and while Mrs. Lane was getting one they asked her husband for arms, and upon his denying that he had any they deliberately shot him through the shoulder, the ball being afterwards cut out below in his back. As they were going out one of the fiends deliberately shot their little girl through the right arm. In the language of the mother, the little child "screamed dreadfully and bled awfully, and looked just as though she had been dipped in a tub of blood." The mother seeing her husband and child thus wounded and bleeding, commenced screaming, whereupon the crowd left.

Jane Goodloe testified before General Stoneman's commission that the mob shot into her house on the evening of that first of May and wounded her in the breast.

ATTEMPTS TO BURN WHITE CHILDREN

The vindictive and revengeful feelings of the mob were not limited to the colored people, but they extended to such white people as had manifested particular friendship to the colored race by interesting themselves in their schools and churches, and in their welfare generally. Mr. and Mrs. Cooper were English people; they had put up a building, a portion of which was to be let for a colored school, which was to be taught by a Mr. Glasgow, who had been a soldier in the Union Army. Mr. Cooper was called an "abolitionist," because they said he was doing too much for the colored people, and spoke occasionally in their chapel. A gang of policemen and citizens came into the neighborhood in a threatening attitude. Being appealed to by Mrs. Cooper to know what they were going to do, they said they were going to kill her husband and Mr. Glasgow, for they would have no abolitionists in the South. While they were talking to her, at some distance from her house, and assuring her that they would not hurt her or her children, the house, with her four little children in it, was deliberately set on fire, and while her husband and Mr. Glasgow attempted to put it out the mob fired at them several times. A policeman headed this crowd of incendiaries, whose intention, Mrs. Cooper thinks, was to burn up her children. The building and all the furniture was burned, and Mr. Cooper fled from the city to save his life.

TEACHERS OF COLORED SCHOOLS

The most intense and unjustifiable prejudice on the part of the people of Memphis seems to have been arrayed against teachers of colored schools and against preachers to colored people. They would not teach the colored people themselves, and seemed to think it a reflection upon them that benevolent persons and societies outside should undertake the work. The preachers seemed to be men of earnest piety and sincere convictions, and to be actuated by the highest and best motives. Many of the teachers of the schools were young ladies from the northern states, graduates of the best northern schools, of intelligence, of education, and of the most unblemished characters, and who, responding to convictions of duty, had, at the call of benevolent individuals and societies, left their homes, gone to Memphis, and entered upon the task of educating and elevating a downtrodden and oppressed race. In the face of scorn and obloquy they proceeded, even at the peril of their own lives, to the work assigned them; and with consciences so void of offense and lives so pure and blameless, that while subject to persecution and insult, neither hatred nor calumny was ever able to stain their reputations or to blacken their characters; and yet these people, guilty of no crime, engaged in a work of benevolence and Christianity, were themselves obliged to flee from the city for personal safety; and as they left, they were guided in their pathway by the light reflected from their burning school-houses.

THE SCHOOLS

At the breaking out of the riots the number of schools was twelve, and the number in attendance was about 1,200, taught by twenty-two teachers. The superintendent of these schools was a Mr. Orin E. Waters, whose testimony was taken by the committee, and is hereby referred to. The teachers were employed by the American Baptist Missionary Association, the Western Freedmen's Aid Commission, the American Missionary Associations, two or three independent associations, and two or three were established independent of any associations. Twelve school-houses, or places where schools were taught, were burned during the riot, and the value of each was estimated at $2,500, besides the apparatus, furniture, &c. Mr. Waters testifies as to the teachers leaving on account of the threats of the mob that they would burn them out and kill them. Their offense was that they were teaching colored children; and although these schools had been going on for three years, there had never been a single instance in which any difficulty had been created on the part of any person connected with them, and the character and conduct of the scholars had been uniformly good. The progress of the scholars in their studies was said to be remarkable. The colored children evinced very great eagerness and interest in their studies. As an instance of the low prejudice against the teachers, your committee quote the following anonymous communication which was sent three or four days after the riots:

MEMPHIS, TENNESSEE, May 6, 1866.

To——:

You will please to notice that we have determined to rid our community of Negro fanatics and philanthropic teachers of our former slaves. You are one of the number, and it will be well for you are absent from the city by the 1st of June. Consult you safety.

ANONYMOUS.

It might also be stated that the mob were not satisfied with burning school-houses and churches, but they burned also a building belonging to the government, used by the Western Freedmen's Aid Commission as a storehouse for supplies for freedmen. The total amount of stores destroyed, and of property belonging to that commission was $4,597.35. Your committee were glad to learn that, to supply the place of the school-houses burned by the mob, Major General Fisk had, on behalf of the Freedmen's Bureau, with commendable energy, built a large school-house for the use of colored schools.

THE CHURCHES BURNED

Four churches were burned during the riots. One was a large brick building; another was a large frame structure, with a brick basement, and two others were used as churches and school-houses. And although all the churches and places of worship of the colored people were destroyed by the mob, no effort whatever seems to have been made by the people of Memphis to supply, even temporarily, the want created. So far as your committee were able to ascertain, no church within the control of the white people was open for their worship. . . .

THE CAUSE OF THE RIOT—THE NEWSPAPERS

As has been stated in this report, the riotous proceedings had their immediate cause in a difficulty between Irish police and colored soldiers. The more remote cause may be found in the prejudice which has grown up between the two races. The feelings of hatred and revenge toward the colored race, which have been fostered by the Irish and by large numbers of people in the south, seem to have been intensified since the Negro became free. The colored race have been subject to great abuse and ill-treatment. In fact, they have no protection from the law whatever. All the testimony shows that it was impossible for a colored man in Memphis to get justice against a white man. Such is the prejudice against the Negro that it is almost impossible to punish a white man by the civil courts for any injury inflicted upon a Negro. It was in the testimony before the committee that several months prior to their arrival in Memphis a Negro was most brutally and inhumanly murdered publicly in the streets by a policeman by the name of Maloney. The officer in command at Memphis, Major General John E. Smith, knowing full well that Maloney would not be punished through the civil tribunals, had him tried by a military commission, by which he was found guilty and sentenced to imprisonment in Nashville. It appears that afterwards the murderer Maloney was brought before United States Judge Trigg, at Nashville, on a writ of *habeas corpus*, and the judge, without giving any notice whatever to General Thomas, that there might be a fair hearing of the question, made haste to discharge him from imprisonment, and he is now at large, "unwhipt of justice." There can be no doubt that the feeling which led to the terrible massacres at Memphis was stimulated by the disloyal press of that city.

Judge Hunter states that he has no doubt but that the mob was stimulated by the newspapers. Reverend Mr. Tade says the effect of the press was to incite the riotous proceedings; and expresses the opinion that the Irish have been used as mere cat's-paws; that the papers published there had every day incited them to the deeds of violence which they committed. He states that the Avalanche is the worst, and that the Argus and Ledger are echoes of it. Witness believed that much of the ill-feeling against men of northern birth, entertaining what are called "radical sentiments," is due to the conduct of the press. Out of the seven daily papers there, five were controlled, in a greater or less degree, by men who have been in the rebel army. He states that the Avalanche, which is the most violent, vindictive, and unscrupulous of all the papers there, and which has done the most to exasperate the people against the Negroes and northern people, claims to have the largest circulation and most patronage of any paper in the city, and to most truly represent the sentiments and opinions of the mass of the people. Your committee caused extracts to be made from these papers, which they have carefully read over. Many of the articles were characterized by a bitter hostility to the government, and by appeals to the lowest and basest prejudices against the colored population; by bitter personal attacks upon northern people residing in Memphis; and, in fact, the whole tenor of the disloyal press was a constant incitation to violence and ill-feeling.

CONDUCT OF THE COLORED SOLDIERS

As great efforts had been made to justify the massacre of the colored people on account of the conduct of the colored soldiers who have been so long stationed at Fort Pickering, your committee deemed it their duty to take much testimony on this subject in order to satisfy themselves as to the facts in the case. That there was bad conduct on the part of some of the soldiers there can be no doubt, and the riotous and lawless conduct of a portion of them on the evening of the 1st of May is without excuse. General Stoneman, in answer to the question as to how these colored troops compared with white troops under similar circumstances, answered as follows: "I must say, in justice to the colored troops, that their conduct compared very favorably with that of the same number of white troops under similar circumstances."

Lieutenants Garrett and Hastings, and others, who had been officers in the colored regiment stationed at Fort Pickering, testified as to their general good conduct, and it was testified that there was no disposition on the part of the colored soldiers to maltreat white people, or to attack them in any way, and that whenever it became necessary for them to make arrests of white citizens it was done in an orderly and proper manner.

The testimony of Captain Thomas J. Dornin, of the 16th regular infantry, is referred to as being particularly full and explicit in regard to the character and conduct of the colored soldiers. He was in Fort Pickering with them during the days of the riot, and was in a position to know the facts in regard to which he testified. The behavior of these colored men under the trying circumstances in which they were placed, seeing their families murdered and their dwellings burned, was such as to extort admiration from all the officers in the fort. With the exception of a feeble attempt on the part of a few to seize some arms to defend their families from the butcheries of the mob, there was the most complete subordination among them, although they had been in point of fact mustered out of the service. In answer as to what he had seen in regard to the riotous conduct of these soldiers, Captain Dornin states:

I never saw any riotous act among them, and one thing I will say for them, that there is no number of white soldiers that I ever saw that could be held in such subjection as they were when their houses were being burned as they were. I could not have expected it; never could have believed it could be done.

In speaking of this matter, Captain Dornin, with the instincts which belong to the true soldier, states that he sympathized with the colored people, and was sorry that the men could not get their arms to defend their wives and families. He said he "sympathized with them as things were going, for they could not defend themselves, and it seemed like a brutish laughter on the part of the mob." Captain D. further states that there were policemen leading the mob and shooting down the colored people, and he himself saw them engaged in carrying off everything they could lay their hands on, and inciting others to do the same.

Captain Allyn, of the sixteenth regular infantry, commanding the post at Memphis, testified before the committee, and gave a very full and detailed account of the riotous proceedings, and the operations of the force under him. His report to the general commanding will be found in the appendix. Captain A. seems to have made the best and most judicious use of the small forces under his command. He states, in regard to the conduct of the colored soldiers, that if his own regiment had been there he does not think it would have been possible to keep them from interfering in favor of the negroes with their arms; and if the negroes had been a regiment of regulars, they would have rushed out unless it could have been prevented by previous knowledge, and by placing a heavy guard over it. Speaking his feelings, he said he should not have blamed them.

THE FEELING TOWARD THE GOVERNMENT

General Stoneman states, in answer to a question as to what was his opinion of the loyalty of the people of Memphis toward the United States, that if the desire to be restored to the Union was considered loyal, he should consider a large majority of the people of Memphis loyal, that far; but if a love of the Union and the flag was considered loyal he would look *upon a large majority of the people of Memphis as not being loyal.* He said there was not that disposition now on the part of the people of Tennessee to recognize existing facts that there was six months previous; that, so far as he could get at it from the press and from the meetings of the people for various purposes, he did not consider them as loyal, if loyalty was to be defined as love for the Union, *as they were six months ago, and that it was growing worse and worse every day.* He states that he knows of only three points where the United States flag is displayed—one at his own headquarters, another at the Freedmen's Bureau, and another is in front of the building used as the printing office for the Memphis Post. He had never seen it displayed at public meetings or places of amusement or theatres, and only sometimes on steamboats coming down the river. Information was conveyed to the general that at the theatre such national airs as "Hail Columbia," "Star-spangled Banner," and "Yankee Doodle" were hissed by the audience, and that the rebel airs were received with applause; he was obliged to write to the manager of the theatre that if national airs were to be met with disapprobation, and the "so-called confederate national airs" should be received with applause by the audience, it would compel him to interfere.

Mr. Stanbrough says that he would no more have raised the United States flag over his mill than he would think of putting a match to his property to burn it up; that he would not for his life think of taking the American flag and marching down Main Street with it; that if a band should go through the streets playing the national airs it would be received with a hiss and a groan. Everybody residing in Memphis knew the flag of our country was not respected, and that while national airs are hissed, when "Dixie" is struck up there is always a shout, and if played for the twentieth time, for every time there is a shout; but there is no "Yankee Doodle" or "Hail Columbia" in Memphis. He says there is not a bit more love for the laws, the Constitution of the United States, or the Union in Memphis than there was in the hottest days of the rebellion, and that the fires of hate burn as hot and as deep down as ever.

General Runkle, of the Freedmen's Bureau, speaks of having seen pictures of rebel generals in all the shop-windows, but of never having seen those of such men as Lincoln, Grant, Sherman, or Farragut displayed, nor even the picture of the name printed in gold letters on the sign-board; that such was the feeling there the people hated the sight of the uniform of a Union officer, and he would not consider it safe for him to be on the streets alone at night in his uniform.

GENERAL CONCLUSIONS

From the testimony taken by your committee, from personal observation and from what they could learn in regard to the state of feeling in Memphis, and, indeed, through that entire section of the country, they are of opinion that there is but little loyalty to the government and flag. The state of the things in the city of Memphis is very much now as it was before the breaking out of the rebellion. Many of the same newspapers published there then are published now, and by many of the same men—by who, during the war, were in the rebel armies fighting for the overthrow of the government. Professing to accept the situation, they seem inspired with as deadly hatred against the government as ever, and are guilty of the same incitation to violence, persecution, and oppression toward the men holding opinions obnoxious to

them, that they were towards the men who were well disposed toward the Union men in 1861. Your committee say, deliberately, that, in their judgment, there will be no safety to loyal men, either white or black, should the troops be withdrawn and no military protection afforded. They believe that the riots and massacres of Memphis are only a specimen of what would take place throughout the entire south, should the government fail to afford adequate military protection. There is everywhere too much envenomed feeling toward the blacks, particularly those who served in the Union armies, and against northern men and Union people generally who love the government, and who desired to see it sustained, its authority vindicated, and who believe that treason is a crime that should be punished. There is no public sentiment in the south sufficiently strong enough to demand and enforce protection to Union men and colored people. The civil-rights bill, so far as your committee could ascertain, is treated as a dead letter. Attorney General Wallace, in flagrant violation of his oath and duty, whose name has been heretofore alluded to in this report, has, according to the newspapers, proclaimed that he will utterly disregard the law.

The hopes based upon this law that the colored people might find protection under it are likely to prove delusive; for, where there is no public opinion to sustain law, but, on the other hand, that public opinion is so overwhelmingly against it, there is no probability of its being executed. Indeed, your committee believe the sentiment of the south which they observed is not a sentiment of full acquiescence in the results of the war, but that there is among them a lingering hope that their favorite doctrine of succession may yet be vindicated. It is the same idea that Jeff. Davis expressed. When he was seeking safety in flight, a traveler remarked to him that the cause was lost. Davis replied: *"It appears so; but the principle for which we contended is bound to reassert itself, though it may be at another time, and in another form."* (Pollard's Southern History of the War, vol. 2, page 582.) They believe in the principle and doctrine of succession. Though they have been beaten by arms, they assert and maintain that the principle is the same, and hope for its vindication hereafter in some way. Recognizing the friendship to them of what was called the "democratic party" in the north during the war, and their efforts to embarrass the government in the prosecution of the war against them, they hope, by combining with them in their political movements, finally to secure by the ballot what they dialed to achieve by arms.

The fact that the chosen guardians of the public peace, the sworn executors of the law for the protection of the lives, liberty, and property of the people, and the reliance of the weak and defenseless in time of danger, were found the foremost in the work of murder and pillage, gives a character of infamy to the whole proceeding which is almost without a parallel in all the annals of history. The dreadful massacre of Fort Pillow, which excited the horror of the country and of the civilized world, was attempted to be palliated on the ground that the garrison was taken after the most desperate resistance, and after having been repeatedly summoned to surrender; that the blood of the assailants had been heated to such a degree and their passions so aroused that there was no controlling them, though it is alleged that some of their officers vainly attempted to do so. But no such ground of palliation can be advanced in the case of the Memphis massacres. After the first troubles on the first evening, there was no pretense of any disturbance by the colored people, or any resistance to the mob, calculated to excite their passions, and what subsequently took place was the result of a cool and mature deliberation to murder and destroy the colored people. Like the massacre of St. Bartholomew, the Memphis massacre had the sanction of official authority; and it is no wonder that the mob, finding itself led by officers of the law, butchered miserably and without resistance every negro it could find, and regretting that death had saved their victims from further insult, exercised on their dead bodies all the rage of the most insensate cruelty.

In view of the fact that the state of public sentiment is such in Memphis that is it conceded that no punishment whatever can be meted out to the perpetrators of these outrages by the civil authorities, and in view of the further fact that the city repudiates any liability for the property, both of the government and individuals, destroyed by the mob, your committee believe it to be the duty of the government to arrest, try, and punish the offenders by military authority; and also by the same authority levy a tax upon the citizens of Memphis sufficient to cover the losses for all property destroyed.

Source: "Memphis Riots and Massacres." U.S. House of Representatives, 30th Congress, 1st Session, Report No. 101, Report of the Select Committee on the Memphis Riots. Washington, D.C.: Government Printing Office, 1866, 13–21, 30–34.

See also: Asbury Park (New Jersey) Riot of 1970; Atlanta (Georgia) Riot of 1906; Atlanta (Georgia) Riot of 1967; Bellingham Riots (1907); Bensonhurst (New York) Incident (1989); Biloxi Beach (Mississippi) Riot of 1960; Black Church Arsons; Bloody Sunday; Boston (Massachusetts) Riots of 1975 and 1976; Brownsville (Texas) Incident of 1906; Charleston (South Carolina) Riot of 1919; Chattanooga (Tennessee) Riot of 1906; Chester and Philadelphia (Pennsylvania) Riots of 1918; Chicago Commission on Race Relations; Chicago (Illinois) Riot of 1919; Cincinnati (Ohio) Riots of 1967 and 1968; Cincinnati (Ohio) Riots of 2001; Cleveland (Ohio) Riot of 1966; Detroit (Michigan) Riot of 1943; Detroit (Michigan) Riot of 1967; East St. Louis (Illinois) Riot of 1917; Election Riots of the 1880s and 1890s; Greensburg (Indiana) Riot of 1906; Greenwood Community (Tulsa, Oklahoma); Harlem (New York) Riot of 1935; Houston (Texas) Mutiny of 1917; Howard Beach (New York) Incident (1986); Johnson-Jeffries Fight of 1910, Riots Following; Knoxville (Tennessee) Riot of 1919; Long Hot Summer Riots (1965–1967); Longview (Texas) Riot of 1919; Los Angeles (California) Riot of 1965; Los Angeles (California) Riots of 1992; Miami (Florida) Riot of 1982; New Bedford (Massachusetts) Riot of 1970; New Orleans (Louisiana) Riot of 1866; New York City Draft Riot of 1863; New York City Riot of 1943; Newark (New Jersey) Riot of 1967; Orangeburg (South Carolina) Massacre of 1968; Philadelphia (Pennsylvania) Riot of 1964; Prison Riots; Race Riots in America; Red Scare and Race Riots; Red Summer Race Riots of 1919; Rosewood (Florida) Riot of 1923; Saint Genevieve (Missouri) Riot of 1930; San Francisco (California) Riot of 1966; Springfield (Ohio) Riot of 1904; Tampa (Florida) Riots of 1987; Texas Southern University Riot of 1967; Tulsa (Oklahoma) Riot of 1921; Washington (D.C.) Riot of 1919; Washington (D.C.) Riots of 1968; Wilmington (North Carolina) Riot of 1898; Zoot Suit Riots

Report of the Federal Grand Jury on the Activities of the Ku Klux Klan in South Carolina (1871)

Introduction

The activities of the Ku Klux Klan in South Carolina in the years 1868–1871 were so notorious as to lead President

Ulysses Grant to suspend the right of habeas corpus in nine South Carolina counties in October 1871. The military was sent in to arrest perpetrators and a grand jury was convened in Columbia, South Carolina, to investigate Klan activities and the Klan organization throughout these counties. Below is an excerpt of the grand jury's report to the judges of the U.S. Circuit Court.

Primary Source

In closing the labors of the present term, the grand jury begs leave to submit the following presentment.

During the whole session we have been engaged in investigations of the most grave and extraordinary character—investigations of the crimes committed by the organization known as the Ku Klux Klan. The evidence elicited has been voluminous, gathered from the victims themselves and their families, as well as those who belong to the Klan and participated in its crimes. The jury has been shocked beyond measure at the developments which have been made in their presence of the number and character of the atrocities committed, producing a state of terror and a sense of utter insecurity among a large portion of the people, especially the colored population. The evidence produced before us has established the following facts:

1. That there has existed since 1868, in many counties of the state, an organization known as the "Ku Klux Klan," or "Invisible Empire of the South," which embraces in its membership a large proportion of the white population of every profession and class.
2. That this Klan is bound together by an oath, administered to its members at the time of their initiation into the order, of which the following is a copy:

Obligation
I [name], before the immaculate Judge of Heaven and Earth, and upon the Holy Evangelists of Almighty God, do, of my own free will and accord, subscribe to the following sacredly binding obligation:

1. We are on the side of justice, humanity, and constitutional liberty, as bequeathed to us in its purity by our forefathers.

2. We oppose and reject the principles of the Radical Party.
3. We pledge mutual aid to each other in sickness, distress, and pecuniary embarrassment.
4. Female friends, widows, and their households shall ever be special objects of our regard and protection.

Any member divulging, or causing to be divulged, any part of the foregoing obligations, shall meet the fearful penalty and traitor's doom, which is Death! Death! Death!

That, in addition to this oath, the Klan has a constitution and bylaws, which provides, among other things, that each member shall furnish himself with a pistol, a Ku Klux gown, and a signal instrument. That the operations of the Klan were executed in the night, and were invariably directed against members of the Republican Party by warnings to leave the country, by whippings, and by murder.

3. That in large portions of the counties of York, Union, and Spartanburgh, to which our attention has been more particularly called in our investigations during part of the time for the last eighteen months, the civil law has been set at defiance and ceased to afford any protection to the citizens.
4. That the Klan, in carrying out the purposes for which it was organized and armed, inflicted summary vengeance on the colored citizens of these counties by breaking into their houses at the dead of night, dragging them from their beds, torturing them in the most inhumane manner, and in many instances murdering them; and this, mainly, on account of their political affiliations. Occasionally, additional reasons operated, but in no instance was the political feature wanting.
5. That for this condition of things, for all these violations of law and order and the sacred rights of citizens, many of the leading men of those counties were responsible. It was proven that large numbers of the most prominent citizens were members of the order. Many of this class attended meetings of the Grand Klan. At a meeting of the Grand Klan held in Spartanburgh County, at which there were representatives from

the various dens of Sparatanburgh, York, Union, and Chester Counties, in this state, besides a number from North Carolina, a resolution was adopted that no raids should be undertaken or anyone whipped or injured by members of the Klan without orders from the Grand Klan. The penalty for violating this resolution was 100 lashes on the bare back for the first offense; and for the second, death.

This testimony establishes the nature of the discipline enforced in the order, and also the fact that many of the men who were openly and publicly speaking against the Klan, and pretending to deplore the work of this murderous conspiracy, were influential members of the order and directing its operations, even in detail.

The jury has been appalled as much at the number of outrages as at their character, it appearing that 11 murders and over 600 whippings have been committed in York County alone. Our investigation in regard to the other counties named has been less full; but it is believed, from the testimony, that an equal or greater number has been committed in Union, and that the number is not greatly less in Spartanburgh and Laurens.

We are of the opinion that the most vigorous prosecution of the parties implicated in these crimes is imperatively demanded; that without this there is great danger that these outrages will be continued, and that there will be no security to our fellow citizens of African descent.

We would say further that unless the strong arm of the government is interposed to punish these crimes committed upon this class of citizen, there is every reason to believe that an organized and determined attempt at retaliation will be made, which can only result in a state of anarchy and bloodshed too terrible to contemplate.

Source: Report of the Federal Grand Jury on the Activities of the Ku Klux Klan in South Carolina, 1871, 42nd Congress, 2nd Session, House Report No. 22, Pt. 1, 48–49.

See also: Aryan Brotherhood; Aryan Nations; Christian Identity Hate Groups; Churches; Hate Crimes in America; Hate Groups in America; Ku Klux Klan; Preachers; White Supremacy

The Chinese Exclusion Act (1882)
Introduction

After the California Gold Rush in 1848, a large number of Chinese workers came to California to be used as cheap labor for mining and railroad construction. However, anti-Chinese sentiment was gradually building in California in parallel to the increase in the number of Chinese workers. The increase in anti-Chinese sentiment in California found a receptive audience among Washington politicians and culminated in the passage of the Chinese Exclusion Act in 1882. The original act was to bar Chinese labor immigration for ten years, but Congress extended the 10-year banning of Chinese immigration twice, in 1892 and 1902, and then indefinitely in 1912. It was repealed in 1943, when China was helping the United States in the fight against Japan.

Primary Source
Forty-Seventh Congress. Session I. 1882

Chapter 126. An act to execute certain treaty stipulations relating to Chinese.

Preamble. Whereas, in the opinion of the Government of the United States the coming of Chinese laborers to this country endangers the good order of certain localities within the territory thereof:

Therefore,
Be it enacted by the Senate and House of Representatives of the United States of America in Congress assembled, That from and after the expiration of ninety days next after the passage of this act, and until the expiration of ten years next after the passage of this act, the coming of Chinese laborers to the United States be, and the same is hereby, suspended; and during such suspension it shall not be lawful for any Chinese laborer to come, or, having so come after the expiration of said ninety days, to remain within the United States.

SEC. 2. That the master of any vessel who shall knowingly bring within the United States on such vessel, and land or permit to be landed, and Chinese laborer, from any foreign port of place, shall be deemed guilty of a misdemeanor, and on conviction thereof shall be punished by a fine of not more than five hundred dollars for each and every such Chinese laborer so brought, and may be also imprisoned for a term not exceeding one year.

SEC. 3. That the two foregoing sections shall not apply to Chinese laborers who were in the United States on the seventeenth day of November, eighteen hundred and eighty, or who shall have come into the same before the expiration of ninety days next after the passage of this act, and who shall produce to such master before going on board such vessel, and shall produce to the collector of the port in the United States at which such vessel shall arrive, the evidence hereinafter in this act required of his being one of the laborers in this section mentioned; nor shall the two foregoing sections apply to the case of any master whose vessel, being bound to a port not within the United States by reason of being in distress or in stress of weather, or touching at any port of the United States on its voyage to any foreign port of place: Provided, That all Chinese laborers brought on such vessel shall depart with the vessel on leaving port.

SEC. 4. That for the purpose of properly identifying Chinese laborers who were in the United States on the seventeenth day of November, eighteen hundred and eighty, or who shall have come into the same before the expiration of ninety days next after the passage of this act, and in order to furnish them with the proper evidence of their right to go from and come to the United States of their free will and accord, as provided by the treaty between the United States and China dated November seventeenth, eighteen hundred and eighty, the collector of customs of the district from which any such Chinese laborer shall depart from the United States shall, in person or by deputy, go on board each vessel having on board any such Chinese laborer and cleared or about to sail from his district for a foreign port, and on such vessel make a list of all such Chinese laborers, which shall be entered in registry-books to be kept for that purpose, in which shall be stated the name, age, occupation, last place of residence, physical marks or peculiarities, and all facts necessary for the identification of each of such Chinese laborers, which books shall be safely kept in the custom-house; and every such Chinese laborer so departing from the United States shall be entitled to, and shall receive, free of any charge or cost upon application therefore, from the collector or his deputy, at the time such list is taken, a certificate, signed by the collector or his deputy and attested by his seal of office, in such form as the Secretary of the Treasury shall prescribe, which certificate shall contain a statement of the name, age, occupation, last place of residence, personal description, and fact of identification of the Chinese laborer to whom the certificate is issued, corresponding with the said list and registry in all particulars. In case any Chinese laborer after having received such certificate shall leave such vessel before her departure he shall deliver his certificate to the master of the vessel, and if such Chinese laborer shall fail to return to such vessel before her departure from port the certificate shall be delivered by the master to the collector of customs for cancellation. The certificate herein provided for shall entitle the Chinese laborer to whom the same is issued to return to and re-enter the United States upon producing and delivering the same to the collector of customs of the district at which such Chinese laborer shall seek to re-enter; and upon delivery of such certificate by such Chinese laborer to the collector of customs at the time of re-entry in the United States, said collector shall cause the same to be filed in the custom house and duly canceled.

SEC. 5. That any Chinese laborer mentioned in section four of this act being in the United States, and desiring to depart from the United States by land, shall have the right to demand and receive, free of charge or cost, a certificate of identification similar to that provided for in section four of this act to be issued to such Chinese laborers as may desire to leave the United States by water; and it is hereby made the duty of the collector of customs of the district next adjoining the foreign country to which said Chinese laborer desires to go to issue such certificate, free of charge or cost, upon application by such Chinese laborer, and to enter the same upon registry-books to be kept by him for the purpose, as provided for in section four of this act.

SEC. 6. That in order to the faithful execution of articles one and two of the treaty in this act before mentioned, every Chinese person other than a laborer who may be entitled by said treaty and this act to come within the United States, and who shall be about to come to the United States, shall be identified as so entitled by the Chinese Government in each case, such identity to be evidenced by a certificate issued under the authority of said government, which certificate shall be in the English language or (if not in the English language) accompanied by a translation into English, stating such right to come, and which certificate shall state the name, title, or official rank, if any, the age, height, and all physical peculiarities, former and present occupation or profession, and place of residence in China of the person to whom the certificate is issued and that such person is entitled conformably to the treaty in this act mentioned to come within the United States. Such certificate shall be prima-facie evidence of the fact set forth therein, and shall be produced to the collector of customs, or his deputy, of the port in the district in the United States at which the person named therein shall arrive.

SEC. 7. That any person who shall knowingly and falsely alter or substitute any name for the name written in such certificate or forge any such certificate, or knowingly utter any forged or fraudulent certificate, or falsely personate any person named in any such certificate, shall be deemed guilty of a misdemeanor; and upon conviction thereof shall be fined in a sum not exceeding one thousand dollars, an imprisoned in a penitentiary for a term of not more than five years.

SEC. 8. That the master of any vessel arriving in the United States from any foreign port or place shall, at the same time he delivers a manifest of the cargo, and if there be no cargo, then at the time of making a report of the entry of vessel pursuant to the law, in addition to the other matter required to be reported, and before landing, or permitting to land, any Chinese passengers, deliver and report to the collector of customs of the district in which such vessels shall have arrived a separate list of all Chinese passengers taken on board his vessel at any foreign port or place, and all such passengers on board the vessel at that time. Such list shall show the names of such passengers (and if accredited officers of the Chinese Government traveling on the business of that government, or their servants, with a note of such facts), and the name and other particulars, as shown by their respective certificates; and such list shall be sworn to by the master in the manner required by law in relation to the manifest of the cargo. Any willful refusal or neglect of any such

master to comply with the provisions of this section shall incur the same penalties and forfeiture as are provided for a refusal or neglect to report and deliver a manifest of cargo.

SEC. 9. That before any Chinese passengers are landed from any such vessel, the collector, or his deputy, shall proceed to examine such passengers, comparing the certificates with the list and with the passengers; and no passenger shall be allowed to land in the United States from such vessel in violation of law.

SEC. 10. That every vessel whose master shall knowingly violate any of the provisions of this act shall be deemed forfeited to the United States, and shall be liable to seizure and condemnation on any district of the United States into which such vessel may enter or in which she may be found.

SEC. 11. That any person who shall knowingly bring into or cause to be brought into the United States by land, or who shall knowingly aid or abet the same, or aid or abet the landing in the United States from any vessel of any Chinese person not lawfully entitled to enter the United States, shall be deemed guilty of a misdemeanor, and shall, on conviction thereof, be fined in a sum not exceeding one thousand dollars, and imprisoned for a term not exceeding one year.

SEC. 12. That no Chinese person shall be permitted to enter the United States by land without producing to the proper officer of customs the certificate in this act required of Chinese persons seeking to land from a vessel. And any Chinese person found unlawfully within the United States shall be caused to be removed therefrom to the country from whence he came, by direction of the United States, after being brought before some justice, judge, or commissioner of a court of the United States and found to be one not lawfully entitled to be or remain in the United States.

SEC. 13. That this act shall not apply to diplomatic and other officers of the Chinese Government traveling upon the business of that government, whose credentials shall be taken as equivalent to the certificate in this act mentioned, and shall exempt them and their body and household servants from the provisions of this act as to other Chinese persons.

SEC. 14. That hereafter no State court or court of the United States shall admit Chinese to citizenship; and all laws in conflict with this act are hereby repealed.

SEC. 15. That the words "Chinese laborers," whenever used in this act, shall be construed to mean both skilled and unskilled laborers and Chinese employed in mining.

Approved, May 6, 1882.

> **Source:** Chinese Exclusion Act. *U.S. Statutes at Large* 22 (1882): 58.

> **See also:** Chinese Exclusion Act of 1882; Immigration Acts; Immigration and Customs Enforcement; Naturalization and Citizenship Process

Excerpt from the Dawes Act (1887)

Introduction

Congress passed the General Allotment Act (Dawes Act) in 1887. The passage of the Act indicates a major change in the U.S. government's policy toward Native Americans from segregation and separation to assimilation. The Act stipulated that each Indian family be given seventy acres of land. Native Americans considered their land belonging to their tribe, as they had no sense of private property. One main goal of allotting certain acres of land to each Indian family was to teach them the capitalist value of private ownership. But a more important, practical goal of the allotment was to take away land from Indian tribes. The federal government took the remaining tribal lands after allotments to Indian families. Moreover, many Indian families lost their allotted land due to their ignorance of complicated paperwork associated with property ownership.

Primary Source

. . .

Chapter 119—An act to provide for the allotment of lands in severalty to Indians on the various reservations, and to extend the protection of the laws of the United States and Territories over the Indians, and for other purposes. Be it enacted, &c., [For substitute for section 1, see 1891, February 28, c. 383, s. 1, post,].

SEC. 2. That all allotments set apart under the provisions of this act shall be selected by the Indians, heads of families selecting for their minor children, and the agents shall select for each orphan child, and in such manner as to embrace the improvements of the Indians making the selection.

Where the improvements of two or more Indians have been made on the same legal subdivision of land, unless they shall otherwise agree, a provisional line may be run dividing said lands between them, and the amount to which each is entitled shall be equalized in the assignment of the remainder of the land to which they are entitled under this act:

Provided, That if any one entitled to an allotment shall fail to make a selection within four years after the President shall direct that allotments may be made on a particular reservation, the Secretary of the Interior may direct the agent of such tribe or band, if such there be, and if there be no agent, then a special agent appointed for that purpose, to make a selection for such Indian, which selection shall be allotted as in cases where selections are made by the Indians, and patents shall issue in like manner.

SEC. 3. That the allotments provided for in this act shall be made by special agents appointed by the President for such purpose, and the agents in charge of the respective reservations on which the allotments are directed to be made, under such rules and regulations as the Secretary of the Interior may from time to time prescribe, and shall be certified by such agents to the Commissioner of Indian Affairs, in duplicate, one copy to be retained in the Indian Office and the other to be transmitted to the Secretary of the Interior for his action, and to be deposited in the General Land Office.

SEC. 4. That where any Indian not residing upon a reservation, or for whose tribe no reservation has been provided by treaty, act of Congress, or executive order, shall make settlement upon any surveyed or un-surveyed lands of the United States not otherwise appropriated, he or she shall be entitled, upon application to the local land office for the district in which the lands are located, to have the same allotted to him or her, and to his or her children, in quantities and manner as provided in this act for Indians residing upon reservations; and when such settlement is made upon unsurveyed lands, the grant to such Indians shall be adjusted upon the survey of the lands so as to conform thereto; and patents shall be issued to them for such lands in the manner and with the restrictions as herein provided.

And the fees to which the officers of such local land-office would have been entitled has such lands been entered under the general laws for the disposition of the public lands shall be paid to them, from any moneys in the Treasury of the United States not otherwise appropriated, upon a statement of an account in their behalf for such fees by the Commissioner of the General Land Office and certification of such account to the Secretary of the Treasury by the Secretary of the Interior.

SEC. 5. That upon the approval of the allotments provided for in this act by the Secretary of the Interior, he shall cause patents to issue therefore in the name of the allottees, which patents shall be of the legal effect, and declare that the United States does and will hold the land thus allotted for the period of twenty-five years, in trust for the sole use and benefit of the Indian to whom such allotment shall have been made, or, in case of his decease, of his heirs according to the laws of the State or Territory where such land is located, and that at the expiration of said period the Untied States will convey the same by patent to said Indian, or his heirs as aforesaid, in fee, discharged of said trust and free of all charge or incumbrance whatsoever: *Provided*, That the President of the United States may in any case in his discretion extend the period.

And if any conveyance shall be made of the lands set apart and allotted as herein provided, or any contract made touching the same, before the expiration of the time above mentioned, such conveyance or contract shall be absolutely null and void:

Provided, That the law of descent and partition in force in the State or Territory where such lands are situate shall apply thereto after patents therefore have been executed and delivered, except as herein otherwise provided; and the laws of the State of Kansas regulating the descent and partition of real estate shall, so far as practicable, apply to all lands in the Indian Territory which may be allotted in severalty under the provisions of this act:

And provided further, that at any time after lands have been allotted to all the Indians of any tribe as herein provided, or sooner if in the opinion of the President it shall be for the best interests of said tribe, it shall be lawful for the Secretary of the Interior to negotiate with such Indian tribe for the purchase and release by said tribe, in conformity with the treaty or statute under which such reservation is held, of such portions of its reservation not allotted as such tribe shall, from time to time, consent to sell, on such terms and conditions as shall be considered just and equitable between the United States and said tribe of Indians, which purchase shall not be complete until ratified by Congress, and the form and manner of executing such release shall also be prescribed by Congress:

Provided however, That all lands adapted to agriculture, with or without irrigation so sold or released to the United States by any Indian tribe shall be held by the United States for the sole purpose of securing homes to actual settlers and shall be disposed of by the United States to actual and bona fide settlers only in tracts not exceeding one hundred and sixty acres to any one person, on such terms as Congress shall prescribe, subject to grants which Congress may make in aid of education:

And provided further, That no patents shall issue therefore except to the person so taking the same as and for a homestead, or his heirs, and after the expiration of five years occupancy thereof as such homestead; and any conveyance of said lands so taken as a homestead, or any contract touching the same, or lien thereon, created prior to the date of such patent, shall be null and void.

Fees of land officers to be paid from Treasury.

Patent to issue, holding lands in trust; conveyance after twenty-five years.

Contracts, conveyances, etc., before end of twenty-five years void.

Laws of descent and partition.

Negotiations by Secretary of Interior for purchase of lands not allotted.

Agricultural lands so purchased to be held for actual settlers, if arable.

Patent to issue only to persons taking for homestead.

And the sums agreed to be paid by the United States as purchase money for any portion of any such reservation shall be held in the Treasury of the United States for the sole use of the tribe or tribes of Indians to whom such reservations belonged; and the same, with interest thereon at three per cent per annum, shall be at all times subject to appropriation by Congress for the education and civilization of such tribe or tribes of Indian or the members thereof.

The patents aforesaid shall be recorded in the General Land Office, and afterward delivered, free of charge, to the allottee entitled thereto.

And if any religious society or other organization is now occupying any of the public lands to which this act is applicable, for religious or educational work among the Indians, the Secretary of the Interior is hereby authorized to confirm such occupation to such society or organization, in quantity not exceeding one hundred and sixty acres in any one tract, so long as the same shall be so occupied, on such terms as he shall deem just; but nothing herein contained shall change or alter any claim of such society for religious or educational purposes theretofore granted by law.

And hereafter in the employment of Indian police, or any other employees in the public service among any of the Indian tribes or bands affected by this act, and where Indians can perform the duties required, those Indians who have availed themselves of the provisions of this act and become citizens of the United States shall be preferred.

SEC. 6. That upon the completion of said allotments and the patenting of the lands to said allottees, each and every member of the respective bands or tribes of Indians to whom allotments have been made shall have the benefit of and be subject to the laws, both civil and criminal, of the State or Territory in which they may reside; and no Territory shall pass or enforce any law denying any such Indian within its jurisdiction the equal protection of the law.

And every Indian born within the territorial limits of the United States to whom allotments shall have been made under the provisions of this act, or under any law or treaty, and every Indian born within the territorial limits of the Untied States who has voluntarily taken up, within said limits, his residence separate and apart from any tribe of Indians therein, and has adopted the habits of civilized life, [and every Indian in Indian Territory,] is hereby declared to be a citizen of the United States, and is entitled to all the rights, privileges, and immunities of such citizens, whether said Indian has been or not, by birth or otherwise, a member of any tribe of Indians within the territorial limits of the United States without in any manner impairing or otherwise affecting the right of any such Indian to tribal or other property.

SEC. 7. That in cases where the use of water for irrigation is necessary to render the lands within any Indian reservation available for agricultural purposes, the Secretary of the Interior be, and he is hereby, authorized to prescribe such rules and regulations as he may deem necessary to secure a just and equal distribution thereof among the Indians residing upon any such reservations; and no other appropriation or grant of water by any riparian proprietor shall be authorized or permitted to the damage of any other riparian proprietor.

SEC. 8. That the provision of this act shall not extend to the territory occupied by the Cherokees, Creeks, Choctaws, Chickasaws, Seminoles, and Osage, Miamies and Peorias, and Sacs and Foxes, in the Indian Territory, nor to any of the reservations of the Seneca Nation of New York Indians in the State of New York; nor to that strip of territory in the State of Nebraska adjoining the Sioux Nation on the south added by executive order.

SEC. 9. That for the purpose of making the surveys and resurveys mentioned in section two of this act, there be, and hereby is, appropriated, of any monies in the Treasury not otherwise appropriated, the sum of one hundred thousand dollars, to be repaid proportionately out of the proceeds of the sales of such land as may be acquired from the Indians under the provisions of this act.

SEC. 10. That nothing in this act contained shall be so construed as to affect the right and power of Congress to grant the right of way through any lands granted to an Indian, or a tribe of Indians, for railroads or other highways, or telegraph lines, for the public use, or to condemn such lands to public uses, upon making just compensation.

SEC. 11. That nothing in this act shall be so construed as to prevent the removal of the Southern Ute Indians from their present reservation in Southwestern Colorado to a new reservation by and with the consent of a majority of the adult male members of said tribe.

Approved, Feb. 8, 1887

Source: Dawes Act of 1887. *U.S. Statutes at Large* 24 (1887): 388-91.

See also: Bureau of Indian Affairs; Dawes Act (1887); Indian Claims Commission; Indian Removal and the Creation of Indian Territory; Indian Reservations. Documents: Andrew Jackson: Indian Removal Message to Congress (1829); Indian Removal Act (1830)

Excerpts from Ida B. Wells' Exposé on Lynching (*The Red Record,* 1895)

Introduction

Noted anti-lynching crusader Ida B. Wells published The Red Record *in 1895. The book, as shown in the excerpt reproduced below, not only provided statistics on lynching, which were mainly gathered from mainstream press accounts, but also offered a detailed overview of the history of lynching in the United States since the Civil War.*

Primary Source

Offenses Charged for Lynching

Suspected arson, 2; stealing, 1; political causes, 1; murder, 45; rape, 29; desperado, 1; suspected incendiarism, 1; train wrecking, 1; enticing servant away, 1; kidnapping, 1; unknown offense, 6; larceny, 1; barn burning, 10; writing letters to a white woman, 1; without cause, 1; burglary, 1; asking white woman to marry, 1; conspiracy, 1; attempted murder, 1; horse stealing, 3; highway robbery, 1; alleged rape, 1; attempted rape, 11; race prejudice, 2; introducing smallpox, 1; giving information, 1; conjuring, 1; incendiarism, 2; arson, 1; assault, 1; no offense, 1; alleged murder, 2; total (colored), 134.

Lynching States

Mississippi, 15; Arkansas, 8; Virginia, 5; Tennessee, 15; Alabama, 12; Kentucky, 12; Texas, 9; Georgia, 19; South Carolina, 5; Florida, 7; Louisiana, 15; Missouri, 4; Ohio, 2; Maryland, 1; West Virginia, 2; Indiana, 1; Kansas, 1; Pennsylvania, 1.

Lynching by Month

January, 11; February, 17; March, 8; April, 36; May, 16; June, 31; July, 21; August, 4; September 17; October, 7; November, 9; December, 20; total colored and white, 197.

Women Lynched

July 24, unknown woman, race prejudice, Sampson County, Miss.; March 6, unknown, woman, unknown offense, Marche, Ark.; Dec. 5, Mrs. Teddy Arthur, unknown cause, Lincoln County, W.Va.

Chapter X. The Remedy

It is a well-established principle of law that every wrong has a remedy. Herein rests our respect for law. The Negro does not claim that all of the one thousand black men, women and children, who have been hanged, shot and burned alive during the past ten years, were innocent of the charges made against them. We have associated too long with the white man not to have copied his vices as well as his virtues. But we do insist that the punishment is not the same for both classes of criminals. In lynching, opportunity is not given the Negro to defend himself against the unsupported accusations of white men and women. The word of the accuser is held true and the excited bloodthirsty mob demands that the rule of law be reversed and instead of proving the accused to be guilty, the victim of their hate and revenge must prove himself innocent. No evidence he can offer will satisfy the mob; he is bound hand and foot and swung into eternity. Then to excuse its infamy, the mob almost invariably reports the monstrous falsehood that its victim made a full confession before he was hanged.

With all military, legal and political power in their hands, only two of the lynching States have attempted a check by exercising the power which is theirs. Mayor Trout, of Roanoke, Virginia, called out the militia in 1893, to protect a Negro prisoner, and in so doing nine men were killed and a number wounded. Then the mayor and militia withdrew, left the Negro to his fate and he was promptly lynched. The businessmen realized the blow to the town's financial interests, [and] called the mayor home. The grand jury indicted and prosecuted the ringleaders of the mob. They were given light sentences, the highest being one of twelve months in State prison. The day he arrived at the penitentiary, he was pardoned by the governor of the State.

The only other real attempt made by the authorities to protect a prisoner of the law, and which was more successful, was that of Gov. McKinley, of Ohio, who sent the militia to Washington Courthouse, O., in October, 1894, and five men were killed and twenty wounded in maintaining the principle that the law must be upheld.

In South Carolina, in April, 1893, Gov. Tillman aided the mob by yielding up to be killed, a prisoner of the law, who had voluntarily placed himself under the Governor's protection. Public sentiment by its representatives has encouraged Lynch Law, and upon the revolution of this sentiment we must depend for its abolition.

Therefore, we demand a fair trial by the law for those accused of crime, and punishment by law after honest conviction. No maudlin sympathy for criminals is solicited, but we do ask that the law shall punish all alike. We earnestly desire those that control the forces which make public sentiment to join with us in the demand. Surely the humanitarian spirit of this country which reaches out to denounce the treatment of the Russian Jews, the Armenian Christians, the laboring poor of Europe, the Siberian exiles and the native women of India—will no longer refuse to lift its voice on this subject. If it were known that the cannibals or the savage Indians had burned three human beings alive in the past two years, the whole of Christendom would be roused to devise ways and means to put a stop to it. Can you remain silent and inactive when such things are done in our own community and country? Is your duty to humanity in the United States less binding?

What can you do, reader, to prevent lynching, to thwart anarchy and promote law and order throughout our land?

1st. You can help disseminate the facts contained in this book by bringing them to the knowledge of every one with whom you come in contact, to the end that public sentiment may be revolutionized. Let the facts speak for themselves, with you as a medium.

2d. You can be instrumental in having churches, missionary societies, Y.M.C.A.'s, W.C.T.U.'s and all Christian and moral forces in connection with your religious and social life, pass resolutions of condemnation and protest every time a lynching takes place; and see that they are sent to the place where these outrages occur.

3d. Bring to the intelligent consideration of Southern people the refusal of capital to invest where lawlessness and mob violence hold sway. Many labor organizations have declared by resolution that they would avoid lynch infested localities as they would the pestilence when seeking new homes. If the South wishes to build up its waste places quickly, there is no better way than to uphold the majesty of the law by enforcing obedience to the same, and meting out the same punishment to all classes of criminals, white as well as black. "Equality before the law," must become a fact as well as a theory before America is truly the "land of the free and the home of the brave."

4th. Think and act on independent lines in this behalf, remembering that after all, it is the white man's civilization and the white man's government which are on trial. This crusade will determine whether that civilization can maintain itself by itself, or whether anarchy shall prevail; whether this Nation shall write itself down a success at self government, or in its deepest humiliation admit its failure complete; whether the precepts and theories of Christianity are professed and practiced by American white people as Golden Rules of thought and action, or adopted as a system of morals to be preached to heathen until they attain to the intelligence which needs the system of Lynch Law.

5th. Congressman Blair [Henry W. Blair, a New Hampshire Republican] offered a resolution in the House of Representatives, August, 1894. The organized life of the country can speedily make this a law by sending resolutions to Congress endorsing Mr. Blair's bill and asking Congress to create the commission. In no better way can the question be settled, and the Negro does not fear the issue. . . .

The belief has been constantly expressed in England that in the United States, which has produced Wm. Lloyd Garrison, Henry Ward Beecher, James Russell Lowell, John G. Whittier and Abraham Lincoln there must be those of their descendants who would take hold of the work of inaugurating an era of law and order. The colored people of this country who have been loyal to the flag believe the same, and strong in that belief have begun this crusade.

> **Source:** Ida B. Wells. *The Red Record: Tabulated Statistics and Alleged Causes of Lynchings in the United States, 1892–1893–1894.* Chicago: Ida B. Wells, 1895.

> **See also:** Anti-Lynching Campaign; Anti-Lynching League; Anti-Lynching Legislation; Lynching. Documents: Excerpts from the NAACP Report (1919); Excerpts from the "Anti-Lynching" Hearings (1920); Excerpts from the Transcripts of *Bee Publishing Company v. State of Nebraska* (1921)

Plessy v. Ferguson (1896)

Introduction

After the federal troops withdrew from the South after the Tilden-Hay Compromise of 1878, Southern states began to develop segregation laws to keep whites and blacks separate. By the 1890s, all Southern states had established various segregation laws that required whites and blacks to use separate facilities in public accommodations, such as trains, buses, motels, parks, and schools. Plessy v. Ferguson (1896) is the most notorious case in which the U.S Supreme Court ruled "equal but separate" facilities (passenger trains) between whites and black was not a violation of the U.S. Constitution (the equal protection of all citizens guaranteed by the Fourteenth Amendment). The Supreme Court decision reflected the segregationist ideology of the time. It was the Brown v. Board of Education case in 1954 that overturned the 1896 decision.

Primary Source

Transcription of the Judgement of the Supreme Court of the United States in *Plessy v. Ferguson*

Supreme Court of the United States,

No. 210, October Term, 1895.

Homer Adolph Plessy,
Plaintiff in Error,
vs.
J. H. Ferguson, Judge of Section "A"
Criminal District Court for the Parish of Orleans

In Error to the Supreme Court of the State of Louisiana

This cause came on to be heard on the transcript of the record from the Supreme Court of the State of Louisiana, and was argued by counsel.

On consideration whereof, It is now here ordered and adjudged by this Court that the judgement of the said Supreme Court, in this cause, be and the same is hereby, affirmed with costs.

per Mr. Justice Brown,

May 18, 1896.

Dissenting:

Mr. Justice Harlan

Transcription of Opinion of the Supreme Court of the United States in *Plessy v. Ferguson*

U.S. Supreme Court

PLESSY v. FERGUSON, **163 U.S. 537 (1896)**

163 U.S. 537

PLESSY

v.

FERGUSON.

No. 210.

May 18, 1896.

This was a petition for writs of prohibition and *certiorari* originally filed in the supreme court of the state by Plessy, the plaintiff in error, against the Hon. John H. Ferguson, judge of the criminal district court for the parish of Orleans, and setting forth, in substance, the following facts:

That petitioner was a citizen of the United States and a resident of the state of Louisiana, of mixed descent, in the proportion of seven-eighths Caucasian and one-eighth African blood; that the mixture of colored blood was not discernible in him, and that he was entitled to every recognition, right, privilege, and immunity secured to the citizens of the United States of the white race by its constitution and laws; that on June 7, 1892, he engaged and paid for a first-class passage on the East Louisiana Railway, from New Orleans to Covington, in the same state, and thereupon entered a passenger train, and took possession of a vacant seat in a coach where passengers of the white race were accommodated; that such railroad company was incorporated by the laws of Louisiana as a common carrier, and was not authorized to distinguish between citizens according to their race, but, notwithstanding this, petitioner was required by the conductor, under penalty of ejection from said train and imprisonment, to vacate said coach, and occupy another seat, in a coach assigned by said company for persons not of the white race, and for no other reason than that petitioner was of the colored race; that, upon petitioner's refusal to comply with such order, he was, with the aid of a police officer, forcibly ejected from said coach, and hurried off to, and imprisoned

in, the parish jail of New Orleans, and there held to answer a charge made by such officer to the effect that he was guilty of having criminally violated an act of the general assembly of the state, approved July 10, 1890, in such case made and provided.

The petitioner was subsequently brought before the recorder of the city for preliminary examination, and committed for trial to the criminal district court for the parish of Orleans, where an information was filed against him in the matter above set forth, for a violation of the above act, which act the petitioner affirmed to be null and void, because in conflict with the constitution of the United States; that petitioner interposed a plea to such information, based upon the unconstitutionality of the act of the general assembly, to which the district attorney, on behalf of the state, filed a demurrer; that, upon issue being joined upon such demurrer and plea, the court sustained the demurrer, overruled the plea, and ordered petitioner to plead over to the facts set forth in the information, and that, unless the judge of the said court be enjoined by a writ of prohibition from further proceeding in such case, the court will proceed to fine and sentence petitioner to imprisonment, and thus deprive him of his constitutional rights set forth in his said plea, notwithstanding the unconstitutionality of the act under which he was being prosecuted; that no appeal lay from such sentence, and petitioner was without relief or remedy except by writs of prohibition and certiorari. Copies of the information and other proceedings in the criminal district court were annexed to the petition as an exhibit.

Upon the filing of this petition, an order was issued upon the respondent to show cause why a writ of prohibition should not issue, and be made perpetual, and a further order that the record of the proceedings had in the criminal cause be certified and transmitted to the supreme court.

To this order the respondent made answer, transmitting a certified copy of the proceedings, asserting the constitutionality of the law, and averring that, instead of pleading or admitting that he belonged to the colored race, the said Plessy declined and refused, either by pleading or otherwise, to admit that he was in any sense or in any proportion a colored man.

The case coming on for hearing before the supreme court, that court was of opinion that the law under which the prosecution was had was constitutional and denied the relief prayed for by the petitioner (*Ex parte Plessy*, 45 La. Ann. 80, 11 South. 948); whereupon petitioner prayed for a writ of error from this court, which was allowed by the chief justice of the supreme court of Louisiana.

Mr. Justice Harlan dissenting.

A. W. Tourgee and S. F. Phillips, for plaintiff in error.

Alex. Porter Morse, for defendant in error.

Mr. Justice BROWN, after stating the facts in the foregoing language, delivered the opinion of the court.

This case turns upon the constitutionality of an act of the general assembly of the state of Louisiana, passed in 1890, providing for separate railway carriages for the white and colored races. Acts 1890, No. 111, p. 152.

The first section of the statute enacts "that all railway companies carrying passengers in their coaches in this state, shall provide equal but separate accommodations for the white, and colored races, by providing two or more passenger coaches for each passenger train, or by dividing the passenger coaches by a partition so as to secure separate accommodations: provided, that this section shall not be construed to apply to street railroads. No person or persons shall be permitted to occupy seats in coaches, other than the ones assigned to them, on account of the race they belong to."

By the second section it was enacted "that the officers of such passenger trains shall have power and are hereby required to assign each passenger to the coach or compartment used for the race to which such passenger belongs; any passenger insisting on going into a coach or compartment to which by race he does not belong, shall be liable to a fine of twenty-five dollars, or in lieu thereof to imprisonment for a period of not more than twenty days in the parish prison, and any officer of any railroad insisting on assigning a passenger to a coach or compartment other than the one set aside for the race to which said passenger belongs, shall be liable to a fine of twenty-five dollars, or in lieu thereof to imprisonment for a period of not more than twenty days in the parish prison; and should any passenger refuse to occupy the coach or compartment to which he or she is assigned by the officer of such railway, said officer shall have power to refuse to carry such passenger on his train, and for such refusal neither he nor the railway company which he represents shall be liable for damages in any of the courts of this state."

The third section provides penalties for the refusal or neglect of the officers, directors, conductors, and employees of railway companies to comply with the act, with a proviso that "nothing in this act shall be construed as applying to nurses attending children of the other race." The fourth section is immaterial.

The information filed in the criminal district court charged, in substance, that Plessy, being a passenger between two stations within the state of Louisiana, was assigned by officers of the company to the coach used for the race to which he belonged, but he insisted upon going into a coach used by the race to which he did not belong. Neither in the information nor plea was his particular race or color averred.

The petition for the writ of prohibition averred that petitioner was seven-eighths Caucasian and one-eighth African blood; that the mixture of colored blood was not discernible in him; and that he was entitled to every right, privilege, and immunity secured to citizens of the United States of the white race; and that, upon such theory, he took possession of a vacant seat in a coach where passengers of the white race were accommodated, and was ordered by the conductor to vacate said coach, and take a seat in another, assigned to persons of the colored race, and, having refused to comply with such demand, he was forcibly ejected, with the aid of a police officer, and imprisoned in the parish jail to answer a charge of having violated the above act.

The constitutionality of this act is attacked upon the ground that it conflicts both with the thirteenth amendment of the constitution, abolishing slavery, and the fourteenth amendment, which prohibits certain restrictive legislation on the part of the states.

1. That it does not conflict with the thirteenth amendment, which abolished slavery and involuntary servitude, except a punishment for crime, is too clear for argument. Slavery implies involuntary servitude,—a state of bondage; the ownership of mankind as a chattel, or, at least, the control of the labor and services of one man for the benefit of another, and the absence of a legal right to the disposal of his own person, property, and services. This amendment was said in the Slaughter-House Cases, 16 Wall. 36, to have been intended primarily to abolish slavery, as it had been previously known in this country, and that it equally forbade Mexican peonage or the Chinese coolie trade, when they amounted to slavery or involuntary servitude, and that the use of the word "servitude" was intended to prohibit the use of all forms of involuntary slavery, of whatever class or name. It was intimated, however, in that case, that this amendment was regarded by the statesmen of that day as insufficient to protect the colored race from certain laws which had been enacted in the Southern states, imposing upon the colored race onerous disabilities and burdens, and curtailing their rights in the pursuit of life, liberty, and property to such an extent that their freedom was of little value; and that the fourteenth amendment was devised to meet this exigency.

So, too, in the Civil Rights Cases, 109 U.S. 3, 3 Sup. Ct. 18, it was said that the act of a mere individual, the owner of an inn, a public conveyance or place of amusement, refusing accommodations to colored people, cannot be justly regarded as imposing any badge of slavery or servitude upon the applicant, but only as involving an ordinary civil injury, properly cognizable by the laws of the state, and presumably subject to redress by those laws until the contrary appears. "It would be running the slavery question into the ground," said Mr. Justice Bradley, "to make it apply to every act of discrimination which a person may see fit to make as to the guests he will entertain, or as to the people he will take into his coach or cab or car, or admit to his concert or theater, or deal with in other matters of intercourse or business."

A statute which implies merely a legal distinction between the white and colored races—a distinction which is founded in the color of the two races, and which must always exist so long as white men are distinguished from the other race by color—has no tendency to destroy the legal equality of the two races, or re-establish a state of involuntary servitude. Indeed, we do not understand that the thirteenth amendment is strenuously relied upon by the plaintiff in error in this connection.

2. By the fourteenth amendment, all persons born or naturalized in the United States, and subject to the jurisdiction thereof, are made citizens of the United States and of the state wherein they reside; and the states are forbidden from making or enforcing any law which shall abridge the privileges or immunities of citizens of the United States, or shall deprive any person of life, liberty, or property without due process of law, or deny to any person within their jurisdiction the equal protection of the laws.

The proper construction of this amendment was first called to the attention of this court in the Slaughter-House Cases, 16 Wall. 36, which involved, however, not a question of race, but one of exclusive privileges. The case did not call for any expression of opinion as to the exact rights it was intended to secure to the colored race, but it was said generally that its main purpose was to establish the citizenship of the negro, to give definitions of citizenship of the United States and of the states, and to protect from the hostile legislation of the states the privileges and immunities of citizens of the United States, as distinguished from those of citizens of the states. The object of the amendment was undoubtedly to enforce the absolute equality of the two races before the law, but, in the nature of things, it could not have been intended to abolish distinctions based upon color, or to enforce social, as distinguished from political, equality, or a commingling of the two races upon terms unsatisfactory to either. Laws permitting, and even requiring, their separation, in places where they are liable to be brought into contact, do not necessarily imply the inferiority of either race to the other, and have been generally, if not universally, recognized as within the competency of the state legislatures in the exercise of their police power. The most common instance of this is connected with the establishment of separate schools for white and colored children, which have been held to be a valid exercise of the legislative power even by courts of states where the political rights of the colored race have been longest and most earnestly enforced.

One of the earliest of these cases is that of *Roberts v. City of Boston*, 5 Cush. 198, in which the supreme judicial court of Massachusetts held that the general school committee of Boston had power to make provision for the instruction of colored children in separate schools established exclusively for them, and to prohibit their attendance upon the other schools. "The great principle," said Chief Justice Shaw, "advanced by the learned and eloquent advocate for the plaintiff [Mr. Charles Sumner], is that, by the constitution and laws of Massachusetts, all persons, without distinction of age or sex, birth or color, origin or condition, are equal before the law. . . . But, when this great principle comes to be applied to the actual and various conditions of persons in society, it will not warrant the assertion that men and women are legally clothed with the same civil and political powers, and that children and adults are legally to have the same functions and be subject to the same treatment; but only that the rights of all, as they are settled and regulated by law, are equally entitled to the paternal consideration and protection of the law for their maintenance and security." It was held that the powers of the committee extended to the establishment of separate schools for children of different ages, sexes and colors, and that they might also establish special schools for poor and neglected children, who have become too old to attend the primary school, and yet have not acquired the rudiments of learning, to enable them to enter the ordinary schools. Similar laws have been enacted by congress under its general power of legislation over the District of Columbia (sections 281–283, 310, 319, Rev. St. D. C.), as well as by the legislatures of many of the states, and have been generally, if not uniformly, sustained by the courts. *State v. McCann*, 21 Ohio St. 210; *Lehew v. Brummell* (Mo. Sup.) 15 S. W. 765; *Ward v. Flood*, 48 Cal. 36; *Bertonneau v. Directors of City Schools*, 3 Woods, 177, Fed. Cas. No. 1,361; *People v. Gallagher*, 93 N. Y. 438; *Cory v. Carter*, 48 Ind. 337; *Dawson v. Lee*, 83 Ky. 49.

Laws forbidding the intermarriage of the two races may be said in a technical sense to interfere with the freedom of contract, and yet have been universally recognized as within the police power of the state. *State v. Gibson*, 36 Ind. 389.

The distinction between laws interfering with the political equality of the negro and those requiring the separation of the two races in schools, theaters, and railway carriages has been frequently drawn by this court. Thus, in *Strauder v. West Virginia*, 100 U.S. 303, it was held that a law of West Virginia limiting to white male persons 21 years of age, and citizens of the state, the right to sit upon juries, was a discrimination which implied a legal inferiority in civil society, which lessened the security of the right of the colored race, and was a step towards reducing them to a condition of servility. Indeed, the right of a colored man that, in the selection of jurors to pass upon his life, liberty, and property, there shall be no exclusion of his race, and no discrimination against them because of color, has been asserted in a number of cases. *Virginia v. Rivers*, 100 U.S. 313; *Neal v. Delaware*, 103 U.S. 370; *Bush v. Com.*, 107 U.S. 110, 1 Sup. Ct. 625; *Gibson v. Mississippi*, 162 U.S. 565, 16 Sup. Ct. 904. So, where the laws of a particular locality or the charter of a particular railway corporation has provided that no person shall be excluded from the cars on account of color, we have held that this meant that persons of color should travel in the same car as white ones, and that the enactment was not satisfied by the company providing cars assigned exclusively to people of color, though they were as good as those which they assigned exclusively to white persons. *Railroad Co. v. Brown*, 17 Wall. 445.

Upon the other hand, where a statute of Louisiana required those engaged in the transportation of passengers among the states to give to all persons traveling within that state, upon vessels employed in that business, equal rights and privileges in all parts of the vessel, without distinction on account of race or color, and subjected to an action for damages the owner of such a vessel who excluded colored passengers on account of their color from the cabin set aside by him for the use of whites, it was held to be, so far as it applied to interstate commerce, unconstitutional and void. *Hall v. De Cuir*, 95 U.S. 485. The court in this case, however, expressly disclaimed that it had anything whatever to do with the statute as a regulation of internal commerce, or affecting anything else than commerce among the states.

In the Civil Rights Cases, 109 U.S. 3, 3 Sup. Ct. 18, it was held that an act of congress entitling all persons within the jurisdiction of the United States to the full and equal enjoyment of the accommodations, advantages, facilities, and privileges of inns, public conveyances, on land or water, theaters, and other places of public amusement, and made applicable to citizens of every race and color, regardless of any previous condition of servitude, was unconstitutional and void, upon the ground that the fourteenth amendment was prohibitory upon the states only, and the legislation authorized to be adopted by congress for enforcing it was not direct legislation on matters respecting which the states were prohibited from making or enforcing certain laws, or doing certain acts, but was corrective legislation, such as might be necessary or proper for counter-acting and redressing the effect of such laws or acts. In delivering the opinion of the court, Mr. Justice Bradley observed that the fourteenth amendment "does not invest congress with power to legislate upon subjects that are within the domain of state legislation, but to provide modes of relief against state legislation or state action of the kind referred to. It does not authorize congress to create a code of municipal law for the regulation of private rights, but to provide modes of redress against the operation of state laws, and the action of state officers, executive or judicial, when these are subversive of the fundamental rights specified in the amendment. Positive rights and privileges are undoubtedly secured by the fourteenth amendment; but they are secured by way of prohibition against state laws and state proceedings affecting those rights and privileges, and by power given to congress to legislate for the purpose of carrying such prohibition into effect; and such legislation must necessarily be predicated upon such supposed state laws or state proceedings, and be directed to the correction of their operation and effect."

Much nearer, and, indeed, almost directly in point, is the case of the *Louisville, N. O. & T. Ry. Co. v. State*, 133 U.S. 587, 10 Sup. Ct. 348, wherein the railway company was indicted for a violation of a statute of Mississippi, enacting that all railroads carrying passengers should provide equal, but separate, accommodations for the white and colored races, by providing two or more passenger cars for each passenger train, or by dividing the passenger cars by a partition, so as to secure separate accommodations. The case was presented in a different aspect from the one under consideration, inasmuch as it was an indictment against the railway company for failing to provide the separate accommodations, but the question considered was the constitutionality of the law. In that case, the supreme court of Mississippi (66 Miss. 662, 6 South. 203) had held that the statute applied solely to commerce within the state, and, that being the construction of the state statute by its highest court, was accepted as conclusive. "If it be a matter," said the court (page 591, 133 U.S., and page 348, 10 Sup. Ct.), "respecting commerce wholly within a state, and not interfering with commerce between the states, then, obviously, there is no violation of the commerce clause of the federal constitution. . . . No question arises under this section as to the power of the state to separate in different compartments interstate passengers, or affect, in any manner, the privileges and rights of such passengers. All that we can consider is whether the state has the power to require that railroad trains within her limits shall have separate accommodations for the two races. That affecting only commerce within the state is no invasion of the power given to congress by the commerce clause."

A like course of reasoning applies to the case under consideration, since the supreme court of Louisiana, in the case of *State v. Judge*, 44 La. Ann. 770, 11 South. 74, held that the statute in question did not apply to interstate passengers, but was confined in its application to passengers traveling exclusively within the borders of the state. The case was decided largely upon the authority of *Louisville, N. O. & T. Ry. Co. v. State*, 66 Miss. 662, 6 South, 203, and affirmed by this court in 133 U.S. 587, 10 Sup. Ct. 348. In the present case no question of interference with interstate commerce can possibly arise, since the East Louisiana Railway appears to have been purely a local line, with both its termini within the state of Louisiana. Similar statutes for the separation of the two races upon public conveyances were held to be constitutional in *Railroad v. Miles*, 55 Pa. St. 209; *Day v. Owen*, 5 Mich. 520; *Railway Co. v. Williams*, 55 Ill. 185; *Railroad Co. v. Wells*, 85 Tenn. 613; 4 S. W. 5; *Railroad Co. v. Benson*, 85 Tenn. 627, 4 S. W. 5; The Sue, 22 Fed. 843; *Logwood v. Railroad Co.*, 23 Fed. 318; *McGuinn v. Forbes*, 37 Fed. 639; *People v. King* (N. Y. App.) 18 N. E. 245; *Houck v. Railway Co.*, 38 Fed. 226; *Heard v. Railroad Co.*, 3 Inter St. Commerce Com. R. 111, 1 Inter St. Commerce Com. R. 428.

While we think the enforced separation of the races, as applied to the internal commerce of the state, neither abridges the privileges or immunities of the colored man, deprives him of his property without due process of law, nor denies him the equal protection of the laws, within the meaning of the fourteenth amendment, we are not prepared to say that the conductor, in assigning passengers to the coaches according to their race, does not act at his peril, or that the provision of the second section of the act that denies to the passenger compensation in damages for a refusal to receive him into the coach in which he properly belongs is a valid exercise of the legislative power. Indeed, we understand it to be conceded by the state's attorney that such part of the act as exempts from liability the railway company and its officers is unconstitutional. The power to assign to a particular coach obviously implies the power to determine to which race the passenger belongs, as well as the power to determine who, under the laws of the particular state, is to be deemed a white, and who a colored, person. This question, though indicated in the brief of the plaintiff in error, does not properly arise upon the record in this case, since the only issue made is as to the unconstitutionality of the act, so far as it requires the railway to provide separate accommodations, and the conductor to assign passengers according to their race.

It is claimed by the plaintiff in error that, in an mixed community, the reputation of belonging to the dominant race, in this instance the white race, is "property," in the same sense that a right of action or of inheritance is property. Conceding this to be so, for the purposes of this case, we are unable to see how this statute deprives him of, or in any way affects his right to, such property. If he be a white man, and assigned to a colored coach, he may have his action for damages against the company for being deprived of his so-called "property." Upon the other hand, if he be a colored man, and be so assigned, he has been deprived of no property, since he is not lawfully entitled to the reputation of being a white man.

In this connection, it is also suggested by the learned counsel for the plaintiff in error that the same argument that will justify the state legislature in requiring railways to provide separate accommodations for the two races will also authorize them to require separate cars to be provided for people whose hair is of a certain color, or who are aliens, or who belong to certain nationalities, or to enact laws requiring colored people to walk upon one side of the street, and white people upon the other, or requiring white men's houses to be painted white, and colored men's black, or their vehicles or business signs to be of different colors, upon the theory that one side of the street is as good as the other, or that a house or vehicle of one color is as good as one of another color. The reply to all this is that every exercise of the police power must be reasonable, and extend only to such laws as are enacted in good faith for the promotion of the public good, and not for the annoyance or oppression of a particular class. Thus, in *Yick Wo v. Hopkins*, 118 U.S. 356, 6 Sup. Ct. 1064, it was held by this court that a municipal ordinance of the city of San Francisco, to regulate the carrying on of public laundries within the limits of the municipality, violated the provisions of the constitution of the United States, if it conferred upon the municipal authorities arbitrary power, at their own will, and without regard to discretion, in the legal sense of the term, to give or withhold consent as to persons or places, without regard to the competency of the persons applying or the propriety of the places selected for the carrying on of the business. It was held to be a covert attempt on the part of the municipality to make an arbitrary and unjust discrimination against the Chinese race. While this was the case of a municipal ordinance, a like principle has been held to apply to acts of a state legislature passed in the exercise of the police power. *Railroad Co. v. Husen*, 95 U.S. 465; *Louisville & N. R. Co. v. Kentucky*, 161 U.S. 677, 16 Sup. Ct. 714, and cases cited on page 700, 161 U.S., and page 714, 16 Sup. Ct.; *Daggett v. Hudson*, 43 Ohio St. 548, 3 N. E. 538; *Capen v. Foster*, 12 Pick. 485; *State v. Baker*, 38 Wis. 71; *Monroe v. Collins*, 17 Ohio St. 665; *Hulseman v. Rems*, 41 Pa. St. 396; *Osman v. Riley*, 15 Cal. 48.

So far, then, as a conflict with the fourteenth amendment is concerned, the case reduces itself to the question whether the statute of Louisiana is a reasonable regulation, and with respect to this there must necessarily be a large discretion on the part of the legislature. In determining the question of reasonableness, it is at liberty to act with reference to the established usages, customs, and traditions of the people, and with a view to the promotion of their comfort, and the preservation of the public peace and good order. Gauged by this standard, we cannot say that a law which authorizes or even requires the separation of the two races in public conveyances is unreasonable, or more obnoxious to the fourteenth amendment than the acts of congress requiring separate schools for colored children in the District of Columbia, the constitutionality of which does not seem to have been questioned, or the corresponding acts of state legislatures.

We consider the underlying fallacy of the plaintiff's argument to consist in the assumption that the enforced separation of the two races stamps the colored race with a badge of inferiority. If this be so, it is not by reason of anything found in the act, but solely because the colored race chooses to put that construction upon it. The argument necessarily assumes that if, as has been more than once the case, and is not unlikely to be so again, the colored race should become the dominant power in the state legislature, and should enact a law in precisely similar terms, it would thereby relegate the white race to an inferior position. We imagine that the white race, at least, would not acquiesce in this assumption. The argument also assumes that social prejudices may be overcome by legislation, and that equal rights cannot be secured to the negro except by an enforced commingling of the two races. We cannot accept this proposition. If the two races are to meet upon terms of social equality, it must be the result of natural affinities, a mutual appreciation of each other's merits, and a voluntary consent of individuals. As was said by the court of appeals of New York in *People v. Gallagher*, 93 N. Y. 438, 448: "This end can neither be accomplished nor promoted by laws which conflict with the general sentiment of the community upon whom they are designed to operate. When the government, therefore, has secured to each of its citizens equal rights before the law, and equal opportunities for improvement and progress, it has accomplished the end for which it was organized, and performed all of the functions respecting social advantages with which it is endowed." Legislation is powerless to eradicate racial instincts, or to abolish distinctions based upon physical differences, and the attempt to do so can only result in accentuating the difficulties of the present situation. If the civil and political rights of both races be equal, one cannot be inferior to the other civilly or politically. If one race be inferior to the other socially, the constitution of the United States cannot put them upon the same plane.

It is true that the question of the proportion of colored blood necessary to constitute a colored person, as distinguished from a white person, is one upon which there is a difference of opinion in the different states; some holding that any visible admixture of black blood stamps the person as belonging to the colored race (*State v. Chavers*, 5 Jones [N. C.] 1); others, that it depends upon the preponderance of blood (*Gray v. State*, 4 Ohio, 354; *Monroe v. Collins*, 17 Ohio St. 665); and still others, that the predominance of white blood must only be in the proportion of three-fourths (*People v. Dean*, 14 Mich. 406; *Jones v. Com.*, 80 Va. 544). But these are questions to be determined under the laws of each state, and are not properly put in issue in this case. Under the allegations of his petition, it may undoubtedly become a question of importance whether, under the laws of Louisiana, the petitioner belongs to the white or colored race.

The judgment of the court below is therefore affirmed.

Mr. Justice BREWER did not hear the argument or participate in the decision of this case.

Mr. Justice HARLAN dissenting.

By the Louisiana statute the validity of which is here involved, all railway companies (other than street-railroad companies) carry passengers in that state are required to have separate but equal accommodations for white and colored persons, "by providing two or more passenger coaches for each passenger train, or by dividing the passenger coaches by a partition so as to secure separate accommodations." Under this statute, no colored person is permitted to occupy a seat in a coach assigned to white persons; nor any white person to occupy a seat in a coach assigned to colored persons. The managers of the railroad are not allowed to exercise any discretion in the premises, but are required to assign each passenger to some coach or compartment set apart for the exclusive use of is race. If a passenger insists upon going into a coach or compartment not set apart for persons of his race, he is subject to be fined, or to be imprisoned in the parish jail. Penalties are prescribed for the refusal or neglect of the officers, directors, conductors, and employees of railroad companies to comply with the provisions of the act.

Only "nurses attending children of the other race" are excepted from the operation of the statute. No exception is made of colored attendants traveling with adults. A white man is not permitted to have his colored servant with him in the same coach, even if his condition of health requires the constant personal assistance of such servant. If a colored maid insists upon riding in the same coach with a white woman whom she has been employed to serve, and who may need her personal attention while traveling, she is subject to be fined or imprisoned for such an exhibition of zeal in the discharge of duty.

While there may be in Louisiana persons of different races who are not citizens of the United States, the words in the act "white and colored races" necessarily include all citizens of the United States of both races residing in that state. So that we have before us a state enactment that compels, under penalties, the separation of the two races in railroad passenger coaches, and makes it a crime for a citizen of either race to enter a coach that has been assigned to citizens of the other race.

Thus, the state regulates the use of a public highway by citizens of the United States solely upon the basis of race.

However apparent the injustice of such legislation may be, we have only to consider whether it is consistent with the constitution of the United States.

That a railroad is a public highway, and that the corporation which owns or operates it is in the exercise of public functions, is not, at this day, to be disputed. Mr. Justice Nelson, speaking for this court in *New Jersey Steam Nav. Co. v. Merchants' Bank*, 6 How. 344, 382, said that a common carrier was in the exercise "of a sort of public office, and has public duties to perform, from which he should not be permitted to exonerate himself without the assent of the parties concerned." Mr. Justice Strong, delivering the judgment of this court in *Olcott v. Supervisors*, 16 Wall. 678, 694, said: "That railroads, though constructed by private corporations, and owned by them, are public highways, has been the doctrine of nearly all the courts ever since such conveniences for passage and transportation have had any existence. Very early the question arose whether a state's right of eminent

domain could be exercised by a private corporation created for the purpose of constructing a railroad. Clearly, it could not, unless taking land for such a purpose by such an agency is taking land for public use. The right of eminent domain nowhere justifies taking property for a private use. Yet it is a doctrine universally accepted that a state legislature may authorize a private corporation to take land for the construction of such a road, making compensation to the owner. What else does this doctrine mean if not that building a railroad, though it be built by a private corporation, is an act done for a public use?" So, in *Township of Pine Grove v. Talcott*, 19 Wall. 666, 676: "Though the corporation [a railroad company] was private, its work was public, as much so as if it were to be constructed by the state." So, in *Inhabitants of Worcester v. Western R. Corp.*, 4 Metc. (Mass.) 564: "The establishment of that great thoroughfare is regarded as a public work, established by public authority, intended for the public use and benefit, the use of which is secured to the whole community, and constitutes, therefore, like a canal, turnpike, or highway, a public easement." "It is true that the real

and personal property, necessary to the establishment and management of the railroad, is vested in the corporation; but it is in trust for the public."

In respect of civil rights, common to all citizens, the constitution of the United States does not, I think, permit any public authority to know the race of those entitled to be protected in the enjoyment of such rights. Every true man has pride of race, and under appropriate circumstances, when the rights of others, his equals before the law, are not to be affected, it is his privilege to express such pride and to take such action based upon it as to him seems proper. But I deny that any legislative body or judicial tribunal may have regard to the race of citizens when the civil rights of those citizens are involved. Indeed, such legislation as that here in question is inconsistent not only with that equality of rights which pertains to citizenship, national and state, but with the personal liberty enjoyed by every one within the United States.

The thirteenth amendment does not permit the withholding or the deprivation of any right necessarily inhering in freedom. It not only struck down the institution of slavery as previously existing in the United States, but it prevents the imposition of any burdens or disabilities that constitute badges of slavery or servitude. It decreed universal civil freedom in this country. This court has so adjudged. But, that amendment having been found inadequate to the protection of the rights of those who had been in slavery, it was followed by the fourteenth amendment, which added greatly to the dignity and glory of American citizenship, and to the security of personal liberty, by declaring that "all persons born or naturalized in the United States, and subject to the jurisdiction thereof, are citizens of the United States and of the state wherein they reside," and that "no state shall make or enforce any law which shall abridge the privileges or immunities of citizens of the United States; nor shall any state deprive any person of life, liberty or property without due process of law, nor deny to any person within its jurisdiction the equal protection of the laws." These two amendments, if enforced according to their true intent and meaning, will protect all the civil rights that pertain to freedom and citizenship. Finally, and to the end that no citizen should be denied, on account of his race, the privilege of participating in the political control of his country, it was declared by the fifteenth amendment that "the right of citizens of the United States to vote shall not be denied or abridged by the United States or by any state on account of race, color or previous condition of servitude."

These notable additions to the fundamental law were welcomed by the friends of liberty throughout the world. They removed the race line from our governmental systems. They had, as this court has said, a common purpose, namely, to secure "to a race recently emancipated, a race that through many generations have been held in slavery, all the civil rights that the superior race enjoy." They declared, in legal effect, this court has further said, "that the law in the states shall be the same for the black as for the white; that all persons, whether colored or white, shall stand equal before the laws of the states; and in regard to the colored race, for whose protection the amendment was primarily designed, that no discrimination shall be made against them by law because of their color." We also said: "The words of the amendment, it is true, are prohibitory, but they contain a necessary implication of a positive immunity or right, most valuable to the colored race,-the right to exemption from unfriendly

legislation against them distinctively as colored; exemption from legal discriminations, implying inferiority in civil society, lessening the security of their enjoyment of the rights which others enjoy; and discriminations which are steps towards reducing them to the condition of a subject race." It was, consequently, adjudged that a state law that excluded citizens of the colored race from juries, because of their race, however well qualified in other respects to discharge the duties of jurymen, was repugnant to the fourteenth amendment. *Strauder v. West Virginia*, 100 U.S. 303, 306, 307 S.; *Virginia v. Rives*, Id. 313; *Ex parte Virginia*, Id. 339; *Neal v. Delaware*, 103 U.S. 370, 386; *Bush v. Com.*, 107 U.S. 110, 116, 1 S. Sup. Ct. 625. At the present term, referring to the previous adjudications, this court declared that "underlying all of those decisions is the principle that the constitution of the United States, in its present form, forbids, so far as civil and political rights are concerned, discrimination by the general government or the states against any citizen because of his race. All citizens are equal before the law." *Gibson v. State*, 162 U.S. 565, 16 Sup. Ct. 904.

The decisions referred to show the scope of the recent amendments of the constitution. They also show that it is not within the power of a state to prohibit colored citizens, because of their race, from participating as jurors in the administration of justice.

It was said in argument that the statute of Louisiana does not discriminate against either race, but prescribes a rule applicable alike to white and colored citizens. But this argument does not meet the difficulty. Every one knows that the statute in question had its origin in the purpose, not so much to exclude white persons from railroad cars occupied by blacks, as to exclude colored people from coaches occupied by or assigned to white persons. Railroad corporations of Louisiana did not make discrimination among whites in the matter of commodation for travelers. The thing to accomplish was, under the guise of giving equal accommodation for whites and blacks, to compel the latter to keep to themselves while traveling in railroad passenger coaches. No one would be so wanting in candor as to assert the contrary. The fundamental objection, therefore, to the statute, is that it interferes with the personal freedom of citizens. "Personal liberty," it has been well said, "consists in the power of locomotion, of changing situation, or removing one's person to whatsoever places one's own inclination may direct, without imprisonment or restraint, unless by due course of law." 1 Bl. Comm. *134. If a white man and a black man choose to occupy the same public conveyance on a public highway, it is their right to do so; and no government, proceeding alone on grounds of race, can prevent it without infringing the personal liberty of each.

It is one thing for railroad carriers to furnish, or to be required by law to furnish, equal accommodations for all whom they are under a legal duty to carry. It is quite another thing for government to forbid citizens of the white and black races from traveling in the same public conveyance, and to punish officers of railroad companies for permitting persons of the two races to occupy the same passenger coach. If a state can prescribe, as a rule of civil conduct, that whites and blacks shall not travel as passengers in the same railroad coach, why may it not so regulate the use of the streets of its cities and towns as to compel white citizens to keep on one side of a street, and black citizens to keep on the other? Why may it not, upon like grounds, punish whites and blacks who ride together in street cars or in open vehicles on a public road or street? Why may it not require sheriffs to assign whites to one side of a court room, and blacks to the other? And why may it not also prohibit the commingling of the two races in the galleries of legislative halls or in public assemblages convened for the consideration of the political questions of the day? Further, if this statute of Louisiana is consistent with the personal liberty of citizens, why may not the state require the separation in railroad coaches of native and naturalized citizens of the United States, or of Protestants and Roman Catholics?

The answer given at the argument to these questions was that regulations of the kind they suggest would be unreasonable, and could not, therefore, stand before the law. Is it meant that the determination of questions of legislative power depends upon the inquiry whether the statute whose validity is questioned is, in the judgment of the courts, a reasonable one, taking all the circumstances into consideration? A statute may be unreasonable merely because a sound public policy forbade its enactment. But I do not understand that the courts have anything to do with the policy or expediency of legislation. A statute may be valid, and yet, upon grounds of public policy, may well be characterized as unreasonable. Mr. Sedgwick correctly states the rule when he says that, the legislative intention being clearly ascertained, "the courts have no other duty to perform than to execute the legislative will, without any regard to their views as to the wisdom or justice of the particular enactment." Sedg. St. & Const. Law, 324. There is a dangerous tendency in these latter days to enlarge the functions of the courts, by means of judicial interference with the will of the people as expressed by the legislature. Our institutions have the distinguishing characteristic that the three departments of government are co-ordinate and separate. Each much keep within the limits defined by the constitution. And the courts best discharge their duty by executing the will of the law-making power, constitutionally expressed, leaving the results of legislation to be dealt with by the people through their representatives. Statutes must always have a reasonable construction. Sometimes they are to be construed strictly, sometimes literally, in order to carry out the legislative will. But, however construed, the intent of the legislature is to be respected if the particular statute in question is valid, although the courts, looking at the public interests, may conceive the statute to be both unreasonable and impolitic. If the power exists to enact a statute, that ends the matter so far as the courts are concerned. The adjudged cases in which statutes have been held to be void, because unreasonable, are those in which the means employed by the legislature were not at all germane to the end to which the legislature was competent.

The white race deems itself to be the dominant race in this country. And so it is, in prestige, in achievements, in education, in wealth, and in power. So, I doubt not, it will continue to be for all time, if it remains true to its great heritage, and holds fast to the principles of constitutional liberty. But in view of the constitution, in the eye of the law, there is in this country no superior, dominant, ruling class of citizens. There is no caste here. Our constitution is color-blind, and neither knows nor tolerates classes among citizens. In respect of civil rights, all citizens are equal before the law. The humblest is the peer of the most powerful. The law regards man as man, and takes no account of his surroundings or of his color when his civil rights as guaranteed by the supreme law of the land are involved. It is therefore to be regretted that this high tribunal, the final expositor of the fundamental law of the land, has reached the conclusion that it is competent for a state to regulate the enjoyment by citizens of their civil rights solely upon the basis of race.

In my opinion, the judgment this day rendered will, in time, prove to be quite as pernicious as the decision made by this tribunal in the Dred Scott Case.

It was adjudged in that case that the descendants of Africans who were imported into this country, and sold as slaves, were not included nor intended to be included under the word "citizens" in the constitution, and could not claim any of the rights and privileges which that instrument provided for and secured to citizens of the United States; that, at time of the adoption of the constitution, they were "considered as a subordinate and inferior class of beings, who had been subjugated by the dominant race, and, whether emancipated or not, yet remained subject to their authority, and had no rights or privileges but such as those who held the power and the government might choose to grant them." 17 How. 393, 404. The recent amendments of the constitution, it was supposed, had eradicated these principles from our institutions. But it seems that we have yet, in some of the states, a dominant race,-a superior class of citizens,—which assumes to regulate the enjoyment of civil rights, common to all citizens, upon the basis of race. The present decision, it may well be apprehended, will not only stimulate aggressions, more or less brutal and irritating, upon the admitted rights of colored citizens, but will encourage the belief that it is possible, by means of state enactments, to defeat the beneficent purposes which the people of the United States had in view when they adopted the recent amendments of the constitution, by one of which the blacks of this country were made citizens of the United States and of the states in which they respectively reside, and whose privileges and immunities, as citizens, the states are forbidden to abridge. Sixty millions of whites are in no danger from the presence here of eight millions of blacks. The destinies of the two races, in this country, are indissolubly linked together, and the interests of both require that the common government of all shall not permit the seeds of race hate to be planted under the sanction of law. What can more certainly arouse race hate, what more certainly create and perpetuate a feeling of distrust between these races, than state enactments which, in fact, proceed on the ground that colored citizens are so inferior and degraded that they cannot be allowed to sit in public coaches occupied by white citizens? That, as all will admit, is the real meaning of such legislation as was enacted in Louisiana.

The sure guaranty of the peace and security of each race is the clear, distinct, unconditional recognition by our governments, national and state, of every right that inheres in civil freedom, and of the equality before the law of all citizens of the United States, without regard to race. State enactments regulating the enjoyment of civil rights upon the basis of race, and cunningly devised to defeat legitimate results of the war, under the pretense of recognizing equality of rights, can have no other result than to render permanent peace impossible, and to keep alive a conflict of races, the continuance of which must do harm to all concerned. This question is not met by the suggestion that social equality cannot exist between the white and black races in this country. That argument, if it can be properly regarded as one, is scarcely worthy of consideration; for social equality no more exists between two races when traveling in a passenger coach or a public highway than when members of the same races sit by each other in a street car or in the jury box, or stand or sit with each other in a political assembly, or when they use in common the streets of a city or town, or when they are in the same room for the purpose of having their names placed on the registry of voters, or when they approach the ballot box in order to exercise the high privilege of voting.

There is a race so different from our own that we do not permit those belonging to it to become citizens of the United States. Persons belonging to it are, with few exceptions, absolutely excluded from our country. I allude to the Chinese race. But, by the statute in question, a Chinaman can ride in the same passenger coach with white citizens of the United States, while citizens of the black race in Louisiana, many of whom, perhaps, risked their lives for the preservation of the Union, who are entitled, by law, to participate in the political control of the state and nation, who are not excluded, by law or by reason of their race, from public stations of any kind, and who have all the legal rights that belong to white citizens, are yet declared to be criminals, liable to imprisonment, if they ride in a public coach occupied by citizens of the white race. It is scarcely just to say that a colored citizen should not object to occupying a public coach assigned to his own race.

He does not object, nor, perhaps, would he object to separate coaches for his race if his rights under the law were recognized. But he does object, and he ought never to cease objecting, that citizens of the white and black races can be adjudged criminals because they sit, or claim the right to sit, in the same public coach on a public highway. The arbitrary separation of citizens, on the basis of race, while they are on a public highway, is a badge of servitude wholly inconsistent with the civil freedom and the equality before the law established by the constitution. It cannot be justified upon any legal grounds.

If evils will result from the commingling of the two races upon public highways established for the benefit of all, they will be infinitely less than those that will surely come from state legislation regulating the enjoyment of civil rights upon the basis of race. We boast of the freedom enjoyed by our people above all other peoples. But it is difficult to reconcile that boast with a state of the law which, practically, puts the brand of servitude and degradation upon a large class of our fellow citizens,-our equals before the law. The thin disguise of "equal" accommodations for passengers in railroad coaches will not mislead any one, nor atone for the wrong this day done.

The result of the whole matter is that while this court has frequently adjudged, and at the present term has recognized the doctrine, that a state cannot, consistently with the constitution of the United States, prevent white and black citizens, having the required qualifications for jury service, from sitting in the same jury box, it is now solemnly held that a state may prohibit white and black citizens from sitting in the same passenger coach on a public highway, or may require that they be separated by a "partition" when in the same passenger coach. May it not now be reasonably expected that astute men of the dominant race, who affect to be disturbed at the possibility that the integrity of the white race may be corrupted, or that its supremacy will be imperiled, by contact on public highways with black people, will endeavor to procure statutes requiring white and black jurors to be separated in the jury box by a "partition," and that, upon retiring from the court room to consult as to their verdict, such partition, if it be a movable one, shall be taken to their consultation room, and set up in such way as to prevent black jurors from coming too close to their brother jurors of the white race. If the "partition" used in the court room happens to be stationary, provision could be made for screens with openings through which jurors of the two races could confer as to their verdict without coming into personal contact with each other. I cannot see but that, according to the principles this day announced, such state legislation, although conceived in hostility to, and enacted for the purpose of humiliating, citizens of the United States of a particular race, would be held to be consistent with the constitution.

I do not deem it necessary to review the decisions of state courts to which reference was made in argument. Some, and the most important, of them, are wholly inapplicable, because rendered prior to the adoption of the last amendments of the constitution, when colored people had very few rights which the dominant race felt obliged to respect. Others were made at a time when public opinion, in many localities, was dominated by the institution of slavery; when it would not have been safe to do justice to the black man; and when, so far as the rights of blacks were concerned, race prejudice was, practically, the supreme law of the land. Those decisions cannot be guides in the era introduced by the recent amendments of the supreme law, which established universal civil freedom, gave citizenship to all born or naturalized in the United States, and residing ere, obliterated the race line from our systems of governments, national and state, and placed our free institutions upon the broad and sure foundation of the equality of all men before the law.

I am of opinion that the state of Louisiana is inconsistent with the personal liberty of citizens, white and black, in that state, and hostile to both the spirit and letter of the constitution of the United States. If laws of like character should be enacted in the several states of the Union, the effect would be in the highest degree mischievous. Slavery, as an institution tolerated by law, would, it is true, have disappeared from our country; but there would remain a power in the states, by sinister legislation, to interfere with the full enjoyment of the blessings of freedom, to regulate civil rights, common to all citizens, upon the basis of race, and to place in a condition of legal inferiority a large body of American citizens, now constituting a part of the political community, called the "People of the United States," for whom, and by whom through representatives, our government is administered. Such a system is inconsistent with the guaranty given by the constitution to each state of a republican form of government, and may be stricken down by congressional action, or by the courts in the discharge of their solemn duty to maintain the supreme law of the land, anything in the constitution or laws of any state to the contrary notwithstanding. For the reason stated, I am constrained to withhold my assent from the opinion and judgment of the majority.

Source: *Plessy v. Ferguson*, 163 U.S. 537 (1896).

See also: Anti-Miscegenation Laws; Black Separatism; De Jure and De Facto Segregation; Desegregation; Greensboro Four; Montgomery Bus Boycott; *Plessy v. Ferguson* (1896); Racial Segregation; Segregation; Segregation, Rural; Segregation, Suburban; Segregation, Voluntary versus Involuntary; Sit-Ins

Excerpt from the Draft Report of the 1898 Wilmington Race Riot Commission (December 2005)

Introduction

Created by the North Carolina Legislature in 2000 to initiate and review research on the causes and course of the race riot that occurred in Wilmington in November 1898, the Wilmington Race Riot Commission issued its 600-page draft report on December 15, 2005. The excerpt from that report reproduced below describes the initial violence that occurred on November 10, 1898. The 13-member Commission concluded that the riot was not a spontaneous event, but was instead fomented by white businessmen and Democratic leaders who sought to overthrow the political power local blacks had won in the elections of 1894 and 1896, when an alliance between local Republicans and local Populists had broken the political dominance the Democrats had exercised in the town since the end of Reconstruction. Democrats had won the election held on November 8, two days before the disorders began, by stuffing ballot boxes and keeping African Americans from the polls through intimidation. The riots only sealed the return to power of white supremacist forces.

Primary Source

Eye of the Storm—Fourth and Harnett Streets
The bloodshed began when black workers from the waterfront industrial yards and Brooklyn residents confronted with armed whites. The point where the peace was fractured was at the corner of Fourth and Harnett Streets in Brooklyn, a mixed race neighborhood on the edge of the predominantly black section of Wilmington.

A group of blacks were gathered on the southwest corner of Fourth and Harnett near Brunje's Saloon in George Heyer's store when armed whites returned to the neighborhood. A streetcar also entered the area loaded with men direct from burning the Record. As the groups exchanged verbal assaults from opposite street corners, whites and blacks alike sought to calm fellow citizens.

Norman Lindsay encouraged his fellow blacks to go home: "For the sake of your lives, your families, your children, and your country, go home and stay there!" After Lindsay's plea, the group of blacks moved to the opposite corner at W.A. Walker's store while the whites took up a position between Brunje's store and St. Matthew's English Lutheran Church. Aaron Lockamy, a newly deputized white police officer, also tried to diffuse the problem by going between the two groups and trying to get them to disperse. He recalled that, while serving as a special policeman during the aftermath of the election, he was stationed in Brooklyn to ensure that the opening of two bars on Fourth Street would be peaceful. Instructed not to arrest anyone by Chief Melton, Lockamy asked the blacks to disperse and go home for their own safety. They refused but moved as a group a bit further away from the corner. Lockamy's inability to disperse the crowd angered the white men at the opposite corner. Lockamy felt he had done all he could in the turf war and went back to his post on Fourth near Brunswick. From this point forward, gunshots rang throughout the city for the next several hours.

White and black witnesses of the activities at the intersection of Fourth and Harnett both claimed that the other side was the responsible party for firing the first shots. There are conflicting viewpoints on first shots and an affidavit, probably taken by Rountree [Attorney George Rountree] was used in the newspapers to counter accounts from black witnesses such as George H. Davis, a black man wounded at Fourth and Harnett and interviewed by reporter Thomas Clawson for the Wilmington *Messenger*. Lockamy went back and forth between the clusters of whites and blacks on opposing corners at Fourth and Harnett at least two times and later said that the only people on the corner that were armed were whites. Notwithstanding the point of origin, once the first shot was fired, whites launched a fusillade of bullets towards the blacks near Walker's store. Several black men fell injured but most were able to get up and run away from the scene. Most accounts agree that three men died instantly at Walker's while two injured men ran around the corner into a home at 411 Harnett. One of these men by the surname of Bizzell died in the house while the other, George H. Davis, was later taken to the hospital on the 11th and survived his wounds. Davis apparently lived at the residence and was wounded in his left thigh and had a bullet lodged between his shoulders. He was found in the house along with a dead black man and three women by reporter Clawson and taken to the hospital on the eleventh. Although Davis recovered, Clawson recalled that after he sent for a white doctor, W.D. McMillan, and a black doctor, T.R. Mask, he thought that "it appeared impossible for one so desperately wounded ever to recover." The rest of the men fled west on Harnett, reportedly firing at whites as they ran. Although it was difficult for black men to purchase weapons in the weeks and months just prior to the election, many already owned weapons for hunting or personal safety. Men identified in papers as wounded at Fourth and Harnett intersection: Alfred White, William Lindsay, Sam McFarland. Men identified as dead at Fourth and Harnett: John Townsend (Townsell?), Charles Lindsay (aka Silas Brown), William Mouzon, John L. Gregory. Whites identified as being at the scene: S. Hill Terry (armed with double-barrel shot gun loaded with buck shot),

Theodore Curtis, N.B. Chadwick (armed with a 16-shot Colt or Remington rifle), Sam Matthews (armed with a .44 caliber Navy rifle), and George Piner.

After the first shots were fired, a streetcar entered the business section in downtown from Brooklyn and the conductor told men gathered there that blacks had shot into the car. Men crowded into the car bound for Brooklyn at the stop on Fourth and Harnett. One of the "first responders" was Captain Donald MacRae of Company K, fresh from the tense situation at Sprunt's Compress [Sprunt's Cotton Compress, where a standoff between whites and blacks had occurred earlier in the day]. MacRae recalled that once he arrived in Brooklyn after hearing reports of fighting, he began to establish a skirmish line with other white men in the area. He was stopped by another man because he was still a Captain of Company K in the U.S. Army and white leaders thought that he should not be involved in case the President investigated the participants.

Having feared the worst in the weeks prior to the election, leaders Roger Moore and Walker Taylor had developed a strategy for quelling violence by stationing contacts throughout the city with instructions to notify Taylor and Moore if trouble ignited. The contact in the Fourth Street area near Harnett was Bernice Moore at his drug store at 901 North Fourth Street. Moore was instructed by J. Alan Taylor of the Secret Nine to sound the "riot alarm" to alert the WLI [Wilmington Light Infantry] and Naval Reserves in the event of violence. As soon as shots were heard, Moore called the armory to inform the leaders there that shots were being fired in Brooklyn. Once the "riot alarm" was sounded, as leader of the WLI, Walker Taylor declared martial law and the WLI and the Naval Reserves began to make their way into the Brooklyn neighborhood.

Taylor had authority to take control because just before Moore's call for backup was received at the armory, a telegram arrived from Governor Russell through the state's Adjutant General that instructed Taylor to "take command of Captain James' company . . . and preserve the peace."

Before the Governor's telegram arrived, Commander George Morton of the Naval Reserves sought approval from a city official to grant the military authority to take over but claimed he could not locate the mayor or police officer. Instead, Morton's men found Deputy Sheriff G.Z. French in his room at the Orton Hotel and requested permission to march his men from his headquarters in Brooklyn. French complied, possibly under duress, and wrote out an order instructing Morton to "use all force at your disposal to quell the existing violation of the peace in this city."

Morton then sent a telegram to the Governor informing him of his plan of action as well as notifying Walker Taylor of his intentions. The Governor later ordered Morton to place his men under the command of Taylor although the transfer of power had already taken place by the time the telegram was received. Morton's men, equipped with Lee magazine rifles and a Hotchkiss rapid firing gun, assembled at the corner of Third and Princess.

As soon as the first shots were fired, a "running firefight" erupted on Harnett, with scores of men, black and white, running in all directions from the intersection, some firing at the opposite side as they ran. William Mayo, a white man who lived at 307 Harnett, was seriously wounded by a stray bullet.

Mayo's wounding presented a rallying point for the whites who then began to retaliate. Because of Mayo, whites fired in unison into a group of black men and another five or six died near the intersection of Harnett and Fourth Streets. Mayo was taken to a nearby drug store for treatment by Dr. John T. Schonwald who lived close to the scene. Mayo's injury was serious but since he received quick care, he survived an otherwise life-threatening injury. Additionally, two other white men, Bert Chadwick and George Piner, were injured and treated alongside Mayo. Mayo's wounding rallied the white men involved in the first scuffle and they began to avenge Mayo as they aimed for any blacks that came into sight. The whites also sought to identify the individual who shot Mayo, perhaps as a means to stop random shootings. Later in the afternoon they pointed to Daniel Wright, who lived nearby at 810 North Third, as the culprit responsible for shooting Mayo as well as shooting George Piner. A manhunt was launched for Wright.

As large groups of white men gathered in the vicinity of Fourth and Harnett—milling about, angry and eager to avenge Mayo's shooting—Wright was identified by a "half breed Indian" who told J. Alan Taylor that he knew who had shot Mayo. Taylor was shown a house where he was told Wright was hiding and that he could be identified by "a missing thumb on his right hand and the possession of an outmoded rifle with a large bore." Captain MacRae remembered the incident with the Indian, saying that he felt the man had a grudge against local blacks. Taylor then sent a group of men led by John S. Watters to capture and identify Wright. Once his house was surrounded, white witnesses claimed Wright went into the attic and shot into the approaching crowd, wounding Will Terry and George Bland.

Wright's home was set afire and he tried to escape but was captured while his wife watched from the street. Once captured, Wright was marched into the street and hit in the head with a length of gas pipe. When he stood back up, someone in the crowd suggested that Wright be hanged from a nearby lamp post. Before a rope could be found, a member of the Citizen's Patrol drove up and suggested that Wright be given the chance to run for his freedom. Wright was given this opportunity but, after he ran about fifty yards, "at least forty guns of all descriptions turned loose on him." Wright was left in the street bleeding and severely wounded with about thirteen gunshot wounds, five of which entered through his shoulders and back, for about a half hour before he was picked up and carried to the hospital. Doctors at the hospital observed that they had never seen anyone with as many gunshot wounds live for as long as Wright did. He held onto life until early the next morning and his body was handed over to undertaker Thomas Rivera for burial after a formal inquest by coroner David Jacobs.

More shots rang throughout the area as more and more whites and blacks filtered into the Brooklyn area. Among the white onlookers was attorney George Rountree. Having just mediated the safety of blacks at Sprunt's Compress, Rountree went to investigate so that if a governmental inquiry took place, he would be prepared to answer questions. Rountree is probably the person responsible for filing the sworn affidavit of William McAllister that was published repeatedly in local and statewide newspapers indicating that a black man was responsible for firing the first shots. Rountree recalled that he and several others attempted to "quiet the situation and to prevent any further shooting," but acknowledged that "at this time I had no influence whatever with the rioters" and was pleased that the arrival of the military "quieted the matter down as quickly as possible."

Source: Wilmington 1898 Race Riot Commission. North Carolina Office of Archives and History. Full text of Draft Report available at: http://www.history.ncdcr.gov/1898-wrrc/report/report.htm.

See also: Asbury Park Riot of 1970; Atlanta Riot of 1906; Atlanta Riot of 1967; Bellingham Riots; Bensonhurst Incident 1989; Biloxi Beach Riot of 1960; Black Church Arsons; Bloody Sunday; Boston Riot of 1975 and 1976; Brownsville Riot of 1906; Charleston Riot of 1919; Chattanooga Riot of 1906; Chester and Philadelphia Riots of 1918; Chicago Commission on Race Relations; Chicago Riot of 1919; Cincinnati Riots of 1967 and 1968; Cincinnati Riot of 2001; Cleveland Riot of 1966; Detroit Riot of 1943; Detroit Riot of 1967; East St. Louis Riot of 1917; Election Riots of the 1880s and 1890s; Greensburg Riot of 1906; Greenwood Community; Harlem Riot of 1935; Houston Mutiny of 1917; Howard Beach Incident 1986; Johnson-Jeffries Fight of 1910; Knoxville Riot of 1919; Long Hot Summer Riots 1965–1967; Longview Riot of 1919; Los Angeles Riot of 1965; Los Angeles Riots of 1992; Miami Riot of 1982; New Bedford Riot of 1970; New Orleans Riot of 1866; New York City Draft Riot of 1863; New York City Riot of 1943; Newark Riot of 1967; Orangeburg Massacre of 1968; Philadelphia Riot of 1964; Prison Riots; Race Riots in America; Red Scare and Race Riots; Red Summer Race Riots of 1919; Rosewood Riot of 1923; Saint Genevieve Riot of 1930; San Francisco Riot of 1966; Springfield Riot of 1904; Tampa Riots of 1987; Texas Southern University Riot of 1967; Tulsa Riot of 1921; Washington, D.C., Riot of 1919; Washington, D.C., Riots of 1968; Wilmington Riot of 1898; Zoot Suit Riots

Thomas Dixon's Preface to His Novel, *The Clansman* (1905)

Introduction

Published in 1905, Thomas Dixon's The Clansman, which was both a novel and a play, became the basis for the pro-Klan view displayed in the second part of D. W. Griffith's controversial 1915 film, The Birth of a Nation. That viewpoint is amply illustrated in Dixon's Preface to The Clansman, which is reprinted here. Through The Clansman, Dixon hoped to support the continuance of racial segregation, which he viewed as vital to the maintenance of stable race relations.

Primary Source

TO THE READER

"THE CLANSMAN" is the second book of a series of historical novels planned on the Race Conflict. "The Leopard's Spots" was the statement in historical outline of the conditions from the enfranchisement of the Negro to his disfranchisement.

"The Clansman" develops the true story of the "Ku Klux Klan Conspiracy," which overturned the Reconstruction régime.

The organization was governed by the Grand Wizard Commander-in-Chief, who lived at Memphis, Tennessee. The Grand Dragon commanded a State, the Grand Titan a Congressional District, the Grand Giant a County, and the Grand Cyclops a Township Den. The twelve volumes of Government reports on the famous Klan refer chiefly to events which occurred after 1870, the date of its dissolution.

The chaos of blind passion that followed Lincoln's assassination is inconceivable to-day. The Revolution it produced in our Government, and the bold attempt of Thaddeus Stevens to Africanize ten great states of the American Union, read now like tales from "The Arabian Nights."

I have sought to preserve in this romance both the letter and the spirit of this remarkable period. The men who enact the drama of fierce revenge into which I have woven a double love-story are historical figures. I have merely changed their names without taking a liberty with any essential historic fact.

In the darkest hour of the life of the South, when her wounded people lay helpless amid rags and ashes under the beak and talon of the Vulture, suddenly from the mists of the mountains appeared a white cloud the size of a man's hand. It grew until its mantle of mystery enfolded the stricken earth and sky. An "Invisible Empire" had risen from the field of Death and challenged the Visible to mortal combat.

How the young South, led by the reincarnated souls of the Clansmen of Old Scotland, went forth under this cover and against overwhelming odds, daring exile, imprisonment, and a felon's death, and saved the life of a people, forms one of the most dramatic chapters in the history of the Aryan race.

Thomas Dixon, Jr.
Dixondale, Va., December 14, 1904.

> **Source:** Thomas Dixon, Jr., *The Clansman: An Historical Romance of the Ku Klux Klan.* New York: Doubleday, Page & Company, 1905.

> **See also:** Aryan Brotherhood; Aryan Nations; Christian Identity Hate Groups; Churches; Hate Crimes in America; Hate Groups in America; Ku Klux Klan; Preachers; White Supremacy

Excerpts from Various Newspaper Accounts of Disorders Following the Jack Johnson–James Jeffries Fight (July 4, 1910)

Introduction

When African American boxer Jack Johnson, then current heavyweight champion, defeated former white champion Jim Jeffries in Reno, Nevada, on July 4, 1910, news of the decision caused racial disorders to erupt in almost a dozen cities across the country as both blacks, proud of their fighter's victory, and whites, angry at their fighter's defeat, responded to the outcome and to each other.

Primary Source

Baltimore
Seventy negroes, half the number women, were arrested tonight in the "black belt" of this city for disorderly celebration of Johnson's victory. One negro was badly cut by another, and two other negroes were assaulted and severely injured by whites in arguments over the big fight.

> **Source:** "Race Clashes in Many Cities." *Washington Post*, July 5, 1910, 11.

Bluefields, West Virginia
Negroes are boisterous at Keystone, W. Va., tonight and are said to be in possession of the town, the police being powerless.

> **Source:** "Racial Clashes Follow Victory of Jack Johnson." *Atlanta Constitution*, July 5, 1910, 2.

Little Rock, Arkansas
Although there have been a number of fights in Little Rock in which whites and blacks clashed, with the latter receiving the worst of the argument in practically all cases, following the announcement of the result of the Jeffries–Johnson fight, no fatalities have occurred. . . . Several fights between whites and negroes started at a local theater, where fight returns were received, but were quickly stopped.

> **Source:** "Racial Clashes Follow Victory of Jack Johnson." *Atlanta Constitution*, July 5, 1910, 2.

Mounds, Illinois
One dead and one mortally wounded is the result of an attempt by four negroes to shoot up the town in honor of Jack Johnson's victory at Reno tonight. A negro constable was killed when he attempted to arrest them.

> **Source:** "Racial Clashes Follow Victory of Jack Johnson." *Atlanta Constitution*, July 5, 1910, 2.

Philadelphia
The announcement of Johnson's victory over Jeffries was followed by numerous clashes in this city between colored men and crowds of white men and boys. In some cases, the blacks, exulting the victory, were the aggressors, but in other cases inoffensive colored men were attacked by riotous whites. . . . Lombard Street, the principal street in the negro section, went wild in celebrating the victory, and a number of fights, in which razors were drawn, resulted. In the suburb of Germantown a crowd of negroes paraded the streets and there were several clashes with white men.

> **Source:** "Eight Killed in Fight Riots." *New York Times*, July 5, 1910, 4.

Pittsburgh

Less than half an hour after the decision of the fight was announced here three riot calls were sent into two police precincts in the negro hill district. Street cars were held up and insulting epithets were hurled at the passengers. The police beat the crowds back with their clubs to permit the passage of street cars. Patrolmen have been summoned to this district from all sections of the city.

Source: "Race Clashes in Many Cities." *Washington Post*, July 5, 1910, 11.

Roanoke, Virginia

Six negroes with broken heads, six white men locked up and one white man, Joe Chockley, with a bullet wound through his skull and probably fatally wounded, is the net result of clashes here tonight following the announcement that Jack Johnson had defeated James J. Jeffries. The trouble started when a negro, who had just heard the news from Reno, said: "Now I guess the white folks will let the negroes alone." A white man replied: "No!" and the two clashed.

Source: "Racial Clashes Follow Victory of Jack Johnson." *Atlanta Constitution*, July 5, 1910, 1.

St. Joseph, Missouri

S.I. Sawyer, a white man who took the part of a negro when the latter was struck by another white man, was mobbed by a crowd of whites immediately following the Johnson–Jeffries fight. Sawyer was rescued by a policeman, and charges that the latter struck him in the face and broke his nose.

Source: "Racial Clashes Follow Victory of Jack Johnson." *Atlanta Constitution*, July 5, 1910, 2.

St. Louis

Rioting in a negro section of St. Louis, at Market Street and Jefferson Avenue, followed quickly upon the announcement that Jack Johnson was the victor in the Reno prize fight. The eighth district police responded to a riot call, but were powerless to cope with the negroes who were blocking traffic and making threats. A second call to the Central district brought out a score of policemen. The negroes were clubbed into submission and dispersed.

Source: "Racial Clashes Follow Victory of Jack Johnson." *Atlanta Constitution*, July 5, 1910, 2.

Shreveport, Louisiana

L.E. Roberts, a conductor of the Iron Mountain railroad is dead; John Anderson, a negro, is dead; his son, Henry Anderson, is dead; an unknown negro woman is dying, shot through the head; one or two negroes are injured, and a race riot is imminent. The authorities have no control over the situation in Madison and East Carroll parishes, and posses are scouring the whole country tonight.

Source: "Eleven Killed in Many Race Riots." *Chicago Tribune*, July 5, 1910, 4.

Wilmington, Delaware

A serious race riot occurred here tonight as the result of an argument over the victory of Johnson. Michael Brown, a white man, was attacked by a gang of negroes and severely injured about the head and cut with a razor. A mob of whites then chased the negroes several blocks. One of the negroes, Benjamin White, fled into a negro apartment house. The mob of whites, which by this time numbered several thousand, bombarded the place with stones.

Source: "Eleven Killed in Many Race Riots." *Chicago Tribune*, July 5, 1910, 4.

See also: Race Riots in America; Sports and Racism

Account of the Riots in East St. Louis, Illinois (July 1917)

Introduction

The National Association for the Advancement of Colored People (NAACP) commissioned W.E.B. Du Bois and Martha Gruening to investigate and report on the riots that had convulsed East St. Louis during the summer of 1917. The following excerpts from their report, which was published in The Crisis, *summarize eyewitness accounts of the horrible atrocities perpetrated on the African American residents of East St. Louis by the white rioters. See also the entries Du Bois, W.E.B.;*

East St. Louis (Illinois) Riot of 1917; National Association for the Advancement of Colored People (NAACP).

Primary Source

A Negro, his head laid open by a great stone-cut, had been dragged to the mouth of the alley on Fourth Street and a small rope was being put about his neck. There was joking comment on the weakness of the rope, and everyone was prepared for what happened when it was pulled over a projecting cable box, a short distance up the pole. It broke, letting the Negro tumble back to his knees, and causing one of the men who was pulling on it to sprawl on the pavement.

An old man, with a cap like those worn by street car conductors, but showing no badge of car service, came out of his house to protest. "Don't you hang that man on this street," he shouted. "I dare you to." He was pushed angrily away, and a rope, obviously strong enough for its purpose, was brought.

Right here I saw the most sickening incident of the evening. To put the rope around the Negro's neck, one of the lynchers stuck his fingers inside the gaping scalp and lifted the Negro's head by it, literally bathing his hand in the man's blood.

"Get hold and pull for East St. Louis!" called a man with a black coat and a new straw hat, as he seized the other end of the rope. The rope was long, but not too long for the number of hands that grasped it, and this time the Negro was lifted to a height of about seven feet from the ground. . . .

A Negro weighing 300 pounds came out of the burning line of dwellings just north and east of the Southern freight house. His hands were elevated and his yellow face was speckled with the awful fear of death.

"Get him!" they cried. Here was a chance to see suffering, something that bullets didn't always make.

So a man in the crowd clubbed his revolver and struck the Negro in the face with it. Another dashed an iron bolt between the Negro's eyes. Still another stood near and battered him with a rock.

Then the giant Negro toppled to the ground. "This is the way," cried one. He ran back a few paces, then ran at the prostrate black at full speed and made a flying leap.

His heels struck right in the middle of the battered face. A girl stepped up and struck the bleeding man with her foot. The blood spurted onto her stockings and men laughed and grunted.

No amount of suffering awakened pity in the hearts of the rioters. . . . A few Negroes, caught on the street, were kicked and shot to death. As flies settled on their terrible wounds, the gaping-mouthed mobsmen forbade the dying blacks to brush them off. Girls with blood on their stockings helped to kick in what had been black faces of the corpses on the street. The first houses were fired shortly after 5 o'clock. These were back of Main Street, between Broadway and Railroad Avenue. Negroes were "flushed" from the burning houses, and ran for their lives, screaming and begging for mercy. A Negro crawled into a shed and fired on the white men. Guardsmen started after him, but when they saw he was armed, turned to the mob and said:

"He's armed, boys. You can have him. A white man's life is worth the lives of a thousand Negroes."

A few minutes later matches were applied to hastily gathered debris piled about the corner of one of the three small houses 100 feet from the first fired. These were back of the International Harvester Company's plant. Eight Negroes fled into the last of the houses and hid in the basement. When roof and walls were about to fall in, an aged Negro woman came out. She was permitted to walk to safety. Three Negro women followed and were not fired upon. Then came four Negro men, and 100 shots were fired at them. They fell. No one ventured out to see if they were dead, as the place had come to resemble No Man's Land, with bullets flying back and forth and sparks from the fires falling everywhere.

A Negro who crawled on hands and knees through the weeds was a target for a volley. The mob then burned back to Main Street and another Negro was spied on a Main Street car. He was dragged to the street and a rioter stood over him, shooting.

The crowd then turned to Black Valley. Here the greatest fire damage was caused.

Flames were soon raging and the shrieking rioters stood about in the streets, made lurid by the flames, and shot and beat Negroes as they fled from burning homes.

They pursued the women who were driven out of the burning homes, with the idea, not of extinguishing their burning clothing, but of inflicting added pain, if possible. They stood around in groups, laughing and jeering, while they witnessed the final writhings of the terror and pain wracked wretches who crawled to the streets to die after their flesh had been cooked in their own homes.

Mrs. Cox saw a Negro beheaded with a butcher's knife by someone in a crowd standing near the Free Bridge. The crowd had to have its jest. So its members laughingly threw the head over one side of the bridge and the body over the other.

A trolley-car came along. The crowd forced its inmates to put their hands out the window. Colored people thus recognized were hauled out of the car to be beaten, trampled on, shot. A little twelve-year-old colored girl fainted—her mother knelt beside her. The crowd surged in on her. When its ranks opened up again Mrs. Cox saw the mother prostrate with a hole as large as one's fist in her head.

Source: W.E.B. Du Bois and Martha Gruening. "Massacre at East St. Louis." *The Crisis*, 14, 1917, 222–238.

See also: Asbury Park (New Jersey) Riot of 1970; Atlanta (Georgia) Riot of 1906; Atlanta (Georgia) Riot of 1967; Bellingham Riots (1907); Bensonhurst (New York) Incident (1989); Biloxi Beach (Mississippi) Riot of 1960; Black Church Arsons; Bloody Sunday; Boston (Massachusetts) Riots of 1975 and 1976; Brownsville (Texas) Incident of 1906; Charleston (South Carolina) Riot of 1919; Chattanooga (Tennessee) Riot of 1906; Chester and Philadelphia (Pennsylvania) Riots of 1918; Chicago Commission on Race Relations; Chicago (Illinois) Riot of 1919; Cincinnati (Ohio) Riots of 1967 and 1968; Cincinnati (Ohio) Riots of 2001; Cleveland (Ohio) Riot of 1966; Detroit (Michigan) Riot of 1943; Detroit (Michigan) Riot of 1967; East St. Louis (Illinois) Riot of 1917; Election Riots of the 1880s and 1890s; Greensburg (Indiana) Riot of 1906; Greenwood Community (Tulsa, Oklahoma); Harlem (New York) Riot of 1935; Houston (Texas) Mutiny of 1917; Howard Beach (New York) Incident (1986); Johnson-Jeffries Fight of 1910, Riots Following; Knoxville (Tennessee) Riot of 1919; Long Hot Summer Riots (1965–1967); Longview (Texas) Riot of 1919; Los Angeles (California) Riot of 1965; Los Angeles (California) Riots of 1992; Miami (Florida) Riot of 1982; New Bedford (Massachusetts) Riot of 1970; New Orleans (Louisiana) Riot of 1866; New York City Draft Riot of 1863; New York City Riot of 1943; Newark (New Jersey) Riot of 1967; Orangeburg (South Carolina) Massacre of 1968; Philadelphia (Pennsylvania) Riot of 1964; Prison Riots; Race Riots in America; Red Scare and Race Riots; Red Summer Race Riots of 1919; Rosewood (Florida) Riot of 1923; Saint Genevieve (Missouri) Riot of 1930; San Francisco (California) Riot of 1966; Springfield (Ohio) Riot of 1904; Tampa (Florida) Riots of 1987; Texas Southern University Riot of 1967; Tulsa (Oklahoma) Riot of 1921; Washington (D.C.) Riot of 1919; Washington (D.C.) Riots of 1968; Wilmington (North Carolina) Riot of 1898; Zoot Suit Riots

A Southern Black Woman's Letter Regarding the Recent Riots in Chicago and Washington (November 1919)

Primary Source

The Washington riot gave me the thrill that comes once in a lifetime. I was alone when I read between the lines of the morning paper that at last our men had stood like men, struck back, were no longer dumb, driven cattle. When I could no longer read for my streaming tears, I stood up, alone in my room, held both hands high over my head and exclaimed aloud: "Oh, I thank God, thank God!" When I remember anything after this, I was prone on my bed, beating the pillow with both fists, laughing and crying, whimpering like a whipped child, for sheer gladness and madness. The pent-up humiliation, grief and horror of a life time—half a century—was being stripped from me. Only colored women of the south know the extreme in suffering and humiliation.

We know how many insults we have borne silently, for we have hidden many of them from our men because we did not want them to die needlessly in our defense; we know the sorrow of seeing our boys and girls grow up, the swift stab of the heart at night to the sound of a strange footstep, the feel of a tigress to spring and claw the white man with his lustful look at our comely daughters, the deep humiliation of sitting in the Jim Crow part of a street car and hear the white man laugh and discuss us, point out the good and bad points of our bodies. God alone knows the many things colored women have borne here in the South in silence.

And, too, a woman loves a strong man, she delights to feel that her man can protect her, fight for her, if necessary, save her.

No woman loves a weakling, a coward, be she white or black, and some of us have been near to thinking our men cowards, but thank God for Washington colored men! All honor to them, for they first blazed the way and right swiftly did Chicago men follow. They put new hope, a new vision in their almost despairing women.

God grant that our men everywhere refrain from strife, provoke no quarrel, but that they protect their women and homes at any cost.

A Southern Colored Woman

I'm sure the editor will understand why I cannot sign my name.

Source: *The Crisis*, XIX, November 1919, 339.

Excerpts from the NAACP Report *Thirty Years of Lynching in the United States: 1889–1918* (1919)

Introduction

Published by the NAACP in 1919, the report Thirty Years of Lynching in the United States: 1889–1918 *was an important part of the organization's strenuous ongoing effort to eradicate the crime of lynching by educating the public to the frequency and brutality of the crime. Written by Martha Gruening and Helen Boardman,* Thirty Years of Lynching *presents facts, figures, and anecdotes on lynching collected by the NAACP. The two excerpts below offer statistics on the types of crimes that were given as reasons for lynchings and the opening of the section from newspaper accounts describing 100 lynchings that had occurred between 1894 and 1918. See also the entries* Lynching; National Association for the Advancement of Colored People (NAACP); Thirty Years of Lynching in the United States: 1889–1918.

Primary Source

Alleged Offenses Which Appear as "Causes" for the Lynchings

Table No. 6 sums up the known facts regarding the alleged offenses committed by the men and women lynched. It is

Table No. 6

	Murder	Rape	Attacks upon Women*	Other Crimes Against the Person	Crimes Against Property	Miscellaneous Crimes	Absence of Crime[†]	Total
Total	1,219	523	250	315	331	438	148	3,224
White	319	46	13	62	121	135	6	702
Per cent. of total whites lynched	45.7	6.6	1.8	8.7	17.4	18.1	1.4	100.0
Negro	900	477	237	253	210	303	142	2,522
Per cent. of total Negroes lynched	35.8	19.0	9.4	9.5	8.3	12.0	5.6	100.0

*This classification includes all cases in which press accounts state that attacks upon women were made, but in which it was not clear whether rape was alleged to have been consummated or attempted.
[†]Under this heading are listed such causes as "testifying against whites," "suing whites," "wrong man lynched," "race prejudice," "defending himself against attack," etc.

to be remembered that the alleged offenses given are pretty loose descriptions of the crimes charged against the mob victims, where actual crime was committed. Of the whites lynched, nearly 46 per cent were accused of murder; a little more than 18 per cent were accused of what have been classified as miscellaneous crimes, *i.e.*, all crimes not otherwise classified; 17.4 per cent were said to have committed crimes against property; 8.7 per cent crimes against the person, other than rape, "attacks upon women," and murder; while 8.4 per cent were accused of rape and "attacks upon women."

Among colored victims, 35.8 per cent were accused of murder; 28.4 per cent or rape and "attacks upon women" (19 per cent of rape and 9.4 per cent of "attacks upon women"); 17.8 per cent of crimes against the person (other than those already mentioned) and against property; 12 per cent were charged with miscellaneous crimes and in 5.6 per cent of cases no crime at all was charged. The 5.6 per cent, classified under "Absence of Crime," does not include a number of cases in which crime was alleged but in which it was afterwards shown conclusively that no crime had been committed. Further, it may fairly be pointed out that in a number of cases where Negroes have been lynched for rape and "attacks upon white women," the alleged attacks rest upon no stronger evidence than "entering the room of a woman" or brushing against her. In such cases as these latter the victims and their friends have often asserted that there was no intention on the part of the victim to attack a white woman or to commit rape. In many cases, of course, the evidence points to *bona fide* attacks upon women.

The Story of One Hundred Lynchings[‡]

To give concreteness and to make vivid the facts of lynching in the United States, we give below in chronological order an account of one hundred lynchings which have occurred in the period from 1894 to 1918. These "stories," as they are technically described in newspaper parlance, have been taken from press accounts and, in a few cases, from the reports of investigations made by the National Association for the Advancement of Colored People. Covering twenty-five years of American history, these accounts serve to present a characteristic picture of the lynching sport, as was picturesquely defined by Henry Watterson.

The last of the stories describes one of the rare events in connection with lynchings, that of the conviction of members of a mob involved in such affairs. In this case no lynching was consummated, it having been prevented by the prompt and public-spirited action of the mayor of the city (Winston-Salem, North Carolina), and members of the "Home Guard" and Federal troops who defended the jail against the mob.

Alabama, 1894

Three Negroes, Tom Black, Johnson Williams and Tony Johnston, were lynched at Tuscumbia, Alabama. They were in the local jail, awaiting trial on the charge of having burnt a barn. A mob of two hundred masked men entered the jail, after having enticed away the jailer with a false message, took the keys from the jailer's wife and secured the three prisoners. They were carried to a near-by bridge. Here a rope was placed around the neck of each victim, the other end being tied to the timbers of the bridge, and they were compelled to jump.

‡ One hundred *persons* lynched, not one hundred occasions on which lynching occurred.

Source: NAACP. *Thirty Years of Lynching in the United States.* National Association for the Advancement of Colored People, 1919, 9, 10, 11, 36.

Source: NAACP. "Thirty Years of Lynching in the United States: 1889–1918." *New York Tribune*, April 23, 1894.

See also: Anti-Lynching Campaign; Anti-Lynching League; Anti-Lynching Legislation; Lynching. Documents: Ida B. Wells Expose on Lynching (1895); The "Anti-Lynching" Hearings Held before the House Judiciary Committee (January 1920); Transcripts of *Bee Publishing Company v. State of Nebraska* Regarding Lynching in September 1919 (November 17, 1921)

Excerpts from the "Anti-Lynching" Hearings Held before the House Judiciary Committee (January 1920)

Introduction

Reproduced below are excerpts of testimony given before the House Judiciary Committee in January 1920. Responding to the many serious race riots that had erupted over the previous three years, and especially during the "Red Summer" of 1919, the committee heard testimony regarding the need for anti-lynching legislation to protect African Americans from the growing racist violence being offered them throughout the country. The hearings accompanied the House's consideration of the Dyer Anti-Lynching Bill, which was introduced into the House in 1918 by Congressman Leonidas Dyer, a Republican from a heavily black district in St. Louis. Although passed by the House in January 1922, the Dyer bill, which made participation in a lynch mob a federal crime, was defeated in the Senate shortly thereafter. No federal anti-lynching legislation was ever passed by Congress. See also the entries Anti-Lynching Legislation; Dyer, Leonidas C.

Primary Source

Statement of Mr. Neval H. Thomas

Mr. Thomas. In the first place, I am representing the National Association for the Advancement of Colored People. Locally we have 7,000 members whom I am representing, and nationally we have 100,000 members in 310 branches, which are organized to oppose just such a recommendation as has been presented here to-day. I do not know where this man comes from—

Mr. Dyer. He says he comes from St. Louis. How long have you lived in St. Louis, Mr. Madden?

Mr. Madden. About two years: I came there from Oklahoma.

Mr. Dyer. I thought so.

Mr. Thomas. I am acquainted with the leaders of thought among colored people all over this country, and I never even heard of this man before. He represents nothing but himself. Beware of any Negro who comes recommending a segregation scheme to you: he is simply seeking to be head of the group if we are segregated. When Woodrow Wilson became President, there were some venal Negro politicians who asked him to segregate the colored clerks in one department, and at the same time everyone presented an application for the leadership of that department; so pay no attention to them. The masses of the colored people are unalterably opposed to segregation. Civilization has been spread and prejudices softened by the contact of peoples with each other. Even President Wilson is on record as saying that you can not hate a man whom you know, although he has segregated men to keep them from knowing, so that they can hate.

We recognize, in the first place that every man is lord of his castle; complete master of his own home. We seek no association, but cooperation with the white people of this country in the up-building of the things which belong to us all. When we go upon a common carrier, we are not seeking contact with the other people, we simply want to travel from place to place; we do not even expect another passenger to say "Good morning" to us. This is an ordinary civil right. The common carrier, like all other institutions, belongs to all of us alike. They are supported by our taxes, protected by the police power of our State, and every one is a taxpayer because the ultimate consumer is the taxpayer. The owner of property does not pay the taxes. He charges enough rent to make a profitable return on his investment, plus the insurance, water rent, and all other expenses, and the tenant pays it. The owner of the property is simply a messenger through whom the tenant sends his taxes to the taxgatherer. Therefore, we have equal rights to all public places, such as the common carrier, the theaters, restaurants, and hotels, and we will never cease to clamor for our rights until we gain admission. What we want the Congress to do, and also the Department of Justice, is to enforce the thirteenth, the fourteenth, and the fifteenth amendments to the Constitution. Even the thirteenth amendment, forbidding slavery and involuntary servitude, is violated in the Southern States by the infamous system of peonage. We demand the ballot, for in a Government where men vote the voter is king, and the disfranchised man is the victim of the man who does vote. We demand the abolition of the infamous "Jim-Crow" car, which was simply made to insult us. We demand admission to all public places, in fact, we demand equality of treatment everywhere, and equality before the law. Again, I say that segregation keeps men apart and is opposed to all sound principles of Government. My own experience in this country and Europe with white people has taught me how segregation works against my people. I have met people in this country and in Europe who were surprised that I could write; that I knew history; that I knew what I was traveling for; could explain a painting or a piece of sculpture or a great work of architecture. They had lived side by side with me for all these years, the segregation had kept them from knowing me. Suppose there were no prejudices in this country, the races would mingle and discover their common humanity, and learn that color is the least of differences among men, and we would have no resulting friction. There are people living right in Boston who have gone over Boston Common, the most historic park in this country, where there is a statue of Crispus Attucks, a Negro, the first to shed his blood in the American Revolution. Nearby is the famous Robert Gould Shaw statue, dedicated to the Fifty-fourth and Fifty-fifth regiments of Negroes in the Civil War, who died like men at Fort Pillow for the preservation of the Union, and yet have never looked up to find how much the colored men of this country have done for it. The system of segregation prevents that mutual interest that should exist between the races; we are all opposed to segregation. The African Methodist Episcopal Church is the largest institution among the Negroes, with 700,000 members. This church issued a declaration of 14 points, the number of which is in imitation on the President's 14 points, and the strongest point in it is a declaration against segregation. This church supports 24 institutions in the South and collects from the pockets of washerwomen $350,000 every year for the education of the Negro youth, and this is in addition to the expense to which colored people are put for education of their own in the South because all the people are taxpayers.

As this great church is against segregation, so are the Baptists and other denominations. The great organization for which I am talking to-day is opposed to it. We are all opposed to it, and this man is simply seeking his own personal gain. The gentleman from Oklahoma asked if we were willing to leave this country and said he believed three-fourths of us would not leave. No. Nine hundred and ninety-nine out of every thousand would not leave. This man has falsely stated that this is a white man's country. He knows nothing of the history of his people. The Negro came here when the white man did, and he has contributed to the upbuilding of this country by this labor, by his suffering, by his sacrifices and blood. There are none of the highest callings he has not entered. In art, the highest calling of man, the greatest name is Henry O. Tanner, a Negro, whose paintings the French Government seeks and purchases and puts in her great art galleries as soon as they are painted. So it is foolish to talk about Americans, and we are not going to leave in spite of our sufferings, but we are going to work out our destiny right here in our own land. We have almost enough law in this country. What we want is enforcement of the law. We have a Constitution with 19 amendments, and with its imperfections, it is the greatest political document that has ever come from the hand of man. What we want Congress to do is to enforce it. Think of it: even the House of Representatives has closed its public restaurants to Negroes, where we have been going for 50 years without friction. This was done at the very time that brave black boys were dying in the trenches in France. This is a new reward to give the returning black soldier for his heroic sacrifices in every part of far-off France. . . .

Statement of Prof. George William Cook, Howard University, Washington, D.C.

Mr. Cook. I have been coming to the Capitol appearing before committees for nigh onto 20 years. I must say that I have never been before a committee where the occasion was of such vast and deep importance as this appearance to-day. You may read it through the inference or read where the inference is given, or you may read it out of the logic of events, that this committee representing the judiciary of the United States in Congress assembled is to-day challenged. The presentation of facts and conditions here to-day are such that if the committee does not take a very serious consideration of it, it is scarcely up to the level of its own duty.

We did not come here to-day simply for the purpose of talking to you. We came here to convince you as we know it, and as we hope to show it to you that this awful carnage of lynching and injustice in so many different ways must be stopped or we have our backs to the wall. My family is broken to-day and let me give you the circumstances. As my wife and I motored from Washington last July, we heard in Baltimore that there was a race riot in Washington. It was Tuesday after Monday the last day of the riot. We hastened here because we had one son, our only child, a young boy whom we found home, and I asked him. "Where were you, George?" "I was in it." "Why were you in it?" "You can not take me out and shoot me like a dog. I am going to die fighting if I have to die." There is an 18-year-old boy. He contemplated that thing, and he said finally, "Papa, I am not going to stay here." He is somewhat of a law unto himself. I said, "Where are you going?" "I am going out of the country." "Where do you propose to go first?" "I think that I will go to Canada and go to school." He went to Canada. These holidays he returned to Washington on a visit and he was not

home two days before he said, "I smelt it as soon as I reached Baltimore and I am going away again."

Now, you may consider that as an isolated case or you may consider it trivial. I have been teaching young colored men for 40 years. I have tested the opinion and growing conviction. I want to say if you want to drive out a pure unadulterated loyalty that has existed in the colored man, just allow this lynching to continue. You are all men of spirit and courage and belong to the Anglo-Saxon race. You would not stand it. You did not stand taxation without representation with very little personal violence attached to it and you were right, and I want to say here as far as I can gauge my people they are loyal to the backbone, they want no disturbance, and they will accept none until forced to. This is our position in the matter.

Why did I speak of that boy? Do you want to drive citizens who are loyal from your shores? You have sent away the undesirables. We are not undesirable; no. You want the labor, but we are going to say and can say that along with that response and the giving of labor we are going to ask for our God-given rights, and it is our duty as far as possible to demand them.

There was a question raised this morning as to loyalty. There seems to be some little idea that possibly the Negro is not quite as loyal as he used to be. The Attorney General of the United States shows that in 30 pages, I read almost all of it night before last and there are some in the South who feel the same way.

Mr. Sumners. Just a moment. I made the statement that there was no evidence. I made the statement that there was no general evidence of disloyalty on the part of the colored man toward the Government. I made that upon my own responsibility.

Mr. Cook. I meant simply the question that came before us. I want to say now, sir, that the colored man is loyal. He is loyal in secret and he is loyal openly, and there is but one way to shake that loyalty. He sings, "My Country, 'Tis of Thee," with all the luster and all of the sincerity that you sing, and there is now but one way to shake that, and that is to continue the lawlessness against him, and when you find him raising his hand in defense it is against the mob. He never voluntarily raises his hand against the Government, never has, never was an assassin, political assassin or menace, never was a traitor, there is not one that betrayed the confidence in all of the wars, and in all you have had he has engaged. There never was one. Therefore, I appeal to you now to help us because we are a weak people, financially, economically, but with all the opposition we have had we are stronger that we were 50 years ago, and it is not only in strength that we would come and ask you, we would come and ask you in our helplessness, that we, as American citizens, in the Thomas Jefferson declaration sense, are willing to die rather than continue our serfdom.

It is only necessary to be a little honest. You gentlemen who have studied the Elaine case understand it. These four brothers were not in the riot. They were out hunting when that treacherous gang came to them and told them they had better go home because they might get into trouble, and "let us have your guns in order that you will not be considered in the mob." They got their guns and then shot them to death. They had not done anything and did not even know a riot was going on in the town. I appeal to every man on this committee and I am sorry they are not here to hear these other gentlemen speak. I am only taking up the raveled ends and appeal to you upon pure justice first, and then on the lower ground of political necessity, to give us our rights. Do not allow your communities to deny the colored man an accounting when he has given his sweat toward the cultivation of the crop. Let him have an accounting and treat him fairly.

We bring this general proposition to you and we can support every one of them by cases upon cases. The most horrible thing of it all in that lynching, when they shot these four brothers to death, that they scarcely knew for what they were being shot. That was a lynching. Now, it is too late, and I am glad to see by the public press, the white press, that the white man is half ashamed of bringing attacks upon women as the great cause for lynching. The record has been too well kept by the *Chicago Tribune* and by *The Crisis*. We know why it is. Men have been lynched for nothing else but wearing the uniform of the United States Government. It was but yesterday that a young man in my class in commercial law said to me: "I will tell you something." I went to him when I came out of the classroom. He said: "I was simply standing in the street down in South Carolina talking when a young white man came up and said, "What are you doing with this on?" He says, "I just came out of the Army." "Well, you can not wear that down here." Can not wear the uniform of the United States Government down there? Just a few feet away they brought up another one and he left for nothing but wearing the uniform. He said he went to the post office for his father's mail and the postmaster said to him, "Do you want the package that is here?" He said, "No, I can not carry that, I will wait for the car to come in." This young man said, "What did you say to me?" I said, "No, I will not take that now." He said, "I want you to know you can not talk that way to me. You must say 'sir' to me, if you propose to stay about here," and started to come out to him. He talked up and said, "If you come after me on a charge like that, one or both of us will report to God to-day."

That is just yesterday. Do you blame the man for saying it. No security from attack upon a colored man even though he had the uniform of the United States Government upon him; this young man in the post office assuming to chastise a man who had given his all for the life of the Government, offered his all, for the protection of the flag of the United States. He said his father said to him, "You had better go. They might take out revenge on me and burn us out." He was not wrong in telling that young man to go away. The other young men had gone away. These cases are not imaginary cases. These have happened.

Now, there are two points I wanted to make. One is will you continue to teach the younger element of 12,000,000 people to ask the question, Is loyalty worth while? One you have driven out of the country. We are bereft of our son, as I have told you. He made up his mind that he would not die like a dog and that he would get out of it. Are you anxious to lose loyal citizens? If the economic condition of the Negro was such, hundreds of them, would migrate upon economic grounds, you may say, and go out as pioneers, but we have been chained down in America for over 300 years, the sweat of our brow has gone into the wealth of the Nation; it is undeniable because the statistics of your own department records will show it. What we ask now is protection under the flag that we have fought to keep aloft in as many wars as you have engaged in. Well might we repeat what Carney said when he returned at Fort Wagner, "The old flag never touched the ground," you have never heard of a Negro color bearer of the United States going to the rear unless ordered there. That is a sample of the feeling of the colored people.

We are born here. "My Country, 'Tis of Thee," I sing. You will find some few colored people, and probably with just convictions, who will not sing it. I sing it. Why? It is my country. Born here, my mother and father before me and my grandmother and grandfather. And what they added in honest industry went to help build up this Nation and to make it strong. It is my country. I will not forsake it. Why? I will treat it very much as I will a leaking house. I will repair the roof. I will not abandon it. The United States to the black man has a leaky roof, and we are here to-day to ask you to repair that roof in order that we may live in comfort and in peace, and the challenge that I spoke of to you was a challenge to you who have not thought the matter out to think it out and come on the side of justice. Let no man go out of here and say the Negroes are arguing for social equality. What some people call social equality we call disdain. I want my company and I never seek other company, which does not want me, and so it is with every self-respecting colored man, but I tell you what else I want, whether you want me or not, I want my civic political rights, and if you call that social equality, I say that you have made a misrepresentation and you give a wrong distinction. For me to be driven to travel from here to New Orleans and forced to ride and sit in a dirty car is what I protest against. I do not protest for social equality. I protest for civil rights, for civic privileges, for a discharge of the contract on the part of the railroad people to give me what I have paid for, and when you allow, as was done Sunday night, a man to step up and put a pistol to the body of an attorney of the District of Columbia and say to him, "You get out of this car or I will shoot you," when you allow that, gentlemen, you are only inviting the downfall of the Republic, because not only will the 12,000,000 finally be affected by that, but the whole Nation will be affected.

Some people speak of the unrest of the Negro. The Negro has always been the most quiet man in the United States. There are a few criminals who are among us, naturally, just like the white criminals, but the unrest in this Nation is not only

with Negroes, and I pray to Almighty God that when the time comes for you to put down unrest in the form of anarchy, that the 12,000,000 of Negroes will have a just cause to be on the side of the United States, and if that is not realized, then may God help, for my country is lost. Do not misunderstand us. We are here to ask you to attempt to do something, even though there is a doubt as to the constitutionality of it. Don't I remember when I walked down to pay my income tax? There were men who said it was unconstitutional before you passed it, and you put it up to the Supreme Court of the United States, and you remember there was some little juggling up there and finally it was declared unconstitutional. Somebody changed. The inveighed against it because there was some doubt. They all said let us do it, and to-day what have you? An amendment to the Constitution for an income tax to be operated. Now, let us for the hope of our common good and of justice to all and for a fair understanding, let us pass some bill that will look toward stopping the greatest crime that you have in the land, that of lynching.

Source: "Anti-Lynching Hearings." Hearings Before the Judiciary Committee, House of Representatives, 66th Congress, 2nd Session, on House Judiciary Resolution 75; House Resolutions 259, 4123, and 11873, Serial No. 14. January 14 and 29, 1920. Part II, Anti-Lynching. Washington, DC: Government Printing Office, 1920, 8–10, 72–75.

See also: Anti-Lynching Campaign; Anti-Lynching League; Anti-Lynching Legislation; Lynching. Documents: Excerpts from Ida B. Wells' Expose on Lynching (1895); The NAACP Report (1919); Excerpts from the Transcripts of *Bee Publishing Company v. State of Nebraska* (November 1921)

Excerpt from the Cook County Coroner's Report Regarding the 1919 Chicago Race Riots (1920)

Introduction

Reproduced below is an excerpt from one of several reports by the Cook County Coroner's Office on the causes and results of a series of race riots that occurred in Chicago in 1917, 1918, and 1919. The passage given here is from the report of the Coroner's Jury investigating the particularly serious riot of July and August 1919. The jury finds the main causes of the riot to be criminal activity on the part of both whites and African Americans, as well as, to a lesser extent, the friction created by a greater mixing of the races resulting from a great influx of African Americans from the South, who came North during World War I seeking work.

Primary Source

The true facts regarding the race riots in the City of Chicago in July and August, 1919, should be presented to set at rest the many grossly exaggerated tales and rumors and the misrepresentations which have been broadcast throughout the City of Chicago and the United States. The number of lives lost, the manner of losing the same, the causes of the riots, and all known facts attending the dark and frightful days beginning July 27, 1919, are matters of vital interest to all orderly citizens who live and work in Chicago and for Chicago. That these facts may become known and studied and analyzed is the purpose of this report.

Five days of terrible heat and passion let loose cost the people of Chicago thirty-eight lives, wounded and maimed several hundred, destroyed property of untold value, filled thousands with awful fright, blemished the good name of our City, and left in its wake fear and apprehension for the future.

Race feeling and distrust reaches far back into the history of the past. While new, perhaps, to Chicago, other cities and communities have tasted of its frightfulness, and yet race antagonism in itself rarely gets beyond bound and control. The real danger lies with the criminal and hoodlum element, white and colored, who are quick to take advantage of any incipient race riot conditions to spread the firebrands of disorder, thieving, arson, lust and murder—and under the cover of large numbers, to give full sway to cowardly animal and criminal instincts.

The riot jury was impaneled July 28, 1919, and our investigations and inquiry have proceeded continuously through one form and another, to the present time.

We have visited hospitals, undertakers, and scenes of the rioting, received statements from the relatives and friends of the victims, attended the exhumation of one body at Lincoln Cemetery for fuller confirmation as to the course of the bullet wound; have held seventy day sessions and twenty night sessions on inquest work, examining approximately four hundred and fifty witnesses, the testimony taken amounting to fifty-five hundred and eighty-four folio pages, typewritten. Twenty men were held to the Grand Jury for murder or manslaughter, one held to court martial for murder. There were seven cases of justifiable homicide. Recommendation that unknown rioters be apprehended and punished was made in eighteen cases. One Police Officer was killed, three men were killed by Police Officers. One case—that of Joseph Lovings, a colored man—is still under investigation.

Homicides, due to the riots, occurred in widely separated localities, on the south, southwest and west sides of the city. Particularly atrocious and cruel murder was committed on the persons of Morris Parel, Walter Parejko, Eugene Temple, David Marcus, Morris Lazzeroni and George L. Wilkins (white men), and Robert Williams, B.F. Hardy, John Mills, William H. Lozier, Oscar Lozier, Louis Taylor, Paul Hardwick and Joseph Lovings (colored men)....

We have no thought of, or desire, to criticize any of the city officials, the State's Attorney or the Police Department. In the grave emergency and riot conditions, we believe they all did their duty, as we conscientiously tried to do ours; nor do we believe that politics, so-called, or catering to the white or colored vote, had much if anything to do with the production of race rioting.

The riots began on the afternoon of July 27, 1919, when Eugene Williams, a colored boy, was drowned at the 29th street bathing beach, having been prevented from landing by stones thrown by a mob of white men and boys. Prior to that afternoon, this beach had been used exclusively by white people. The colored people contested the right of the white people thereto, and a pitched battle was fought with stones thrown between two mobs, the drowning of Williams being the result. The report of his death spread with great rapidity through the colored residence district, and the report was in general that he had been stoned to death in the water. Evidence disclosed that no stones struck the boy, that an attempt was made to stone him and stones were thrown in his direction. He was drowned—probably by reason of exhaustion due to the inability to land. However, the reports caused a white heat of passion and desire for reprisal among a large proportion of the colored population, and the riot spread.

July 27, 2 men were killed or sustained injuries causing death.

July 28, 17 men were killed or sustained injuries causing death.

July 29, 11 men were killed or sustained injuries causing death.

July 30, 5 men were killed or sustained injuries causing death.

July 31, 1 man was killed or sustained injuries causing death.

One George R. Fleming, white, was slain by a soldier, white, August 5th.

By August the 1st, the riots had subsided, the situation being well under control of the police and the soldiery, normal conditions being in part restored.

Incomplete police reports covering the five days of the rioting, show that one police officer was killed and thirty-nine wounded or injured; twenty-three colored men and fourteen white men killed; two hundred and ninety-one white and colored citizens wounded or injured. We have no report of white or colored women outraged and but few women were mistreated during the rioting. No evidence of drunkenness was presented.

To review the circumstances of all the thirty-eight homicides would be tiresome to the reader and serve no good purpose. As illustrating all of them we will review briefly the cases of Eugene Temple, a white man, and Joseph Lovings, a colored man. All verdicts rendered are on record in the Coroner's Office.

Eugene Temple, a reputable citizen and proprietor of the Columbia Laundry, located at 3642 South State Street, stepped from the doorway of his place of business, accompanied by his wife and another lady, and was thus upon the sidewalk about to enter his automobile. He was leisurely

approached by three colored men, who grabbed him, one on either side, at his back. While securely held by two of the men, the third man lifted up Mr. Temple's left arm and plunged a sharp and long knife, evidently a stiletto, through his heart. Then they as leisurely walked away, leaving their victim dead upon the sidewalk. Apparently, this was a cold blooded, calculated murder, without the element of race passion. There was evidence that some attempt had been made to rob him at the same time. These men have not been apprehended and presumably are walking the streets of Chicago, a constant and continual menace.

The slaying of Joseph Lovings, colored, was an atrocious, savage crime. He, a defenseless man, caught like a rat in a trap, by a surrounding mob, was dragged from his place of concealment and refuge, beaten, skull fractured, and shot fourteen times—left lying a bruised and broken semblance of a man, on the grass plot in front of a city home in the heart of the west side. This crime has not a single redeeming feature. It particularly illustrates the savage animal nature of a mob. To hunt down, apprehend and punish the dastardly criminals who killed this man, is the duty, not alone of the Police Department, but of every citizen who values the security of life. No wonder that reports of this crime grew to large proportions as it spread. It was published by the press of this and other large cities that he had been sprayed with gasoline and burned alive. Comments were made in Congress at Washington regarding the rumor. It gives us satisfaction to say that this rumor, from our investigation, is false and unsubstantiated—but the subtraction of this rumor mitigates the crime but a very slight degree.

Persistent reports have been circulated that the total number of deaths far exceeded thirty-eight. Intelligent citizens have approached the Coroner and members of this jury and gave their opinion that the number of deaths was far in excess of the number found. These reports were freely handed about and believed.

We have made a thorough investigation to verify or disprove these reports. Bubbly Creek has been the favorite cemetery for the undiscovered dead, and our inquiry has been partly directed to that stream. In our inquiry we have been assisted by the Stock Yard officials and workers, by adjacent property owners and residents, by private detective bureaus, the Police Department, Department of Health, State's Attorney's Office, by observing and intelligent colored citizens, and by other agencies, and we are firmly of the opinion that these reports, so widely circulated, are erroneous, misleading and without foundation in fact, the race riot victims numbering thirty-eight, and no more, nor are there any colored citizens reported to us as missing.

It has been said that the importation of colored labor from the South, congesting the south side residence district, caused ill feeling and friction, and was one of the causes of the rioting. The labor situation was a war condition; at the same time taking thousands of young men from the factory and shop for war service. Labor was needed, and employers turned to the South as their source of supply. Neither the Government, the employer nor

the southern laborer is to be criticized for that condition. And while some friction was produced, we doubt very much whether it was in any considerable measure productive of the rioting.

Nevertheless, it was unfortunate that negroes in large numbers, and unacquainted with northern ways, were induced to come or did come to the City of Chicago without adequate steps being taken to properly house and care for them. Naturally they gathered in the south division, where others of their race were to be found, and where there was congestion, abominable housing, and bad sanitary conditions. This, with the inadequate transportation facilities, notably in the rush hour, which resulted daily in the mixing of white and colored in the overcrowded street cars and elevated trains, tending to friction and bad feeling, can be readily understood.

These conditions can and should be changed. We believe that a representative committee of white and colored people, working together, could suggest and bring about the necessary and advisable changes.

The movement of the southern negro to the North, and mainly to the large northern cities, has brought the race problem to the North. It is serious indeed, but not necessarily a great danger, unless we allow it to become so. The problem is new to the North and must be solved by northern people. This problem is so large and entails such serious consequences that this jury feels itself powerless to do more than suggest its seriousness to the civilized thinking people of the North, both white and colored, in the hope that the initiative may be taken in the solution of the race problem, which is here now and here to stay.

In our investigations, numerous visits were made to the home district of the colored population, and we observed the housing conditions of which we had heard much.

Overcrowded and unmistakably bad living conditions were found, and we were impressed with the fact that the colored people justifiably for cleanliness and health had moved in considerable numbers to the east of Michigan Avenue and to the south of 39th Street, encroaching on the residence districts of the white people. The streets mentioned have been the boundaries voluntarily accepted by the colored population to within the past few years. The inrush of colored labor from the South caused congestion and resulted in a movement of considerable extent into the white neighborhoods where homes were purchased or leased.

Unquestionably this movement was encouraged by unscrupulous dealers in real estate, both white and colored, who were interested solely in the profits to be derived.

In our opinion the situation described was not a vital or material cause of the riot, but the rioting certainly awakened the public to the changing conditions of the south side residence district, and thoughtful men must consider that unless some remedy is found and applied, the situation is fruitful of unsettled and inharmonious relations in the future.

Source: Cook County (Illinois) Coroner. *The Race Riots: Biennial Report 1918–1919 and Official Record of Inquests on the Victims of the Race Riots of July and August, 1919, Whereby Fifteen White Men and Twenty-three Colored Men Lost Their Lives and Several Hundred Were Injured.* Chicago, 1920, 19–22.

See also: Asbury Park (New Jersey) Riot of 1970; Atlanta (Georgia) Riot of 1906; Atlanta (Georgia) Riot of 1967; Bellingham Riots (1907); Bensonhurst (New York) Incident (1989); Biloxi Beach (Mississippi) Riot of 1960; Black Church Arsons;

Bloody Sunday; Boston (Massachusetts) Riots of 1975 and 1976; Brownsville (Texas) Incident of 1906; Charleston (South Carolina) Riot of 1919; Chattanooga (Tennessee) Riot of 1906; Chester and Philadelphia (Pennsylvania) Riots of 1918; Chicago Commission on Race Relations; Chicago (Illinois) Riot of 1919; Cincinnati (Ohio) Riots of 1967 and 1968; Cincinnati (Ohio) Riots of 2001; Cleveland (Ohio) Riot of 1966; Detroit (Michigan) Riot of 1943; Detroit (Michigan) Riot of 1967; East St. Louis (Illinois) Riot of 1917; Election Riots of the 1880s and 1890s; Greensburg (Indiana) Riot of 1906; Greenwood Community (Tulsa, Oklahoma); Harlem (New York) Riot of 1935; Houston (Texas) Mutiny of 1917; Howard Beach (New York) Incident (1986); Johnson-Jeffries Fight of 1910, Riots Following; Knoxville (Tennessee) Riot of 1919; Long Hot Summer Riots (1965–1967); Longview (Texas) Riot of 1919; Los Angeles (California) Riot of 1965; Los Angeles (California) Riots of 1992; Miami (Florida) Riot of 1982; New Bedford (Massachusetts) Riot of 1970; New Orleans (Louisiana) Riot of 1866; New York City Draft Riot of 1863; New York City Riot of 1943; Newark (New Jersey) Riot of 1967; Orangeburg (South Carolina) Massacre of 1968; Philadelphia (Pennsylvania) Riot of 1964; Prison Riots; Race Riots in America; Red Scare and Race Riots; Red Summer Race Riots of 1919; Rosewood (Florida) Riot of 1923; Saint Genevieve (Missouri) Riot of 1930; San Francisco (California) Riot of 1966; Springfield (Ohio) Riot of 1904; Tampa (Florida) Riots of 1987; Texas Southern University Riot of 1967; Tulsa (Oklahoma) Riot of 1921; Washington (D.C.) Riot of 1919; Washington (D.C.) Riots of 1968; Wilmington (North Carolina) Riot of 1898; Zoot Suit Riots

Excerpt from the Final Report of the Grand Jury on the Tulsa Race Riot (June 25, 1921)

Introduction

In this excerpt from their final report, the grand jury charged with investigating the causes of the 1921 Tulsa riot places full blame for the violence on African Americans and completely exonerates whites of any part in starting the disorders. See also the entries on Tulsa (Oklahoma) Riot of 1921; Tulsa Race Riot Commission.

Primary Source

To the Honorable Judge Valjean Biddison, of the District Court, Tulsa County:

We, the grand jurors summoned by you to make an investigation of the cause of the recent riot, and other violations of the law in Tulsa and Tulsa County, beg leave to submit to you the following report, in addition to indictments and accusations which are already in your hands.

We first desire to state that we have examined a great many witnesses in our effort to arrive at the facts; we have advertised that we desired the full information of every citizen who knew facts: We have heard every one who requested to be heard in addition to the many who were summoned to appear; we have weighed the evidence impartially; we have sought to do justice to every individual and to carry out the instructions of the honorable court.

We find that the recent race riot was the direct result of an effort on the part of a certain group of colored men who appeared at the courthouse on the night of May 31, 1921, for the purpose of protecting one Dick Rowland then and now in the custody of the sheriff of Tulsa County for an alleged assault upon a young white woman. We have not been able to find any evidence either from white or colored citizens that any organized attempt was made or planned to take from the sheriff's custody any prisoner; the crowd assembled about the courthouse being purely spectators and curiosity seekers resulting from rumors circulated about the city. There was no mob spirit among the whites, no talk of lynching and no arms. The assembly was quiet until the arrival of armed negroes, which precipitated and was the direct cause of the entire affair.

While we find the presence of the armed negroes was the direct cause of the riot, we further find that there existed indirect causes more vital to the public interest than the direct cause. Among these were agitation among the negroes of social equality, and the laxity of law enforcement on the part of the officers of the city and county.

We find that certain propaganda and more or less agitation had been going on among the colored population for some time. This agitation resulted in the accumulation of firearms among the people and the storage of quantities of ammunition, all of which was accumulative in the minds of the negro which led them as a people to believe in equal rights, social equality and their ability to demand the same. We are glad to exonerate the great majority of the colored people who neither had knowledge of or part in either the agitation or the accumulation of arms or ammunition, and recognize the possibility of such a fact as even in as public a place as a church without the rank and file of the people having knowledge of the same. We have sought to ascertain the names of the particular parties who took part and the indictments returned show our findings.

Source: "Final Report of the Grand Jury on the Tulsa Race Riot." *Tulsa World*, June 26, 1921, 1, 8.

See also: Asbury Park (New Jersey) Riot of 1970; Atlanta (Georgia) Riot of 1906; Atlanta (Georgia) Riot of 1967; Bellingham Riots (1907); Bensonhurst (New York) Incident (1989); Biloxi Beach (Mississippi) Riot of 1960; Black Church Arsons; Bloody Sunday; Boston (Massachusetts) Riots of 1975 and 1976; Brownsville (Texas) Incident of 1906; Charleston (South Carolina) Riot of 1919; Chattanooga (Tennessee) Riot of 1906; Chester and Philadelphia (Pennsylvania) Riots of 1918; Chicago Commission on Race Relations; Chicago (Illinois) Riot of 1919; Cincinnati (Ohio) Riots of 1967 and 1968; Cincinnati (Ohio) Riots of 2001; Cleveland (Ohio) Riot of 1966; Detroit (Michigan) Riot of 1943; Detroit (Michigan) Riot of 1967; East St. Louis (Illinois) Riot of 1917; Election Riots of the 1880s and 1890s; Greensburg (Indiana) Riot of 1906; Greenwood Community (Tulsa, Oklahoma); Harlem (New York) Riot of 1935; Houston (Texas) Mutiny of 1917; Howard Beach (New York) Incident (1986); Johnson-Jeffries Fight of 1910, Riots Following; Knoxville (Tennessee) Riot of 1919; Long Hot Summer Riots (1965–1967); Longview (Texas) Riot of 1919; Los Angeles (California) Riot of 1965; Los Angeles (California) Riots of 1992; Miami (Florida) Riot of 1982; New Bedford (Massachusetts) Riot of 1970; New Orleans (Louisiana) Riot of 1866; New York City Draft Riot of 1863; New York City Riot of 1943; Newark (New Jersey) Riot of 1967; Orangeburg (South Carolina) Massacre of 1968; Philadelphia (Pennsylvania) Riot of 1964; Prison Riots; Race Riots in America; Red Scare and Race Riots; Red Summer Race Riots of 1919; Rosewood (Florida) Riot of 1923; Saint Genevieve (Missouri) Riot of 1930; San Francisco (California) Riot of 1966; Springfield (Ohio) Riot of 1904; Tampa (Florida) Riots of 1987; Texas Southern University Riot of 1967; Tulsa (Oklahoma) Riot of 1921; Washington (D.C.) Riot of 1919; Washington (D.C.) Riots of 1968; Wilmington (North Carolina) Riot of 1898; Zoot Suit Riots

Excerpts from the Transcripts of *Bee Publishing Company v. State of Nebraska* Regarding the Lynching That Occurred in Omaha in September 1919 (November 17, 1921)

Introduction

Filed on November 17, 1921, Bee Publishing Company v. State of Nebraska *concerns an appeal by the publisher of the* Omaha Bee *of his conviction for constructive contempt of court in publishing an article that allegedly attempted to sway public opinion on behalf of a* Bee *reporter who was awaiting trial on charges of arson. The charges against the reporter arose from his alleged activities during a September 1919 riot that concluded with the lynching of a black man being held on a rape charge and the subsequent burning of the courthouse from which he was taken by the mob. The excerpts from the trial transcripts that are reproduced below describe the riot and the events following that led to the arrest of the* Bee *reporter and the publication of the offending article.*

Primary Source

On November 11, 1919, the Bee Publishing Company, a corporation, Victor Rosewater, and John H. Moore, defendants, were jointly informed against by the county attorney for Douglas County, under Section 8236, Rev. St. 1913, and charged with a willful attempt to obstruct the proceedings and hinder the due administration of justice in a suit, then lately pending and undetermined, by the publication of a certain article in the *Omaha Sunday Bee*, November 9, 1919. Moore was acquitted, but the Bee Publishing Company and Rosewater were both found guilty of contempt and were each separately fined $1,000 and costs. They have brought the case here for review.

The exhibits and the evidence tend to show that the facts out of which this suit arose, and which form the basis of the newspaper story in question, are substantially these:

On the afternoon and night of Sunday, September 28, 1919, the Douglas County courthouse in Omaha was beset by a riotously assembled mob made up of several thousand persons who came together for the unconcealed purpose of lynching an inmate of the jail, who was suspected of having made an attempt to commit a heinous offense against a defenseless woman. The mob overpowered the police force and other of the city officials, all of whom were assisted by many law-abiding citizens, but to no avail, in an endeavor to restore order. The object of the mob's fury was seized and lynched, the courthouse was fired and in large part destroyed, and with it most of its contents, before the mob dispersed. Within a short time after the fire, namely, November 6, 1919, John H. Moore, a *Bee* reporter, was indicted by a grand jury specially called by the district court to inquire into the facts leading up to and connected with the riot and the fire. The indictment charged Moore with conspiring with others to commit arson. Two boys, named Morris and Thorpe, were suspected of being implicated in the riot and were arrested. While under arrest they testified before the grand jury and informed that body that they saw Moore, on the afternoon of the riot, leading a gang of boys to the courthouse, carrying gasoline and oils for the purpose of aiding in the conflagration. It was mainly on this evidence that the indictment against Moore was based.

Subsequently, and while the Moore case, pursuant to the indictment, was pending and undetermined in the district court, Morris and Thorpe furnished affidavits which in effect stated that their testimony before the grand jury with respect to Moore was false, and that it was obtained by coercion and intimidation practiced upon them, while under arrest, by certain members of the Omaha police force, and by promise of immunity from prosecution. The article that is set out in the information and that appears as an exhibit in the *Omaha Bee* of Sunday November 9, 1919, and other like exhibits, purport to give an account of some of the circumstances attending the fire and the alleged unfair methods under which the testimony that implicated Moore was obtained. The article, or newspaper story in question, covers about two columns of the newspaper exhibit of Sunday, November 9, and about six pages of legal cap in the information. It is too extended to be fully reproduced in this opinion.

The following headlines that precede the article that is incorporated in the information are in large display type:

Boys Disclose the Frame-up—Promised Freedom by Police—Captain Haze Offered Liberty to Prisoners for False Testimony Before Grand Jury, They Declare in Affidavits—Rotten Police Methods Laid Bare by Youths—Admit They Never Saw Bee Man They Testified Against Until After Case Had Been Framed by Detectives.

The excerpts in ordinary brevier type follow:

Captain of Police Henry P. Haze "framed up" the malicious and false testimony submitted to the grand jury upon which J. Harry Moore, reporter for the Bee, was indicted Friday, on a charge of conspiracy to commit arson in connection with the riot of September 28th. This statement was made to a reporter for the *Bee*, in the county jail yesterday by Ernest Morris and Harold Thorpe, confessed members of the mob, upon whose evidence the indictment against the reporter was returned. Both Morris and Thorpe made affidavits to the effect that Haze prevailed upon them to perjure themselves in order to convict Moore, whose investigations as a newspaper man have resulted in sensational and startling revelations against the Omaha police department, upon a promise that they would not be required to serve their full sentences in jail for rioting. They were told they would be released from jail as soon as the reporter had been tried and sent to the penitentiary. When the boys told Captain Haze they never had laid their eyes on the *Bee* reporter, the policeman replied that he would arrange it so they could see the man.

The article goes on to say that the boys changed their minds, and that Morris informed a reporter that after they got to thinking about it in jail they agreed they "did not want to be a party to a frame-up on an innocent man," and decided to "expose Captain Haze and the other detective." The writer of the article then observed that the other witness who testified against reporter Moore before the grand jury was a notorious bootlegger and a former policeman. Then follow the affidavits of Morris and Thorpe, that were printed as a part of the objectionable article, that purport to substantiate the foregoing statements, and many other statements of like import that appear in the article in question. Besides the foregoing excerpts, the article elsewhere, as it appears in the information, proceeds to vilify the police department generally, and the police officers who testified before the grand jury, and who would of necessity be witnesses at the coming trial against Moore in the district court. It proceeds to say that whether the police commissioner or the chief of police "had a hand in the frame-up on the reporter (Moore) Morris and Thorpe were unable to say." Continuing, the article observed that the commissioner always approved of Captain Haze's methods, and that the chief of police was known to have offered to promote a certain police officer if he succeeded in "getting" the *Bee* reporter.

Taylor Kennerly was the managing editor of the *Bee* when the objectionable article was published, and as the head of the editorial department he directed the news policy of the paper. He said that Rosewater never gave him any orders with respect to his work, and if he, the witness, was absent the city editor or the news editor determined what articles should appear. He testified that as a general proposition a communication or a reporter's story, before publication, was edited by one of six or seven men called copy readers, day editors, night editors, or telegraph editors.

It plainly appears that the article seriously reflected upon the integrity of the witnesses who appeared before the grand jury and who would in all probability testify in the district court. It took sides as between the state and the defendant, and opinions in respect of the merits were expressed. Violent comment was indulged in respecting the evidence, and the innocence of the accused was declared. Upon its face it is apparent that a bold attempt was made to mold public opinion favorable to Moore in advance of his trial, the Bee having an extensive circulation, not only throughout the state, but in the city and in Douglas County as well, the vicinity from which the jurors would be drawn and before whom Moore would be subsequently tried. Clearly an inflammatory harangue, in the locality where the trial was to be had, so worded, would tend to hinder the due administration of justice. That a publication so worded and so circulated, under the circumstances that prevailed at the place of its publication, constitutes constructive contempt of court is well settled.

Source: *Bee Publishing Company v. State of Nebraska; Victor Rosewater v. State of Nebraska*, Nos. 21314, 21315, Supreme Court of Nebraska, 107 Neb. 74; 185 N.W. 339 (1921).

See also: Anti-Lynching Campaign; Anti-Lynching League; Anti-Lynching Legislation; Lynching. Documents: Excerpts from Ida B. Wells's Exposé on Lynching (1895); Excerpts from the NAACP Report (1919); Excerpts from the "Anti-Lynching Hearings" (1920)

Excerpts of Testimony from *Laney v. United States* Describing Events during the Washington, D.C., Riot of July 1919 (December 3, 1923)

Primary Source

Decided on December 3, 1923, *Laney v. United States* involved an appeal by William Laney, an African American man convicted of manslaughter in the death of a white man during the July 1919 riots in Washington, D.C. Laney sought a new trial based on the trial court's refusal to allow him to assert a defense based on self-defense. The excerpts of testimony reproduced below include Laney's description of what happened on the night of July 21, 1919, as well as the supporting statement of his lady friend, Mattie Burke. The appeals court refused to overturn Laney's conviction, believing that he could have escaped without further incident, but instead deliberately exposed himself to the crowd to provoke further violence.

VAN ORSDEL, Associate Justice. This appeal is from a verdict and judgment of the Supreme Court of the District of Columbia, adjudging appellant, defendant below [William Laney], guilty of the crime of manslaughter. The indictment charged the defendant with the crime of murder in the first degree, growing out of the killing of one Kenneth Crall, during a race riot in Washington on July 21, 1919.

The defense interposed was self-defense, and a large number of assignments of error are based upon the refusal of the court to grant certain prayers offered by the defendant relating to the law of self-defense. The court instructed the jury on this subject, but we think it will be unnecessary for us to consider the assignments of error in relation to the prayers offered, since in our opinion, viewing the evidence in the most favorable aspect, self-defense does not enter into the case.

Defendant testified as follows:

On the night of the 21st of July, 1919, I went to the theater with Mattie Burke, and came back and went up on Seventh Street at the request of Teresa Dobbins, to get Florence and Garfield Wood. On my return to 617 Massachusetts Avenue, as I got to the corner where the Home Savings Bank is located, a large crowd that was there started to yelling "Catch the nigger!" and "Kill the nigger!" and started to chase me. I ran ahead of them down Massachusetts Avenue. When I got near to 617 Massachusetts Avenue, I pulled out my gun and the crowd stopped chasing me. I went into the back yard, and while trying to fix the safety on my gun it went off. I then put the gun in my pocket and went to the front again, intending to go back to my place of employment. The mob was attacking a house across the street, and were coming both ways on Massachusetts Avenue, from the direction of Sixth and from the direction of Seventh Street. While I was in the areaway between 617 and 619, the mob came across from the south side of the street, firing and hollering "Let's kill the nigger!" The mob was firing at me, and I shot in the direction towards Seventh Street. I fired to protect my life. I fired three shots. My pistol had eight bullets in it at first. There were four bullets in it when it was taken by the officials; three bullets having been fired in the front yard and one in the back yard.

The witness Mattie Burke testified, in relation to the movements of the defendant, as follows:

Later he came running back, with a mob chasing him, throwing sticks and stones at him, hollering "Catch the nigger!" I think Mr. Laney had his gun in his hand while he was running, but I did not see him do anything with it. He ran into the areaway between 615 and 617. The crowd, consisting of 100 or more men, then started after a house on the opposite side of the street. At that time William Laney went into the back yard and tried his gun. I was with him in the back yard at the time. Then we came out to the front again. After attacking the house on the opposite side of the street, the mob gathered in the car track as though they were coming toward 617, and then Laney fired his gun. After Laney had escaped through the back way, the crowd began to break into the house, and then I escaped myself over the back fence, and I did not see any more.

It is clearly apparent from the above testimony that, when defendant escaped from the mob into the back yard of the Ferguson place, he was in a place of comparative safety, from which, if he desired to go home, he could have gone by the back way, as he subsequently did. The mob had turned its attention to a house on the opposite side of the street. According to Laney's testimony, there was shooting going on in the street. His appearance on the street at that juncture could mean nothing but trouble for him. Hence, when he adjusted his gun and stepped out into the areaway, he had every reason to believe that his presence there would provoke trouble. We think his conduct in adjusting his revolver and going into the areaway was such as to deprive him of any right to involve the pleas of self-defense. Of course, the extent to which a person assailed may go, under a given state of facts involving self-defense, is always a question of fact for the jury; but whether or not self-defense can be invoked under the evidence adduced is a question of law for the court to determine. If the facts, in the judgment of the court, are not such as to admit of this defense, the issue should not be left to the mere speculation of the jury.

Source: *Laney v. United States*, No. 4000, Court of Appeals of the District of Columbia, 54 App. D.C. 56; 294 F. 412 (1923).

See also: Asbury Park Riot of 1970; Atlanta Riot of 1906; Atlanta Riot of 1967; Bellingham Riots; Bensonhurst Incident 1989; Biloxi Beach Riot of 1960; Black Church Arsons; Bloody Sunday; Boston Riot of 1975 and 1976; Brownsville Riot of 1906; Charleston Riot of 1919; Chattanooga Riot of 1906; Chester and Philadelphia Riots of 1918; Chicago Commission on Race Relations; Chicago Riot of 1919; Cincinnati Riots of 1967 and 1968; Cincinnati Riot of 2001; Cleveland Riot of 1966; Detroit Riot of 1943; Detroit Riot of 1967; East St. Louis Riot of 1917; Election Riots of the 1880s and 1890s; Greensburg Riot of 1906; Greenwood Community; Harlem Riot of 1935; Houston Mutiny of 1917; Howard Beach Incident 1986; Johnson-Jeffries Fight of 1910; Knoxville Riot of 1919; Long Hot Summer Riots 1965–1967; Longview Riot of 1919; Los Angeles Riot of 1965; Los Angeles Riots of 1992; Miami Riot of 1982; New Bedford Riot of 1970; New Orleans Riot of 1866; New York City Draft Riot of 1863; New York City Riot of 1943; Newark Riot of 1967; Orangeburg Massacre of 1968; Philadelphia Riot of 1964; Prison Riots; Race Riots in America; Red Scare and Race Riots; Red Summer Race Riots of 1919; Rosewood Riot of 1923; Saint Genevieve Riot of 1930; San Francisco Riot of 1966; Springfield Riot of 1904; Tampa Riots of 1987; Texas Southern University

Riot of 1967; Tulsa Riot of 1921; Washington, D.C., Riot of 1919; Washington, D.C., Riots of 1968; Wilmington Riot of 1898; Zoot Suit Riots

The National Origins Act of 1924 (Johnson-Reed Act)

Introduction

This is the most racist U.S. immigration law. It intended to favor Northern and Western European countries in immigrant visas and to restrict the number of immigrants from Southern and Eastern European countries. It also completely banned the immigration of non-Europeans who were not eligible for citizenship. As a result, the number of immigrants from Southern and Eastern European, predominantly non-Protestant, countries, was drastically reduced, and Asian immigration almost came to an end.

Primary Source

Sixty Eighth Congress. Sess. I. Ch. 185, 190. 1924.

Be it enacted by the Senate and House of Representatives of the United States of America in Congress assembled, That this Act may be cited as the "Immigration Act of 1924."

SEC. 2. (a) A consular officer upon the application of any immigrant (as defined in section 3) may (under the conditions hereinafter prescribed and subject to the limitations prescribed in this Act or regulations made thereunder as to the number of immigration visas which may be issued by such officer) issue to such immigrant an immigration visa which shall consist of one copy of the application provided for in section 7, visaed by such consular officer. Such visa shall specify (1) the nationality of the immigrant; (2) whether he is a quota immigrant (as defined in section 5) or a non-quota immigrant (as defined in section 4); (3) the date on which the validity of the immigration visa shall expire; and such additional information necessary to the proper enforcement of the immigration laws and the naturalization laws as may be by regulations prescribed.

(b) The immigrant shall furnish two copies of his photograph to the consular officer. One copy shall be permanently attached by the consular officer to the immigration visa and the other copy shall be disposed of as may be by regulations prescribed.

(c) The validity of an immigration visa shall expire at the end of such period, specified in the immigration visa, not exceeding four months, as shall be by regulations prescribed. In the case of a immigrant arriving in the United States by water, or arriving by water in foreign contiguous territory on a continuous voyage to the United States, if the vessel, before the expiration of the validity of his immigration visa, departed from the last port outside the United States and outside foreign contiguous territory at which the immigrant embarked, and if the immigrant proceeds on a continuous voyage to the United States, then, regardless of the time of his arrival in the United States, the validity of his immigration visa shall not be considered to have expired.

(d) If an immigrant is required by any law, or regulations or orders made pursuant to law, to secure the visa of his passport by a consular officer before being permitted to enter the United States, such immigrant shall not be required to secure any other visa of his passport than the immigration visa issued under this Act, but a record of the number and date of his immigration visa shall be noted on his passport without charge therefor. This subdivision shall not apply to an immigrant who is relieved, under subdivision (b) of section 13, from obtaining an immigration visa.

(e) The manifest or list of passengers required by the immigration laws shall contain a place for entering thereon the date, place of issuance, and number of the immigration visa of each immigrant. The immigrant shall surrender his immigration visa to the immigration officer at the port of inspection, who shall at the time of inspection indorse on the immigration visa the date, the port of entry, and the name of the vessel, if any, on which the immigrant arrived. The immigration visa shall be transmitted forthwith by the immigration officer in charge at the port of inspection to the Department of Labor under regulations prescribed by the Secretary of Labor.

(f) No immigration visa shall be issued to an immigrant if it appears to the consular officer, from statements in the application, or in the papers submitted therewith, that the immigrant is inadmissible to the United States under the immigration laws, nor shall such immigration visa be issued if the application fails to comply with the provisions of this Act, nor shall such immigration visa be issued if the consular officer knows or has reason to believe that the immigrant is inadmissible to the United States under the immigration laws.

(g) Nothing in this Act shall be construed to entitle an immigrant, to whom an immigration visa has been issued, to enter the United States, if, upon arrival in the United States, he is found to be inadmissible to the United States under the immigration laws. The substance of this subdivision shall be printed conspicuously upon every immigration visa.

(h) A fee of $9 shall be charged for the issuance of each immigration visa, which shall be covered into the Treasury as miscellaneous receipts.

Definition of Immigrant.

SEC. 3. When used in this Act the term "immigrant" means an alien departing from any place outside the United States destined for the United States, except (1) a government official, his family, attendants, servants, and employees, (2) an alien visiting the United States temporarily as a tourist or temporarily for business or pleasure, (3) an alien in continuous transit through the United States, (4) an alien lawfully admitted to the United States who later goes in transit from one part of the United States to another through foreign contiguous territory, (5) a bona fide alien seaman serving as such on a vessel arriving at a port of the United States and seeking to enter temporarily the United States solely in the pursuit of his calling as a seaman, and (6) an alien entitled to enter the United States solely to carry on trade under and in pursuance of the provisions of a present existing treaty of commerce and navigation.

Non-quota Immigrants.

SEC. 4. When used in this Act the term "non-quota immigrant" means—

(a) An immigrant who is the unmarried child under 18 years of age, or the wife, of a citizen of the United States who resides therein at the time of the filing of a petition under section 9;

(b) An immigrant previously lawfully admitted to the United States, who is returning from a temporary visit abroad;

(c) An immigrant who was born in the Dominion of Canada, Newfoundland, the Republic of Mexico, the Republic of Cuba, the Republic of Haiti, the Dominican Republic, the Canal Zone, or an independent country of Central or South America, and his wife, and his unmarried children under 18 years of age, if accompanying or following to join him;

(d) An immigrant who continuously for at least two years immediately preceding the time of his application for admission to the United States has been, and who seeks to enter the United States solely for the purpose of, carrying on the vocation of minister of any religious denomination, or professor of a college, academy, seminary, or university; and his wife, and his unmarried children under 18 years of age, if accompanying or following to join him; or

(e) An immigrant who is a bona fide student at least 15 years of age and who seeks to enter the United States solely for the purpose of study at an accredited school, college, academy, seminary, or university, particularly designated by him and approved by, the Secretary of Labor, which shall have agreed to report to the Secretary of Labor the termination of attendance of each immigrant student, and if any such institution of learning fails to make such reports promptly the approval shall be withdrawn.

Exclusion from United States.

SEC. 13. (a) No immigrant shall be admitted to the United States unless he (1) has an unexpired immigration visa or was born subsequent to the issuance of the immigration visa of the accompanying parent, (2) is of the nationality specified in the visa in the immigration visa, (3) is a non-quota immigrant if specified in the visa in the immigration visa as such, and (4) is otherwise admissible under the immigration laws.

(b) In such classes of cases and under such conditions as may be by regulations prescribed immigrants who have been legally admitted to the United States and who depart therefrom temporarily may be admitted to the United States without being required to obtain an immigration visa.

(c) No alien ineligible to citizenship shall be admitted to the United States unless such alien (1) is admissible as a non-quota immigrant under the provisions of subdivision (b), (d), or (e) of section 4, or (2) is the wife, or the unmarried child under 18 years of age, of an immigrant admissible under such subdivision (d), and is accompanying or following to join him, or (3) is not an immigrant as defined in section 3.

(d) The Secretary of Labor may admit to the United States any otherwise admissible immigrant not admissible under clause (2) or (3) of subdivision (a) of this section, if satisfied that such inadmissibility was not known to, and could not have been ascertained by the exercise of reasonable diligence by, such immigrant prior to the departure of the vessel from the last port outside the United States and outside foreign contiguous territory or, in the case of an immigrant coming from foreign contiguous territory, prior to the application of the immigrant for admission.

(e) No quota immigrant shall be admitted under subdivision (d) if the entire number of immigration visas which may be issued to quota immigrants of the same nationality for the fiscal year already been issued. If such entire number of immigration visas has not been issued, then the Secretary of State, upon the admission of a quota immigrant under subdivision (d), shall reduce by one the number of immigration visas which may be issued to quota immigrants of the same nationality during the fiscal year in which such immigrant is admitted; but if the Secretary of State finds that it will not be practicable to make such reduction before the end of such fiscal year, then such immigrant shall not be admitted.

(f) Nothing in this section shall authorize the remission or refunding of a fine, liability to which has accrued under section 16.

Deportation

SEC. 14. Any alien who at any time after entering the United States is found to have been at the time of entry not entitled under this Act to enter the United States, or to have remained therein for a longer time than permitted under this Act or regulations made thereunder, shall be taken into custody and deported in the same manner as provided for in sections 19 and 20 of the Immigration Act of 1917: Provided, That the Secretary of Labor may, under such conditions and restrictions as to support and care as he may deem necessary, permit permanently to remain in the United States, any alien child who, when under sixteen years of age was heretofore temporarily admitted to the United States and who is now within the United States and either of whose parents is a citizen of the United States.

Maintenance of Exempt Status.

SEC. 15. The admission to the United States of an alien excepted from the class of immigrants by clause (2), (3), (4), (5), or (6) of section 3, or declared to be a non-quota immigrant by subdivision (e) of section 4, shall be for such time as may be by regulations prescribed, and under such conditions as may be by regulations prescribed (including, when deemed necessary for the classes mentioned in clauses (2), (3), (4), or (6) of section 3, the giving of bond with sufficient surety, in such sum and containing such conditions as may be by regulations prescribed) to insure that, at the expiration of such time or upon subdivision (d), and is accompanying or following to join him, or (3) is not an immigrant as defined in section 3.

(d) The Secretary of Labor may admit to the United States any otherwise admissible immigrant not admissible under clause (2) or (3) of subdivision (a) of this section, if satisfied that such inadmissibility was not known to, and could not have been ascertained by the exercise of reasonable diligence by, such immigrant prior to the departure of the vessel from the last port outside the United States and outside foreign contiguous territory or, in the case of an immigrant coming from foreign contiguous territory, prior to the application of the immigrant for admission.

(e) No quota immigrant shall be admitted under subdivision (d) if the entire number of immigration visas which may be issued to quota immigrants of the same nationality for the fiscal year already been issued. If such entire number of immigration visas has not been issued, then the Secretary of State, upon the admission of a quota immigrant under subdivision (d), shall reduce by one the number of immigration visas which may be issued to quota immigrants of the same nationality during the fiscal year in which such immigrant is admitted; but if the Secretary of State finds that it will not be practicable to make such reduction before the end of such fiscal year, then such immigrant shall not be admitted.

(f) Nothing in this section shall authorize the remission or refunding of a fine, liability to which has accrued under section 16. failure to maintain the status under which he was admitted, he will depart from the United States.

SEC 28. As used in this Act—

(a) The term "United States," when used in a geographical sense, means the States, the Territories of Alaska and Hawaii, the District of Columbia, Porto Rico, and the Virgin Islands; and the term "continental United States" means the States and the District of Columbia;

(b) The term "alien" includes any individual not a native-born or naturalized citizen of the United States, but this definition shall not be held to include Indians of the United States not taxed, nor citizens of the islands under the jurisdiction of the United States;

(c) The term "ineligible to citizenship," when used in reference to any individual, includes an individual who is debarred from becoming a citizen of the United States under section 2169 of the Revised Statutes, or under section 14 of the Act entitled "An Act to execute certain treaty stipulations relating to Chinese," approved May 6, 1882, or under section 1996, 1997, or 1998 of the Revised Statutes, as amended, or

under section 2 of the Act entitled "An Act to authorize the President to increase temporarily the Military Establishment of the United States," approved May 18, 1917, as amended, or under law amendatory of, supplementary to, or in substitution for, any of such sections;

(d) The term "immigration visa" means an immigration visa issued by a consular officer under the provisions of this Act;

(e) The term "consular officer" means any consular or diplomatic officer of the United States designated, under regulations prescribed under this Act, for the purpose of issuing immigration visas under this Act. In case of the Canal Zone and the insular possessions of the United States the term "consular officer" (except as used in section 24) means an officer designated by the President, or by his authority, for the purpose of issuing immigration visas under this Act;

(f) The term "Immigration Act of 1917" means the Act of February 5, 1917, entitled "An Act to regulate the immigration of aliens to, and the residence of aliens in, the United States";

(g) The term "immigration laws" includes such Act, this Act, and all laws, conventions, and treaties of the United States relating to the immigration, exclusion, or expulsion of aliens;

(h) The term "person" includes individuals, partnerships, corporations, and associations;

(i) The term "Commissioner General" means the Commissioner General of Immigration;

(j)The term "application for admission" has reference to the application for admission to the United States and not to the application for the issuance of the immigration visa;

(k) The term "permit" means a permit issued under section 10;

(l) The term "unmarried," when used in reference to any as of any time, means an individual who at such time is not married, whether or not previously married;

1472   Excerpts from the Mayor's Commission on Conditions in Harlem

(m) The terms "child," "father," and "mother," do not include child or parent by adoption unless the adoption took place before January 1, 1924;

(n) The terms "wife" and "husband" do not include a wife husband by reason of a proxy or picture marriage.

> **Source:** The National Origins Act of 1924. *The Statutes at Large of the United States of America, from December, 1923 to March, 1925.* Vol. XLII, part 1, 153–69. Washington, DC: Government Printing Office, 1925.

> **See also:** 287g Delegation of Immigration Authority; Anchor Baby; Anti-Immigrant Sentiment; Immigration Acts; Immigration and Customs Enforcement; Operation Wetback; Unauthorized Immigration; United States Border Patrol

Excerpts from the Mayor's Commission on Conditions in Harlem (1935)

Introduction

In response to the race riots that erupted in Harlem in March 1935, New York mayor Fiorella LaGuardia appointed a commission to investigate the cause of the violence. Including among its members the distinguished African American sociologist E. Franklin Frazier, the commission dismissed the notion that communists and other outside agitators had started the riots, and concluded instead that the main causes of the disorders were racial discrimination, unemployment, and police brutality. Because Mayor LaGuardia refused to release the report, it was first made public by the New York Amsterdam News, *a leading African American newspaper.*

Primary Source

At about 2:30 on the afternoon of March 19, 1935, Lino Rivera, a 16-year-old colored boy, stole a knife from a counter in the rear of E.H. Kress and Company on 125th Street. He was seen by the manager of the store, Jackson Smith, and an assistant, Charles Hurley, who were on the balcony at the time. Mr. Hurley and another employee overtook the boy before he was able to make his escape through the front door. When the two men took the knife from Rivera's

pocket and threatened him with punishment, the boy in his fright tried to cling to a pillar and bit the hands of his captors. Rivera was finally taken to the front entrance, where Mounted Patrolman Donahue was called. The boy was then taken back into the store by the officer, who asked the manager if an arrest was desired. While Mr. Smith, the manager, instructed the officer to let the culprit go free—as he had done in many cases before—an officer from the Crime Prevention Bureau was sent to the store.

This relatively unimportant case of juvenile pilfering would never had acquired the significance which it later took on had not a fortuitous combination of subsequent events made it the spark that set aflame the smoldering resentments of the people of Harlem against racial discrimination and poverty in the midst of plenty. Patrolman Donahue, in order to avoid the curious and excited spectators, took the boy through the basement to the rear entrance on 124th Street. But his act only confirmed the outcry of a hysterical Negro woman that they had taken "the boy to the basement to beat him up." Likewise, the appearance of the ambulance which had been summoned to dress the wounded hands of the boy's captors not only seemed to substantiate her charge, but, when it left empty, gave color to another rumor that that the boy was dead. By an odd trick of fate, still another incident furnished the final confirmation of the rumor of the boy's death to the excited throng of shoppers. A hearse which was usually kept in a garage opposite the store on 124th Street was parked in front of the store entrance while the driver entered the store to see his brother-in-law. The rumor of the death of the boy, which became now to the aroused Negro shoppers an established fact, awakened the deep-seated sense of wrongs and denials and even memories of injustices in the South. One woman was heard to cry out that the treatment was "just like down south where they lynch us." The deep sense of wrong expressed in this remark was echoed in the rising resentment which turned the hundred or more shoppers into an indignant crowd.

The sporadic attempts on the part of the police to assure the crowd within the store that no harm had been done the boy fell upon unbelieving ears, partly because no systematic attempt was made to let representatives of the crowd determine the truth for themselves, and partly because of the attitude of the policemen. According to the testimony of one policeman, a committee of women from among the shoppers was permitted to search the basement, but these women have never been located. On the other hand, when the crowd became too insistent about learning the fate of the boy, the police told them that it was none of their business and attempted to shove them towards the door. This only tended to infuriate the crowd and was interpreted by them as further evidence of the suppression of a wronged race. At 5:30 it became necessary to close the store.

The closing of the store did not stay the rumors that were current inside. With incredible swiftness the feelings and attitude of the outraged crowd of shoppers was communicated to those on 125th Street and soon all of Harlem was repeating the rumor that a Negro boy had been murdered in the basement of Kress' store. The first sign of the reaction of the community appeared when a group of men attempted to start a public meeting at a nearby corner. When the police ordered the group to move from the corner, they set up a stand in front of Kress' store. A Negro who acted as chairman introduced a white speaker. Scarcely had the speaker uttered the first words of his address to the crowd when someone threw a missile through the window of Kress' store. This was the signal for the police to drag the speaker from the stand and disperse the crowd. Immediately, the crowd reassembled across the street and another speaker attempted to address the crowd from a perch on a lamppost. He was pulled down from his post and arrested along with the other speaker on a charge of "unlawful assemblage." . . . the extreme barbarity which was shown towards at least one of these speakers was seemingly motivated by the fact that these policemen who made derogatory and threatening remarks concerning Negroes were outraged because white men dared to take the part of Negroes. . . . These actions on the part of the police only tended to arouse resentment in the crowd which was increasing all the time along 125th Street. From 125th Street the crowds spread to Seventh Avenue and Lenox Avenue and the smashing of windows and looting of shops gathered momentum as the evening and the night came on. . . .

From its inception, as we have pointed out, the outbreak was a spontaneous and unpremeditated action on the part, first,

of women shoppers in Kress' store and, later, of the crowds on 125th Street that had been formed as the result of the rumor of a boy's death in the store. As the fever of excitement based upon this rumor spread to other sections of the community, other crowds, formed by many unemployed standing about the streets and other on-lookers, sprang up spontaneously. At no time does it seem that these crowds were under the direction of any single individual or that they acted as a part of a conspiracy against law and order. The very susceptibility which the people in the community showed towards this rumor—which was more or less vague, depending on the circumstances under which it was communicated—was due to the feeling of insecurity produced by years of unemployment and deep-seated resentment against the many forms of discrimination which they had suffered as a racial minority.

While it is difficult to estimate the actual number of persons who participated in the outburst, it does not seem, from available sources of information, that more than a few thousand were involved. These were not concentrated at any time in one place. Crowds formed here and there as the rumors spread. When a crowd was dispersed by the police, it often re-formed again. These crowds constantly changed their make-up. When bricks thrown through store windows brought the police, the crowds would often dissolve, only to gather again and continue their assaults upon property. Looting often followed the smashing of store windows. The screaming of sirens, the sound of pistol shots and the cracking of glass created in many a need for destruction and excitement. Rubbish, flowerpots, or any objects at hand were tossed from windows into the street. People seized property when there was no possible use which it would serve. They acted as if there were a chance to seize what rightfully belonged to them, but had long been withheld. The crowds showed various needs and changed their mood from time to time.

Some of the destruction was carried on in a playful spirit. Even the looting, which has furnished many an amusing take, was sometimes done in the spirit of children taking preserves from a closet to which they have accidentally found the key. The mood of these crowds was determined in many cases by the attitude of the police toward their unruly conduct. But, in the end, neither the threats nor the reassurances of the police could restrain these spontaneous outbursts until the crowds had spent themselves in giving release to their pent-up emotions.

Source: Mayor's Commission on Conditions in Harlem. *The Negro in Harlem: A Report on the Social and Economic Conditions Responsible for the Outbreak of March 19, 1935.* LaGuardia, Fiorello. Papers. Municipal Archives, New York, NY.

See also: Asbury Park Riot of 1970; Atlanta Riot of 1906; Atlanta Riot of 1967; Bellingham Riots; Bensonhurst Incident 1989; Biloxi Beach Riot of 1960; Black Church Arsons; Bloody Sunday; Boston Riot of 1975 and 1976; Brownsville Riot of 1906; Charleston Riot of 1919; Chattanooga Riot of 1906; Chester and Philadelphia Riots of 1918; Chicago Commission on Race Relations; Chicago Riot of 1919; Cincinnati Riots of 1967 and 1968; Cincinnati Riot of 2001; Cleveland Riot of 1966; Detroit Riot of 1943; Detroit Riot of 1967; East St. Louis Riot of 1917; Election Riots of the 1880s and 1890s; Greensburg Riot of 1906; Greenwood Community; Harlem Riot of 1935; Houston Mutiny of 1917; Howard Beach Incident 1986; Johnson-Jeffries Fight of 1910; Knoxville Riot of 1919; Long Hot Summer Riots 1965–1967; Longview Riot of 1919; Los Angeles Riot of 1965; Los Angeles Riots of 1992; Miami Riot of 1982; New Bedford Riot of 1970; New Orleans Riot of 1866; New York City Draft Riot of 1863; New York City Riot of 1943; Newark Riot of 1967; Orangeburg Massacre of 1968; Philadelphia Riot of 1964; Prison Riots; Race Riots in America; Red Scare and Race Riots; Red Summer Race Riots of 1919; Rosewood Riot of 1923; Saint Genevieve Riot of 1930; San Francisco Riot of 1966; Springfield Riot of 1904; Tampa Riots of 1987; Texas Southern University Riot of 1967; Tulsa Riot of 1921; Washington, D.C., Riot of 1919; Washington, D.C., Riots of 1968; Wilmington Riot of 1898; Zoot Suit Riots

Executive Order 9066 (February 1942)

Introduction

In February 1942, President Franklin D. Roosevelt ordered the establishment of internment camps and the forced evacuation of people of Japanese ancestry settled in the West Coast, with the exception of Hawaii. By this order, more than 100,000 Japanese Americans, including many U.S.-born citizens of Japanese ancestry, were interned in 10 camps established in the West.

Although the U.S. government's ostensible reason for their internment was the possibility of Japanese Americans engaging in espionage activities to help Japan in the Pacific War, there was no evidence that Japanese Americans were involved in such espionage activities. Many scholars have indicated that racial prejudice against Japanese Americans and white farmers' jealousy of Japanese Americans' success in farming in California led to political lobbies that contributed to the decision to intern Japanese Americans during the war in the Pacific.

Primary Source

Authorizing the Secretary of War to Prescribe Military Areas.

Whereas, The successful prosecution of the war requires every possible protection against espionage and against sabotage to national defense material, national defense premises, and national defense utilities as defined in Section 4, Act of April 20, 1918, 40 Stat. 533, as amended by the Act of November 30, 1940, 54 Stat. 1220, and the Act of August 21, 1941, 55 Stat.

655 (U.S.C., Title 50, Sec 104):

Now, therefore, by virtue of the authority vested in me as President of the United States, and Commander in Chief of the Army and Navy, I hereby authorize and direct the Secretary of War, and the Military Commanders whom he may from time to time designate, whenever he or any designated Commander deems such action necessary or desirable, to prescribe military areas in such places and of such extent as he or the appropriate Military Commander may determine, from which any or all persons may be excluded, and with respect to which, the right of any person to enter, remain in, or leave shall be subject to whatever restrictions the Secretary of War or the appropriate Military Commander may determine, from which any or all persons may be excluded, and with respect to which, the right of any person to enter, remain in, or leave shall be subject to whatever restrictions the Secretary of War or the appropriate Military Commander may impose in his discretion. The Secretary of War is hereby authorized to provide for residents of any such area who are excluded therefrom, such transportation, food, shelter, and other accommodations as may be necessary, in the judgment of the Secretary of War or the said Military Commander, and until other arrangements are made, to accomplish the purpose of this order. The designation of military areas in any region or locality shall supersede designations of prohibited and restricted areas by the Attorney General under the Proclamation of December 7 and 8, 1941, and shall supersede the responsibility and authority of the Attorney General under the said Proclamations in respect of such prohibited and restricted areas.

I hereby further authorize and direct the Secretary of War and said Military Commanders to take such other steps as he or the appropriate Military Commander may deem advisable to enforce compliance with the restrictions applicable to each Military area hereinabove authorized to be designated, including the use of Federal troops and other Federal Agencies, with authority to accept assistance of state and local agencies.

I hereby further authorize and direct all Executive Departments, independent establishments and other Federal Agencies, to assist the Secretary of War or the said Military Commanders in carrying out this Executive Order, including the furnishing of medical aid, hospitalization, food, clothing, transportation, use of land, shelter, and other supplies, equipment, utilities, facilities, and services.

This order shall not be construed as modifying or limiting in any way the authority heretofore granted under Executive Order 8972 dated December 12, 1941, nor shall it be construed as limiting or modifying the duty and responsibility of the Federal Bureau of Investigation, with respect to the investigation of alleged acts of sabotage or the duty and responsibility of the Attorney General and the Department of Justice under the Proclamation of December 7 and 8, 1941, prescribing regulations for the conduct and control of alien enemies, except as such duty and responsibility is superseded by the designation of military areas hereunder.

Franklin D. Roosevelt
The White House, February 19, 1942.

> **Source:** Executive Order 9066, February 19, 1942; General Records of the United States Government; Record Group 11; National Archives.

See also: Japanese Americans, Redress Movement for; Japanese Internment; World War II

Brown v. Board of Education (May 1954)

Introduction

In May 1954, the U.S. Supreme Court concluded in the case of Brown v. the Board of Education *that "in the field of public education, the doctrine of 'separate but equal' has no place" and that "separate facilities are inherently unequal." Thus, the 1954 Supreme Court ruling destroyed the doctrine of separate but unequal facilities supported by the Supreme Court in the 1896* Plessy v. Ferguson *case. The decision came to have the revolutionary impact of dismantling institutionalized segregation practices not only in education, but in other areas such as public transportation.*

Primary Source

Supreme Court of the United States
347 U.S. 483
Argued December 9, 1952
Reargued December 8, 1953
Decided May 17, 1954

APPEAL FROM THE UNITED STATES DISTRICT COURT FOR THE DISTRICT OF KANSAS*

Syllabus

Segregation of white and Negro children in the public schools of a State solely on the basis of race, pursuant to state laws permitting or requiring such segregation, denies to Negro children the equal protection of the laws guaranteed by the Fourteenth Amendment—even though the physical facilities and other "tangible" factors of white and Negro schools may be equal.

(a) The history of the Fourteenth Amendment is inconclusive as to its intended effect on public education.

(b) The question presented in these cases must be determined not on the basis of conditions existing when the

Fourteenth Amendment was adopted, but in the light of the full development of public education and its present place in American life throughout the Nation.

(c) Where a State has undertaken to provide an opportunity for an education in its public schools, such an opportunity is a right which must be made available to all on equal terms.

(d) Segregation of children in public schools solely on the basis of race deprives children of the minority group of equal educational opportunities, even though the physical facilities and other "tangible" factors may be equal.

(e) The "separate but equal" doctrine adopted in *Plessy v. Ferguson*, 163 U.S. 537, has no place in the field of public education.

(f) The cases are restored to the docket for further argument on specified questions relating to the forms of the decrees.

Opinion

MR. CHIEF JUSTICE WARREN delivered the opinion of the Court.

These cases come to us from the States of Kansas, South Carolina, Virginia, and Delaware. They are premised on different facts and different local conditions, but a common legal question justifies their consideration together in this consolidated opinion.

In each of the cases, minors of the Negro race, through their legal representatives, seek the aid of the courts in obtaining admission to the public schools of their community on a nonsegregated basis. In each instance, they had been denied admission to schools attended by white children under laws requiring or permitting segregation according to race. This segregation was alleged to deprive the plaintiffs of the equal protection of the laws under the Fourteenth Amendment. In each of the cases other than the Delaware case, a three-judge federal district court denied relief to the plaintiffs on the so-called "separate but equal" doctrine announced by this Court in *Plessy v. Ferguson*, 163 U.S. 537. Under that doctrine, equality of treatment is accorded when the races

are provided substantially equal facilities, even though these facilities be separate. In the Delaware case, the Supreme Court of Delaware adhered to that doctrine, but ordered that the plaintiffs be admitted to the white schools because of their superiority to the Negro schools.

The plaintiffs contend that segregated public schools are not "equal" and cannot be made "equal," and that hence they are deprived of the equal protection of the laws. Because of the obvious importance of the question presented, the Court took jurisdiction. Argument was heard in the 1952 Term, and reargument was heard this Term on certain questions propounded by the Court.

Reargument was largely devoted to the circumstances surrounding the adoption of the Fourteenth Amendment in 1868. It covered exhaustively consideration of the Amendment in Congress, ratification by the states, then-existing practices in racial segregation, and the views of proponents and opponents of the Amendment. This discussion and our own investigation convince us that, although these sources cast some light, it is not enough to resolve the problem with which we are faced. At best, they are inconclusive. The most avid proponents of the post-War Amendments undoubtedly intended them to remove all legal distinctions among "all persons born or naturalized in the United States." Their opponents, just as certainly, were antagonistic to both the letter and the spirit of the Amendments and wished them to have the most limited effect. What others in Congress and the state legislatures had in mind cannot be determined with any degree of certainty.

An additional reason for the inconclusive nature of the Amendment's history with respect to segregated schools is the status of public education at that time. In the South, the movement toward free common schools, supported by general taxation, had not yet taken hold. Education of white children was largely in the hands of private groups. Education of Negroes was almost nonexistent, and practically all of the race were illiterate. In fact, any education of Negroes was forbidden by law in some states. Today, in contrast, many Negroes have achieved outstanding success in the arts and sciences, as well as in the business and professional world. It is true that public school education at the time of the Amendment had advanced further in the North, but the effect of the Amendment on Northern States was generally ignored in the congressional debates. Even in the North, the conditions of public education did not approximate those existing today. The curriculum was usually rudimentary; ungraded schools were common in rural areas; the school term was but three months a year in many states, and compulsory school attendance was virtually unknown. As a consequence, it is not surprising that there should be so little in the history of the Fourteenth Amendment relating to its intended effect on public education.

In the first cases in this Court construing the Fourteenth Amendment, decided shortly after its adoption, the Court interpreted it as proscribing all state-imposed discriminations against the Negro race. The doctrine of "separate but equal" did not make its appearance in this Court until 1896 in the case of *Plessy v. Ferguson*, supra, involving not education but transportation. American courts have since labored with the doctrine for over half a century. In this Court, there have been six cases involving the "separate but equal" doctrine in the field of public education. In *Cumming v. County Board of Education*, 175 U.S. 528, and *Gong Lum v. Rice*, 275 U.S. 78, the validity of the doctrine itself was not challenged. In more recent cases, all on the graduate school level, inequality was found in that specific benefits enjoyed by white students were denied to Negro students of the same educational qualifications. *Missouri ex rel. Gaines v. Canada*, 305 U.S. 337; *Sipuel v. Oklahoma*, 332 U.S. 631; *Sweatt v. Painter*, 339 U.S. 629; *McLaurin v. Oklahoma State Regents*, 339 U.S. 637. In none of these cases was it necessary to reexamine the doctrine to grant relief to the Negro plaintiff. And in *Sweatt v. Painter*, supra, the Court expressly reserved decision on the question whether *Plessy v. Ferguson* should be held inapplicable to public education.

In the instant cases, that question is directly presented. Here, unlike *Sweatt v. Painter*, there are findings below that the Negro and white schools involved have been equalized, or are being equalized, with respect to buildings, curricula, qualifications and salaries of teachers, and other "tangible" factors. Our decision, therefore, cannot turn on merely a comparison of these tangible factors in the Negro and white schools involved in each of the cases. We must look instead to the effect of segregation itself on public education.

In approaching this problem, we cannot turn the clock back to 1868, when the Amendment was adopted, or even to 1896, when *Plessy v. Ferguson* was written. We must consider public education in the light of its full development and its present place in American life throughout the Nation. Only in this way can it be determined if segregation in public schools deprives these plaintiffs of the equal protection of the laws.

Today, education is perhaps the most important function of state and local governments. Compulsory school attendance laws and the great expenditures for education both demonstrate our recognition of the importance of education to our democratic society. It is required in the performance of our most basic public responsibilities, even service in the armed forces. It is the very foundation of good citizenship. Today it is a principal instrument in awakening the child to cultural values, in preparing him for later professional training, and in helping him to adjust normally to his environment. In these days, it is doubtful that any child may reasonably be expected to succeed in life if he is denied the opportunity of an education. Such an opportunity, where the state has undertaken to provide it, is a right which must be made available to all on equal terms.

We come then to the question presented: Does segregation of children in public schools solely on the basis of race, even though the physical facilities and other "tangible" factors may be equal, deprive the children of the minority group of equal educational opportunities? We believe that it does.

In *Sweatt v. Painter*, supra, in finding that a segregated law school for Negroes could not provide them equal educational opportunities, this Court relied in large part on "those qualities which are incapable of objective measurement but which make for greatness in a law school." In *McLaurin v. Oklahoma State Regents*, supra, the Court, in requiring that a Negro admitted to a white graduate school be treated like all other students, again resorted to intangible considerations: "his ability to study, to engage in discussions and exchange views with other students, and, in general, to learn his profession." Such considerations apply with added force to children in grade and high schools. To separate them from others of similar age and qualifications solely because of their race generates a feeling of inferiority as to their status in the community that may affect their hearts and minds in a way unlikely ever to be undone. The effect of this separation on their educational opportunities was well stated by a finding in the Kansas case by a court which nevertheless felt compelled to rule against the Negro plaintiffs:

Segregation of white and colored children in public schools has a detrimental effect upon the colored children. The impact is greater when it has the sanction of the law, for the policy of separating the races is usually interpreted as denoting the inferiority of the negro group. A sense of inferiority affects the motivation of a child to learn. Segregation with the sanction of law, therefore, has a tendency to [retard] the educational and mental development of negro children and to deprive them of some of the benefits they would receive in a racial[ly] integrated school system.

Whatever may have been the extent of psychological knowledge at the time of *Plessy v. Ferguson*, this finding is amply supported by modern authority. Any language in *Plessy v. Ferguson* contrary to this finding is rejected.

We conclude that, in the field of public education, the doctrine of "separate but equal" has no place. Separate educational facilities are inherently unequal. Therefore, we hold that the plaintiffs and others similarly situated for whom the actions have been brought are, by reason of the segregation complained of, deprived of the equal protection of the laws guaranteed by the Fourteenth Amendment. This disposition makes unnecessary any discussion whether such segregation also violates the Due Process Clause of the Fourteenth Amendment.

Because these are class actions, because of the wide applicability of this decision, and because of the great variety of local conditions, the formulation of decrees in these cases presents problems of considerable complexity. On reargument, the consideration of appropriate relief was necessarily subordinated to the primary question—the constitutionality of segregation in public education. We have now announced

that such segregation is a denial of the equal protection of the laws. In order that we may have the full assistance of the parties in formulating decrees, the cases will be restored to the docket, and the parties are requested to present further argument on Questions 4 and 5 previously propounded by the Court for the reargument this term. The Attorney General of the United States is again invited to participate. The Attorneys General of the states requiring or permitting segregation in public education will also be permitted to appear as amici curiae upon request to do so by September 15, 1954, and submission of briefs by October 1, 1954.

It is so ordered.

* Together with No. 2, *Briggs et al. v. Elliott et al.*, on appeal from the United States District Court for the Eastern District of South Carolina, argued December 9–10, 1952, reargued December 7–8, 1953; No. 4, *Davis et al. v. County School Board of Prince Edward County, Virginia, et al.*, on appeal from the United States District Court for the Eastern District of Virginia, argued December 10, 1952, reargued December 7–8, 1953, and No. 10, *Gebhart et al. v. Belton et al.*, on certiorari to the Supreme Court of Delaware, argued December 11, 1952, reargued December 9, 1953.

Source: *Brown v. Board of Education.* 347 U.S. 483 (1954).

See also: American Apartheid; *Bolling v. Sharpe* (1954); *Brown v. Board of Education* (1954); *Brown v. Board of Education* Legal Groundwork; Busing; *Cooper v. Aaron* (1958); *Cumming v. Richmond County Board of Education* (1899); Desegregation; Education; Gray Commission; Little Rock Nine; *Plessy v. Ferguson* (1896); School Segregation; Segregation; Separate But Equal Doctrine

Méndez v. Westminster (1954)

Introduction

The following is an excerpt from the decision of the U.S. Court of Appeals for the Ninth Circuit on one of the most important segregation cases in Mexican American history. This case, filed in 1945, was spearheaded by Gonzalo Méndez, a native of Mexico, and his wife Felicita Méndez, a native of Puerto

Rico. The controversy came to a head when the Méndezes tried to enroll their children in the Westminster Elementary School. They refused to receive an inferior education for their children; the community filed a suit against four Southern California school districts on behalf of 5,000 Mexican American families who demanded equal protection under the Fourteenth Amendment. The case later served as legal precedent for Brown v. Board of Education *(1954) that ended de jure segregation and established that separate was not equal.*

Primary Source

UNITED STATES CIRCUIT COURT OF APPEALS, NINTH CIRCUIT

161 F.2d 774; 1947 U.S. App. LEXIS 2835

April 14, 1947

The court found that the segregation as alleged in the petition has been for several years past and is practiced under regulations, customs, and usages adopted more or less as a common plan and enforced by respondent-appellants throughout the mentioned school districts; that petitioners are citizens of the United States, of Mexican ancestry, of good moral habits, free from infectious disease or any other disability, and are fully qualified to attend and use the public school facilities; that respondents occupy official positions as alleged in the petition.

In both written and oral argument, our attention has been directed to the cases in which the highest court of the land has upheld state laws providing for limited segregation of the great races of mankind. . . .

It is argued by appellants that we should reverse the judgment in this case upon the authority of the segregation cases . . . because the Supreme Court has upheld the right of the states to provide for segregation upon the requirement that equal facilities be furnished each segregated group. Appellees argue that the segregation cases do not rule the instant case. There is argument in two of the amicus curiae briefs that we should strike out independently on the whole question of segregation, on the ground that recent world stirring events have set men to the reexamination of concepts

considered fixed. Of course, judges as well as all others must keep abreast of the times but judges must ever be on their guard lest they rationalize outright legislation under the too free use of the power to interpret. We are not tempted by the siren who calls to us that the sometimes slow and tedious ways of democratic legislation [are] no longer respected in a progressive society. For reasons presently to be stated, we are of the opinion that the segregation cases do not rule the instant case and that is reason enough for not responding to the argument that we should consider them in the light of the amicus curiae briefs. In the first place we are aware of no authority justifying any segregation fiat by an administrative or executive decree as every case cited to us is based upon a legislative act. The segregation in this case is without legislative support and comes into fatal collision with the legislation of the state.

The State of California has a statewide free school system governed by general law, the local application of which by necessity is to a considerable extent, under the direction of district and city school boards or trustees, superintendents, and teachers. Section 16601 of the California Educational Code requires the parent of any child between the ages of eight and sixteen years to send him to the full-time day school. There are some few exceptions, but none of them are pertinent here. There are no exceptions based upon the ancestry of the child other than those contained in Secs. 8003, 8004, Calif.Ed.C. (both repealed as of 90 days after June 14, 1947), which includes Indians under certain conditions and children of Chinese, Japanese, or Mongolian parentage. As to these, there are laws requiring them in certain cases to attend separate schools. *Expressio Unius Est Exclusio Alterius.* It may appropriately be noted that the segregation so provided for and the segregation referred to in the cited cases includes only children of parents belonging to one or another of the great races of mankind. It is interesting to note at this juncture of the case that the parties stipulated that there is no question as to race segregation in the case. Amicus curiae brief writers, however, do not agree that this is so. Nowhere in any California law is there a suggestion that any segregation can be made of children within one of the great races. Thus it is seen that there is a substantial difference in our case from those which have been decided by the Supreme Court, a difference which possibly could be held as placing our case outside the scope of such decisions. However, we are not put to this choice as the state law permits of segregation only as we have stated, that is, it is definitely confined to Indians and certain named Asiatics. That the California law does not include the segregation of school children because of their Mexican blood, is definitely and affirmatively indicated as the trial judge pointed out, by the fact that legislative action has been taken by the State of California to admit to her schools, children [of] citizens of a foreign country, living across the border. Calif.Ed.C. §§ 16004, 16005. Mexico is the only foreign country on any California boundary.

It follows that the acts of respondents were and are entirely without authority of California law, notwithstanding their performance has been and is under color or pretense of California law. Therefore, conceding for the argument that California could legally enact a law authorizing the segregation as practiced, the fact stands out unchallengeable that California has not done so but to the contrary has enacted laws wholly inconsistent with such practice. By enforcing the segregation of school children of Mexican descent against their will, and contrary to the laws of California, respondents have violated the federal law as provided in the Fourteenth Amendment to the Federal Constitution by depriving them of liberty and property without due process of law and by denying to them the equal protection of the laws.

It may be said at this point that the practice of California law in California State Courts, and this may be so but the idea is of no relevancy. Mr. Justice Douglas made this point clear in the case of *Screws v. United States*, supra, when he said that the Fourteenth Amendment does not come into play merely because the federal law or the state law under which the officer purports to act is violated. "It is applicable when and only when someone is deprived of a federal right by that action." And it is as appropriate for us to say here, what Mr. Justice Douglas said in a like situation in the cited case, "We agree that when this statute is applied (in our case when Sec. 41(14) of 28 U.S.C.A. is applied) it should be construed so as to respect the proper balance between the states and the federal government in law enforcement." Punishment for the act would be legal under either or both federal and state governments. *United States v. Lanza*, 260 U.S. 377, S.Ct. 103,

71 L.Ed. 270, 48 A.L.R. 1102. However, since the practice complained of has continued for several consecutive years, apparent to California executive and peace officers, and continues, it cannot be said that petitioners violated Mr. Justice Douglas' admonition in taking their action in a federal court.

In the view of the case we have herein taken the contention that the Findings of Fact do not support the Conclusions of Law and the Judgment is wholly unmeritorious. The pleadings, findings, and judgment in this case refer to children of "Mexican and Latin descent and extraction," but it does not appear that any segregation of school children other than those of Mexican descent was practiced. Therefore, we have confined our comment thereto. If the segregation of all children of Latin descent and extraction in addition to those of Mexican descent were included in the practice and the plan, its illegality would, of course, be upon the same basis as that herein found. In addition, however, the impossibility of there being any reason for the inclusion in the segregation plan of all children of Latin descent and extraction and the palpable impossibility of its enforcement would brand any such plan void on its face.

Affirmed.

Source: *Mendez, et al v. Westminster School District*. 64 F.Supp. 544 (C.D. Cal. 1946).

See also: Chicano Movement; Civil Rights Movement; Desegregation; School Segregation; Segregation

The Civil Rights Act of 1964

Introduction

As a result of the civil rights movement in the latter half of the 1950s and early 1960s, Congress passed the Civil Rights Act of 1964 to end practices of racial segregation and other forms of racial discrimination. It was the most comprehensive legislation in American history that sought to end racial discrimination in the public arena. Its main objective was to end formal discrimination based on race, color, and/or national origin in various areas, such as voting, public accommodation, education, and employment.

Primary Source

An Act

To enforce the constitutional right to vote, to confer jurisdiction upon the district courts of the United States to provide injunctive relief against discrimination in public accommodations, to authorize the Attorney General to institute suits to protect constitutional rights in public facilities and public education, to extend the Commission on Civil Rights, to prevent discrimination in federally assisted programs, to establish a Commission on Equal Employment Opportunity, and for other purposes.

Be it enacted by the Senate and House of Representatives of the United States of America in Congress assembled, That this Act may be cited as the "Civil Rights Act of 1964."

Title I—Voting Rights
Title II—Injunctive Relief against Discrimination in Places of Public Accommodation

SEC. 201. (a) All persons shall be entitled to the full and equal enjoyment of the goods, services, facilities, and privileges, advantages, and accommodations of any place of public accommodation, as defined in this section, without discrimination or segregation on the ground of race, color, religion, or national origin.

(b) Each of the following establishments which serves the public is a place of public accommodation within the meaning of this title if its operations affect commerce, or if discrimination or segregation by it is supported by State action:

(1) any inn, hotel, motel, or other establishment which provides lodging to transient guests, other than an establishment located within a building which contains not more than five rooms for rent or hire and which is actually occupied by the proprietor of such establishment as his residence;

(2) any restaurant, cafeteria, lunchroom, lunch counter, soda fountain, or other facility principally engaged in selling food for consumption on the premises, including, but not limited to, any such facility located on the premises of any retail establishment; or any gasoline station;

(3) any motion picture house, theater, concert hall, sports arena, stadium or other place of exhibition or entertainment; and

(4) any establishment (A) (i) which is physically located within the premises of any establishment otherwise covered by this subsection, or (ii) within the premises of which is physically located any such covered establishment, and (B) which holds itself out as serving patrons of such covered establishment.

(c) The operations of an establishment affect commerce within the meaning of this title if (1) it is one of the establishments described in paragraph (1) of subsection (b); (2) in the case of an establishment described in paragraph (2) of subsection (b), it serves or offers to serve interstate travelers or a substantial portion of the food which it serves, or gasoline or other products which it sells, has moved in commerce; (3) in the case of an establishment described in paragraph (3) of subsection (b), it customarily presents films, performances, athletic teams, exhibitions, or other sources of entertainment which move in commerce; and (4) in the case of an establishment described in paragraph (4) of subsection (b), it is physically located within the premises of, or there is physically located within its premises, an establishment the operations of which affect commerce within the meaning of this subsection. For purposes of this section, "commerce" means travel, trade, traffic, commerce, transportation, or communication among the several States, or between the District of Columbia and any State, or between any foreign country or any territory or possession and any State or the District of Columbia, or between points in the same State but through any other State or the District of Columbia or a foreign country.

(d) Discrimination or segregation by an establishment is supported by State action within the meaning of this title if such discrimination or segregation (1) is carried on under color of any law, statute, ordinance, or regulation; or (2) is carried on under color of any custom or usage required or enforced by officials of the State or political subdivision thereof; or (3) is required by action of the State or political subdivision thereof.

(e) The provisions of this title shall not apply to a private club or other establishment not in fact open to the public, except to the extent that the facilities of such establishment are made available to the customers or patrons of an establishment within the scope of subsection (b).

SEC. 202. All persons shall be entitled to be free, at any establishment or place, from discrimination or segregation of any kind on the ground of race, color, religion, or national origin, if such discrimination or segregation is or purports to be required by any law, statute, ordinance, regulation, rule, or order of a State or any agency or political subdivision thereof.

SEC. 203. No person shall (a) withhold, deny, or attempt to withhold or deny, or deprive or attempt to deprive, any person of any right or privilege secured by section 201 or 202, or (b) intimidate, threaten, or coerce, or attempt to intimidate, threaten, or coerce any person with the purpose of interfering with any right or privilege secured by section 201 or 202, or (c) punish or attempt to punish any person for exercising or attempting to exercise any right or privilege secured by section 201 or 202.

SEC. 204. (a) Whenever any person has engaged or there are reasonable grounds to believe that any person is about to engage in any act or practice prohibited by section 203, a civil action for preventive relief, including an application for a permanent or temporary injunction, restraining order, or other order, may be instituted by the person aggrieved and, upon timely application, the court may, in its discretion, permit the Attorney General to intervene in such civil action if he certifies that the case is of general public importance. Upon application by the complainant and in such circumstances as the court may deem just, the court may appoint an attorney for such complainant and may authorize the commencement of the civil action without the payment of fees, costs, or security.

(b) In any action commenced pursuant to this title, the court, in its discretion, may allow the prevailing party, other than the United States, a reasonable attorney's fee as part of the costs, and the United States shall be liable for costs the same as a private person.

(c) In the case of an alleged act or practice prohibited by this title which occurs in a State, or political subdivision of a State, which has a State or local law prohibiting such act or practice and establishing or authorizing a State or local authority to grant or seek relief from such practice or to institute criminal proceedings with respect thereto upon receiving notice thereof, no civil action may be brought under subsection (a) before the expiration of thirty days after written notice of such alleged act or practice has been given to the appropriate State or local authority by registered mail or in person, provided that the court may stay proceedings in such civil action pending the termination of State or local enforcement proceedings.

(d) In the case of an alleged act or practice prohibited by this title which occurs in a State, or political subdivision of a State, which has no State or local law prohibiting such act or practice, a civil action may be brought under subsection (a): Provided, That the court may refer the matter to the Community Relations Service established by title X of this Act for as long as the court believes there is a reasonable possibility of obtaining voluntary compliance, but for not more than sixty days: Provided further, That upon expiration of such sixty-day period, the court may extend such period for an additional period, not to exceed a cumulative total of one hundred and twenty days, if it believes there then exists a reasonable possibility of securing voluntary compliance.

SEC. 205. The Service is authorized to make a full investigation of any complaint referred to it by the court under section 204(d) and may hold such hearings with respect thereto as may be necessary. The Service shall conduct any hearings with respect to any such complaint in executive session, and shall not release any testimony given therein except by agreement of all parties involved in the complaint with the permission of the court, and the Service shall endeavor to bring about a voluntary settlement between the parties.

SEC. 206. (a) Whenever the Attorney General has reasonable cause to believe that any person or group of persons is engaged in a pattern or practice of resistance to the full enjoyment of any of the rights secured by this title, and that the pattern or practice is of such a nature and is intended to deny the full exercise of the rights herein described, the Attorney General may bring a civil action in the appropriate district court of the United States by filing with it a complaint (1) signed by him (or in his absence the Acting Attorney General), (2) setting forth facts pertaining to such pattern or practice, and (3) requesting such preventive relief, including an application for a permanent or temporary injunction, restraining order or other order against the person or persons responsible for such pattern or practice, as he deems necessary to insure the full enjoyment of the rights herein described.

(b) In any such proceeding the Attorney General may file with the clerk of such court a request that a court of three judges be convened to hear and determine the case. Such request by the Attorney General shall be accompanied by a certificate that, in his opinion, the case is of general public importance.

A copy of the certificate and request for a three-judge court shall be immediately furnished by such clerk to the chief judge of the circuit (or in his absence, the presiding circuit judge of the circuit) in which the case is pending. Upon receipt of the copy of such request it shall be the duty of the chief judge of the circuit or the presiding circuit judge, as the case may be, to designate immediately three judges in such circuit, of whom at least one shall be a circuit judge and another of whom shall be a district judge of the court in which the proceeding was instituted, to hear and determine such case, and it shall be the duty of the judges so designated to assign the case for hearing at the earliest practicable date, to participate in the hearing and determination thereof, and to cause the case to be in every way expedited. An appeal from the final judgment of such court will lie to the Supreme Court.

In the event the Attorney General fails to file such a request in any such proceeding, it shall be the duty of the chief judge of the district (or in his absence, the acting chief judge) in which the case is pending immediately to designate a judge in such district to hear and determine the case. In the event that no judge in the district is available to hear and determine the case, the chief judge of the district, or the acting chief judge, as the case may be, shall certify this fact to the chief judge of the circuit (or in his absence, the acting chief judge) who shall then designate a district or circuit judge of the circuit to hear and determine the case.

It shall be the duty of the judge designated pursuant to this section to assign the case for hearing at the earliest practicable date and to cause the case to be in every way expedited.

SEC. 207. (a) The district courts of the United States shall have jurisdiction of proceedings instituted pursuant to this title and shall exercise the same without regard to whether the aggrieved party shall have exhausted any administrative or other remedies that may be provided by law.

(b) The remedies provided in this title shall be the exclusive means of enforcing the rights based on this title, but nothing in this title shall preclude any individual or any State or local agency from asserting any right based on any other Federal or State law not inconsistent with this title, including any statute or ordinance requiring nondiscrimination in public establishments or accommodations, or from pursuing any remedy, civil or criminal, which may be available for the vindication or enforcement of such right.

Discrimination because of Race, Color, Religion, Sex, or National Origin

SEC. 703. (a) It shall be an unlawful employment practice for an employer—

(1) to fail or refuse to hire or to discharge any individual, or otherwise to discriminate against any individual with respect to his compensation, terms, conditions, or privileges of employment, because of such individual's race, color, religion, sex, or national origin; or

(2) to limit, segregate, or classify his employees in any way which would deprive or tend to deprive any individual of employment opportunities or otherwise adversely affect his status as an employee, because of such individual's race, color, religion, sex, or national origin.

(b) It shall be an unlawful employment practice for an employment agency to fail or refuse to refer for employment, or otherwise to discriminate against, any individual because of his race, color, religion, sex, or national origin, or to classify or refer for employment any individual on the basis of his race, color, religion, sex, or national origin.

(c) It shall be an unlawful employment practice for a labor organization—

(1) to exclude or to expel from its membership, or otherwise to discriminate against, any individual because of his race, color, religion, sex, or national origin;

(2) to limit, segregate, or classify its membership, or to classify or fail or refuse to refer for employment any individual, in any way which would deprive or tend to deprive any individual of employment opportunities, or would limit such employment opportunities or otherwise adversely affect his status as an employee or as an applicant for employment, because of such individual's race, color, religion, sex, or national origin; or

(3) to cause or attempt to cause an employer to discriminate against an individual in violation of this section.

(d) It shall be an unlawful employment practice for any employer, labor organization, or joint labor-management committee controlling apprenticeship or other training or retraining, including on-the-job training programs to discriminate against any individual because of his race, color, religion, sex, or national origin in admission to, or employment in, any program established to provide apprenticeship or other training.

(e) Notwithstanding any other provision of this title, (1) it shall not be an unlawful employment practice for an employer to hire and employ employees, for an employment agency to classify, or refer for employment any individual, for a labor organization to classify its membership or to classify or refer for employment any individual, or for an employer, labor organization, or joint labor-management committee controlling apprenticeship or other training or retraining programs to admit or employ any individual in any such program, on the basis of his religion, sex, or national origin in those certain instances where religion, sex, or national origin is a bona fide occupational qualification reasonably necessary to the normal operation of that particular business or enterprise, and (2) it shall not be an unlawful employment practice for a school, college, university, or other educational institution or institution of learning to hire and employ employees of a particular religion if such school, college, university, or other educational institution or institution of learning is, in whole or in substantial part, owned, supported, controlled, or managed by a particular religion or by a particular religious corporation, association, or society, or if the curriculum of such school, college, university, or other educational institution or institution of learning is directed toward the propagation of a particular religion.

(f) As used in this title, the phrase "unlawful employment practice" shall not be deemed to include any action or measure taken by an employer, labor organization, joint labor-management committee, or employment agency with respect to an individual who is a member of the Communist Party of the United States or of any other organization required to register as a Communist-action or Communist-front organization by final order of the Subversive Activities Control Board pursuant to the Subversive Activities Control Act of 1950.

(g) Notwithstanding any other provision of this title, it shall not be an unlawful employment practice for an employer to fail or refuse to hire and employ any individual for any position, for an employer to discharge any individual from any position, or for an employment agency to fail or refuse to refer any individual for employment in any position, or for a labor organization to fail or refuse to refer any individual for employment in any position, if—

(1) the occupancy of such position, or access to the premises in or upon which any part of the duties of such position is performed or is to be performed, is subject to any requirement imposed in the interest of the national security of the United States under any security program in effect pursuant to or administered under any statute of the United States or any Executive order of the President; and

(2) such individual has not fulfilled or has ceased to fulfill that requirement.

(h) Notwithstanding any other provision of this title, it shall not be an unlawful employment practice for an employer to apply different standards of compensation, or different terms, conditions, or privileges of employment pursuant to a bona fide seniority or merit system, or a system which measures earnings by quantity or quality of production or to employees who work in different locations, provided that such differences are not the result of an intention to discriminate because of race, color, religion, sex, or national origin, nor shall it be an unlawful employment practice for an employer to give and to act upon the results of any professionally developed ability test provided that such test, its administration or action upon the results is not designed, intended or used to discriminate because of race, color, religion, sex or national origin. It shall not be an unlawful employment practice under this title for any employer to differentiate upon the basis of sex in determining the amount of the wages or compensation paid or to be paid to employees of such employer if such differentiation is authorized by the provisions of section 6(d) of the Fair Labor Standards Act of 1938, as amended (29 U.S.C. 206(d)).

(i) Nothing contained in this title shall apply to any business or enterprise on or near an Indian reservation with respect to any publicly announced employment practice of such business or enterprise under which a preferential treatment is given to any individual because he is an Indian living on or near a reservation.

(j) Nothing contained in this title shall be interpreted to require any employer, employment agency, labor organization, or joint labor-management committee subject to this title to grant preferential treatment to any individual or to any group because of the race, color, religion, sex, or national origin of such individual or group on account of an imbalance which may exist with respect to the total number or percentage of persons of any race, color, religion, sex, or national origin employed by any employer, referred or classified for employment by any employment agency or labor organization, admitted to membership or classified by any labor organization, or admitted to, or employed in, any apprenticeship or other training program, in comparison with the total number or percentage of persons of such race, color, religion, sex, or national origin in any community, State, section, or other area, or in the available work force in any community, State, section, or other area.

Approved July 2, 1964.

LEGISLATIVE HISTORY

HOUSE REPORTS: Nos. 914, 914 pt. 2 (Comm. on the Judiciary).

CONGRESSIONAL RECORD, Vol. 110 (1964):

Jan. 31; Feb. 1, 3–8: Considered in House.

Feb. 10: Considered and passed House.

Feb. 26: Senate placed bill on calendar.

Mar. 9–14, 16–21, 23–25: Senate debated motion to consider bill.

Mar. 26: Senate agreed to motion to consider bill.

Mar. 30, 31; Apr. 1–3, 6–11, 13–18, 20–25, 27–30; May 1, 2, 4–8, 11–16, 18–22, 25–28; June 1–6: Considered in Senate.

June 8: Motion for cloture filed in Senate.

June 9: Considered in Senate.

June 10: Senate adopted motion for cloture.

June 11–13, 15–18: Considered in Senate.

June 19: Considered and passed Senate, amended.

July 2: House concurred in Senate amendments.

> **Source:** Civil Rights Act of 1964. Public Law 88–352. *U.S. Statutes at Large* 78 (1964): 241.

> **See also:** Civil Rights Act of 1875; Civil Rights Act of 1957; Civil Rights Act of 1964; Civil Rights Act of 1968; Civil Rights Movement

Excerpt from the Immigration and Naturalization Act of 1965

Introduction

The Immigration and Naturalization Act of 1965 is the most liberal immigration act. It abolished discrimination in immigration based on race, national origin, and religion; allowed every country to send quota immigrants up to 20,000 per year and additional nonquota immigrants for unmarried children, spouses, and parents of U.S. citizens; and set three main criteria for immigration to the United States: family connections to those already in the United States, possession of occupational skills needed in the U.S. labor market, and vulnerability to persecution in the home country due to their religious or political ideology. Fully enforced in 1968, it has altered U.S. immigration patterns drastically. More than 85 percent of immigrants since 1968 have originated from non-European countries, mostly from Latin American and Asian countries.

Primary Source

An Act

To amend the Immigration and Naturalization Act, and for other purposes.

Be it enacted by the Senate and House of Representatives of the United States of America in Congress assembled, That section 201 of the Immigration and Naturalization Act (66 Stat. 175; 8 U.S.C. 1151) be amended to read as follows:

SEC. 201. (a) Exclusive of special immigrants defined in section 101(a)(27), and of the immediate relatives of United States citizens specified in subsection (b) of this section, the number of aliens who may be issued immigrant visas or who may otherwise acquire the status of an alien lawfully admitted to the United States for permanent residence, or who may, pursuant to section 203(a)(7) enter conditionally, (i) shall not in any of the first three quarters of any fiscal year exceed a total of 45,000 and (ii) shall not in any fiscal year exceed a total of 170,000.

(b) The "immediate relatives" referred to in subsection (a) of this section shall mean the children, spouses, and parents of a citizen of the United States: Provided, That in the case

of parents, such citizen must be at least twenty-one years of age. The immediate relatives specified in this subsection who are otherwise qualified for admission as immigrants shall be admitted as such, without regard to the numerical limitations in this Act.

(c) During the period from July 1, 1965, through June 30, 1968, the annual quota of any quota area shall be the same as that which existed for that area on June 30, 1965. The Secretary of State shall, not later than on the sixtieth day immediately following the date of enactment of this subsection and again on or before September 1, 1966, and September 1, 1967, determine and proclaim the amount of quota numbers which remain unused at the end of the fiscal year ending on June 30, 1965, June 30, 1966, and June 30, 1967, respectively, and are available for distribution pursuant to subsection (d) of this section.

(d) Quota numbers not issued or otherwise used during the previous fiscal year, as determined in accordance with subsection (c) hereof, shall be transferred to an immigration pool. Allocation of numbers from the pool and from national quotas shall not together exceed in any fiscal year the numerical limitations in subsection (a) of this section. The immigration pool shall be made available to immigrants otherwise admissible under the provisions of this Act who are unable to obtain prompt issuance of a preference visa due to oversubscription of their quotas, or subquotas as determined by the Secretary of State. Visas and conditional entries shall be allocated from the immigration pool within the percentage limitations and in the order of priority specified in section 203 without regard to the quota to which the alien is chargeable.

(e) The immigration pool and the quotas of quota areas shall terminate June 30, 1968. Thereafter immigrants admissible under the provisions of this Act who are subject to the numerical limitations of subsection (a) of this section shall be admitted in accordance with the percentage limitations and in the order of priority specified in section 203.

SEC. 2. Section 202 of the Immigration and Naturalization Act (66 Stat. 175; 8 U.S.C. 1152) is amended to read as follows:

(a) No person shall receive any preference or priority or be discriminated against in the issuance of an immigrant visa because of his race, sex, nationality, place of birth, or place of residence, except as specifically provided in section 101(a)(27), section 201(b), and section 203: Provided, That the total number of immigrant visas and the number of conditional entries made available to natives of any single foreign state under paragraphs (1) through (8) of section 203(a) shall not exceed 20,000 in any fiscal year: Provided further, That the foregoing proviso shall not operate to reduce the number of immigrants who may be admitted under the quota of any quota area before June 30, 1968.

(b) Each independent country, self-governing dominion, mandated territory, and territory under the international trusteeship system of the United Nations, other than the United States and its outlying possessions shall be treated as a separate foreign state for the purposes of the numerical limitation set forth in the proviso to subsection (a) of this section when approved by the Secretary of State. All other inhabited lands shall be attributed to a foreign state specified by the Secretary of State. For the purposes of this Act the foreign state to which an immigrant is chargeable shall be determined by birth within such foreign state except that (1) an alien child, when accompanied by his alien parent or parents, may be charged to the same foreign state as the accompanying parent or of either accompanying parent if such parent has received or would be qualified for an immigrant visa, if necessary to prevent the separation of the child from the accompanying parent or parents, and if the foreign state to which such parent has been or would be chargeable has not exceeded the numerical limitation set forth in the proviso to subsection (a) of this section for that fiscal year; (2) if an alien is chargeable to a different foreign state from that of his accompanying spouse, the foreign state to which such alien is chargeable may, if necessary to prevent the separation of husband and wife, be determined by the foreign state of the accompanying spouse, if such spouse has received or would be qualified for an immigrant visa and if the foreign state to which such spouse has been or would be chargeable has not exceeded the numerical limitation set forth in the proviso to subsection (a) of this section for that fiscal year; (3) an alien born in the United States shall be considered as having been born in the country of which he is a citizen or subject, or if he is not a citizen or subject of any country then in the last foreign country in which he had his residence as determined by the consular officer; (4) an alien born within any foreign state in which neither of his parents was born and in which neither of his parents had a residence at the time of such alien's birth may be charged to the foreign state of either parent.

(c) Any immigrant born in a colony or other component or dependent area of a foreign state unless a special immigrant as provided in section 101(a)(27) or an immediate relative of a United States citizen as specified in section 201(b), shall be chargeable, for the purpose of limitation set forth in section 202(a), to the foreign state, except that the number of persons born in any such colony or other component or dependent area overseas from the foreign state chargeable to the foreign state in any one fiscal year shall not exceed 1 per centum of the maximum number of immigrant visas available to such foreign state.

(d) In the case of any change in the territorial limits of foreign states, the Secretary of State shall, upon recognition of such change, issue appropriate instructions to all diplomatic and consular offices.

Source: Immigration and Naturalization Act of 1965. U.S. Statutes at Large, Public Law, 89–236 (1965): 911–922

See also: 287g; Anchor Baby; Anti-Immigrant Sentiment; Immigration Act of 1965; Immigration and Customs Enforcement; National Origin Immigration Act of 1924; Operation Wetback; Unauthorized Immigration; Undocumented Immigrants; United States Border Patrol

Excerpts from the Moynihan Report (March 1965)

Introduction

In March 1965, Daniel Patrick Moynihan, the undersecretary of labor policy planning in the Johnson administration, published a study titled The Negro Family: The Case for National Action. *The study, which was informally known as the Moynihan Report, looked at the potential for social advancement available to contemporary African Americans and found that the social and familial structures of African Americans were weak and highly dependent on white society. The following excerpts from the Moynihan Report look at what Moynihan and his researchers saw as the causes of the problem and some possible means for improvement.*

Primary Source

The United States is approaching a new crisis in race relations.

In the decade that began with the school desegregation decision of the Supreme Court, and ended with the passage of the Civil Rights Act of 1964, the demand of Negro Americans for full recognition of their civil rights was finally met.

The effort, no matter how savage and brutal, of some State and local governments to thwart the exercise of those rights is doomed. The nation will not put up with it—least of all the Negroes. The present moment will pass. In the meantime, a new period is beginning.

In this new period the expectations of the Negro Americans will go beyond civil rights. Being Americans, they will now expect that in the near future equal opportunities for them as a group will produce roughly equal results, as compared with other groups. This is not going to happen. Nor will it happen for generations to come unless a new and special effort is made.

There are two reasons. First, the racist virus in the American blood stream still afflicts us: Negroes will encounter serious personal prejudice for at least another generation. Second, three centuries of sometimes unimaginable mistreatment have taken their toll on the Negro people. The harsh fact is that as a group, at the present time, in terms of ability to win out in the competitions of American life, they are not equal to most of those groups with which they will be competing. Individually, Negro Americans reach the highest peaks of achievement. But collectively, in the spectrum of American ethnic and religious and regional groups, where some get plenty and some get none, where some send eighty percent of their children to college and others pull them out of school at the 8th grade, Negroes are among the weakest.

The most difficult fact for white Americans to understand is that in these terms the circumstances of the Negro American community in recent years has probably been getting worse, not better.

Indices of dollars of income, standards of living, and years of education deceive. The gap between the Negro and most other groups in American society is widening.

The fundamental problem, in which this is most clearly the case, is that of family structure. The evidence—not final, but powerfully persuasive—is that the Negro family in the urban ghettos is crumbling. A middle-class group has managed to save itself, but for vast numbers of the unskilled, poorly educated city working class the fabric of conventional social relationships has all but disintegrated. There are indications that the situation may have been arrested in the past few years, but the general post-war trend is unmistakable. So long as this situation persists, the cycle of poverty and disadvantage will continue to repeat itself.

The thesis of this paper is that these events, in combination, confront the nation with a new kind of problem. Measures that have worked in the past, or would work for most groups in the present, will not work here. A national effort is required that will give a unity of purpose to the many activities of the Federal government in this area, directed to a new kind of national goal: the establishment of a stable Negro family structure.

This would be a new departure for Federal policy. And a difficult one. But it almost certainly offers the only possibility of resolving in our time what is, after all, the nation's oldest, and most intransigent, and now its most dangerous social problem. What Gunnar Myrdal said in *An American Dilemma* remains true today: "America is free to chose whether the Negro shall remain her liability or become her opportunity."

CHAPTER III. THE ROOTS OF THE PROBLEM

Slavery
The most perplexing question abut American slavery, which has never been altogether explained, and which indeed most

Americans hardly know exists, has been stated by Nathan Glazer as follows: "Why was American slavery the most awful the world has ever known?" The only thing that can be said with certainty is that this is true: it was.

American slavery was profoundly different from, and in its lasting effects on individuals and their children, indescribably worse than, any recorded servitude, ancient or modern. The peculiar nature of American slavery was noted by Alexis de Tocqueville and others, but it was not until 1948 that Frank Tannenbaum, a South American specialist, pointed to the striking differences between Brazilian and American slavery. The feudal, Catholic society of Brazil had a legal and religious tradition which accorded the slave a place as a human being in the hierarchy of society—a luckless, miserable place, to be sure, but a place withal. In contrast, there was nothing in the tradition of English law or Protestant theology which could accommodate to the fact of human bondage—the slaves were therefore reduced to the status of chattels—often, no doubt, well cared for, even privileged chattels, but chattels nevertheless.

Glazer, also focusing on the Brazil–United States comparison, continues.

In Brazil, the slave had many more rights than in the United States: he could legally marry, he could, indeed had to, be baptized and become a member of the Catholic Church, his family could not be broken up for sale, and he had many days on which he could either rest or earn money to buy his freedom. The Government encouraged manumission, and the freedom of infants could often be purchased for a small sum at the baptismal font. In short: the Brazilian slave knew he was a man, and that he differed in degree, not in kind, from his master.

[In the United States,] the slave was totally removed from the protection of organized society (compare the elaborate provisions for the protection of slaves in the Bible), his existence as a human being was given no recognition by any religious or secular agency, he was totally ignorant of and completely cut off from his past, and he was offered absolutely no hope for the future. His children could be sold, his marriage was not recognized, his wife could be violated or sold (there was something comic about calling the woman with whom the master permitted him to live a "wife"), and he could also be subject, without redress, to frightful barbarities—there were presumably as many sadists among slaveowners, men and women, as there are in other groups. The slave could not, by law, be taught to read or write; he could not practice any religion without the permission of his master, and could never meet with his fellows, for religious or any other purposes, except in the presence of a white; and finally, if a master wished to free him, every legal obstacle was used to thwart such action. This was not what slavery meant in the ancient world, in medieval and early modern Europe, or in Brazil and the West Indies.

More important, American slavery was also awful in its effects. If we compared the present situation of the American Negro with that of, let us say, Brazilian Negroes (who were slaves 20 years longer), we begin to suspect that the differences are the result of very different patterns of slavery. Today the Brazilian Negroes are Brazilians; though most are poor and do the hard and dirty work of the country, as Negroes do in the United States, they are not cut off from society. They reach into its highest strata, merging there—in smaller and smaller numbers, it is true, but with complete acceptance—with other Brazilians of all kinds. The relations between Negroes and whites in Brazil show nothing of the mass irrationality that prevails in this country.

Stanley M. Elkins, drawing on the aberrant behavior of the prisoners in Nazi concentration camps, drew an elaborate parallel between the two institutions. This thesis has been summarized as follows by Thomas Pettigrew:

Both were closed systems, with little chance of manumission, emphasis on survival, and a single, omnipresent authority. The profound personality change created by Nazi internment, as independently reported by a number of psychologists and psychiatrists who survived, was toward childishness and total acceptance of the SS guards as father-figures—a syndrome strikingly similar to the "Sambo" caricature of the Southern slave. Nineteenth-century racists readily believed that the "Sambo" personality was simply an inborn racial type. Yet no African anthropological data have ever shown any personality type resembling Sambo; and the concentration camps molded the equivalent personality pattern in a wide variety of Caucasian prisoners. Nor was Sambo merely a product of "slavery" in the abstract, for the less devastating Latin American system never developed such a type.

Extending this line of reasoning, psychologists point out that slavery in all its forms sharply lowered the need for achievement in slaves. . . . Negroes in bondage, stripped of their African heritage, were placed in a completely dependent role. All of their rewards came, not from individual initiative and enterprise, but from absolute obedience—a situation that severely depresses the need for achievement among all peoples. Most important of all, slavery vitiated family life. . . . Since many slaveowners neither fostered Christian marriage among their slave couples nor hesitated to separate them on the auction block, the slave household often developed a fatherless matrifocal (mother-centered) pattern.

The Reconstruction

With the emancipation of the slaves, the Negro American family began to form in the United States on a widespread scale. But it did so in an atmosphere markedly different from that which has produced the white American family.

The Negro was given liberty, but not equality. Life remained hazardous and marginal. Of the greatest importance, the Negro male, particularly in the South, became an object of intense hostility, an attitude unquestionably based in some measure of fear.

When Jim Crow made its appearance towards the end of the 19th century, it may be speculated that it was the Negro male who was most humiliated thereby; the male was more likely to use public facilities, which rapidly became segregated once the process began, and just as important, segregation, and the submissiveness it exacts, is surely more destructive to the male than to the female personality. Keeping the Negro "in his place" can be translated as keeping the Negro male in his place: the female was not a threat to anyone.

Unquestionably, these events worked against the emergence of a strong father figure. The very essence of the male animal, from the bantam rooster to the four-star general, is to strut. Indeed, in 19th century America, a particular type of exaggerated male boastfulness became almost a national style. Not for the Negro male. The "sassy nigger [sic]" was lynched.

In this situation, the Negro family made but little progress toward the middle-class pattern of the present time. Margaret Mead has pointed out that while "In every known human society, everywhere in the world, the young male learns that when he grows up one of the things which he must do in order to be a full member of society is to provide food for some female and her young." This pattern is not immutable, however: it can be broken, even though it has always eventually reasserted itself.

Within the family, each new generation of young males learn the appropriate nurturing behavior and superimpose upon their biologically given maleness this learned parental role. When the family breaks down—as it does under slavery, under certain forms of indentured labor and serfdom, in periods of extreme social unrest during wars, revolutions, famines, and epidemics, or in periods of abrupt transition from one type of economy to another—this delicate line of transmission is broken. Men may flounder badly in these periods, during which the primary unit may again become mother and child, the biologically given, and the special conditions under which man has held his social traditions in trust are violated and distorted.

E. Franklin Frazier makes clear that at the time of emancipation Negro women were already "accustomed to playing the dominant role in family and marriage relations" and that this role persisted in the decades of rural life that followed.

Urbanization

Country life and city life are profoundly different. The gradual shift of American society from a rural to an urban basis over the past century and a half has caused abundant strains, many of which are still much in evidence. When this shift occurs suddenly, drastically, in one or two generations, the effect is immensely disruptive of traditional social patterns.

It was this abrupt transition that produced the wild Irish slums of the 19th Century Northeast. Drunkenness, crime, corruption, discrimination, family disorganization, juvenile delinquency were the routine of that era. In our own time, the same sudden transition has produced the Negro slum—different from, but hardly better than its predecessors, and fundamentally the result of the same process.

Negroes are now more urbanized than whites.

Negro families in the cities are more frequently headed by a woman than those in the country. The difference between the white and Negro proportions of families headed by a woman is greater in the city than in the country.

The promise of the city has so far been denied the majority of Negro migrants, and most particularly the Negro family.

In 1939, E. Franklin Frazier described its plight movingly in that part of *The Negro Family* entitled "In the City of Destruction":

The impact of hundreds of thousands of rural southern Negroes upon northern metropolitan communities presents a bewildering spectacle. Striking contrasts in levels of civilization and economic well-being among these newcomers to modern civilization seem to baffle any attempt to discover order and direction in their mode of life.

In many cases, of course, the dissolution of the simple family organization has begun before the family reaches the northern city. But, if these families have managed to preserve their integrity until they reach the northern city, poverty, ignorance, and color force them to seek homes in deteriorated slum areas from which practically all institutional life has disappeared. Hence, at the same time that these simple rural families are losing their internal cohesion, they are being freed from the controlling force of public opinion and communal institutions. Family desertion among Negroes in cities appears, then, to be one of the inevitable consequences of the impact of urban life on the simple family organization and folk culture which the Negro has evolved in the rural South. The distribution of desertions in relation to the general economic and cultural organization of Negro communities that have grown up in our American cities shows in a striking manner the

influence of selective factors in the process of adjustment to the urban environment.

Frazier concluded his classic study, *The Negro Family*, with the prophecy that the "travail of civilization is not yet ended."

First, it appears that the family which evolved within the isolated world of the Negro folk will become increasingly disorganized. Modern means of communication will break down the isolation of the world of the black folk, and, as long as the bankrupt system of southern agriculture exists, Negro families will continue to seek a living in the towns and cities of the country. They will crowd the slum areas of southern cities or make their way to northern cities where their family life will become disrupted and their poverty will force them to depend upon charity.

In every index of family pathology—divorce, separation, and desertion, female family head, children in broken homes, and illegitimacy—the contrast between the urban and rural environment for Negro families is unmistakable.

Harlem, into which Negroes began to move early in this century, is the center and symbol of the urban life of the Negro American. Conditions in Harlem are not worse, they are probably better than in most Negro ghettos. The social disorganization of central Harlem, comprising ten health areas, was thoroughly documented by the HARYOU report, save for the illegitimacy rates. These have now been made available to the Labor Department by the New York City Department of Health. There could hardly be a more dramatic demonstration of the crumbling—the breaking—of the family structure on the urban frontier.

Unemployment and Poverty
The impact of unemployment on the Negro family, and particularly on the Negro male, is the least understood of all the developments that have contributed to the present crisis. There is little analysis because there has been almost no inquiry.

Unemployment, for whites and nonwhites alike, has on the whole been treated as an economic phenomenon, with almost no attention paid for at least a quarter-century to social and personal consequences.

In 1940, Edward Wight Bakke described the effects of unemployment on family structure in terms of six stages of adjustment. Although the families studied were white, the pattern would clearly seem to be a general one, and apply to Negro families as well.

The first two stages end with the exhaustion of credit and the entry of the wife into the labor force. The father is no longer the provider and the elder children become resentful.

The third stage is the critical one of commencing a new day-to-day existence. At this point two women are in charge:

Consider the fact that relief investigators or case workers are normally women and deal with the housewife. Already suffering a loss in prestige and authority in the family because of his failure to be the chief bread winner, the male head of the family feels deeply this obvious transfer of planning for the family's well-being to two women, one of them an outsider. His role is reduced to that of errand boy to and from the relief office.

If the family makes it through this stage Bakke finds that it is likely to survive, and the rest of the process is one of adjustment. The critical element of adjustment was not welfare payments, but work.

Having observed our families under conditions of unemployment with no public help, or with that help coming from direct [sic] and from work relief, we are convinced that after the exhaustion of self-produced resources, work relief is the only type of assistance which can restore the strained bonds of family relationship in a way which promises the continued functioning of that family in meeting the responsibilities imposed upon it by our culture.

Work is precisely the one thing the Negro family head in such circumstances has not received over the past generation.

The fundamental, overwhelming fact is that Negro unemployment, with the exception of a few years during World War II and the Korean War, has continued at disaster levels for 35 years.

Once again, this is particularly the case in the northern urban areas to which the Negro population has been moving.

The 1930 Census (taken in the spring, before the Depression was in full swing) showed Negro unemployment at 6.1 percent, as against 6.6 percent for whites. But taking out the South reversed the relationship: white 7.4 percent, nonwhite 11.5 percent.

By 1940, the 2 to 1 white-Negro unemployment relationship that persists to this day had clearly emerged. Taking out the South again, whites were 14.8 percent, nonwhites 29.7 percent.

Since 1929, the Negro worker has been tremendously affected by the movements of the business cycle and of employment. He has been hit worse by declines than whites, and proportionately helped more by recoveries.

From 1951 to 1963, the level of the Negro male unemployment was on a long-run rising trend, while at the same time following the short-run ups and downs of the business cycle. During the same period, the number of broken families in the Negro world was also on a long-run rise, with intermediate ups and downs.

[The data reveal] that the series move in the same directions—up and down together, with a long-run rising trend—but that the peaks and troughs are 1 year out of phase. Thus unemployment peaks 1 year before broken families, and so on. By plotting these series in terms of deviation from trend, and moving the unemployment curve 1 year ahead, we see the clear relation of the two otherwise seemingly unrelated series of events; the cyclical swings in unemployment have their counterpart in increases and decreases in separations.

The effect of recession unemployment on divorces further illustrates the economic roots of the problem. The nonwhite divorce rates dipped slightly in high unemployment years like 1954–55, 1958, and 1961–62. . . .

Divorce is expensive: those without money resort to separation or desertion. While divorce is not a desirable goal for a society, it recognizes the importance of marriage and family, and for children some family continuity and support is more likely when the institution of the family has been so recognized.

The conclusion from these and similar data is difficult to avoid: During times when jobs were reasonably plentiful (although at no time during this period, save perhaps the first 2 years, did the unemployment rate for Negro males drop to anything like a reasonable level) the Negro family became stronger and more stable. As jobs became more and more difficult to find, the stability of the family became more and more difficult to maintain.

This relation is clearly seen in terms of the illegitimacy rates of census tracts in the District of Columbia compared with male unemployment rates in the same neighborhoods.

In 1963, a prosperous year, 29.2 percent of all Negro men in the labor force were unemployed at some time during the year. Almost half of these men were out of work 15 weeks or more.

The impact of poverty on Negro family structure is no less obvious, although again it may not be widely acknowledged. There would seem to be an American tradition, agrarian in its origins but reinforced by that family morality and stability decline as income and social position rise. Over the years this may have provided some consolation to the poor, but there is little evidence that it is true. On the contrary, higher family incomes are unmistakably associated with greater family stability—which comes first may be a matter for conjecture, but the conjunction of the two characteristics is unmistakable.

The Negro family is no exception. In the District of Columbia, for example, census tracts with median incomes over $8,000 had an illegitimacy rate one-third that of tracts in the category under $4,000.

The Wage System
The American wage system is conspicuous in the degree to which it provides high incomes for individuals, but is rarely adjusted to insure that family, as well as individual needs are met. Almost without exception, the social welfare and social insurance systems of other industrial democracies provide for some adjustment or supplement of a worker's income to provide for the extra expenses of those with families. American arrangements do not, save for income tax deductions.

The Federal minimum wage of $1.25 per hour provides a basic income for an individual, but an income well below the poverty line for a couple, much less a family with children.

The 1965 Economic Report of the President revised the data on the number of persons living in poverty in the United States to take account of the varying needs of families of different sizes, rather than using a flat cut off at the $3,000 income level. The resulting revision illustrated the significance of family size. Using these criteria, the number of poor families is smaller, but the number of large families who are poor increases, and the number of children in poverty rises by more than one-third—from 11 million to 15 million. This means that one-fourth of the Nation's children live in families that are poor.

A third of these children belong to families in which the father was not only present, but was employed the year round. In overall terms, median family income is lower for large families than for small families. Families of six or more children have median incomes 24 percent below families with three. (It may be added that 47 percent of young men who fail the Selective Service education test come from families of six or more.)

During the 1950–60 decade of heavy Negro migration to the cities of the North and West, the ratio of nonwhite to white family income in cities increased from 57 to 63 percent. Corresponding declines in the ratio in the rural nonfarm and farm areas kept the national ratio virtually unchanged. But between 1960 and 1963, median nonwhite family income slipped from 55 percent to 53 percent of white income. The drop occurred in three regions, with only the South, where a larger proportion of Negro families have more than one earner, showing a slight improvement.

Because in general terms Negro families have the largest number of children and the lowest incomes, many Negro fathers literally cannot support their families. Because the father is either not present, is unemployed, or makes such a low wage, the Negro woman goes to work. Fifty-six percent of Negro women, age 25 to 64, are in the work force, against 42 percent of white women. This dependence on the mother's income undermines the position of the father and deprives the children of the kind of attention, particularly in school matters, which is now a standard feature of middle-class upbringing.

The Dimensions Grow

The dimensions of the problems of Negro Americans are compounded by the present extraordinary growth in Negro population. At the founding of the nation, and into the first decade of the 19th century, 1 American in 5 was a Negro. The proportion declined steadily until it was only 1 in 10 by 1920, where it held until the 1950's, when it began to rise. Since 1950, the Negro population has grown at a rate of 2.4 percent per year compared with 1.7 percent for the total population. If this rate continues, in seven years 1 American in 8 will be nonwhite.

These changes are the result of a declining Negro death rate, now approaching that of the nation generally, and a fertility rate that grew steadily during the postwar period. By 1959, the ratio of white to nonwhite fertility rates reached 1:1.42. Both the white and nonwhite fertility rates have declined since 1959, but the differential has not narrowed.

Family size increased among nonwhite families between 1950 and 1960—as much for those without fathers as for those with fathers. Average family size changed little among white families, with a slight increase in the size of husband-wife families balanced by a decline in the size of families without fathers.

Negro women not only have more children, but have them earlier. Thus in 1960, there were 1,247 ever children born per thousand ever-married nonwhite women 15 to 19 years of age, as against only 725 among white women, a ratio of 1.7:1. The Negro fertility rate overall is now 1.4 times the white, but what might be called the generation rate is 1.7 times the white.

This population growth must inevitably lead to an unconcealable crisis in Negro unemployment. The most conspicuous failure of the American social system in the past 10 years has been its inadequacy in providing jobs for Negro youth. Thus, in January 1965 the unemployment rate for Negro teenagers stood at 29 percent. This problem will now become steadily more serious.

During the rest of the 1960's the nonwhite civilian population 14 years of age and over will increase by 20 percent—more than double the white rate. The nonwhite labor force will correspondingly increase 20 percent in the next 6 years, double the rate of increase in the nonwhite labor force of the past decade.

As with the population as a whole, there is much evidence that children are being born most rapidly in those Negro families with the least financial resources. This is an ancient pattern, but because the needs of children are greater today it is very possible that the education and opportunity gap between the offspring of these families and those of stable middle-class unions is not closing, but is growing wider.

A cycle is at work; too many children too early make it most difficult for the parents to finish school. (In February, 1963, 38 percent of the white girls who dropped out of school did so because of marriage or pregnancy, as against 49 percent of nonwhite girls.) An Urban League study in New York reported that 44 percent of girl dropouts left school because of pregnancy.

Low education levels in turn produce low income levels, which deprive children of many opportunities, and so the cycle repeats itself.

CHAPTER V. THE CASE FOR NATIONAL ACTION

The object of this study has been to define a problem, rather than propose solutions to it. We have kept within these confines for three reasons.

First, there are many persons, within and without the Government, who do not feel the problem exists, at least in any serious degree. These persons feel that, with the legal obstacles to assimilation out of the way, matters will take care of themselves in the normal course of events. This is a fundamental issue, and requires a decision within the government.

Second, it is our view that the problem is so inter-related, one thing with another, that any list of program proposals would necessarily be incomplete, and would distract attention from the main point of inter-relatedness. We have shown a clear relation between male employment, for example, and the number of welfare dependent children. Employment in turn reflects educational achievement, which depends in large part on family stability, which reflects employment. Where we should break into this cycle, and how, are the most difficult domestic questions facing the United States. We must first reach agreement on what the problem is, then we will know what questions must be answered.

Third, it is necessary to acknowledge the view, held by a number of responsible persons, that this problem may in fact be out of control. This is a view with which we emphatically and totally disagree, but the view must be acknowledged. The persistent rise in Negro educational achievement is probably the main trend that belies this thesis. On the other hand our study has produced some clear indications that the situation may indeed have begun to feed on itself. It may be noted, for example, that for most of the post-war period male Negro unemployment and the number of new AFDC [Aid to Families with Dependent Children] cases rose and fell together as if connected by a chain from 1948 to 1962. The correlation between the two series of data was an astonishing .91. (This would mean that 83 percent of the rise and fall in AFDC cases can be statistically ascribed to the rise and fall in the unemployment rate.) In 1960, however, for the first time, unemployment declined, but the number of new AFDC cases rose. In 1963 this happened a second time. In 1964 a third. The possible implications of these and other data are serious enough that they, too, should be understood before program proposals are made.

However, the argument of this paper does lead to one central conclusion: Whatever the specific elements of a national effort designed to resolve this problem, those elements must be coordinated in terms of one general strategy.

What then is that problem? We feel the answer is clear enough. Three centuries of injustice have brought about deep-seated structural distortions in the life of the Negro American. At this point, the present tangle of pathology is capable of perpetuating itself without assistance from the white world. The cycle can be broken only if these distortions are set right.

In a word, a national effort towards the problems of Negro Americans must be directed towards the question of family structure. The object should be to strengthen the Negro family so as to enable it to raise and support its members as do other families. After that, how this group of Americans chooses to run its affairs, take advantage of its opportunities, or fail to do so, is none of the nation's business.

The fundamental importance and urgency of restoring the Negro American Family structure has been evident for some time. E. Franklin Frazier put it most succinctly in 1950:

As the result of family disorganization a large proportion of Negro children and youth have not undergone the socialization which only the family can provide. The disorganized families have failed to provide for their emotional needs and have not provided the discipline and habits which are necessary for personality development. Because the disorganized family has failed in its function as a socializing agency, it has handicapped the children in their relations to the institutions in the community. Moreover, family disorganization has been partially responsible for a large amount of juvenile delinquency and adult crime among Negroes. Since the widespread family disorganization among Negroes has resulted from the failure of the father to play the role in family life required by American society, the mitigation of this problem must await those changes in the Negro and American society which will enable the Negro father to play the role required of him.

Nothing was done in response to Frazier's argument. Matters were left to take care of themselves, and as matters will, grew worse not better. The problem is now more serious, the obstacles greater. There is, however, a profound change for the better in one respect. The President has committed the nation to an all out effort to eliminate poverty wherever it exists, among whites or Negroes, and a militant, organized, and responsible Negro movement exists to join in that effort.

Such a national effort could be stated thus:

The policy of the United States is to bring the Negro American to full and equal sharing in the responsibilities and rewards of citizenship. To this end, the programs of the Federal government bearing on this objective shall be designed to have the effect, directly or indirectly, of enhancing the stability and resources of the Negro American family.

Source: *The Negro Family: The Case for National Action.* Office of Planning and Research, United States Department of Labor (March, 1965). Full text available at: www.dol.gov/oasam/programs/history/webid-meynihan.htm.

See also: Civil Rights Act of 1964; Race Relations Cycle

Excerpt from the Governor's Commission Report on the Watts Riots (December 1965)

Introduction

Reproduced here is an excerpt from the report, titled "Violence in the City—An End or a Beginning?" compiled by the commission appointed by California governor Edmund G. Brown to investigate the causes and course of the riots that erupted in the Watts district of Los Angeles in August 1965. The governor also charged the commission, which was chaired by John A. McCone, with developing recommendations for how to avoid similar violence in the future. The following excerpt describes how the riot started and grew.

Primary Source

144 HOURS IN AUGUST 1965

The Frye Arrests
On August 11, 1965, California Highway Patrolman Lee W. Minikus, a Caucasian, was riding his motorcycle along 122nd Street, just south of the Los Angeles City boundary, when a passing Negro motorist told him he had just seen a car that was being driven recklessly. Minikus gave chase and pulled the car over at 116th and Avalon, in a predominantly Negro neighborhood, near but not in Watts. It was 7:00 P.M.

The driver was Marquette Frye, a 21-year-old Negro, and his older brother, Ronald, 22, was a passenger. Minikus asked Marquette to get out and take the standard Highway Patrol sobriety test. Frye failed the test, and at 7:05 P.M., Minikus told him he was under arrest. He radioed for his motorcycle partner, for a car to take Marquette to jail, and a tow truck to take the car away.

They were two blocks from the Frye home, in an area of two-story apartment buildings and numerous small family residences. Because it was a very warm evening, many of the residents were outside.

Ronald Frye, having been told he could not take the car when Marquette was taken to jail, went to get their mother so that she could claim the car. They returned to the scene about 7:15 P.M. as the second motorcycle patrolman, the patrol car, and tow truck arrived. The original group of 25 to 50 curious spectators had grown to 250 to 300 persons.

Mrs. Frye approached Marquette and scolded him for drinking. Marquette, who until then had been peaceful and cooperative, pushed her away and moved toward the crowd, cursing and shouting at the officers that they would have to kill him to take him to jail. The patrolmen pursued Marquette and he resisted.

The watching crowd became hostile, and one of the patrolmen radioed for more help. Within minutes, three more highway patrolmen arrived.

Minikus and his partner were now struggling with both Frye brothers. Mrs. Frye, now belligerent, jumped on the back of one of the officers and ripped his shirt. In an attempt to subdue Marquette, one officer swung at his shoulder with a night stick, missed, and struck him on the forehead, inflicting a minor cut. By 7:23 P.M., all three of the Fryes were under arrest, and other California Highway Patrolmen and, for the first time, Los Angeles police officers had arrived in response to the call for help.

Officers on the scene said there were now more than 1,000 persons in the crowd. About 7:25 P.M., the patrol car with the prisoners, and the tow truck pulling the Frye car, left the scene. At 7:31 P.M., the Fryes arrived at a nearby sheriff's substation.

Undoubtedly the situation at the scene of the arrest was tense. Belligerence and resistance to arrest called for forceful action by the officers. This brought on hostility from Mrs. Frye and some of the bystanders, which, in turn, caused increased actions by the police. Anger at the scene escalated and, as in all such situations, bitter recriminations from both sides followed.

Considering the undisputed facts, the Commission finds that the arrest of the Fryes was handled efficiently and expeditiously. The sobriety test administered by the California Highway Patrol and its use of a transportation vehicle for the prisoner and a tow truck to remove his car are in accordance with the practices of other law enforcement agencies, including the Los Angeles Police Department.

The Spitting Incident
As the officers were leaving the scene, someone in the crowd spat on one of them. They stopped withdrawing and two highway patrolmen went into the crowd and arrested a young Negro woman and a man who was said to have been inciting the crowd to violence when the officers were arresting her. Although the wisdom of stopping the withdrawal to make these arrests has been questioned, the Commission finds no basis for criticizing the judgment of the officers on the scene.

Following these arrests, all officers withdrew at 7:40 P.M. As the last police car left the scene, it was stoned by the now irate mob.

As has happened so frequently in riots in other cities, inflated and distorted rumors concerning the arrests spread quickly to adjacent areas. The young woman arrested for spitting was wearing a barber's smock, and the false rumor spread throughout the area that she was pregnant and had been abused by police. Erroneous reports were also circulated concerning the treatment of the Fryes at the arrest scene.

The crowd did not disperse, but ranged in small groups up and down the street, although never more than a few blocks from the arrest scene. Between 8:15 P.M. and midnight, the mob stoned automobiles, pulled Caucasian motorists out of their cars and beat them, and menaced a police field command post which had been set up in the area. By 1:00 A.M., the outbreak seemed to be under control but, until early morning hours, there were sporadic reports of unruly mobs, vandalism, and rock throwing. Twenty-nine persons were arrested.

A Meeting Misfires
On Thursday morning, there was an uneasy calm, but it was obvious that tensions were still high. A strong expectancy of further trouble kept the atmosphere tense in the judgment of both police and Negro leaders. The actions by many individuals, both Negro and white, during Thursday, as well as at other times, to attempt to control the riots are commendable. We have heard many vivid and impressive accounts of the work of Negro leaders, social workers, probation officers, churchmen, teachers, and businessmen in their attempts to persuade the people to desist from their illegal activities, to stay in their houses and off the street, and to restore order.

However, the meeting called by the Los Angeles County Human Relations Commission, at the request of county officials, for the purpose of lowering the temperature misfired. That meeting was held beginning about 2:00 P.M. in an auditorium at Athens Park, eleven blocks from the scene of the arrest. It brought together every available representative of neighborhood groups and Negro leaders to discuss the problem. Members of the press, television, and radio covered the meeting. Various elected officials participated and members of the Los Angeles Police Department, Sheriff's Office and District Attorney's Office were in attendance as observers.

Several community leaders asked members of the audience to use their influence to persuade area residents to stay home Thursday evening. Even Mrs. Frye spoke and asked the crowd to "help me and others calm this situation down so that we will not have a riot tonight." But one Negro high school youth ran to the microphones and said the rioters would attack adjacent white areas that evening. This inflammatory remark was widely reported on television and radio, and it was seldom balanced by reporting of the many responsible statements made at the meeting. Moreover, it appears that the tone and conduct of the meeting shifted, as the meeting was in progress, from attempted persuasion with regard to the maintenance of law and order to a discussion of the grievances felt by the Negro.

Following the main meeting, certain leaders adjourned to a small meeting where they had discussions with individuals representing youth gangs and decided upon a course of action. They decided to propose that Caucasian officers be withdrawn from the troubled area, and that Negro officers in civilian clothes and unmarked cars be substituted.

Members of this small group then went to see Deputy Chief of Police Roger Murdock at the 77th Street Station, where the proposals were rejected by him at about 7:00 P.M. They envisaged an untested method of handling a serious situation that was rapidly developing. Furthermore, the proposal to use only Negro officers ran counter to the policy of the Police Department, adopted over a period of time at the urging of Negro leaders, to deploy Negro officers throughout the city and not concentrate them in the Negro area. Indeed, when the proposal came the police had no immediate means of determining where the Negro officers on the forces were stationed. At this moment, rioting was breaking out again, and the police felt that their established procedures were the only way to handle what was developing as another night of rioting. Following those procedures, the police decided to set up a perimeter around the center of trouble and keep all crowd activity within that area.

An Alert Is Sounded
About 5:00 P.M. Thursday, after receiving a report on the Athens Park meeting, Police Chief William H. Parker called Lt. Gen. Roderic Hill, the Adjutant General of the California National Guard in Sacramento, and told him that the Guard might be needed. This step was taken pursuant to a procedure instituted by Governor Brown and agreed upon in 1963 and 1964 between the Los Angeles Police Department, the Governor and the Guard. It was an alert that the Guard might be needed.

Pursuant to the agreed-upon procedure, General Hill sent Colonel Robert Quick to Los Angeles to work as liaison officer. He also alerted the commanders of the 40th Armored Division located in Southern California to the possibility of being called. In addition, in the absence of Governor Brown who was in Greece, he called the acting Governor, Lieutenant Governor Glenn Anderson, in Santa Barbara, and informed him of the Los Angeles situation.

The Emergency Control Center at Police Headquarters—a specially outfitted command post—was opened at 7:30 P.M. on Thursday. That day, one hundred and ninety deputy sheriffs were asked for and assigned. Between 6:45 and 7:15 P.M., crowds at the scene of the trouble of the night before had grown to more than 1,000. Firemen who came into the area to fight fires in three overturned automobiles were shot at and bombarded with rocks. The first fire in a commercial establishment was set only one block from the location of the Frye arrests, and police had to hold back rioters as firemen fought the blaze.

Shortly before midnight, rock-throwing and looting crowds for the first time ranged outside the perimeter. Five hundred police officers, deputy sheriffs and highway patrolmen used various techniques, including fender-to-fender sweeps by police cars, in seeking to disperse the mob. By 4:00 A.M. Friday, the police department felt that the situation was at least for the moment under control. At 5:09 A.M., officers were withdrawn from emergency perimeter control.

During the evening on Thursday, Lt. Gov. Anderson had come to his home in suburban Los Angeles from Santa Barbara. While at his residence, he was informed that there were as many as 8,000 rioters in the streets. About 1:00 A.M. Friday, he talked by phone to John Billett of his staff and with General Hill, and both advised him that police officials felt the situation was nearing control. About 6:45 A.M., at Lt. Gov. Anderson's request, Billet called the Emergency Control Center and was told by Sergeant Jack Eberhardt, the intelligence officer on duty, that "the situation was rather well in hand," and this information was promptly passed on to Anderson. Anderson instructed Billett to keep in touch with him and left Los Angeles at 7:25 A.M. for a morning meeting of the Finance Committee of the Board of Regents of the University of California in Berkeley, and an afternoon meeting of the full Board.

Friday, the 13th

Around 8:00 A.M., crowds formed again in the vicinity of the Frye arrests and in the adjacent Watts business area, and looting resumed. Before 9:00 A.M., Colonel Quick called General Hill in Sacramento from the Emergency Control Center and told him riot activity was intensifying.

At approximately 9:15 A.M., Mayor Sam Yorty and Chief Parker talked on the telephone, and they decided, at that time, to call the Guard. Following this conversation, Mayor Yorty went to the airport and boarded a 10:05 flight to keep a speaking engagement at the Commonwealth Club in San Francisco. Mayor Yorty told our Commission that "by about 10:00 or so, I have to decide whether I am going to disappoint that audience in San Francisco and maybe make my city look rather ridiculous if the rioting doesn't start again, and the mayor has disappointed that crowd." The Mayor returned to the City at 3:35 P.M.

The riot situation was canvassed in a Los Angeles Police Department staff meeting held at 9:45 A.M. where Colonel Quick, of the California National Guard, was in attendance, along with police officials. At 10:00 A.M., according to Colonel Quick, Chief Parker said, "It looks like we are going to have to call the troops. We will need a thousand men." Colonel Quick has said that Chief Parker did not specifically ask him to get the National Guard. On the other hand, Chief Parker has stated that he told Colonel Quick that he wanted the National Guard and that Quick indicated that he would handle the request.

In any event, at 10:15 A.M., Colonel Quick informed General Hill by telephone that Chief Parker would probably request 1,000 national guardsmen. General Hill advised Colonel Quick to have Chief Parker call the Governor's office in Sacramento. At 10:50 A.M., Parker made the formal request for the National Guard to Winslow Christian, Governor Brown's executive secretary, who was then in Sacramento, and Christian accepted the request.

By mid-morning, a crowd of 3,000 had gathered in the commercial section of Watts and there was general looting in that district as well as in adjacent business areas. By the time the formal request for the Guard had been made, ambulance drivers and firemen were refusing to go into the riot area without an armed escort.

Calling the Guard

At approximately 11:00 A.M., Christian reached Lt. Gov. Anderson by telephone in Berkeley and relayed Chief Parker's request. Lt. Gov. Anderson did not act on the request at that time. We believe that this request from the chief law enforcement officer of the stricken city for the National Guard should have been honored without delay. If the Lieutenant Governor was in doubt about conditions in Los Angeles, he should, in our view, have confirmed Chief Parker's estimate by telephoning National Guard officers in Los Angeles. Although we are mindful that it was natural and prudent for the

Lieutenant Governor to be cautious in acting in the absence of Governor Brown, we feel that, in this instance, he hesitated when he should have acted.

Feeling that he wished to consider the matter further, Lt. Gov. Anderson returned to Los Angeles by way of Sacramento. A propeller-driven National Guard plane picked him up at Oakland at 12:20 P.M., and reached McClellan Air Force Base, near Sacramento, at 1:00 P.M. Anderson met with National Guard officers and civilian staff members and received various suggestions, ranging from advice from Guard officers that he commit the Guard immediately to counsel from some civilian staff members that he examine the situation in Los Angeles and meet with Chief Parker before acting. Although Anderson still did not reach a decision to commit the Guard, he agreed with Guard officers that the troops should be assembled in the Armories at 5 P.M., which he had been told by General Hill was the earliest hour that it was feasible to do so. Hill then ordered 2,000 men to be at the armories by that hour. Anderson's plane left Sacramento for Los Angeles at 1:35 P.M. and arrived at 3:35 P.M.

At the time Lt. Gov. Anderson and General Hill were talking in Sacramento, approximately 856 Guardsmen in the 3rd

Brigade were in the Long Beach area 12 miles to the south, while enroute from San Diego, outfitted with weapons, to summer camp at Camp Roberts. We feel it reasonable to conclude, especially since this unit was subsequently used in the curfew area, that further escalation of the riots might have been averted if these Guardsmen had been diverted promptly and deployed on station throughout the riot area by early or mid-afternoon Friday.

Friday afternoon, Hale Champion, State Director of Finance, who was in the Governor's office in Los Angeles, reached Governor Brown in Athens. He briefed the Governor on the current riot situation, and Brown said he felt the Guard should be called immediately, that the possibility of a curfew should be explored, and that he was heading home as fast as possible.

Early Friday afternoon, rioters jammed the streets, began systematically to burn two blocks of 103rd Street in Watts, and drove off firemen by sniper fire and by throwing missiles. By late afternoon, gang activity began to spread the disturbance as far as fifty and sixty blocks to the north.

Lieutenant Governor Anderson arrived at the Van Nuys Air National Guard Base at 3:35 P.M. After talking with Hale Champion who urged him to call the Guard, Anderson ordered General Hill to commit the troops. At 4:00 P.M., he announced this decision to the press. At 5:00 P.M., in the Governor's office downtown, he signed the proclamation officially calling the Guard.

By 6:00 P.M., 1,336 National Guard troops were assembled in the armories. These troops were enroute to two staging areas in the rioting area by 7:00 P.M. However, neither the officials of the Los Angeles Police Department nor officers of the Guard deployed any of the troops until shortly after 10:00 P.M. Having in mind these delays, we believe that law enforcement agencies and the National Guard should develop contingency plans so that in future situations of emergency, there will be a better method at hand to assure the early commitment of the National Guard and the rapid deployment of the troops.

The first death occurred between 6:00 and 7:00 P.M. Friday, when a Negro bystander, trapped on the street between police and rioters, was shot and killed during an exchange of gunfire.

The Worst Night
Friday was the worst night. The riot moved out of the Watts area and burning and looting spread over wide areas of Southeast Los Angeles several miles apart. At 1:00 A.M. Saturday, there were 100 engine companies fighting fires in the area. Snipers shot at firemen as they fought new fires. That night, a fireman was crushed and killed on the fire line by a falling wall, and a deputy sheriff was killed when another sheriff's shotgun was discharged in a struggle with rioters.

Friday night, the law enforcement officials tried a different tactic. Police officers made sweeps on foot, moving en masse along streets to control activity and enable firemen to fight fires. By midnight, Friday, another 1,000 National Guard troops were marching shoulder to shoulder clearing the streets. By 3:00 A.M. Saturday, 3,356 guardsmen were on the streets, and the number continued to increase until the full commitment of 13,900 guardsmen was reached by midnight on Saturday. The maximum commitment of the Los Angeles Police Department during the riot period was 934 officers; the maximum for the Sheriff's Office was 719 officers.

Despite the new tactics and added personnel, the area was not under control at any time on Friday night, as major calls of looting, burning, and shooting were reported every two to three minutes. On throughout the morning hours of Saturday and during the long day, the crowds of looters and patterns of burning spread out and increased still further until it became necessary to impose a curfew on the 46.5 square-mile area on Saturday.

Lieutenant Governor Anderson appeared on television early Saturday evening to explain the curfew, which made it a crime for any unauthorized persons to be on the streets in the curfew area after 8:00 P.M.

The Beginning of Control
Much of the Saturday burning had been along Central Avenue. Again using sweep tactics, the guardsmen and police were able to clear this area by 3:30 P.M. Guardsmen rode "shotgun" on the fire engines and effectively stopped the

sniping and rock throwing at firemen. Saturday evening, road blocks were set up in anticipation of the curfew. The massive show of force was having some effect although there was still riot activity and rumors spread regarding proposed activity in the south central area.

When the curfew started at 8:00 P.M., police and guardsmen were able to deal with the riot area as a whole. Compared with the holocaust of Friday evening, the streets were relatively quiet. The only major exception was the burning of a block of stores on Broadway between 46th and 48th Streets. Snipers again prevented firemen from entering the area, and while the buildings burned, a gun battle ensued between law enforcement officers, the Guard, and the snipers.

During the day Sunday, the curfew area was relatively quiet. Because many markets had been destroyed, food distribution was started by churches, community groups, and government agencies. Governor Brown, who had returned Saturday night, personally toured the area, talking to residents. Major fires were under control but there were new fires and some rekindling of old ones. By Tuesday, Governor Brown was able to lift the curfew and by the following Sunday, only 252 guardsmen remained.

Coordination between the several law enforcement agencies during the period of the riot was commendable. When the California Highway Patrol called for help on Wednesday evening, the Los Angeles Police Department responded immediately. When the situation grew critical Thursday evening, the Los Angeles Sheriff's Office committed substantial forces without hesitation. Indeed, the members of all law enforcement agencies—policemen, sheriff's officers, highway Patrolmen, city Marshals—and the Fire Departments as well—worked long hours, in harmony and with conspicuous bravery, to quell the disorder. However, the depth and the seriousness of the situation were not accurately appraised in the early stages, and the law enforcement forces committed and engaged in the several efforts to bring the riots under control on Thursday night and all day Friday proved to be inadequate. It required massive force to subdue the riot, as demonstrated by the effectiveness of the Guard when it moved into position late Friday night and worked in coordination with the local law enforcement units.

Other Areas Affected

As the word of the South Los Angeles violence was flashed almost continuously by all news media, the unrest spread. Although outbreaks in other areas were minor by comparison with those in South Central Los Angeles, each one held dangerous potential. San Diego, 102 miles away, had three days of rioting and 81 people were arrested. On Friday night, there was rioting in Pasadena, 12 miles from the curfew zone. There, liquor and gun stores were looted and Molotov cocktails and fire bombs were thrown at police cars. Only prompt and skillful handling by the police prevented this situation from getting out of control.

Pacoima, 20 miles north, had scattered rioting, looting, and burning. There was burning in Monrovia, 25 miles east. On Sunday night, after the curfew area was quiet, there was an incident in Long Beach, 12 miles south. About 200 guardsmen and Los Angeles police assisted Long Beach police in containing a dangerous situation which exploded when a policeman was shot when another officer's gun discharged as he was being attacked by rioters. Several fires were set Sunday night in the San Pedro-Wilmington area, 12 miles south.

Was There a Pre-established Plan?

After a thorough examination, the Commission has concluded that there is no reliable evidence of outside leadership or pre-established plans for the rioting. The testimony of law enforcement agencies and their respective intelligence officers supports this conclusion. The Attorney General, the District Attorney, and the Los Angeles police have all reached the conclusion that there is no evidence of a pre-plan or a pre-established central direction of the rioting activities. This finding was submitted to the Grand Jury by the District Attorney.

This is not to say that there was no agitation or promotion of the rioting by local groups or gangs which exist in pockets throughout the south central area. The sudden appearance of Molotov cocktails in quantity and the unexplained movement of men in cars through the areas of great destruction support the conclusion that there was organization and planning after the riots commenced. In addition, on that tense Thursday, inflammatory handbills suddenly appeared in Watts. But this cannot be identified as a master plan by one group; rather it appears to have been the work of several gangs, with membership of young men ranging in age from 14 to 35 years. All of these activities intensified the rioting and caused it to spread with increased violence from one district to another in the curfew area.

The Grim Statistics

The final statistics are staggering. There were 34 persons killed and 1,032 reported injuries, including 90 Los Angeles police officers, 136 firemen, 10 national guardsmen, 23 persons from other governmental agencies, and 773 civilians; 118 of the injuries resulted from gunshot wounds. Of the 34 killed, one was a fireman, one was a deputy sheriff, and one a Long Beach policeman.

In the weeks following the riots, Coroner's Inquests were held regarding thirty-two of the deaths. The Coroner's jury ruled that twenty-six of the deaths were justifiable homicide, five were homicidal, and one was accidental. Of those ruled justifiable homicide, the jury found that death was caused in sixteen instances by officers of the Los Angeles Police Department and in seven instances by the National Guard.

The Coroner's Inquest into one of the deaths was canceled at the request of the deceased's family. There was no inquest into the death of the deputy sheriff because of pending criminal proceedings.

A legal memorandum analyzing the procedures followed in the inquests, which was prepared at the request of the Commission, has been forwarded to the appropriate public officials for their consideration.

It has been estimated that the loss of property attributable to the riots was over $40 million. More than 600 buildings were damaged by burning and looting. Of this number, more than 200 were totally destroyed by fire. The rioters concentrated primarily on food markets, liquor stores, furniture stores, clothing stores, department stores, and pawn shops. Arson arrests numbered 27 and 10 arson complaints were filed, a relatively small number considering that fire

department officials say that all of the fires were incendiary in origin. Between 2,000 and 3,000 fire alarms were recorded during the riot, 1,000 of these between 7:00 A.M. on Friday and 7:00 A.M. on Saturday. We note with interest that no residences were deliberately burned, that damage to schools, libraries, churches and public buildings was minimal, and that certain types of business establishments, notably service stations and automobile dealers, were for the most part unharmed.

There were 3,438 adults arrested, 71% for burglary and theft. The number of juveniles arrested was 514, 81% for burglary and theft. Of the adults arrested, 1,232 had never been arrested before; 1,164 had a "minor" criminal record (arrest only or convictions with sentence of 90 days or less); 1,042 with "major" criminal record (convictions with sentence of more than 90 days). Of the juveniles arrested, 257 had never been arrested before; 212 had a "minor" criminal record; 43 had a "major" criminal record. Of the adults arrested, 2,057 were born in 16 southern states whereas the comparable figure for juveniles was 131. Some of the juveniles arrested extensively damaged the top two floors of an auxiliary jail which had been opened on the Saturday of the riots.

Those involved in the administration of justice—judges, prosecutors, defense counsel, and others—merit commendation for the steps they took to cope with the extraordinary responsibility thrust on the judicial system by the riots. By reorganizing calendars and making special assignments, the Los Angeles Superior and Municipal Courts have been able to meet the statutory deadlines for processing the cases of those arrested. Court statistics indicate that by November 26, the following dispositions had been made of the 2,278 felony cases filed against adults: 856 were found guilty; 155 were acquitted; 641 were disposed of prior to trial, primarily by dismissal; 626 are awaiting trial. Of the 1,133 misdemeanor cases filed, 733 were found guilty, 81 were acquitted, 184 dismissed and 135 are awaiting trial.

The Police and Sheriff's Department have long known that many members of gangs, as well as others, in the south central area possessed weapons and knew how to use them. However, the extent to which pawn shops, each one of which possessed an inventory of weapons, were the immediate target of looters, leads to the conclusion that a substantial number of the weapons used were stolen from these shops. During the riots, law enforcement officers recovered 851 weapons. There is no evidence that the rioters made any attempt to steal narcotics from pharmacies in the riot area even though some pharmacies were looted and burned.

Overwhelming as are the grim statistics, the impact of the August rioting on the Los Angeles community has been even greater. The first weeks after the disorders brought a flood tide of charges and recriminations, Although this has now ebbed, the feeling of fear and tension persists, largely unabated, throughout the community. A certain slowness in the rebuilding of the fired structures has symbolized the difficulty in mending relationships in our community which were so severely fractured by the August nightmare.

Source: Governor's Commission on the Los Angeles Riots. *Violence in the City—An End or a Beginning?* Los Angeles: The Commission, 1965.

See also: Asbury Park Riot of 1970; Atlanta Riot of 1906; Atlanta Riot of 1967; Bellingham Riots; Bensonhurst Incident 1989; Biloxi Beach Riot of 1960; Black Church Arsons; Bloody Sunday; Boston Riot of 1975 and 1976; Brownsville Riot of 1906; Charleston Riot of 1919; Chattanooga Riot of 1906; Chester and Philadelphia Riots of 1918; Chicago Commission on Race Relations; Chicago Riot of 1919; Cincinnati Riots of 1967 and 1968; Cincinnati Riot of 2001; Cleveland Riot of 1966; Detroit Riot of 1943; Detroit Riot of 1967; East St. Louis Riot of 1917; Election Riots of the 1880s and 1890s; Greensburg Riot of 1906; Greenwood Community; Harlem Riot of 1935; Houston Mutiny of 1917; Howard Beach Incident 1986; Johnson-Jeffries Fight of 1910; Knoxville Riot of 1919; Long Hot Summer Riots 1965–1967; Longview Riot of 1919; Los Angeles Riot of 1965; Los Angeles Riots of 1992; Miami Riot of 1982; New Bedford Riot of 1970; New Orleans Riot of 1866; New York City Draft Riot of 1863; New York City Riot of 1943; Newark Riot of 1967; Orangeburg Massacre of 1968; Philadelphia Riot of 1964; Prison Riots; Race Riots in America; Red Scare and Race Riots; Red Summer Race Riots of 1919; Rosewood Riot of 1923; Saint Genevieve Riot of 1930; San Francisco Riot of 1966; Springfield Riot of 1904; Tampa Riots of 1987; Texas Southern University Riot of 1967; Tulsa Riot of 1921; Washington, D.C., Riot of 1919; Washington, D.C., Riots of 1968; Wilmington Riot of 1898; Zoot Suit Riots

Voting Rights Act of 1965
Introduction
In the Jim Crow era, Southern states deprived African Americans of voting rights by imposing a few qualifications for voting, such as a literacy test, poll tax, and grandfather clause. Congress passed the Voting Rights Act in 1965 to eliminate all qualifications or prerequisites for voting imposed by states.

Primary Source
Eighty-ninth Congress of the United States of America at the First Session

Begun and held at the City of Washington on Monday, the fourth day of January, One thousand nine hundred and sixty-five.

An Act to enforce the fifteenth amendment to the Constitution of the United States, and for other purposes.

Be it enacted by the Senate and House of Representatives of the United States of America in Congress assembled, That this Act shall be known as the "Voting Rights Act of 1965."

SEC. 2. No voting qualifications or prerequisite to voting, or standard, practice, or procedure shall be imposed or applied by any State or political subdivision to deny or abridge the right of any citizen of the United States to vote on account of race or color.

SEC. 3. (a) Whenever the Attorney General institutes a proceeding under any statute to enforce the guarantees of the fifteenth amendment in any State or political subdivision the court shall authorize the appointment of Federal examiners by the United States Civil Service Commission in accordance with section 6 to serve for such period of time and for such political subdivisions as the court shall determine is appropriate to enforce the guarantees of the fifteenth amendment (1) as part of any interlocutory order if the court determines that the appointment of such examiners is necessary to enforce such guarantees or (2) as part of any final judgment if the court finds that violations of the fifteenth amendment justifying equitable relief have occurred in such State or subdivision: Provided, That the court need not authorize the appointment of examiners if any incidents of denial or abridgement of the right to vote on account of race or color (1) have been few in number and have been promptly and effectively corrected by State or local action, (2) the continuing effect of such incidents has been eliminated, and (3) there is no reasonable probability of their recurrence in the future.

(b) If in a proceeding instituted by the Attorney General under any statute to enforce the guarantees of the fifteenth amendment in any State or political subdivision the court finds that a test or device has been used for the purpose or with the effect of denying or abridging the right of any citizen of the United States to vote on account of race or color, it shall suspend the use of tests and devices in such State or political subdivisions as the court shall determine is appropriate and for such period as it deems necessary.

(c) If in any proceeding instituted by the Attorney General under any statute to enforce the guarantees of the fifteenth amendment in any State or political subdivision the court finds that violations of the fifteenth amendment justifying equitable relief have occurred within the territory of such State or political subdivisions, the court in addition to such relief as it may grant, shall retain jurisdiction for such period as it may deem appropriate and during such period no voting qualification or prerequisite to voting, or standard, practice, or procedure with respect to voting different from that in force or effect at the time the proceeding was commenced shall be enforced unless and until the court finds that such qualifications, prerequisite, standard, practice, or procedure does not have the purpose and will not have the effect of denying or abridging the right to vote on account of race or color: Provided, That such qualification, prerequisite, standard, practice, or procedure has been submitted by the chief legal officer or other appropriate official of such State or subdivision to the Attorney General and the Attorney General has not interposed an objection within sixty days after such submission, except that neither the court's findings not the Attorney General's failure to object shall bar a subsequent action to enjoin enforcement of such qualifications, prerequisite, standard, practice, or procedure.

SEC. 4. (a) To assure that the right of citizens of the United States to vote is not denied or abridged on account of race or color, no citizen shall be denied the right to vote in any Federal, State, or local election because of his failure to comply with any test or device in any State with respect to which the determinations have been made under subsection (b) or in any political subdivision with respect to which such determinations have been made as a separate unit, unless the United States District Court for the District of Columbia in an action for a declaratory judgment brought by such State or subdivision against the United States has determined that no such test or device has been used during the five years preceding the filing of the action for the purpose or with the effect of denying or abridging the right to vote on account of race or color: Provided, That no such declaratory judgment shall issue with respect to any plaintiff for a period of five years after the entry of a final judgment of any court of the United States, other than the denial of a declaratory judgment under this section, whether entered prior to or after the enactment of this Act, determining that denials or abridgments of the right to vote on account of race or color through the use of such tests or devices have occurred anywhere in the territory of such plaintiff. An action pursuant to this subsection shall be heard and determined by a court of three judges in accordance with the provisions of section 2284 of title 28 of the United States Code and any appeal shall lie to the Supreme Court. The court shall retain jurisdiction of any action pursuant to this subsection for five years after judgment and shall reopen the action upon motion of the Attorney General alleging that a test or device has been used for the purpose or with the effect of denying or abridging the right to vote on account of race or color. If the Attorney General determines that he has no reason to believe that any such test or device has been used during the five years preceding the filing of the action for the purpose or with the effect of denying or abridging the right to vote on account of race or color, he shall consent to the entry of such judgment.

(b) The provisions of subsection (a) shall apply in any State or in any political subdivision of a state which (1) the Attorney General determines maintained on November 1, 1964, any test or device, and with respect to when (2) the Director of the Census determines that less than 50 per centum of the persons of voting age residing therein were registered on

November 1, 1964, or that less than 50 per centum of such persons voted in the presidential election of November 1964. A determination or certification of the Attorney General or of the Director of the Census under this section or under section 6 or section 13 shall not be reviewable in any court and shall be effective upon publication in the Federal Register.

(c) The phrase "test or device" shall mean any requirement that a person as a prerequisite for voting or registration for voting (1) demonstrates the ability to read, write, understand, or interpret any matter, (2) demonstrates any educational achievement of his knowledge of any particular subject, (3) possess good moral character, or (4) prove his qualification by the voucher of registered voters or members of any other class.

(d) For purposes of this section no State or political subdivision shall be determined to have engaged in the use of tests or devices for the purpose or with the effect of denying or abridging the right to vote on account of race or color if (1) incidents of such use have been few in number and have been promptly and effectively corrected by State or local action, (2) the continuing effect of such incidents has been eliminated, and (3) there is no reasonable probability of their recurrence in the future.

(e) (1) Congress hereby declares that to secure the rights under the fourteenth amendment of persons educated in American-flag schools in which the predominant classroom language was other than English, it is necessary to prohibit the States from conditioning the right to vote of such persons on ability to read, write, understand, or interpret any matter in the English language.

(2) No person who demonstrates that he has successfully completed the sixth primary grade in a public school in, or a private school accredited by, any State or territory, the District of Columbia, or the Commonwealth of Puerto Rico in which the predominant classroom language was other than English, shall be denied the right to vote in any Federal, State, or local election because of his inability to read, write, understand, or interpret any matter in the English language, except that in States in which State law provides that a different level of education is presumptive of literacy, he shall demonstrate

that he has successfully completed an equivalent level of education in a public school in, or a private school accredited by, any State or territory, the District of Columbia, or the Commonwealth of Puerto Rico in which the predominant classroom language was other than English. . . .

Source: Voting Rights Act of 1965. Public Law 89–110. Enrolled Acts and Resolutions of Congress, 1789-; General Records of the United States Government; Record Group 11; National Archives.

See also: Voting and Race; Voting Rights Act of 1965

Executive Order 11246 (1965), as Amended

Introduction

Executive Order 11246, issued by President Lyndon B. Johnson in September 1965, laid the groundwork for affirmative-action policy. It mandated contracts with the government to include a nondiscrimination clause and federal contractors with 100 or more employees to take "affirmative action" to achieve the goal of nondiscrimination in employment, promotion, recruitment, and related areas. It required contractors and their subcontractors to submit compliance reports with information on the practices, policies, programs, and racial composition of their work force.

Primary Source

Executive Order 11246—Equal Employment Opportunity

Source: The provisions of Executive Order 11246 of September 24, 1965, appear at 30 FR 12319, 12935, 3 CFR, 1964–1965 Comp., p. 339, unless otherwise noted.

Under and by virtue of the authority vested in me as President of the United States by the Constitution and statutes of the United States, it is ordered as follows:

Part I—Nondiscrimination in Government Employment

[Part I superseded by EO 11478 of Aug. 8, 1969, 34 FR 12985, 3 CFR, 1966–1970 Comp., p. 803]

Part II—Nondiscrimination in Employment by Government Contractors and Subcontractors

Subpart A—Duties of the Secretary of Labor

SEC. 201. The Secretary of Labor shall be responsible for the administration and enforcement of Parts II and III of this Order. The Secretary shall adopt such rules and regulations and issue such orders as are deemed necessary and appropriate to achieve the purposes of Parts II and III of this Order.

[Sec. 201 amended by EO 12086 of Oct. 5, 1978, 43 FR 46501, 3 CFR, l978 Comp., p. 230]

Subpart B—Contractors' Agreements

SEC. 202. Except in contracts exempted in accordance with Section 204 of this Order, all Government contracting agencies shall include in every Government contract hereafter entered into the following provisions:

During the performance of this contract, the contractor agrees as follows:

(1) The contractor will not discriminate against any employee or applicant for employment because of race, color, religion, sex, or national origin. The contractor will take affirmative action to ensure that applicants are employed, and that employees are treated during employment, without regard to their race, color, religion, sex or national origin. Such action shall include, but not be limited to the following: employment, upgrading, demotion, or transfer; recruitment or recruitment advertising; layoff or termination; rates of pay or other forms of compensation; and selection for training, including apprenticeship. The contractor agrees to post in conspicuous places, available to employees and applicants for employment, notices to be provided by the contracting officer setting forth the provisions of this nondiscrimination clause.

(2) The contractor will, in all solicitations or advancements for employees placed by or on behalf of the contractor, state that all qualified applicants will receive consideration for employment without regard to race, color, religion, sex or national origin.

(3) The contractor will send to each labor union or representative of workers with which he has a collective bargaining agreement or other contract or understanding, a notice, to be provided by the agency contracting officer, advising the labor union or workers' representative of the contractor's commitments under Section 202 of Executive Order No. 11246 of September 24, 1965, and shall post copies of the notice in conspicuous places available to employees and applicants for employment.

(4) The contractor will comply with all provisions of Executive Order No. 11246 of Sept. 24, 1965, and of the rules, regulations, and relevant orders of the Secretary of Labor.

(5) The contractor will furnish all information and reports required by Executive Order No. 11246 of September 24, 1965, and by the rules, regulations, and orders of the Secretary of Labor, or pursuant thereto, and will permit access to his books, records, and accounts by the contracting agency and the Secretary of Labor for purposes of investigation to ascertain compliance with such rules, regulations, and orders.

(6) In the event of the contractor's noncompliance with the nondiscrimination clauses of this contract or with any of such rules, regulations, or orders, this contract may be cancelled, terminated, or suspended in whole or in part and the contractor may be declared ineligible for further Government contracts in accordance with procedures authorized in Executive Order No. 11246 of Sept. 24, 1965, and such other sanctions may be imposed and remedies invoked as provided in Executive Order No. 11246 of September 24, 1965, or by rule, regulation, or order of the Secretary of Labor, or as otherwise provided by law.

(7) The contractor will include the provisions of paragraphs (1) through (7) in every subcontract or purchase order unless exempted by rules, regulations, or orders of the Secretary of Labor issued pursuant to Section 204 of Executive Order No. 11246 of September 24, 1965, so that such provisions will be binding upon each subcontractor or vendor. The contractor

will take such action with respect to any subcontract or purchase order as may be directed by the Secretary of Labor as a means of enforcing such provisions including sanctions for noncompliance: Provided, however, that in the event the contractor becomes involved in, or is threatened with, litigation with a subcontractor or vendor as a result of such direction, the contractor may request the United States to enter into such litigation to protect the interests of the United States. [Sec. 202 amended by EO 11375 of Oct. 13, 1967, 32 FR 14303, 3 CFR, 1966–1970 Comp., p. 684, EO 12086 of Oct. 5, 1978, 43 FR 46501, 3 CFR, 1978 Comp., p. 230]

SEC. 203. Each contractor having a contract containing the provisions prescribed in Section 202 shall file, and shall cause each of his subcontractors to file, Compliance Reports with the contracting agency or the Secretary of Labor as may be directed. Compliance Reports shall be filed within such times and shall contain such information as to the practices, policies, programs, and employment policies, programs, and employment statistics of the contractor and each subcontractor, and shall be in such form, as the Secretary of Labor may prescribe.

(b) Bidders or prospective contractors or subcontractors may be required to state whether they have participated in any previous contract subject to the provisions of this Order, or any preceding similar Executive order, and in that event to submit, on behalf of themselves and their proposed subcontractors, Compliance Reports prior to or as an initial part of their bid or negotiation of a contract.

(c) Whenever the contractor or subcontractor has a collective bargaining agreement or other contract or understanding with a labor union or an agency referring workers or providing or supervising apprenticeship or training for such workers, the Compliance Report shall include such information as to such labor union's or agency's practices and policies affecting compliance as the Secretary of Labor may prescribe: Provided, That to the extent such information is within the exclusive possession of a labor union or an agency referring workers or providing or supervising apprenticeship or training and such labor union or agency shall refuse to furnish such information to the contractor, the contractor shall so certify to the Secretary of Labor as

part of its Compliance Report and shall set forth what efforts he has made to obtain such information.

(d) The Secretary of Labor may direct that any bidder or prospective contractor or subcontractor shall submit, as part of his Compliance Report, a statement in writing, signed by an authorized officer or agent on behalf of any labor union or any agency referring workers or providing or supervising apprenticeship or other training, with which the bidder or prospective contractor deals, with supporting information, to the effect that the signer's practices and policies do not discriminate on the grounds of race, color, religion, sex or national origin, and that the signer either will affirmatively cooperate in the implementation of the policy and provisions of this Order or that it consents and agrees that recruitment, employment, and the terms and conditions of employment under the proposed contract shall be in accordance with the purposes and provisions of the order. In the event that the union, or the agency shall refuse to execute such a statement, the Compliance Report shall so certify and set forth what efforts have been made to secure such a statement and such additional factual material as the Secretary of Labor may require.

[Sec. 203 amended by EO 11375 of Oct. 13, 1967, 32 FR 14303, 3 CFR, 1966–1970 Comp., p. 684; EO 12086 of Oct. 5, 1978, 43 FR 46501, 3 CFR, 1978 Comp., p. 230]

SEC. 204 (a) The Secretary of Labor may, when the Secretary deems that special circumstances in the national interest so require, exempt a contracting agency from the requirement of including any or all of the provisions of Section 202 of this Order in any specific contract, subcontract, or purchase order.

(b) The Secretary of Labor may, by rule or regulation, exempt certain classes of contracts, subcontracts, or purchase orders (1) whenever work is to be or has been performed outside the United States and no recruitment of workers within the limits of the United States is involved; (2) for standard commercial supplies or raw materials; (3) involving less than specified amounts of money or specified numbers of workers; or (4) to the extent that they involve subcontracts below a specified tier.

(c) Section 202 of this Order shall not apply to a Government contractor or subcontractor that is a religious corporation, association, educational institution, or society, with respect to the employment of individuals of a particular religion to perform work connected with the carrying on by such corporation, association, educational institution, or society of its activities. Such contractors and subcontractors are not exempted or excused from complying with the other requirements contained in this Order.

(d) The Secretary of Labor may also provide, by rule, regulation, or order, for the exemption of facilities of a contractor that are in all respects separate and distinct from activities of the contractor related to the performance of the contract: provided, that such an exemption will not interfere with or impede the effectuation of the purposes of this Order: and provided further, that in the absence of such an exemption all facilities shall be covered by the provisions of this Order.

[Sec. 204 amended by EO 13279 of Dec. 16, 2002, 67 FR 77141, 3 CFR, 2002 Comp., pp. 77141–77144]

Subpart C—Powers and Duties of the Secretary of Labor and the Contracting Agencies

SEC. 205. The Secretary of Labor shall be responsible for securing compliance by all Government contractors and subcontractors with this Order and any implementing rules or regulations. All contracting agencies shall comply with the terms of this Order and any implementing rules, regulations, or orders of the Secretary of Labor. Contracting agencies shall cooperate with the Secretary of Labor and shall furnish such information and assistance as the Secretary may require.

[Sec. 205 amended by EO 12086 of Oct. 5, 1978, 43 FR 46501, 3 CFR, 1978 Comp., p. 230]

SEC. 206. The Secretary of Labor may investigate the employment practices of any Government contractor or subcontractor to determine whether or not the contractual provisions specified in Section 202 of this Order have been violated. Such investigation shall be conducted in accordance with the procedures established by the Secretary of Labor.

(b) The Secretary of Labor may receive and investigate complaints by employees or prospective employees of a Government contractor or subcontractor which allege discrimination contrary to the contractual provisions specified in Section 202 of this Order.

[Sec. 206 amended by EO 12086 of Oct. 5, 1978, 43 FR 46501, 3 CFR, 1978 Comp., p. 230]

SEC. 207. The Secretary of Labor shall use his/her best efforts, directly and through interested Federal, State, and local agencies, contractors, and all other available instrumentalities to cause any labor union engaged in work under Government contracts or any agency referring workers or providing or supervising apprenticeship or training for or in the course of such work to cooperate in the implementation of the purposes of this Order. The Secretary of Labor shall, in appropriate cases, notify the Equal Employment Opportunity Commission, the Department of Justice, or other appropriate Federal agencies whenever it has reason to believe that the practices of any such labor organization or agency violate Title VI or Title VII of the Civil Rights Act of 1964 or other provision of Federal law.

[Sec. 207 amended by EO 12086 of Oct. 5, 1978, 43 FR 46501, 3 CFR, 1978 Comp., p. 230]

SEC. 208. The Secretary of Labor, or any agency, officer, or employee in the executive branch of the Government designated by rule, regulation, or order of the Secretary, may hold such hearings, public or private, as the Secretary may deem advisable for compliance, enforcement, or educational purposes.

(b) The Secretary of Labor may hold, or cause to be held, hearings in accordance with Subsection of this Section prior to imposing, ordering, or recommending the imposition of penalties and sanctions under this Order. No order for debarment of any contractor from further Government contracts under Section 209(6) shall be made without affording the contractor an opportunity for a hearing.

Subpart D—Sanctions and Penalties

SEC. 209. In accordance with such rules, regulations, or orders as the Secretary of Labor may issue or adopt, the Secretary may:

(1) Publish, or cause to be published, the names of contractors or unions which it has concluded have complied or have failed to comply with the provisions of this Order or of the rules, regulations, and orders of the Secretary of Labor.

(2) Recommend to the Department of Justice that, in cases in which there is substantial or material violation or the threat of substantial or material violation of the contractual provisions set forth in Section 202 of this Order, appropriate proceedings be brought to enforce those provisions, including the enjoining, within the limitations of applicable law, of organizations, individuals, or groups who prevent directly or indirectly, or seek to prevent directly or indirectly, compliance with the provisions of this Order.

(3) Recommend to the Equal Employment Opportunity Commission or the Department of Justice that appropriate proceedings be instituted under Title VII of the Civil Rights Act of 1964.

(4) Recommend to the Department of Justice that criminal proceedings be brought for the furnishing of false information to any contracting agency or to the Secretary of Labor as the case may be.

(5) After consulting with the contracting agency, direct the contracting agency to cancel, terminate, suspend, or cause to be cancelled, terminated, or suspended, any contract, or any portion or portions thereof, for failure of the contractor or subcontractor to comply with equal employment opportunity provisions of the contract. Contracts may be cancelled, terminated, or suspended absolutely or continuance of contracts may be conditioned upon a program for future compliance approved by the Secretary of Labor.

(6) Provide that any contracting agency shall refrain from entering into further contracts, or extensions or other modifications of existing contracts, with any noncomplying contractor, until such contractor has satisfied the Secretary of Labor that such contractor has established and will carry out personnel and employment policies in compliance with the provisions of this Order.

(b) Pursuant to rules and regulations prescribed by the Secretary of Labor, the Secretary shall make reasonable efforts, within a reasonable time limitation, to secure compliance with the contract provisions of this Order by methods of conference, conciliation, mediation, and persuasion before proceedings shall be instituted under subsection (a)(2) of this Section, or before a contract shall be cancelled or terminated in whole or in part under subsection (a)(5) of this Section.

[Sec. 209 amended by EO 12086 of Oct. 5, 1978, 43 FR 46501, 3 CFR, 1978 Comp., p. 230]

SEC. 210. Whenever the Secretary of Labor makes a determination under Section 209, the Secretary shall promptly notify the appropriate agency. The agency shall take the action directed by the Secretary and shall report the results of the action it has taken to the Secretary of Labor within such time as the Secretary shall specify. If the contracting agency fails to take the action directed within thirty days, the Secretary may take the action directly.

[Sec. 210 amended by EO 12086 of Oct. 5, 1978, 43 FR 46501, 3 CFR, 1978 Comp., p. 230]

SEC. 211. If the Secretary shall so direct, contracting agencies shall not enter into contracts with any bidder or prospective contractor unless the bidder or prospective contractor has satisfactorily complied with the provisions of this Order or submits a program for compliance acceptable to the Secretary of Labor.

[Sec. 211 amended by EO 12086 of Oct. 5, 1978, 43 FR 46501, 3 CFR, 1978 Comp., p. 230]

SEC. 212. When a contract has been cancelled or terminated under Section 209(a)(5) or a contractor has been debarred from further Government contracts under Section 209(a)(6) of this Order, because of noncompliance with the contract provisions specified in Section 202 of this Order, the Secretary of Labor shall promptly notify the Comptroller General of the United States.

[Sec. 212 amended by EO 12086 of Oct. 5, 1978, 43 FR 46501, 3 CFR, 1978 Comp., p. 230]

Subpart E—Certificates of Merit

SEC. 213. The Secretary of Labor may provide for issuance of a United States Government Certificate of Merit to employers or labor unions, or other agencies which are or may hereafter be engaged in work under Government contracts, if the Secretary is satisfied that the personnel and employment practices of the employer, or that the personnel, training, apprenticeship, membership, grievance and representation, upgrading, and other practices and policies of the labor union or other agency conform to the purposes and provisions of this Order.

SEC. 214. Any Certificate of Merit may at any time be suspended or revoked by the Secretary of Labor if the holder thereof, in the judgment of the Secretary, has failed to comply with the provisions of this Order.

SEC. 215. The Secretary of Labor may provide for the exemption of any employer, labor union, or other agency from any reporting requirements imposed under or pursuant to this Order if such employer, labor union, or other agency has been awarded a Certificate of Merit which has not been suspended or revoked.

Part III—Nondiscrimination Provisions in Federally Assisted Construction Contracts

SEC. 301. Each executive department and agency, which administers a program involving Federal financial assistance shall require as a condition for the approval of any grant, contract, loan, insurance, or guarantee thereunder, which may involve a construction contract, that the applicant for Federal assistance undertake and agree to incorporate, or cause to be incorporated, into all construction contracts paid for in whole or in part with funds obtained from the Federal Government or borrowed on the credit of the Federal Government pursuant to such grant, contract, loan, insurance, or guarantee, or undertaken pursuant to any Federal program involving such grant, contract, loan, insurance, or guarantee, the provisions prescribed for Government contracts by Section 202 of this Order or such modification thereof, preserving in substance the contractor's obligations thereunder, as may be approved by the Secretary of Labor, together with such additional provisions as the Secretary deems appropriate to establish and protect the interest of the United States in the enforcement of those obligations. Each such applicant shall also undertake and agree (1) to assist and cooperate actively with the Secretary of Labor in obtaining the compliance of contractors and subcontractors with those contract provisions and with the rules, regulations and relevant orders of the Secretary, (2) to obtain and to furnish to the Secretary of Labor such information as the Secretary may require for the supervision of such compliance, (3) to carry out sanctions and penalties for violation of such obligations imposed upon contractors and subcontractors by the Secretary of Labor pursuant to Part II, Subpart D, of this Order, and (4) to refrain from entering into any contract subject to this Order, or extension or other modification of such a contract with a contractor debarred from Government contracts under Part II, Subpart D, of this Order.

[Sec. 301 amended by EO 12086 of Oct. 5, 1978, 43 FR 46501, 3 CFR, 1978 Comp., p. 230]

SEC. 302. "Construction contract" as used in this Order means any contract for the construction, rehabilitation, alteration, conversion, extension, or repair of buildings, highways, or other improvements to real property.

(b) The provisions of Part II of this Order shall apply to such construction contracts, and for purposes of such application the administering department or agency shall be considered the contracting agency referred to therein.

(c) The term "applicant" as used in this Order means an applicant for Federal assistance or, as determined by agency regulation, other program participant, with respect to whom an application for any grant, contract, loan, insurance, or guarantee is not finally acted upon prior to the effective date of this Part, and it includes such an applicant after he/she becomes a recipient of such Federal assistance.

SEC. 303. The Secretary of Labor shall be responsible for obtaining the compliance of such applicants with their undertakings under this Order. Each administering department and agency is directed to cooperate with the Secretary of Labor and to furnish the Secretary such information and assistance as the Secretary may require in the performance of the Secretary's functions under this Order.

(b) In the event an applicant fails and refuses to comply with the applicant's undertakings pursuant to this Order, the Secretary of Labor may, after consulting with the administering department or agency, take any or all of the following actions: (1) direct any administering department or agency to cancel, terminate, or suspend in whole or in part the agreement, contract or other arrangement with such applicant with respect to which the failure or refusal occurred; (2) direct any administering department or agency to refrain from extending any further assistance to the applicant under the program with respect to which the failure or refusal occurred until satisfactory assurance of future compliance has been received by the Secretary of Labor from such applicant; and (3) refer the case to the Department of Justice or the Equal Employment Opportunity Commission for appropriate law enforcement or other proceedings.

(c) In no case shall action be taken with respect to an applicant pursuant to clause (1) or (2) of subsection (b) without notice and opportunity for hearing.

[Sec. 303 amended by EO 12086 of Oct. 5, 1978, 43 FR 46501, 3 CFR, 1978 Comp., p. 230]

SEC. 304. Any executive department or agency which imposes by rule, regulation, or order requirements of nondiscrimination in employment, other than requirements imposed pursuant to this Order, may delegate to the Secretary of Labor by agreement such responsibilities with respect to compliance standards, reports, and procedures as would tend to bring the administration of such requirements into conformity with the administration of requirements imposed under this Order: Provided, That actions to effect compliance by recipients of Federal financial assistance with requirements imposed pursuant to Title VI of the Civil Rights Act of 1964 shall be taken in conformity with the procedures and limitations prescribed in Section 602 thereof and the regulations of the administering department or agency issued thereunder.

Part IV—Miscellaneous

SEC. 401. The Secretary of Labor may delegate to any officer, agency, or employee in the Executive branch of the Government, any function or duty of the Secretary under Parts II and III of this Order.

[Sec. 401 amended by EO 12086 of Oct. 5, l978, 43 FR 46501, 3 CFR, 1978 Comp., p. 230]

SEC. 402. The Secretary of Labor shall provide administrative support for the execution of the program known as the "Plans for Progress."

SEC. 403. Executive Orders Nos. 10590 (January 19, 1955), 10722 (August 5, 1957), 10925 (March 6, 1961), 11114 (June 22, 1963), and 11162 (July 28, 1964), are hereby superseded and the President's Committee on Equal Employment Opportunity established by Executive Order No. 10925 is hereby abolished. All records and property in the custody of the Committee shall be transferred to the Office of Personnel Management and the Secretary of Labor, as appropriate.

(b) Nothing in this Order shall be deemed to relieve any person of any obligation assumed or imposed under or pursuant to any Executive Order superseded by this Order. All rules, regulations, orders, instructions, designations, and other directives issued by the President's Committee on Equal Employment Opportunity and those issued by the heads of various departments or agencies under or pursuant to any of the Executive orders superseded by this Order, shall, to the extent that they are not inconsistent with this Order, remain in full force and effect unless and until revoked or superseded by appropriate authority. References in such directives to provisions of the superseded orders shall be deemed to be references to the comparable provisions of this Order.

[Sec. 403 amended by EO 12107 of Dec. 28, 1978, 44 FR 1055, 3 CFR, 1978 Comp., p, 264]

SEC. 404. The General Services Administration shall take appropriate action to revise the standard Government contract forms to accord with the provisions of this Order and of the rules and regulations of the Secretary of Labor.

SEC. 405. This Order shall become effective thirty days after the date of this Order.

> **Source:** Executive Order 11246, As Amended, 1965; Office of Federal Contract Compliance Programs (OFCCP); United States Department of Labor.

> **See also:** Affirmative Action

Excerpts from Cyrus R. Vance's Report on the Riots in Detroit (July–August 1967)

Introduction

Cyrus R. Vance, a special assistant to the secretary of defense, was sent to Detroit by the Johnson administration in July 1967 to coordinate the federal response to the riot with state and local authorities. The following excerpts from Vance's official report on his activities describe the actions taken by authorities to quell the disorders; it is not a description of the disorders themselves or an attempt to determine the causes of the riot. After three years of what would be known as the Long Hot Summer Riots (1965–1967), Vance's purpose was to gather information that could help the government respond more effectively to similar urban disorders in the future.

Primary Source

I. Introduction

This report covers the Federal activities connected with the riots in Detroit, Michigan, during the period 23 July through 2 August 1967. Its purpose is to recount the sequence of events, to summarize the experience gained, and to focus upon the problems encountered, both resolved and unresolved, for consideration in planning for or conducting future operations of a similar nature. This report does not treat with the underlying causes of the loss of law and order in Detroit, which required Federal intervention.

My participation commenced shortly after 1100 on Monday, 24 July. The facts with respect to the period prior to my participation have been taken from the records of the Department of Justice and the Department of Defense.

II. Narrative of Events

The first contact between city and state officials in Detroit and Attorney General Clark occurred Sunday night, 23 July at 2355. Mayor Cavanagh, who was with Governor Romney at the time, called the Attorney General at his home and said a very dangerous situation existed in the city. The Attorney General promptly relayed this information to Secretary of the Army Resor.

At 0240 on Monday, Governor Romney called the Attorney General at his home and said he thought he might need Army troops to quell the rioting. Mr. Clark said he would begin the alert so that the Army could make preparations and be ready promptly if needed. Immediately upon the completion of this conversation, the Attorney General again called Secretary Resor to inform him of the situation and of the need for the Army to commence preparations.

The Attorney General called the President, at about 0300, to advise him of the disorders in Detroit.

At 0340 the Attorney General called Governor Romney, who reported that the situation was about the same and that he still might need help from the Army. The Attorney General said the Army could be present by late morning, if necessary.

At this point, the Attorney General proceeded to his office, where he called Secretary Resor at 0420. The Army Secretary stated that General Moore, of the Michigan National Guard, believed the Guard could handle the situation. Secretary Resor also said that the Army could place troops in Detroit before noon, if necessary.

The Attorney General called Secretary Resor at 0450 to review the situation and again at 0500. On this latter occasion, Secretary Resor said General Simmons, the Commanding General of the 46th Infantry Division, Michigan National Guard, had toured the riot area and believed that the Guard could handle the situation. Secretary Resor said he was informed that 2,000 Guardsmen were in the area, 3,000 more would be there by noon and another 3,000 were not yet called from a reserve force. The Secretary also reported again that General Moore believed the Guard could handle the situation. He reported that Inspector Gage of the Detroit Police was of the same view.

Attorney General Clark called Governor Romney at 0515 and relayed the information that General Simmons, General Moore and Inspector Gage felt the situation was under control and could be handled locally. The Governor replied that rather than take any chance, he should get Federal help. He said he had just told the press that Federal troops were requested. The Attorney General said that a written request for Federal troops would be desirable before their commitment. He advised the Governor that he would have to exhaust his resources and be prepared to say that there was a state of insurrection in Michigan or that there was domestic violence he was unable to suppress. The Governor replied that he would talk to General Simmons and advise the Attorney General later of his decision. He said the situation at that time was not as bad as it had been in Watts or Newark. He also said he appreciated the assistance he had been given.

The Attorney General called Secretary Resor at 0535 to report this conversation with Governor Romney. At 0550 Secretary Resor called the Attorney General to say that 2,400 troops from Fort Bragg, North Carolina, and 2,400 from Fort Campbell, Kentucky, were in a position to move into Selfridge Air Base, Michigan, by noon, if ordered to do so within the next 10 or 15 minutes. At 0640 the Secretary informed Mr. Clark that 2,190 National Guardsmen were in Detroit and it was estimated 5,000 would be there by noon.

Governor Romney called the Attorney General at 0650 to say that major looting continued and new fires were breaking out. He stated that no one could say whether the situation was contained or not. He said he was going out to look the situation over and would call back in an hour. The Attorney General told Governor Romney that if Federal troops were used, it would probably be necessary to Federalize the National Guard. The Attorney General went on to say that the Governor should not ask for the troops unless they were needed. He also stated that the Army had troops in a state of readiness to move and that the Governor would need to decide within three hours to ask for the troops if they were to arrive in daylight.

Mr. Clark called Secretary Resor at 0700 to report his conversation with Governor Romney.

At 0855 the Governor called the Attorney General and read a statement *recommending* the use of Federal troops. Mr. Clark replied that, under the Constitution and other laws, it would be necessary for the Governor to *request* the use of Federal troops, and to give assurances that a full commitment of State resources had been made and that he was unable to suppress the violence. Governor Romney answered that he understood and would get in touch with the Attorney General as soon as he could.

At 0915 Secretary Resor informed Mr. Clark that General Throckmorton would be in command of the Army troops if they were to be used.

At 0935 the Attorney General briefed the President.

At 0945 Governor Romney called the Attorney General and read a draft of a telegram to the President requesting troops. The Attorney General said the telegram was adequate and that if the Governor decided to send it, he should do so quickly. The Governor said a decision would be made promptly.

Mr. Clark relayed the gist of this conversation to Secretary Resor at 1000 and then to the President at 1010. The President instructed the Attorney General to tell Secretary Resor to move full speed ahead. Mr. Clark did so at 1015.

At 1046 Governor Romney sent the President the telegram he had read to the Attorney General. The telegram was received by the President at 1056 and he replied at 1105 with a wire informing Governor Romney that he was dispatching Federal troops.

At 1155 the Attorney General, then at the White House, reached Governor Romney and read the President's telegram to him. The Governor said it was very helpful. The Attorney General informed him that I would be in charge of the Federal operations. Thereupon I took the phone and talked briefly with the Governor.

At approximately 1100 I had received a telephone call at home from Secretary McNamara who said that he was at the White House with the President and wished to know whether it would be possible for me to go to Detroit in connection with the riots which had started on Sunday. I replied affirmatively, and told him that I would come to the White House as soon as possible.

I arrived at the White House at about 1150 and went to the Cabinet Room where a meeting was in progress. Among those present at the meeting were the President, Secretary McNamara, Attorney General Clark, Deputy Attorney General Christopher, Assistant Attorney General Doar and Mr. Wilkins, the Director of the Department of Justice Community Relations Service.

Secretary McNamara summarized the situation and gave me two telegrams to read. One was from Governor Romney; the second was the response from the President. . . . Governor Romney's telegram stated that as Governor of the State of Michigan he was officially requesting the immediate deployment of Federal troops into Michigan to assist state and local authorities in re-establishing law and order in the City of Detroit. His telegram stated "there is reasonable doubt that we can suppress the existing looting, arson and sniping without the assistance of Federal troops. Time could be of the essence." The President's telegram stated that he had directed the troops, which had been requested by the Governor, to proceed at once to Selfridge Air Force Base. The President's telegram further stated that these troops would be available for immediate deployment as required to support and assist city and state police and Michigan National Guard forces. The telegram also stated that I was being sent as Special Assistant to the Secretary of Defense to confer with Governor Romney and Mayor Cavanagh and to make specific plans for providing such support and assistance as might be necessary.

At 1155, as reported above, Attorney General Clark read to Governor Romney over the telephone the text of the telegram from the President which had been dispatched. I spoke briefly to Governor Romney and told him I would be catching a special military aircraft as soon as possible, and hoped to be in Detroit within 1½ to 2 hours. I asked if he could have a car available at Selfridge Air Force Base to take me to downtown Detroit immediately to meet with him and Mayor Cavanagh. He said he would arrange this.

The President made it very clear to me that he was delegating to me all the responsibility which he could under the Constitution and laws enacted by the Congress and that I should take such action as I believed necessary after I evaluated the situation in Detroit. He asked that I keep Secretary McNamara informed. Secretary McNamara then asked me to designate the individuals whom I wished to take with me to Detroit. I designated Mr. Christopher, Mr. Doar, Mr. Wilkins, Mr. Fitt, General Counsel of the Army; Mr. Henkin, Deputy Assistant Secretary of Defense for Public Affairs; and Colonel Elder.

At approximately 1220 I reached General Throckmorton by telephone at Fort Bragg, and told him to commence as soon as possible the deployment of the already alerted and waiting troops from Fort Bragg, and Fort Campbell, to Selfridge Air Force Base, approximately 25 miles outside of Detroit. I asked General Throckmorton to meet me at Selfridge, and told him we would then proceed together to meet with the Governor and Mayor and their staffs in downtown Detroit.

At 1335, as soon as we could assemble our team, the other members and I departed National Airport for Selfridge. On the plane, we reviewed the facts which were then available and the mission that had been assigned to us. Specific assignments were made to each member of the team for the collection of detailed information which would be needed to form the basis of an objective, comprehensive and independent appraisal of the situation in Detroit and of the Federal support and assistance which might be required. Members of my team present at this time included Mr. Christopher, Mr. Doar, Mr. Wilkins, Mr. Henkin, Mr. Fitt, and Colonel Elder.

I arrived at Selfridge at 1510 and was met by General Throckmorton, who had arrived shortly before from Fort Bragg. We conferred briefly and agreed to put all incoming troops on a 30-minute alert so they would be able to move instantly into Detroit if required. We also confirmed that the necessary transportation was being assembled to move the troops rapidly into the city should they be needed. This transportation consisted primarily of city buses which had been hired by the Fifth Army. We placed a telephone call to find out where Governor Romney and Mayor Cavanagh were located. I was informed that they were at the Detroit Police Headquarters in downtown Detroit. General Throckmorton changed into civilian clothes and we immediately proceeded by police car to that building, arriving at about 1625.

We met at Police Headquarters with Governor Romney and Mayor Cavanagh; Detroit Commissioner of Police Girardin; Colonel Davids of the Michigan State Police; Major General Simmons, Commanding General of the 46th National Guard Division; and Major General Schnippke, Adjutant General of the State of Michigan, and other members of the Governor's and Mayor's staffs.

Mayor Cavanagh reported that there had been 483 fires with 23 still burning on the west side and 6 on the east side; that 1,800 arrests had been made and that detention facilities were being strained. He said that between 800 and 900 Detroit policemen were on the streets at that time (3,000 of the Detroit Police Force normally being assigned to street duty, all shifts). Mayor Cavanagh further stated that he believed local forces were inadequate to cope with the situation, and that there had been intelligence reports that there would be attacks on Monday night on the homes of middle-class Negroes, and that they, in turn, were arming themselves.

Governor Romney asked General Simmons to brief me on the deployment of the Michigan National Guard. General Simmons reported that a substantial number of Guardsmen had not been deployed into the streets and that they were awaiting instructions. I asked him what they were waiting for, and was informed that they were waiting for us. General Throckmorton and I recommended that they immediately deploy additional Guard units into the streets. General Simmons left the room to take such action.

Governor Romney further indicated there were 730 State Police available in Detroit. He said that he felt Federal troops would be necessary to quell the riots. I asked Governor Romney whether he was stating that there was a condition of insurrection or domestic violence which state and local law enforcement forces could not control. Governor Romney replied that he was not prepared to so state but had said "there was reasonable doubt" as to whether the situation could be controlled by state and local law enforcement agencies. He said that he did not wish to state that there was an insurrection because he had been advised that such action might result in the voiding of insurance policies. I pointed out that the commitment of Federal troops to the streets presented grave legal issues and that it was necessary, under the law, to have a finding that a condition of insurrection or domestic violence existed and that local law enforcement agencies could not control the situation prior to the commitment of Federal troops. He did not state that either of those conditions existed. I then requested that space be made available for our headquarters and that it be as close as possible to offices being used by the Mayor and the Police Commissioner. This request was filled immediately.

Governor Romney and Mayor Cavanagh suggested that we take a tour of the city with them to assess the situation. I concurred in this suggestion and said that I wished to make a personal evaluation of the situation on the ground in the riot-torn areas of the city.

At about 1730, Governor Romney, Mayor Cavanagh, General Throckmorton, Mr. Christopher, Mr. Doar and I departed on an automobile tour of the areas of the city which had suffered the most from the rioting, looting and burning. This tour covered a period of about an hour and three-quarters. Our tour took us through all the hardest-hit areas.

In a few areas, fires were burning but they appeared to be coming under the control of fire fighting equipment on the scene. Furthermore, there were large areas of the city where only an occasional window was broken or store burned out. In the downtown business district there was no evidence of lawlessness. The only incident during our tour of the city was a flat tire.

Upon our return to Police Headquarters, I received preliminary reports from the local Federal agencies (i.e., the FBI, the U.S. Attorney's Office and the Community Relations Service) and the members of my party.

These reports indicated that the situation was much quieter than the preceding day. The information available at this time was fragmentary and in oral form, and left much to be desired. Colonel Elder soon thereafter began to assemble data from all sources—principally the local police—on the number of incidents, both current and for the period prior to our arrival, in order to provide a sounder basis for our subsequent assessments of the situation. This compilation proved invaluable.

I was informed that there was a delegation of community leaders who wished to meet with Governor Romney, Mayor Cavanagh and me. We met with this group at about 1930. The group consisted of approximately 15 community leaders, including Congressman Diggs and Congressman Conyers. The meeting was chaired by Mr. Damon Keith, a lawyer and Chairman of the Michigan Civil Rights Commission. Mr. Keith stated at the outset of the meeting that time was short and that the fundamental issue on which the community leaders wished to express their views was the question of whether Federal troops should be deployed in the city. To the best of my recollection, about eight of those present spoke. Congressman Diggs was the first to speak, stating he believed the situation demanded immediate deployment of Federal troops into the city. Congressman Conyers then spoke, saying he did not believe the situation was sufficiently critical to justify the deployment of Federal troops at that time, and that he felt the deployment of Federal troops into the city might inflame rather than quiet the situation. He also said that he believed the rioting had passed its peak and was on the downturn. Of those who spoke, the majority were in favor of the immediate deployment of troops and the remainder were opposed. I closed the meeting by thanking the community leaders for the expression of their views on this critical question and stated that while I tended to agree with Congressman Conyers, I had not finally made up my mind and wished to meet briefly with my staff to review all available evidence prior to making a decision.

General Throckmorton and I and the members of my staff, after reviewing the available evidence, concluded unanimously that there was an insufficient basis at that time to justify the deployment of Federal troops into the city. We gave special weight to two points. First, the incident rate as reflected in the figures now available was about one-third of what it had been the previous day and was holding approximately level.... Second, there were now three times as many National Guard troops in the city as on the previous day and it was not clear that law and order could not be re-established with this additional force.

At approximately 2015 Governor Romney, Mayor Cavanagh and I held a joint press conference. I stated publicly that I had just met with a group of community leaders and also had completed a tour of the city with Governor Romney and Mayor Cavanagh. I said with respect to the evening we hoped very much that the situation would quiet down and that by tomorrow morning people would be able to return to work. I told the newsmen that Federal troops were moving into Selfridge Air Force Base and that we hoped it would not be necessary for them to be used. I said that the City of Detroit and the State of Michigan had an excellent police force and National Guard. I noted that these forces were on the streets at the present time, and said I was hopeful that it would be possible to contain the situation during the night without the necessity of using Federal troops. I further said the Governor, the Mayor and I would continue to follow the situation throughout the entire night and that I would take whatever action might be required.

Governor Romney then stated that he thought the situation was more hopeful that night as a result of these basic facts— number one, the Army was at Selfridge and available to give assistance if necessary; number two, the effort throughout the community, including the police and National Guard, was better organized than the night before; number three, about three times as many National Guardsmen were available for duty in the streets as the night before; and, number four, the fire fighting organization, including units from adjacent communities, unlike the preceding night, was ... available to deal with that aspect of the situation. He also cited a rising desire on the part of people throughout the community to see the disorder and lawlessness ended. The Governor urged everyone in the community to work for the restoration of law and order and the reestablishment of community life on a peaceful basis, and suggested it might be possible the next day to lift the emergency bans. Mayor Cavanagh stated that although he saw some hopeful signs that didn't exist yesterday, he would still like to see the Federal troops committed at this point.

Following the news conference, we returned to our headquarters room, which was located immediately adjacent to the Press Room and to the Police Commissioner's office, from which Mayor Cavanagh was operating. Governor Romney had an office a few doors away on the same floor. Shortly after the press conference at about 2030, Governor Romney came into my office and stated privately that it would soon be dark and that he felt strongly that Federal troops should be deployed into the city before nightfall. I told him that I was still not satisfied that the situation could not be controlled by the local law enforcement agencies but that we would follow the matter on a continuous basis as the evening developed. General Throckmorton and I continued to follow the reports of incidents, both by type and number, on a one-half hour basis as reports were received from the police and other sources. Between this time and 2100, the incident rate data began to climb. . . . Most of the incidents, as reported over the police net, were cases of arson or looting. As the incident rate continued to increase, General Throckmorton and I decided at about 2130 that we should move three battalions of paratroopers to the Fairgrounds within the Metropolitan area of Detroit so they might be more readily available in case they should have to be deployed into the streets. General Throckmorton gave the necessary orders to implement this decision. During the next hour and one-half the incidents throughout the city, as reported over police radio, continued a steady rise.

Just before 2300, General Throckmorton and I, after further consultation with Governor Romney and Mayor Cavanagh, determined that the local law enforcement agencies could not control the situation. The Governor and the Mayor both now informed me that they had committed all available police and National Guard forces. At approximately 2310, I

recommended to the President, with the concurrence of all of the members of my team, that Federal troops be deployed into the streets.

At 2320, the President signed the Proclamation and Executive Order authorizing the use of Federal troops in the City of Detroit and Federalizing the Army and Air National Guard of the State of Michigan. I made a public statement at a news conference about 2325 announcing the action which was being taken; General Throckmorton immediately took command of all the military forces. He ordered the deployment of Regular U.S. Army forces into the eastern half of the city, with the responsibility for the western half assigned to the Michigan National Guard. The rules of engagement issued to all troops under Federal control were to use the minimum force necessary to restore law and order. Specifically the troop commanders were instructed to apply force in the following order of priority:

A. Unloaded rifles with bayonets fixed and sheathed
B. Unloaded rifles with bare bayonets fixed
C. Riot control agent CS—tear gas
D. Loaded rifles with bare bayonets fixed

Immediately after the President signed the Executive Order, General Throckmorton called Major General Simmons to inform him that he was under General Throckmorton's command and requested him to stand by at his headquarters for a visit, and to send a liaison officer to General Throckmorton's office at Police Headquarters. General Throckmorton then drove to the Fairgrounds where he contacted Major General Seitz, Commander of the Federal troops (Task Force 82) and instructed him to assume responsibility from the 46th Division (National Guard) for the restoration of law and order in the eastern half of the city—east of Woodward Avenue. The time of changeover would be mutually agreed upon by the commanders concerned.

From the Fairgrounds, General Throckmorton preceded to the 46th Division CP at the Artillery Guard Armory where he issued instructions to General Simmons, relieving him of responsibility for the east side of town and charged him with retaining responsibility for the west side. Prior to General

Throckmorton's departure from the 46th Division CP, General Seitz arrived to coordinate with General Simmons.

During the inspection tour which we had taken with the Mayor and Governor commencing at 1730, we visited three areas which had been harder hit by the disturbances than any others. These were in the 2d Precinct along Grand River Avenue, the area around 12th Street north of Grand River Avenue in the 10th Precinct and the area around Mack Avenue in the 5th Precinct in the eastern part of the city. . . . Of the three areas, 12th Street had been the hardest hit; however, as it became dark the incidents in the eastern half of the city began to increase over those in the western part of the city. Thus, at the time the decision was made to assign TF 82 to the eastern portion of the city, it appeared that the Regular troops were taking over the most active sector. Other factors influencing the decision to assign the eastern portion to TF 82 were the closer proximity of eastern Detroit to Selfridge and the proximity of the 46th Division CP to western Detroit.

At 0410 on Tuesday, 25 July, TF 82 completed relief of the 46th National Guard Division elements in that portion of the city east of Woodward Avenue, and the remainder of the Federal troops were moved from Selfridge to the Fairgrounds. . . .

At 0225, General Throckmorton and I made a statement to the press outlining the situation and delineating the areas of responsibility of the Federal and National Guard troop units. General Throckmorton and I made another tour of the city beginning at 0330. On our return we held another press conference at 0520 at Police Headquarters. Our objective was to keep the public fully informed of all developments connected with the restoration of law and order to Detroit.

Based on the situation as I saw it then, I proposed to Governor Romney and Mayor Cavanagh that a joint announcement be made to the effect that Detroit industrial plants, businesses and offices should be reopened that day. They concurred and such a statement was released at 0703.

Throughout the morning of Tuesday, 25 July, the members of my group and I participated in a series of discussions with state and city officials and community leaders concerning health and medical problems; food distribution; emergency shelter needs; processing, confinement and disposition of persons in arrest; and other matters which required consideration at once in order to begin and expedite the return to normal.

Early Tuesday morning, on the basis of a deteriorating situation in other parts of Michigan, Governor Romney requested the release of 250 National Guard troops for use outside of the Detroit area. He said he also wanted to remove 250 State Police for use elsewhere in the State. These actions were taken. Throughout Tuesday and Wednesday further releases of National Guard and police to State control were made. Adjustments also were made in troop dispositions within the city to take account of changes in the situation in Detroit and nearby areas.

The incident rate on Tuesday during daylight hours ran at about half the rate for Monday. Although it rose sharply again in the evening, the peak rate at 2300 was only 166 per hour versus 231 at the same hour on Monday. There were 11 deaths between noon on Tuesday and daylight Wednesday and about 60 fires were reported between 2100 and midnight, a rate well above normal.

On Wednesday night, Mayor Cavanagh, Governor Romney and I all agreed that it was essential that we assure the leadership of the city that law and order was being re-established and that we urge the leadership to mobilize to take the necessary steps to begin to rebuild the city. A list of those to be invited to attend a meeting on Thursday was prepared by the staffs of the Mayor and the Governor and telegrams were sent out asking them to attend a meeting on Thursday at 1500.

In view of the improved situation which existed early Thursday morning, the first steps of restoring full responsibility for the maintenance of law and order to the state and local authorities were initiated. As an initial step, General Throckmorton and I agreed that an order should be issued that bayonets be sheathed and ammunition removed from the weapons of the Regular Army and National Guard troops. This was done. An announcement of the lifting of the curfew and the easing of gasoline restrictions was made by the Governor at 1000 Thursday, 27 July. The lifting of curfew, however, was withdrawn later that day by the Governor because of the congestion caused by "spectators, gawkers and photographers" in the damaged areas.

On Thursday, additional attention was given to the definition of the tasks that needed to be performed to get the stricken city moving again. The meeting of several hundred community leaders was held at 1615 that day for the purpose of discussing how best to organize to meet this challenge. General Throckmorton and I gave brief situation reports on the status of law and order and on Federal actions being taken to provide for emergency food, health and safety needs. Following remarks made by a number of participants, Governor Romney announced the appointment of Mr. Joseph L. Hudson, Jr. to head a broadly based committee of community leaders to proceed with the development of recovery plans for the city.

By Friday morning, the situation had improved sufficiently so that, after coordination with Governor Romney and Mayor Cavanagh, the first steps could be taken in the withdrawal of Federal troops from Detroit. Units of TF 82 were withdrawn from the First, Seventh and Thirteenth Precincts and were assembled at City Airport and the Fairgrounds. Their sectors were taken over by National Guard troops of the 46th Infantry Division. The 5th precinct remained under the responsibility of the Regular U.S. Army forces.

I met with Governor Romney and Mayor Cavanagh on Friday morning, in accordance with the President's telegram of 27 July to discuss further the emergency health, food and safety needs of the citizens of Detroit. At 1200 we announced results of these discussions at a joint press conference. These matters are discussed further in a later section of the report.

At 1230, Mr. Christopher, Mr. Doar and I met with Governor Romney, Mayor Cavanagh and state, city and county legal and judicial authorities to review the problems associated with the large numbers of persons in custody and awaiting disposition. These matters are discussed in some detail later in the report.

On Saturday morning, 29 July, I returned to Washington to report to the President and to attend the first meeting of the President's National Advisory Commission on Civil Disorders.

Following my meeting with the Commission, a news conference was held at which I announced the Small Business Administration's declaration of Detroit as a disaster area. This declaration had the effect of authorizing low interest (3%) long-term (30 year) loans for repairing or replacing small businesses, homes and personal property destroyed or damaged by the riots.

I returned to Detroit at 2040 that night and met with my group to discuss further plans. Deputy Attorney General Christopher returned to Washington upon my arrival in Detroit.

On Sunday, I met with Mr. Phillips, Regional Director of the SBA with responsibility for the Detroit area, to discuss the actions needed to carry out the previous day's SBA declaration of Detroit as a disaster area. Mr. Phillips agreed to open a temporary office in the riot-torn 12th Street area, to consider opening an additional office in the most heavily damaged area on the east side, to supplement his personnel in the Detroit area, and to hold a press conference with me in Police Headquarters on Monday morning to announce the special arrangements which had been made. These arrangements were completed on Sunday and an announcement was made at 0935 on Monday morning. On Wednesday, 2 August, Mr. Moot, Administrator designate of the SBA, visited Detroit with members of his staff for further discussions of the SBA program and its potential contribution to the city's recovery.

During Monday, Tuesday and Wednesday, Federal troops were withdrawn progressively from the Detroit area and the TF 82 sectors were taken over by the 46th Division. On Monday, the last units of TF 82 were withdrawn from the streets of Detroit and three battalions were moved to Selfridge Air Force Base with the remaining four held in assembly areas at the City Airport and the Fairgrounds. On Tuesday, four battalions were airlifted to their home stations at Fort Campbell and all remaining battalions were assembled at Selfridge Air

Force Base from which they were airlifted to Fort Bragg on Wednesday. The 46th National Guard Division was de-Federalized and returned to the control of the State of Michigan (to operate under the State Police Director) at 1200 on Wednesday, 2 August, as the last units of TF 82 were being returned home.

The curfew was relaxed concurrently with the withdrawal of Federal troops; the effective period was 2400 to 0530 on Monday night–Tuesday morning and it was discontinued entirely on Wednesday. Liquor sales, which had been suspended, were resumed outside curfew hours beginning on Monday. The return of the control of the city to the National Guard and local authorities, and the relaxation of curfew and the restriction on liquor sales, did not result in any increase in incident rates. These rates had lessened each day, reaching a low of 280 incidents in 24 hours on Tuesday, 1 August.

On Monday, 31 July, I met with Mr. Crook, Director of Volunteers in Service to America (VISTA) and Mr. Brabson, VISTA Program Officer, to review the VISTA program in support of Detroit's recovery. . . .

My principal activities and those of my staff on Monday, Tuesday, and Wednesday, 31 July–2 August, were to meet and talk with as wide a segment of the citizens of Detroit as possible in order to gain additional insights into the problems which had caused the riots and those which had grown from them. Although these meetings proved highly productive, they did not lead me to any simple conclusions with respect to the problems which Detroit must meet and overcome; they convinced me anew of the tangled economic, sociological, and psychological origins of the riots and of the enormity of the related tasks to be performed.

At 0935 on Wednesday, 2 August, General Throckmorton and I held a final press conference in the Police Headquarters press room. At that time we announced that "law and order have been restored to Detroit . . . responsibility for maintaining law and order in Detroit will be returned at noon to state authorities."

At 2110 I departed from Detroit, arriving in Washington with my mission completed at 2310.

Source: Transcript, Final Report of Cyrus R. Vance, Special Assistant to the Secretary of Defense, Concerning the Detroit Riots, July 23 through August 2, 1967, 1–27, LBJ Library. Online: http://www.lbjlib.utexas.edu/johnson/archives.hom/oralhistory.hom/vance-c/detroitreport.asp. Accessed April 24, 2013.

See also: Asbury Park Riot of 1970; Atlanta Riot of 1906; Atlanta Riot of 1967; Bellingham Riots; Bensonhurst Incident 1989; Biloxi Beach Riot of 1960; Black Church Arsons; Bloody Sunday; Boston Riot of 1975 and 1976; Brownsville Riot of 1906; Charleston Riot of 1919; Chattanooga Riot of 1906; Chester and Philadelphia Riots of 1918; Chicago Commission on Race Relations; Chicago Riot of 1919; Cincinnati Riots of 1967 and 1968; Cincinnati Riot of 2001; Cleveland Riot of 1966; Detroit Riot of 1943; Detroit Riot of 1967; East St. Louis Riot of 1917; Election Riots of the 1880s and 1890s; Greensburg Riot of 1906; Greenwood Community; Harlem Riot of 1935; Houston Mutiny of 1917; Howard Beach Incident 1986; Johnson-Jeffries Fight of 1910; Knoxville Riot of 1919; Long Hot Summer Riots 1965–1967; Longview Riot of 1919; Los Angeles Riot of 1965; Los Angeles Riots of 1992; Miami Riot of 1982; New Bedford Riot of 1970; New Orleans Riot of 1866; New York City Draft Riot of 1863; New York City Riot of 1943; Newark Riot of 1967; Orangeburg Massacre of 1968; Philadelphia Riot of 1964; Prison Riots; Race Riots in America; Red Scare and Race Riots; Red Summer Race Riots of 1919; Rosewood Riot of 1923; Saint Genevieve Riot of 1930; San Francisco Riot of 1966; Springfield Riot of 1904; Tampa Riots of 1987; Texas Southern University Riot of 1967; Tulsa Riot of 1921; Washington, D.C., Riot of 1919; Washington, D.C., Riots of 1968; Wilmington Riot of 1898; Zoot Suit Riots

Bilingual Education Act (1968)

Introduction

The Bilingual Education Act, which was passed in 1968, marked the first time that Congress mandated the creation and funding of bilingual programs in public schools. Sponsored by Sen. Ralph Yarborough of Texas, who was concerned with the number of Spanish-speaking children in his state that were educationally disadvantaged by having English-only instruction in school, the act is also known as Title II of the Elementary and Secondary Education Act. Bilingual programs have come under increasing scrutiny in the late 1990s because of their expense and apparent lack of success.

Primary Source

Sec. 7401. Short title

This part may be cited as the "Bilingual Education Act."

Sec. 7402. Findings, policy, and purpose

(a) Findings. The Congress finds that—

(1) language-minority Americans speak virtually all world languages plus many that are indigenous to the United States;

(2) there are large and growing numbers of children and youth of limited-English proficiency, many of whom have a cultural heritage that differs from that of their English-proficient peers;

(3) the presence of language-minority Americans is related in part to Federal immigration policies;

(4) many language-minority Americans are limited in their English proficiency, and many have limited education and income;

(5) limited English proficient children and youth face a number of challenges in receiving an education that will enable such children and youth to participate fully in American society, including—

(A) segregated education programs;

(B) disproportionate and improper placement in special education and other special programs due to the use of inappropriate evaluation procedures;

(C) the limited-English proficiency of their own parents, which hinders the parents' ability to fully participate in the education of their children; and

(D) a shortage of teachers and other staff who are professionally trained and qualified to serve such children and youth;

(6) Native Americans and Native American languages (as such terms are defined in section 2902 of title 25), including native residents of the outlying areas, have a unique status under Federal law that requires special policies within the broad purposes of this chapter to serve the education needs of language minority students in the United States;

(7) institutions of higher education can assist in preparing teachers, administrators and other school personnel to understand and build upon the educational strengths and needs of language-minority and culturally diverse student enrollments;

(8) it is the purpose of this subchapter to help ensure that limited English proficient students master English and develop high levels of academic attainment in content areas;

(9) quality bilingual education programs enable children and youth to learn English and meet high academic standards including proficiency in more than one language;

(10) as the world becomes increasingly interdependent and as international communication becomes a daily occurrence in government, business, commerce, and family life, multilingual skills constitute an important national resource which deserves protection and development;

(11) educational technology has the potential for improving the education of language-minority and limited English proficient students and their families, and the Federal Government should foster this development;

(12) parent and community participation in bilingual education programs contributes to program effectiveness;

(13) research, evaluation, and data-collection capabilities in the field of bilingual education need to be strengthened so that educators and other staff can better identify and promote those programs, program implementation strategies, and instructional practices that result in effective education of limited English proficient children;

(14) the use of a child or youth's native language and culture in classroom instruction can—

(A) promote self-esteem and contribute to academic achievement and learning English by limited English proficient children and youth;

(B) benefit English-proficient children and youth who also participate in such programs; and

(C) develop our Nation's national language resources, thus promoting our Nation's competitiveness in the global economy;

(15) the Federal Government, as exemplified by title VI of the Civil Rights Act of 1964 (42 U.S.C. 2000d et seq.) and section 1703(f) of this title, has a special and continuing obligation to ensure that States and local school districts take appropriate action to provide equal educational opportunities to children and youth of limited-English proficiency; and

(16) the Federal Government also, as exemplified by the Federal Government's efforts under this subchapter, has a special and continuing obligation to assist States and local school districts in developing the capacity to provide programs of instruction that offer limited English proficient children and youth an equal educational opportunity.

(b) Policy. The Congress declares it to be the policy of the United States, in order to ensure equal educational opportunity for all children and youth and to promote educational excellence, to assist State and local educational agencies, institutions of higher education and community-based organizations to build their capacity to establish, implement, and sustain programs of instruction for children and youth of limited-English proficiency.

(c) Purpose. The purpose of this part is to educate limited English proficient children and youth to meet the same rigorous standards for academic performance expected of all children and youth, including meeting challenging State content standards and challenging State student performance standards in academic areas by—

(1) developing systemic improvement and reform of educational programs serving limited English proficient students through the development and implementation of exemplary bilingual education programs and special alternative instruction programs;

(2) developing bilingual skills and multicultural understanding;

(3) developing the English of such children and youth and, to the extent possible, the native language skills of such children and youth;

(4) providing similar assistance to Native Americans with certain modifications relative to the unique status of Native American languages under Federal law;

(5) developing data collection and dissemination, research, materials development, and technical assistance which is focused on school improvement for limited English proficient students; and

(6) developing programs which strengthen and improve the professional training of educational personnel who work with limited English proficient students.

Sec. 7403. Authorization of appropriations

(a) In general. For the purpose of carrying out this part, there are authorized to be appropriated $215,000,000 for the fiscal year 1995 and such sums as may be necessary for each of the four succeeding fiscal years.

(b) Distribution. From the sums appropriated under subsection (a) of this section for any fiscal year, the Secretary shall reserve not less than 25 percent of such funds for such year to carry out subpart 3 of this part.

Sec. 7404. Native American and Alaska Native children in school

(a) Eligible entities. For the purpose of carrying out programs under this part for individuals served by elementary, secondary, and postsecondary schools operated predominately for Native American or Alaska Native children and youth, an Indian tribe, a tribally sanctioned educational authority, a Native Hawaiian or Native American Pacific Islander native language education organization, or an elementary or secondary school that is operated or funded by the Bureau of Indian Affairs shall be considered to be a local educational agency as such term is used in this part, subject to the following qualifications:

(1) "Indian tribe" defined. The term "Indian tribe" means any Indian tribe, band, nation, or other organized group or community, including any Alaska Native village or regional or village corporation as defined in or established pursuant to the Alaska Native Claims Settlement Act (43 U.S.C. 1601 et seq.), that is recognized for the special programs and services provided by the United States to Indians because of their status as Indians.

(2) "Tribally sanctioned educational authority" defined. The term "tribally sanctioned educational authority" means—

(A) any department or division of education operating within the administrative structure of the duly constituted governing body of an Indian tribe; and

(B) any nonprofit institution or organization that is—

(i) chartered by the governing body of an Indian tribe to operate any such school or otherwise to oversee the delivery of educational services to members of that tribe; and

(ii) approved by the Secretary for the purpose of this section.

(b) Eligible entity application. Notwithstanding any other provision of this part, each eligible entity described in subsection (a) of this section shall submit any application for assistance under this part directly to the Secretary along with timely comments on the need for the proposed program.

7405. Residents of territories and freely associated nations.
SUBPART 1—BILINGUAL EDUCATION CAPACITY AND DEMONSTRATION GRANTS

Sec. 7421. Financial assistance for bilingual education

The purpose of this subpart is to assist local educational agencies, institutions of higher education, and community-based organizations, through the grants authorized under sections 7422, 7423, 7424, and 7425 of this title to—

(1) develop and enhance their capacity to provide high-quality instruction through bilingual education or special alternative instruction programs to children and youth of limited-English proficiency; and

(2) to help such children and youth—

(A) develop proficiency in English, and to the extent possible, their native language; and

(B) meet the same challenging State content standards and challenging State student performance standards expected for all children and youth as required by section 6311(b) of this title.

Sec. 7422. Program development and implementation grants

(a) Purpose. The purpose of this section is to develop and implement new comprehensive, coherent, and successful bilingual education or special alternative instructional programs for limited English proficient students, including programs of early childhood education, kindergarten through twelfth grade education, gifted and talented education, and vocational and applied technology education.

(b) Program authorized.

(1) Authority.

(A) The Secretary is authorized to award grants to eligible entities having applications approved under section 7426 of this title to enable such entities to carry out activities described in paragraph (2).

(B) Each grant under this section shall be awarded for a period of three years.

(2) Authorized activities

(A) Grants awarded under this section shall be used to improve the education of limited English proficient students and their families by—

(i) developing and implementing comprehensive preschool, elementary, or secondary bilingual education or special alternative instructional programs that are coordinated with other relevant programs and services to meet the full range of educational needs of limited English proficient students; and

(ii) providing inservice training to classroom teachers, administrators, and other school or community-based organizational personnel to improve the instruction and assessment of language-minority and limited English proficient students.

(B) Grants under this section may be used to improve the education of limited English proficient students and their families by—

(i) implementing family education programs and parent outreach and training activities designed to assist parents to become active participants in the education of their children;

(ii) improving the instructional program for limited English proficient students by identifying, acquiring, and upgrading curriculum, instructional materials, educational software and assessment procedures and, if appropriate, applying educational technology;

(iii) compensating personnel, including teacher aides who have been specifically trained, or are being trained, to provide services to children and youth of limited-English proficiency;

(iv) providing tutorials and academic or career counseling for children and youth of limited-English proficiency; and

(v) providing such other activities, related to the purposes of this part, as the Secretary may approve.

(c) "Eligible entity" defined. For the purpose of this section the term "eligible entity" means—

(1) one or more local educational agencies;

(2) one or more local educational agencies in collaboration with an institution of higher education, community-based organization or local or State educational agency; or

(3) a community-based organization or an institution of higher education which has an application approved by the local educational agency to develop and implement early childhood education or family education programs or to conduct an instructional program which supplements the educational services provided by a local educational agency.

(d) Due consideration. In awarding grants under this section, the Secretary shall give due consideration to the need for early childhood education, elementary education, and secondary education programs.

Sec. 7423. Program enhancement projects

(a) Purpose. The purpose of this section is to carry out highly focused, innovative, locally designed projects to expand or enhance existing bilingual education or special alternative instructional programs for limited English proficient students.

(b) Program authorized.

(1) Authority.

(A) The Secretary is authorized to award grants to eligible entities having applications approved under section 7426 of this title to enable such entities to carry out activities described in paragraph (2).

(B) Each grant under this section shall be awarded for a period of two years.

(2) Authorized activities

(A) Grants under this section shall be used for providing inservice training to classroom teachers, administrators, and other school or community-based organization personnel to improve the instruction and assessment of language-minority and limited English proficient students.

(B) Grants under this section may be used for—

(i) implementing family education programs and parent outreach and training activities designed to assist parents to become active participants in the education of their children;

(ii) improving the instructional program for limited English proficient students by identifying, acquiring, and upgrading curriculum, instructional materials, educational software and assessment procedures and, if appropriate, applying educational technology;

(iii) compensating personnel, including teacher aides who have been specifically trained, or are being trained, to provide services to children and youth of limited-English proficiency;

(iv) providing tutorials and academic or career counseling for children and youth of limited-English proficiency;

(v) providing intensified instruction; and

(vi) providing such other activities, related to the purposes of this part, as the Secretary may approve.

(c) "Eligible entity" defined. For the purpose of this section the term "eligible entity" means—

(1) one or more local educational agencies;

(2) one or more local educational agencies in collaboration with an institution of higher education, community-based organization or local or State educational agency; or

(3) a community-based organization or an institution of higher education which has an application approved by the local educational agency to enhance early childhood education or family education programs or to conduct an instructional program which supplements the educational services provided by a local educational agency.

Sec. 7424. Comprehensive school grants

(a) Purpose. The purpose of this section is to provide financial assistance to eligible entities to implement schoolwide bilingual education programs or special alternative instruction programs for reforming, restructuring, and upgrading all relevant programs and operations, within an individual school, that serve all (or virtually all) children and youth of limited-English proficiency in schools with significant concentrations of such children and youth.

(b) Program authorized.

(1) Authority.

(A) The Secretary is authorized to award grants to eligible entities having applications approved under section 7426 of this title to enable such entities to carry out activities described in paragraph (3).

(B) Each grant under this section shall be awarded for five years.

(2) Termination. The Secretary shall terminate grants to eligible entities under this section if the Secretary determines that—

(A) the program evaluation required by section 7433 of this title indicates that students in the schoolwide program are not being taught to and are not making adequate progress toward achieving challenging State content standards and challenging State student performance standards; or

(B) in the case of a program to promote dual language facility, such program is not promoting such facility.

(3) Authorized activities. Grants under this section may be used to improve the education of limited English proficient students and their families by—

(A) implementing family education programs and parent outreach and training activities designed to assist parents to become active participants in the education of their children;

(B) improving the instructional program for limited English proficient students by identifying, acquiring and upgrading curriculum, instructional materials, educational software and assessment procedures and, if appropriate, applying educational technology;

(C) compensating personnel, including teacher aides who have been specifically trained, or are being trained, to provide services to children and youth of limited-English proficiency;

(D) providing tutorials and academic or career counseling for children and youth of limited-English proficiency;

(E) providing intensified instruction; and

(F) providing such other activities, related to the purposes of this part, as the Secretary may approve.

(4) Special rule. A grant recipient, before carrying out a program assisted under this section, shall plan, train personnel, develop curriculum, and acquire or develop materials.

(c) "Eligible entity" defined. For the purpose of this section the term "eligible entity" means—

(1) one or more local educational agencies; or

(2) one or more local educational agencies in collaboration with an institution of higher education, community-based organizations or a local or State educational agency.

Sec. 7425. Systemwide improvement grants

(a) Purpose. The purpose of this section is to implement districtwide bilingual education programs or special alternative instruction programs to improve, reform, and upgrade relevant programs and operations, within an entire local educational agency, that serve a significant number of children and youth of limited-English proficiency in local educational agencies with significant concentrations of such children and youth.

(b) Program authorized.

(1) Authority.

(A) The Secretary is authorized to award grants to eligible entities having applications approved under section 7426 of this title to enable such entities to carry out activities described in paragraphs (3) and (4).

(B) Each grant under this section shall be awarded for 5 years.

(2) Termination. The Secretary shall terminate grants to eligible entities under this section if the Secretary determines that—

(A) the program evaluation required by section 7433 of this title indicates that students in the program are not being taught to and are not making adequate progress toward achieving challenging State content standards and challenging State student performance standards; or

(B) in the case of a program to promote dual language facility, such program is not promoting such facility.

(3) Preparation. Grants under this section may be used during the first 12 months exclusively for activities preparatory to the delivery of services.

(4) Uses. Grants under this section may be used to improve the education of limited English proficient students and their families by reviewing, restructuring, and upgrading—

(A) educational goals, curriculum guidelines and content, standards and assessments;

(B) personnel policies and practices including recruitment, certification, staff development, and assignment;

(C) student grade-promotion and graduation requirements;

(D) student assignment policies and practices;

(E) family education programs and parent outreach and training activities designed to assist parents to become active participants in the education of their children;

(F) the instructional program for limited English proficient students by identifying, acquiring and upgrading curriculum, instructional materials, educational software and assessment procedures and, if appropriate, applying educational technology;

(G) tutorials and academic or career counseling for children and youth of limited-English proficiency; and

(H) such other activities, related to the purposes of this part, as the Secretary may approve.

(c) "Eligible entity" defined. For the purpose of this section the term "eligible entity" means—

(1) one or more local educational agencies; or

(2) one or more local educational agencies in collaboration with an institution of higher education, community-based organizations or a local or State educational agency.

Sec. 7426. Applications

(a) In general.

(1) Secretary. To receive a grant under this subpart, an eligible entity shall submit an application to the Secretary at such time, in such form, and containing such information as the Secretary may require.

(2) State educational agency. An eligible entity, with the exception of schools funded by the Bureau of Indian Affairs, shall submit a copy of its application under this section to the State educational agency.

(b) State review and comments.

(1) Deadline. The State educational agency, not later than 45 days after receipt of an application under this section, shall review the application and transmit such application to the Secretary.

(2) Comments.

(A) Regarding any application submitted under this subchapter, the State educational agency shall—

(i) submit to the Secretary written comments regarding all such applications; and

(ii) submit to each eligible entity the comments that pertain to such entity.

(B) For purposes of this subpart, such comments shall address how the eligible entity—

(i) will further the academic achievement of limited English proficient students served pursuant to a grant received under this subpart; and

(ii) how the grant application is consistent with the State plan submitted under section 6311 of this title.

(c) Eligible entity comments. An eligible entity may submit to the Secretary comments that address the comments submitted by the State educational agency.

(d) Comment consideration. In making grants under this subpart the Secretary shall take into consideration comments made by a State educational agency.

(e) Waiver. Notwithstanding subsection (b) of this section, the Secretary is authorized to waive the review requirement of subsection (b) of this section if a State educational agency can demonstrate that such review requirement may impede such agency's ability to fulfill the requirements of participation in the State grant program, particularly such agency's data collection efforts and such agency's ability to provide technical assistance to local educational agencies not receiving funds under this chapter.

(f) Required documentation. Such application shall include documentation that the applicant has the qualified personnel required to develop, administer, and implement the proposed program.

(g) Contents.

(1) In general. An application for a grant under this subpart shall contain the following:

(A) A description of the need for the proposed program, including data on the number of children and youth of limited-English proficiency in the school or school district to be served and the characteristics of such children and youth, such as language spoken, dropout rates, proficiency in English and the native language, academic standing in relation to the English-proficient peers of such children and youth, and, where applicable, the recency of immigration.

(B) A description of the program to be implemented and how such program's design—

(i) relates to the linguistic and academic needs of the children and youth of limited-English proficiency to be served;

(ii) is coordinated with other programs under this chapter, the Goals 2000: Educate America Act (20 U.S.C. 5801 et seq.) and other Acts, as appropriate, in accordance with section 8856 of this title;

(iii) involves the parents of the children and youth of limited-English proficiency to be served;

(iv) ensures accountability in achieving high academic standards; and

(v) promotes coordination of services for the children and youth of limited-English proficiency to be served and their families.

(C) A description, if appropriate, of the applicant's collaborative activities with institutions of higher education, community-based organizations, local or State educational agencies, private schools, nonprofit organizations, or businesses in carrying out the proposed program.

(D) An assurance that the applicant will not reduce the level of State and local funds that the applicant expends for bilingual education or special alternative instruction programs if the applicant receives an award under this subpart.

(E) An assurance that the applicant will employ teachers in the proposed program that, individually or in combination, are proficient in English, including written, as well as oral, communication skills.

(F) A budget for grant funds.

(2) Additional information. Each application for a grant under section 7424 or 7425 of this title shall—

(A) describe—

(i) current services the applicant provides to children and youth of limited-English proficiency;

(ii) what services children and youth of limited-English proficiency will receive under the grant that such children or youth will not otherwise receive;

(iii) how funds received under this subpart will be integrated with all other Federal, State, local, and private resources that may be used to serve children and youth of limited-English proficiency;

(iv) specific achievement and school retention goals for the children and youth to be served by the proposed program and how progress toward achieving such goals will be measured; and

(v) current family education programs if applicable; and

(B) provide assurances that—

(i) the program funded will be integrated with the overall educational program; and

(ii) the application has been developed in consultation with an advisory council, the majority of whose members are parents and other representatives of the children and youth to be served in such programs.

(h) Approval of applications. An application for a grant under this subpart may be approved only if the Secretary determines that—

(1) the program will use qualified personnel, including personnel who are proficient in the language or languages used for instruction;

(2) in designing the program for which application is made, the needs of children in nonprofit private elementary and secondary schools have been taken into account through consultation with appropriate private school officials and, consistent with the number of such children enrolled in such schools in the area to be served whose educational needs are of the type and whose language and grade levels are of a similar type to those which the program is intended to address, after consultation with appropriate private school officials, provision has been made for the participation of such children on a basis comparable to that provided for public school children;

(3) student evaluation and assessment procedures in the program are valid, reliable, and fair for limited English proficient students, and that limited English proficient students who are disabled are identified and served in accordance with the requirements of the Individuals with Disabilities Education Act (20 U.S.C. 1400 et seq.);

(4) Federal funds made available for the project or activity will be used so as to supplement the level of State and local funds that, in the absence of such Federal funds, would have been expended for special programs for children of limited English proficient individuals and in no case to supplant such State and local funds, except that nothing in this paragraph shall be construed to preclude a local educational agency from using funds under this subchapter for activities carried out under an order of a court of the United States or of any State respecting services to be provided such children, or to carry out a plan approved by the Secretary as adequate under title VI of the Civil Rights Act of 1964 (42 U.S.C. 2000d et seq.) with respect to services to be provided such children;

(5) the assistance provided under the application will contribute toward building the capacity of the applicant to provide a program on a regular basis, similar to that proposed for assistance, which will be of sufficient size, scope, and quality to promise significant improvement in the education of students of limited-English proficiency, and that the applicant will have the resources and commitment to continue the program when assistance under this subpart is reduced or no longer available; and

(6) the applicant provides for utilization of the State and national dissemination sources for program design and in dissemination of results and products.

(i) Priorities and special rules.

(1) Priority. The Secretary shall give priority to applications which provide for the development of bilingual proficiency both in English and another language for all participating students.

(2) Special alternative instructional program. Grants for special alternative instructional programs under this subpart shall not exceed 25 percent of the funds provided for any type of grant under any section, or of the total funds provided, under this subpart for any fiscal year.

(3) Special rule. Notwithstanding paragraph (2), the Secretary may award grants under this subpart for special alternative instructional programs if an applicant has demonstrated that the applicant cannot develop and implement a bilingual education program for the following reasons:

(A) Where the diversity of the limited English proficient students' native languages and the small number of students speaking each respective language makes bilingual education impractical.

(B) Where, despite documented efforts, the applicant has not been able to hire qualified instructional personnel who are able to communicate in the students' native language.

(4) Consideration. In approving applications under this subpart, the Secretary shall give consideration to the degree to which the program for which assistance is sought involves the collaborative efforts of institutions of higher education, community-based organizations, the appropriate local and State educational agency, or businesses.

(5) Due consideration. The Secretary shall give due consideration to applications providing training for personnel participating in or preparing to participate in the program which will assist such personnel in meeting State and local certification requirements and that, to the extent possible, describe how college or university credit will be awarded for such training.

Sec. 7427. Intensified instruction

In carrying out this subpart, each grant recipient may intensify instruction for limited English proficient students by—

(1) expanding the educational calendar of the school in which such student is enrolled to include programs before and after school and during the summer months;

(2) expanding the use of professional and volunteer aids;

(3) applying technology to the course of instruction; and

(4) providing intensified instruction through supplementary instruction or activities, including educationally enriching extracurricular activities, during times when school is not routinely in session.

Sec. 7428. Capacity building

Each recipient of a grant under this subpart shall use the grant in ways that will build such recipient's capacity to continue to offer high-quality bilingual and special alternative education programs and services to children and youth of limited-English proficiency once Federal assistance is reduced or eliminated.

Sec. 7429. Subgrants

A local educational agency that receives a grant under this subpart may, with the approval of the Secretary, make a subgrant to, or enter into a contract with, an institution of higher education, a nonprofit organization, or a consortium of such entities to carry out an approved program, including a program to serve out-of-school youth.

Sec. 7430. Priority on funding

The Secretary shall give priority to applications under this subpart that describe a program that—

(1) enrolls a large percentage or large number of limited English proficient students;

(2) takes into account significant increases in limited English proficient children and youth, including such children and youth in areas with low concentrations of such children and youth; and

(3) ensures that activities assisted under this subpart address the needs of school systems of all sizes and geographic areas, including rural and urban schools.

Sec. 7431. Coordination with other programs

In order to secure the most flexible and efficient use of Federal funds, any State receiving funds under this subpart shall coordinate its program with other programs under this chapter, the Goals 2000: Educate America Act (20 U.S.C. 5801 et seq.), and other Acts, as appropriate, in accordance with section 8856 of this title.

Sec. 7432. Programs for Native Americans and Puerto Rico

Programs authorized under this part that serve Native American children, Native Pacific Island children, and children in the Commonwealth of Puerto Rico, notwithstanding any other provision of this part, may include programs of instruction, teacher training, curriculum development, evaluation, and testing designed for Native American children and youth learning and studying Native American languages and children and youth of limited-Spanish proficiency, except that one outcome of such programs serving Native American children shall be increased English proficiency among such children.

Sec. 7433. Evaluations

(a) Evaluation. Each recipient of funds under this subpart shall provide the Secretary with an evaluation, in the form prescribed by the Secretary, of such recipient's program every two years.

(b) Use of evaluation. Such evaluation shall be used by a grant recipient—

(1) for program improvement;

(2) to further define the program's goals and objectives; and

(3) to determine program effectiveness.

(c) Evaluation components. Evaluations shall include—

(1) how students are achieving the State student performance standards, if any, including data comparing children and youth of limited-English proficiency with nonlimited English proficient children and youth with regard to school retention, academic achievement, and gains in English (and, where applicable, native language) proficiency;

(2) program implementation indicators that provide information for informing and improving program management and effectiveness, including data on appropriateness of curriculum in relationship to grade and course requirements, appropriateness of program management, appropriateness of the program's staff professional development, and appropriateness of the language of instruction;

(3) program context indicators that describe the relationship of the activities funded under the grant to the overall school program and other Federal, State, or local programs serving children and youth of limited-English proficiency; and

(4) such other information as the Secretary may require.

7434. Construction. SUBPART 2—RESEARCH, EVALUATION, AND DISSEMINATION

Sec. 7451. Authority

(a) In general. The Secretary is authorized to conduct data collection, dissemination, research, and ongoing program evaluation activities in accordance with the provisions of this subpart for the purpose of improving bilingual education and special alternative instruction programs for children and youth of limited-English proficiency.

(b) Competitive awards. Research and program evaluation activities carried out under this subpart shall be supported through competitive grants, contracts and cooperative agreements awarded institutions of higher education, nonprofit organizations, and State and local educational agencies.

(c) Administration. The Secretary shall conduct data collection, dissemination, and ongoing program evaluation activities authorized by this subpart through the Office of Bilingual Education and Minority Language Affairs.

Sec. 7452. Research

(a) Administration. The Secretary shall conduct research activities authorized by this subpart through the Office of Educational Research and Improvement in coordination and collaboration with the Office of Bilingual Education and Minority Language Affairs.

(b) Requirements. Such research activities—

(1) shall have a practical application to teachers, counselors, paraprofessionals, school administrators, parents, and others involved in improving the education of limited English proficient students and their families;

(2) may include research on effective instructional practices for multilingual classes, and on effective instruction strategies to be used by teachers and other staff who do not know the native language of a limited English proficient child or youth in their classrooms;

(3) may include establishing (through the National Center for Education Statistics in consultation with experts in bilingual education, second language acquisition, and English-as-a-second-language) a common definition of "limited English proficient student" for purposes of national data collection; and

(4) shall be administered by individuals with expertise in bilingual education and the needs of limited English proficient students and their families.

(c) Field-initiated research.

(1) In general. The Secretary shall reserve not less than 5 percent of the funds made available to carry out this section for field-initiated research conducted by current or recent recipients of grants under this subpart or subpart 1 of this part who have received such grants within the previous five years. Such research may provide for longitudinal studies of students or teachers in bilingual education, monitoring the education of such students from entry in bilingual education through secondary school completion.

(2) Applications. Applicants for assistance under this subsection may submit an application for such assistance to the Secretary at the same time as applications are submitted under this subpart or subpart 1 of this part. The Secretary shall complete a review of such applications on a timely basis to allow research and program grants to be coordinated when recipients are awarded two or more such grants.

(d) Consultation. The Secretary shall consult with agencies and organizations that are engaged in bilingual education research and practice, or related research, and bilingual education researchers and practitioners to identify areas of study and activities to be funded under this section.

(e) Data collection. The Secretary shall provide for the continuation of data collection on limited English proficient students as part of the data systems operated by the Department.

Sec. 7453. Academic excellence awards

(a) Awards. The Secretary may make grants to, and enter into contracts and cooperative agreements with, State and local educational agencies, nonprofit organizations, and institutions of higher education to promote the adoption and implementation of bilingual education, special alternative instruction programs, and professional development programs that demonstrate promise of assisting children and youth of limited-English proficiency to meet challenging State standards.

(b) Applications.

(1) In general. Each entity desiring an award under this section shall submit an application to the Secretary in such form, at such time, and containing such information and assurances as the Secretary may reasonably require.

(2) Peer review. The Secretary shall use a peer review process, using effectiveness criteria that the Secretary shall establish, to review applications under this section.

(c) Use of funds. Funds under this section shall be used to enhance the capacity of States and local education agencies to provide high quality academic programs for children and youth of limited-English proficiency, which may include—

(1) completing the development of such programs;

(2) professional development of staff participating in bilingual education programs;

(3) sharing strategies and materials; and

(4) supporting professional networks.

(d) Coordination. Recipients of funds under this section shall coordinate the activities assisted under this section with activities carried out by comprehensive regional assistance centers assisted under part A of subchapter XIII of this chapter.

Sec. 7454. State grant program

(a) State grant program. The Secretary is authorized to make an award to a State educational agency that demonstrates, to the satisfaction of the Secretary, that such agency, through such agency's own programs and other Federal education programs, effectively provides for the education of children and youth of limited-English proficiency within the State.

(b) Payments. The amount paid to a State educational agency under subsection (a) of this section shall not exceed 5 percent of the total amount awarded to local educational agencies within the State under subpart 1 of this part for the previous fiscal year, except that in no case shall the amount paid by the Secretary to any State educational agency under this subsection for any fiscal year be less than $100,000.

(c) Use of funds.

(1) In general. A State educational agency shall use funds awarded under this section for programs authorized by this section to—

(A) assist local educational agencies in the State with program design, capacity building, assessment of student performance, and program evaluation; and

(B) collect data on the State's limited English proficient populations and the educational programs and services available to such populations.

(2) Exception. States which do not, as of October 20, 1994, have in place a system for collecting the data described in subparagraph (B) of paragraph (1) for all students in such State, are not required to meet the requirement of such subparagraph. In the event such State develops a system for collecting data on the educational programs and services available to all students in the State, then such State shall comply with the requirement of paragraph (1)(B).

(3) Training. The State educational agency may also use funds provided under this section for the training of State educational agency personnel in educational issues affecting limited English proficient children and youth.

(4) Special rule. Recipients of funds under this section shall not restrict the provision of services under this section to federally funded programs.

(d) State consultation. A State educational agency receiving funds under this section shall consult with recipients of grants under this subchapter and other individuals or organizations involved in the development or operation of programs serving limited English proficient children or youth to ensure that such funds are used in a manner consistent with the requirements of this subchapter.

(e) Applications. A State educational agency desiring to receive funds under this section shall submit an application to the Secretary in such form, at such time, and containing such information and assurances as the Secretary may require.

(f) Supplement not supplant. Funds made available under this section for any fiscal year shall be used by the State educational agency to supplement and, to the extent practical, to increase to the level of funds that would, in the absence of such funds, be made available by the State for the purposes described in this section, and in no case to supplant such funds.

(g) Report to Secretary. State educational agencies receiving awards under this section shall provide for the annual submission of a summary report to the Secretary describing such State's use of such funds.

Sec. 7455. National Clearinghouse for Bilingual Education

(a) Establishment. The Secretary shall establish and support the operation of a National Clearinghouse for Bilingual Education, which shall collect, analyze, synthesize, and disseminate information about bilingual education and related programs.

(b) Functions. The National Clearinghouse for Bilingual Education shall—

(1) be administered as an adjunct clearinghouse of the Educational Resources Information Center Clearinghouses system of clearinghouses supported by the Office of Educational Research and Improvement;

(2) coordinate its activities with Federal data and information clearinghouses and dissemination networks and systems;

(3) develop a data base management and monitoring system for improving the operation and effectiveness of federally funded bilingual education programs; and

(4) develop, maintain, and disseminate, through comprehensive regional assistance centers described in part A of subchapter XIII of this chapter if appropriate, a listing by geographical area of education professionals, parents, teachers, administrators, community members and others who are native speakers of languages other than English for use as a resource by local educational agencies and schools

in the development and implementation of bilingual education programs.

7456. Instructional materials development. SUBPART 3—PROFESSIONAL DEVELOPMENT

Sec. 7471. Purpose

The purpose of this subpart is to assist in preparing educators to improve the educational services for limited English proficient children and youth by supporting professional development programs and the dissemination of information on appropriate instructional practices for such children and youth.

Sec. 7472. Training for all teachers program

(a) Purpose. The purpose of this section is to provide for the incorporation of courses and curricula on appropriate and effective instructional and assessment methodologies, strategies and resources specific to limited English proficient students into preservice and inservice professional development programs for teachers, pupil services personnel, administrators and other education personnel in order to prepare such individuals to provide effective services to limited English proficient students.

(b) Authorization.

(1) Authority. The Secretary is authorized to award grants to institutions of higher education, local educational agencies, and State educational agencies or to nonprofit organizations which have entered into consortia arrangements with one of such institutions or agencies.

(2) Duration. Each grant under this section shall be awarded for a period of not more than five years.

(c) Permissible activities. Activities conducted under this section may include the development of training programs in collaboration with other programs such as programs authorized under subchapters I and II of this chapter, and under the Head Start Act (42 U.S.C. 9831 et seq.).

Sec. 7473. Bilingual education teachers and personnel grants

(a) Purpose. The purpose of this section is to provide for—

(1) preservice and inservice professional development for bilingual education teachers, administrators, pupil services personnel, and other educational personnel who are either involved in, or preparing to be involved in, the provision of educational services for children and youth of limited-English proficiency; and

(2) national professional development institutes that assist schools or departments of education in institutions of higher education to improve the quality of professional development programs for personnel serving, preparing to serve, or who may serve, children and youth of limited-English proficiency.

(b) Priority. The Secretary shall give priority in awarding grants under this section to institutions of higher education, in consortia with local or State educational agencies, that offer degree programs which prepare new bilingual education teachers in order to increase the availability of educators to provide high-quality education to limited English proficient students.

(c) Authorization.

(1) The Secretary is authorized to award grants for not more than five years to institutions of higher education which have entered into consortia arrangements with local or State educational agencies to achieve the purposes of this section.

(2) The Secretary is authorized to make grants for not more than five years to State and local educational agencies for inservice professional development programs.

Sec. 7474. Bilingual education career ladder program

(a) Purpose. The purpose of this section is—

(1) to upgrade the qualifications and skills of noncertified educational personnel, especially educational paraprofessionals, to meet high professional standards, including

certification and licensure as bilingual education teachers and other educational personnel who serve limited English proficient students, through collaborative training programs operated by institutions of higher education and local and State educational agencies; and

(2) to help recruit and train secondary school students as bilingual education teachers and other educational personnel to serve limited English proficient students.

(b) Authorization.

(1) In general. The Secretary is authorized to award grants for bilingual education career ladder programs to institutions of higher education applying in consortia with local or State educational agencies, which consortia may include community-based organizations or professional education organizations.

(2) Duration. Each grant under this section shall be awarded for a period of not more than five years.

(c) Permissive activities. Grants awarded under this section may be used—

(1) for the development of bilingual education career ladder program curricula appropriate to the needs of the consortium participants;

(2) to provide assistance for stipends and costs related to tuition, fees and books for enrolling in courses required to complete the degree and certification requirements to become bilingual education teachers; and

(3) for programs to introduce secondary school students to careers in bilingual education teaching that are coordinated with other activities assisted under this section.

(d) Special consideration. The Secretary shall give special consideration to applications under this section which provide for—

(1) participant completion of baccalaureate and master's degree teacher education programs, and certification

requirements and may include effective employment placement activities;

(2) development of teacher proficiency in English a second language, including demonstrating proficiency in the instructional use of English and, as appropriate, a second language in classroom contexts;

(3) coordination with the Federal TRIO programs under chapter 1 of part A of title IV of the Higher Education Act of 1965 (20 U.S.C. 1070a et seq.), the National Mini Corps under subpart 1 of part F of title V of such Act, the Teacher Corps program under subpart 3 of part C of title V of such Act, and the National Community and Service Trust Act of 1993 programs, and other programs for the recruitment and retention of bilingual students in secondary and post-secondary programs to train to become bilingual educators; and

(4) the applicant's contribution of additional student financial aid to participating students.

Sec. 7475. Graduate fellowships in bilingual education program

(a) Authorization.

(1) In general. The Secretary may award fellowships for masters, doctoral, and post-doctoral study related to instruction of children and youth of limited-English proficiency in such areas as teacher training, program administration, research and evaluation, and curriculum development, and for the support of dissertation research related to such study.

(2) Number. For fiscal year 1994 not less than 500 fellowships leading to a master's or doctorate degree shall be awarded under this section.

(3) Information. The Secretary shall include information on the operation and the number of fellowships awarded under the fellowship program in the evaluation required under section 7479 of this title.

(b) Fellowship requirements.

(1) In general. Any person receiving a fellowship under this section shall agree to—

(A) work in an activity related to the program or in an activity such as an activity authorized under this part, including work as a bilingual education teacher, for a period of time equivalent to the period of time during which such person receives assistance under this section; or

(B) repay such assistance.

(2) Regulations. The Secretary shall establish in regulations such terms and conditions for such agreement as the Secretary deems reasonable and necessary and may waive the requirement of paragraph (1) in extraordinary circumstances.

(c) Priority. In awarding fellowships under this section the Secretary may give priority to institutions of higher education that demonstrate experience in assisting fellowship recipients find employment in the field of bilingual education.

Sec. 7476. Application

(a) In general.

(1) Secretary. To receive an award under this subpart, an eligible entity shall submit an application to the Secretary at such time, in such form, and containing such information as the Secretary may require.

(2) Consultation and assessment. Each such application shall contain a description of how the applicant has consulted with, and assessed the needs of, public and private schools serving children and youth of limited-English proficiency to determine such school's need for, and the design of, the program for which funds are sought.

(3) Special rule.

(A) An application for a grant under subsection (a) of this section from an applicant who proposes to conduct a master's- or doctoral-level program with funds received under

this section shall provide an assurance that such program will include, as a part of the program, a training practicum in a local school program serving children and youth of limited-English proficiency.

(B) A recipient of a grant under subsection (a) of this section may waive the requirement of a training practicum for a degree candidate with significant experience in a local school program serving children and youth of limited-English proficiency.

(4) State educational agency. An eligible entity, with the exception of schools funded by the Bureau of Indian Affairs, shall submit a copy of the application under this subsection to the State educational agency.

(b) State review and comments.

(1) Deadline. The State educational agency, not later than 45 days after receipt of such application copy, shall review the application and transmit such application to the Secretary.

(2) Comments.

(A) Regarding any application submitted under this subpart, the State educational agency shall—

(i) submit to the Secretary written comments regarding all such applications; and

(ii) submit to each eligible entity the comments that pertain to such entity.

(B) For purposes of this subpart, comments shall address how the eligible entity—

(i) will further the academic achievement of limited English proficient students served pursuant to a grant received under this subpart; and

(ii) how the grant application is consistent with the State plan submitted under section 6311 of this title.

(3) Waiver. Notwithstanding paragraphs (1) and (2), the Secretary is authorized to waive the review requirement if a

State educational agency can demonstrate that such review requirement may impede such agency's ability to fulfill the requirements of participation in the State grant program, particularly such agency's data collection efforts and such agency's ability to provide technical assistance to local educational agencies not receiving funds under this chapter.

(c) Eligible entity comments. An eligible entity may submit to the Secretary comments that address the comments submitted by the State educational agency.

(d) Comment consideration. In making awards under this subpart the Secretary shall take into consideration comments made by a State educational agency.

(e) Special rule.

(1) Outreach and technical assistance. The Secretary shall provide for outreach and technical assistance to institutions of higher education eligible for assistance under title III of the Higher Education Act of 1965 (20 U.S.C. 1051 et seq.) and institutions of higher education that are operated or funded by the Bureau of Indian Affairs to facilitate the participation of such institutions in activities under this part.

(2) Distribution rule. In making awards under this subpart, the Secretary, consistent with subsection (d) of this section, shall ensure adequate representation of Hispanic-serving institutions that demonstrate competence and experience in the programs and activities authorized under this subpart and are otherwise qualified.

Sec. 7477. Program requirements

Activities conducted under this subpart shall assist educational personnel in meeting State and local certification requirements for bilingual education and, wherever possible, shall lead toward the awarding of college or university credit.

Sec. 7478. Stipends

The Secretary shall provide for the payment of such stipends (including allowances for subsistence and other expenses for such persons and their dependents), as the Secretary determines to be appropriate, to persons participating in training programs under this subpart.

Sec. 7479. Program evaluations

Each recipient of funds under this subpart shall provide the Secretary with an evaluation of the program assisted under this subpart every two years. Such evaluation shall include data on—

(1) post-program placement of persons trained in a program assisted under this subpart;

(2) how the training relates to the employment of persons served by the program;

(3) program completion; and

(4) such other information as the Secretary may require.

7480. Use of funds for second language competence. SUBPART 4—TRANSITION

Sec. 7491. Special rule

Notwithstanding any other provision of law, no recipient of a grant under title VII of this Act (as such title was in effect on the day preceding October 20, 1994) shall be eligible for fourth- and fifth-year renewals authorized by section 7021(d)(1)(C) of such title (as such section was in effect on the day preceding October 20, 1994).

Source: Bilingual Education Act. *U.S. Statutes at Large* 81 (1968): 816–820.

See also: Bilingual Education; English-Only Movement; Immigration. Document: Proposition 227 (1998)

Excerpt from the Kerner Commission Report (1968)

Introduction

The Kerner Commission was formed by President Lyndon B. Johnson in July 1967 to investigate the causes and implications of full-scale urban riots in black sections of major American cities in 1967. The report, issued in 1968, stated that pervasive racial discrimination and segregation in employment, education, and housing had excluded African Americans from the benefits of economic progress. It concluded that racial segregation and racial inequality were the major causes of race riots. It recommended sweeping changes to moderate racial inequality so that further race riots could be prevented.

Primary Source

The Reservoir of Grievances in the Negro Community

Our examination of the background of the surveyed disorders revealed a typical pattern of deeply held grievances which were widely shared by many members of the Negro community. The specific content of the expressed grievances varied somewhat from city to city. But in general, grievances among Negroes in all the cities related to prejudice, discrimination, severely disadvantaged living condition, and a general sense of frustration about their inability to change those conditions. Specific events or incidents exemplified and reinforced the shared sense of grievance. News of such incidents spread quickly throughout the community and added to the reservoir. Grievances about police practices, unemployment and underemployment, housing, and other objective conditions in the ghetto were aggravated in the minds of many Negroes by the inaction of municipal authorities.

Out of this reservoir of grievance and frustration, the riot process began in the cities which we surveyed.

Precipitating Incidents

In virtually every case a single triggering or precipitating incident can be identified as having immediately preceded within a few hours and in generally the same location—the outbreak of disorder. But this incident was usually a relatively minor, even trivial one, by itself substantially disproportionate to the scale of violence that followed. Often it was an incident of a type which had occurred frequently in the same community in the past without provoking violence.

We found that violence was generated by an increasingly disturbed social atmosphere, in which typically not one,

but a series of incidents occurred over a period of weeks or months prior to the outbreak of disorder. Most cities had three or more such incidents. Houston had 10 over a 5-month period. These earlier or prior were linked in the minds of many Negroes to the preexisting reservoir of underlying grievances. With each such incident, frustration and tension grew until at some point a final incident, often similar to the incidents preceding it, occurred and was followed almost immediately by violence.

As we see it, the prior incidents and the reservoir of underlying grievances contributed to a cumulative process of mounting tension that spilled over into violence when the final incident occurred.

This chain describes the central trend in the disorders we surveyed and not necessarily all aspects of the riots or of all rioters. For example, incidents have not always increased tension; and tension has not always resulted in violence. We conclude only that the processes did occur in the disorders we examined.

Similarly, we do not suggest that all rioters shared the conditions or grievances of their Negro neighbors: some may deliberately have exploited the chaos created out of the frustration of others; some may have been drawn into the melee merely because they identified with, or wished to emulate, others. Some who shared the adverse conditions and grievances did not riot.

We found that the majority of the rioters did share the adverse conditions and grievances, although they did not necessarily articulate in their own minds the connection between that background and their actions.

The Profile of a Rioter

The typical rioter in the summer of 1967 was a Negro, unmarried male between the ages of 15 and 24. He was in many ways very different from the stereotype. He was not a migrant. He was born in the state and was a lifelong resident of the city in which the riot took place. Economically his position was about the same as his Negro neighbors who did not actively participate in the riot. Although he had not, usually, graduated from high school, he was somewhat better educated than the average inner-city Negro, having at least attended high school for a time.

Nevertheless he was more likely to be working in a menial or low status job as an unskilled laborer. If he was employed, he was not working full time and his employment was frequently interrupted by periods of unemployment.

He feels strongly that he deserves a better job and that he is barred from achieving it, not because of lack of training, ability, or ambition, but because of discrimination by employers.

He rejects the white bigot stereotype of the Negro as ignorant and shiftless. He takes great pride in his race and believes that in some respects Negroes are superior to whites. He is extremely hostile to whites, but his hostility is more apt to be a product of social and economic class than of race; he is almost equally hostile toward middle class Negroes.

He is substantially better informed about politics than Negroes who were not involved in the riots. He is more likely to be actively engaged in civil rights efforts, but is extremely distrustful of the political system and of political leaders.

The Profile of the Counterrioter

The typical counterrioter, who risked injury and arrest to walk the streets urging rioters to cool it, was an active supporter of existing social institutions. He was, for example, far more likely than either the rioter or the noninvolved to feel that his country is worth defending in a major war. His actions and his attitudes reflected his substantially greater stake in the social system; he was considerably better educated and more affluent than either the rioter or the noninvolved. He was somewhat more likely than the rioter, but less likely than the noninvolved, to have been a migrant. In all other respects he was identical to the noninvolved.

The Pattern of Disadvantage

Social and economic conditions in the riot cities constituted a clear pattern of severe disadvantage for Negroes as compared with whites, whether the Negroes lived in the disturbance area or outside of it. When ghetto conditions are compared with those for whites in the suburbs, the relative disadvantage for Negroes is even greater.

In all the cities surveyed, the Negro population increased between 1950 and 1960 at a median rate of 75 percent.

Meanwhile the white population decreased in more than half the cities including six which experienced the most severe disturbances in 1967. The increase in nonwhite population in four of these cities was so great that their total population increased despite the decrease in white population. These changes were attributable in large part to heavy in-migration of Negroes from rural poverty areas and movement of whites from the central cities to the suburbs.

Source: Kerner Commission Report. Washington, DC: Government Printing Office, 1968, 73–77.

See also: Asbury Park (New Jersey) Riot of 1970; Atlanta (Georgia) Riot of 1906; Atlanta (Georgia) Riot of 1967; Bellingham Riots (1907); Bensonhurst (New York) Incident (1989); Biloxi Beach (Mississippi) Riot of 1960; Black Church Arsons; Bloody Sunday; Boston (Massachusetts) Riots of 1975 and 1976; Brownsville (Texas) Incident of 1906; Charleston (South Carolina) Riot of 1919; Chattanooga (Tennessee) Riot of 1906; Chester and Philadelphia (Pennsylvania) Riots of 1918; Chicago Commission on Race Relations; Chicago (Illinois) Riot of 1919; Cincinnati (Ohio) Riots of 1967 and 1968; Cincinnati (Ohio) Riots of 2001; Cleveland (Ohio) Riot of 1966; Detroit (Michigan) Riot of 1943; Detroit (Michigan) Riot of 1967; East St. Louis (Illinois) Riot of 1917; Election Riots of the 1880s and 1890s; Greensburg (Indiana) Riot of 1906; Greenwood Community (Tulsa, Oklahoma); Harlem (New York) Riot of 1935; Houston (Texas) Mutiny of 1917; Howard Beach (New York) Incident (1986); Johnson-Jeffries Fight of 1910, Riots Following; Knoxville (Tennessee) Riot of 1919; Long Hot Summer Riots (1965–1967); Longview (Texas) Riot of 1919; Los Angeles (California) Riot of 1965; Los Angeles (California) Riots of 1992; Miami (Florida) Riot of 1982; New Bedford (Massachusetts) Riot of 1970; New Orleans (Louisiana) Riot of 1866; New York City Draft Riot of 1863; New York City Riot of 1943; Newark (New Jersey) Riot of 1967; Orangeburg (South Carolina) Massacre of 1968; Philadelphia (Pennsylvania) Riot of 1964; Prison Riots; Race Riots in America; Red Scare and Race Riots; Red Summer Race Riots of 1919; Rosewood (Florida) Riot of 1923; Saint Genevieve (Missouri) Riot of 1930; San Francisco

(California) Riot of 1966; Springfield (Ohio) Riot of 1904; Tampa (Florida) Riots of 1987; Texas Southern University Riot of 1967; Tulsa (Oklahoma) Riot of 1921; Washington (D.C.) Riot of 1919; Washington (D.C.) Riots of 1968; Wilmington (North Carolina) Riot of 1898; Zoot Suit Riots

Furman v. Georgia (1972)

Introduction

In Furman v. Georgia, *the Supreme Court ruled in a five-to-four per curiam opinion that the death penalty, as then administered, was in violation of the Eighth Amendment's guarantee against cruel and unusual punishment. Juries had convicted Furman for murder and two other individuals for rape—all three were African American—and then imposed the death penalty. The Court's decision halted not only those executions but also all scheduled executions in states that sanctioned capital punishment at the time.*

Primary Source

PER CURIAM

Petitioner in No. 69–5003 was convicted of murder in Georgia and was sentenced to death pursuant to Ga. Code Ann. 26-1005 (Supp. 1971) (effective prior to July 1, 1969). Petitioner in No. 69-5030 was convicted of rape in Georgia and was sentenced to death pursuant to Ga. Code Ann. 26-1302 (Supp. 1971) (effective prior to July 1, 1969). Petitioner in No. 69-5031 was convicted of rape in Texas and was sentenced to death pursuant to Tex. Penal Code, Art. 1189 (1961). Certiorari was granted limited to the following question: "Does the imposition and carrying out of the death penalty in [these cases] constitute cruel and unusual punishment in violation of the Eighth and Fourteenth Amendments?" The Court holds that the imposition and carrying out of the death penalty in these cases constitute cruel and unusual punishment in violation of the Eighth and Fourteenth Amendments. The judgment in each case is therefore reversed insofar as it leaves undisturbed the death sentence imposed, and the cases are remanded for further proceedings.

So ordered.

MR. JUSTICE DOUGLAS, concurring.

In these three cases the death penalty was imposed, one of them for murder, and two for rape. In each, the determination of whether the penalty should be death or a lighter punishment was left by the State to the discretion of the judge or of the jury. In each of the three cases, the trial was to a jury. They are here on petitions for certiorari which we granted limited to the question whether the imposition and execution of the death penalty constitute "cruel and unusual punishment" within the meaning of the Eighth Amendment as applied to the States by the Fourteenth. I vote to vacate each judgment, believing that the exaction of the death penalty does violate the Eighth and Fourteenth Amendments.

That the requirements of due process ban cruel and unusual punishment is now settled. It is also settled that the proscription of cruel and unusual punishments forbids the judicial imposition of them as well as their imposition by the legislature.

Congressman Bingham, in proposing the Fourteenth Amendment, maintained that "the privileges or immunities of citizens of the United States," as protected by the Fourteenth Amendment, included protection against "cruel and unusual punishments":

[M]any instances of State injustice and oppression have already occurred in the State legislation of this Union, of flagrant violations of the guaranteed privileges of citizens of the United States, for which the national Government furnished and could furnish by law no remedy whatever. Contrary to the express letter of your Constitution, "cruel and unusual punishments" have been inflicted under State laws within this Union upon citizens not only for crimes committed, but for sacred duty done, for which and against which the Government of the United States had provided no remedy, and could provide none.

Whether the privileges and immunities route is followed or the due process route, the result is the same.

It has been assumed in our decisions that punishment by death is not cruel, unless the manner of execution can be said to be inhuman and barbarous. It is also said in our opinions that the proscription of cruel and unusual punishments "is not fastened to the obsolete, but may acquire meaning as public opinion becomes enlightened by a humane justice." A like statement was made in *Trop v. Dulles*, that the Eighth Amendment "must draw its meaning from the evolving standards of decency that mark the progress of a maturing society."

The generality of a law inflicting capital punishment is one thing. What may be said of the validity of a law on the books and what may be done with the law in its application do, or may, lead to quite different conclusions.

It would seem to be incontestable that the death penalty inflicted on one defendant is "unusual" if it discriminates against him by reason of his race, religion, wealth, social position, or class, or if it is imposed under a procedure that gives room for the play of such prejudices.

There is evidence that the provision of the English Bill of Rights of 1689, from which the language of the Eighth Amendment was taken, was concerned primarily with selective or irregular application of harsh penalties, and that its aim was to forbid arbitrary and discriminatory penalties of a severe nature:

The words "cruel and unusual" certainly include penalties that are barbaric. But the words, at least when read in light of the English proscription against selective and irregular use of penalties, suggest that it is "cruel and unusual" to apply the death penalty—or any other penalty—selectively to minorities whose numbers are few, who are outcasts of society, and who are unpopular, but whom society is willing to see suffer though it would not countenance general application of the same penalty across the board.

What the legislature may not do for all classes uniformly and systematically a judge or jury may not do for a class that prejudice sets apart from the community.

There is increasing recognition of the fact that the basic theme of equal protection is implicit in "cruel and unusual" punishments. "A penalty . . . should be considered

'unusually' imposed if it is administered arbitrarily or discriminatorily." The same authors add that "[t]he extreme rarity with which applicable death penalty provisions are put to use raises a strong inference of arbitrariness." The President's Commission on Law Enforcement and Administration of Justice recently concluded: "Finally, there is evidence that the imposition of the death sentence and the exercise of dispensing power by the courts and the executive follow discriminatory patterns. The death sentence is disproportionately imposed, and carried out on the poor, the Negro, and the members of unpopular groups."

A study of capital cases in Texas from 1924 to 1968 reached the following conclusions: "Application of the death penalty is unequal: most of those executed were poor, young, and ignorant."

Seventy-five of the 460 cases involved codefendants, who, under Texas law, were given separate trials. In several instances where a white and a Negro were co-defendants, the white was sentenced to life imprisonment or a term of years, and the Negro was given the death penalty.

Another ethnic disparity is found in the type of sentence imposed for rape. The Negro convicted of rape is far more likely to get the death penalty than a term sentence, whereas whites and Latins are far more likely to get a term sentence than the death penalty.

Warden Lewis E. Lawes of Sing Sing said:

Not only does capital punishment fail in its justification, but no punishment could be invented with so many inherent defects. It is an unequal punishment in the way it is applied to the rich and to the poor. The defendant of wealth and position never goes to the electric chair or to the gallows. Juries do not intentionally favour the rich, the law is theoretically impartial, but the defendant with ample means is able to have his case presented with every favourable aspect, while the poor defendant often has a lawyer assigned by the court. Sometimes such assignment is considered part of political patronage; usually the lawyer assigned has had no experience whatever in a capital case.

Former Attorney General Ramsey Clark has said, "It is the poor, the sick, the ignorant, the powerless and the hated who are executed." One searches our chronicles in vain for the execution of any member of the affluent strata of this society. The Leopolds and Loebs are given prison terms, not sentenced to death.

Jackson, a black, convicted of the rape of a white woman, was 21 years old. A court-appointed psychiatrist said that Jackson was of average education and average intelligence, that he was not an imbecile, or schizophrenic, or psychotic, that his traits were the product of environmental influences, and that he was competent to stand trial. Jackson had entered the house after the husband left for work. He held scissors against the neck of the wife, demanding money. She could find none, and a struggle ensued for the scissors, a battle which she lost, and she was then raped, Jackson keeping the scissors pressed against her neck. While there did not appear to be any long-term traumatic impact on the victim, she was bruised and abrased in the struggle, but was not hospitalized. Jackson was a convict who had escaped from a work gang in the area, a result of a three-year sentence for auto theft. He was at large for three days and during that time had committed several other offenses—burglary, auto theft, and assault and battery.

Furman, a black, killed a householder while seeking to enter the home at night. Furman shot the deceased through a closed door. He was 26 years old and had finished the sixth grade in school. Pending trial, he was committed to the Georgia Central State Hospital for a psychiatric examination on his plea of insanity tendered by court-appointed counsel. The superintendent reported that a unanimous staff diagnostic conference had concluded "that this patient should retain his present diagnosis of Mental Deficiency, Mild to Moderate, with Psychotic Episodes associated with Convulsive Disorder." The physicians agreed that "at present the patient is not psychotic, but he is not capable of cooperating with his counsel in the preparation of his defense"; and the staff believed "that he is in need of further psychiatric hospitalization and treatment."

Later, the superintendent reported that the staff diagnosis was Mental Deficiency, Mild to Moderate, with Psychotic Episodes associated with Convulsive Disorder. He concluded, however, that Furman was "not psychotic at present, knows right from wrong and is able to cooperate with his counsel in preparing his defense."

Branch, a black, entered the rural home of a 65-year-old widow, a white, while she slept and raped her, holding his arm against her throat. Thereupon he demanded money, and for 30 minutes or more, the widow searched for money, finding little. As he left, Jackson said if the widow told anyone what happened, he would return and kill her. The record is barren of any medical or psychiatric evidence showing injury to her as a result of Branch's attack.

He had previously been convicted of felony theft and found to be a borderline mental deficient and well below the average IQ of Texas prison inmates. He had the equivalent of five and a half years of grade school education. He had a "dull intelligence," and was in the lowest fourth percentile of his class.

We cannot say from facts disclosed in these records that these defendants were sentenced to death because they were black. Yet our task is not restricted to an effort to divine what motives impelled these death penalties. Rather, we deal with a system of law and of justice that leaves to the uncontrolled discretion of judges or juries the determination whether defendants committing these crimes should die or be imprisoned. Under these laws, no standards govern the selection of the penalty. People live or die, dependent on the whim of one man or of 12.

Those who wrote the Eighth Amendment knew what price their forebears had paid for a system based not on equal justice, but on discrimination. In those days, the target was not the blacks or the poor, but the dissenters, those who opposed absolutism in government, who struggled for a parliamentary regime, and who opposed governments' recurring efforts to foist a particular religion on the people. But the tool of capital punishment was used with vengeance against the opposition and those unpopular with the regime. One cannot read this history without realizing that the desire for equality was reflected in the ban against "cruel and unusual punishments" contained in the Eighth Amendment.

In a Nation committed to equal protection of the laws there is no permissible "caste" aspect of law enforcement. Yet we know that the discretion of judges and juries in imposing the death penalty enables the penalty to be selectively applied, feeding prejudices against the accused if he is poor and despised, and lacking political clout, or if he is a member of a suspect or unpopular minority, and saving those who by social position may be in a more protected position. In ancient Hindu law a Brahman was exempt from capital punishment, and, under that law, "[g]enerally, in the law books, punishment increased in severity as social status diminished." We have, I fear, taken in practice the same position, partially as a result of making the death penalty discretionary and partially as a result of the ability of the rich to purchase the services of the most respected and most resourceful legal talent in the Nation.

The high service rendered by the "cruel and unusual" punishment clause of the Eighth Amendment is to require legislatures to write penal laws that are evenhanded, nonselective, and nonarbitrary, and to require judges to see to it that general laws are not applied sparsely, selectively, and spottily to unpopular groups.

A law that stated that anyone making more than $50,000 would be exempt from the death penalty would plainly fall, as would a law that in terms said that blacks, those who never went beyond the fifth grade in school, those who made less than $3,000 a year, or those who were unpopular or unstable should be the only people executed. A law which, in the overall view, reaches that result in practice has no more sanctity than a law which in terms provides the same.

Thus, these discretionary statutes are unconstitutional in their operation. They are pregnant with discrimination, and discrimination is an ingredient not compatible with the idea of equal protection of the laws that is implicit in the ban on "cruel and unusual" punishments.

Any law which is nondiscriminatory on its face may be applied in such a way as to violate the Equal Protection Clause of the Fourteenth Amendment. Such conceivably might be the fate of a mandatory death penalty, where equal or lesser sentences were imposed on the elite, a harsher one on the minorities or members of the lower castes. Whether a mandatory death penalty would otherwise be constitutional is a question I do not reach.

I concur in the judgments of the Court.

Source: *Furman v. Georgia*, 408 U.S. 238 (1972).

See also: *Batson v. Kentucky* (1986); Crime and Race; *McCleskey v. Kemp* (1987); Racial Disparities in Capital Punishment; Sentencing Disparities

Boldt Decision (1974)

Introduction

Officially titled United States v. State of Washington, *the Boldt Decision established a system by which Native Americans were allowed up to 50 percent of the salmon and other fish returning to the waters of fishing sites guaranteed them by treaties signed during the 1850s.*

Primary Source

UNITED STATES of America, Plaintiff, Quinault Tribe of Indians on its own behalf and on behalf of the Queets Band of Indians, et al., Intervenor-Plaintiffs, v. STATE OF WASHINGTON, Defendant, Thor C. Tollefson, Director, Washington State Department of Fisheries, et al., Intervenor-Defendants

Civ. No. 9213

UNITED STATES DISTRICT COURT FOR THE WESTERN DISTRICT OF WASHINGTON, TACOMA DIVISION

384 F. Supp. 312; 1974 U.S. Dist. LEXIS 12291 February 12, 1974 . . .

STATEMENT OF THE CASE

GEORGE H. BOLDT, Senior District Judge.

In September, 1970 the United States, on its own behalf and as trustee for several Western Washington Indian Tribes, later joined as intervenor plaintiffs by additional tribes, filed the complaint initiating this action against the State of Washington. Shortly later the State Department of Fisheries (Fisheries) and the State Game Commission (Game), their respective directors, and the Washington Reef Net Owners Association (Reef Net Owners) were included as defendants. By state statute Fisheries is charged with exercising regulatory authority over fishing for all anadromous food fish. Regulation of anadromous steelhead trout is vested in Game. Plaintiffs seek a declaratory judgment pursuant to 28 U.S.C. §§ 2201 and 2202 concerning off reservation treaty right fishing within the case area by plaintiff tribes, which long has been and now is in controversy, and for injunctive relief to provide enforcement of those fishing rights as they previously have been or herein may be judicially determined. The case area is that portion of the State of Washington west of the Cascade Mountains and north of the Columbia River drainage area, and includes the American portion of the Puget Sound watershed, the watersheds of the Olympic Peninsula north of the Grays Harbor watershed, and the offshore waters adjacent to those areas. . . .

More than a century of frequent and often violent controversy between Indians and non-Indians over treaty right fishing has resulted in deep distrust and animosity on both sides. This has been inflamed by provocative, sometimes illegal, conduct of extremists on both sides and by irresponsible demonstrations instigated by non-resident opportunists. . . .

The ultimate objective of this decision is to determine every issue of fact and law presented and, at long last, thereby finally settle, either in this decision or on appeal thereof, as many as possible of the divisive problems of treaty right fishing which for so long have plagued all of the citizens of this area, and still do.

I. ESTABLISHED BASIC FACTS AND LAW . . .

The "Constitution . . . of the United States . . . and all Treaties made, or which shall be made, under the Authority of the United States, shall be the supreme Law of the Land; and the Judges in every State shall be bound thereby, any Thing in the Constitution or Laws of any State to the Contrary notwithstanding." . . .

3. The United States Supreme Court in Missouri (252 U.S. p. 434, 40 S. Ct. p. 384) stated:

"Valid treaties of course 'are as binding within the territorial limits of the States as they are elsewhere throughout the dominion of the United States.' *Baldwin v. Franks,* 120 U.S. 678, 683, 7 S. Ct. 656, 30 L. Ed. 766."

4. Each of the basic fact and law issues in this case must be considered and decided in accordance with the treaty language reserving fishing rights to the plaintiff tribes, interpreted in the spirit and manner directed in the above quoted language of the United States Supreme Court. Each treaty in this case contains a provision substantially identical to that in the Medicine Creek treaty: "The right of taking fish, at all usual and accustomed grounds and stations, is further secured to said Indians, in common with all citizens of the territory, and of erecting temporary houses for the purpose of curing, . . ."

5. "The right to resort to the [usual and accustomed] fishing places in controversy was a part of larger rights possessed by the Indians, upon the exercise of which there was not a shadow of impediment, and which were not much less necessary to the existence of the Indians than the atmosphere they breathed. . . . [The] treaty was not a grant of rights to the Indians but a grant of right from them—a reservation of those not granted."

"And surely it was within the competency of the Nation to secure to the Indians such a remnant of the great rights they possessed as 'taking fish at all usual and accustomed places.'" . . .

6. ". . . [The] [treaty] negotiations were with the tribe. They reserved rights, however, to every individual Indian, as though named therein. . . . And the right was intended to be continuing against the United States and its grantees as well as against the State and its grantees." That those rights are also reserved to the descendants of treaty Indians, without limitation in time, excepting as Congress may determine,

has been recognized and applied by the United States Supreme Court from the first to the latest decision of that court involving Indian treaty fishing rights. . . .

7. An exclusive right of fishing was reserved by the tribes within the area and boundary waters of their reservations, wherein tribal members might make their homes if they chose to do so. The tribes also reserved the right to off reservation fishing "at all usual and accustomed grounds and stations" and agreed that "all citizens of the territory" might fish at the same places "in common with" tribal members. The tribes and their members cannot rescind that agreement or limit non-Indian fishing pursuant to the agreement. However, off reservation fishing by other citizens and residents of the state is not a right but merely a privilege which may be granted, limited or withdrawn by the state as the interests of the state or the exercise of treaty fishing rights may require. . . .

III. STATE REGULATION OF OFF RESERVATION TREATY RIGHT FISHING

There is neither mention nor slightest intimation in the treaties themselves, in any of the treaty negotiation records or in any other credible evidence, that the Indians who represented the tribes in the making of the treaties, at that time or any time afterward, understood or intended that the fishing rights reserved by the tribes as recorded in the above quoted language would, or ever could, authorize the "citizens of the territory" or their successors, either individually or through their territorial or state government, to qualify, restrict or in any way interfere with the full exercise of those rights. All of the evidence is overwhelmingly to the contrary, particularly in the vivid showing in the record that the treaty Indians pleaded for and insisted upon retaining the exercise of those rights as essential to their survival. They were given unqualified assurance of that by Governor Stevens himself without any suggestion that the Indians' exercise of those rights might some day, without authorization of Congress, be subjected to regulation by non-Indian citizens through their territorial or state government. . . .

These measures and others make plain the intent and philosophy of Congress to increase rather than diminish or limit the exercise of tribal self-government.

The right to fish for all species available in the waters from which, for so many ages, their ancestors derived most of their subsistence is the single most highly cherished interest and concern of the present members of plaintiff tribes, with rare exceptions even among tribal members who personally do not fish or derive therefrom any substantial amount of their subsistence. The right to fish, as reserved in the treaties of plaintiff tribes, certainly is the treaty provision most frequently in controversy and litigation involving all of the tribes and numerous of their individual members for many years past.

The philosophy of Congress referred to above and the evidence in this case as a whole clearly indicate to this court that the time has now arrived, and this case presents an appropriate opportunity, to take a step toward applying congressional philosophy to Indian treaty right fishing in a way that will not be inconsistent with Puyallup-I and Puyallup-II and also will provide ample security for the interest and purposes of conservation. . . .

CONCLUSIONS OF LAW . . .

17. Admission of the State of Washington into the Union upon an equal footing with the original states had no effect upon the treaty rights of the Plaintiff tribes. Such admission imposed upon the State, equally with other states, the obligation to observe and carry out the provisions of treaties of the United States. . . .

DECLARATORY JUDGMENT AND DECREE . . .

B. Treaty Fishing Rights

- 10. Each of the plaintiff tribes listed below is a Treaty Tribe. The list given below is a declaration only as to those 14 Indian entities which have been represented on the plaintiff side in this case. A Treaty Tribe occupies the status of a party to one or more of the Stevens treaties and therefore holds for the benefit of its members a reserved right to harvest anadromous fish at all usual and accustomed places outside reservation boundaries, in common with others:

Hoh Tribe of Indians;

Lummi Indian Tribe;

Makah Indian Tribe;

Muckleshoot Indian Tribe;

Nisqually Indian Community of the Nisqually
Reservation;

Puyallup Tribe of the Puyallup Reservation;

Quileute Indian Tribe;

Quinault Tribe of Indians;

Sauk-Suiattle Indian Tribe;

Skokomish Indian Tribe;

Squaxin Island Tribe of Indians;

Stillaguamish Tribe of Indians;

Upper Skagit River Tribe;

Confederated Tribes and Bands of the Yakima Indian
   Nation

- 11. The right of a Treaty Tribe to harvest anadromous fish outside reservation boundaries arises from a provision which appears in each of the Stevens treaties and which, with immaterial variations, states: The right of taking fish, at all usual and accustomed grounds and stations, is further secured to said Indians, in common with all citizens of the Territory. . . .

- 12. It is the responsibility of all citizens to see that the terms of the Stevens treaties are carried out, so far as possible, in accordance with the meaning they were understood to have by the tribal representatives at the councils, and in a spirit which generously recognizes the full obligation of this nation to protect the interests of a dependent people. . . .

- 15. The treaty-secured rights to resort to the usual and accustomed places to fish were a part of larger rights possessed by the treating Indians, upon the exercise of which there was not a shadow of impediment, and which were not much less necessary to their existence than the atmosphere they breathed. The treaty was not a grant of rights to the treating Indians, but a grant of rights from them, and a reservation of those not granted. In the Stevens treaties, such reservations were not of particular parcels of land, and could not be expressed in deeds, as dealings between private individuals. The reservations were in large areas of territory, and

the negotiations were with the tribes. The treaties reserved rights, however, to every individual Indian, as though described therein. There was an exclusive right of fishing reserved within certain boundaries. There was a right outside of those boundaries reserved for exercise "in common with citizens of the Territory."

- 16. The Stevens treaties do not reserve to the Treaty Tribes any specific manner, method or purpose of taking fish; nor do the treaties prohibit any specific manner, method or purpose. Just as non-Indians may continue to take advantage of improvements in fishing techniques, the Treaty Tribes may, in exercising their rights to take anadromous fish, utilize improvements in traditional fishing methods, such for example as nylon nets and steel hooks.

- 17. The exercise of a Treaty Tribe's right to take anadromous fish outside of reservation boundaries is limited only by geographical extent of the usual and accustomed places, the limits of the harvestable stock and the number of fish which non-treaty fishermen shall have an opportunity to catch, as provided in the Decision of the Court.

- 18. Because the right of each Treaty Tribe to take anadromous fish arises from a treaty with the United States, that right is preserved and protected under the supreme law of the land, does not depend on State law, is distinct from rights or privileges held by others, and may not be qualified by any action of the State.

- 19. The treaty phrase "in common with" does not secure any treaty right or privilege to anyone other than the Treaty Tribes, nor does that phrase qualify any Indian's treaty right to fish, except as provided in the Decision of the Court.

- 20. Except for tribes now or hereafter entitled to self-regulation of tribal fishing, as provided in the Decision of the Court, the right of a Treaty Tribe to take anadromous fish may be regulated by an appropriate exercise of State power. To be appropriate, such regulation must:
  1. Not discriminate against the Treaty Tribe's reserved right to fish;
  2. Meet appropriate standards of substantive and procedural due process; and

3. Be shown by the State to be both reasonable and necessary to preserve and maintain the resource. When State law or regulations affect the volume of anadromous fish available for harvest by a Treaty Tribe at usual and accustomed places, such regulations must be designed so as to carry out the purposes of the treaty provision securing to the Tribe the right to take fish.

- 21. If any person shows identification, as provided in the Decision of the Court, that he is exercising the fishing rights of a Treaty Tribe and if he is fishing in a usual and accustomed place, he is protected under federal law against any State action which affects the time, place, manner, purpose or volume of his harvest of anadromous fish, unless the State has previously established that such action is an appropriate exercise of its power.

- 22. The application of currently effective laws and regulations of the State of Washington specified in the Conclusions of Law which affect the time, place, manner and volume of off-reservation harvest of anadromous fish by Treaty Tribes is unlawful for the reasons also stated in the Conclusions of Law. . . .

- Therefore, it is hereby Ordered, adjudged and decreed that the State of Washington; Thor C. Tollefson, Director, Washington State Department of Fisheries; Carl Crouse, Director, Washington Department of Game; The Washington State Game Commission; the Washington Reef Net Owners Association, their agents, officers, employees, successors in interest; and all persons acting in concert or participation with any of them ("defendants") are permanently enjoined and restrained to obey, to respect and to comply with all rulings of this court in its Final Decision #I and with each provision of this injunction, subject only to such modifications as may be approved as a part of an interim program.

- 1. Defendants shall:

- 1. fully and fairly recognize each of the plaintiff tribes as a tribe holding all rights described and declared as to it in Final Decision #I and accord to each the tribal rights and powers recognized as to it in that decision;

2. fully observe and to the best of their ability carry out the provisions and purposes of the treaties cited in paragraph 1 of the Findings of Fact;

3. conform their regulatory action and enforcement to each and all of the standards set forth in Final Decision #I;

4. recognize the fishing rights in the case area of any treaty tribe not a party to this case to the full extent declared in Final Decision #I as to the plaintiff tribes and perform all acts and duties set forth in this injunction with respect to such additional treaty tribe upon the agreement of defendants or determination by the court that the tribe is a treaty tribe.

- 2. Defendants shall not interfere with or regulate or attempt to regulate the treaty right fishing of members of the Yakima Indian Nation or Quinault Tribe or any other treaty tribe during any period for which said tribe has been or is hereafter determined pursuant to Final Decision #I to be entitled to self-regulate such fishing by its members without any state regulation thereof; provided however that monitoring by the state as stated as a condition for self-regulation may be exercised by the state and in case of a threat to the resource, the defendants may apply to the court for the exercise of regulatory authority;

- 3. Defendants shall not interfere with or regulate or attempt to regulate the treaty right fishing of members of any treaty tribe during any period not covered by paragraph 2 above as to such tribe unless the state first shows to the satisfaction of such tribe or this court that such regulation conforms to the requirements of Final Decision #I and this injunction. . . .

- 11. The state defendants shall not adopt regulations or enforce any statutes or regulations affecting the volume of anadromous fish available for harvest by a treaty tribe at usual and accustomed places unless such regulations are designed so as to carry out the purposes of the treaty provisions securing to the tribe the right to take fish.

- 12. Except as otherwise provided by paragraph 19 hereof, the state defendants shall not adopt or enforce any regulations that affect the harvest by the tribe on future runs unless there first has been a full, fair and public consideration and determination in accordance with the requirements of the Washington Administrative Procedures Act and regulations under it.

- 13. The state defendants shall not regulate or restrain the exercise of treaty fishing rights of plaintiff tribes and their members by use of a state statute or regulation of broad applicability instead of one specific as to time, place, species and gear.

- 14. The state defendants shall not adopt or enforce any regulation which effectively limits the harvest by treaty tribes on future runs unless the state's regulatory scheme provides an opportunity for treaty tribes and their members to take, at their off-reservation usual and accustomed fishing places, by reasonable means feasible to them, an equal share of the harvestable number of each species of fish that may be taken by all fishermen; provided that for the present time defendants shall not be required to achieve mathematical precision in so allocating the fish; Provided further that in order to approach more nearly the principle of equal sharing, the fish which Indian treaty fishermen shall have an opportunity to catch shall include not only an equal share of the total number of fish of any species which are within the regulatory jurisdiction of the State of Washington but shall also include an additional amount or quantity of fish which shall be determined by agreement of the parties or by approval of this court, to reflect the substantially disproportionate numbers of fish, many of which might otherwise be available for harvest by Indian treaty right fishermen, caught by non-treaty fishermen in marine areas closely adjacent to, but beyond the territorial waters of the state, or outside the jurisdiction of the state although within Washington waters; . . .

  - 21. Defendants shall in no manner limit, restrict or inhibit the time, place, manner, volume or purpose of the disposition by a member of a plaintiff tribe of fish harvested according to his rights and the rights and powers of his tribe, as declared and adjudged in Final Decision #I, or interfere with any person purchasing, attempting to purchase, transporting, receiving for shipment, processing or reselling, fish taken pursuant to the exercise of such rights. . . .

INTERIM PLAN AND STAY ORDER PENDING FINAL DECISION ON APPEAL

The court having considered the need for an interim plan and having considered the interim proposal, now hereby orders that the following interim plan shall be in effect and shall be binding upon all parties to this litigation except as to tribes determined to be self-regulating. In making this order the court does so reserving jurisdiction to make further modifications if the court deems them necessary and further orders a stay of portions of the injunction, final decision No. 1 and the decree of February 12, 1974.

The court now, therefore, orders, adjudges and decrees:

(1) Effective June 1, 1974, all off-reservation fishing areas in the case area are closed to Indian treaty fishing except to the extent that tribes adopt and file with the court and the defendants tribal regulations for the fishing activities of their members and specifying the areas to be opened to fishing by tribal members. Indians who engage in fishing activities not in accordance with those tribal regulations shall be subject to the same provisions of the state law as non-Indians engaging in fishing activities. . . .

Source: *United States v. State of Washington* (Boldt Decision). 384 F. Supp. 312; U.S. Dist. LEXIS 12291 (W.D. Wash. 1974).

See also: Bureau of Indian Affairs; Dawes Act; Indian Claims Commission; Indian Reservations. Document: Indian Removal Act (1830)

Lau v. Nichols (1974)

Introduction

In Lau v. Nichols, *the U.S. Supreme Court ruled that students of Chinese ancestry in San Francisco were not receiving an equal educational experience. About 1,800 non-English-speaking Chinese students were not given instruction in English, denying them equal educational opportunity according to the ruling. To force students to know English before entering the public school system would, according to the majority opinion, "make a mockery of public education." The Court did not rely on the Fourteenth Amendment as it was urged, however. The majority relied, instead, on the Civil Rights Act (1964).*

Primary Source

MR. JUSTICE DOUGLAS delivered the opinion of the Court.

The San Francisco, California, school system was integrated in 1971 as a result of a federal court decree. See *Lee v. Johnson*. The District Court found that there are 2,856 students of Chinese ancestry in the school system who do not speak English. Of those who have that language deficiency, about 1,000 are given supplemental courses in the English language. About 1,800, however, do not receive that instruction.

This class suit brought by non-English-speaking Chinese students against officials responsible for the operation of the San Francisco Unified School District seeks relief against the unequal educational opportunities, which are alleged to violate, inter alia, the Fourteenth Amendment. No specific remedy is urged upon us. Teaching English to the students of Chinese ancestry who do not speak the language is one choice. Giving instructions to this group in Chinese is another. There may be others. Petitioners ask only that the Board of Education be directed to apply its expertise to the problem and rectify the situation.

The District Court denied relief. The Court of Appeals affirmed, holding that there was no violation of the Equal Protection Clause of the Fourteenth Amendment or of 601 of the Civil Rights Act of 1964, which excludes from participation in federal financial assistance, recipients of aid which discriminate against racial groups. One judge dissented. A hearing en banc was denied, two judges dissenting.

We granted the petition for certiorari because of the public importance of the question presented.

The Court of Appeals reasoned that "[e]very student brings to the starting line of his educational career different advantages and disadvantages caused in part by social, economic and cultural background, created and continued completely apart from any contribution by the school system." Yet in our view the case may not be so easily decided. This is a public school system of California and 71 of the California Education Code states that "English shall be the basic language of instruction in all schools." That section permits a school district to determine "when and under what circumstances instruction may be given bilingually." That section also states as "the policy of the state" to insure "the mastery of English by all pupils in the schools." And bilingual instruction is authorized "to the extent that it does not interfere with the systematic, sequential, and regular instruction of all pupils in the English language."

Moreover, 8573 of the Education Code provides that no pupil shall receive a diploma of graduation from grade 12 who has not met the standards of proficiency in "English," as well as other prescribed subjects. Moreover, by 12101 of the Education Code (Supp. 1973) children between the ages of six and 16 years are (with exceptions not material here) "subject to compulsory full-time education."

Under these state-imposed standards there is no equality of treatment merely by providing students with the same facilities, textbooks, teachers, and curriculum; for students who do not understand English are effectively foreclosed from any meaningful education.

Basic English skills are at the very core of what these public schools teach. Imposition of a requirement that, before a child can effectively participate in the educational program, he must already have acquired those basic skills is to make a mockery of public education. We know that those who do not understand English are certain to find their classroom experiences wholly incomprehensible and in no way meaningful.

We do not reach the Equal Protection Clause argument which has been advanced but rely solely on 601 of the Civil Rights Act of 1964, to reverse the Court of Appeals.

That section bans discrimination based "on the ground of race, color, or national origin," in "any program or activity receiving Federal financial assistance." The school district involved in this litigation receives large amounts of federal financial assistance. The Department of Health, Education, and Welfare (HEW), which has authority to promulgate regulations prohibiting discrimination in federally assisted school systems, in 1968 issued one guideline that "[s]chool systems are responsible for assuring that students of a particular race, color, or national origin are not denied the opportunity to obtain the education generally obtained by other students in the system." In 1970 HEW made the guidelines more specific, requiring school districts that were federally funded "to rectify the language deficiency in order to open" the instruction to students who had "linguistic deficiencies."

By 602 of the Act HEW is authorized to issue rules, regulations, and orders to make sure that recipients of federal aid under its jurisdiction conduct any federally financed projects consistently with 601. HEW's regulations, 45 CFR 80.3 (b) (1), specify that the recipients may not

(ii) Provide any service, financial aid, or other benefit to an individual which is different, or is provided in a different manner, from that provided to others under the program; . . .

(iv) Restrict an individual in any way in the enjoyment of any advantage or privilege enjoyed by others receiving any service, financial aid, or other benefit under the program.

Discrimination among students on account of race or national origin that is prohibited includes "discrimination . . . in the availability or use of any academic . . . or other facilities of the grantee or other recipient."

Discrimination is barred which has that effect even though no purposeful design is present: a recipient "may not . . . utilize criteria or methods of administration which have the effect of subjecting individuals to discrimination" or have "the effect of defeating or substantially impairing accomplishment of the objectives of the program as respect individuals of a particular race, color, or national origin."

It seems obvious that the Chinese-speaking minority receive fewer benefits than the English-speaking majority from respondents' school system which denies them a meaningful opportunity to participate in the educational program—all earmarks of the discrimination banned by the regulations. In 1970 HEW issued clarifying guidelines, which include the following:

Where inability to speak and understand the English language excludes national origin-minority group children from effective participation in the educational program offered by a school district, the district must take affirmative steps to rectify the language deficiency in order to open its instructional program to these students.

Any ability grouping or tracking system employed by the school system to deal with the special language skill needs of national origin-minority group children must be designed to meet such language skill needs as soon as possible and must not operate as an educational deadend or permanent track.

Respondent school district contractually agreed to "comply with title VI of the Civil Rights Act of 1964 . . . and all requirements imposed by or pursuant to the Regulation" of HEW which are "issued pursuant to that title" and also immediately to "take any measures necessary to effectuate this agreement." The Federal Government has power to fix the terms on which its money allotments to the States shall be disbursed. *Oklahoma v. CSC.* Whatever may be the limits of that power, *Steward Machine Co. v. Davis,* they have not been reached here. Senator Humphrey, during the floor debates on the Civil Rights Act of 1964, said:

Simple justice requires that public funds, to which all taxpayers of all races contribute, not be spent in any fashion which encourages, entrenches, subsidizes, or results in racial discrimination.

We accordingly reverse the judgment of the Court of Appeals and remand the case for the fashioning of appropriate relief.

Reversed and remanded.

Source: *Lau v. Nichols*, 414 U.S. 563 (1974).

See also: Education and African Americans; Educational Achievement Gap; Racial Stigmatization

Albermarle Paper Co. v. Moody (1975)

Introduction

In Albemarle Paper Co. v. Moody, *the Supreme Court decided that the Albemarle Paper Company owed its workers back pay*

and should revise or end pre-employment tests that created discriminatory effects because the tests were not sufficiently job related. The questions arose concerning the enforcement of the Civil Rights Act of 1964, because African American employees were locked into lower seniority positions with little opportunity to advance, and employment tests were not concerned with job-related skills. The court's decision made clear that employers would be held responsible for discriminatory practices, arguing that the threat of forced back pay, for example, would be incentive enough to end discriminatory employment procedures.

Primary Source

MR. JUSTICE STEWART delivered the opinion of the Court.

These consolidated cases raise two important questions under Title VII of the Civil Rights Act of 1964, 78 Stat. 253, as amended by the Equal Employment Opportunity Act of 1972, 86 Stat. 103, 42 U.S.C. 2000e et seq. (1970 ed. and Supp. III): First: When employees or applicants for employment have lost the opportunity to earn wages because an employer has engaged in an unlawful discriminatory employment practice, what standards should a federal district court follow in deciding whether to award or deny backpay? Second: What must an employer show to establish that pre-employment tests racially discriminatory in effect, though not in intent, are sufficiently "job related" to survive challenge under Title VII?

I.

The respondents—plaintiffs in the District Court—are a certified class of present and former Negro employees at a paper mill in Roanoke Rapids, N.C.; the petitioners—defendants in the District Court—are the plant's owner, the Albemarle Paper Co., and the plant employees' labor union, Halifax Local No. 425. In August 1966, after filing a complaint with the Equal Employment Opportunity Commission (EEOC), and receiving notice of their right to sue, the respondents brought a class action in the United States District Court for the Eastern District of North Carolina, asking permanent injunctive relief against "any policy, practice, custom or usage" at the plant that violated Title VII. The respondents assured the court that the suit involved no claim for any monetary awards on a class basis, but in

June 1970, after several years of discovery, the respondents moved to add a class demand for backpay. The court ruled that this issue would be considered at trial.

At the trial, in July and August 1971, the major issues were the plant's seniority system, its program of employment testing, and the question of backpay. In its opinion of November 9, 1971, the court found that the petitioners had "strictly segregated" the plant's departmental "lines of progression" prior to January 1, 1964, reserving the higher paying and more skilled lines for whites. The "racial identifiability" of whole lines of progression persisted until 1968, when the lines were reorganized under a new collective-bargaining agreement. The court found, however, that this reorganization left Negro employees "'locked' in the lower paying job classifications." The formerly "Negro" lines of progression had been merely tacked on to the bottom of the formerly "white" lines, and promotions, demotions, and layoffs continued to be governed—where skills were "relatively equal"—by a system of "job seniority." Because of the plant's previous history of overt segregation, only whites had seniority in the higher job categories. Accordingly, the court ordered the petitioners to implement a system of "plantwide" seniority.

The court refused, however, to award backpay to the plaintiff class for losses suffered under the "job seniority" program. The court explained:

In the instant case there was no evidence of bad faith non-compliance with the Act. It appears that the company as early as 1964 began active recruitment of blacks for its Maintenance Apprentice Program. Certain lines of progression were merged on its own initiative, and as judicial decisions expanded the then existing interpretations of the Act, the defendants took steps to correct the abuses without delay....

In addition, an award of back pay is an equitable remedy.... The plaintiffs' claim for back pay was filed nearly five years after the institution of this action. It was not prayed for in the pleadings. Although neither party can be charged with deliberate dilatory tactics in bringing this cause to trial, it is apparent that the defendants would be substantially prejudiced by the granting of such affirmative relief. The defendants might have chosen to exercise unusual zeal in having this court determine their rights at an earlier date had they known that back pay would be at issue.

The court also refused to enjoin or limit Albemarle's testing program. Albemarle had required applicants for employment in the skilled lines of progression to have a high school diploma and to pass two tests, the Revised Beta Examination, allegedly a measure of nonverbal intelligence, and the Wonderlic Personnel Test (available in alternative Forms A and B), allegedly a measure of verbal facility. After this Court's decision in *Griggs v. Duke Power Co.* (1971), and on the eve of trial. Albemarle engaged an industrial psychologist to study the "job relatedness" of its testing program. His study compared the test scores of current employees with supervisorial judgments of their competence in ten job groupings selected from the middle or top of the plant's skilled lines of progression. The study showed a statistically significant correlation with supervisorial ratings in three job groupings for the Beta Test, in seven job groupings for either Form A or Form B of the Wonderlic Test, and in two job groupings for the required battery of both the Beta and the Wonderlic Tests. The respondents' experts challenged the reliability of these studies, but the court concluded:

The personnel tests administered at the plant have undergone validation studies and have been proven to be job related. The defendants have carried the burden of proof in proving that these tests are "necessary for the safe and efficient operation of the business" and are, therefore, permitted by the Act. However, the high school education requirement used in conjunction with the testing requirements is unlawful in that the personnel tests alone are adequate to measure the mental ability and reading skills required for the job classifications.

The petitioners did not seek review of the court's judgment, but the respondents appealed the denial of a backpay award and the refusal to enjoin or limit Albemarle's use of pre-employment tests. A divided Court of Appeals for the Fourth Circuit reversed the judgment of the District Court, ruling that backpay should have been awarded and that use of the tests should have been enjoined (1973). As for backpay,

the Court of Appeals held that an award could properly be requested after the complaint was filed and that an award could not be denied merely because the employer had not acted in "bad faith,":

Because of the compensatory nature of a back pay award and the strong congressional policy embodied in Title VII, a district court must exercise its discretion as to back pay in the same manner it must exercise discretion as to attorney fees under Title II of the Civil Rights Act. . . . Thus, a plaintiff or a complaining class who is successful in obtaining an injunction under Title VII of the Act should ordinarily be awarded back pay unless special circumstances would render such an award unjust. *Newman v. Piggie Park Enterprises . . .* (1968). (Footnote omitted.)

As for the pre-employment tests, the Court of Appeals held that it was error to approve a validation study done without job analysis, to allow Albemarle to require tests for 6 lines of progression where there has been no validation study at all, and to allow Albemarle to require a person to pass two tests for entrance into 7 lines of progression when only one of those tests was validated for that line of progression.

In so holding the Court of Appeals "gave great deference" to the "Guidelines on Employee Selection Procedures," which the EEOC has issued "as a workable set of standards for employers, unions and employment agencies in determining whether their selection procedures conform with the obligations contained in title VII . . . ."

We granted certiorari because of an evident Circuit conflict as to the standards governing awards of backpay6 and as to the showing required to establish the "job relatedness" of pre-employment tests.

II.
Whether a particular member of the plaintiff class should have been awarded any backpay and, if so, how much, are questions not involved in this review. The equities of individual cases were never reached. Though at least some of the members of the plaintiff class obviously suffered a loss of wage opportunities on account of Albemarle's unlawfully discriminatory system of job seniority, the District Court

decided that no backpay should be awarded to anyone in the class. The court declined to make such an award on two stated grounds: the lack of "evidence of bad faith non-compliance with the Act," and the fact that "the defendants would be substantially prejudiced" by an award of backpay that was demanded contrary to an earlier representation and late in the progress of the litigation. Relying directly on *Newman v. Piggie Park Enterprises* (1968), the Court of Appeals reversed, holding that backpay could be denied only in "special circumstances." The petitioners argue that the Court of Appeals was in error—that a district court has virtually unfettered discretion to award or deny backpay, and that there was no abuse of that discretion here.

Piggie Park Enterprises, supra, is not directly in point. The Court held there that attorneys' fees should "ordinarily" be awarded—i. e., in all but "special circumstances"—to plaintiffs successful in obtaining injunctions against discrimination in public accommodations, under Title II of the Civil Rights Act of 1964. While the Act appears to leave Title II fee awards to the district court's discretion, the court determined that the great public interest in having injunctive actions brought could be vindicated only if successful plaintiffs, acting as "private attorneys general," were awarded attorneys' fees in all but very unusual circumstances. There is, of course, an equally strong public interest in having injunctive actions brought under Title VII, to eradicate discriminatory employment practices. But this interest can be vindicated by applying the *Piggie Park* standard to the attorneys' fees provision of Title VII, 42 U.S.C. 2000e-5 (k), see *Northcross v. Memphis Board of Education* (1973). For guidance as to the granting and denial of backpay, one must, therefore, look elsewhere.

The petitioners contend that the statutory scheme provides no guidance, beyond indicating that backpay awards are within the District Court's discretion. We disagree. It is true that backpay is not an automatic or mandatory remedy; like all other remedies under the Act, it is one which the courts "may" invoke. The scheme implicitly recognizes that there may be cases calling for one remedy but not another, and—owing to the structure of the federal judiciary—these choices are, of course, left in the first instance to the district courts. However, such discretionary choices are not left to a

court's "inclination, but to its judgment; and its judgment is to be guided by sound legal principles." *United States v. Burr* (CC Va. 1807) (Marshall, C. J.). The power to award backpay was bestowed by Congress, as part of a complex legislative design directed at a historic evil of national proportions. A court must exercise this power "in light of the large objectives of the Act," *Hecht Co. v. Bowles* (1944). That the court's discretion is equitable in nature, see *Curtis v. Loether* (1974), hardly means that it is unfettered by meaningful standards or shielded from thorough appellate review. In *Mitchell v. DeMario Jewelry* (1960), this Court held, in the face of a silent statute, that district courts enjoyed the "historic power of equity" to award lost wages to workmen unlawfully discriminated against under 17 of the Fair Labor Standards Act of 1938. The Court simultaneously noted that "the statutory purposes [leave] little room for the exercise of discretion not to order reimbursement."

It is true that "[e]quity eschews mechanical rules . . . [and] depends on flexibility." *Holmberg v. Armbrecht* (1946). But when Congress invokes the Chancellors conscience to further transcendent legislative purposes, what is required is the principled application of standards consistent with those purposes and not "equity [which] varies like the Chancellor's foot." Important national goals would be frustrated by a regime of discretion that "produce[d] different results for breaches of duty in situations that cannot be differentiated in policy." *Moragne v. States Marine Lines* (1970).

The District Court's decision must therefore be measured against the purposes which inform Title VII. As the Court observed in *Griggs v. Duke Power Co.* the primary objective was a prophylactic one: "It was to achieve equality of employment opportunities and remove barriers that have operated in the past to favor an identifiable group of white employees over other employees."

Backpay has an obvious connection with this purpose. If employers faced only the prospect of an injunctive order, they would have little incentive to shun practices of dubious legality. It is the reasonably certain prospect of a backpay award that "provide[s] the spur or catalyst which causes employers and unions to self-examine and to self-evaluate their employment practices and to endeavor to eliminate, so far as possible, the last vestiges of an unfortunate and igno-minious page in this country's history." *United States v. N. L. Industries, Inc.* (CA8 1973).

It is also the purpose of Title VII to make persons whole for injuries suffered on account of unlawful employment discrimination. This is shown by the very fact that Congress took care to arm the courts with full equitable powers. For it is the historic purpose of equity to "secur[e] complete justice," *Brown v. Swann* (1836); see also *Porter v. Warner Holding Co.* (1946). "[W]here federally protected rights have been invaded, it has been the rule from the beginning that courts will be alert to adjust their remedies so as to grant the necessary relief." *Bell v. Hood* (1946). Title VII deals with legal injuries of an economic character occasioned by racial or other antiminority discrimination. The terms "complete justice" and "necessary relief" have acquired a clear meaning in such circumstances. Where racial discrimination is concerned, "the [district] court has not merely the power but the duty to render a decree which will so far as possible eliminate the discriminatory effects of the past as well as bar like discrimination in the future." *Louisiana v. United States* (1965). And where a legal injury is of an economic character

[t]he general rule is, that when a wrong has been done, and the law gives a remedy, the compensation shall be equal to the injury. The latter is the standard by which the former is to be measured. The injured party is to be placed, as near as may be, in the situation he would have occupied if the wrong had not been committed. *Wicker v. Hoppock* (1867).

The "make whole" purpose of Title VII is made evident by the legislative history. The backpay provision was expressly modeled on the backpay provision of the National Labor Relations Act. Under that Act, "[m]aking the workers whole for losses suffered on account of an unfair labor practice is part of the vindication of the public policy which the Board enforces." *Phelps Dodge Corp. v. NLRB* (1941). See also *Nathanson v. NLRB* (1952); *NLRB v. Rutter-Rex Mfg. Co.* (1969). We may assume that Congress was aware that the Board since its inception, has awarded backpay as a matter of course—not randomly or in the exercise of a standard-less discretion, and not merely where employer violations

are peculiarly deliberate, egregious, or inexcusable. Furthermore, in passing the Equal Employment Opportunity Act of 1972, Congress considered several bills to limit the judicial power to award backpay. These limiting efforts were rejected, and the backpay provision was re-enacted substantially in its original form. A Section-by-Section Analysis introduced by Senator Williams to accompany the Conference Committee Report on the 1972 Act strongly reaffirmed the "make whole" purpose of Title VII:

The provisions of this subsection are intended to give the courts wide discretion exercising their equitable powers to fashion the most complete relief possible. In dealing with the present section 706 (g) the courts have stressed that the scope of relief under that section of the Act is intended to make the victims of unlawful discrimination whole, and that the attainment of this objective rests not only upon the elimination of the particular unlawful employment practice complained of, but also requires that persons aggrieved by the consequences and effects of the unlawful employment practice be, so far as possible, restored to a position where they would have been were it not for the unlawful discrimination.

As this makes clear, Congress' purpose in vesting a variety of "discretionary" powers in the courts was not to limit appellate review of trial courts, or to invite inconsistency and caprice, but rather to make possible the "fashion[ing] [of] the most complete relief possible."

It follows that, given a finding of unlawful discrimination, backpay should be denied only for reasons which, if applied generally, would not frustrate the central statutory purposes of eradicating discrimination throughout the economy and making persons whole for injuries suffered through past discrimination. The courts of appeals must maintain a consistent and principled application of the backpay provision, consonant with the twin statutory objectives, while at the same time recognizing that the trial court will often have the keener appreciation of those facts and circumstances peculiar to particular cases.

The District Court's stated grounds for denying backpay in this case must be tested against these standards. The first ground was that Albemarle's breach of Title VII had not been in "bad faith." This is not a sufficient reason for denying backpay. Where an employer has shown bad faith—by maintaining a practice which he knew to be illegal or of highly questionable legality—he can make no claims whatsoever on the Chancellor's conscience. But, under Title VII, the mere absence of bad faith simply opens the door to equity; it does not depress the scales in the employer's favor. If backpay were awardable only upon a showing of bad faith, the remedy would become a punishment for moral turpitude, rather than a compensation for workers' injuries. This would read the "make whole" purpose right out of Title VII, for a worker's injury is no less real simply because his employer did not inflict it in "bad faith." Title VII is not concerned with the employer's "good intent or absence of discriminatory intent" for "Congress directed the thrust of the Act to the consequences of employment practices, not simply the motivation." *Griggs v. Duke Power Co.* See also *Watson v. City of Memphis* (1963); *Wright v. Council of City of Emporia* (1972). To condition the awarding of backpay on a showing of "bad faith" would be to open an enormous chasm between injunctive and backpay relief under Title VII. There is nothing on the face of the statute or in its legislative history that justifies the creation of drastic and categorical distinctions between those two remedies.

The District Court also grounded its denial of backpay on the fact that the respondents initially disclaimed any interest in backpay, first asserting their claim five years after the complaint was filed. The court concluded that the petitioners had been "prejudiced" by this conduct. The Court of Appeals reversed on the ground "that the broad aims of Title VII require that the issue of back pay be fully developed and determined even though it was not raised until the post-trial stage of litigation."

It is true that Title VII contains no legal bar to raising backpay claims after the complaint for injunctive relief has been filed, or indeed after a trial on that complaint has been had. Furthermore, Fed. Rule Civ. Proc. 54 (c) directs that "every final judgment shall grant the relief to which the party in whose favor it is rendered is entitled, even if the party has not demanded such relief in his pleadings."

But a party may not be "entitled" to relief if its conduct of the cause has improperly and substantially prejudiced the other party. The respondents here were not merely tardy, but also inconsistent, in demanding backpay. To deny backpay because a particular cause has been prosecuted in an eccentric fashion, prejudicial to the other party, does not offend the broad purposes of Title VII. This is not to say, however, that the District Court's ruling was necessarily correct. Whether the petitioners were in fact prejudiced, and whether the respondents' trial conduct was excusable, are questions that will be open to review by the Court of Appeals, if the District Court, on remand, decides again to decline to make any award of backpay. But the standard of review will be the familiar one of whether the District Court was "clearly erroneous" in its factual findings and whether it "abused" its traditional discretion to locate "a just result" in light of the circumstances peculiar to the case, *Langnes v. Green* (1931). On these issues of procedural regularity and prejudice, the "broad aims of Title VII" provide no ready solution.

III.

In *Griggs v. Duke Power Co.* (1971), this Court unanimously held that Title VII forbids the use of employment tests that are discriminatory in effect unless the employer meets "the burden of showing that any given requirement [has] . . . a manifest relationship to the employment in question." This burden arises, of course, only after the complaining party or class has made out a prima facie case of discrimination, i. e., has shown that the tests in question select applicants for hire or promotion in a racial pattern significantly different from that of the pool of applicants. See *McDonnell Douglas Corp. v. Green* (1973). If an employer does then meet the burden of proving that its tests are "job related," it remains open to the complaining party to show that other tests or selection devices, without a similarly undesirable racial effect, would also serve the employer's legitimate interest in "efficient and trustworthy workmanship." Such a showing would be evidence that the employer was using its tests merely as a "pretext" for discrimination. In the present case, however, we are concerned only with the question whether Albemarle has shown its tests to be job related.

The concept of job relatedness takes on meaning from the facts of the *Griggs* case. A power company in North Carolina had reserved its skilled jobs for whites prior to 1965. Thereafter, the company allowed Negro workers to transfer to skilled jobs, but all transferees—white and Negro—were required to attain national median scores on two tests: "[T]he Wonderlic Personnel Test, which purports to measure general intelligence, and the Bennett Mechanical Comprehension Test. Neither was directed or intended to measure the ability to learn to perform a particular job or category of jobs. . . .

". . . Both were adopted, as the Court of Appeals noted, without meaningful study of their relationship to job-performance ability. Rather, a vice president of the Company testified, the requirements were instituted on the Company's judgment that they generally would improve the overall quality of the work force."

The Court took note of "the inadequacy of broad and general testing devices as well as the infirmity of using diplomas or degrees as fixed measures of capability," and concluded:

Nothing in the Act precludes the use of testing or measuring procedures; obviously they are useful. What Congress has forbidden is giving these devices and mechanisms controlling force unless they are demonstrably a reasonable measure of job performance. . . . What Congress has commanded is that any tests used must measure the person for the job and not the person in the abstract.

Like the employer in *Griggs*, Albemarle uses two general ability tests, the Beta Examination, to test nonverbal intelligence, and the Wonderlic Test (Forms A and B), the purported measure of general verbal facility which was also involved in the *Griggs* case. Applicants for hire into various skilled lines of progression at the plant are required to score 100 on the Beta Exam and 18 on one of the Wonderlic Test's two alternative forms.

The question of job relatedness must be viewed in the context of the plant's operation and the history of the testing program. The plant, which now employs about 650 persons, converts raw wood into paper products. It is organized into a number of functional departments, each with one or more distinct lines of progression, the theory being that workers can move up the line as they acquire the necessary skills. The

number and structure of the lines have varied greatly over time. For many years, certain lines were themselves more skilled and paid higher wages than others, and until 1964 these skilled lines were expressly reserved for white workers. In 1968, many of the unskilled "Negro" lines were "end-tailed" onto skilled "white" lines, but it apparently remains true that at least the top jobs in certain lines require greater skills than the top jobs in other lines. In this sense, at least, it is still possible to speak of relatively skilled and relatively unskilled lines.

In the 1950's while the plant was being modernized with new and more sophisticated equipment, the Company introduced a high school diploma requirement for entry into the skilled lines. Though the Company soon concluded that this requirement did not improve the quality of the labor force, the requirement was continued until the District Court enjoined its use. In the late 1950's the Company began using the Beta Examination and the Bennett Mechanical Comprehension Test (also involved in the *Griggs* case) to screen applicants for entry into the skilled lines. The Bennett Test was dropped several years later, but use of the Beta Test continued.

The Company added the Wonderlic Tests in 1963, for the skilled lines, on the theory that a certain verbal intelligence was called for by the increasing sophistication of the plant's operations. The Company made no attempt to validate the test for job relatedness, and simply adopted the national "norm" score of 18 as a cut-off point for new job applicants. After 1964, when it discontinued overt segregation in the lines of progression, the Company allowed Negro workers to transfer to the skilled lines if they could pass the Beta and Wonderlic Tests, but few succeeded in doing so. Incumbents in the skilled lines, some of whom had been hired before adoption of the tests, were not required to pass them to retain their jobs or their promotion rights. The record shows that a number of white incumbents in high-ranking job groups could not pass the tests.

Because departmental reorganization continued up to the point of trial, and has indeed continued since that point, the details of the testing program are less than clear from the record. The District Court found that, since 1963, the Beta and Wonderlic Tests have been used in 13 lines of progression, within eight departments. Albemarle contends that at present the tests are used in only eight lines of progression, within four departments.

Four months before this case went to trial, Albemarle engaged an expert in industrial psychology to "validate" the job relatedness of its testing program. He spent a half day at the plant and devised a "concurrent validation" study, which was conducted by plant officials, without his supervision. The expert then subjected the results to statistical analysis. The study dealt with 10 job groupings, selected from near the top of nine of the lines of progression. Jobs were grouped together solely by their proximity in the line of progression; no attempt was made to analyze jobs in terms of the particular skills they might require. All, or nearly all, employees in the selected groups participated in the study—105 employees in all, but only four Negroes. Within each job grouping, the study compared the test scores of each employee with an independent "ranking" of the employee, relative to each of his coworkers, made by two of the employee's supervisors. The supervisors, who did not know the test scores, were asked to "determine which ones they felt irrespective of the job that they were actually doing, but in their respective jobs, did a better job than the person they were rating against . . . ."

For each job grouping, the expert computed the "Phi coefficient" of statistical correlation between the test scores and an average of the two supervisorial rankings. Consonant with professional conventions, the expert regarded as "statistically significant" any correlation that could have occurred by chance only five times, or fewer, in 100 trials. On the basis of these results, the District Court found that "[t]he personnel tests administered at the plant have undergone validation studies and have been proven to be job related." Like the Court of Appeals, we are constrained to disagree.

The EEOC has issued "Guidelines" for employers seeking to determine, through professional validation studies, whether their employment tests are job related. These Guidelines draw upon and make reference to professional standards of test validation established by the American Psychological Association. The EEOC Guidelines are not administrative "regulations" promulgated pursuant to formal procedures established by the Congress. But, as this Court has heretofore noted, they do constitute "[t]he administrative interpretation of the Act by the enforcing agency," and consequently they are "entitled to great deference." *Griggs v. Duke Power Co.* See also *Espinoza v. Farah Mfg. Co.* (1973).

The message of these Guidelines is the same as that of the *Griggs* case—that discriminatory tests are impermissible unless shown, by professionally acceptable methods, to be "predictive of or significantly correlated with important elements of work behavior which comprise or are relevant to the job or jobs for which candidates are being evaluated."

Measured against the Guidelines, Albemarle's validation study is materially defective in several respects:

(1) Even if it had been otherwise adequate, the study would not have "validated" the Beta and Wonderlic test battery for all of the skilled lines of progression for which the two tests are, apparently, now required. The study showed significant correlations for the Beta Exam in only three of the eight lines. Though the Wonderlic Test's Form A and Form B are in theory identical and interchangeable measures of verbal facility, significant correlations for one form but not for the other were obtained in four job groupings. In two job groupings neither form showed a significant correlation. Within some of the lines of progression, one form was found acceptable for some job groupings but not for others. Even if the study were otherwise reliable, this odd patchwork of results would not entitle Albemarle to impose its testing program under the Guidelines. A test may be used in jobs other than those for which it has been professionally validated only if there are "no significant differences" between the studied and unstudied jobs. The study in this case involved no analysis of the attributes of, or the particular skills needed in, the studied job groups. There is accordingly no basis for concluding that "no significant differences" exist among the lines of progression, or among distinct job groupings within the studied lines of progression. Indeed, the study's checkered results appear to compel the opposite conclusion.

(2) The study compared test scores with subjective supervisorial rankings. While they allow the use of supervisorial rankings in test validation, the Guidelines quite plainly contemplate that the rankings will be elicited with far more care

than was demonstrated here. Albemarle's supervisors were asked to rank employees by a "standard" that was extremely vague and fatally open to divergent interpretations. As previously noted, each "job grouping" contained a number of different jobs, and the supervisors were asked, in each grouping, to "determine which ones [employees] they felt irrespective of the job that they were actually doing, but in their respective jobs, did a better job than the person they were rating against . . . ."

There is no way of knowing precisely what criteria of job performance the supervisors were considering, whether each of the supervisors was considering the same criteria or whether, indeed, any of the supervisors actually applied a focused and stable body of criteria of any kind. There is, in short, simply no way to determine whether the criteria actually considered were sufficiently related to the Company's legitimate interest in job-specific ability to justify a testing system with a racially discriminatory impact.

(3) The Company's study focused, in most cases, on job groups near the top of the various lines of progression. In *Griggs v. Duke Power Co.*, supra, the Court left open "the question whether testing requirements that take into account capability for the next succeeding position or related future promotion might be utilized upon a showing that such long-range requirements fulfill a genuine business need." The Guidelines take a sensible approach to this issue, and we now endorse it:

If job progression structures and seniority provisions are so established that new employees will probably, within a reasonable period of time and in a great majority of cases, progress to a higher level, it may be considered that candidates are being evaluated for jobs at that higher level. However, where job progression is not so nearly automatic, or the time span is such that higher level jobs or employees' potential may be expected to change in significant ways, it shall be considered that candidates are being evaluated for a job at or near the entry level.

The fact that the best of those employees working near the top of a line of progression score well on a test does not necessarily mean that that test, or some particular cutoff score on the test, is a permissible measure of the minimal

qualifications of new workers entering lower level jobs. In drawing any such conclusion, detailed consideration must be given to the normal speed of promotion, to the efficacy of on-the-job training in the scheme of promotion, and to the possible use of testing as a promotion device, rather than as a screen for entry into low-level jobs. The District Court made no findings on these issues. The issues take on special importance in a case, such as this one, where incumbent employees are permitted to work at even high-level jobs without passing the company's test battery.

(4) Albemarle's validation study dealt only with job-experienced, white workers; but the tests themselves are given to new job applicants, who are younger, largely inexperienced, and in many instances nonwhite. The APA Standards state that it is "essential" that "[t]he validity of a test should be determined on subjects who are at the age or in the same educational or vocational situation as the persons for whom the test is recommended in practice."

The EEOC Guidelines likewise provide that "[d]ata must be generated and results separately reported for minority and nonminority groups wherever technically feasible." In the present case, such "differential validation" as to racial groups was very likely not "feasible," because years of discrimination at the plant have insured that nearly all of the upper level employees are white. But there has been no clear showing that differential validation was not feasible for lower level jobs. More importantly, the Guidelines provide:

If it is not technically feasible to include minority employees in validation studies conducted on the present work force, the conduct of a validation study without minority candidates does not relieve any person of his subsequent obligation for validation when inclusion of minority candidates becomes technically feasible.

. . . [E]vidence of satisfactory validity based on other groups will be regarded as only provisional compliance with these guidelines pending separate validation of the test for the minority group in question.

For all these reasons, we agree with the Court of Appeals that the District Court erred in concluding that Albemarle had proved the job relatedness of its testing program and that the respondents were consequently not entitled to equitable relief. The outright reversal by the Court of Appeals implied that an injunction should immediately issue against all use of testing at the plant. Because of the particular circumstances here, however, it appears that the more prudent course is to leave to the District Court the precise fashioning of the necessary relief in the first instance. During the appellate stages of this litigation, the plant has apparently been amending its departmental organization and the use made of its tests. The appropriate standard of proof for job relatedness has not been clarified until today. Similarly, the respondents have not until today been specifically apprised of their opportunity to present evidence that even validated tests might be a "pretext" for discrimination in light of alternative selection procedures available to the Company. We also note that the Guidelines authorize provisional use of tests, pending new validation efforts, in certain very limited circumstances. Whether such circumstances now obtain is a matter best decided, in the first instance, by the District Court. That court will be free to take such new evidence, and to exercise such control of the Company's use and validation of employee selection procedures, as are warranted by the circumstances and by the controlling law.

Accordingly, the judgment is vacated, and these cases are remanded to the District Court for proceedings consistent with this opinion.

It is so ordered.

Source: *Albemarle Paper Co. v. Moody.* 422 U.S. 405 (1975).

See also: Civil Rights Act of 1964. Document: Civil Rights Act of 1964

American Indian Religious Freedom Act (1978)

Introduction

Enacted on August 11, 1978, the American Indian Religious Freedom Act offers safeguards for Native Americans' traditional religious practices and religions. After the U.S. Supreme Court ruled in Department of Human Services of Oregon v. Smith (1990), and Oregon v. Black (1988) that this law did not allow Native Americans to use the illegal drug peyote in their religious services, Congress amended the act in 1994 to extend such protection.

Primary Source

Resolved by the Senate and House of Representatives of the United States of America in Congress assembled,

That henceforth it shall be the policy of the United States to protect and preserve for American Indians their inherent fight of freedom to believe, express and exercise the traditional religions of the American Indian, Eskimo, Aleut, and Native Hawaiians, including but not limited to access to sites, use and possession of sacred objects, and the freedom to worship through ceremonials and traditional rites.

An Act To emend the American Indian Religious Freedom Act to provide for the traditional use of peyote by Indians for religious purposes, and for other purposes.

Be it enacted by the Senate and House of Representatives of the United States of America in Congress assembled,

SECTION 1. SHORT TITLE. This Act may be cited as the "American Indian Religious Freedom Act Amendments of 1994."

SECTION 2. TRADITIONAL INDIAN RELIGIOUS USE OF THE PEYOTE SACRAMENT. The Act of August 11, 1978 (42 U.S.C. 1996), commonly referred to as the "American Indian Religious Freedom Act," is amended by adding at the end thereof the following new section:

SECTION 3.

a. The Congress finds and declares that

1. for many Indian people, the traditional ceremonial use of the peyote cactus as a religious sacrament has for centuries been integral to a way of life, and significant in perpetuating Indian tribes and cultures;

2. since 1965, this ceremonial use of peyote by Indians has been protected by Federal regulation;

3. while at least 28 States have enacted laws which are similar to, or are in conformance with, the Federal regulation which protects the ceremonial use of peyote by Indian religious practitioners, 22 States have not done so, and this lack of uniformity has created hardship for Indian people who participate in such religious ceremonies;

4. the Supreme Court of the United States, in the case of *Employment Division v. Smith*, 494 U.S. 872 (1990), held that the First Amendment does not protect Indian practitioners who use peyote in Indian religious ceremonies, and also raised uncertainty whether this religious practice would be protected under the compelling State interest standard; and

5. the lack of adequate and clear legal protection for the religious use of peyote by Indians may serve to stigmatize and marginalize Indian tribes and cultures, and increase the risk that they will be exposed to discriminatory treatment.

b. 1. Notwithstanding any other provision of law, the use, possession, or transportation of peyote by an Indian for bona fide traditional ceremonial purposes in connection with the practice of a traditional Indian religion is lawful, and shall not be prohibited by the United States or any State. No Indian shall be penalized or discriminated against on the basis of such use, possession or transportation, including, but not limited to, denial of otherwise applicable benefits under public assistance programs.

2. This section does not prohibit such reasonable regulation and registration by the Drug Enforcement Administration of those persons who cultivate, harvest, or distribute peyote as may be consistent with the purposes of this Act.

3. This section does not prohibit application of the provisions of section 481.111 of Vernon's Texas Health and Safety Code Annotated, in effect on the date of enactment of this section, insofar as those provisions pertain to the cultivation, harvest, and distribution of peyote.

4. Nothing in this section shall prohibit any Federal department or agency, in carrying out its statutory responsibilities and functions, from promulgating regulations establishing reasonable limitations on the use or ingestion of peyote prior to or during the performance of duties by sworn law enforcement officers or personnel directly involved in public transportation or any other safety-sensitive positions where the performance of such duties may be adversely affected by such use or ingestion. Such regulations shall be adopted only after consultation with representatives of traditional Indian religions for which the sacramental use of peyote is integral to their practice. Any regulation promulgated pursuant to this section shall be subject to the balancing test set forth in section 3 of the Religious Freedom Restoration Act (Public Law 103-141; 42 U.S.C.2000bb-1).

5. This section shall not be construed as requiring prison authorities to permit, nor shall it be construed to prohibit prison authorities from permitting, access to peyote by Indians while incarcerated within Federal or State prison facilities.

6. Subject to the provisions of the Religious Freedom Restoration Act (Public Law 103-141; 42 U.S.C. 2000bb-1), this section shall not be construed to prohibit States from enacting or enforcing reasonable traffic safety laws or regulations.

7. Subject to the provisions of the Religious Freedom Restoration Act (Public Law 103-141; 42 USC 2000bb-1), this section does not prohibit the Secretary of Defense from promulgating regulations establishing reasonable limitations on the use, possession, transportation, or distribution of peyote to promote military readiness, safety, or compliance with international law or laws of other countries. Such regulations shall be adopted only after consultation with representatives of traditional Indian religions for which the sacramental use of peyote is integral to their practice.

c. For purposes of this section—

1. the term "Indian" means a member of an Indian tribe;

2. the term "Indian tribe" means any tribe, band, nation, pueblo, or other organized group or community of Indians,

including any Alaska Native village (as defined in, or established pursuant to, the Alaska Native Claims Settlement Act [43 U.S.C. 1601 et seq.]), which is recognized as eligible for the special programs and services provide by the United States to Indians because of their status as Indians;

3. the term "Indian religion" means any religion—A. which is practiced by Indians; and B. the origin and interpretation of which is from within a traditional Indian culture or community; and

4. the term "State" means any State of the United States and any political subdivision thereof.

d. Nothing in this section shall be construed as abrogating, diminishing, or otherwise affecting—

1. the inherent rights of any Indian tribe;

2. the rights, express or implicit, of any Indian tribe which exist under treaties, Executive orders, and laws of the United States;

3. the inherent right of Indians to practice their religions; and

4. the right of Indians to practice their religions under any Federal or State law.

> **Source:** American Indian Religious Freedom Act. Public Law No. 95–341, 92 *U.S. Statues at Large* (1978): 469.

> **See also:** Cultural Genocide; Indian Reservations; Native Americans, Conquest of

Regents of the University of California v. Bakke (1978)

Introduction

The Regents of the University of California v. Bakke *case, in which a white student rejected from medical school sued because the school's affirmative action program gave* preference to minority students, was the first U.S. Supreme Court test of affirmative action. Twice in the early 1970s, a gifted student named Alan P. Bakke applied for entrance to the medical school at the University of California, Davis. Twice, he was turned down. Bakke was not alone in his situation. Admission to the Davis Medical School was highly prized, and more than 26 applicants were turned down for every one who was accepted. But Bakke, who was white, felt that the university's admission program unfairly discriminated against him because of his race.

Primary Source

Mr. Justice POWELL announced the judgment of the Court.

This case presents a challenge to the special admissions program of . . . the Medical School of the University of California at Davis, which is designed to assure the admission of a specified number of students from certain minority groups. . . .

For the reasons stated in the following opinion, I believe that so much of the judgment of the California court as holds petitioner's special admissions program unlawful and directs that respondent be admitted to the Medical School must be affirmed. For the reasons expressed in a separate opinion, my Brothers the Chief Justice, Mr. Justice STEWART, Mr. Justice REHNQUIST, and Mr. Justice STEVENS concur in this judgment.

I also conclude for the reasons stated in the following opinion that the portion of the court's judgment enjoining petitioner from according any consideration to race in its admissions process must be reversed. For reasons expressed in separate opinions, my Brothers Mr. Justice BRENNAN, Mr. Justice WHITE, Mr. Justice MARSHALL, and Mr. Justice BLACKMUN concur in this judgment.

Affirmed in part and reversed in part.

I

The Medical School of the University of California at Davis opened in 1968. . . . In 1971, the size of the entering class was increased to 100 students, a level at which it remains.

No admissions program for disadvantaged or minority students existed when the school opened, and the first class contained three Asians but no blacks, no Mexican-Americans, and no American Indians. Over the next two years, the faculty devised a special admissions program to increase the representation of "disadvantaged" students in each Medical School class. The special program consisted of a separate admissions system operating in coordination with the regular admissions process. . . .

The special admissions program operated with a separate committee, a majority of whom were members of minority groups. On the 1973 application form, candidates were asked to indicate whether they wished to be considered as "economically and/or educationally disadvantaged" applicants; on the 1974 form the question was whether they wished to be considered as members of a "minority group," which the Medical School apparently viewed as "Blacks," "Chicanos," "Asians," and "American Indians." . . . If these questions were answered affirmatively, the application was forwarded to the special admissions committee. No formal definition of "disadvantaged" was ever produced, but the chairman of the special committee screened each application to see whether it reflected economic or educational deprivation. . . .

Allan Bakke is a white male who applied to the Davis Medical School. . . .

Bakke's 1974 application was completed early in the year. His student interviewer gave him an overall rating of 94, finding him "friendly, well tempered, conscientious and delightful to speak with." His faculty interviewer was, by coincidence, the same Dr. Lowrey to whom he had written in protest of the special admissions program. Dr. Lowrey found Bakke "rather limited in his approach" to the problems of the medical profession and found disturbing Bakke's "very definite opinions which were based more on his personal viewpoints than upon a study of the total problem." Dr. Lowrey gave Bakke the lowest of his six ratings, an 86; his total was 549 out of 600. Again, Bakke's application was rejected. . . . In both years, applicants were admitted under the special program with grade point averages, MCAT scores, and benchmark scores significantly lower than Bakke's.

After the second rejection, Bakke filed the instant suit in the Superior Court of California. . . . He alleged that the Medical School's special admissions program operated to exclude him from the school on the basis of his race. . . . The trial court found that the special program operated as a racial quota, because minority applicants in the special program were rated only against one another and 16 places in the class of 100 were reserved for them. Declaring that the University could not take race into account in making admissions decisions, the trial court held the challenged program violative of the Federal Constitution, the State Constitution, and Title VI. . . .

B

The language of [Title VI], like that of the Equal Protection Clause, is majestic in its sweep:

No person in the United States shall, on the ground of race, color, or national origin, be excluded from participation in, be denied the benefits of, or be subjected to discrimination under any program or activity receiving Federal financial assistance.

The concept of "discrimination," like the phrase "equal protection of the laws," is susceptible of varying interpretations. . . .

[T]he legislation's supporters [refused] precisely to define the term "discrimination." Opponents sharply criticized this failure, but proponents of the bill merely replied that the meaning of "discrimination" would be made clear by reference to the Constitution or other existing law. For example, Senator Humphrey noted the relevance of the Constitution:

As I have said, the bill has a simple purpose. That purpose is to give fellow citizens—Negroes—the same rights and opportunities that white people take for granted. This is no more than what was preached by the prophets, and by Christ Himself. It is no more than what our Constitution guarantees.

In view of the clear legislative intent, Title VI must be held to proscribe only those racial classifications that would violate the Equal Protection Clause or the Fifth Amendment. . . .

IV

We have held that in "order to justify the use of a suspect classification, a State must show that its purpose or interest is both constitutionally permissible and substantial, and that its use of the classification is "necessary . . . to the accomplishment of its purpose or the safeguarding of its interest." . . . The special admissions program purports to serve the purposes of: (i) "reducing the historic deficit of traditionally disfavored minorities in medical schools and in the medical profession"; (ii) countering the effects of societal discrimination; (iii) increasing the number of physicians who will practice in communities currently underserved; and (iv) obtaining the educational benefits that flow from an ethnically diverse student body. It is necessary to decide which, if any, of these purposes is substantial enough to support the use of a suspect classification.

A

. . . The fourth goal asserted by petitioner is the attainment of a diverse student body. This clearly is a constitutionally permissible goal for an institution of higher education. Academic freedom, though not a specifically enumerated constitutional right, long has been viewed as a special concern of the First Amendment. The freedom of a university to make its own judgments as to education includes the selection of its student body. . . .

Ethnic diversity, however, is only one element in a range of factors a university properly may consider in attaining the goal of a heterogeneous student body. Although a university must have wide discretion in making the sensitive judgments as to who should be admitted, constitutional limitations protecting individual rights may not be disregarded. Respondent urges—and the courts below have held—that petitioner's dual admissions program is a racial classification that impermissibly infringes his rights under the Fourteenth Amendment. As the interest of diversity is compelling in the context of a university's admissions program, the question remains whether the program's racial classification is necessary to promote this interest.

V

A

It may be assumed that the reservation of a specified number of seats in each class for individuals from the preferred ethnic groups would contribute to the attainment of considerable ethnic diversity in the student body. But petitioner's argument that this is the only effective means of serving the interest of diversity is seriously flawed. . . .

The experience of other university admissions programs, which take race into account in achieving the educational diversity valued by the First Amendment, demonstrates that the assignment of a fixed number of places to a minority group is not a necessary means toward that end. An illuminating example is found in the Harvard College program:

In recent years Harvard College has expanded the concept of diversity to include students from disadvantaged economic, racial and ethnic groups. Harvard College now recruits not only Californians or Louisianans but also blacks and Chicanos and other minority students. . . .

In practice, this new definition of diversity has meant that race has been a factor in some admission decisions. When the Committee on Admissions reviews the large middle group of applicants who are "admissible" and deemed capable of doing good work in their courses, the race of an applicant may tip the balance in his favor just as geographic origin or a life spent on a farm may tip the balance in other candidates' cases. A farm boy from Idaho can bring something to Harvard College that a Bostonian cannot offer. Similarly, a black student can usually bring something that a white person cannot offer. . . .

In such an admissions program, race or ethnic background may be deemed a "plus" in a particular applicant's file, yet it does not insulate the individual from comparison with all other candidates for the available seats. . . .

This kind of program treats each applicant as an individual in the admissions process. The applicant who loses out on the last available seat to another candidate receiving a "plus" on the basis of ethnic background will not have been foreclosed from all consideration for that seat simply because he was not the right color or had the wrong surname. It would mean only that his combined qualifications, which may have included similar nonobjective factors, did not outweigh those of the other applicant. His qualifications would have been weighed fairly and competitively, and he would have no basis to complain of unequal treatment under the Fourteenth Amendment.

In summary, it is evident that the Davis special admissions program involves the use of an explicit racial classification never before countenanced by this Court. It tells applicants who are not Negro, Asian, or Chicano that they are totally excluded from a specific percentage of the seats in an entering class. No matter how strong their qualifications, quantitative and extracurricular, including their own potential for contribution to educational diversity, they are never afforded the chance to compete with applicants from the preferred groups for the special admissions seats. At the same time, the preferred applicants have the opportunity to compete for every seat in the class.

The fatal flaw in petitioner's preferential program is its disregard of individual rights as guaranteed by the Fourteenth Amendment. Such rights are not absolute. But when a State's distribution of benefits or imposition of burdens hinges on ancestry or the color of a person's skin, that individual is entitled to a demonstration that the challenged classification is necessary to promote a substantial state interest. Petitioner has failed to carry this burden. For this reason, that portion of the California court's judgment holding petitioner's special admissions program invalid under the Fourteenth Amendment must be affirmed.

Opinion of Mr. Justice BRENNAN, Mr. Justice WHITE, Mr. Justice MARSHALL, and Mr. Justice BLACKMUN, concurring in the judgment in part and dissenting in part.

The Court today . . . affirms the constitutional power of Federal and State Governments to act affirmatively to achieve equal opportunity for all. The difficulty of the issue presented—whether government may use race-conscious programs to redress the continuing effects of past discrimination and the mature consideration which each of our Brethren has brought to it have resulted in many opinions, no single one speaking for the Court. But this should not and must not mask the central meaning of today's opinions: Government may take race into account when it acts not to demean or insult any racial group, but to remedy disadvantages cast on minorities by past racial prejudice, at least when appropriate findings have been made by judicial, legislative, or administrative bodies with competence to act in this area.

The Chief Justice and our Brothers STEWART, REHNQUIST, and STEVENS, have concluded that Title VI of the Civil Rights Act of 1964, prohibits programs such as that at the Davis Medical School. On this statutory theory alone, they would hold that respondent Allan Bakke's rights have been violated and that he must, therefore, be admitted to the Medical School. Our Brother POWELL, reaching the Constitution, concludes that, although race may be taken into account in university admissions, the particular special admissions program used by petitioner, which resulted in the exclusion of respondent Bakke, was not shown to be necessary to achieve petitioner's stated goals. Accordingly, these Members of the Court form a majority of five affirming the judgment of the Supreme Court of California insofar as it holds that respondent Bakke "is entitled to an order that he be admitted to the University." . . .

I

Our Nation was founded on the principle that "all Men are created equal." Yet candor requires acknowledgment that the Framers of our Constitution, to forge the 13 Colonies into one Nation, openly compromised this principle of equality with its antithesis: slavery. The consequences of this compromise are well known and have aptly been called our "American Dilemma." Still, it is well to recount how recent the time has been, if it has yet come, when the promise of our principles has flowered into the actuality of equal opportunity for all regardless of race or color.

The Fourteenth Amendment, the embodiment in the Constitution of our abiding belief in human equality, has been the law of our land for only slightly more than half its 200 years. And for half of that half, the Equal Protection Clause of the Amendment was largely moribund. . . .

Against this background, claims that law must be "color-blind" or that the datum of race is no longer relevant to public policy must be seen as aspiration rather than as description of reality. This is not to denigrate aspiration; for reality rebukes us that race has too often been used by those who would stigmatize and oppress minorities. Yet we cannot . . . let color blindness become myopia which masks the reality that many "created equal" have been treated within our lifetimes as inferior both by the law and by their fellow citizens.

. . .

Unquestionably, we have held that a government practice or statute which restricts "fundamental rights" or which contains "suspect classifications" is to be subjected to "strict scrutiny" and can be justified only if it furthers a compelling government purpose and, even then, only if no less restrictive alternative is available. But no fundamental right is involved here. Nor do whites as a class have any of the "traditional indicia of suspectness: the class is not saddled with such disabilities, or subjected to such a history of purposeful unequal treatment, or relegated to such a position of political powerlessness as to command extraordinary protection from the majoritarian political process" (see *United States v. Carolene Products Co.*) . . .

On the other hand, the fact that this case does not fit neatly into our prior analytic framework for race cases does not mean that it should be analyzed by applying the very loose rational-basis standard of review that is the very least that is always applied in equal protection cases. . . . Instead, a number of considerations—developed in gender-discrimination cases but which carry even more force when applied to racial classifications—lead us to conclude that racial classifications designed to further remedial purposes "must serve important governmental objectives and must be substantially related to achievement of those objectives." . . .

Davis' articulated purpose of remedying the effects of past societal discrimination is, under our cases, sufficiently important to justify the use of race-conscious admissions programs where there is a sound basis for concluding that minority underrepresentation is substantial and chronic, and that the handicap of past discrimination is impeding access of minorities to the Medical School. . . .

The "Harvard" program, as those employing it readily concede, openly and successfully employs a racial criterion for the purpose of ensuring that some of the scarce places in institutions of higher education are allocated to disadvantaged minority students. That the Harvard approach does not also make public the extent of the preference and the precise workings of the system while the Davis program employs a specific, openly stated number, does not condemn the latter plan for purposes of Fourteenth Amendment adjudication. It may be that the Harvard plan is more acceptable to the public than is the Davis "quota." If it is, any State, including California, is free to adopt it in preference to a less acceptable alternative, just as it is generally free, as far as the Constitution is concerned, to abjure granting any racial preferences in its admissions program. But there is no basis for preferring a particular preference program simply because in achieving the same goals that the Davis Medical School is pursuing, it proceeds in a manner that is not immediately apparent to the public.

Mr. Justice MARSHALL:

I agree with the judgment of the Court only insofar as it permits a university to consider the race of an applicant in making admissions decisions. I do not agree that petitioner's admissions program violates the Constitution. For it must be remembered that, during most of the past 200 years, the Constitution as interpreted by this Court did not prohibit the most ingenious and pervasive forms of discrimination against the Negro. Now, when a state acts to remedy the effects of that legacy of discrimination, I cannot believe that this same Constitution stands as a barrier.

I

A

Three hundred and fifty years ago, the Negro was dragged to this country in chains to be sold into slavery. Uprooted from his homeland and thrust into bondage for forced labor, the slave was deprived of all legal rights. It was unlawful to teach him to read; he could be sold away from his family and friends at the whim of his master; and killing or maiming him was not a crime. The system of slavery brutalized and dehumanized both master and slave. . . .

The status of the Negro as property was officially erased by his emancipation at the end of the Civil War. But the long-awaited emancipation, while freeing the Negro from slavery, did not bring him citizenship or equality in any meaningful way. Slavery was replaced by a system of "laws which imposed upon the colored race onerous disabilities and burdens, and curtailed their rights in the pursuit of life, liberty, and property to such an extent that their freedom was of little value" (*Slaughter-House Cases*). Despite the passage of the Thirteenth, Fourteenth, and Fifteenth Amendments, the Negro was systematically denied the rights those Amendments were supposed to secure. The combined actions and inactions of the State and Federal Governments maintained Negroes in a position of legal inferiority for another century after the Civil War. . . .

The position of the Negro today in America is the tragic but inevitable consequence of centuries of unequal treatment. Measured by any benchmark of comfort or achievement, meaningful equality remains a distant dream for the Negro.

A Negro child today has a life expectancy which is shorter by more than five years than that of a white child. The Negro child's mother is over three times more likely to die of complications in childbirth, and the infant mortality rate for Negroes is nearly twice that for whites. The median income of the Negro family is only 60% that of the median of a white family, and the percentage of Negroes who live in families with incomes below the poverty line is nearly four times greater than that of whites.

When the Negro child reaches working age, he finds that America offers him significantly less than it offers his white counterpart. For Negro adults, the unemployment rate is twice that of whites, and the unemployment rate for Negro teenagers is nearly three times that of white teenagers. A Negro male who completes four years of college can expect a median annual income of merely $110 more than a white male who has only a high school diploma. Although Negroes represent 11.5% of the population, they are only 1.2% of the lawyers and judges, 2% of the physicians, 2.3% of the dentists, 1.1 % of the engineers and 2.6% of the college and university professors.

The relationship between those figures and the history of unequal treatment afforded to the Negro cannot be denied.

At every point from birth to death the impact of the past is reflected in the still disfavored position of the Negro.

In light of the sorry history of discrimination and its devastating impact on the lives of Negroes, bringing the Negro into the mainstream of American life should be a state interest of the highest order. To fail to do so is to ensure that America will forever remain a divided society. . . .

It is plain that the Fourteenth Amendment was not intended to prohibit measures designed to remedy the effects of the Nation's past treatment of Negroes. The Congress that passed the Fourteenth Amendment is the same Congress that passed the 1866 Freedmen's Bureau Act, an Act that provided many of its benefits only to Negroes (Act of July 16, 1866). Although the Freedmen's Bureau legislation provided aid for refugees, thereby including white persons within some of the relief measures, the bill was regarded, to the dismay of many Congressmen, as "solely and entirely for the freedmen, and to the exclusion of all other persons." Indeed, the bill was bitterly opposed on the ground that it "undertakes to make the negro in some respects . . . superior . . . and gives them favors that the poor white boy in the North cannot get." The bill's supporters defended it—not by rebutting the claim of special treatment—but by pointing to the need for such treatment. . . .

Since the Congress that considered and rejected the objections to the 1866 Freedmen's Bureau Act concerning special relief to Negroes also proposed the Fourteenth Amendment, it is inconceivable that the Fourteenth Amendment was intended to prohibit all race-conscious relief measures. . . .

While I applaud the judgment of the Court that a university may consider race in its admissions process, it is more than a little ironic that, after several hundred years of class-based discrimination against Negroes, the Court is unwilling to hold that a class-based remedy for that discrimination is permissible. In declining to so hold, today's judgment ignores the fact that for several hundred years Negroes have been discriminated against, not as individuals, but rather solely because of the color of their skins. It is unnecessary in 20th-century America to have individual Negroes demonstrate that they have been victims of racial discrimination;

the racism of our society has been so pervasive that none, regardless of wealth or position, has managed to escape its impact. The experience of Negroes in America has been different in kind, not just in degree, from that of other ethnic groups. It is not merely the history of slavery alone but also that a whole people were marked as inferior by the law. And that mark has endured. The dream of America as the great melting pot has not been realized for the Negro; because of his skin color he never even made it into the pot. . . .

I fear that we have come full circle. After the Civil War our Government started several "affirmative action" programs. This Court in the *Civil Rights Cases* and *Plessy v. Ferguson* destroyed the movement toward complete equality. For almost a century no action was taken, and this nonaction was with the tacit approval of the courts. Then we had *Brown v. Board of Education* and the Civil Rights Acts of Congress, followed by numerous affirmative-action programs. Now, we have this Court again stepping in, this time to stop affirmative-action programs of the type used by the University of California.

Source: *Regents of the University of California v. Bakke*, 438 U.S. 265 (1978).

See also: Affirmative Action; *Berea College v. Kentucky*; College Admissions, Discrimination in; Education; Ethnic Retention and School Performance; UC Berkeley Bake Sale

Summary of the Immigration Reform and Control Act (Simpson-Mazzoli Act) (1986)

Introduction

The 1965 Immigration and Nationality Act was a defeat for nativists committed to the ideals of National Origins, strict quotas for immigrants from—according to restrictionists—the least desirable nationalities. It kept "Third World" immigrants, with the exception of Latin Americans, out of the country. But the act was only a partial loss for nativists because, for the first time, Latin Americans immigrants were put on a quota. As nonwhite immigrants poured into the country beginning in

the 1970s, nativists sent up an alarm and pressured politicos to pass anti-immigration laws. The most obvious immigrant was the Mexican whose undocumented immigration accelerated in the 1970s. By the mid-1980s the nativists gathered momentum as right-wing think tanks married this issue with campaigns against bilingual education, English only, and affirmative action. These nativist forces made immigration restriction a political wedge issue. In Congress, legislators such as Alan Simpson from Wyoming and Peter Rodino of New Jersey sponsored nativist bills in their respective chambers. In 1986, Romano Mazzoli of Kentucky had replaced Rodino in the House of Representatives as cosponsor, and the Simpson-Mazzoli Act, also known as the Immigration Reform and Control Act (IRCA), passed amendments to the Immigration and Nationality Act of 1952. Anti-immigrant forces won: those knowingly employing undocumented workers would face financial and other penalties, and additional funds would be used for border patrol. The law also provided amnesty for undocumented residents who had been in the country for a certain period of time. The following are excerpts from that important law that gave documents to 2.7 million immigrants.

Primary Source

SUMMARY AS OF:

10/14/1986—Conference report filed in House. (There are 4 other summaries)

(Conference report filed in House, H. Rept. 99–1000)

IMMIGRATION REFORM AND CONTROL ACT OF 1986

Title I: Control of Illegal Immigration—Part A: Employment—Amends the Immigration and Nationality Act to make it unlawful for a person or other entity to: (1) hire (including through subcontractors), recruit, or refer for a fee for U.S. employment any alien knowing that such person is unauthorized to work, or any person without verifying his or her work status; or (2) continue to employ an alien knowing of such person's unauthorized work status.

Makes verification compliance (including the use of State employment agency documentation) an affirmative defense to any hiring or referral violation.

Establishes an employment verification system. Requires: (1) the employer to attest, on a form developed by the Attorney General, that the employee's work status has been verified by examination of a passport, birth certificate, social security card, alien documentation papers, or other proof; (2) the worker to similarly attest that he or she is a U.S. citizen or national, or authorized alien; and (3) the employer to keep such records for three years in the case of referral or recruitment, or the later of three years or one year after employment termination in the case of hiring.

States that nothing in this Act shall be construed to authorize a national identity card or system.

Directs the President to monitor and evaluate the verification system and implement changes as necessary within 60 days after notifying the appropriate congressional committees (within two years for a major change). Prohibits implementation of a major change unless the Congress provides funds for such purpose. Authorizes related demonstration projects of up to three years.

Limits the use of such verification system or any required identification document to enforcing this Act and not for other law enforcement purposes.

Directs the Attorney General to establish complaint and investigation procedures which shall provide for: (1) individuals and entities to file written, signed complaints regarding potential hiring violations; (2) INS investigations of complaints with substantial probability of validity; (3) Department of Justice–initiated investigations; and (4) designation of a specific INS unit to prosecute such violations.

Sets forth employer sanction provisions. Provides for a six-month period of public education during which no employment violation penalties shall be imposed.

Provides for a subsequent 12-month period during which violators shall be issued warning citations. Defers enforcement for seasonal agricultural services.

Provides, at the end of such citation period, for graduated first- and subsequent-offense civil penalties, injunctive

remedies, or criminal penalties (for pattern of practice violations). Subjects violators to graduated civil penalties for related paperwork violations.

Directs the Attorney General to provide notice and, upon request, an administrative hearing in the case of a disputed penalty. States that: (1) judicial review of a final administrative penalty shall be in the U.S. court of appeals; and (2) suits to collect unpaid penalties shall be filed in U.S. district courts.

Makes it unlawful for an employer to require an employee to provide any type of financial guarantee or indemnity against any potential employment liability. Subjects violators, after notice and hearing opportunity, to a civil penalty for each violation and the return of any such amounts received.

States that such employer sanction provisions preempt State and local laws.

Requires the General Accounting Office (GAO) to submit to the Congress and to a specially created task force three annual reports regarding the operation of the employer sanction program, including a determination of whether a pattern of national origin discrimination has resulted. States that if the GAO report makes such a determination: (1) the task force shall so report to the Congress; and (2) the House and the Senate shall hold hearings within 60 days.

Terminates employer sanctions 30 days after receipt of the last GAO report if: (1) GAO finds a widespread pattern of discrimination has resulted from the employer sanctions; and (2) the Congress enacts a joint resolution within such 30-day period approving such findings.

Amends the Migrant and Seasonal Agricultural Worker Protection Act to subject farm labor contractors to the requirements of this Act, beginning seven months after enactment.

Directs the Attorney General, in consultation with the Secretary of Labor and the Secretary of Health and Human Services, to conduct a study of the use of a telephone system to verify the employment status of job applicants. Requires related congressional reports.

Directs the Comptroller General to: (1) investigate ways to reduce counterfeiting of social security account number cards; and (2) report to the appropriate congressional committees within one year.

Directs the Secretary of Health and Human Services, acting through the Social Security Administration and in cooperation with the Attorney General and the Secretary of Labor, to: (1) conduct a study of the feasibility of establishing a social security number validation system; and (2) report to the appropriate congressional committees within two years.

Makes it an unfair immigration-related employment practice for an employer of three or more persons to discriminate against any individual (other than an unauthorized alien) with respect to hiring, recruitment, firing, or referral for fee, because of such individual's origin or citizenship (or intended citizenship) status. States that it is not an unfair immigration-related employment practice to hire a U.S. citizen or national over an equally qualified alien.

Requires that complaints of violations of an immigration-related employment practice be filed with the Special Counsel for Immigration-Related Unfair Employment Practices (established by this Act) within the Department of Justice. Prohibits the overlap of immigration-related discrimination complaints and discrimination complaints filed with the Equal Employment Opportunity Commission.

Authorizes the Special Counsel to: (1) investigate complaints and determine (within 120 days) whether to bring such complaints before a specially trained administrative law judge; and (2) initiate investigations and complaints. Permits private actions if the Special Counsel does not file a complaint within such 120-day period. Sets forth related administrative provisions.

Makes it illegal to fraudulently misuse or manufacture entry or work documents.

Part B: Improvement of Enforcement and Services—States that essential elements of the immigration control and reform program established by this Act are increased enforcement and administrative activities of the Border Patrol, the Immigration and Naturalization Service (INS), and other appropriate Federal agencies.

Authorizes increased FY [fiscal year] 1987 and 1988 appropriations for: (1) INS; and (2) the Executive Office of Immigration Review. Obligates increased funding in FY 1987 and 1988 for the border patrol.

Directs the Attorney General, from funds appropriated to the Department of Justice for INS, to provide for improved immigration and naturalization services and for enhanced community outreach and in-service personnel training.

Authorizes additional appropriations for wage and hour enforcement.

Revises the criminal penalties for the unlawful transportation of unauthorized aliens into the United States.

Authorizes a $35,000,000 immigration emergency fund to be established in the Treasury for necessary enforcement activities and related State and local reimbursements.

Permits the owner or operator of a railroad line, international bridge, or toll road to request the Attorney General to inspect and approve measures taken to prevent aliens from illegally crossing into the United States. States that such approved measures shall be prima facie evidence of compliance with obligations under such Act to prevent illegal entries.

Expresses the sense of the Congress that the immigration laws of the United States should be vigorously enforced, while taking care to protect the rights and safety of U.S. citizens and aliens.

Requires INS to have an owner's consent or a warrant before entering a farm or outdoor operations to interrogate persons to determine if undocumented aliens are present.

Prohibits the adjustment of status to permanent resident for violators of (nonimmigrant) visa terms.

Title II: Legalization—Directs the Attorney General to adjust to temporary resident status those aliens who: (1) apply within 18 months; (2) establish that they entered the United States before January 1, 1982, and have resided here continuously in an unlawful status (including Cuban/Haitian entrants) since such date; and (3) are otherwise admissible.

Authorizes similar status adjustment for specified aliens who entered legally as nonimmigrants but whose period of authorized stay ended before January 1, 1982. (States that in the case of exchange visitors, the two-year foreign residence requirement must have been met or waived.)

Prohibits the legalization of persons: (1) convicted of a felony or three or more misdemeanors in the United States; or (2) who have taken part in political, religious, or racial persecution. Requires an alien applying for temporary resident status to register under the Military Selective Service Act, if such Act so requires.

Directs the Attorney General to adjust the status of temporary resident aliens to permanent resident if the alien: (1) applies during the one-year period beginning with the 19th month following the grant of temporary resident status; (2) has established continuous residence in the United States since the grant of temporary resident status; (3) is otherwise admissible and has not been convicted of a felony or three or more misdemeanors committed in the United States; and (4) either meets the minimum requirements for an understanding of English and a knowledge of American history and government, or demonstrates the satisfactory pursuit of a course of study in these subjects. (Authorizes an exemption from such language and history requirement for individuals 65 years of age or older.)

Specifies circumstances in which the Attorney General may terminate an alien's temporary resident status. Permits travel abroad and employment during such period.

Authorizes the filing of status adjustment applications with the Attorney General or designated voluntary or governmental agencies. Directs the Attorney General to work with such agencies to: (1) disseminate program information; and (2) process aliens. Provides for the confidential treatment of application records. Establishes criminal penalties (fines, imprisonment, or both) for: (1) violations of such confidentiality; and (2) false application statements. Provides for application fees.

Waives numerical limitations, labor certification, and other specified entry violations for such aliens. Permits the Attorney General to waive other grounds for exclusion (except criminal, most drug-related, and security grounds) to assure family unity or when otherwise in the national interest.

Requires the Attorney General to provide an alien otherwise eligible but unregistered who is apprehended before the end of the application period, an opportunity to apply for the legalization program before deportation or exclusion proceedings are begun. States that such alien shall be authorized to work in the United States pending disposition of the case.

Provides for administrative and judicial review of a determination respecting an application for adjustment of status under this Act.

Makes legalized aliens (other than Cuban/Haitian entrants) ineligible for Federal financial assistance, Medicaid (with certain exceptions), or food stamps for five years following a grant of temporary resident status and for five years following a grant of permanent resident status (permits aid to the aged, blind, or disabled). States that programs authorized under the National School Lunch Act, the Child Nutrition Act of 1966, the Vocational Education Act of 1963, chapter 1 of the Education Consolidation and Improvement Act of 1981, the Headstart-Follow Through Act, the Job Training Partnership Act, title IV of the Higher Education Act of 1965, the Public Health Service Act, and titles V, XVI, and XX of the Social Security Act shall not be construed as prohibited assistance. Continues assistance to aliens under the Refugee Education Assistance Act of 1980 without regard to adjustment of status.

Requires the Attorney General to disseminate information regarding the legalization program.

Establishes procedures for the status adjustment to permanent resident of certain Cuban and Haitian entrants who arrived in the United States before January 1, 1982.

Updates from June 30, 1948, to January 1, 1972, the registry date for permanent entry admissions records.

Authorizes FY 1988 through 1991 appropriations for State legalization impact assistance grants. Permits States to spend unused funds through FY 1994. Prohibits offsets for Medicaid and supplemental security income costs. Bases State amounts on the number of legalized aliens and related expenditures. Permits States to use such funds to reimburse public assistance, health, and education costs. Limits reimbursement to actual costs.

Title III: Reform of Legal Immigration—Part A: Temporary Agricultural Workers—Separates temporary agricultural labor from other temporary labor for purposes of nonimmigrant (H-2A visa) worker provisions.

Requires an employer H-2A visa petition to certify that: (1) there are not enough local U.S. workers for the job; and (2) similarly employed U.S. workers' wages and working conditions will not be adversely affected. Authorizes the Secretary of Labor to charge application fees.

Prohibits the Secretary from approving such petition if: (1) the job is open because of a strike or lock-out; (2) the employer violated temporary worker admissions terms; (3) in a case where such workers are not covered by State workers' compensation laws, the employer has not provided equivalent protection at no cost to such workers; or (4) the employer has not made regional recruitment efforts in the traditional or expected labor supply.

Provides with regard to agricultural worker applications that: (1) the Secretary may not require such an application to be filed more than 60 days before needed; (2) the employer shall be notified in writing within seven days if the application requires perfecting; (3) the Secretary shall approve an acceptable application not later than 20 days before needed; and (4) the employer shall provide or secure housing meeting appropriate Federal, State, or local standards, including making provision for family housing for employees principally engaged in the range production of livestock.

Provides that for three years, labor certifications for specified employers shall require such an employer to hire qualified U.S. workers who apply until the end of 50 percent of the H-2A workers' contract work period. Requires the Secretary, six months before the end of such period, to consider the advisability of continuing such requirement and to issue regulations (in the absence of enacting legislation) three months before the end of such period.

States that employers shall not be liable for specified employment penalties if H-2A workers are dismissed in order to meet such 50 percent requirement.

Permits agricultural producer associations to file H-2A petitions.

Provides for expedited administrative appeals of denied certifications.

Prohibits the entry of an alien as an H-2A worker if he or she has violated a term of admission within the previous five years.

Authorizes permanent appropriations beginning with FY 1987 for the purposes of: (1) recruiting domestic workers for temporary labor and services which might otherwise be performed by nonimmigrants and agricultural transition workers; and (2) monitoring terms and conditions under which such individuals are employed.

Authorizes permanent appropriations beginning in FY 1987 to enable the Secretary to make determinations and certifications.

Expresses the sense of the Congress that the President should establish an advisory commission to consult with Mexico and other appropriate countries and advise the Attorney General regarding the temporary worker program.

Establishes a special agricultural worker adjustment program. Provides for permanent resident adjustment for aliens who: (1) apply during a specified 18-month period; (2) have performed at least 90 man-days of seasonal agricultural work during the 12-month period ending May 1, 1986; and (3) are admissible as immigrants. Sets forth adjustment dates based upon periods of work performed in the United States. Authorizes travel and employment during such temporary residence period.

Authorizes applications to be made inside the United States with the Attorney General or designated entities and outside the United States through consular offices. Provides for confidentiality and limited access to such information. Establishes criminal penalties for false application information, and makes an alien so convicted inadmissible for U.S. entry.

Exempts such admissions from numerical entry limitations.

Permits waiver of exclusion (except for specified criminal, drug offense, public charge, Nazi persecution, and national security grounds) for humanitarian or family purposes, or when in the national interest.

Provides for a temporary stay of exclusion or deportation (and authority to work) for apprehended aliens who are able to establish a nonfrivolous claim for status adjustment.

Provides for a single level of administrative appellate review of such status adjustment applications. Limits such review of the order of exclusion or deportation.

Defines "seasonal agricultural services" as the performance of fieldwork related to growing fruits and vegetables of every kind and other perishable commodities as defined in regulations by the Secretary of Agriculture.

Directs the Secretaries of Agriculture and of Labor, jointly before each fiscal year (beginning in FY 1990 and ending in FY 1993) to determine whether additional special agricultural workers should be admitted because of a shortage of such workers in the United States. Sets forth factors to be considered in making such determinations.

Authorizes associations and groups of employers to request additional admissions due to emergency or unforeseen circumstances. Authorizes groups of special agricultural workers to request decreased admissions due to worker oversupply. Requires the Secretaries to make request determinations within 21 days.

Sets forth numerical limitations for such admissions beginning with FY 1990.

Provides for the deportation of newly admitted special agricultural workers who do not perform 60 man-days of seasonal agricultural work in each of the first two years after entry. Prohibits naturalization of such workers unless they have performed 60 man-days of such work in each of five fiscal years.

Treats temporary agricultural workers and special agricultural workers as "eligible legalized aliens" for purposes of Federal assistance to State and local entities for specified costs associated with such workers during their first five years in the United States.

Establishes a 12-member Commission on Agricultural Workers to review the special agricultural worker provisions, the impact of the legalization and employer sanctions on agricultural labor, and other aspects of agricultural labor. Requires a report to the Congress within five years. Authorizes appropriations. Terminates the Commission at the end of the 63-month period beginning with the month after the month of enactment of this Act.

States that specified agricultural workers shall be eligible for legal assistance under the Legal Service Corporation Act.

Part B: Other Changes in the Immigration Law—Increases the annual colonial quota from 600 visas to 5,000 visas.

Includes within the definition of "special immigrant": (1) unmarried sons and daughters and surviving spouses of employees of certain international organizations; and (2) specified retirees of such organizations ("I" status) and their spouses.

Grants nonimmigrant status to: (1) parents of children receiving "I" status while they are minors; and (2) other children of such parents or a surviving "I" status spouse.

Authorizes the three-year pilot visa waiver program for up to eight countries providing similar benefits to U.S. visitors.

Requires such visitors to the United States to: (1) have a nonrefundable roundtrip ticket; and (2) stay in the United States for not more than 90 days.

Authorizes an additional 5,000 nonpreference visas in each of FY 1987 and 1988 with preference being given to nationals of countries who were adversely affected by Public Law 89–236 (1965 immigration amendments).

Includes the relationship between an illegitimate child and its natural father within the definition of "child" for purposes of status, benefits, or privilege under such Act.

States that for suspension of deportation purposes, an alien shall not be considered to have failed to maintain continuous physical presence in the United States if the absence did not meaningfully interrupt the continuous physical presence.

Prohibits for one year the admission of nonimmigrant alien crew members to perform services during a strike against the employer for whom such aliens intend to work.

Title IV: Reports—Directs the President to transmit to the Congress: (1) not later than January 1, 1989, and not later than January 1 of every third year thereafter, a comprehensive immigration-impact report; and (2) annual reports for three years on unauthorized alien employment and the temporary agricultural worker (H-2A) program.

Directs the Attorney General and the Secretary of State to jointly monitor the visa waiver program established by this Act, and report to the Congress within two years.

Directs the President to submit to the Congress an initial and a second report (three years after the first report) on the impact of the legalization program.

Directs the Attorney General to report to the Congress within 90 days regarding necessary improvements for INS.

Expresses the sense of the Congress that the President should consult with the President of Mexico within 90 days regarding the implementation of this Act and its possible effect on the United States or Mexico.

Title V: State Assistance for Incarceration Costs of Illegal Aliens and Certain Cuban Nationals—Directs the Attorney General to reimburse States for the costs incurred in incarcerating certain illegal aliens and Cuban nationals convicted of felonies. Authorizes appropriations.

Title VI: Commission for the Study of International Migration and Cooperative Economic Development—Establishes a 12-member Commission for the Study of International Migration and Cooperative Economic Development to examine, in consultation with Mexico and other Western Hemisphere sending countries, conditions which contribute to unauthorized migration to the United States and trade and investment programs to alleviate such conditions. Requires a report to the President and to the Congress within three years. Terminates the Commission upon filing of such report, except that the Commission may function for up to 30 additional days to conclude its affairs.

Title VII: Federal Responsibility for Deportable and Excludable Aliens Convicted of Crimes—Provides for the expeditious deportation of aliens convicted of crimes.

Provides for the identification of Department of Defense facilities that could be made available to incarcerate deportable or excludable aliens.

Source: The Immigration Reform and Control Act (Simpson-Mazzoli Act), Pub.L. 99–603, 100 Stat. 3359.

See also: 287g; Anchor Baby; Anti-immigrant Sentiment; Immigration Act of 1965; Immigration and Customs Enforcement; National Origin Immigration Act of 1924; Operation Wetback; Proposition 187; Unauthorized Immigration; Undocumented Immigrants; United States Border Patrol

California v. Cabazon Band of Mission Indians (1987)

Introduction

In this case, the U.S. Supreme Court upheld the right of Native Americans on reservations to conduct gambling free of state control, despite the fact that California claims civil

and criminal jurisdiction under Public Law 280. In California, according to a number of court rulings, state criminal jurisdiction is concurrent with that of Native American governments. This case arose after California asserted a right to regulate gambling (including card games and bingo) on the reservations of the Cabazon and Morongo bands of Mission Indians.

Primary Source

Justice White (for the Court):

The Cabazon and Morongo Bands of Mission Indians, federally recognized Indian Tribes, occupy reservations in Riverside County, California. [Footnote 1. . . . The Cabazon Band has 25 enrolled members and the Morongo Band . . . approximately 730. . . . Each Band, pursuant to an ordinance approved by the [U.S.] Secretary of the Interior, conducts bingo games on its reservation. The Cabazon Band has also opened a card club at which draw poker and other card games are played. The games are open to the public and are played predominantly by non-Indians coming onto the reservations. The games are a major source of employment for tribal members, and the profits are the Tribes' sole source of income. The State of California seeks to apply to the two Tribes [a California Penal Code provision that] . . . does not entirely prohibit the playing of bingo but permits it [only] when the games are operated and staffed by members of designated charitable organizations who may not be paid for their services. Profits must be kept in special accounts and used only for charitable purposes; prizes may not exceed $250 per game. Asserting that the bingo games on the two reservations violated each of these restrictions, California insisted that the Tribes comply with state law. Riverside County also sought to apply its local [o]rdinance . . . regulating bingo, as well as its [o]rdinance . . . prohibiting the playing of draw poker and the other card games. . . .

[The Ninth Circuit U.S. Court of Appeals], applying what it thought to be the civil/criminal dichotomy [of] Bryan[,] . . . [has drawn] a distinction between state "criminal/prohibitory" laws and state "civil/regulatory" laws: [I]f the intent of a state law is generally to prohibit certain conduct, it falls within Public Law 280's grant of criminal jurisdiction, but if

the state law generally permits the conduct at issue, subject to regulation, it must be classified as civil/regulatory and Public Law 280 does not authorize its enforcement on an Indian reservation. The shorthand test is whether the conduct at issue violates the State's public policy. Inquiring into the nature of [the California bingo statute], the Court of Appeals held that it was regulatory rather than prohibitory. . . .

We are persuaded that the prohibitory/regulatory distinction is consistent with Bryan's construction of Public Law 280. It is not a bright-line rule [and] . . . an argument of some weight may be made that the bingo statute is prohibitory rather than regulatory. But . . . we are reluctant to disagree with [the Court of Appeals'] view of the nature and intent of the state law at issue here. . . .

This case . . . involves a state burden on tribal Indians in the context of their dealings with non-Indians since the question is whether the State may prevent the Tribes from making available high stakes bingo games to non-Indians coming from outside the reservations. . . . [S]tate authority . . . "is preempted . . . if it interferes . . . with federal and tribal interests reflected in federal law, unless the state interests at stake are sufficient to justify the assertion of state authority." [*New Mexico v. Mescalero Apache Tribe* 1983, 333–334] The inquiry is to proceed in light of traditional notions of Indian sovereignty and the congressional goal of Indian self-government, including its "overriding goal" of encouraging tribal self-sufficiency and economic development. [*Mescalero* 1983, 334–335]

These are important federal interests. They were reaffirmed by [President Ronald Reagan's] 1983 Statement on Indian Policy. More specifically, the Department of the Interior, which has the primary responsibility for carrying out the Federal Government's trust obligations to Indian tribes, [and also the Department of Health and Human Services and the Department of Housing and Urban Development,] ha[ve] sought to implement these policies by promoting tribal bingo enterprises. . . .

These policies and actions, which demonstrate the Government's approval and active promotion of tribal bingo enterprises, are of particular relevance in this case. The Cabazon and Morongo Reservations contain no natural resources which can be exploited. The tribal games at present provide the sole source of revenues for the operation of the tribal governments and the provision of tribal services. They are also the major sources of employment on the reservations. Self-determination and economic development are not within reach if the Tribes cannot raise revenues and provide employment for their members. The Tribes' interests obviously parallel the federal interests. . . .

The [other] interest asserted by the State to justify the imposition of its bingo laws on the Tribes is in preventing the infiltration of the tribal games by organized crime. To the extent that the State seeks to prevent any and all bingo games from being played on tribal lands while permitting regulated, off-reservation games, this asserted interest is irrelevant. . . . The State insists that the high stakes offered at tribal games are attractive to organized crime, whereas the controlled games authorized under California law are not. This is surely a legitimate concern, but we are unconvinced that it is sufficient. . . . California does not allege any present criminal involvement in the Cabazon and Morongo enterprises. . . . [F]ar from any action being taken [by the Federal Government] evidencing this concern[,]. . . the prevailing federal policy continues to support these tribal enterprises, including those of the Tribes involved in this case.

We conclude that the State's interest in preventing the infiltration of the tribal bingo enterprises by organized crime does not justify state regulation of [those] enterprises in light of the compelling federal and tribal interests supporting them.

Source: *California v. Cabazon Band of Mission Indians.* 480 U.S. 202 (1987).

See also: Indian Reservations; Reservations and Casinos

Native American Graves Protection and Repatriation Act (1990)

Introduction

Approved by Congress on November 16, 1990, this act seeks to protect long-neglected Native American burial sites and encourage the return of Native American artifacts to their originating tribes.

Primary Source

An Act to provide for the protection of Native American graves, and for other purposes.

Be it enacted by the Senate and the House of Representatives of the United States of America in Congress assembled,

Section 1. Short Title.

This Act may be cited as the "Native American Graves Protection and Repatriation Act."

Section 2. Definitions.

For purposes of this Act, the term—

(1) "burial site" means any natural or prepared physical location, whether originally below, on, or above the surface of the earth, into which as a part of the death rite or ceremony of a culture, individual human remains are deposited.

(2) "cultural affiliation" means that there is a relationship of shared group identity which can be reasonably traced historically or prehistorically between a present day Indian tribe or Native Hawaiian organization and an identifiable earlier group.

(3) "cultural items" means human remains and—

(A) "associated funerary objects" which shall mean objects that, as a part of the death rite or ceremony of a culture, are reasonably believed to have been placed with individual human remains either at the time of death or later, and both the human remains and associated funerary objects are presently in the possession or control of a Federal agency or museum, except that other items exclusively made for burial purposes or to contain human remains shall be considered as associated funerary objects.

(B) "unassociated funerary objects" which shall mean objects that, as a part of the death rite or ceremony of a culture, are reasonably believed to have been placed with individual human remains either at the time of death or later, where the remains are not in the possession or control of the Federal agency or museum and the objects can be identified by a preponderance of the evidence, as having been removed from a specific burial site of an individual culturally affiliated with a particular Indian tribe.

(C) "sacred objects" which shall mean specific ceremonial objects which are needed by traditional Native American religious leaders for the practice of traditional Native American religions by their present day adherents, and

(D) "cultural patrimony" which shall mean an object having ongoing historical, traditional, or cultural importance central to the Native American group or culture itself, rather than property owned by an individual Native American, and which, therefore, cannot be alienated, appropriated, or conveyed by any individual regardless of whether or not the individual is a member of the Indian tribe or Native Hawaiian organization and such object shall have been considered inalienable by such Native American group at the time the object was separated from such group.

(4) "Federal agency" means any department, agency, or instrumentality of the United States. Such term does not include the Smithsonian Institution.

(5) "Federal lands" means any land other than tribal lands which are controlled or owned by the United States, including lands selected by but not yet conveyed to Alaska Native Corporations and groups organized pursuant to the Alaska Native Claims Settlement Act of 1971.

(6) "Hui Malama I Na Kupuna O Hawai'i Nei" means the nonprofit, Native Hawaiian organizations incorporated under the laws of the States of Hawaii by that name on April 17, 1989, for the purpose of providing guidance and expertise in decisions dealing with Native Hawaiian cultural issues, particularly burial issues.

(7) "Indian tribe" means any tribe, band, nation, or other organized group or community of Indians, including any Alaska Native village (as defined in, or established pursuant to, the Alaska Native Claims Settlement Act), which is recognized as eligible for the special programs and services provided by the United States to Indians because of their status as Indians.

(8) "museum" means any institution or State or local government agency (including any institution of higher learning) that receives Federal funds and has possession of, or control over, Native American cultural items. Such term does not include the Smithsonian Institution or any other Federal agency.

(9) "Native American" means of, or relating to, a tribe, people, or culture that is indigenous to the United States.

(10) "Native Hawaiian" means any individual who is a descendant of the aboriginal people who, prior to 1778, occupied and exercised sovereignty in the area that now constitutes the State of Hawaii.

(11) "Native Hawaiian organization" means any organization which—

(A) serves and represents the interests of Native Hawaiians,

(B) has as a primary and states purpose the provision of services to Native Hawaiians, and

(C) has expertise in Native Hawaiian Affairs, and shall include the Office of Hawaiian Affairs and Hui Malama I Na Kupuna O Hawai'i Nei.

(12) "Office of Hawaiian Affairs" means the Office of Hawaiian Affairs established by the constitution of the State of Hawaii.

(13) "rights of possession" means possession obtained with the voluntary consent of an individual or group that had authority of alienation. The original acquisition of a Native American unassociated funerary object, sacred object or object of cultural patrimony from an Indian tribe or Native Hawaiian organization with the voluntary consent of an

individual or group with authority to alienate such object is deemed to give right of possession of that object, unless the phrase so defined would, as applied in section 7(c), result in a Fifth Amendment taking by the United States as determined by the United States Claims Court pursuant to 28 U.S.C. 1491 in which event the "right of possession" shall be as provided under otherwise applicable property law. The original acquisition of Native American human remains and associated funerary objects which were excavated, exhumed, or otherwise obtained with full knowledge and consent of the next of kin or the official governing body of the appropriate culturally affiliated Indian tribe or Native Hawaiian organization is deemed to give right of possession to those remains.

(14) "Secretary" means the Secretary of the Interior.

(15) "tribal land" means—

(A) all lands within the exterior boundaries of any Indian reservation;

(B) all dependent Indian communities;

(C) any lands administered for the benefit of Native Hawaiians pursuant to the Hawaiian Homes Commission Act, 1920, and section 4 of Public Law 86-3.

Section 3. Ownership.

(a) Native American Human Remains and Objects. The ownership or control of Native American cultural items which are excavated or discovered on Federal or tribal lands after the date of enactment of this Act shall be (with priority given in the order listed)—

(1) in the case of Native American human remains and associated funerary objects, in the lineal descendants of the Native American; or

(2) in any case in which such lineal descendants cannot be ascertained, and in the case of unassociated funerary objects, sacred objects, and objects of cultural patrimony—

(A) in the Indian tribe or Native Hawaiian organization on whose tribal land such objects or remains were discovered;

(B) in the Indian tribe or Native Hawaiian organization which has the closest cultural affiliation with such remains or objects and which, upon notice, states a claim for such remains or objects; or

(C) if the cultural affiliation of the objects cannot be reasonably ascertained and if the objects were discovered on Federal land that is recognized by a final judgment of the Indian Claims Commission or the United States Court of Claims as the aboriginal land of some Indian tribe—

(1) in the Indian tribe that is recognized as aboriginally occupying the area in which the objects were discovered, if upon notice, such tribe states a claim for such remains or objects, or

(2) if it can be shown by a preponderance of the evidence that a different tribe has a stronger cultural relationship with the remains or objects than the tribe or organization specified in paragraph (1), in the Indian tribe that has the strongest demonstrated relationship, if upon notice, such tribe states a claim for such remains or objects.

(b) Unclaimed Native American Human Remains and Objects. Native American cultural items not claimed under subsection (a) shall be disposed of in accordance with regulations promulgated by the Secretary in consultation with the review committee established under section 8, Native American groups, representatives of museums and the scientific community.

(c) Intentional Excavation and Removal of Native American Human Remains and Objects. The intentional removal from or excavation of Native American cultural items from Federal or tribal lands for purposes of discovery, study, or removal of such items is permitted only if—

(1) such items are excavated or removed pursuant to a permit issued under section 4 of the Archaeological Resources

Protection Act of 1979 (93 Stat. 721; 16 U.S.C. 470aa et seq.) which shall be consistent with this Act;

(2) such items are excavated or removed after consultation with or, in the case of tribal lands, consent of the appropriate (if any) Indian tribe or Native Hawaiian organization;

(3) the ownership and right of control of the disposition of such items shall be as provided in subsections (a) and (b); and

(4) proof of consultation or consent under paragraph (2) is shown.

(d) Inadvertent Discovery of Native American Remains and Objects.

(1) Any person who knows, or has reason to know, that such person has discovered Native American cultural items on Federal or tribal lands after the date of enactment of this Act shall notify, in writing, the Secretary of the Department, or head of any other agency or instrumentality of the United States, having primary management authority with respect to Federal lands and the appropriate Indian tribe or Native Hawaiian organization with respect to tribal lands, if known or readily ascertainable, and, in the case of lands that have been selected by an Alaska Native Corporation or group organized pursuant to the Alaska Native Claims Settlement Act of 1971, the appropriate corporation or group. If the discovery occurred in connection with an activity, including (but not limited to) construction, mining, logging, and agriculture, the person shall cease the activity in the area of the discovery, make a reasonable effort to protect the items discovered before resuming such activity, and provide notice under this subsection. Following the notification under this subsection, and upon certification by the Secretary of the department or the head of any agency or instrumentality of the United States or the appropriate Indian tribe or Native Hawaiian organization that notification has been received, the activity may resume after 30 days of such certification.

(2) The disposition of and control over any cultural items excavated or removed under this subsection shall be determined as provided for in this section.

(3) If the Secretary of the Interior consents, the responsibilities (in whole or in part) under paragraphs (1) and (2) of the Secretary of any department (other than the Department of the Interior) or the head of any other agency or instrumentality may be delegated to the Secretary with respect to any land managed by such other Secretary or agency head.

(e) Relinquishment. Nothing in this section shall prevent the governing body of an Indian tribe or Native Hawaiian organization from expressly relinquishing control over any Native American human remains, or title to or control over any funerary object, or sacred object.

Section 4. Illegal Trafficking.

(a) Illegal Trafficking. Chapter 53 of title 18, United States Code, is amended by adding at the end thereof the following new section:

"Section 1170. Illegal Trafficking in Native American Human Remains and Cultural Items

"(a) Whoever knowingly sells, purchases, uses for profit, or transports for sale or profit, the human remains of a Native American without the right of possession to those remains as provided in the Native American Graves Protection and Repatriation Act shall be fined in accordance with this title, or imprisoned not more than 12 months, or both, and in the case of a second or subsequent violation, be fined in accordance with this title, or imprisoned not more than 5 years, or both.

"(b) Whoever knowingly sells, purchases, uses for profit, or transports for sale or profit any Native American cultural items obtained in violation of the Native American Grave Protection and Repatriation Act shall be fined in accordance with this title, imprisoned not more than one year. or both, and in the case of a second or subsequent violation. be fined in accordance with this title, imprisoned not more than 5 years, or both."

(b) Table of Contents. The table of contents for chapter 53 of title 18, United States Code, is amended by adding at the end thereof the following new item:

"Section 1170. Illegal Trafficking in Native American Human Remains and Cultural Items."

Section 5. Inventory for Human Remains and Associated Funerary Objects.

(a) In General. Each Federal agency and each museum which has possession or control over holdings or collections of Native American human remains and associated funerary objects shall compile an inventory of such items and, to the extent possible based on information possessed by such museum or Federal agency, identify the geographical and cultural affiliation of such item.

(b) Requirements.

(1) The inventories and identifications required under subsection (a) shall be—

(A) completed in consultation with tribal government and Native Hawaiian organization officials and traditional religious leaders;

(B) completed by not later than the date that is 5 years after the date of enactment of this Act, and

(C) made available both during the time they are being conducted and afterward to a review committee established under section 8.

(2) Upon request by an Indian tribe or Native Hawaiian organization which receives or should have received notice, a museum or Federal agency shall supply additional available documentation to supplement the information required by subsection (a) of this section. The term "documentation" means a summary of existing museum or Federal agency records, including inventories or catalogues, relevant studies, or other pertinent data for the limited purpose of determining the geographical origin, cultural affiliation, and basic facts surrounding acquisition and accession of Native American human remains and associated funerary objects subject to this section. Such term does not mean, and this Act shall not be construed to be an authorization for, the initiation of new scientific studies of such remains and associated funerary objects or other means of acquiring or preserving additional scientific information from such remains and objects.

(c) Extension of Time for Inventory. Any museum which has made a good faith effort to carry out an inventory and identification under this section, but which has been unable to complete the process, may appeal to the Secretary for an extension of the time requirements set forth in subsection (b)(1)(B). The Secretary may extend such time requirements for any such museum upon a finding of good faith effort. An indication of good faith shall include the development of a plan to carry out the inventory and identification process.

(d) Notification.

(1) If the cultural affiliation of any particular Native American human remains or associated funerary objects is determined pursuant to this section, the Federal agency or museum concerned shall, not later than 6 months after the completion of the inventory, notify the affected Indian tribes or Native Hawaiian organizations.

(2) The notice required by paragraph (1) shall include information—

(A) which identifies each Native American human remains or associated funerary objects and the circumstances surrounding its acquisition:

(B) which lists the human remains or associated funerary objects that are clearly identifiable as to tribal origin; and

(C) which lists the Native American human remains and associated funerary objects that are not clearly identifiable as being culturally affiliated with that Indian tribe or Native Hawaiian organization, but which, given the totality of circumstances surrounding acquisition of the remains or objects, are determined by a reasonable belief to be remains or objects culturally affiliated with the Indian tribe or Native Hawaiian organization.

(3) A copy of each notice provided under paragraph (1) shall be sent to the Secretary who shall publish each notice in the Federal Register.

(e) Inventory. For the purposes of this section, the term 'inventory' means a simple itemized list that summarizes the information called for by this section.

Section 6. Summary For Unassociated Funerary Objects, Sacred Objects, and Cultural Patrimony.

(a) In General. Each Federal agency or museum which has possession or control over holdings or collections of Native American unassociated funerary objects, sacred objects, or objects of cultural patrimony shall provide a written summary of such objects based upon available information held by such agency or museum. The summary shall describe the scope of the collection, kinds of objects included, reference to geographical location, means and period of acquisition and cultural affiliation, where readily ascertainable.

(b) Requirements.

(1) The summary required under subsection (a) shall be—

(A) in lieu of an object-by-object inventory;

(B) followed by consultation with tribal government and Native Hawaiian organization officials and traditional religious leaders; and

(C) completed by not later than the date that is 3 years after the date of enactment of this Act.

(2) Upon request, Indian Tribes and Native Hawaiian organizations shall have access to records, catalogues, relevant studies or other pertinent data for the limited purposes of determining the geographic origin, cultural affiliation, and basic facts surrounding acquisition and accession of Native American objects subject to this section. Such information shall be provided in a reasonable manner to be agreed upon by all parties.

Section 7. Repatriation.

(a) Repatriation of Native American Human Remains and Objects Possessed or Controlled by Federal Agencies and Museums.

(1) If, pursuant to section 5, the cultural affiliation of Native American human remains and associated funerary objects with a particular Indian tribe or Native Hawaiian organization is established, then the Federal agency or museum. upon the request of a known lineal descendant of the Native American or of the tribe or organization and pursuant to subsections (b) and (e) of this section, shall expeditiously return such remains and associated funerary objects.

(2) If, pursuant to section 6, the cultural affiliation with a particular Indian tribe or Native Hawaiian organization is shown with respect to unassociated funerary objects, sacred objects or objects of cultural patrimony, then the Federal agency or museum, upon the request of the Indian tribe or Native Hawaiian organization and pursuant to subsections (b), (c) and (e) of this section, shall expeditiously return such objects.

(3) The return of cultural items covered by this Act shall be in consultation with the requesting lineal descendant or tribe or organization to determine the place and manner of delivery of such items.

(4) Where cultural affiliation of Native American human remains and funerary objects has not been established in an inventory prepared pursuant to section 5, or the summary pursuant to section 6, or where Native American human remains and funerary objects are not included upon any such inventory, then, upon request and pursuant to subsections (b) and (e) and, in the case of unassociated funerary objects, subsection (c), such Native American human remains and funerary objects shall be expeditiously returned where the requesting Indian tribe or Native Hawaiian organization can show cultural affiliation by a preponderance of the evidence based upon geographical, kinship, biological, archaeological, anthropological, linguistic, folkloric, oral traditional, historical, or other relevant information or expert opinion.

(5) Upon request and pursuant to subsections (b), (c) and (e), sacred objects and objects of cultural patrimony shall be expeditiously returned where—

(A) the requesting party is the direct lineal descendant of an individual who owned the sacred object;

(B) the requesting Indian tribe or Native Hawaiian organization can show that the object was owned or controlled by the tribe or organization; or

(C) the requesting Indian tribe or Native Hawaiian organization can show that the sacred object was owned or controlled by a member thereof, provided that in the case where a sacred object was owned by a member thereof, there are no identifiable lineal descendants of said member or the lineal descendants, upon notice, have failed to make a claim for the object under this Act.

(b) Scientific Study. If the lineal descendant, Indian tribe, or Native Hawaiian organization requests the return of culturally affiliated Native American cultural items, the Federal agency or museum shall expeditiously return such items unless such items are indispensable for completion of a specific scientific study, the outcome of which would be of major benefit to the United States. Such items shall be returned by no later than 90 days after the date on which the scientific study is completed.

(c) Standard of Repatriation. If a known lineal descendant or an Indian tribe or Native Hawaiian organization requests the return of Native American unassociated funerary objects, sacred objects or objects of cultural patrimony pursuant to this Act and presents evidence which, if standing alone before the introduction of evidence to the contrary, would support a finding that the Federal agency or museum did not have the right of possession, then such agency or museum shall return such objects unless it can overcome such inference and prove that it has a right of possession to the objects.

(d) Sharing of Information by Federal Agencies and Museums. Any Federal agency or museum shall share what information it does possess regarding the object in question with the known lineal descendant, Indian tribe, or Native Hawaiian organization to assist in making a claim under this section,

(e) Competing Claims. Where there are multiple requests for repatriation of any cultural item and, after complying with the requirements of this Act, the Federal agency or museum cannot clearly determine which requesting party is the most appropriate claimant, the agency or museum may retain such item until the requesting parties agree upon its disposition or the dispute is otherwise resolved pursuant to the provisions of this Act or by a court of competent jurisdiction.

(f) Museum Obligation. Any museum which repatriates any item in good faith pursuant to this Act shall not be liable for claims by an aggrieved party or for claims of breach of fiduciary duty, public trust, or violations of state law that are inconsistent with the provisions of this Act.

Section 8. Review Committee.

(a) Establishment. Within 120 days after the date of enactment of this Act the Secretary shall establish a committee to monitor and review the implementation of the inventory and identification process and repatriation activities required under sections 5, 6 and 7.

(b) Membership.

(1) The Committee established under subsection (a) shall be composed of 7 members,

(A) 3 of whom shall be appointed by the Secretary from nominations submitted by Indian tribes, Native Hawaiian organizations, and traditional Native American religious leaders with at least 2 of such persons being traditional Indian religious leaders;

(B) 3 of whom shall be appointed by the Secretary from nominations submitted by national museum organizations and scientific organizations; and

(C) 1 who shall be appointed by the Secretary from a list of persons developed and consented to by all of the members appointed pursuant to subparagraphs (A) and (B).

(2) The Secretary may not appoint Federal officers or employees to the committee.

(3) In the event vacancies shall occur, such vacancies shall be filled by the Secretary in the same manner as the

original appointment within 90 days of the occurrence of such vacancy.

(4) Members of the committee established under subsection (a) shall serve without pay, but shall be reimbursed at a rate equal to the daily rate for GS-18 of the General Schedule for each day (including travel time) for which the member is actually engaged in committee business. Each member shall receive travel expenses, including per diem in lieu of subsistence, in accordance with sections 5702 and 5703 of title 5, United States Code.

(c) Responsibilities. The committee established under subsection (a) shall be responsible for—

(1) designating one of the members of the committee as chairman;

(2) monitoring the inventory and identification process conducted under sections 5 and 6 to ensure a fair, objective consideration and assessment of all available relevant information and evidence;

(3) upon the request of any affected party, reviewing and making findings related to—

(A) the identity or cultural affiliation of cultural items, or

(B) the return of such items;

(4) facilitating the resolution of any disputes among Indian tribes, Native Hawaiian organizations, or lineal descendants and Federal agencies or museums relating to the return of such items including convening the parties to the dispute if deemed desirable;

(5) compiling an inventory of culturally unidentifiable human remains that are in the possession or control of each Federal agency and museum and recommending specific actions for developing a process for disposition of such remains;

(6) consulting with Indian tribes and Native Hawaiian organizations and museums on matters within the scope of the work of the committee affecting such tribes or organizations;

(7) consulting with the Secretary in the development of regulations to carry out this Act;

(8) performing such other related functions as the Secretary may assign to the committee; and

(9) making recommendations, if appropriate, regarding future care of cultural items which are to be repatriated.

(d) Any records and findings made by the review committee pursuant to this Act relating to the identity or cultural affiliation of any cultural items and the return of such items may be admissible in any action brought under section 15 of this Act.

(e) Recommendations and Report. The committee shall make the recommendations under paragraph (c)(5) in consultation with Indian tribes and Native Hawaiian organizations and appropriate scientific and museum groups.

(f) Access. The Secretary shall ensure that the committee established under subsection (a) and the members of the committee have reasonable access to Native American cultural items under review and to associated scientific and historical documents.

(g) Duties of Secretary. The Secretary shall—

(1) establish such rules and regulations for the committee as may be necessary, and

(2) provide reasonable administrative and staff support necessary for the deliberations of the committee.

(h) Annual Report. The committee established under subsection (a) shall submit an annual report to the Congress on the progress made, and any barriers encountered, in implementing this section during the previous year.

(i) Termination. The committee established under subsection (a) shall terminate at the end of the 120-day period beginning on the day the Secretary certifies, in a report submitted to Congress, that the work of the committee has been completed.

Section 9. Penalty.

(a) Penalty. Any museum that fails to comply with the requirements of this Act may be assessed a civil penalty by the Secretary of the Interior pursuant to procedures established by the Secretary through regulation. A penalty assessed under this subsection shall be determined on the record after opportunity for an agency hearing. Each violation under this subsection shall be a separate offense.

(b) Amount of Penalty. The amount of a penalty assessed under subsection (a) shall be determined under regulations promulgated pursuant to this Act, taking into account, in addition to other factors—

(1) the archaeological, historical, or commercial value of the item involved:

(2) the damages suffered, both economic and noneconomic, by an aggrieved party, and

(3) the number of violations that have occurred.

(c) Actions to Recover Penalties. If any museum fails to pay Courts, an assessment of a civil penalty pursuant to a final order of the Secretary that has been issued under subsection (a) and not appealed or after a final judgment has been rendered on appeal of such order, the Attorney General may institute a civil action in an appropriate district court of the United States to collect the penalty. In such action, the validity and amount of such penalty shall not be subject to review.

(d) Subpoenas. In hearings held pursuant to subsection (a), subpoenas may be issued for the attendance and testimony of witnesses and the production of relevant papers, books, and documents. Witnesses so summoned shall be paid the same fees and mileage that are paid to witnesses in the courts of the United States.

Section 10. Grants.

(a) Indian Tribes and Native Hawaiian Organizations. The Secretary is authorized to make grants to Indian tribes and Native Hawaiian organizations for the purpose of assisting such tribes and organizations in the repatriation of Native American cultural items.

(b) Museums. The Secretary is authorized to make grants to museums for the purpose of assisting the museums in conducting the inventories and identification required under sections 5 and 6.

Section 11. Savings Provisions.

Nothing in this Act shall be construed to—

(1) limit the authority of any Federal agency or museum to—

(A) return or repatriate Native American cultural items to Indian tribes, Native Hawaiian organizations, or individuals, and

(B) enter into any other agreement with the consent of the culturally affiliated tribe or organization as to the disposition of, or control over, items covered by this Act;

(2) delay actions on repatriation requests that are pending on the date of enactment of this Act;

(3) deny or otherwise affect access to any court;

(4) limit any procedural or substantive right which may otherwise be secured to individuals or Indian tribes or Native Hawaiian organizations; or

(5) limit the application of any State or Federal law pertaining to theft or stolen property.

Section 12. Special Relationship Between Federal Government and Indian Tribes.

This Act reflects the unique relationship between the Federal Government and Indian tribes and Native Hawaiian organizations and should not be construed to establish a precedent with respect to any other individual, organization or foreign government.

Section 13. Regulations.

The Secretary shall promulgate regulations to carry out this Act within 12 months of enactment.

Section 14. Authorization of Appropriations.

There is authorized to be appropriated such sums as may be necessary to carry out this Act.

Section 15. Enforcement.

The United States district courts shall have jurisdiction over any action brought by any person alleging a violation of this Act and shall have the authority to issue such orders as may be necessary to enforce the provisions of this Act.

> **Source:** Native American Graves Protection and Repatriation Act. Public Law 101–601, *U.S. Statutes at Large* 104 (1990): 3048.
>
> **See also:** Cultural Genocide; Indian Reservations; Native Americans, Conquest of

Board of Education v. Dowell (1991)

Introduction

The case of Board of Education v. Dowell *considered the terms under which a school district might be released from a busing order even though the district's schools may have become resegregated through housing patterns. The Supreme Court ruled in the school district's favor, stating that court-ordered busing regulations were not intended to "operate in perpetuity." This ruling had several significant features, as the Court examined whether the school district had made a good faith effort to eradicate segregation, its record in complying with earlier desegregation and busing orders, and whether or not the continuation of such orders were practicable.*

Primary Source

CHIEF JUSTICE REHNQUIST delivered the opinion of the Court.

Petitioner Board of Education of Oklahoma City (Board) sought dissolution of a decree entered by the District Court imposing a school desegregation plan. The District Court granted relief over the objection of respondents Robert L. Dowell, et al., black students and their parents. The Court of Appeals for the Tenth Circuit reversed, holding that the Board would be entitled to such relief only upon "'[n]othing less than a clear showing of grievous wrong evoked by new and unforeseen conditions. . . .'" We hold that the Court of Appeals' test is more stringent than is required either by our cases dealing with injunctions or by the Equal Protection Clause of the Fourteenth Amendment.

I.

This school desegregation litigation began almost 30 years ago. In 1961, respondents, black students and their parents, sued the Board to end *de jure* segregation in the public schools. In 1963, the District Court found that Oklahoma City had intentionally segregated both schools and housing in the past, and that Oklahoma City was operating a "dual" school system—one that was intentionally segregated by race. *Dowell v. School Board of Oklahoma City Public Schools* (WD Okla.). In 1965, the District Court found that the Board's attempt to desegregate by using neighborhood zoning failed to remedy past segregation because residential segregation resulted in one-race schools. Residential segregation had once been state imposed, and it lingered due to discrimination by some realtors and financial institutions. The District Court found that school segregation had caused some housing segregation. In 1972, finding that previous efforts had not been successful at eliminating state imposed segregation, the District Court ordered the Board to adopt the "Finger Plan," under which kindergarteners would be assigned to neighborhood schools unless their parents opted otherwise; children in grades 1–4 would attend formerly all-white schools, and thus black children would be bused to those schools; children in grade five would attend formerly all black schools, and thus white children would be bused to those schools; students in the upper grades would be bused to various areas in order to maintain integrated schools; and in integrated neighborhoods there would be stand-alone schools for all grades.

In 1977, after complying with the desegregation decree for five years, the Board made a "Motion to Close Case." The District Court held in its "Order Terminating Case:"

The Court has concluded that [the Finger Plan] worked, and that substantial compliance with the constitutional requirements has been achieved. The School Board, under the oversight of the Court, has operated the Plan properly, and the Court does not foresee that the termination of its jurisdiction will result in the dismantlement of the Plan or any affirmative action by the defendant to undermine the unitary system so slowly and painfully accomplished over the 16 years during which the cause has been pending before this court. . . .

The School Board, as now constituted, has manifested the desire and intent to follow the law. The court believes that the present members and their successors on the Board will now and in the future continue to follow the constitutional desegregation requirements.

Now sensitized to the constitutional implications of its conduct and with a new awareness of its responsibility citizens of all races, the Board is entitled to pursue in good faith its legitimate policies without the continuing constitutional supervision of this Court. . . .

Jurisdiction in this case is terminated ipso facto, subject only to final disposition of any case now pending on appeal.

This unpublished order was not appealed.

In 1984, the Board faced demographic changes that led to greater burdens on young black children. As more and more neighborhoods became integrated, more stand-alone schools were established, and young black students had to be bused further from their inner-city homes to outlying white areas. In an effort to alleviate this burden and to increase parental involvement, the Board adopted the Student Reassignment Plan (SRP), which relied on neighborhood assignments for students in grades K-4 beginning in the 1985–1986 school year. Busing continued for students in grades 5–12. Any student could transfer from a school where he or she was in the majority to a school where he or she would be in the minority. Faculty and staff integration was retained, and an "equity officer" was appointed.

In 1985, respondents filed a "Motion to Reopen the Case," contending that the school district had not achieved

"unitary" status and that the SRP was a return to segregation. Under the SRP, 11 of 64 elementary schools would be greater than 90% black, 22 would be greater than 90% white plus other minorities, and 31 would be racially mixed. The District Court refused to reopen the case, holding that its 1977 finding of unitariness was res judicata as to those who were then parties to the action, and that the district remained unitary. *Dowell v. Board of Education of Oklahoma City Public Schools* (WD Okla. 1985). The District Court found that the Board, administration, faculty, support staff, and student body were integrated, and transportation, extracurricular activities and facilities within the district were equal and nondiscriminatory. Because unitariness had been achieved, the District Court concluded that court-ordered desegregation must end.

The Court of Appeals for the Tenth Circuit reversed, *Dowell v. Board of Education of Oklahoma City Public Schools* (1986). It held that, while the 1977 order finding the district unitary was binding on the parties, nothing in that order indicated that the 1972 injunction itself was terminated. The court reasoned that the finding that the system was unitary merely ended the District Court's active supervision of the case, and, because the school district was still subject to the desegregation decree, respondents could challenge the SRP. The case was remanded to determine whether the decree should be lifted or modified.

On remand, the District Court found that demographic changes made the Finger Plan unworkable, that the Board had done nothing for 25 years to promote residential segregation, and that the school district had bused students for more than a decade in good-faith compliance with the court's orders. The District Court found that present residential segregation was the result of private decisionmaking and economics, and that it was too attenuated to be a vestige of former school segregation. It also found that the district had maintained its unitary status, and that the neighborhood assignment plan was not designed with discriminatory intent. The court concluded that the previous injunctive decree should be vacated, and the school district returned to local control.

The Court of Appeals again reversed, holding that "'an injunction takes on a life of its own, and becomes an edict quite independent of the law it is meant to effectuate.'" That court approached the case "not so much as one dealing with desegregation, but as one dealing with the proper application of the federal law on injunctive remedies." Relying on *United States v. Swift & Co.* (1932), it held that a desegregation decree remains in effect until a school district can show "grievous wrong evoked by new and unforeseen conditions," and "'dramatic changes in conditions unforeseen at the time of the decree that . . . impose extreme and unexpectedly oppressive hardships on the obligor.'" Given that a number of schools would return to being primarily one-race schools under the SRP, circumstances in Oklahoma City had not changed enough to justify modification of the decree. The Court of Appeals held that, despite the unitary finding, the Board had the "'affirmative duty . . . not to take any action that would impede the process of disestablishing the dual system and its effects.'" (quoting *Dayton Bd. of Education v. Brinkman* [1979]).

We granted the Board's petition for certiorari, to resolve a conflict between the standard laid down by the Court of Appeals in this case and that laid down in *Spangler v. Pasadena City Board of Education* (CA9 1979), and *Riddick v. School Bd. of Norfolk* (CA4 1986). We now reverse the Court of Appeals.

II.

We must first consider whether respondents may contest the District Court's 1987 order dissolving the injunction which had imposed the desegregation decree. Respondents did not appeal from the District Court's 1977 order finding that the school system had achieved unitary status, and petitioners contend that the 1977 order bars respondents from contesting the 1987 order. We disagree, for the 1977 order did not dissolve the desegregation decree, and the District Court's unitariness finding was too ambiguous to bar respondents from challenging later action by the Board.

The lower courts have been inconsistent in their use of the term "unitary." Some have used it to identify a school district that has completely remedied all vestiges of past discrimination. See, e.g., *United States v. Overton* (CA5 1987); *Riddick v. School Bd. of Norfolk*, supra; *Vaughns v. Board*

of Education of Prince George's Cty. (CA4 1985). Under that interpretation of the word, a unitary school district is one that has met the mandate of *Brown v. Board of Education* (1955), and *Green v. New Kent County School Board* (1968). Other courts, however, have used "unitary" to describe any school district that has currently desegregated student assignments, whether or not that status is solely the result of a court-imposed desegregation plan. In other words, such a school district could be called unitary and nevertheless still contain vestiges of past discrimination. That there is such confusion is evident in *Georgia State Conference of Branches of NAACP v. Georgia* (CA11 1985), where the Court of Appeals drew a distinction between a "unitary school district" and a district that has achieved "unitary status." The court explained that a school district that has not operated segregated schools as proscribed by *Green v. New Kent County School Board,* supra, and *Swann v. Charlotte-Mecklenburg Bd. of Education* (1971), "for a period of several years" is unitary, but that a school district cannot be said to have achieved "unitary status" unless it "has eliminated the vestiges of its prior discrimination and has been adjudicated as such through the proper judicial procedures." *Georgia State Conference*, supra.

We think it is a mistake to treat words such as "dual" and "unitary" as if they were actually found in the Constitution. The constitutional command of the Fourteenth Amendment is that "[n]o State shall . . . deny to any person . . . the equal protection of the laws." Courts have used the terms "dual" to denote a school system which has engaged in intentional segregation of students by race, and "unitary" to describe a school system which has been brought into compliance with the command of the Constitution. We are not sure how useful it is to define these terms more precisely, or to create subclasses within them. But there is no doubt that the differences in usage described above do exist. The District Court's 1977 order is unclear with respect to what it meant by unitary, and the necessary result of that finding. We therefore decline to overturn the conclusion of the Court of Appeals that, while the 1977 order of the District Court did bind the parties as to the unitary character of the district, it did not finally terminate the Oklahoma City school litigation. In *Pasadena City Bd of Education v. Spangler* (1976), we held that a school board is entitled to a rather precise statement of its obligations under a desegregation decree. If such a decree is to be terminated or dissolved, respondents as well as the school board are entitled to a like statement from the court.

III.

The Court of Appeals relied upon language from this Court's decision in *United States v. Swift and Co.*, supra, for the proposition that a desegregation decree could not be lifted or modified absent a showing of "grievous wrong evoked by new and unforeseen conditions." It also held that "compliance alone cannot become the basis for modifying or dissolving an injunction," relying on *United States v. W.T. Grant Co.* (1953). We hold that its reliance was mistaken.

In *Swift*, several large meatpacking companies entered into a consent decree whereby they agreed to refrain forever from entering into the grocery business. The decree was by its terms effective in perpetuity. The defendant meatpackers and their allies had, over a period of a decade, attempted, often with success in the lower courts, to frustrate operation of the decree. It was in this context that the language relied upon by the Court of Appeals in this case was used.

United States v. United Shoe Machinery Corp. (1968), explained that the language used in *Swift* must be read in the context of the continuing danger of unlawful restraints on trade which the Court had found still existed. "*Swift* teaches . . . a decree may be changed upon an appropriate showing, and it holds that it may not be changed . . . if the purposes of the litigation as incorporated in the decree . . . have not been fully achieved." In the present case, a finding by the District Court that the Oklahoma City School District was being operated in compliance with the commands of the Equal Protection Clause of the Fourteenth Amendment, and that it was unlikely that the Board would return to its former ways, would be a finding that the purposes of the desegregation litigation had been fully achieved. No additional showing of "grievous wrong evoked by new and unforeseen conditions" is required of the school board.

In *Milliken v. Bradley* (1977) (Milliken II), we said:

[F]ederal-court decrees must directly address and relate to the constitutional violation itself. Because of this inherent limitation upon federal judicial authority, federal-court decrees exceed appropriate limits if they are aimed at eliminating a condition that does not violate the Constitution or does not flow from such a violation. . . .

From the very first, federal supervision of local school systems was intended as a temporary measure to remedy past discrimination. *Brown* considered the "complexities arising from the transition to a system of public education freed of racial discrimination" in holding that the implementation of desegregation was to proceed "with all deliberate speed." *Green* also spoke of the "transition to a unitary, nonracial system of public education."

Considerations based on the allocation of powers within our federal system, we think, support our view that quoted language from *Swift* does not provide the proper standard to apply to injunctions entered in school desegregation cases. Such decrees, unlike the one in *Swift*, are not intended to operate in perpetuity. Local control over the education of children allows citizens to participate in decisionmaking, and allows innovation so that school programs can fit local needs. *Milliken v. Bradley* (1974) (Milliken I); *San Antonio Independent School District v. Rodriguez* (1973). The legal justification for displacement of local authority by an injunctive decree in a school desegregation case is a violation of the Constitution by the local authorities. Dissolving a desegregation decree after the local authorities have operated in compliance with it for a reasonable period of time properly recognizes that "necessary concern for the important values of local control of public school systems dictates that a federal court's regulatory control of such systems not extend beyond the time required to remedy the effects of past intentional discrimination." *Spangler v. Pasadena City Bd. of Education* (Kennedy, J., concurring).

The Court of Appeals, as noted, relied for its statement that "compliance alone cannot become the basis for modifying or dissolving an injunction" on our decision in *United States v. W.T. Grant Co.*, supra. That case, however, did not involve the dissolution of an injunction, but the question of whether an injunction should be issued in the first place. This Court observed that a promise to comply with the law on the part of a wrongdoer did not divest a district court of its power to enjoin the wrongful conduct in which the defendant had previously engaged.

A district court need not accept at face value the profession of a school board which has intentionally discriminated that it will cease to do so in the future. But in deciding whether to modify or dissolve a desegregation decree, a school board's compliance with previous court orders is obviously relevant. In this case, the original finding of de jure segregation was entered in 1963, the injunctive decree from which the Board seeks relief was entered in 1972, and the Board complied with the decree in good faith until 1985. Not only do the personnel of school boards change over time, but the same passage of time enables the district court to observe the good faith of the school board in complying with the decree. The test espoused by the Court of Appeals would condemn a school district, once governed by a board which intentionally discriminated, to judicial tutelage for the indefinite future. Neither the principles governing the entry and dissolution of injunctive decrees, nor the commands of the Equal Protection Clause of the Fourteenth Amendment require any such Draconian result.

Petitioners urge that we reinstate the decision of the District Court terminating the injunction, but we think that the preferable course is to remand the case to that court so that it may decide, in accordance with this opinion, whether the Board made a sufficient showing of constitutional compliance as of 1985, when the SRP was adopted, to allow the injunction to be dissolved. The District Court should address itself to whether the Board had complied in good faith with the desegregation decree since it was entered, and whether the vestiges of past discrimination had been eliminated to the extent practicable.

In considering whether the vestiges of de jure segregation had been eliminated as far as practicable, the District Court should look not only at student assignments, but "to every facet of school operations—faculty, staff, transportation, extracurricular activities and facilities." Green. See also Swann ("[E]xisting policy and practice with regard to faculty, staff, transportation, extracurricular activities, and facilities" are "among the most important indicia of a segregated system").

After the District Court decides whether the Board was entitled to have the decree terminated, it should proceed to decide respondent's challenge to the SRP. A school district which has been released from an injunction imposing a desegregation plan no longer requires court authorization for the promulgation of policies and rules regulating matters such as assignment of students and the like, but it of course remains subject to the mandate of the Equal Protection Clause of the Fourteenth Amendment. If the Board was entitled to have the decree terminated as of 1985, the District Court should then evaluate the Board's decision to implement the SRP under appropriate equal protection principles. See *Washington v. Davis* (1976); *Arlington Heights v. Metropolitan Housing Development Corp.* (1977).

The judgment of the Court of Appeals is reversed, and the case is remanded to the District Court for further proceedings consistent with this opinion.

It is so ordered.

Source: *Board of Education v. Dowell* 498 U.S. 237 (1991).

See also: American Apartheid; *Bolling v. Sharpe* (1954); *Brown v. Board of Education* (1954); *Brown v. Board of Education* Legal Groundwork; Busing; *Cooper v. Aaron* (1958); *Cumming v. Richmond County Board of Education* (1899); Desegregation; Education; Gray Commission; Little Rock Nine; *Plessy v. Ferguson* (1896); School Segregation; Segregation; Separate But Equal Doctrine

Progress Report of the Presidential Task Force on Los Angeles Recovery (May 1992)

Introduction

Reproduced below is the initial progress report of the task force of cabinet undersecretaries and other federal officials appointed by President George H. W. Bush to assess how

the federal government could best assist the recovery pro-cess in Los Angeles in the first weeks following the 1992 riots. Released barely two weeks after the end of the riots, this report mainly describes conditions in the riot zone immediately after the disorders ended and the first steps taken by federal, state, and local officials to begin the economic recovery of the affected areas.

Primary Source
Members of the Task Force:
David T. Kearns, Co-chairman
Deputy Secretary
U.S. Department of Education
Washington, D.C.

Alfred A. DelliBovi, Co-chairman
Deputy Secretary
U.S. Department of Housing and Urban Development
Washington, D.C.

Robert E. Grady
Deputy Director-designate
Office of Management and Budget
Executive Office of the President
Washington, D.C.

Delbert Spurlock
Deputy Secretary
U.S. Department of Labor
Washington, D.C.

Arnold Tompkins
Assistant Secretary for Management and Budget
U.S. Department of Health and Human Services
Washington, D.C.

Robert S. Mueller, III.
Assistant Attorney General
Criminal Division
U.S. Department of Justice
Washington, D.C.

Oscar Wright
Regional Administrator

Small Business Administration
San Francisco, California

Linda Peterson
Regional Administrator
Office of Personnel Management
Los Angeles, California

Jay Lefkowitz
Office of Cabinet Affairs
The White House
Washington, D.C.

William Medigovich
Federal Coordinating Officer
Federal Emergency Management Agency
Los Angeles, California

Earl Fields
Chairman
Federal Executive Board
Long Beach, California

Gretchen Pagel
Office of National Service
The White House
Washington, D.C.

Presidential Task Force on Los Angeles Recovery
May 12, 1992
The President
The White House

Dear Mr. President:
On Monday, May 4, 1992, in response to the civil unrest in the city of Los Angeles and Los Angeles County, California, you directed that a task force of Cabinet Deputy Secretaries and other key Federal officials be sent immediately to Los Angeles to assist in the recovery process.

Attached is a progress report on what that task force has accomplished in the past eight days. We hope that our efforts to date have assisted in easing the effects of this tragedy, and in ensuring the prompt delivery of Federal, state, county, and city services.

We have been struck in conducting our work by the genuine desire for prompt recovery, and by the cooperative spirit that has sprung from the ashes of the Los Angeles fires.

The work of this task force is ongoing and will continue. We will report again to you in the weeks and months ahead. While our work has been focused on process and implementation issues, we would be pleased to give you and your Cabinet impressions and input as you develop programs and legislation to assist large urban centers. Thank you for the opportunity to serve in this important mission.

Respectfully,
Alfred A. DelliBovi
Co-chairman
David T. Kearns
Co-chairman

Progress Report of the Presidential Task Force on Los Angeles Recovery

I. Overview and Highlights

On Monday, May 4th, the President established a task force of Cabinet Deputies and other key Federal officials to assist in the recovery of Los Angeles. The purpose of the task force was limited and straightforward: to knock down barriers to the speedy delivery of services to the citizens of greater Los Angeles who suffered as a result of the disturbances there, and to bring quickly to the area those Federal resources and programs which could help address the immediate problems facing the affected area.

The Federal role represented by the task force was not to supplant state and local efforts to rebuild Los Angeles, but rather to ensure a coordinated response and to make the Federal government a helpful partner—assisting in every way possible the state, county, and city governments, and the private sector, in rebuilding their community.

Examples of the work accomplished by the task force include:

- Assisting in the establishment of 7 Disaster Application Centers (DACS) to provide "one-stop shopping" for residents and businesses in need of disaster assistance and Federal, state, or local services. As demand for the services grew, the task force helped arrange for a mobile facility to expand the space available at one DAC and for the opening of an eighth DAC in an area in need.
- Removing roadblocks to the provision of FEMA and SBA assistance to those who suffered fire or looting losses due to the disturbance.
- Cutting red tape and providing special assistance to small businesses in the provision of SBA disaster loans. The task force brought in minority business specialists to help small businesses prepare loan applications and IRS personnel to assist in the prompt recovery of tax returns. The task force helped create a special expedited process at the Treasury Department for clearing SBA loan checks, and removed a hurdle for very small businesses by creating a much simplified test of the requirement that they seek credit elsewhere before applying to the SBA.
- Responding to the language problem which naturally arises in a diverse community such as Los Angeles. The task force helped arrange for the hiring of about 60 bilingual aides to assist applicants. When a shortage of Spanish-speaking assistants arose, ten were hired on the same day.
- Helping to speed the delivery of a full array of Federal services to the Los Angeles area, including rental assistance for those who were displaced from their homes, unemployment assistance for those who lost their jobs, food for those in areas with shortages, emergency funds for those who did not receive Social Security checks, and crisis counseling for those affected by the disturbance. On Monday, May 11th, three days after the opening of the application centers, FEMA mailed the first disaster housing assistance checks to applicants.

II. The Mission of the Task Force

One might think of the Federal response to the civil unrest that occurred in Los Angeles as encompassing three phases.

One phase was the restoration of peace and the rule of law in the immediate term. A second phase is the provision of necessary assistance and services to those who suffered losses or disruption of services as a result of the disturbance. A third phase is the crafting of a long-term policy strategy for addressing the underlying problems facing urban America.

The work of this task force has been focused on the second phase. The task force did not participate in or direct any law enforcement activities, although in the aftermath of the disturbance, the task force leadership has worked closely with Robert Mueller, the Assistant Attorney General, Criminal Division, and with Governor Wilson to coordinate appropriately with law enforcement. Nor is the task force a policy-making body.

This task force has sought to work with the state, county, and city governments, as well as private sector and non-profit entities, in speeding the delivery of services to the people of Los Angeles. The task force worked to bring quickly to the Los Angeles area those programs which the Federal government can deliver right now, under existing statutory authority and using existing funds, to help those victimized by the violence.

Most importantly, the mission of the task force has been to knock down any extraneous barriers to the efficient delivery of services to the people of Los Angeles city and county. Too often, the processes and paperwork of the Federal government are a source of frustration to citizens who confront them. The goal of this task force was to ease that frustration in every way possible—and to deliver assistance to the people who need it in record time.

III. THE PROCESS

Meeting Schedule
Upon arrival in Los Angeles on Monday night May 4th, members of the task force met with Governor Pete Wilson and his staff. Governor Wilson also met with the full task force on Tuesday morning May 5th to offer his assessment of the situation. At that meeting, he designated the State of California's Director of Emergency Services, Richard Andrews, as liaison with the task force.

Also on Tuesday morning, task force representatives met with Los Angeles Mayor Tom Bradley and Deputy Mayor Linda Griego. Bradley appointed Deputy Mayor Griego as liaison and she met with the full task force on Tuesday to identify specific problems the city had encountered that could be addressed by task force actions.

The task force coordinated by telephone on Tuesday with Los Angeles County Chief Administrative officer Richard Dixon, who designated Sheriff's Lieutenant Ben Nottingham as the County's liaison with the task force. On Wednesday, May 6th, representatives of the task force met with the Chairman of the Los Angeles County Board of Supervisors, Supervisor Deane Dana, Los Angeles County Sheriff Sherman Block, Supervisor Michael Antonovich, Mr. Dixon, and other representatives of the county.

On the afternoon of Tuesday, May 5th, the task force met with Mr. Peter Ueberroth, who had been appointed by Mayor Bradley and Governor Wilson to chair Rebuild L.A., a long-term effort to promote recovery by encouraging private sector investment in affected areas of greater Los Angeles.

On Friday, May 8th, at the invitation of its President, Councilman John Ferraro, representative of the task force presented a briefing to the Los Angeles City Council, and subsequently met with various members of the Council.

Throughout the week, members of the task force took the opportunity to meet with members of the community, including the mayors of Compton, Inglewood, Long Beach, and Linwood, City of Los Angeles Superintendent of Schools Bill Anton, Los Angeles County Superintendent of Schools Stuart Godholt, President of the Los Angeles Urban League John Mack, various members of the clergy, representatives of the police and firefighting forces, and affected businessmen and women. In addition, members of the task force toured affected areas and neighborhoods at various times throughout the week.

The task force briefed the President on two occasions: upon his arrival in Los Angeles on Wednesday night, May 6th, and again on Thursday evening, May 7th. Also in attendance at one or both of these briefings was Governor Wilson, Mayor

Bradley, U.S. Senator John Seymour, Supervisor Dana, Councilman Ferraro, Secretary of Health and Human Services Louis Sullivan, Secretary of Housing and Urban Development Jack Kemp, and Administrator of the Small Business Administration Patricia Saiki.

Coordination Mechanisms

The task force has coordinated its activities closely with the state, county, and city governments. Since Tuesday, May 5th, senior task force representatives have participated in a daily conference call with officials of the state, city, county, the Small Business Administration (SBA) and FEMA. This conference call has made possible an immediate, coordinated response, on a daily basis, to problems that are occurring in the field. This daily conference call will continue for the foreseeable future.

For the past week in Los Angeles, the task force met at the beginning and at the end of each working day.

IV. ASSESSMENT OF THE SITUATION IN LOS ANGELES

While the greater Los Angeles community sustained significant damage as a result of the rioting, the task force was impressed by the pervasive signs of hope that have arisen in the wake of this tragedy. Every member of the task force was struck by the genuine desire, at every level of government and throughout the community, to cooperate in working toward the quick recovery of Los Angeles.

The nature of the damage which resulted from the thousands of fires set during the rioting was different from that sustained in Watts, Detroit, and other riots in the 1960s. While the damage was extensive and indeed staggering, relatively few residences were burned: HUD estimates that approximately 250–300 families lost their homes as a result of fires related to the disturbance.

The principal physical damage sustained during the rioting was the destruction and/or looting of several thousand businesses. Preliminary estimates by city and county building and safety experts are that 5,000 structures in the greater Los Angeles area were either damaged or destroyed. The businesses housed in these structures provided essential services

to the citizens of South Central, Crenshaw, Koreatown, Compton, Inglewood, Long Beach and other areas of greater Los Angeles. The task force believes that an urgent priority is to encourage re-investment in these neighborhoods.

Because many of the businesses which were destroyed or looted were small, family-owned businesses, without the staff or facilities for extensive recordkeeping, the task force recognized that these businesses might encounter special difficulties in completing the paperwork necessary to apply for SBA disaster loans and FEMA disaster assistance.

Further, given the emotionally charged nature of the disaster and the attendant tensions in the community, the task force was eager to minimize any additional frustration which might result from delays in processing and receiving disaster assistance. Two key objectives of the task force were therefore to assist in the application process and to streamline the approval process for these types of assistance.

The record-keeping problems of small business had the potential to be exacerbated by language barriers in the culturally diverse community of Los Angeles. The languages spoken by affected business owners ranged from English to Korean to Spanish to Persian to Armenian to Thai to Mandarin Chinese. Throughout the week, the task force worked to surmount this barrier by marshalling the resources necessary to provide effective translation services.

V. DISASTER ASSISTANCE

On Saturday, May 2nd, in response to a request from Governor Wilson on that same date, the President declared that a major disaster exists in the County and City of Los Angeles. This declaration made Federal disaster-related funding available for individuals, businesses' and local governments who had suffered as a result of the civil disturbance.

Specifically, as a result of the President's declaration, SBA is making available direct, low-interest loans to homeowners, renters, businesses and non-profit organizations who suffered losses. These include physical disaster loans to help rebuild and replace uninsured property, and economic industry loans to provide small businesses with the working capital to replace inventory and otherwise resume normal operations.

FEMA is providing temporary housing and grants to individuals and families whose homes and property were damaged in the disaster, and who cannot qualify for SBA loans. In addition, FEMA provides grants to local governments to cover the costs of repairing public buildings and facilities and the overtime salaries of state and local workers who had to respond to the disaster.

This SBA and FEMA assistance constitutes the lion's share of the Federal assistance made available to respond to urgent, short-term recovery needs. In the past, the application and approval process for these programs has been the source of some frustration. The task force was and is committed to removing any unnecessary bureaucratic barriers to the efficient functioning of this process. The specific goal of the task force is to provide this FEMA and SBA assistance in record time.

To aid in the task of minimizing confusion for a local population already under stress, the task force worked with the state, county, and city governments to establish centers that would provide all key services under one roof. Under this "one stop shopping" approach, a citizen could find information on and make application for SBA loans; FEMA grants; emergency food, clothing, shelter, and medical assistance; individual and family grants; tax assistance; and crisis counseling—all at one location.

On Friday, May 8th, seven DACS were opened throughout the affected areas of greater Los Angeles to provide this "one-stop shopping" service. One measure of the success of the task force is this: on Monday, May 11th, three days after the opening of the application centers, FEMA mailed its first disaster housing assistance checks to victims of the disturbance.

Breaking Down Language Barriers
The task force recognized that language differences could constitute an important barrier to the efficient delivery of services in such a culturally diverse community as Los Angeles. As a result, FEMA, SBA, and the task force worked to tap a range of resources to provide sufficient numbers of linguistic specialists in the DACS. FEMA and SBA enlisted the services of Korean-speaking assistants to aid the many Korean-American business owners affected by the disaster. On Friday, May 8th, it became clear that a shortage of Spanish-speaking assistants existed at the Ardmore DAC site. FEMA redeployed several assistants to that site, and hired ten additional Spanish speaking aides that day.

In total, approximately 60 bilingual aides have been hired to date to ease the language problem.

In order to minimize the time between the actual disaster and the receipt of disaster assistance, the task force took several actions to reduce red tape and assist applicants.

Speeding Delivery of SBA Disaster Assistance Loans
Many of the businesses affected by the rioting were small businesses without extensive records. In order to receive disaster assistance loans, businesses must furnish tax returns from the past three years; an itemized list of losses; proof of operation of a business at a particular location, such as a copy of a deed, lease, or mortgage; a brief history of the business; and financial statements for the past three years.

For many of the businesses in the affected areas of Los Angeles, it is difficult to meet these requirements. To help such applicants, the task force:

- Arranged for the placement of specialists from the Minority Business Development Agency (MBDA) in each of the DACS. These specialists are providing technical assistance to businesses in preparing such required items as the business history and the profit and loss statements from the past three years. MBDA arranged to have its services provided in several languages.
- Arranged for the placement of representatives of the IRS in each of the DACS, to speed the process of recovering tax returns from IRS headquarters in those cases in which the applicants' copies of the tax returns are missing or destroyed. In addition, the task force worked with the IRS headquarters in Washington to ensure that expedited treatment is given to any request

to retrieve tax returns in cases related to the situation in Los Angeles.

Another requirement of the SBA for disaster loan applicants is that they demonstrate that they sought and were unable to secure credit elsewhere. In the case of many of the small businesses in South Central and other affected areas of Los Angeles, it is safe to assume that availability of credit was a major difficulty for them even prior to the disturbance—that they would be unable to secure such credit. In response, the task force:

- Developed through SBA a simplified "credit elsewhere" test. This is a major time saver in the application process, which for thousands of businesses will cut weeks from the time it takes to receive an SBA disaster loan.

The length of time required to process SBA disaster loan applications and actually provide checks to affected businesses has been a source of frustration in past disasters. To reduce that frustration, the task force:

- Established a special expedited process with the U.S. Treasury Department to speed approval of check writing for the Small Business Administration.

Delivering FEMA Assistance Fairly and Efficiently
The city and state governments expressed concern that, due to the wording of the disaster declaration, FEMA and SBA might be in the position of providing disaster assistance to those who had suffered losses or damage due to fire, but not to those who had suffered losses or damage due to looting. The task force:

- Worked with FEMA to clarify the interpretation of the President's disaster declaration. Under the clarification, FEMA declared that, "'Fires during a period of civil unrest means all *fire-related damages or hardships* which occurred during the major disaster." (emphasis added) Further, FEMA stated that "where it is not feasible to differentiate among the causes of civil unrest . . . or where it appears that damages or hardships may be in any way the effect of fires or

fire-related circumstances, all damage is considered to be related to fires." This interpretation should allow agencies to provide assistance to all those who suffered damages as a result of the civil disturbance.

Creating Additional DACs
The task force has sought to be flexible in accommodating the demand for assistance in the community and to reduce undue waiting time in the DACS.

When indications of long waiting times at the Ardmore Recreation Center DAC in Koreatown arose on Friday, May 8th, the task force:

- Worked with FEMA and the state government to move a mobile DAC to the site, expanding the available space by 720 square feet.

When the need for additional application facilities in the Crenshaw area was identified during the first weekend of operations of the DACS, the task force:

- Worked to establish a new DAC site at 4030 Crenshaw Boulevard in Los Angeles. This new DAC was opened at 10:00 am on Monday, May 11th.

The task force is prepared to remain flexible as new demand for disaster recovery services arises.

VI. ASSISTANCE PROVIDED BY OTHER FEDERAL AGENCIES

In addition to FEMA and SBA, other Federal agencies have worked to provide quickly a range of other services and types of assistance in response to the disturbance in Los Angeles. Some examples follow.

Agriculture
In response to spot shortages of food in certain neighborhoods, the U.S. Department of Agriculture (USDA) sent over 27,000 boxes of cereal, over 58,000 cans of infant formula, over 1,500 six-pound boxes of nonfat dry milk, and other foodstuffs to Los Angeles area food banks.

A USDA survey revealed that private sector donations to food banks soared in the wake of Los Angeles disturbance, and that distribution outlets in the area had been increased, thanks to the participation of churches and other non-profit institutions in the community.

The USDA survey revealed that there was no marked increase in food stamp demand in the wake of the disturbance. Nevertheless new requests from individuals affected by the disturbances will be put on a special fast track. Because several outlets authorized to accept food stamps were closed or destroyed, red tape was cut so that new food stamp authorization applications from retail outlets are being processed in one day.

At least fifty stores authorized to receive vouchers in the Women, Infants and Children (WIC) program were closed or destroyed. In response, USDA issued instructions to allow WIC coupons to be valid at any authorized vendor.

Commerce
The Department of Commerce has provided both business and economic development assistance in the wake of the Los Angeles disturbance.

In addition to placing its representatives in the DACs to assist in the preparation of applications by small minority businesses, the Minority Business Development Agency (MBDA) operates two Minority Business Development Centers in the Los Angeles areas.

The Commerce Department is in the process of making available approximately $25 million in Economic Development Administration (EDA) funds to assist in the recovery process. Six to ten million dollars will be made available to the county and city governments for bridge loans to businesses to be used for purposes such as cleanup, demolition, and restoration of inventory, machinery and equipment, or building structures.

Another $2 to 3 million is expected to be provided to Rebuild LA, chaired by Peter Ueberroth, to help set up and operate this non-profit organization, whose mission is to assist in the economic recovery of greater Los Angeles by attracting job-creating private sector investment.

Approximately $1 to 2 million is expected to be provided to the Los Angeles Convention and Visitors Bureau, to help reinvigorate international tourism to the Los Angeles area. This is the second largest industry in the area, employing 360,000 southern Californians, eighty percent of whom are minorities.

Finally, EDA is discussing $5.5 million in defense adjustment grants for Los Angeles County, to assist areas where defense contracts were terminated. Some of these grants could be used for seed capital for technology companies which are spinoffs from defense-related companies.

Education
The Department of Education is taking steps to speed the availability of-approximately $1.2 billion in formula grants to the State of California, and to work with the state to optimize the suballocation of these grants in order to address conditions related to the disturbances.

Education is working with college student aid administrators to allow them to use "special condition" procedures in the Pell Grant program to take into account any loss of family income due to the disturbances.

In addition, a special desk has been set up at Education's Federal Student Aid Information Center to handle inquiries from Los Angeles students on how to apply for student aid or how to reflect loss of assets or income due to the disturbances in the application. This desk will be serviced by an "800" phone number.

Health and Human Services
Within 24 hours of the disturbance, the Department of Health and Human Services (HHS), through the Social Security Administration, ordered the use of emergency check-writing authority to make payments of up to $200 for those elderly poor or low income, disabled children whose Supplemental Security Income (SSI) checks were not received as a result of the disturbance. HHS also put in place procedures

to speed the replacement of any welfare or disability check lost as a result of the disturbance.

HHS dispatched experts from the National Institute of Mental Health to assess mental health assistance needs and requirements. Mental health and crisis counseling is available in the DACS. Epidemiologist from the Centers for Disease Control were brought in to investigate the health effects of the disturbance—including those related to environmental safety (chemical and biohazards), health control (sanitation and clean water), and other questions.

Housing and Urban Development
The Department of Housing and Urban Development (HUD) immediately made available Section 8 rental assistance vouchers to those families who have been displaced by fires related to the disturbance.

HUD is also making available 32 HUD-owned homes, with a dollar value of $2.3 million, for use in the affected areas. These homes will be leased to the city for one dollar per month. HUD issued a new rule this past week to provide priority contracting for businesses that are at least 51 percent resident owned. This means that a higher proportion of contracts for work performed for HUD will go to businesses which are representative of the area in which the work is to be performed.

On Wednesday, May 6th, HUD announced that it will approve requests to allow the early release of over $92 million in Community Development Block Grant (CDBG) funds to the city and County of Los Angeles that were scheduled to be released on July 1st.

On Thursday, May 7th, HUD signed an interagency memorandum of understanding with the Department of Labor to better coordinate Labor's job training efforts with HUD's HOPE and other public housing initiatives.

On Friday, May 8th, HUD announced the availability of $1.5 million in Technical Assistance program grants for low- and moderate-income young people (between the ages of 14 and 21) to help them acquire the skills and knowledge they need to start and operate successful small businesses.

The Resolution Trust Corporation (RTC) has made available to HUD a list of properties available in the affected area of Los Angeles. HUD has been working to match these properties to local needs, and leases could be signed later this week.

Labor
The Department of Labor provided $2 million in emergency grants to hire and pay the wages of workers who were dislocated as a result of the disturbance.

Labor also launched a demonstration project to use unemployment insurance benefit payments to support entrepreneurship efforts by unemployment insurance claimants.

Labor also provided about $2 million for several types of training assistance. One grant would establish "one-stop shopping" skill centers to provide vocational training and employment-related assistance to affected areas. Another would finance an expansion of a program operated by the Community Youth Gang Services which allows area youth to participate in community service projects as an alternative to incarceration. A third would finance youth apprenticeship model programs for African American and Hispanic males. And a fourth would provide training funds to supplement local economic development efforts.

Office of Personnel Management
The Director of the Office of Personnel Management (OPM) authorized the conduct of a special Combined Federal Campaign effort among Federal employees in the Los Angeles area to help generate contributions to non-profit organizations involved in the recovery effort. OPM has also taken steps in the past week to increase job opportunities and to provide job counseling and stress counseling in the Los Angeles area.

VII. CONTINUATION OF THE WORK OF THE TASK FORCE

The work of the task force will continue beyond the efforts of this first week. The task force is committed to implementing fully the President's directive to work with the state, county, and city, and with the private sector, to ensure the swift delivery of needed assistance and services to the people of Los Angeles.

The task force has established a structure and a set of processes to see that this directive is carried out in the weeks and months ahead.

With the return of most Deputy Secretaries to Washington, the conference calls with State, county, city, and on-site Federal representatives are nevertheless continuing. Deputy Secretary DelliBovi has returned to Los Angeles this week. Deputy Secretary Schnabel will arrive later in the week. The task force co-chairs, Deputy Secretaries Kearns and Delli-Bovi, plan to continue alternate visits to Los Angeles for as long as such visits are helpful.

Each of the agencies represented on the task force has stationed a representative to remain in Los Angeles. Some of these representatives will be moved to the site of the current Federal/State/Local coordinating office in Pasadena to ensure maximum coordination.

The task force co-chairmen are now in the process of identifying a task force leader to lead the task force in Los Angeles on a day-to-day basis. This leader will report regularly to the co-chairmen.

In six weeks, the task force has agreed to reconvene in Los Angeles to assess the state of the recovery effort, to meet again with state, local, and private sector officials, and to determine what additional actions are necessary.

The task force will work diligently to support state, county, city, and private sector efforts to help Los Angeles recover, and to make sure that the Federal government is a constructive partner in that recovery.

VIII. CONCLUSION

Throughout greater Los Angeles, members of the task force witnessed inspiring signs of hope in the wake of the tragic violence. Store owners whose shops had been looted only days earlier rushed to replace inventory, placed plywood over their shattered windows, and proudly painted "Open for Business" in bold letters on their newly installed plywood facades.

Volunteers poured into the affected areas from all over the city—indeed from all over the country. Mayor Bradley estimated that 50,000 volunteers had assisted in the cleanup of Los Angeles in the days following the disturbances.

On one street corner in South Central, against a backdrop of a burned out shopping center, a man opened a flower stand, in one first small step of hope and recovery.

One firefighter who had served 27 years earlier in combating the fires of Watts, predicted and observed "a much quicker recovery" than that which followed the Watts disturbances, because, he said, of "the total commitment to cleanup and recovery on the part of the local people."

From the ashes of this recovery, the members of the task force found blossoming a springtime of hope. Its most important feature was a near-consensus on the types of measures that are needed not only to restore Los Angeles but to make its neighborhoods stronger than they were before this incident happened.

While there is much about which to be encouraged, the task force found that this is a *very* tough situation. It is estimated that unemployment in the affected area *prior* to the disturbance was far higher than the national average, perhaps more than triple the national rate. Mayor Bradley estimates that many thousands of jobs were lost as a result of the disturbance—some permanently.

Virtually everyone the task force spoke to believed that private sector investment in these neighborhoods, investment which can create jobs in the community, was the most urgent priority. Virtually everyone the task force spoke to believed that residents of these affected areas must be given a greater equity stake in success—the opportunity to accumulate assets without penalty—from the welfare system, the opportunity to own and manage their own homes, the opportunity to live in neighborhoods free from crime and drugs. What the Federal government can provide is incentives to encourage investment that will create jobs and build local assets.

The members of the task force believe that in this emergent consensus lie the seeds of a truly complete recovery for Los Angeles, and for all of America's cities.

Source: Progress Report of the Presidential Task Force on Los Angeles Recovery. Washington, DC: The Task Force, 1992.

See also: Asbury Park Riot of 1970; Atlanta Riot of 1906; Atlanta Riot of 1967; Bellingham Riots; Bensonhurst Incident 1989; Biloxi Beach Riot of 1960; Black Church Arsons; Bloody Sunday; Boston Riot of 1975 and 1976; Brownsville Riot of 1906; Charleston Riot of 1919; Chattanooga Riot of 1906; Chester and Philadelphia Riots of 1918; Chicago Commission on Race Relations; Chicago Riot of 1919; Cincinnati Riots of 1967 and 1968; Cincinnati Riot of 2001; Cleveland Riot of 1966; Detroit Riot of 1943; Detroit Riot of 1967; East St. Louis Riot of 1917; Election Riots of the 1880s and 1890s; Greensburg Riot of 1906; Greenwood Community; Harlem Riot of 1935; Houston Mutiny of 1917; Howard Beach Incident 1986; Johnson-Jeffries Fight of 1910; Knoxville Riot of 1919; Long Hot Summer Riots 1965–1967; Longview Riot of 1919; Los Angeles Riot of 1965; Los Angeles Riots of 1992; Miami Riot of 1982; New Bedford Riot of 1970; New Orleans Riot of 1866; New York City Draft Riot of 1863; New York City Riot of 1943; Newark Riot of 1967; Orangeburg Massacre of 1968; Philadelphia Riot of 1964; Prison Riots; Race Riots in America; Red Scare and Race Riots; Red Summer Race Riots of 1919; Rosewood Riot of 1923; Saint Genevieve Riot of 1930; San Francisco Riot of 1966; Springfield Riot of 1904; Tampa Riots of 1987; Texas Southern University Riot of 1967; Tulsa Riot of 1921; Washington, D.C., Riot of 1919; Washington, D.C., Riots of 1968; Wilmington Riot of 1898; Zoot Suit Riots

Shaw v. Reno (1993)

Introduction

Shaw v. Reno *was the landmark case in which the Supreme Court ruled that states may not draw the boundaries of congressional districts simply on the basis of race. In the 1990 census, North Carolina became entitled to create a 12th congressional district. Because North Carolina had not sent an African American to Congress in the 20th century, the state General Assembly drew up plans for 12 seats, one of which was a so-called majority-minority seat, in which a majority of the voters were racial or ethnic minorities. By the provisions of Title 5 of the Voting Rights Act of 1965, under which a state found to have discriminated in the past must submit their reapportionment plans to either the U.S. District Court for the District of Columbia or the attorney general, the original apportionment plan was thrown out by the Justice*

Department so that a second so-called minority seat could be created. The General Assembly went back and redrew the plans, making for a second "majority-minority" seat.

Primary Source

JUSTICE O'CONNOR delivered the opinion of the Court.

This case involves two of the most complex and sensitive issues this Court has faced in recent years: the meaning of the constitutional "right" to vote, and the propriety of race-based state legislation designed to benefit members of historically disadvantaged racial minority groups. As a result of the 1990 census, North Carolina became entitled to a 12th seat in the United States House of Representatives. The General Assembly enacted a reapportionment plan that included one majority-black congressional district. After the Attorney General of the United States objected to the plan pursuant to 5 of the Voting Rights Act of 1965 . . . as amended . . . , the General Assembly passed new legislation creating a second majority-black district. Appellants allege that the revised plan, which contains district boundary lines of dramatically irregular shape, constitutes an unconstitutional racial gerrymander. The question before us is whether appellants have stated a cognizable claim.

I.

The voting age population of North Carolina is approximately 78% white, 20% black, and 1% Native American; the remaining 1% is predominantly Asian. . . . The black population is relatively dispersed; blacks constitute a majority of the general population in only 5 of the State's 100 counties. . . . Geographically, the State divides into three regions: the eastern Coastal Plain, the central Piedmont Plateau, and the western mountains. . . . The largest concentrations of black citizens live in the Coastal Plain, primarily in the northern part. . . . The General Assembly's first redistricting plan contained one majority-black district centered in that area of the State.

Forty of North Carolina's one hundred counties are covered by 5 of the Voting Rights Act of 1965 . . . , which prohibits a jurisdiction subject to its provisions from implementing changes in a "standard, practice, or procedure with respect to voting" without federal authorization. . . . The jurisdiction must obtain either a judgment from the United States District Court for the District of Columbia declaring that the proposed change "does not have the purpose and will not have the effect of denying or abridging the right to vote on account of race or color" or administrative preclearance from the Attorney General. . . . Because the General Assembly's reapportionment plan affected the covered counties, the parties agree that 5 applied. . . . The State chose to submit its plan to the Attorney General for preclearance.

The Attorney General, acting through the Assistant Attorney General for the Civil Rights Division, interposed a formal objection to the General Assembly's plan. The Attorney General specifically objected to the configuration of boundary lines drawn in the south-central to southeastern region of the State. In the Attorney General's view, the General Assembly could have created a second majority-minority district "to give effect to black and Native American voting strength in this area" by using boundary lines "no more irregular than [those] found elsewhere in the proposed plan," but failed to do so for "pretextual reasons." . . .

Under 5, the State remained free to seek a declaratory judgment from the District Court for the District of Columbia notwithstanding the Attorney General's objection. It did not do so. Instead, the General Assembly enacted a revised redistricting plan . . . that included a second majority-black district. The General Assembly located the second district not in the south-central to southeastern part of the State, but in the north-central region along Interstate 85. . . .

The first of the two majority-black districts contained in the revised plan, District 1, is somewhat hook shaped. Centered in the northeast portion of the State, it moves southward until it tapers to a narrow band; then, with finger-like extensions, it reaches far into the southern-most part of the State near the South Carolina border. District 1 has been compared to a "Rorschach inkblot test," *Shaw v. Barr* . . . (1992) . . . , and a "bug splattered on a windshield," *Wall Street Journal*, Feb. 4, 1992.

The second majority-black district, District 12, is even more unusually shaped. It is approximately 160 miles long and, for much of its length, no wider than the I-85 corridor. It winds in snake like fashion through tobacco country, financial centers, and manufacturing areas "until it gobbles in enough enclaves of black neighborhoods." . . . Northbound and southbound drivers on I-85 sometimes find themselves in separate districts in one county, only to "trade" districts when they enter the next county. Of the 10 counties through which District 12 passes, 5 are cut into 3 different districts; even towns are divided. At one point, the district remains contiguous only because it intersects at a single point with two other districts before crossing over them. . . . One state legislator has remarked that "'[i] f you drove down the interstate with both car doors open, you'd kill most of the people in the district.'" *Washington Post* Apr. 20, 1993. . . . The district even has inspired poetry: "Ask not for whom the line is drawn; it is drawn to avoid thee." . . .

The Attorney General did not object to the General Assembly's revised plan. But numerous North Carolinians did. The North Carolina Republican Party and individual voters brought suit in Federal District Court, alleging that the plan constituted an unconstitutional political gerrymander under *Davis v. Bandemer* . . . (1986). That claim was dismissed, see *Pope v. Blue* . . . , and this Court summarily affirmed. . . .

Shortly after the complaint in *Pope v. Blue* was filed, appellants instituted the present action in the United States District Court for the Eastern District of North Carolina. Appellants alleged not that the revised plan constituted a political gerrymander, nor that it violated the "one person, one vote" principle, see *Reynolds v. Sims* . . . (1964), but that the State had created an unconstitutional racial gerrymander. Appellants are five residents of Durham County, North Carolina, all registered to vote in that county. Under the General Assembly's plan, two will vote for congressional representatives in District 12 and three will vote in neighboring District 2. Appellants sued the Governor of North Carolina, the Lieutenant Governor, the Secretary of State, the Speaker of the North Carolina House of Representatives, and members of the North Carolina State Board of Elections (state appellees), together with two federal officials, the Attorney General and the Assistant Attorney General for the Civil Rights Division (federal appellees).

Appellants contended that the General Assembly's revised reapportionment plan violated several provisions of the United States Constitution, including the Fourteenth Amendment. They alleged that the General Assembly deliberately "create[d] two Congressional Districts in which a majority of black voters was concentrated arbitrarily—without regard to any other considerations, such as compactness, contiguousness, geographical boundaries, or political subdivisions" with the purpose "to create Congressional Districts along racial lines" and to assure the election of two black representatives to Congress. . . . Appellants sought declaratory and injunctive relief against the state appellees. They sought similar relief against the federal appellees, arguing, alternatively, that the federal appellees had misconstrued the Voting Rights Act or that the Act itself was unconstitutional.

The three-judge District Court granted the federal appellees' motion to dismiss. . . . The court agreed unanimously that it lacked subject matter jurisdiction by reason of 14(b) of the Voting Rights Act . . . , which vests the District Court for the District of Columbia with exclusive jurisdiction to issue injunctions against the execution of the Act and to enjoin actions taken by federal officers pursuant thereto. . . . Two judges also concluded that, to the extent appellants challenged the Attorney General's preclearance decisions, their claim was foreclosed by this Court's holding in *Morris v. Gressette* . . . (1977). . . .

By a 2-to-1 vote, the District Court also dismissed the complaint against the state appellees. The majority found no support for appellants' contentions that race-based districting is prohibited by Article I, 4, or Article I, 2, of the Constitution, or by the Privileges and Immunities Clause of the Fourteenth Amendment. It deemed appellants' claim under the Fifteenth Amendment essentially subsumed within their related claim under the Equal Protection Clause. . . . That claim, the majority concluded, was barred by *United Jewish Organizations of Williamsburgh, Inc. v. Carey* . . . (1977) (*UJO*).

The majority first took judicial notice of a fact omitted from appellants' complaint: that appellants are white. It rejected the argument that race-conscious redistricting to benefit minority voters is per se unconstitutional. The majority also

rejected appellants' claim that North Carolina's reapportionment plan was impermissible. The majority read *UJO* to stand for the proposition that a redistricting scheme violates white voters' rights only if it is "adopted with the purpose and effect of discriminating against white voters . . . on account of their race." . . . The purposes of favoring minority voters and complying with the Voting Rights Act are not discriminatory in the constitutional sense, the court reasoned, and majority-minority districts have an impermissibly discriminatory effect only when they unfairly dilute or cancel out white voting strength. Because the State's purpose here was to comply with the Voting Rights Act, and because the General Assembly's plan did not lead to proportional underrepresentation of white voters statewide, the majority concluded that appellants had failed to state an equal protection claim. . . .

Chief Judge Voorhees agreed that race-conscious redistricting is not per se unconstitutional, but dissented from the rest of the majority's equal protection analysis. He read JUSTICE WHITE's opinion in *UJO* to authorize race-based reapportionment only when the State employs traditional districting principles such as compactness and contiguity. . . . North Carolina's failure to respect these principles, in Judge Voorhees' view, "augur[ed] a constitutionally suspect, and potentially unlawful, intent" sufficient to defeat the state appellees' motion to dismiss. . . .

We noted probable jurisdiction. . . .

II.

A. "The right to vote freely for the candidate of one's choice is of the essence of a democratic society. . . ." *Reynolds v. Sims.* . . . For much of our Nation's history, that right sadly has been denied to many because of race. The Fifteenth Amendment, ratified in 1870 after a bloody Civil War, promised unequivocally that "[t]he right of citizens of the United States to vote" no longer would be "denied or abridged . . . by any State on account of race, color, or previous condition of servitude." . . .

But "[a] number of states . . . refused to take no for an answer and continued to circumvent the fifteenth amendment's prohibition through the use of both subtle and blunt instruments, perpetuating ugly patterns of pervasive racial discrimination." . . . Ostensibly race-neutral devices such as literacy tests with "grandfather" clauses and "good character" provisos were devised to deprive black voters of the franchise. Another of the weapons in the States' arsenal was the racial gerrymander—"the deliberate and arbitrary distortion of district boundaries . . . for [racial] purposes." . . . In the 1870's, for example, opponents of Reconstruction in Mississippi "concentrated the bulk of the black population in a 'shoestring' Congressional district running the length of the Mississippi River, leaving five others with white majorities." . . . Some 90 years later, Alabama redefined the boundaries of the city of Tuskegee "from a square to an uncouth twenty-eight-sided figure" in a manner that was alleged to exclude black voters, and only black voters, from the city limits. *Gomillion v. Lightfoot* . . . (1960).

Alabama's exercise in geometry was but one example of the racial discrimination in voting that persisted in parts of this country nearly a century after ratification of the Fifteenth Amendment. See *South Carolina v. Katzenbach* . . . (1966). In some States, registration of eligible black voters ran 50% behind that of whites. . . . Congress enacted the Voting Rights Act of 1965 as a dramatic and severe response to the situation. The Act proved immediately successful in ensuring racial minorities access to the voting booth; by the early 1970's, the spread between black and white registration in several of the targeted Southern States had fallen to well below 10%. . . .

But it soon became apparent that guaranteeing equal access to the polls would not suffice to root out other racially discriminatory voting practices. Drawing on the "one person, one vote" principle, this Court recognized that "[t]he right to vote can be affected by a dilution of voting power as well as by an absolute prohibition on casting a ballot." *Allen v. State Bd. of Elections* . . . (1969). . . . Where members of a racial minority group vote as a cohesive unit, practices such as multimember or at-large electoral systems can reduce or nullify minority voters' ability, as a group, "to elect the candidate of their choice." . . . Accordingly, the Court held that such schemes violate the Fourteenth Amendment when they are adopted with a discriminatory

purpose and have the effect of diluting minority voting strength. See, e.g., *Rogers v. Lodge* . . . (1982); *White v. Regester* . . . (1973). Congress, too, responded to the problem of vote dilution. In 1982, it amended 2 of the Voting Rights Act to prohibit legislation that results in the dilution of a minority group's voting strength, regardless of the legislature's intent. . . . see *Thornburg v. Gingles* . . . (1986) (applying amended 2 to vote-dilution claim involving multimember districts); see also *Voinovich v. Quilter* . . . (1993) (single-member districts).

B. It is against this background that we confront the questions presented here. In our view, the District Court properly dismissed appellants' claims against the federal appellees. Our focus is on appellants' claim that the State engaged in unconstitutional racial gerrymandering. That argument strikes a powerful historical chord: it is unsettling how closely the North Carolina plan resembles the most egregious racial gerrymanders of the past.

An understanding of the nature of appellants' claim is critical to our resolution of the case. In their complaint, appellants did not claim that the General Assembly's reapportionment plan unconstitutionally "diluted" white voting strength. They did not even claim to be white. Rather, appellants' complaint alleged that the deliberate segregation of voters into separate districts on the basis of race violated their constitutional right to participate in a "color-blind" electoral process. . . .

Despite their invocation of the ideal of a "color-blind" Constitution, see *Plessy v. Ferguson* . . . (1896) . . . , appellants appear to concede that race-conscious redistricting is not always unconstitutional. . . . That concession is wise: this Court never has held that race-conscious state decision-making is impermissible in all circumstances. What appellants object to is redistricting legislation that is so extremely irregular on its face that it rationally can be viewed only as an effort to segregate the races for purposes of voting, without regard for traditional districting principles and without sufficiently compelling justification. For the reasons that follow, we conclude that appellants have stated a claim upon which relief can be granted under the Equal Protection Clause. . . .

III.

A. The Equal Protection Clause provides that "[n]o State shall . . . deny to any person within its jurisdiction the equal protection of the laws." U.S. Const., Amdt. 14, 1. Its central purpose is to prevent the States from purposefully discriminating between individuals on the basis of race. *Washington v. Davis* . . . (1976). Laws that explicitly distinguish between individuals on racial grounds fall within the core of that prohibition.

No inquiry into legislative purpose is necessary when the racial classification appears on the face of the statute. See *Personnel Administrator of Mass. v. Feeney* . . . (1979). Accord, *Washington v. Seattle School Dist. No. 1* . . . (1982). Express racial classifications are immediately suspect because, "[a] bsent searching judicial inquiry . . . , there is simply no way of determining what classifications are "benign" or "remedial" and what classifications are in fact motivated by illegitimate notions of racial inferiority or simple racial politics." *Richmond v. J.A. Croson Co.* . . . (1989) . . . ; . . . see also *UJO* . . . ("[A] purportedly preferential race assignment may in fact disguise a policy that perpetuates disadvantageous treatment of the plan's supposed beneficiaries").

Classifications of citizens solely on the basis of race "are by their very nature odious to a free people whose institutions are founded upon the doctrine of equality." *Hirabayashi v. United States* . . . (1943). Accord, *Loving v. Virginia* . . . (1967). They threaten to stigmatize individuals by reason of their membership in a racial group and to incite racial hostility. *Croson* . . . ; *UJO* . . . ("[E]ven in the pursuit of remedial objectives, an explicit policy of assignment by race may serve to stimulate our society's latent race consciousness, suggesting the utility and propriety of basing decisions on a factor that ideally bear no relationship to an individual's worth or needs"). Accordingly, we have held that the Fourteenth Amendment requires state legislation that expressly distinguishes among citizens because of their race to be narrowly tailored to further a compelling governmental interest. See, e.g., *Wygant v. Jackson Bd. of Ed.* . . . (1986). . . .

These principles apply not only to legislation that contains explicit racial distinctions, but also to those "rare" statutes that, although race neutral, are, on their face, "unexplainable on grounds other than race." *Arlington Heights v. Metropolitan Housing Development Corp.* . . . (1977). As we explained in *Feeney*:

A racial classification, regardless of purported motivation, is presumptively invalid and can be upheld only upon an extraordinary justification. *Brown v. Board of Education* . . . ; *McLaughlin v. Florida.* . . . This rule applies as well to a classification that is ostensibly neutral but is an obvious pretext for racial discrimination. *Yick Wo v. Hopkins* . . . ; *Guinn v. United States* . . . ; compare *Lane v. Wilson* . . . ; *Gomillion v. Lightfoot.* . . .

B. Appellants contend that redistricting legislation that is so bizarre on its face that it is "unexplainable on grounds other than race," *Arlington Heights* . . . , demands the same close scrutiny that we give other state laws that classify citizens by race. Our voting rights precedents support that conclusion.

In *Guinn v. United States* . . . (1915), the Court invalidated under the Fifteenth Amendment a statute that imposed a literacy requirement on voters but contained a "grandfather clause" applicable to individuals and their lineal descendants entitled to vote "on [or prior to] January 1, 1866." . . . The determinative consideration for the Court was that the law, though ostensibly race neutral, on its face "embod[ied] no exercise of judgment and rest[ed] upon no discernible reason" other than to circumvent the prohibitions of the Fifteenth Amendment. . . . In other words, the statute was invalid because, on its face, it could not be explained on grounds other than race.

The Court applied the same reasoning to the "uncouth twenty-eight-sided" municipal boundary line at issue in Gomillion. Although the statute that redrew the city limits of Tuskegee was race neutral on its face, plaintiffs alleged that its effect was impermissibly to remove from the city virtually all black voters and no white voters. The Court reasoned:

If these allegations upon a trial remained uncontradicted or unqualified, the conclusion would be irresistible, tantamount for all practical purposes to a mathematical demonstration, that the legislation is solely concerned with segregating white and colored voters by fencing Negro citizens out of town so as to deprive them of their preexisting municipal vote. . . .

The majority resolved the case under the Fifteenth Amendment. . . . Justice Whittaker, however, concluded that the "unlawful segregation of races of citizens" into different voting districts was cognizable under the Equal Protection Clause. . . . This Court's subsequent reliance on *Gomillion* in other Fourteenth Amendment cases suggests the correctness of Justice Whittaker's view. See, e.g., *Feeney* . . . ; *Whitcomb v. Chavis* . . . (1971); see also *Mobile v. Bolden* . . . (1980) . . . (*Gomillion*'s holding "is compelled by the Equal Protection Clause"). *Gomillion* thus supports appellants' contention that district lines obviously drawn for the purpose of separating voters by race require careful scrutiny under the Equal Protection Clause regardless of the motivations underlying their adoption.

The Court extended the reasoning of *Gomillion* to congressional districting in *Wright v. Rockefeller* . . . (1964). At issue in *Wright* were four districts contained in a New York apportionment statute. The plaintiffs alleged that the statute excluded nonwhites from one district and concentrated them in the other three. . . . Every member of the Court assumed that the plaintiffs' allegation that the statute "segregate[d] eligible voters by race and place of origin" stated a constitutional claim. . . . The Justices disagreed only as to whether the plaintiffs had carried their burden of proof at trial. The dissenters thought the unusual shape of the district lines could "be explained only in racial terms." . . . The majority, however, accepted the District Court's finding that the plaintiffs had failed to establish that the districts were in fact drawn on racial lines. Although the boundary lines were somewhat irregular, the majority reasoned, they were not so bizarre as to permit of no other conclusion. Indeed, because most of the nonwhite voters lived together in one area, it would have been difficult to construct voting districts without concentrations of nonwhite voters. . . .

Wright illustrates the difficulty of determining from the face of a single-member districting plan that it purposefully distinguishes between voters on the basis of race. A reapportionment statute typically does not classify persons at all; it classifies tracts of land, or addresses. Moreover, redistricting differs from other kinds of state decision-making in that the legislature always is aware of race when it draws district lines, just as it is aware of age, economic status, religious and political persuasion, and a variety of other demographic factors. That sort of race consciousness does not lead inevitably to impermissible race discrimination. As *Wright* demonstrates, when members of a racial group live together in one community, a reapportionment plan that concentrates members of the group in one district and excludes them from others may reflect wholly legitimate purposes. The district lines may be drawn, for example, to provide for compact districts of contiguous territory, or to maintain the integrity of political subdivisions. See *Reynolds* . . . (recognizing these as legitimate state interests).

The difficulty of proof, of course, does not mean that a racial gerrymander, once established, should receive less scrutiny under the Equal Protection Clause than other state legislation classifying citizens by race. Moreover, it seems clear to us that proof sometimes will not be difficult at all. In some exceptional cases, a reapportionment plan may be so highly irregular that, on its face, it rationally cannot be understood as anything other than an effort to "segregat[e] . . . voters" on the basis of race. *Gomillion*, in which a tortured municipal boundary line was drawn to exclude black voters, was such a case. So, too, would be a case in which a State concentrated a dispersed minority population in a single district by disregarding traditional districting principles such as compactness, contiguity, and respect for political subdivisions. We emphasize that these criteria are important not because they are constitutionally required—they are not, compare *Gaffney v. Cummings* . . . (1973)—but because they are objective factors that may serve to defeat a claim that a district has been gerrymandered on racial lines. Compare *Karcher v. Daggett* . . . (1983) . . . ("One need not use Justice Stewart's classic definition of obscenity—'I know it when I see it'—as an ultimate standard for judging the constitutionality of a gerrymander to recognize that dramatically irregular shapes may have sufficient probative force to call for an explanation.") . . .

Put differently, we believe that reapportionment is one area in which appearances do matter. A reapportionment plan that includes in one district individuals who belong to the same race, but who are otherwise widely separated by geographical and political boundaries, and who may have little in common with one another but the color of their skin, bears an uncomfortable resemblance to political apartheid. It reinforces the perception that members of the same racial group—regardless of their age, education, economic status, or the community in which they live—think alike, share the same political interests, and will prefer the same candidates at the polls. We have rejected such perceptions elsewhere as impermissible racial stereotypes. See, e.g., *Holland v. Illinois* . . . (1990) ("[A] prosecutor's assumption that a black juror may be presumed to be partial simply because he is black . . . violates the Equal Protection Clause" . . .); see also *Edmonson v. Leesville Concrete Co.* . . . (1991) ("If our society is to continue to progress as a multiracial democracy, it must recognize that the automatic invocation of race stereotypes retards that progress and causes continued hurt and injury"). By perpetuating such notions, a racial gerrymander may exacerbate the very patterns of racial bloc voting that majority-minority districting is sometimes said to counteract.

The message that such districting sends to elected representatives is equally pernicious. When a district obviously is created solely to effectuate the perceived common interests of one racial group, elected officials are more likely to believe that their primary obligation is to represent only the members of that group, rather than their constituency as a whole. This is altogether antithetical to our system of representative democracy. As Justice Douglas explained in his dissent in *Wright v. Rockefeller* nearly 30 years ago:

> Here the individual is important, not his race, his creed, or his color. The principle of equality is at war with the notion that District A must be represented by a Negro, as it is with the notion that District B must be represented by a Caucasian, District C by a Jew, District D by a Catholic, and so on. . . . That system, by whatever name it is called, is a divisive force in a community, emphasizing differences between candidates and voters that are irrelevant in the constitutional sense. . . .

When racial or religious lines are drawn by the State, the multiracial, multireligious communities that our Constitution seeks to weld together as one become separatist; antagonisms that relate to race or to religion, rather than to political issues, are generated; communities seek not the best representative, but the best racial or religious partisan. Since that system is at war with the democratic ideal, it should find no footing here. . . .

For these reasons, we conclude that a plaintiff challenging a reapportionment statute under the Equal Protection Clause may state a claim by alleging that the legislation, though race neutral on its face, rationally cannot be understood as anything other than an effort to separate voters into different districts on the basis of race, and that the separation lacks sufficient justification. It is unnecessary for us to decide whether or how a reapportionment plan that, on its face, can be explained in nonracial terms successfully could be challenged. Thus, we express no view as to whether "the intentional creation of majority-minority districts, without more," always gives rise to an equal protection claim. . . . We hold only that, on the facts of this case, appellants have stated a claim sufficient to defeat the state appellees' motion to dismiss.

C. The dissenters consider the circumstances of this case "functionally indistinguishable" from multimember districting and at-large voting systems, which are loosely described as "other varieties of gerrymandering." . . . We have considered the constitutionality of these practices in other Fourteenth Amendment cases, and have required plaintiffs to demonstrate that the challenged practice has the purpose and effect of diluting a racial group's voting strength. See, e.g., *Rogers v. Lodge* . . . (1982) (at-large system); *Mobile v. Bolden* . . . (1980) (same); *White v. Regester* . . . (1973) (multimember districts); *Whitcomb v. Chavis* . . . (1971) (same). . . . At-large and multimember schemes, however, do not classify voters on the basis of race. Classifying citizens by race, as we have said, threatens special harms that are not present in our vote-dilution cases. It therefore warrants different analysis.

JUSTICE SOUTER apparently believes that racial gerrymandering is harmless unless it dilutes a racial group's voting strength. . . . As we have explained, however, reapportionment legislation that cannot be understood as anything other than an effort to classify and separate voters by race injures voters in other ways. It reinforces racial stereotypes and threatens to undermine our system of representative democracy by signaling to elected officials that they represent a particular racial group, rather than their constituency as a whole.... JUSTICE SOUTER does not adequately explain why these harms are not cognizable under the Fourteenth Amendment.

The dissenters make two other arguments that cannot be reconciled with our precedents. First, they suggest that a racial gerrymander of the sort alleged here is functionally equivalent to gerrymanders for nonracial purposes, such as political gerrymanders.... This Court has held political gerrymanders to be justiciable under the Equal Protection Clause. See *Davis v. Bandemer*.... But nothing in our case law compels the conclusion that racial and political gerrymanders are subject to precisely the same constitutional scrutiny. In fact, our country's long and persistent history of racial discrimination in voting—as well as our Fourteenth Amendment jurisprudence, which always has reserved the strictest scrutiny for discrimination on the basis of race, see supra, at 10–12—would seem to compel the opposite conclusion.

Second, JUSTICE STEVENS argues that racial gerrymandering poses no constitutional difficulties when district lines are drawn to favor the minority, rather than the majority.... We have made clear, however, that equal protection analysis "is not dependent on the race of those burdened or benefited by a particular classification." *Croson*.... Accord, *Wygant*.... Indeed, racial classifications receive close scrutiny even when they may be said to burden or benefit the races equally. See *Powers v. Ohio* ... (1991) ("It is axiomatic that racial classifications do not become legitimate on the assumption that all persons suffer them in equal degree").

Finally, nothing in the Court's highly fractured decision in *UJO*—on which the District Court almost exclusively relied, and which the dissenters evidently believe controls . . . — forecloses the claim we recognize today. *UJO* concerned New York's revision of a reapportionment plan to include additional majority-minority districts in response to the

Attorney General's denial of administrative preclearance under 5. In that regard, it closely resembles the present case. But the cases are critically different in another way. The plaintiffs in *UJO*—members of a Hasidic community split between two districts under New York's revised redistricting plan—did not allege that the plan, on its face, was so highly irregular that it rationally could be understood only as an effort to segregate voters by race. Indeed, the facts of the case would not have supported such a claim. Three Justices approved the New York statute, in part, precisely because it adhered to traditional districting principles:

> [W]e think it . . . permissible for a State, employing sound districting principles such as compactness and population equality, to attempt to prevent racial minorities from being repeatedly outvoted by creating districts that will afford fair representation to the members of those racial groups who are sufficiently numerous and whose residential patterns afford the opportunity of creating districts in which they will be in the majority. . . .

As a majority of the Justices construed the complaint, the *UJO* plaintiffs made a different claim: that the New York plan impermissibly "diluted" their voting strength. Five of the eight Justices who participated in the decision resolved the case under the framework the Court previously had adopted for vote-dilution cases. Three Justices rejected the plaintiffs' claim on the grounds that the New York statute "represented no racial slur or stigma with respect to whites or any other race" and left white voters with better than proportional representation.... Two others concluded that the statute did not minimize or cancel out a minority group's voting strength, and that the State's intent to comply with the Voting Rights Act, as interpreted by the Department of Justice, "foreclose[d] any finding that [the State] acted with the invidious purpose of discriminating against white voters." ...

The District Court below relied on these portions of *UJO* to reject appellants' claim.... In our view, the court used the wrong analysis. *UJO*'s framework simply does not apply where, as here, a reapportionment plan is alleged to be so irrational on its face that it immediately offends principles of racial equality. *UJO* set forth a standard under which white voters can establish unconstitutional vote dilution. But it did not purport to overrule *Gomillion* or *Wright*. Nothing in the decision precludes white voters (or voters of any other race) from bringing the analytically distinct claim that a reapportionment plan rationally cannot be understood as anything other than an effort to segregate citizens into separate voting districts on the basis of race without sufficient justification. Because appellants here stated such a claim, the District Court erred in dismissing their complaint.

IV.

JUSTICE SOUTER contends that exacting scrutiny of racial gerrymanders under the Fourteenth Amendment is inappropriate because reapportionment "nearly always require[s] some consideration of race for legitimate reasons." . . . "As long as members of racial groups have [a] commonality of interest" and "racial bloc voting takes place," he argues, "legislators will have to take race into account" in order to comply with the Voting Rights Act, JUSTICE SOUTER's reasoning is flawed.

Earlier this Term, we unanimously reaffirmed that racial bloc voting and minority-group political cohesion never can be assumed, but specifically must be proved in each case in order to establish that a redistricting plan dilutes minority voting strength in violation of 2. See *Growe v. Emison* . . . (1993) ("Unless these points are established, there neither has been a wrong nor can be a remedy"). That racial bloc voting or minority political cohesion may be found to exist in some cases, of course, is no reason to treat all racial gerrymanders differently from other kinds of racial classification. JUSTICE SOUTER apparently views racial gerrymandering of the type presented here as a special category of "benign" racial discrimination that should be subject to relaxed judicial review. . . . As we have said, however, the very reason that the Equal Protection Clause demands strict scrutiny of all racial classifications is because, without it, a court cannot determine whether or not the discrimination truly is "benign." . . . Thus, if appellants' allegations of a racial gerrymander are not contradicted on remand, the District Court must determine whether the General Assembly's reapportionment plan satisfies strict scrutiny. We therefore

consider what that level of scrutiny requires in the reapportionment context.

The state appellees suggest that a covered jurisdiction may have a compelling interest in creating majority-minority districts in order to comply with the Voting Rights Act. The States certainly have a very strong interest in complying with federal antidiscrimination laws that are constitutionally valid as interpreted and as applied. But in the context of a Fourteenth Amendment challenge, courts must bear in mind the difference between what the law permits and what it requires.

For example, on remand, North Carolina might claim that it adopted the revised plan in order to comply with the 5 "nonretrogression" principle. Under that principle, a proposed voting change cannot be precleared if it will lead to "a retrogression in the position of racial minorities with respect to their effective exercise of the electoral franchise." *Beer v. United States* . . . (1976). In *Beer*, we held that a reapportionment plan that created one majority-minority district where none existed before passed muster under 5 because it improved the position of racial minorities. . . . see also *Richmond v. United States* . . . (1975) (annexation that reduces percentage of blacks in population satisfies 5 where postannexation districts "fairly reflect" current black voting strength).

Although the Court concluded that the redistricting scheme at issue in *Beer* was nonretrogressive, it did not hold that the plan, for that reason, was immune from constitutional challenge. The Court expressly declined to reach that question. . . . Indeed, the Voting Rights Act and our case law make clear that a reapportionment plan that satisfies 5 still may be enjoined as unconstitutional. . . . (neither a declaratory judgment by the District Court for the District of Columbia nor preclearance by the Attorney General "shall bar a subsequent action to enjoin enforcement" of new voting practice); *Allen* . . . (after preclearance, "private parties may enjoin the enforcement of the new enactment . . . in traditional suits attacking its constitutionality"). Thus, we do not read *Beer* or any of our other 5 cases to give covered jurisdictions carte blanche to engage in racial gerrymandering in the name of nonretrogression. A reapportionment plan would not be narrowly tailored to the goal of avoiding retrogression if the State went beyond what was reasonably necessary to avoid retrogression. Our conclusion is supported by the plurality opinion in *UJO,* in which four Justices determined that New York's creation of additional majority-minority districts was constitutional because the plaintiffs had failed to demonstrate that the State "did more than the Attorney General was authorized to require it to do under the nonretrogression principle of *Beer.*" . . .

Before us, the state appellees contend that the General Assembly's revised plan was necessary not to prevent retrogression, but to avoid dilution of black voting strength in violation of 2, as construed in *Thornburg v. Gingles* . . . (1986). In *Gingles,* the Court considered a multimember redistricting plan for the North Carolina State Legislature. The Court held that members of a racial minority group claiming 2 vote dilution through the use of multimember districts must prove three threshold conditions: that the minority group "is sufficiently large and geographically compact to constitute a majority in a single-member district," that the minority group is "politically cohesive," and that "the white majority votes sufficiently as a bloc to enable it . . . usually to defeat the minority's preferred candidate" . . . We have indicated that similar preconditions apply in 2 challenges to single-member districts. See *Voinovich v. Quilter* . . . ; *Growe v. Emison* . . . .

Appellants maintain that the General Assembly's revised plan could not have been required by 2. They contend that the State's black population is too dispersed to support two geographically compact majority-black districts, as the bizarre shape of District 12 demonstrates, and that there is no evidence of black political cohesion. They also contend that recent black electoral successes demonstrate the willingness of white voters in North Carolina to vote for black candidates. Appellants point out that blacks currently hold the positions of State Auditor, Speaker of the North Carolina House of Representatives, and chair of the North Carolina State Board of Elections. They also point out that, in 1990, a black candidate defeated a white opponent in the Democratic Party run off for a United States Senate seat before being defeated narrowly by the Republican incumbent in the general election. Appellants further argue that, if 2 did

require adoption of North Carolina's revised plan, 2 is to that extent unconstitutional. These arguments were not developed below, and the issues remain open for consideration on remand.

The state appellees alternatively argue that the General Assembly's plan advanced a compelling interest entirely distinct from the Voting Rights Act. We previously have recognized a significant state interest in eradicating the effects of past racial discrimination. See, e.g., *Croson* . . . ; *Wygant.* . . . But the State must have a "'strong basis in evidence for [concluding] that remedial action [is] necessary.'" *Croson* . . . (quoting *Wygant* . . .).

The state appellees submit that two pieces of evidence gave the General Assembly a strong basis for believing that remedial action was warranted here: the Attorney General's imposition of the 5 preclearance requirement on 40 North Carolina counties, and the Gingles District Court's findings of a long history of official racial discrimination in North Carolina's political system and of pervasive racial bloc voting. The state appellees assert that the deliberate creation of majority-minority districts is the most precise way—indeed the only effective way—to overcome the effects of racially polarized voting. This question also need not be decided at this stage of the litigation. We note, however, that only three Justices in *UJO* were prepared to say that States have a significant interest in minimizing the consequences of racial bloc voting apart from the requirements of the Voting Rights Act. And those three Justices specifically concluded that race-based districting, as a response to racially polarized voting, is constitutionally permissible only when the State "employ[s] sound districting principles," and only when the affected racial group's "residential patterns afford the opportunity of creating districts in which they will be in the majority." . . .

V.

Racial classifications of any sort pose the risk of lasting harm to our society. They reinforce the belief, held by too many for too much of our history, that individuals should be judged by the color of their skin. Racial classifications with respect to voting carry particular dangers. Racial gerrymandering, even for remedial purposes, may balkanize us into competing racial factions; it threatens to carry us further from the goal of a political system in which race no longer matters—a goal that the Fourteenth and Fifteenth Amendments embody, and to which the Nation continues to aspire. It is for these reasons that race-based districting by our state legislatures demands close judicial scrutiny.

In this case, the Attorney General suggested that North Carolina could have created a reasonably compact second majority-minority district in the south-central to southeastern part of the State. We express no view as to whether appellants successfully could have challenged such a district under the Fourteenth Amendment. We also do not decide whether appellants' complaint stated a claim under constitutional provisions other than the Fourteenth Amendment. Today we hold only that appellants have stated a claim under the Equal Protection Clause by alleging that the North Carolina General Assembly adopted a reapportionment scheme so irrational on its face that it can be understood only as an effort to segregate voters into separate voting districts because of their race, and that the separation lacks sufficient justification. If the allegation of racial gerrymandering remains uncontradicted, the District Court further must determine whether the North Carolina plan is narrowly tailored to further a compelling governmental interest. Accordingly, we reverse the judgment of the District Court and remand the case for further proceedings consistent with this opinion.

It is so ordered.

Source: *Shaw v. Reno*, 509 U.S. 630 (1993).

See also: Voting and Race; Voting Rights Act of 1965. Document: Voting Rights Act of 1965

Proposition 187 (1994)

Introduction

Passed in California with nearly 60 percent of the popular vote in November 1994, Proposition 187 withdrew many social services from illegal aliens living in California, *representing a conservative shift in the state against illegal immigration. The proposition was extremely controversial and sparked numerous protests throughout the state. The initiative was almost immediately challenged in the federal courts, which have subsequently ruled almost all of its provisions unconstitutional.*

Primary Source

Section 1. Findings and Declaration.

The People of California find and declare as follows: That they have suffered and are suffering economic hardship caused by the presence of illegal aliens in this state. That they have suffered and are suffering personal injury and damage caused by the criminal conduct of illegal aliens in this state. That they have a right to the protection of their government from any person or persons entering this country unlawfully. Therefore, the People of California declare their intention to provide for cooperation between their agencies of state and local government with the federal government, and to establish a system of required notification by and between such agencies to prevent illegal aliens in the United States from receiving benefits or public services in the State of California.

Section 2. Manufacture, Distribution or Sale of False Citizenship or Resident Alien Documents: Crime and Punishment.

Section 113. is added to the Penal Code, to read:

Section 113. Any person who manufactures, distributes or sells false documents to conceal the true citizenship or resident alien status of another person is guilty of a felony, and shall be punished by imprisonment in the state prison for five years or by a fine of seventy-five thousand dollars ($75,000).

Section 3. Use of False Citizenship or Resident Alien Documents: Crime and Punishment.

Section 114. is added to the Penal Code, to read:

Section 114. Any person who uses false documents to conceal his or her true citizenship or resident alien status is guilty of a felony, and shall be punished by imprisonment in the state prison for five years or by a fine of twenty-five thousand dollars ($25,000).

Section 4. Law Enforcement Cooperation with INS.

Section 834b is added to the Penal Code, to read:

Section 834b.

(a) Every law enforcement agency in California shall fully cooperate with the United States Immigration and Naturalization Service regarding any person who is arrested if he or she is suspected of being present in the United States in violation of federal immigration laws.

(b) With respect to any such person who is arrested, and suspected of being present in the United States in violation of federal immigration laws, every law enforcement agency shall do the following:

(1) Attempt to verify the legal status of such person as a citizen of the United States, an alien lawfully admitted as a permanent resident, an alien lawfully admitted for a temporary period of time or as an alien who is present in the United States in violation of immigration laws. The verification process may include, but shall not be limited to, questioning the person regarding his or her date and place of birth, and entry into the United States, and demanding documentation to indicate his or her legal status.

(2) Notify the person of his or her apparent status as an alien who is present in the United States in violation of federal immigration laws and inform him or her that, apart from any criminal justice proceedings, he or she must either obtain legal status or leave the United States.

(3) Notify the Attorney General of California and the United States Immigration and Naturalization Service of the apparent illegal status and provide any additional information that may be requested by any other public entity.

(c) Any legislative, administrative, or other action by a city, county, or other legally authorized local governmental entity with jurisdictional boundaries, or by a law enforcement agency, to prevent or limit the cooperation required by subdivision (a) is expressly prohibited.

Section 5. Exclusion of Illegal Aliens from Public Social Services.

Section 10001.5. is added to the Welfare and Institutions Code, to read:

Section 10001.5.

(a) In order to carry out the intention of the People of California that only citizens of the United States and aliens lawfully admitted to the United States may receive the benefits of public social services and to ensure that all persons employed in the providing of those services shall diligently protect public funds from misuse, the provisions of this section are adopted.

(b) A person shall not receive any public social services to which he or she may be otherwise entitled the legal status of that person has been verified as one of the following:

(1) A citizen of the United States.

(2) An alien lawfully admitted as a permanent resident.

(3) An alien lawfully admitted for a temporary period of time.

(c) If any public entity in this state to whom a person has applied for public social services determines or reasonably suspects, based upon the information provided to it, that the person is an alien in the United States in violation of federal law, the following procedures shall be followed by the public entity:

(1) The entity shall not provide the person with benefits or services.

(2) The entity shall, in writing, notify the person of his or her apparent illegal immigration status, and that the person must either obtain legal status or leave the United States.

(3) The entity shall also notify the State Director of Social Services, the Attorney General of California and the United States Immigration and Naturalization Service of the apparent illegal status, and shall provide any additional information that may be requested by any other public entity.

Section 6. Exclusion of Illegal Aliens from Publicly Funded Health Care.

Chapter 1.3 (commencing with Section 130) is added to Part 1 of Division 1 of the Health and Safety Code, to read:

CHAPTER 1.3. PUBLICLY-FUNDED HEALTH CARE SERVICES

Section 130. In order to carry out the intention of the People of California that, excepting emergency medical care as required by federal law, only citizens of the United States and aliens lawfully admitted to the United States may receive the benefits of publicly-funded health care, and to ensure that all persons employed in the providing of those services shall diligently protect public funds from misuse, the provisions of this section are adopted.

(b) A person shall not receive any health care services from a publicly-funded health care facility, to which he or she is otherwise entitled until the legal status of that person has been verified as one of the following:

(1) A citizen of the United States.

(2) An alien lawfully admitted as a permanent resident.

(3) An alien lawfully admitted for a temporary period of time.

(c) If any publicly-funded health care facility in this state from whom a person seeks health care services, other than emergency medical care as required by federal law, determines or reasonably suspects, based upon the information provided to it, that the person is an alien in the United States in violation of federal law, the following procedures shall be followed by the facility:

(1) The facility shall not provide the person with services.

(2) The facility shall, in writing, notify the person of his or her apparent illegal immigration status, and that the person must either obtain legal status or leave the United States.

(3) The facility shall also notify the State Director of Health Services, the Attorney General of California and the United States Immigration and Naturalization Service of the apparent illegal status, and shall provide any additional information that may be requested by any other public entity.

(d) For purposes of this section "publicly-funded health care facility" shall be defined as specified in Section 1200 and 1250 of the Health and Safety Code as of January 1, 1993.

Section 7. Exclusion of Illegal Aliens From Public Elementary and Secondary Schools.

Section 48215. is added to the Education Code to read:

Section 48215.

(a) No public elementary or secondary school shall admit, or permit the attendance of, any child who is not a citizen of the United States, an alien lawfully admitted as a permanent resident, or a person who is otherwise authorized under federal law to be present in the United States.

(b) Commencing January 1, 1995, each school district shall verify the legal status of each child enrolling in the school district for the first time in order to ensure the enrollment or attendance only of citizens, aliens lawfully admitted as permanent residents, or persons who are otherwise authorized to be present in the United States.

(c) By January 1, 1996, each school district shall have verified the legal status of each child already enrolled and in attendance in the school district in order to ensure the enrollment or attendance only of citizens, aliens lawfully admitted as permanent residents, or persons who are otherwise authorized under federal law to be present in the United States.

(d) By January 1, 1995, each school district shall also have verified the legal status of each parent or guardian of each child referred to in subdivision (b) and (c) above, to determine whether such parent or guardian is one of the following:

(1) A citizen of the United States.

(2) An alien lawfully admired as a permanent resident.

(3) An alien admitted lawfully for a temporary period of time.

(e) Each school district shall provide information to the State Superintendent of Public Instruction, the Attorney General of California and the United States Immigration and Naturalization Service regarding any enrollee or pupil, or parent or guardian, attending a public elementary or secondary school in the school district determined or reasonably suspected to be in violation of federal immigration laws within forty five days after becoming aware of an apparent violation. The notice shall also be provided to the parent or legal guardian of the enrollee or pupil, and shall state that an existing pupil may not continue to attend the school after ninety calendar days from the date of the notice, unless legal status is established.

(f) For each child who cannot establish legal status in the United States, each school district shall continue to provide education for a period of ninety days from the date of the notice. Such ninety day period shall be utilized to accomplish an orderly transition to a school in the child's country of origin. Each school district shall fully cooperate in this transition effort to ensure that the educational needs of the child are best served for that period of time.

Section 8. Exclusion of Illegal Aliens from Public Post-secondary Educational Institutions.

Section 66010.8. is added to the Education Code, to read:

Section 660 10.8.

(a) No public institution of post-secondary education shall admit, enroll, or permit the attendance of any person who is not a citizen of the United States, an alien lawfully admitted as a permanent resident, in the United States, or a person who is otherwise authorized under federal law to be present in the United States.

(b) Commencing with the first term or semester that begins after January 1, 1995, and at the commencement of each term or semester thereafter, each public post-secondary educational institution shall verify the status of each person enrolled or in attendance at that institution in order to ensure the enrollment or attendance only of United States citizens, aliens lawfully admitted as permanent residents in the United States, and persons who are otherwise authorized under federal law to be present in the United States.

(c) No later than 45 days after the admissions officer of a public post-secondary educational institution becomes aware of the application, enrollment, or attendance of a person determined to be, or who is under reasonable suspicion of being, in the United States in violation of federal immigration laws, that officer shall provide that information to the State Superintendent of Public Instruction, the Attorney General of California and the United States Immigration and Naturalization Service. The information shall also be provided to the applicant, enrollee, or person admitted.

Section 9. Attorney General Cooperation with the INS.

Section 53069.65. is added to the Government Code, to read:

53059.55. Whenever the state or a city, or a county, or any other legally authorized local governmental entity with jurisdictional boundaries reports the presence of a person who is suspected of being present in the United States in violation of federal immigration laws to the Attorney General of California, that report shall be transmitted to the United States Immigration and Naturalization Service. The Attorney General shall be responsible for maintaining on-going and accurate records of such reports, and shall provide any additional information that may be requested by any other government entity.

Section 10. Amendment and Severability.

The statutory provisions contained in this measure may not be amended by the Legislature except to further its purposes by statute passed in each house by roll call vote entered in the journal, two-thirds of the membership concurring, or by a statute that becomes effective only when approved by the voters. In the event that any portion of this act or the application thereof to any person or circumstance is held invalid, that invalidity shall not affect any other provision or application of the act, which can be given effect without the invalid provision or application, and to that end the provisions of this act are severable.

Source: California Proposition 187(1994). Text available at the University of Southern California Archives, http://www.usc.edu/.

See also: 287g Delegation of Immigration Authority; Anchor Baby; Anti-Immigrant Sentiment; Immigration Acts; Immigration and Customs Enforcement; National Origins Act of 1924; Operation Wetback; Unauthorized Immigration; United States Border Patrol

Glass Ceiling Commission: Summary of Recommendations (1995)

Introduction

In late November 1995, the Glass Ceiling Commission released this report, outlining how both government and business in the United States discriminated against women and minorities at the management level (the so-called glass ceiling that prevents them from being promoted to positions of authority). The commission had been established by the Civil Rights Act of 1991 and was composed of 21 bipartisan and congressional appointed officials. The excerpt below summarizes the commission's 12 recommendations to break the glass ceiling.

Primary Source

Business:

Demonstrate CEO commitment. Eliminating the glass ceiling requires that the CEO communicate visible and continuing commitment to workforce diversity throughout the organization. The Commission recommends that all CEOs and boards of directors set companywide policies that actively promote diversity programs and policies that remove artificial barriers at every level.

Include diversity in all strategic business plans and hold line managers accountable for progress. Businesses customarily establish short- and long-term objectives and measure progress in key business areas. The Commission recommends that all corporations include in their strategic business plans efforts to achieve diversity both at the senior management level and throughout the workforce. Additionally, performance appraisals, compensation incentives and other evaluation measures must reflect a line manager's ability to set a high standard and demonstrate progress toward breaking the glass ceiling.

Use affirmative action as a tool. Affirmative action is the deliberate undertaking of positive steps to design and implement employment procedures that ensure the employment system provides equal opportunity to all. The Commission recommends that corporate America use affirmative action as a tool ensuring that all qualified individuals have equal access and opportunity to compete based on ability and merit.

Select, promote and retain qualified individuals. Traditional prerequisites and qualifications for senior management and board of director positions focus too narrowly on conventional sources and experiences. The Commission recommends that organizations expand their vision and seek candidates from non-customary sources, backgrounds and experiences, and that the executive recruiting industry work with businesses to explore ways to expand the universe of qualified candidates.

Prepare minorities and women for senior positions. Too often, minorities and women find themselves channeled into staff positions that provide little access and visibility to corporate decisionmakers, and removed from strategic business decisions. The Commission recommends that organizations expand access to core areas of the business and to various developmental experiences, and establish formal mentoring programs that provide career guidance and support to prepare minorities and women for senior positions.

Educate the corporate ranks. Organizations cannot make members of society blind to differences in color, culture or gender, but they can demand and enforce merit-based practice and behavior internally. The Commission recommends that companies provide formal training at regular intervals on company time to sensitize and familiarize all employees about the strengths and challenges of gender, racial, ethnic and cultural differences.

Initiate work/life and family-friendly policies. Work/life and family friendly policies, although they benefit all employees, are an important step in an organization's commitment to hiring, retaining and promoting both men and women. The Commission recommends that organizations adopt policies that recognize and accommodate the balance between work and family responsibilities that impact the lifelong career paths of all employees.

Adopt high performance workplace practices. There is a positive relationship between corporate financial performance, productivity and the use of high performance workplace practices. The Commission recommends that all companies adopt high performance workplace practices, which fall under the categories of skills and information; participation, organization and partnership; and compensation, security and work environment.

Government:

Lead by example. Government at all levels must be a leader in the quest to make equal opportunity a reality for minorities and women. The Commission recommends that all government agencies, as employers, increase their efforts to eliminate internal glass ceilings by examining their practices for promoting qualified minorities and women to senior management and decisionmaking positions.

Strengthen enforcement of anti-discrimination laws. Workplace discrimination presents a significant glass ceiling barrier for minorities and women. The Commission recommends that Federal enforcement agencies increase their efforts to enforce existing laws by expanding efforts to end systemic discrimination and challenging multiple discrimination. The Commission also recommends evaluating effectiveness and efficiency and strengthening interagency coordination as a way of furthering the effort. Additionally, updating anti-discrimination regulations, strengthening and expanding corporate management reviews and improving the complaint processing system play major roles in ending discrimination. Finally, the Commission recommends making sure that enforcement agencies have adequate resources to enforce anti-discrimination laws.

Improve data collection. Accurate data on minorities and women can show where progress is or is not being made in breaking glass ceiling barriers. The Commission recommends that relevant government agencies revise the collection of data by refining existing data categories and improving the specificity of data collected. All government agencies that collect data must break it out by race and gender, and avoid double counting of minority women, in order to develop a clear picture of where minorities an women are in the workforce.

Increase disclosure of diversity data. Public disclosure of diversity data—specifically, data on the most senior positions—is an effective incentive to develop and maintain innovative, effective programs to break glass ceiling barriers. The Commission recommends that both the public and private sectors work toward increased public disclosure of diversity data.

Source: U.S. Glass Ceiling Commission. *A Solid Investment: Making Full Use of the Nation's Human Capital* (Final Report of the Commission). Washington, DC: Government Printing Office, 1995.

See also: Affirmative Action; *Alexander v. Sandoval*; Blacks, Wage Discrimination; Day Laborers; Domestic Work; Fair Employment Practices Commission; Garment Workers; Hiring Practices; Labor Movement, Racism in; Labor Unions; Migrant Workers; Racial Earnings Gap

Church Arson Prevention Act (1996)

Introduction

Signed into law by President Bill Clinton on July 3, 1996, this legislation was passed by Congress in response to a series of attacks against churches that especially targeted predominantly African American congregations. In 1988, Congress had approved a statute mandating federal jurisdiction in cases of religious vandalism in which property damage exceeded $10,000. Proposed by senators Edward Kennedy and Lauch Faircloth and representatives Henry Hyde and John Conyers Jr., the Church Arson Prevention Act was designed to further deter church arson by increasing the authority of federal prosecution; imposing stricter penalties for arson, vandalism, or other acts of destruction on places of religious worship; and authorizing federal assistance in the rebuilding process. The following is the full text of the act.

Primary Source

An Act to amend title 18, United States Code, to clarify the Federal jurisdiction over offenses relating to damage to religious property.

Be it enacted by the Senate and House of Representatives of the United States of America in Congress assembled,

SECTION 1. SHORT TITLE.

This Act may be cited as the "Church Arson Prevention Act of 1996."

SEC. 2. FINDINGS.

The Congress finds the following:

(1) The incidence of arson or other destruction or vandalism of places of religious worship, and the incidence of violent interference with an individual's lawful exercise or attempted exercise of the right of religious freedom at a place of religious worship pose a serious national problem.

(2) The incidence of arson of places of religious worship has recently increased, especially in the context of places of religious worship that serve predominantly African American congregations.

(3) Changes in Federal law are necessary to deal properly with this problem.

(4) Although local jurisdictions have attempted to respond to the challenges posed by such acts of destruction or damage to religious property, the problem is sufficiently serious, widespread, and interstate in scope to warrant Federal intervention to assist State and local jurisdictions.

(5) Congress has authority, pursuant to the Commerce Clause of the Constitution, to make acts of destruction or damage to religious property a violation of Federal law.

(6) Congress has authority, pursuant to section 2 of the 13th amendment to the Constitution, to make actions of private citizens motivated by race, color, or ethnicity that interfere with the ability of citizens to hold or use religious property without fear of attack, violations of Federal criminal law.

SEC. 3. PROHIBITION OF VIOLENT INTERFERENCE WITH RELIGIOUS WORSHIP.

Section 247 of title 18, United States Code, is amended—

(1) in subsection (a), by striking "subsection (c) of this section" and inserting "subsection (d)";

(2) by redesignating subsections (c), (d), and (e), as subsections (d), (e), and (f), respectively;

(3) by striking subsection (b) and inserting the following:

"(b) The circumstances referred to in subsection (a) are that the offense is in or affects interstate or foreign commerce.

"(c) Whoever intentionally defaces, damages, or destroys any religious real property because of the race, color, or ethnic characteristics of any individual associated with that religious property, or attempts to do so, shall be punished as provided in subsection (d).";

(4) in subsection (d), as redesignated—

(A) in paragraph (2)—

(i) by inserting "to any person, including any public safety officer performing duties as a direct or proximate result of conduct prohibited by this section," after "bodily injury"; and

(ii) by striking "ten years" and inserting "20 years";

(B) by redesignating paragraphs (2) and (3) as paragraphs (3) and (4), respectively;

(C) by inserting after paragraph (1) the following: "(2) if bodily injury results to any person, including any public safety officer performing duties as a direct or proximate result of conduct prohibited by this section, and the violation is by means of fire or an explosive, a fine under this title or imprisonment for not more that 40 years, or both;";

(5) in subsection (f), as redesignated—

(A) by striking "religious property" and inserting "religious real property" both places it appears; and

(B) by inserting ", including fixtures or religious objects contained within a place of religious worship" before the period; and

(6) by adding at the end the following new subsection: "(g) No person shall be prosecuted, tried, or punished for any noncapital offense under this section unless the indictment is found or the information is instituted not later than 7 years after the date on which the offense was committed."

SEC. 4. LOAN GUARANTEE RECOVERY FUND.

(a) In General.—

(1) In general.—Using amounts described in paragraph (2), the Secretary of Housing and Urban Development (referred to as the "Secretary") shall make guaranteed loans to financial institutions in connection with loans made by such institutions to assist organizations described in section 501(c)(3) of the Internal Revenue Code of 1986 that have been damaged as a result of acts of arson or terrorism in accordance with such procedures as the Secretary shall establish by regulation.

(2) Use of credit subsidy.—Notwithstanding any other provision of law, for the cost of loan guarantees under this section, the Secretary may use not more than $5,000,000 of the amounts made available for fiscal year 1996 for the credit subsidy provided under the General Insurance Fund and the Special Risk Insurance Fund.

(b) Treatment of Costs.—The costs of guaranteed loans under this section, including the cost of modifying loans, shall be as defined in section 502 of the Congressional Budget Act of 1974.

(c) Limit on Loan Principal.—Funds made available under this section shall be available to subsidize total loan principal, any part of which is to be guaranteed, not to exceed $10,000,000.

(d) Terms and Conditions.—The Secretary shall—

(1) establish such terms and conditions as the Secretary considers to be appropriate to provide loan guarantees under this section, consistent with section 503 of the Credit Reform Act; and

(2) include in the terms and conditions a requirement that the decision to provide a loan guarantee to a financial institution and the amount of the guarantee does not in any way depend on the purpose, function, or identity of the organization to which the financial institution has made, or intends to make, a loan.

SEC. 5. COMPENSATION OF VICTIMS; REQUIREMENT OF INCLUSION IN LIST OF CRIMES ELIGIBLE FOR COMPENSATION.

Section 1403(d)(3) of the Victims of Crime Act of 1984 (42 U.S.C. 10602(d)(3)) is amended by inserting "crimes, whose victims suffer death or personal injury, that are described in section 247 of title 18, United States Code," after "includes."

SEC. 6. AUTHORIZATION FOR ADDITIONAL PERSONNEL TO ASSIST STATE AND LOCAL LAW ENFORCEMENT.

There are authorized to be appropriated to the Department of the Treasury and the Department of Justice, including the Community Relations Service, in fiscal years 1996 and 1997 such sums as are necessary to increase the number of personnel, investigators, and technical support personnel to investigate, prevent, and respond to potential violations of sections 247 and 844 of title 18, United States Code.

SEC. 7. REAUTHORIZATION OF HATE CRIMES STATISTICS ACT.

The first section of the Hate Crimes Statistics Act (28 U.S.C. 534 note) is amended—

(1) in subsection (b), by striking "for the calendar year 1990 and each of the succeeding 4 calendar years" and inserting "for each calendar year"; and

(2) in subsection (c), by striking "1994" and inserting "2002."

SEC. 8. SENSE OF THE CONGRESS.

The Congress—

(1) commends those individuals and entities that have responded with funds to assist in the rebuilding of places of worship that have been victimized by arson; and

(2) encourages the private sector to continue these efforts so that places of worship that are victimized by arson, and their affected communities, can continue the rebuilding process with maximum financial support from private individuals, businesses, charitable organizations, and other non-profit entities.

Approved July 3, 1996.

Source: Church Arson Prevention Act. Title 18, U.S.C., Section 247 (1996).

See also: Aryan Brotherhood; Aryan Nations; Christian Identity Hate Groups; Hate Crimes in America; Hate Groups in America; Ku Klux Klan; Preachers; White Supremacy

Proposition 227 (1998)

Introduction

The following is the full text of Proposition 227, a ballot initiative passed by California voters in June 1998 that essentially required that all public school classes—with the exception of foreign language classes—be taught in English. Although the law permits some exceptions, its passage marked a clear effort to end bilingual education programs in California. It also led to immediate legal challenges from the Mexican American Legal Defense and Educational Fund and the American Civil Liberties Union, which argued that the legislation violated the Equal Opportunities Act of 1974 and the Fourteenth Amendment to the U.S. Constitution.

Primary Source

SECTION 1. Chapter 3 (commencing with Section 300) is added to Part 1 of the Education Code, to read:

Chapter 3. English Language Education for Immigrant Children

Article 1. Findings and Declarations

300. The People of California find and declare as follows:

(a) Whereas, The English language is the national public language of the United States of America and of the State of California, is spoken by the vast majority of California residents, and is also the leading world language for science, technology, and international business, thereby being the language of economic opportunity; and

(b) Whereas, Immigrant parents are eager to have their children acquire a good knowledge of English, thereby allowing them to fully participate in the American Dream of economic and social advancement; and

(c) Whereas, The government and the public schools of California have a moral obligation and a constitutional duty to provide all of California's children, regardless of their ethnicity or national origins, with the skills necessary to become productive members of our society, and of these skills, literacy in the English language is among the most important; and

(d) Whereas, The public schools of California currently do a poor job of educating immigrant children, wasting financial resources on costly experimental language programs whose failure over the past two decades is demonstrated by the current high drop-out rates and low English literacy levels of many immigrant children; and

(e) Whereas, Young immigrant children can easily acquire full fluency in a new language, such as English, if they are heavily exposed to that language in the classroom at an early age.

(f) Therefore, It is resolved that: all children in California public schools shall be taught English as rapidly and effectively as possible.

Article 2. English Language Education

305. Subject to the exceptions provided in Article 3 (commencing with Section 310), all children in California public schools shall be taught English by being taught in English. In particular, this shall require that all children be placed in English language classrooms. Children who are English learners shall be educated through sheltered English immersion during a temporary transition period not normally intended to exceed one year. Local schools shall be permitted to place in the same classroom English learners of different ages but whose degree of English proficiency is similar. Local schools shall be encouraged to mix together in the same classroom English learners from different native-language groups but with the same degree of English fluency. Once English learners have acquired a good working knowledge of English, they shall be transferred to English

language mainstream classrooms. As much as possible, current supplemental funding for English learners shall be maintained, subject to possible modification under Article 8 (commencing with Section 335) below.

306. The definitions of the terms used in this article and in Article 3 (commencing with Section 310) are as follows:

(a) "English learner" means a child who does not speak English or whose native language is not English and who is not currently able to perform ordinary classroom work in English, also known as a Limited English Proficiency or LEP child.

(b) "English language classroom" means a classroom in which the language of instruction used by the teaching personnel is overwhelmingly the English language, and in which such teaching personnel possess a good knowledge of the English language.

(c) "English language mainstream classroom" means a classroom in which the pupils either are native English language speakers or already have acquired reasonable fluency in English.

(d) "Sheltered English immersion" or "structured English immersion" means an English language acquisition process for young children in which nearly all classroom instruction is in English but with the curriculum and presentation designed for children who are learning the language.

(e) "Bilingual education/native language instruction" means a language acquisition process for pupils in which much or all instruction, textbooks, and teaching materials are in the child's native language.

Article 3. Parental Exceptions

310. The requirements of Section 305 may be waived with the prior written informed consent, to be provided annually, of the child's parents or legal guardian under the circumstances specified below and in Section 311. Such informed consent shall require that said parents or legal guardian personally visit the school to apply for the waiver

and that they there be provided a full description of the educational materials to be used in the different educational program choices and all the educational opportunities available to the child. Under such parental waiver conditions, children may be transferred to classes where they are taught English and other subjects through bilingual education techniques or other generally recognized educational methodologies permitted by law. Individual schools in which 20 pupils or more of a given grade level receive a waiver shall be required to offer such a class; otherwise, they must allow the pupils to transfer to a public school in which such a class is offered.

311. The circumstances in which a parental exception waiver may be granted under Section 310 are as follows:

(a) Children who already know English: the child already possesses good English language skills, as measured by standardized tests of English vocabulary comprehension, reading, and writing, in which the child scores at or above the state average for his or her grade level or at or above the 5th grade average, whichever is lower; or

(b) Older children: the child is age 10 years or older, and it is the informed belief of the school principal and educational staff that an alternate course of educational study would be better suited to the child's rapid acquisition of basic English language skills; or

(c) Children with special needs: the child already has been placed for a period of not less than thirty days during that school year in an English language classroom and it is subsequently the informed belief of the school principal and educational staff that the child has such special physical, emotional, psychological, or educational needs that an alternate course of educational study would be better suited to the child's overall educational development. A written description of these special needs must be provided and any such decision is to be made subject to the examination and approval of the local school superintendent, under guidelines established by and subject to the review of the local Board of Education and ultimately the State Board of Education. The existence of such special needs shall not compel

issuance of a waiver, and the parents shall be fully informed of their right to refuse to agree to a waiver.

Article 4. Community-Based English Tutoring

315. In furtherance of its constitutional and legal requirement to offer special language assistance to children coming from backgrounds of limited English proficiency, the state shall encourage family members and others to provide personal English language tutoring to such children, and support these efforts by raising the general level of English language knowledge in the community. Commencing with the fiscal year in which this initiative is enacted and for each of the nine fiscal years following thereafter, a sum of fifty million dollars ($50,000,000) per year is hereby appropriated from the General Fund for the purpose of providing additional funding for free or subsidized programs of adult English language instruction to parents or other members of the community who pledge to provide personal English language tutoring to California school children with limited English proficiency.

316. Programs funded pursuant to this section shall be provided through schools or community organizations. Funding for these programs shall be administered by the Office of the Superintendent of Public Instruction, and shall be disbursed at the discretion of the local school boards, under reasonable guidelines established by, and subject to the review of, the State Board of Education.

Article 5. Legal Standing and Parental Enforcement

320. As detailed in Article 2 (commencing with Section 305) and Article 3 (commencing with Section 310), all California school children have the right to be provided with an English language public education. If a California school child has been denied the option of an English language instructional curriculum in public school, the child's parent or legal guardian shall have legal standing to sue for enforcement of the provisions of this statute, and if successful shall be awarded normal and customary attorney's fees and actual damages, but not punitive or consequential damages. Any school board member or other elected official or public

school teacher or administrator who willfully and repeatedly refuses to implement the terms of this statute by providing such an English language educational option at an available public school to a California school child may be held personally liable for fees and actual damages by the child's parents or legal guardian.

Article 6. Severability

325. If any part or parts of this statute are found to be in conflict with federal law or the United States or the California State Constitution, the statute shall be implemented to the maximum extent that federal law, and the United States and the California State Constitution permit. Any provision held invalid shall be severed from the remaining portions of this statute.

Article 7. Operative Date

330. This initiative shall become operative for all school terms which begin more than sixty days following the date on which it becomes effective.

Article 8. Amendment

335. The provisions of this act may be amended by a statute that becomes effective upon approval by the electorate or by a statute to further the act's purpose passed by a two-thirds vote of each house of the Legislature and signed by the Governor.

Article 9. Interpretation

340. Under circumstances in which portions of this statute are subject to conflicting interpretations, Section 300 shall be assumed to contain the governing intent of the statute.

Source: California Proposition 227 (1998). Text available at the University of Southern California Archives, http://www.usc.edu/.

See also: Bilingual Education; English-Only Movement.

Excerpts from the Preliminary and Final Reports of the Oklahoma Commission to Study the Tulsa Race Riot of 1921 (2000–2001)

Introduction

Formed in 1997, the Tulsa Race Riot Commission was charged with determining exactly what happened during the May 1921 riot that devastated the African American Greenwood district of Tulsa, Oklahoma. The commission undertook both a historical and an archeological analysis of the event and, as indicated below in the cover letter to its preliminary report released in 2000, recommended that reparations be paid to survivors of the riot. Also reproduced below are excerpts of the final report of the commission, which was compiled by Danney Goble and released in 2001.

Primary Source

Letter Introducing the Commission's Preliminary Report, February 7, 2000

The Honorable Frank Keating
Governor of the State of Oklahoma
State Capitol Building
Oklahoma City, OK 73105

Dear Governor Keating:
The Tulsa Race Riot Commission, established by House Joint Resolution No. 1035, is pleased to submit the following preliminary report.

The primary goal of collecting historical documentation on the Tulsa Race Riot of 1921 has been achieved. Attachment A is a summary listing of the record groups that have been gathered and stored at the Oklahoma Historical Society. Also included are summaries of some reports and the full text of selected documents to illustrate the breadth and scope of the collecting process. However, the Commission has not yet voted on historical findings, so these materials do not necessarily represent conclusions of the Commission.

At the last meeting, held February 4, 2000, the Commission voted on three actions. They are:

1. The Issue of Restitution

Whereas, the process of historical analysis by this Commission is not yet complete,

And Whereas, the archeological investigation into casualties and mass burials is not yet complete,

And Whereas, we have seen a continuous pattern of historical evidence that the Tulsa Race Riot of 1921 was the violent consequence of racial hatred institutionalized and tolerated by official federal, state, county, and city policy,

And Whereas, government at all levels has the moral and ethical responsibility of fostering a sense of community that bridges divides of ethnicity and race,

And Whereas, by statute we are to make recommendations regarding whether or not reparations can or should be made to the Oklahoma Legislature, the Governor of the State of Oklahoma, and the Mayor and City Council of Tulsa,

That, we, the 1921 Tulsa Race Riot Commission, recommend that restitution to the historic Greenwood Community, in real and tangible form, would be good public policy and do much to repair the emotional as well as physical scars of this most terrible incident in our shared past.

2. The Issue of Suggested Forms of Restitution in Priority Order

The Commission recommends

1. Direct payment of reparations to survivors of the Tulsa Race Riot
2. Direct payment of reparations to descendants of the survivors of the Tulsa Race Riot
3. A scholarship fund available to students affected by the Tulsa Race Riot
4. Establishment of an economic development enterprise zone in the historic area of the Greenwood District
5. A memorial for the reburial of any human remains found in the search for unmarked graves of riot victims

3. The Issue of an Extension of the Tulsa Race Riot Commission

The Commission hereby endorses and supports House Bill 2468, which extends the life of the Commission in order to finish the historical report on the Tulsa Race Riot of 1921.

We, the members of the Tulsa Race Riot Commission, respectfully submit these findings for your consideration.

COMMISSIONERS:	CHAIRMAN:
Currie Ballard, Coyle	T. D. "Pete" Churchwell, Tulsa
Dr. Bob Blackburn, Oklahoma City	
Joel Burns, Tulsa	SPONSORS:
Vivian Clark, Tulsa	Sen. Maxine Horner, Tulsa
Rep. Abe Deutschendorf, Lawton	Rep. Donn Ross, Tulsa
Eddie Faye Gates, Tulsa	
Jim Lloyd, Tulsa	ADVISORS:
Sen. Robert Milacek, Wauikomis	Dr. John Hope Franklin, Durham NC
Jimmie L. White, Jr., Checotah	Dr. Scott Ellsworth, Portland OR

Final Report of the Oklahoma Commission to Study the Tulsa Race Riot of 1921. Compiled by Danney Goble

The 1921 Tulsa Race Riot Commission originated in 1997 with House Joint Resolution No. 1035. The act twice since has been amended, first in 1998, and again two years later.

The final rewriting passed each legislative chamber in March and became law with Governor Frank Keating's signature on April 6, 2000.

In that form, the State of Oklahoma extended the commission's authority beyond that originally scheduled, to February 28, 2001.

The statute also charged the commission to produce, on that date, "a final report of its findings and recommendations" and to submit that report "in writing to the Governor, the Speaker of the House of Representatives, the President Pro Tempore of the Senate, and the Mayor and each member of the City Council of the City of Tulsa, Oklahoma." This is that report. It accounts for and completes the work of the 1921 Tulsa Race Riot Commission.

A series of papers accompanies the report. Some are written by scholars of national stature, others by experts of international acclaim. Each addresses at length and in depth issues of expressed legislative interest and matters of enormous public consequence. As a group, they comprise a uniquely special and a uniquely significant contribution that must be attached to this report and must be studied carefully along with it.

Nonetheless, the supporting documents are not the report, itself. The scholars' essays have their purposes; this commission's report has another. Its purpose is contained in the statutes that first created this commission, that later extended its life, and that each time gave it the same set of mandates. That is why this report is an accounting, presented officially and offered publicly, of how Oklahoma's 1921 Tulsa Race Riot Commission has conducted its business and addressed its statutory obligations.

Its duties were many, and each presented imposing challenges. Not least was the challenge of preparing this report. Lawmakers scheduled its deadline and defined its purpose, and this report meets their requirements. At the same time, four years of intense study and personal sacrifice surely entitle commission members to add their own expectations. Completely reasonable and entirely appropriate, their desires deserve a place in their report as well.

Together, then, both the law's requirements and the commissioners' resolves guide this report. Designed to be both concise and complete, this is the report that law requires the 1921 Tulsa Race Riot Commission to submit to those who represent the people. Designed to be both compelling and convincing, this also is the report that the 1921 Tulsa Race Riot Commission chooses to offer the people whom both lawmakers and the commissioners serve.

The Commission shall consist of eleven (11) members. . . .

The legislative formula for commission membership assured it appropriate if unusual composition. As an official state inquiry, the state's interest was represented through the executive, legislative, and administrative branches. The governor was to appoint six members, three from names submitted by the Speaker of the House, three from nominees provided by the Senate President Pro Tempore.

Two state officials—the directors of the Oklahoma Human Rights Commission (OHRC) and of the Oklahoma Historical Society (OHS)—also were to serve as ex officio members, either personally or through their designees.

Reflecting Tulsa's obvious interest, the resolution directed the city's mayor to select the commission's final three members. Similar to the gubernatorial appointments, they were to come from names proposed by Tulsa's City Commission. One of the mayor's appointees had to be "a survivor of the 1921 Tulsa Race Riot incident"; two had to be current residents of the historic Greenwood community, the area once devastated by the "incident." The commission began with two ex officio members and ended with two others. After Gracie Monson resigned in March 2000, Kenneth Kendricks replaced her as OHRC's interim director and its representative to the commission. Blake Wade directed the historical society until Dr. Bob Blackburn succeeded him in 1999. Blackburn had been Wade's designated representative to the commission anyway. In fact, the commission had made him its chairman, a position he would hold until June 2000.

Governor Frank Keating's six appointees included two legislators, each from a different chamber, each from an opposite party, each a former history teacher. Democrat Abe Deutschendorf's participation in the debate over the original house resolution echoed his lingering interest in history and foretold his future devotion to this inquiry. As a history teacher, Robert Milacek had included Tulsa's race riot in his classes. Little did he know that he, himself, would contribute to that history as a Republican legislator, but he has.

Governor Keating turned to metropolitan Tulsa for two appointees. T.D. "Pete" Churchwell's father serviced African American businesses in the Greenwood district, and Churchwell has maintained concern for that community and with the 1921 riot that nearly destroyed it. He was Blackburn's replacement as chairman during the commission's closing months. Although born in Oklahoma City, Jim Lloyd and his family moved to Turley (the community just north of Greenwood) when he was three. Raised in Tulsa, he graduated from Nathan Hale and the University of Tulsa's College of Law. He now practices law in Sand Springs and lives in Tulsa.

The governor's other appointees entered the inquiry less with geographical than with professional connections to Tulsa and its history. Currie Ballard lives in Coyle and serves neighboring Langston University as historian-in-residence. Holding a graduate degree in history, Jimmie White teaches it and heads the social science division for Connors State College.

Tulsa Mayor Susan Savage appointed the commission's final three members. If only five in 1921, Joe Burns met the law's requirement that one mayoral appointee be a survivor of the 1921 "incident." He brought the commission not faint childhood memories but seasoned wisdom rooted in eight decades of life in the Greenwood community and with Greenwood's people.

As the resolution specified, Mayor Savage's other two appointees live in contemporary Greenwood, but neither took a direct route to get there. Eddie Faye Gates's path began in Preston, Oklahoma, passed through Alabama's Tuskegee Institute, and crisscrossed two continents before it reached Tulsa in 1968. She spent the next twenty-four years teaching its youngsters and has devoted years since researching and writing her own memoirs and her community's history. Vivian Clark-Adams's route took nearly as many twists and turns, passing through one military base after another until her father retired and the family came to Oklahoma in 1961. Trained at the University of Tulsa, Dr. Vivian Clark-Adams serves Tulsa Community College as chair of the liberal arts division for its southeast campus.

In the November 1997, organizing meeting, commissioners voted to hire clerical assistants and expert consultants through the OHS. (The legislature had added $50,000 to the agency's base appropriations for just such purposes.) They then scheduled their second meeting for December 5 to accommodate the most appropriate and most eminent of all possible authorities.

John Hope Franklin is the son of Greenwood attorney B.C. Franklin, a graduate of Tulsa's Booker T. Washington High School (Fisk and Harvard, too), and James B. Duke Professor of History Emeritus at Duke University. Recipient of scores of academic and literary awards, not to mention more than a hundred honorary doctorates, Franklin came back for another honor. He received the Peggy V. Helmerich Distinguished Author Award on December 4 and stayed to meet and help the commission on the fifth.

Commissioners were delighted to learn that Franklin was anxious to serve, even if he confessed the contributions limited by age (he was eighty-two at the time) and other obligations. They enthusiastically made John Hope Franklin their first consultant, and they instantly took his advice for another. Dr. Scott Ellsworth, a native Tulsan now living in Oregon, was a Duke graduate who already had written a highly regarded study of the riot. Ellsworth became the second consultant chosen; he thereafter emerged first in importance.

As its work grew steadily more exacting and steadily more specialized, the commission turned to more experts. Legal scholars, archeologists, anthropologists, forensic specialists, geophysicists—all of these and more blessed this commission with technical expertise impossible to match and unimaginable otherwise. As a research group, they brought a breadth of vision and a depth of training that made Oklahoma's commission a model of state inquiry.

Ten consultants eventually provided them expert advice, but the commissioners always expected to depend mostly on their own resources, maybe with just a little help from just a few of their friends. Interested OHS employees were a likely source. Sure enough, a half-dozen or so pitched in to search the agency's library and archives for riot-related materials.

That was help appreciated, if not entirely unexpected. What was surprising—stunning, really—was something else that happened in Oklahoma City. As the commission's work attracted interest and gathered momentum, Bob Blackburn noticed something odd: an unusual number of people were volunteering to work at the historical society. Plain, ordinary citizens, maybe forty or fifty of them, had asked to help the commission as unpaid researchers in the OHS collections.

At about that time, Dick Warner decided that he had better start making notes on the phone calls he was fielding for the Tulsa County Historical Society. People were calling in, wanting to contribute to the inquiry, and they just kept calling. After two months, his log listed entries for 148 local calls. Meanwhile, Scott Ellsworth was back in Oregon, writing down information volunteered by some of the three hundred callers who had reached him by long distance.

Most commission meetings were in Tulsa, each open to any and all. Oklahoma's Open Meetings Law required no less, but this commission's special nature yielded much more. It seemed that every time the commissioners met at least one person (usually several) greeted them with at least something (usually a lot) that the commission needed.

Included were records and papers long presumed lost, if their existence had been known at all. Some were official documents, pulled together and packed away years earlier. Uncovered and examined, they took the commission back in time, back to the years just before and just after 1921. Some were musty legal records saved from the shredders. Briefs filed, dockets set, lawsuits decided—each opened an avenue into another corner of history. Pages after pages laid open the city commission's deliberations and decisions as they affected the Greenwood area. Overlooked records from the National Guard offered overlooked perspectives and illuminated them with misplaced correspondence, lost after-action reports, obscure field manuals, and self-typed accounts from men who were on duty at the riot. Maybe there was a family's treasured collection of yellowed newspaper clippings; an envelope of faded photographs; a few carefully folded letters, all hand written, each dated 1921.

One meaning of all of this is obvious, so obvious that this report pauses to affirm it.

Many have questioned why or even if anyone would be interested now in events that happened in one city, one time, one day, long ago. What business did today's state lawmakers have in something so old, so local, and so deservedly forgotten? Surely no one cares, not anymore.

An answer comes from hundreds and hundreds of voices. They tell us that what happened in 1921 in Tulsa is as alive today as it was back then. What happened in Tulsa stays as important and remains as unresolved today as in 1921. What happened there still exerts its power over people who never lived in Tulsa at all.

How else can one explain the thousands of hours volunteered by hundreds of people, all to get this story told and get it told right? How else can one explain the regional, national, even international attention that has been concentrated on a few short hours of a mid-sized city's history? As the introductory paper by Drs. Franklin and Ellsworth recounts, the Tulsa disaster went largely unacknowledged for a half-century or more. After a while, it was largely forgotten.

Eventually it became largely unknown. So hushed was mention of the subject that many pronounced it the final victim of a conspiracy, this a conspiracy of silence.

That silence is shattered, utterly and permanently shattered. Whatever else this commission has achieved or will achieve, it already has made that possible. Regional, national, and international media made it certain. The *Dallas Morning News*, the *Los Angeles Times*, the *New York Times*, National Public Radio (NPR), every American broadcast television network, cable outlets delivering Cinemax and the History Channel to North America, the British Broadcasting Corporation—this merely begins the attention that the media focused upon this commission and its inquiry. Many approached it in depth (NPR twice has made it the featured daily broadcast). Most returned to it repeatedly (the *New York Times* had carried at least ten articles as of February 2000). All considered it vital public information.

Some—including some commission members—thought at least some of the coverage was at least somewhat unbalanced. They may have had a point, but that is not the point.

Here is the point: The 1921 Tulsa Race Riot Commission is pleased to report that this past tragedy has been extensively aired, that it is now remembered, and that it will never again be unknown.

The Commission shall undertake a study to [include] the identification of persons. . . .

No one is certain how many participated in the 1921 riot. No one is certain how many suffered how much for how long. Certainty is reserved for a single quantifiable fact. Every year there remain fewer and fewer who experienced it personally.

Legislation authorizing this commission directed that it seek and locate those survivors.

Specifically, it was to identify any personable to "provide adequate proof to the Commission" that he or she was an "actual resident" of "the 'Greenwood' area or community" at the time of the riot. The commission was also to identify any person who otherwise "sustained an identifiable loss . . . resulting from the . . . 1921 Tulsa Race Riot."

Some considered this the commission's most difficult assignment, some its most important duty, some its most compelling purpose. They all were right, and had Eddie Faye Gates not assumed personal and experienced responsibility for that mandate, this commission might have little to report. Because she did, however, it principally reports what she and those who worked with her were able to accomplish in the commission's name.

Commissioner Gates's presence gave this commission a considerable and welcomed head start. She already had included several riot victims among the early pioneers whom she had interviewed for *They Came Searching: How Blacks Sought the Promised Land in Tulsa.* The book finished, she had an informal list of survivors, but the list kept changing.

Death erased one name after another. Others appeared. Many were of old people who had left Oklahoma years, even decades, ago; but she heard about them and patiently tracked them down. As lawmakers were authorizing this inquiry, the count stood at thirteen, nineteen if all the leads eventually panned out. No one presumed that even nineteen was close to final, but no one knew what the accurate total might be either.

At its very first organizing meeting on November 14, 1997, this commission established a "subcommittee on survivors," headed by Commissioner Gates and including Commissioner Burns and Dr. Clark-Adams. From that moment onward, that subcommittee has aggressively and creatively pursued every possible avenue to identify every possible survivor.

Letters sent over Dr. Ellsworth's signature to *Jet* and *Ebony* magazines urged readers to contact the commission if they knew of any possibilities. From *Gale's Directory of Publications*, Commissioner Gates targeted the nation's leading African American newspapers (papers like the *Chicago Defender* and the *Pittsburgh Courier*), appealing publicly for survivors or to anyone who might know of one. The commission's website, created and maintained by the Oklahoma Historical Society, prominently declared a determination to identify and register every survivor, everywhere. For affirmation, it posted the official forms used as the subcommittee's records, including instructions for their completion and submission.

An old-fashioned, intensely personal web turned out to be more productive than the thoroughly modern, entirely electronic Internet.

Like historical communities everywhere, modern Greenwood maintains a rich, if informal, social network. Sometimes directly, sometimes distantly, it connects Greenwood's people, sometimes young, sometimes old. Anchoring its interstices are the community's longest residents, its most active citizens, and its most prominent leaders.

One quality or another would describe some members of this commission. After all, these are the very qualifications that lawmakers required for their appointments. Others share those same qualities and a passion for their community's history as well. Curtis Lawson, Robert Littlejohn, Hannibal Johnson, Dr. Charles Christopher, Mable Rice, Keith Jemison, Robert and Blanchie Mayes—all are active in the North Tulsa Historical Society, all are some of the community's most respected citizens, and all are among this commission's most valuable assets.

The initial published notices had early results. Slowly they began to compound upon themselves. The first stories in the national and international media introduced a multiplying factor. Thereafter, each burst of press attention seemed to increase what was happening geometrically. People were contacting commissioners, some coming forward as survivors, more suggesting where or how they might be found. Names came in, first a light sprinkle, next a shower, then a downpour, finally a flood.

Old city directories, census reports, and other records verified some claims, but they could confirm only so much. After all, these people had been children, some of them infants, back in 1921. After eighty years, could any one remember the kind of details—addresses, telephone numbers, property descriptions, rental agreements, business locations— someone else could verify with official documents? Not likely. In fact, these were exactly the kind of people most likely to have been ignored or lost in every public record. Officially, they might have never existed.

Except that they did, and one who looked long enough and hard enough and patiently enough could confirm it—that is, if one knew where to look and whom to ask.

That is what happened. Name-by-name, someone found somebody who actually knew each person. In fact, that is how many names surfaced: a credible figure in the community knew how to find older relatives, former neighbors,

or departed friends. Others could be confirmed with equal authority. Maybe someone knew the claimant's family or knew someone that did. If a person claimed to be kin to someone or offered some small detail, surely someone else knew that relative or remembered the same detail as well. Some of those details might even be verified through official documents.

It was a necessary process but slow and delicate, too. As of June 1998, twenty-nine survivors had been identified, contacted, and registered. (The number did not include sixteen identified as descendants of riot victims.) It took another fourteen months for the total to reach sixty-one. It would have been higher, except that three of the first twenty-nine had died in those months. This deadline had an ominous and compelling meaning.

Work immediately shifted through higher gears. In March 2000, the identification process finished for forty-one survivors then living in or near Tulsa. Just a few more still needed to be contacted. The real work remaining, however, involved a remarkable number of survivors who had turned up outside of Oklahoma. Following a recent flurry of media attention, more than sixty out-of-state survivors had been located. They lived everywhere from California to Florida, one in Paris, France! All of that work is complete.

As the commission submits its report, 118 persons have been identified, contacted, and registered as living survivors of the 1921 Tulsa Race Riot. (Another 176 persons also have been registered as descendants of riot victims.) The 1921 Tulsa Race Riot Commission thereby has discharged the mandate regarding the identification of persons.

The Commission shall . . . gather information, identify and interview witnesses . . . , preserve testimony and records obtained, [and] examine and copy documents . . . having historical significance.

Whatever else this commission already has achieved or soon will inspire, one accomplishment will remain indefinitely. Until recently, the Tulsa race riot has been the most important least known event in the state's entire history. Even the most resourceful of scholars stumbled as they neared it for it was dimly lit by evidence and the evidentiary record faded more with every passing year.

That is not now and never will be true again.

These few hours—from start to finish, the actual riot consumed less than sixteen hours—may now comprise the most thoroughly documented moments ever to have occurred in Oklahoma. This commission's work and the documentary record it leaves behind shines upon them a light too bright to ignore.

The Oklahoma Historical Society was searching its existing materials and aggressively pursuing more before this commission ever assembled. By the November 1997, organizing meeting, Bob Blackburn was ready to announce that the society already had ordered prints from every known source of every known photograph taken of the riot. He was contacting every major archival depository and research library in the country to request copies of any riot-related materials they might hold themselves. Experienced OHS professionals were set to research important but heretofore neglected court and municipal records.

This was news welcomed by commission members. It assured early momentum for the job ahead, and it complemented work that some of them were already doing. Eddie Faye Gates, for one, had pulled out every transcript of every interview that she had made with a riot witness, and she was anxious to make more. Jim Lloyd was another. Lloyd already had found and copied transcripts from earlier interviews, including some with Tulsa police officers present at the riot. He also had a hunch that a fellow who knew his way around a court house just might turn up all sorts of information.

That is how it began, but that was just the beginning. In the months ahead, Larry O'Dell and other OHS employees patiently excavated mountains of information, one pebble at a time, as it were. They then pieced together tiny bits of fact, carefully fitting one to another.

One by one, completed puzzles emerged. Arranged in different dimensions, they made magic: a vision of Greenwood long since vanished.

Master maps, both of the community on the eve of the riot and of the post-riot residue, identified every single piece of property. For each parcel, a map displayed any structure present, its owner and its use. If commercial, what firms were there, who owned them, what businesses they were in. If residential, whether it was rented or owned. If the former, the landlord's name. If the latter, whether it was mortgaged (if so, to whom and encumbered by what debt). For both, lists identified each of its occupants by name.

It was not magic; it was more. Larry O'Dell had rebuilt Greenwood from records he and other researchers had examined and collected for the commission. Every building permit granted, every warranty deed recorded, every property appraisal ordered, every damage claim filed, every death certificate issued, every burial record maintained— the commission had copies of every single record related to Greenwood at the time of the riot.

Some it had only because Jim Lloyd was right. Able to navigate a courthouse, he ran across complete records for some 150 civil suits filed after the race riot. No one remembered that they even existed; they had been misplaced for thirty-five years. When Jim Lloyd uncovered and saved them, they were scheduled for routine shredding.

The commission gathered the most private of documents as well. Every form registering every survivor bears notes recording information taken from every one of 118 persons. With Kavin Ross operating the camera, Eddie Faye Gates videotaped interviews with about half of the survivors. Each is available on one of nine cassettes preserved by the commission; full transcripts are being completed for all. Sympathetic collectors turned over transcripts of another fifty or more. Some had been packed away for twenty, even thirty years.

Others, including several resourceful amateur historians, reproduced and gave the commission what amounted to complete documentary collections. There were sets of municipal records, files from state agencies, reports kept by social services, press clippings carefully bound, privately owned photographs never publicly seen.

People who had devoted years to the study of one or more aspects of the riot supplied evidence they had found and presented conclusions they had reached. Beryl Ford followed the commission's work as a Tulsan legendary for his devotion to his city and its history. William O'Brien attended nearly every commission meeting, sometimes to ask questions, sometimes to answer them, once to deliver his own full report on the riot. Robert Norris prepared smaller, occasional reports on military topics.

He also dug up and turned over files from National Guard records. Others located affidavits filed with the State Supreme Court. The military reports usually had been presumed lost; the legal papers always had been assumed unimportant.

Commissioners were surprised to receive so much new evidence and pleased to see that it contributed so much. They were delighted to note that so much came from black sources, that it documented black experiences and recorded black observations.

It had not always been that way. Too many early journalists and historians had dismissed black sources as unreliable. Too few early librarians and archivists had preserved black sources as important. Both thereby condemned later writers and scholars to a never ending game of hide-and-go-seek, the rules rigged so no one could win.

This commission's work changes the game forever. Every future scholar will have access to everything everyone ever had when the original source was white. In fact, they will have a lot more of it. They also will have more from sources few had before when the original source was black.

Because they will, the community future scholars will behold [that] the property they will describe was a community of black people, occupied by black people. The public records they will examine involved black people and affected black people. Objects they will touch came from black people. Interviews they will hear and transcripts they will read were recorded from black people. The evidence they will explore reveals experiences of black people.

Consider what so much new information and what so many new sources can mean for future historians. Consider what it already has meant for one.

Read closely Scott Ellsworth's accompanying essay, "The Tulsa Riot," a rather simple title, as titles go. Much more sophisticated is the title he gave the book he wrote in 1982, *Death in a Promised Land: The Tulsa Race Riot of 1921*.

It is fair that they have different titles. They tell somewhat different stories in somewhat different ways. The chief difference is that the one titled so simply tells a tale much more sophisticated.

For one thing, it is longer. The report attached here filled 115 typed pages in the telling; the comparable portion of the book prints entirely in 25 pages. The report has to be longer because it has more to report, stories not told in the first telling. It offers more because it draws upon more evidence. The report packs 205 footnotes with citations for its story; 50 did the job for the first one.

Within that last difference is the difference that causes every other difference. To write this report, Scott Ellsworth used evidence he did not have—no one had it—as recently as 1982. He cites that new evidence at least 148 times. He had information from black sources accessible now because of this commission.

That knowledge contributed to Scott Ellsworth's citations from black newspapers, black interviews, or black writings. He cites black sources at least 272 times.

No wonder the two are different. From now on, everything can be different. They almost have to be.

Before there was this commission, much was known about the Tulsa race riot. More was unknown. It was buried somewhere, lost somewhere, or somewhere undiscovered. No longer.

Old records have been reopened, missing files have been recovered, new sources have been found. Still being assembled and processed by the Oklahoma Historical Society, their total volume passed ten thousand pages some time ago and well may reach twenty thousand by the time everything is done.

The dimensions of twenty thousand pages can be measured physically. Placed side-by-side, they would reach across at least ten yards of library shelving, filling every inch with new information. The significance of these twenty thousand pages has to be gauged vertically and metaphorically though. Stacked high, they amount to a tower of new knowledge. Rising to reach a new perspective, they offer visions never seen before.

The 1921 Tulsa Race Riot Commission thereby has discharged the mandate to gather and preserve a record of historical significance.

The Commission shall . . . develop a historical record of the 1921 Tulsa Race Riot. . . .

The commission's first substantive decision was to greet this obligation with a series of questions, and there was compelling reason why.

Eighty years after the fact, almost as many unresolved questions surround the race riot as did in 1921—maybe even more. Commissioners knew that no "historical record" would be complete unless it answered the most enduring of those questions—or explain why not. That was reason enough for a second decision: Commissioners agreed to seek consultants, respected scholars, and other experts to investigate those questions and offer answers.

Their findings follow immediately, all without change or comment, each just as the commission received it. Accompanying papers present what scholars and others consider the best answers to hard questions. The reports define their questions, either directly or implicitly, and usually explain why they need answers. The authors give answers, but they present them with only the confidence and exactly the precision they can justify.

Most retrace the route they followed to reach their positions. All advance their positions openly. If they sense themselves in hostile territory, some stake their ground and defend it.

The commissioners harbor no illusion that every reader will accept their every answer to every question. They know better. Why should everyone else? None of them do. All eleven have reservations, some here, some there. Some dispute this point; some deny that one. Some suggest other possibilities. Some insist upon positions squarely opposite the scholars'.

None of that matters. However they divide over specifics, they also are united on principles. Should any be in need, they endorse and recommend the route they took to reach their own consensus. The way around an enraged showdown and the shortest path to a responsible solution is the line that passes through points ahead. Each point marks a big question and an important answer. Study them carefully.

What was the total value of property destroyed in the Tulsa race riot, both in 1921's dollars and in today's? Larry O'Dell has the numbers. Any one of them could be a little off, probably none by very much. Could a lawyer argue, and might a judge decree, that citizens living now had a duty to make that good, had to repay those losses, all because of something that happened eighty years ago? Alfred Brophy can make the case, and he does.

Over eight decades, some Tulsans (mostly black Tulsans) have insisted that whites attacked Greenwood from the air, even bombed it from military airplanes. Other Tulsans (mostly white Tulsans) have denied those claims; many have never even heard them. In a sense, it is a black-or-white question, but Richard S. Warner demonstrates that it has no black-or-white answer.

He proves it absolutely false that military planes could have employed military weapons on Greenwood. He also proves it absolutely true that civilian aircraft did fly over the riot area. Some were there for police reconnaissance, some for photography, some for other legitimate purposes.

He also thinks it reasonable to believe that others had less innocent use. It is probable that shots were fired and that incendiary devices were dropped, and these would have contributed to riot-related deaths or destruction. How much? No one will ever know: History permits no black-or-white answer.

Can modern science bring light to old, dark rumors about a mass grave, at least one, probably more, somewhere in Tulsa? Could those rumors be true? If true, where is one? Robert L. Brooks and Alan H. Witten have answers. Yes, science can address those rumors. Yes, there are many reasons to believe that mass graves exist. Where? They can

point precisely to the single most likely spot. They can explain why scientists settle on that one—explain it clearly enough and completely enough to convince non-scientists, too. Without making a scratch on the ground, they can measure how deep it has to be, how thick, how wide, how long. Were the site to be exhumed and were it to yield human remains, what would anyone learn? Quite a bit if Lesley Rankin-Hill and Phoebe Stubblefield were to examine them.

How many people were killed, anyway? At the time, careful calculations varied almost as much as did pure guesses—forty, fifty, one hundred, two hundred, three hundred, maybe more. After a while, it became hard to distinguish the calculations from the guesses. By now, the record has become so muddied that even the most careful and thorough scientific investigation can offer no more than a preliminary possible answer.

Clyde Collins Snow's inquiry is just as careful and just as thorough as one might expect from this forensic anthropologist of international reputation, and preliminary is the word that he insists upon for his findings. By the most conservative of all possible methods, he can identify thirty-eight riot victims, and he provides the cause of death and the burial site for each of them. He even gives us the names of all but the four burned beyond recognition.

That last fact is their defining element. Thirty-eight is only the number of dead that Snow can identify individually. It says nothing of those who lost their lives in the vicious riot and lost their personal identities in records never kept or later destroyed. An accurate death count would just begin

at thirty-eight; it might end well into the hundreds. Snow explains why as many as 150 might have to be added for one reason, 18 more for an other reason. What neither he nor anyone can ever know is how many to add for how many reasons. That is why there will never be a better answer to the question of how many died than this: How many? Too many.

For some questions there will never be answers even that precise. Open for eighty years and open now, they will remain open forever because they are too large to be filled by the evidence at hand.

Some of the hardest questions surround the evidence, itself. Evidence amounting to personal statements—things said to have been seen, heard, or otherwise observed—raises an entire set of questions in itself. Surely some statements are more credible than others, but how credible is that? Most evidence is incomplete; it may be suggestive but is it dispositive? Evidence often inspires inference, but is the inference reasonable or even possible? Evidence is usually ambiguous, does it mean this or does it mean that? Almost every piece of evidence requires an interpretation, but is only one interpretation possible? Responsibilities will be assigned, decisions will be evaluated, judgments will be offered—on what basis?

These are not idle academic musings. On the contrary: This small set of questions explains why so many specific questions remain open. They explain how people—reasonable, fair-minded, well-intended people—can disagree so often about so much.

Consider a question as old as the riot itself. At the time, many said that this was no spontaneous eruption of the rabble; it was planned and executed by the elite. Quite a few people—including some members of this commission—have since studied the question and are persuaded that this is so, that the Tulsa race riot was the result of a conspiracy. This is a serious position and a provable position—if one looks at certain evidence in certain ways.

Others—again, including members of this commission—have studied the same question and examined the same evidence, but they have looked at it in different ways. They see there no proof of conspiracy. Selfish desires surely. Awful effects certainly. But not a conspiracy. Both sides have evidence that they consider convincing, but neither side can convince the other.

Another nagging question involves the role of the Ku Klux Klan. Everyone who has studied the riot agrees that the Klan was present in Tulsa at the time of the riot and that it had been for some time. Everyone agrees that within months of the riot Tulsa's Klan chapter had be come one of the nation's largest and most powerful, able to dictate its will with the ballot as well as the whip.

Everyone agrees that many of the city's most prominent men were klansmen in the early 1920s and that some remained klansmen through out the decade. Everyone agrees that Tulsa's atmosphere reeked with a Klan-like stench that oozed through the robes of the Hooded Order.

Does this mean that the Klan helped plan the riot? Does it mean that the Klan helped execute it? Does it mean that the Klan, as an organization, had any role at all? Or does it mean that any time thousands of whites assembled—especially if they assembled to assault blacks—that odds were there would be quite a few Klansmen in the mix? Does the presence of those individuals mean that the institution may have been an instigator or the agent of a plot? Maybe both? Maybe neither? Maybe nothing at all? Not everyone agrees on that.

Nor will they ever. Both the conspiracy and the Klan questions remain what they always have been and probably what they always will be. Both are examples of nearly every problem inherent to historical evidence. How reliable is this oral tradition? What conclusions does that evidence permit? Are these inferences reasonable? How many ways can this be interpreted? And so it must go on. Some questions will always be disputed because other questions block the path to their answers. That does not mean there will be no answers, just that there will not be one answer per one question. Many questions will have two, quite a few even more. Some answers will never be proven. Some will never be disproved. Accept it: Some things can never be known.

That is why the complete record of what began in the late evening of May 31 and continued through the morning of June 1 will never quite escape those hours, themselves. They forever are darkened by night or enshrouded by day.

But history has a record of things certain for the hours between one day's twilight and the next day's afternoon. These things:

- Black Tulsans had every reason to believe that Dick Rowland would be lynched after his arrest on charges later dismissed and highly suspect from the start.
- They had cause to believe that his personal safety, like the defense of themselves and their community, depended on them alone.
- As hostile groups gathered and their confrontation worsened, municipal and county authorities failed to take actions to calm or contain the situation.
- At the eruption of violence, civil officials selected many men, all of them white and some of them participants in that violence, and made those men their agents as deputies.
- In that capacity, deputies did not stem the violence but added to it, often through overt acts themselves illegal.
- Public officials provided firearms and ammunition to individuals, again all of them white.
- Units of the Oklahoma National Guard participated in the mass arrests of all or nearly all of Greenwood's residents, removed them to other parts of the city, and detained them in holding centers.
- Entering the Greenwood district, people stole, damaged or destroyed personal property left behind in homes and businesses.
- People, some of them agents of government, also deliberately burned or otherwise destroyed homes credibly estimated to have numbered 1,256, along with virtually every other structure—including churches, schools, businesses, even a hospital and library—in the Greenwood district.
- Despite duties to preserve order and to protect property, no government at any level offered adequate resistance, if any at all, to what amounted to the destruction of the neighborhood referred to commonly as "Little Africa" and politely as the "Negro quarter."

- Although the exact total can never be determined, credible evidence makes it probable that many people, likely numbering between one and three hundred, were killed during the riot.
- Not one of these criminal acts was then or ever has been prosecuted or punished by government at any level, municipal, county, state, or federal.
- Even after the restoration of order it was official policy to release a black detainee only upon the application of a white person, and then only if that white person agreed to accept responsibility for that detainee's subsequent behavior.
- As private citizens, many whites in Tulsa and neighboring communities did extend invaluable assistance to the riot's victims, and the relief efforts of the American Red Cross in particular provided a model of human behavior at its best.
- Although city and county government bore much of the cost for Red Cross relief, neither contributed substantially to Greenwood's rebuilding; in fact, municipal authorities acted initially to impede rebuilding.
- In the end, the restoration of Greenwood after its systematic destruction was left to the victims of that destruction.

These things are not myths, not rumors, not speculations, not questioned. They are the historical record.

The 1921 Tulsa Race Riot Commission thereby has discharged the mandate to develop a historical record of the 1921 Tulsa Race Riot.

The final report of the Commission's findings and recommendations . . . may contain specific recommendations about whether or not reparations can or should be made and the appropriate methods. . . .

Unlike those quoted before, these words give this commission not an obligation but an opportunity. Nearly every commissioner intends to seize it.

A short letter sent to Governor Frank Keating as a preliminary report in February, 2000 declared the majority's view

that reparations could and should be made. "Good public policy," that letter said, required no less. This report maintains the same, and this report makes the case.

Case, reparations—the words, themselves, seem to summon images of lawyers and courtrooms, along with other words, words like culpability, damages, remedies, restitution. Each is a term used in law, with strict legal meaning.

Sometimes commissioners use those words, too, and several agree—firmly agree—that those words describe accurately what happened in 1921 and fit exactly what should happen now.

Those, however, are their personal opinions, and the commissioners who hold them do so as private citizens. Even the most resolute of its members recognizes that this commission has a very different role. This commission is neither court nor judge, and its members are not a jury.

The commission has no binding legal authority to assign culpability, to determine damages, to establish a remedy, or to order either restitution or reparations. In fact, it has no judicial authority whatsoever.

It also has no reason or need for such authority. Any judgments that it might offer would be without effect and meaning. Its words would as well be cast to the winds. Any recommendations that it might offer neither have nor need judicial status at all. Statutes grant this commission its authority to make recommendations and the choice of how—or even if—to exercise that authority.

The commission's majority is determined to exercise its discretion and to declare boldly and directly their purpose: to recommend, independent of what law allows, what these commissioners believe is the right thing to do. They propose to do that in a dimension equal to their purpose. Courts have other purposes, and law operates in a different dimension. Mistake one for the other—let this commission assume what rightly belongs to law—does worse than miss the point. It ruins it.

Think of the difference this way. We will never know exactly how many were killed during the Tulsa race riot, but take at random any twenty-five from that unknown total. What we say of those we might say for everyone of the others, too.

Considering the twenty-five to be homicides, the law would approach those as twenty-five acts performed by twenty-five people (or thereabouts) who, with twenty-five motives, committed twenty-five crimes against twenty-five persons. That they occurred within hours and within a few blocks of each other is irrelevant. It would not matter even if the same person committed two, three, ten of the murders on the same spot, moments apart. Each was a separate act, and each (were the law to do its duty) merits a separate consequence. Law can apprehend it no other way.

Is there no other way to understand that? Of course there is. There is a far better way.

Were these twenty-five crimes or one? Did each have a separate motive, or was there a single intent? Were twenty-five individuals responsible, those and no one else? The burning of 1,256 homes—if we understand these as 1,256 acts of arson committed by 1,256 criminals driven by 1,256 desires, if we understand it that way, do we understand anything at all? These were not any number of multiple acts of homicide; this was one act of horror. If we must name the fires, call it outrage, for it was one. For both, the motive was not to injure hundreds of people, nearly all unseen, almost all unknown. The intent was to intimidate one community, to let it be known and let it be seen. Those who pulled the triggers, those who struck the matches—they alone were law breakers. Those who shouted encouragement and those who stood silently by—they were responsible.

These are the qualities that place what happened in Tulsa outside the realm of law—and not just in Tulsa, either. Lexington, Sapulpa, Norman, Shawnee, Lawton, Claremore, Perry; Waurika, Dewey, and Marshall—earlier purges in every one already had targeted entire black communities, marking every child, woman, and man for exile.

There is no count of how many those people numbered, but there is no need to know that. Know that there, too, something more than a bad guy had committed something more than a crime against something more than a person. Not

someone made mad by lust, not a person gripped by rage, not a heartbroken party of romance gone sour, not one or any number of individuals but a collective body—acting as one body—had coldly and deliberately and systematically assaulted one victim, a whole community, intending to eliminate it as a community. If other black communities heard about it and learned their lessons, too, so much the better; a little intimidation went a long way.

All of this happened years before, most fifteen or twenty years before Dick Rowland landed in jail, but they remained vivid in the recent memories of Greenwood's younger adults.

This, or something quite like it, was almost always what happened when the subject was race.

Here was nothing as amorphous as racism. Here were discrete acts—one act, one town—each consciously calculated to have a collective effect not against a person but against a people.

And is that not also the way of Oklahoma's voting laws at the time? The state had amended its constitution and crafted its laws not to keep this person or that person or a whole list of persons from voting. Lengthen that list to the indefinite, write down names to the infinite—one still will not reach the point. For that, one line, one word is enough. The point was to keep a race, as a race, away from the polls.

Jim Crow laws—the segregation commands of Oklahoma's statutes and of its constitution—worked that way, too. Their object was not to keep some exhausted mother and her two young children out of a "white car" on a train headed somewhere like Checotah and send them walking six miles home. (Even if John Hope Franklin could recall that about his own mother and sister and himself as he accepted the Helmerich Award some three-quarters of a century afterwards.) No, the one purpose was to keep one race "in its place." When Laura Nelson was lynched years earlier in Okemah, it was not to punish her by death. It was to terrify the living. Why else would the lynchers have taken (and printed and copied and posted and distributed) that photograph of her hanging from the bridge, her little boy dangling beside her?

The lynchers knew the purpose; the photographer just helped it along. The purpose had not changed much by 1921, when another photographer snapped another picture, a long shot showing Greenwood's ruin, smoke rising from fires blazing in the background. "RUNING THE NEGRO OUT OF TULSA" someone wrote across it, candor atoning for misspelling. No doubt there. No shame either.

Another photograph probably was snapped the same day but from closer range. It showed what just days before must have been a human being, maybe one who had spent a warm day in late May working and talking and laughing. On this day, though, it was only a grotesque, blackened form, a thing, really, its only sign of humanity the charred remains of arms and hands forever raised, as if in useless supplication.

Shot horizontally, that particular photo still turns up from time to time in the form of an early use: as a postcard. People must have thought it a nice way to send a message.

It still sends a message, too big to be jotted down in a few lines; but, then, this message is not especially nice either. The message is that here is an image of more than a single victim of a single episode in a single city. This image preserves the symbol of a story, preserves it in the same way that the story was told: in black-and-white.

See those two photos and understand that the Tulsa race riot was the worst event in that city's history—an event without equal and without excuse. Understand, too, that it was the worst explosion of violence in this state's history—an episode late to be acknowledged and still to be repaired. But understand also that it was part of a message usually announced not violently at all, but calmly and quietly and deliberately.

Who sent the message? Not one person but many acting as one. Not a "mob"; it took forms too calculated and rational for that word. Not "society"; that word is only a mask to conceal responsibility within a fog of imprecision. Not "whites," because this never spoke for all whites; sometimes it spoke for only a few. Not "America," because the federal government was, at best, indifferent to its black citizens and, at worse, oblivious of them.

Fifty years or so after the Civil War, Uncle Sam was too complacent to crusade for black rights and too callous to care. Let the states handle that—states like Oklahoma.

Except that it really was not "Oklahoma" either. At least, it was not all of Oklahoma. It was just one Oklahoma, one Oklahoma that is distinguishable from another Oklahoma partly by purpose. This Oklahoma had the purpose of keeping the other Oklahoma in its place, and that place was subordinate. That, after all, was the object of suffrage requirements and segregation laws. No less was it the intent behind riots and lynchings, too. One Oklahoma was putting the other Oklahoma in its place.

One Oklahoma also had the power to effect its purpose, and that power had no need to rely on occasional explosions of rage. Simple violence is, after all, the weapon of simple people, people with access to no other instruments of power at all. This Oklahoma had access to power more subtle, more regular, and more formal than that. Indeed, its ready access to such forms of power partially defined that Oklahoma.

No, that Oklahoma is not the same as government, used here as a rhetorical trick to make one accountable for the acts of the other. Government was never the essence of that Oklahoma. Government was, however, always its potential instrument. Having access to government, however employed, if employed at all—just having it—defined this Oklahoma and was the essence of its power.

The acts recounted here reveal that power in one form or another, often several. The Tulsa race riot is one example, but only an example and only one. Put along side it earlier, less publicized pogroms—for that is what they were—in at least ten other Oklahoma towns. Include the systematic disfranchisement of the black electorate through constitutional amendment in 1910, reaffirmed through state statute in 1916.

Add to that the constitution's segregation of Oklahoma's public schools, the First Legislature's segregation of its public transportation, local segregation of Oklahoma neighborhoods through municipal ordinances in Tulsa and elsewhere, even the statewide segregation of public telephones by order of the corporation commission. Do not forget to include the lynchings of twenty-three African-Americans in twelve Oklahoma towns during the ten years leading to 1921. Stand back and look at those deeds now.

In some government participated in the deed.
In some government performed the deed.
In none did government prevent the deed.
In none did government punish the deed.

And that, in the end, is what this inquiry and what these recommendations are all about.

Make no mistake about it: There are members of this commission who are convinced that there is a compelling argument in law to order that present governments make monetary payment for past governments' unlawful acts. Professor Alfred Brophy presses one form of that argument; there doubtless are others.

This is not that legal argument but another one altogether. This is a moral argument. It holds that there are moral responsibilities here and that those moral responsibilities require moral responses now.

It gets down to this: The 1921 riot is, at once, a representative historical example and a unique historical event. It has many parallels in the pattern of past events, but it has no equal for its violence and its completeness. It symbolizes so much endured by so many for so long. It does it, however, in one way that no other can: in the living flesh and blood of some who did endure it.

These paradoxes hold answers to questions often asked: Why does the state of Oklahoma or the city of Tulsa owe anything to anybody? Why should any individual tolerate now spending one cent of one tax dollar over what happened so long ago? The answer is that these are not even the questions. This is not about individuals at all—not anymore than the race riot or anything like it was about individuals.

This is about Oklahoma—or, rather, it is about two Oklahomas. It must be about that because that is what the Tulsa race riot was all about, too. That riot proclaimed that there were two Oklahomas; that one claimed the right to push down, push out, and push under the other; and that it had the power to do that.

That is what the Tulsa race riot has been all about for so long afterwards, why it has lingered not as a past event but lived as a present entity. It kept on saying that there remained two Oklahomas; that one claimed the right to be dismissive of, ignorant of, and oblivious to the other; and that it had the power to do that.

That is why the Tulsa race riot can be about something else. It can be about making two Oklahomas one—but only if we understand that this is what reparation is all about. Because the riot is both symbolic and singular, reparations become both singular and symbolic, too.

Compelled not legally by courts but extended freely by choice, they say that individual acts of reparation will stand as symbols that fully acknowledge and finally discharge a collective responsibility.

Because we must face it: There is no way but by government to represent the collective, and there is no way but by reparations to make real the responsibility.

Does this commission have specific recommendations about whether or not reparations can or should be made and the appropriate methods? Yes, it surely does.

When commissioners went looking to do the right thing, that is what nearly all of them found and what they recommended in last year's preliminary report. To be sure they had found the right thing, they have used this formal report to explore once more the distant terrain of the Tulsa race riot and the forbidding territory in which it lies. Now, they are certain. Reparations are the right thing to do.

What else is there to do? What else is there to find?

Source: "Final Report of the Oklahoma Commission to Study the Tulsa Race Riot of 1921." Oklahoma, 2000–2001. Full text available at http://www.ok-history.mus.ok.us/trrc/freport.htm.

See also: Asbury Park Riot of 1970; Atlanta Riot of 1906; Atlanta Riot of 1967; Bellingham Riots; Bensonhurst Incident 1989; Biloxi Beach Riot of 1960; Black Church Arsons; Bloody Sunday; Boston Riot of 1975 and 1976; Brownsville Riot of 1906; Charleston Riot of 1919; Chattanooga Riot of 1906; Chester and Philadelphia Riots of 1918; Chicago Commission on Race Relations; Chicago Riot of 1919; Cincinnati Riots of 1967 and 1968; Cincinnati Riot of 2001; Cleveland Riot of 1966; Detroit Riot of 1943; Detroit Riot of 1967; East St. Louis Riot of 1917; Election Riots of the 1880s and 1890s; Greensburg Riot of 1906; Greenwood Community; Harlem Riot of 1935; Houston Mutiny of 1917; Howard Beach Incident 1986; Johnson-Jeffries Fight of 1910; Knoxville Riot of 1919; Long Hot Summer Riots 1965–1967; Longview Riot of 1919; Los Angeles Riot of 1965; Los Angeles Riots of 1992; Miami Riot of 1982; New Bedford Riot of 1970; New Orleans Riot of 1866; New York City Draft Riot of 1863; New York City Riot of 1943; Newark Riot of 1967; Orangeburg Massacre of 1968; Philadelphia Riot of 1964; Prison Riots; Race Riots in America; Red Scare and Race Riots; Red Summer Race Riots of 1919; Rosewood Riot of 1923; Saint Genevieve Riot of 1930; San Francisco Riot of 1966; Springfield Riot of 1904; Tampa Riots of 1987; Texas Southern University Riot of 1967; Tulsa Riot of 1921; Washington, D.C., Riot of 1919; Washington, D.C., Riots of 1968; Wilmington Riot of 1898; Zoot Suit Riots

Grutter v. Bollinger (2003)

Introduction

This court case was brought by Barbara Grutter, whose application to the University of Michigan's Law School was denied; she argued that she was rejected because of the school's discriminatory admissions policies that used race as a predominant factor. Upholding the law school's admission policy, the U.S. Supreme Court ruled that the school has a "compelling interest in attaining a diverse student body," noting that the law school broadly defined diversity beyond racial considerations. According to the majority opinion, race could be considered a factor, among others, in the overall assessment of candidates since the law school's policies did not include quotas or fixed numbers. This court case, along with Gratz v. Bollinger *(2003), challenged the use of racial preferences in application processes at the University of Michigan. Decided on the same day, the two cases marked the first time the U.S. Supreme Court ruled on race-based admissions in institutions*

of higher education since 1978. Below is the full text of the opinion of the Court in Grutter v. Bollinger *(2003).*

Primary Source

JUSTICE O'CONNOR delivered the opinion of the Court.

This case requires us to decide whether the use of race as a factor in student admissions by the University of Michigan Law School (Law School) is unlawful.

I.

A.

The Law School ranks among the Nation's top law schools. It receives more than 3,500 applications each year for a class of around 350 students. Seeking to "admit a group of students who individually and collectively are among the most capable," the Law School looks for individuals with "substantial promise for success in law school" and "a strong likelihood of succeeding in the practice of law and contributing in diverse ways to the well-being of others." App. 110. More broadly, the Law School seeks "a mix of students with varying backgrounds and experiences who will respect and learn from each other." *Ibid.* In 1992, the dean of the Law School charged a faculty committee with crafting a written admissions policy to implement these goals. In particular, the Law School sought to ensure that its efforts to achieve student body diversity complied with this Court's most recent ruling on the use of race in university admissions. See *Regents of Univ. of Cal. v. Bakke*, 438 U. S. 265 (1978). Upon the unanimous adoption of the committee's report by the Law School faculty, it became the Law School's official admissions policy.

The hallmark of that policy is its focus on academic ability coupled with a flexible assessment of applicants' talents, experiences, and potential "to contribute to the learning of those around them." App. 111. The policy requires admissions officials to evaluate each applicant based on all the information available in the file, including a personal statement, letters of recommendation, and an essay describing the ways in which the applicant will contribute to the life and diversity of the Law School. *Id.*, at 83–84, 114–121.

In reviewing an applicant's file, admissions officials must consider the applicant's undergraduate grade point average (GPA) and Law School Admission Test (LSAT) score because they are important (if imperfect) predictors of academic success in law school. *Id.*, at 112. The policy stresses that "no applicant should be admitted unless we expect that applicant to do well enough to graduate with no serious academic problems." *Id.*, at 111.

The policy makes clear, however, that even the highest possible score does not guarantee admission to the Law School. *Id.*, at 113. Nor does a low score automatically disqualify an applicant. *Ibid.* Rather, the policy requires admissions officials to look beyond grades and test scores to other criteria that are important to the Law School's educational objectives. *Id.*, at 114. So-called "'soft' variables" such as "the enthusiasm of recommenders, the quality of the undergraduate institution, the quality of the applicant's essay, and the areas and difficulty of undergraduate course selection" are all brought to bear in assessing an "applicant's likely contributions to the intellectual and social life of the institution." *Ibid.*

The policy aspires to "achieve that diversity which has the potential to enrich everyone's education and thus make a law school class stronger than the sum of its parts." *Id.*, at 118. The policy does not restrict the types of diversity contributions eligible for "substantial weight" in the admissions process, but instead recognizes "many possible bases for diversity admissions." *Id.*, at 118, 120. The policy does, however, reaffirm the Law School's longstanding commitment to "one particular type of diversity," that is, "racial and ethnic diversity with special reference to the inclusion of students from groups which have been historically discriminated against, like African-Americans, Hispanics and Native Americans, who without this commitment might not be represented in our student body in meaningful numbers." *Id.*, at 120. By enrolling a "'critical mass' of [underrepresented] minority students," the Law School seeks to "ensur[e] their ability to make unique contributions to the character of the Law School." *Id.*, at 120–121.

The policy does not define diversity "solely in terms of racial and ethnic status." *Id.*, at 121. Nor is the policy "insensitive to the competition among all students for admission to the [L]aw [S]chool." *Ibid.* Rather, the policy seeks to guide admissions officers in "producing classes both diverse and academically outstanding, classes made up of students who promise to continue the tradition of outstanding contribution by Michigan Graduates to the legal profession." *Ibid.*

B.

Petitioner Barbara Grutter is a white Michigan resident who applied to the Law School in 1996 with a 3.8 GPA and 161 LSAT score. The Law School initially placed petitioner on a waiting list, but subsequently rejected her application. In December 1997, petitioner filed suit in the United States District Court for the Eastern District of Michigan against the Law School, the Regents of the University of Michigan, Lee Bollinger (Dean of the Law School from 1987 to 1994, and President of the University of Michigan from 1996 to 2002), Jeffrey Lehman (Dean of the Law School), and Dennis Shields (Director of Admissions at the Law School from 1991 until 1998). Petitioner alleged that respondents discriminated against her on the basis of race in violation of the Fourteenth Amendment; Title VI of the Civil Rights Act of 1964, 78 Stat. 252, 42 U. S. C. § 2000d; and Rev. Stat. § 1977, as amended, 42 U. S. C. § 1981.

Petitioner further alleged that her application was rejected because the Law School uses race as a "predominant" factor, giving applicants who belong to certain minority groups "a significantly greater chance of admission than students with similar credentials from disfavored racial groups." App. 33–34. Petitioner also alleged that respondents "had no compelling interest to justify their use of race in the admissions process." *Id.*, at 34. Petitioner requested compensatory and punitive damages, an order requiring the Law School to offer her admission, and an injunction prohibiting the Law School from continuing to discriminate on the basis of race. *Id.*, at 36. Petitioner clearly has standing to bring this lawsuit. *Northeastern Fla. Chapter, Associated Gen. Contractors of America v. Jacksonville*, 508 U. S. 656, 666 (1993).

The District Court granted petitioner's motion for class certification and for bifurcation of the trial into liability and damages phases. The class was defined as "'all persons who

(A) applied for and were not granted admission to the University of Michigan Law School for the academic years since (and including) 1995 until the time that judgment is entered herein; and (B) were members of those racial or ethnic groups, including Caucasian, that Defendants treated less favorably in considering their applications for admission to the Law School.'" App. to Pet. for Cert. 191a–192a.

The District Court heard oral argument on the parties' cross-motions for summary judgment on December 22, 2000. Taking the motions under advisement, the District Court indicated that it would decide as a matter of law whether the Law School's asserted interest in obtaining the educational benefits that flow from a diverse student body was compelling. The District Court also indicated that it would conduct a bench trial on the extent to which race was a factor in the Law School's admissions decisions, and whether the Law School's consideration of race in admissions decisions constituted a race-based double standard.

During the 15-day bench trial, the parties introduced extensive evidence concerning the Law School's use of race in the admissions process. Dennis Shields, Director of Admissions when petitioner applied to the Law School, testified that he did not direct his staff to admit a particular percentage or number of minority students, but rather to consider an applicant's race along with all other factors. *Id.,* at 206a. Shields testified that at the height of the admissions season, he would frequently consult the so-called "daily reports" that kept track of the racial and ethnic composition of the class (along with other information such as residency status and gender). *Id.,* at 207a. This was done, Shields testified, to ensure that a critical mass of underrepresented minority students would be reached so as to realize the educational benefits of a diverse student body. *Ibid.* Shields stressed, however, that he did not seek to admit any particular number or percentage of underrepresented minority students. *Ibid.*

Erica Munzel, who succeeded Shields as Director of Admissions, testified that "'critical mass'" means "'meaningful numbers'" or "'meaningful representation,'" which she understood to mean a number that encourages underrepresented minority students to participate in the classroom and not feel isolated. *Id.,* at 208a–209a. Munzel stated there is no number, percentage, or range of numbers or percentages that constitute critical mass. *Id.,* at 209a. Munzel also asserted that she must consider the race of applicants because a critical mass of underrepresented minority students could not be enrolled if admissions decisions were based primarily on undergraduate GPAs and LSAT scores. *Ibid.*

The current Dean of the Law School, Jeffrey Lehman, also testified. Like the other Law School witnesses, Lehman did not quantify critical mass in terms of numbers or percentages. *Id.,* at 211a. He indicated that critical mass means numbers such that underrepresented minority students do not feel isolated or like spokespersons for their race. *Ibid.* When asked about the extent to which race is considered in admissions, Lehman testified that it varies from one applicant to another. *Ibid.* In some cases, according to Lehman's testimony, an applicant's race may play no role, while in others it may be a "'determinative'" factor. *Ibid.*

The District Court heard extensive testimony from Professor Richard Lempert, who chaired the faculty committee that drafted the 1992 policy. Lempert emphasized that the Law School seeks students with diverse interests and backgrounds to enhance classroom discussion and the educational experience both inside and outside the classroom. *Id.,* at 213a. When asked about the policy's "'commitment to racial and ethnic diversity with special reference to the inclusion of students from groups which have been historically discriminated against,'" Lempert explained that this language did not purport to remedy past discrimination, but rather to include students who may bring to the Law School a perspective different from that of members of groups which have not been the victims of such discrimination. *Ibid.* Lempert acknowledged that other groups, such as Asians and Jews, have experienced discrimination, but explained they were not mentioned in the policy because individuals who are members of those groups were already being admitted to the Law School in significant numbers. *Ibid.*

Kent Syverud was the final witness to testify about the Law School's use of race in admissions decisions. Syverud was a professor at the Law School when the 1992 admissions policy was adopted and is now Dean of Vanderbilt Law School. In addition to his testimony at trial, Syverud submitted several expert reports on the educational benefits of diversity. Syverud's testimony indicated that when a critical mass of underrepresented minority students is present, racial stereotypes lose their force because nonminority students learn there is no "'minority viewpoint'" but rather a variety of viewpoints among minority students. *Id.*, at 215a.

In an attempt to quantify the extent to which the Law School actually considers race in making admissions decisions, the parties introduced voluminous evidence at trial. Relying on data obtained from the Law School, petitioner's expert, Dr. Kinley Larntz, generated and analyzed "admissions grids" for the years in question (1995–2000). These grids show the number of applicants and the number of admittees for all combinations of GPAs and LSAT scores. Dr. Larntz made "'cell-by-cell'" comparisons between applicants of different races to determine whether a statistically significant relationship existed between race and admission rates. He concluded that membership in certain minority groups "'is an extremely strong factor in the decision for acceptance,'" and that applicants from these minority groups " 'are given an extremely large allowance for admission' " as compared to applicants who are members of nonfavored groups. *Id.*, at 218a–220a. Dr. Larntz conceded, however, that race is not the predominant factor in the Law School's admissions calculus. 12 Tr. 11–13 (Feb. 10, 2001).

Dr. Stephen Raudenbush, the Law School's expert, focused on the predicted effect of eliminating race as a factor in the Law School's admission process. In Dr. Raudenbush's view, a race-blind admissions system would have a "'very dramatic,'" negative effect on underrepresented minority admissions. App. to Pet. for Cert. 223a. He testified that in 2000, 35 percent of underrepresented minority applicants were admitted. *Ibid.* Dr. Raudenbush predicted that if race were not considered, only 10 percent of those applicants would have been admitted. *Ibid.* Under this scenario, underrepresented minority students would have constituted 4 percent of the entering class in 2000 instead of the actual figure of 14.5 percent. *Ibid.*

In the end, the District Court concluded that the Law School's use of race as a factor in admissions decisions was unlawful. Applying strict scrutiny, the District Court determined that the Law School's asserted interest in assembling a diverse student body was not compelling because "the attainment of a racially diverse class . . . was not recognized as such by *Bakke* and it is not a remedy for past discrimination." *Id.*, at 246a. The District Court went on to hold that even if diversity were compelling, the Law School had not narrowly tailored its use of race to further that interest. The District Court granted petitioner's request for declaratory relief and enjoined the Law School from using race as a factor in its admissions decisions. The Court of Appeals entered a stay of the injunction pending appeal.

Sitting en banc, the Court of Appeals reversed the District Court's judgment and vacated the injunction. The Court of Appeals first held that Justice Powell's opinion in *Bakke* was binding precedent establishing diversity as a compelling state interest. According to the Court of Appeals, Justice Powell's opinion with respect to diversity constituted the controlling rationale for the judgment of this Court under the analysis set forth in *Marks v. United States*, 430 U. S. 188 (1977). The Court of Appeals also held that the Law School's use of race was narrowly tailored because race was merely a "potential 'plus' factor" and because the Law School's program was "virtually identical" to the Harvard admissions program described approvingly by Justice Powell and appended to his *Bakke* opinion. 288 F. 3d 732, 746, 749 (CA6 2002).

Four dissenting judges would have held the Law School's use of race unconstitutional. Three of the dissenters, rejecting the majority's Marks analysis, examined the Law School's interest in student body diversity on the merits and concluded it was not compelling. The fourth dissenter, writing separately, found it unnecessary to decide whether diversity was a compelling interest because, like the other dissenters, he believed that the Law School's use of race was not narrowly tailored to further that interest.

We granted certiorari, 537 U. S. 1043 (2002), to resolve the disagreement among the Courts of Appeals on a question of national importance: Whether diversity is a compelling interest that can justify the narrowly tailored use of race in selecting applicants for admission to public universities. Compare *Hopwood v. Texas*, 78 F. 3d 932 (CA5 1996) (*Hopwood I*) (holding that diversity is not a compelling state interest), with *Smith v. University of Wash. Law School*, 233 F. 3d 1188 (CA9 2000) (holding that it is).

II.

A.

We last addressed the use of race in public higher education over 25 years ago. In the landmark *Bakke* case, we reviewed a racial set-aside program that reserved 16 out of 100 seats in a medical school class for members of certain minority groups. 438 U. S. 265 (1978). The decision produced six separate opinions, none of which commanded a majority of the Court. Four Justices would have upheld the program against all attack on the ground that the government can use race to "remedy disadvantages cast on minorities by past racial prejudice." *Id.*, at 325 (joint opinion of Brennan, White, Marshall, and Blackmun, JJ., concurring in judgment in part and dissenting in part). Four other Justices avoided the constitutional question altogether and struck down the program on statutory grounds. *Id.*, at 408 (opinion of Stevens, J., joined by Burger, C. J., and Stewart and Rehnquist, JJ., concurring in judgment in part and dissenting in part). Justice Powell provided a fifth vote not only for invalidating the set-aside program, but also for reversing the state court's injunction against any use of race whatsoever. The only holding for the Court in *Bakke* was that a "State has a substantial interest that legitimately may be served by a properly devised admissions program involving the competitive consideration of race and ethnic origin." *Id.*, at 320. Thus, we reversed that part of the lower court's judgment that enjoined the university "from any consideration of the race of any applicant." *Ibid.*

Since this Court's splintered decision in *Bakke*, Justice Powell's opinion announcing the judgment of the Court has served as the touchstone for constitutional analysis of race-conscious admissions policies. Public and private universities across the Nation have modeled their own admissions programs on Justice Powell's views on permissible race-conscious policies. See, *e. g.*, Brief for Judith Areen et al. as *Amici Curiae* 12–13 (law school admissions programs employ "methods designed from and based on Justice Powell's opinion in *Bakke*"); Brief for Amherst College et al. as *Amici Curiae* 27 ("After *Bakke*, each of the *amici* (and undoubtedly other selective colleges and universities as well) reviewed their admissions procedures in light of Justice Powell's opinion . . . and set sail accordingly"). We therefore discuss Justice Powell's opinion in some detail.

Justice Powell began by stating that "[t]he guarantee of equal protection cannot mean one thing when applied to one individual and something else when applied to a person of another color. If both are not accorded the same protection, then it is not equal." *Bakke*, 438 U. S., at 289–290. In Justice Powell's view, when governmental decisions "touch upon an individual's race or ethnic background, he is entitled to a judicial determination that the burden he is asked to bear on that basis is precisely tailored to serve a compelling governmental interest." *Id.*, at 299. Under this exacting standard, only one of the interests asserted by the university survived Justice Powell's scrutiny.

First, Justice Powell rejected an interest in "'reducing the historic deficit of traditionally disfavored minorities in medical schools and in the medical profession'" as an unlawful interest in racial balancing. *Id.*, at 306–307. Second, Justice Powell rejected an interest in remedying societal discrimination because such measures would risk placing unnecessary burdens on innocent third parties "who bear no responsibility for whatever harm the beneficiaries of the special admissions program are thought to have suffered." *Id.*, at 310. Third, Justice Powell rejected an interest in "increasing the number of physicians who will practice in communities currently underserved," concluding that even if such an interest could be compelling in some circumstances the program under review was not "geared to promote that goal." *Id.*, at 306, 310.

Justice Powell approved the university's use of race to further only one interest: "the attainment of a diverse student body." *Id.*, at 311. With the important proviso that "constitutional limitations protecting individual rights may not be disregarded," Justice Powell grounded his analysis in the academic freedom that "long has been viewed as a special concern of the First Amendment." *Id.*, at 312, 314. Justice Powell emphasized that nothing less than the "'nation's future depends upon leaders trained through wide exposure' to the ideas and mores of students as diverse as this Nation of many peoples." *Id.*, at 313 (quoting *Keyishian v. Board of Regents of Univ. of State of N. Y.*, 385 U. S. 589, 603 [1967]). In seeking the "right to select those students who will contribute the most to the 'robust exchange of ideas,'" a university seeks "to achieve a goal that is of paramount importance in the fulfillment of its mission." 438 U. S., at 313. Both "tradition and experience lend support to the view that the contribution of diversity is substantial." *Ibid.*

Justice Powell was, however, careful to emphasize that in his view race "is only one element in a range of factors a university properly may consider in attaining the goal of a heterogeneous student body." *Id.*, at 314. For Justice Powell, "[i]t is not an interest in simple ethnic diversity, in which a specified percentage of the student body is in effect guaranteed to be members of selected ethnic groups," that can justify the use of race. *Id.*, at 315. Rather, "[t]he diversity that furthers a compelling state interest encompasses a far broader array of qualifications and characteristics of which racial or ethnic origin is but a single though important element." *Ibid.*

In the wake of our fractured decision in *Bakke*, courts have struggled to discern whether Justice Powell's diversity rationale, set forth in part of the opinion joined by no other Justice, is nonetheless binding precedent under *Marks*. In that case, we explained that "[w]hen a fragmented Court decides a case and no single rationale explaining the result enjoys the assent of five Justices, the holding of the Court may be viewed as that position taken by those Members who concurred in the judgments on the narrowest grounds." 430 U. S., at 193 (internal quotation marks and citation omitted). As the divergent opinions of the lower courts demonstrate, however, "[t]his test is more easily stated than applied to the various opinions supporting the result in [*Bakke*]." *Nichols v. United States*, 511 U. S. 738, 745–746 (1994). Compare, *e. g., Johnson v. Board of Regents of Univ. of Ga.*, 263 F. 3d 1234 (CA11 2001) (Justice Powell's diversity rationale was

not the holding of the Court); *Hopwood v. Texas*, 236 F. 3d 256, 274–275 (CA5 2000) (*Hopwood II*) (same); *Hopwood I*, 78 F. 3d 932 (CA5 1996) (same), with *Smith v. University of Wash. Law School*, 233 F. 3d, at 1199 (Justice Powell's opinion, including the diversity rationale, is controlling under *Marks*).

We do not find it necessary to decide whether Justice Powell's opinion is binding under *Marks*. It does not seem "useful to pursue the *Marks* inquiry to the utmost logical possibility when it has so obviously baffled and divided the lower courts that have considered it." *Nichols v. United States, supra*, at 745–746. More important, for the reasons set out below, today we endorse Justice Powell's view that student body diversity is a compelling state interest that can justify the use of race in university admissions.

B.

The Equal Protection Clause provides that no State shall "deny to any person within its jurisdiction the equal protection of the laws." U. S. Const., Amdt. 14, § 2. Because the Fourteenth Amendment "protect[s] *persons*, not *groups*," all "governmental action based on race—a *group* classification long recognized as in most circumstances irrelevant and therefore prohibited—should be subjected to detailed judicial inquiry to ensure that the *personal* right to equal protection of the laws has not been infringed." *Adarand Constructors, Inc. v. Peña*, 515 U. S. 200, 227 (1995) (emphasis in original; internal quotation marks and citation omitted). We are a "free people whose institutions are founded upon the doctrine of equality." *Loving v. Virginia*, 388 U. S. 1, 11 (1967) (internal quotation marks and citation omitted). It follows from that principle that "government may treat people differently because of their race only for the most compelling reasons." *Adarand Constructors, Inc. v. Peña*, 515 U. S., at 227.

We have held that all racial classifications imposed by government "must be analyzed by a reviewing court under strict scrutiny." *Ibid.* This means that such classifications are constitutional only if they are narrowly tailored to further compelling governmental interests. "Absent searching judicial inquiry into the justification for such race-based measures," we have no way to determine what "classifications are 'benign' or 'remedial' and what classifications are in fact motivated by illegitimate notions of racial inferiority or simple racial politics." *Richmond v. J. A. Croson Co.*, 488 U. S. 469, 493 (1989) (plurality opinion). We apply strict scrutiny to all racial classifications to "'smoke out' illegitimate uses of race by assuring that [government] is pursuing a goal important enough to warrant use of a highly suspect tool." *Ibid.* Strict scrutiny is not "strict in theory, but fatal in fact." *Adarand Constructors, Inc. v. Peña*, supra, at 237 (internal quotation marks and citation omitted). Although all governmental uses of race are subject to strict scrutiny, not all are invalidated by it. As we have explained, "whenever the government treats any person unequally because of his or her race, that person has suffered an injury that falls squarely within the language and spirit of the Constitution's guarantee of equal protection." 515 U. S., at 229–230. But that observation "says nothing about the ultimate validity of any particular law; that determination is the job of the court applying strict scrutiny." *Id.*, at 230. When race-based action is necessary to further a compelling governmental interest, such action does not violate the constitutional guarantee of equal protection so long as the narrow-tailoring requirement is also satisfied.

Context matters when reviewing race-based governmental action under the Equal Protection Clause. See *Gomillion v. Lightfoot*, 364 U. S. 339, 343–344 (1960) (admonishing that, "in dealing with claims under broad provisions of the Constitution, which derive content by an interpretive process of inclusion and exclusion, it is imperative that generalizations, based on and qualified by the concrete situations that gave rise to them, must not be applied out of context in disregard of variant controlling facts"). In *Adarand Constructors, Inc. v. Peña*, we made clear that strict scrutiny must take "'relevant differences' into account." 515 U. S., at 228. Indeed, as we explained, that is its "fundamental purpose." *Ibid.* Not every decision influenced by race is equally objectionable, and strict scrutiny is designed to provide a framework for carefully examining the importance and the sincerity of the reasons advanced by the governmental decisionmaker for the use of race in that particular context.

III.

A.

With these principles in mind, we turn to the question whether the Law School's use of race is justified by a compelling state interest. Before this Court, as they have throughout this litigation, respondents assert only one justification for their use of race in the admissions process: obtaining "the educational benefits that flow from a diverse student body." Brief for Respondent Bollinger et al. i. In other words, the Law School asks us to recognize, in the context of higher education, a compelling state interest in student body diversity.

We first wish to dispel the notion that the Law School's argument has been foreclosed, either expressly or implicitly, by our affirmative-action cases decided since *Bakke*. It is true that some language in those opinions might be read to suggest that remedying past discrimination is the only permissible justification for race-based governmental action. See, *e. g.*, *Richmond v. J. A. Croson Co., supra*, at 493 (plurality opinion) (stating that unless classifications based on race are "strictly reserved for remedial settings, they may in fact promote notions of racial inferiority and lead to a politics of racial hostility"). But we have never held that the only governmental use of race that can survive strict scrutiny is remedying past discrimination. Nor, since *Bakke*, have we directly addressed the use of race in the context of public higher education. Today, we hold that the Law School has a compelling interest in attaining a diverse student body.

The Law School's educational judgment that such diversity is essential to its educational mission is one to which we defer. The Law School's assessment that diversity will, in fact, yield educational benefits is substantiated by respondents and their amici. Our scrutiny of the interest asserted by the Law School is no less strict for taking into account complex educational judgments in an area that lies primarily within the expertise of the university. Our holding today is in keeping with our tradition of giving a degree of deference to a university's academic decisions, within constitutionally prescribed limits. See *Regents of Univ. of Mich. v. Ewing*, 474 U. S. 214, 225 (1985); *Board of Curators of Univ.*

of Mo. v. Horowitz, 435 U. S. 78, 96, n. 6 (1978); *Bakke*, 438 U. S., at 319, n. 53 (opinion of Powell, J.).

We have long recognized that, given the important purpose of public education and the expansive freedoms of speech and thought associated with the university environment, universities occupy a special niche in our constitutional tradition. See, *e. g.*, *Wieman v. Updegraff*, 344 U. S. 183, 195 (1952) (Frankfurter, J., concurring); *Sweezy v. New Hampshire*, 354 U. S. 234, 250 (1957); *Shelton v. Tucker*, 364 U. S. 479, 487 (1960); *Keyishian v. Board of Regents of Univ. of State of N. Y.*, 385 U. S., at 603. In announcing the principle of student body diversity as a compelling state interest, Justice Powell invoked our cases recognizing a constitutional dimension, grounded in the First Amendment, of educational autonomy: "The freedom of a university to make its own judgments as to education includes the selection of its student body." *Bakke, supra*, at 312. From this premise, Justice Powell reasoned that by claiming "the right to select those students who will contribute the most to the 'robust exchange of ideas,'" a university "seek[s] to achieve a goal that is of paramount importance in the fulfillment of its mission." 438 U. S., at 313 (quoting *Keyishian v. Board of Regents of Univ. of State of N. Y., supra*, at 603). Our conclusion that the Law School has a compelling interest in a diverse student body is informed by our view that attaining a diverse student body is at the heart of the Law School's proper institutional mission, and that "good faith" on the part of a university is "presumed" absent "a showing to the contrary." 438 U. S., at 318–319.

As part of its goal of "assembling a class that is both exceptionally academically qualified and broadly diverse," the Law School seeks to "enroll a 'critical mass' of minority students." Brief for Respondent Bollinger et al. 13. The Law School's interest is not simply "to assure within its student body some specified percentage of a particular group merely because of its race or ethnic origin." *Bakke*, 438 U. S., at 307 (opinion of Powell, J.). That would amount to outright racial balancing, which is patently unconstitutional. *Ibid.*; *Freeman v. Pitts*, 503 U. S. 467, 494 (1992) ("Racial balance is not to be achieved for its own sake"); *Richmond v. J. A. Croson Co.*, 488 U. S., at 507. Rather, the Law School's concept of critical mass is defined by reference to the educational benefits that diversity is designed to produce.

These benefits are substantial. As the District Court emphasized, the Law School's admissions policy promotes "cross-racial understanding," helps to break down racial stereotypes, and "enables [students] to better understand persons of different races." App. to Pet. for Cert. 246a. These benefits are "important and laudable," because "classroom discussion is livelier, more spirited, and simply more enlightening and interesting" when the students have "the greatest possible variety of backgrounds." *Id.*, at 246a, 244a.

The Law School's claim of a compelling interest is further bolstered by its *amici*, who point to the educational benefits that flow from student body diversity. In addition to the expert studies and reports entered into evidence at trial, numerous studies show that student body diversity promotes learning outcomes, and "better prepares students for an increasingly diverse workforce and society, and better prepares them as professionals." Brief for American Educational Research Association et al. as *Amici Curiae* 3; see, *e. g.*, W. Bowen & D. Bok, *The Shape of the River* (1998); *Diversity Challenged: Evidence on the Impact of Affirmative Action* (G. Orfield & M. Kurlaender eds. 2001); *Compelling Interest: Examining the Evidence on Racial Dynamics in Colleges and Universities* (M. Chang, D. Witt, J. Jones, & K. Hakuta eds. 2003).

These benefits are not theoretical but real, as major American businesses have made clear that the skills needed in today's increasingly global marketplace can only be developed through exposure to widely diverse people, cultures, ideas, and viewpoints. Brief for 3M et al. as *Amici Curiae* 5; Brief for General Motors Corp. as *Amicus Curiae* 3–4. What is more, high-ranking retired officers and civilian leaders of the United States military assert that, "[b]ased on [their] decades of experience," a "highly qualified, racially diverse officer corps . . . is essential to the military's ability to fulfill its principle mission to provide national security." Brief for Julius W. Becton, Jr., et al. as *Amici Curiae* 5. The primary sources for the Nation's officer corps are the service academies and the Reserve Officers Training Corps (ROTC), the latter comprising students already admitted to participating colleges and universities. *Ibid.* At present, "the military cannot achieve an officer corps that is *both* highly qualified and racially diverse unless the service academies and the ROTC used limited race-conscious recruiting and admissions policies." *Ibid.* (emphasis in original). To fulfill its mission, the military "must be selective in admissions for training and education for the officer corps, and it must train and educate a highly qualified, racially diverse officer corps in a racially diverse educational setting." *Id.*, at 29 (emphasis in original). We agree that "[i]t requires only a small step from this analysis to conclude that our country's other most selective institutions must remain both diverse and selective." *Ibid.*

We have repeatedly acknowledged the overriding importance of preparing students for work and citizenship, describing education as pivotal to "sustaining our political and cultural heritage" with a fundamental role in maintaining the fabric of society. *Plyler v. Doe*, 457 U. S. 202, 221 (1982). This Court has long recognized that "education . . . is the very foundation of good citizenship." *Brown v. Board of Education*, 347 U. S. 483, 493 (1954). For this reason, the diffusion of knowledge and opportunity through public institutions of higher education must be accessible to all individuals regardless of race or ethnicity. The United States, as *amicus curiae*, affirms that "[e]nsuring that public institutions are open and available to all segments of American society, including people of all races and ethnicities, represents a paramount government objective." Brief for United States as *Amicus Curiae* 13. And, "[n]owhere is the importance of such openness more acute than in the context of higher education." *Ibid.* Effective participation by members of all racial and ethnic groups in the civic life of our Nation is essential if the dream of one Nation, indivisible, is to be realized.

Moreover, universities, and in particular, law schools, represent the training ground for a large number of our Nation's leaders. *Sweatt v. Painter*, 339 U. S. 629, 634 (1950) (describing law school as a "proving ground for legal learning and practice"). Individuals with law degrees occupy roughly half the state governorships, more than half the seats in the United States Senate, and more than a third of the seats in the United States House of Representatives. See Brief for Association of American Law Schools as *Amicus Curiae* 5–6. The pattern is even more striking when it comes to highly selective law schools. A handful of these schools accounts for 25 of the 100 United States Senators, 74 United States Courts of Appeals judges, and nearly 200 of the more than 600 United States District Court judges. *Id.*, at 6.

In order to cultivate a set of leaders with legitimacy in the eyes of the citizenry, it is necessary that the path to leadership be visibly open to talented and qualified individuals of every race and ethnicity. All members of our heterogeneous society must have confidence in the openness and integrity of the educational institutions that provide this training. As we have recognized, law schools "cannot be effective in isolation from the individuals and institutions with which the law interacts." See *Sweatt v. Painter*, *supra*, at 634. Access to legal education (and thus the legal profession) must be inclusive of talented and qualified individuals of every race and ethnicity, so that all members of our heterogeneous society may participate in the educational institutions that provide the training and education necessary to succeed in America.

The Law School does not premise its need for critical mass on "any belief that minority students always (or even consistently) express some characteristic minority viewpoint on any issue." Brief for Respondent Bollinger et al. 30. To the contrary, diminishing the force of such stereotypes is both a crucial part of the Law School's mission, and one that it cannot accomplish with only token numbers of minority students. Just as growing up in a particular region or having particular professional experiences is likely to affect an individual's views, so too is one's own, unique experience of being a racial minority in a society, like our own, in which race unfortunately still matters. The Law School has determined, based on its experience and expertise, that a "critical mass" of underrepresented minorities is necessary to further its compelling interest in securing the educational benefits of a diverse student body.

B.

Even in the limited circumstance when drawing racial distinctions is permissible to further a compelling state interest, government is still "constrained in how it may pursue that end: [T]he means chosen to accomplish the [government's] asserted purpose must be specifically and narrowly framed to accomplish that purpose." *Shaw v. Hunt*, 517 U. S. 899, 908 (1996) (internal quotation marks and citation omitted). The purpose of the narrow tailoring requirement is to ensure that "the means chosen 'fit' th[e] compelling goal so closely that there is little or no possibility that the motive for the classification was illegitimate racial prejudice or stereotype." *Richmond v. J. A. Croson Co.*, 488 U. S., at 493 (plurality opinion).

Since *Bakke*, we have had no occasion to define the contours of the narrow-tailoring inquiry with respect to race-conscious university admissions programs. That inquiry must be calibrated to fit the distinct issues raised by the use of race to achieve student body diversity in public higher education. Contrary to Justice Kennedy's assertions, we do not "abando[n] strict scrutiny," see *post*, at 394 (dissenting opinion). Rather, as we have already explained, *supra*, at 327, we adhere to *Adarand*'s teaching that the very purpose of strict scrutiny is to take such "relevant differences into account." 515 U. S., at 228 (internal quotation marks omitted).

To be narrowly tailored, a race-conscious admissions program cannot use a quota system—it cannot "insulat[e] each category of applicants with certain desired qualifications from competition with all other applicants." *Bakke*, 438 U. S., at 315 (opinion of Powell, J.). Instead, a university may consider race or ethnicity only as a "'plus' in a particular applicant's file," without "insulat[ing] the individual from comparison with all other candidates for the available seats." *Id.*, at 317. In other words, an admissions program must be "flexible enough to consider all pertinent elements of diversity in light of the particular qualifications of each applicant, and to place them on the same footing for consideration, although not necessarily according them the same weight." *Ibid.*

We find that the Law School's admissions program bears the hallmarks of a narrowly tailored plan. As Justice Powell made clear in *Bakke*, truly individualized consideration demands that race be used in a flexible, nonmechanical way. It follows from this mandate that universities cannot establish quotas for members of certain racial groups or put members of those groups on separate admissions tracks. See *id.*, at 315–316. Nor can universities insulate applicants who belong to certain racial or ethnic groups from the competition for admission. *Ibid.* Universities can, however, consider race or ethnicity more flexibly as a "plus" factor in the

context of individualized consideration of each and every applicant. *Ibid.*

We are satisfied that the Law School's admissions program, like the Harvard plan described by Justice Powell, does not operate as a quota. Properly understood, a "quota" is a program in which a certain fixed number or proportion of opportunities are "reserved exclusively for certain minority groups." *Richmond v. J. A. Croson Co.*, *supra*, at 496 (plurality opinion). Quotas "'impose a fixed number or percentage which must be attained, or which cannot be exceeded,'" *Sheet Metal Workers v. EEOC*, 478 U. S. 421, 495 (1986) (O'Connor, J., concurring in part and dissenting in part), and "insulate the individual from comparison with all other candidates for the available seats," *Bakke*, *supra*, at 317 (opinion of Powell, J.). In contrast, "a permissible goal . . . require[s] only a good-faith effort . . . to come within a range demarcated by the goal itself," *Sheet Metal Workers v. EEOC*, *supra*, at 495, and permits consideration of race as a "plus" factor in any given case while still ensuring that each candidate "compete[s] with all other qualified applicants," *Johnson v. Transportation Agency, Santa Clara Cty.*, 480 U. S. 616, 638 (1987).

Justice Powell's distinction between the medical school's rigid 16-seat quota and Harvard's flexible use of race as a "plus" factor is instructive. Harvard certainly had minimum goals for minority enrollment, even if it had no specific number firmly in mind. See *Bakke*, *supra*, at 323 (opinion of Powell, J.) ("10 or 20 black students could not begin to bring to their classmates and to each other the variety of points of view, backgrounds and experiences of blacks in the United States"). What is more, Justice Powell flatly rejected the argument that Harvard's program was "the functional equivalent of a quota" merely because it had some "'plus'" for race, or gave greater "weight" to race than to some other factors, in order to achieve student body diversity. 438 U. S., at 317–318.

The Law School's goal of attaining a critical mass of underrepresented minority students does not transform its program into a quota. As the Harvard plan described by Justice Powell recognized, there is of course "some relationship between numbers and achieving the benefits to be derived from a diverse student body, and between numbers and providing a reasonable environment for those students admitted." *Id.*, at 323. "[S]ome attention to numbers," without more, does not transform a flexible admissions system into a rigid quota. *Ibid.* Nor, as Justice Kennedy posits, does the Law School's consultation of the "daily reports," which keep track of the racial and ethnic composition of the class (as well as of residency and gender), "sugges[t] there was no further attempt at individual review save for race itself" during the final stages of the admissions process. See *post*, at 392 (dissenting opinion). To the contrary, the Law School's admissions officers testified without contradiction that they never gave race any more or less weight based on the information contained in these reports. Brief for Respondent Bollinger et al. 43, n. 70 (citing App. in Nos. 01–1447 and 01–1516 (CA6), p. 7336). Moreover, as Justice Kennedy concedes, see *post*, at 390, between 1993 and 1998, the number of African-American, Latino, and Native-American students in each class at the Law School varied from 13.5 to 20.1 percent, a range inconsistent with a quota.

The Chief Justice believes that the Law School's policy conceals an attempt to achieve racial balancing, and cites admissions data to contend that the Law School discriminates among different groups within the critical mass. *Post*, at 380–386 (dissenting opinion). But, as the Chief Justice concedes, the number of underrepresented minority students who ultimately enroll in the Law School differs substantially from their representation in the applicant pool and varies considerably for each group from year to year. See *post*, at 385 (dissenting opinion).

That a race-conscious admissions program does not operate as a quota does not, by itself, satisfy the requirement of individualized consideration. When using race as a "plus" factor in university admissions, a university's admissions program must remain flexible enough to ensure that each applicant is evaluated as an individual and not in a way that makes an applicant's race or ethnicity the defining feature of his or her application. The importance of this individualized consideration in the context of a race-conscious admissions program is paramount. See *Bakke*, 438 U. S., at 318, n. 52 (opinion of Powell, J.) (identifying the "denial . . . of th[e] right to individualized consideration" as the "principal evil" of the medical school's admissions program).

Here, the Law School engages in a highly individualized, holistic review of each applicant's file, giving serious consideration to all the ways an applicant might contribute to a diverse educational environment. The Law School affords this individualized consideration to applicants of all races. There is no policy, either *de jure* or *de facto*, of automatic acceptance or rejection based on any single "soft" variable. Unlike the program at issue in *Gratz v. Bollinger, ante*, p. 244, the Law School awards no mechanical, predetermined diversity "bonuses" based on race or ethnicity. See *ante*, at 271–272 (distinguishing a race-conscious admissions program that automatically awards 20 points based on race from the Harvard plan, which considered race but "did not contemplate that any single characteristic automatically ensured a specific and identifiable contribution to a university's diversity"). Like the Harvard plan, the Law School's admissions policy "is flexible enough to consider all pertinent elements of diversity in light of the particular qualifications of each applicant, and to place them on the same footing for consideration, although not necessarily according them the same weight." *Bakke, supra*, at 317 (opinion of Powell, J.).

We also find that, like the Harvard plan Justice Powell referenced in *Bakke*, the Law School's race-conscious admissions program adequately ensures that all factors that may contribute to student body diversity are meaningfully considered alongside race in admissions decisions. With respect to the use of race itself, all underrepresented minority students admitted by the Law School have been deemed qualified. By virtue of our Nation's struggle with racial inequality, such students are both likely to have experiences of particular importance to the Law School's mission, and less likely to be admitted in meaningful numbers on criteria that ignore those experiences. See App. 120.

The Law School does not, however, limit in any way the broad range of qualities and experiences that may be considered valuable contributions to student body diversity. To the contrary, the 1992 policy makes clear "[t]here are many possible bases for diversity admissions," and provides examples of admittees who have lived or traveled widely abroad, are fluent in several languages, have overcome personal adversity and family hardship, have exceptional records of extensive community service, and have had successful careers in other fields. *Id.*, at 118–119. The Law School seriously considers each "applicant's promise of making a notable contribution to the class by way of a particular strength, attainment, or characteristic—*e. g.*, an unusual intellectual achievement, employment experience, nonacademic performance, or personal background." *Id.*, at 83–84. All applicants have the opportunity to highlight their own potential diversity contributions through the submission of a personal statement, letters of recommendation, and an essay describing the ways in which the applicant will contribute to the life and diversity of the Law School.

What is more, the Law School actually gives substantial weight to diversity factors besides race. The Law School frequently accepts nonminority applicants with grades and test scores lower than underrepresented minority applicants (and other nonminority applicants) who are rejected. See Brief for Respondent Bollinger et al. 10; App. 121–122. This shows that the Law School seriously weighs many other diversity factors besides race that can make a real and dispositive difference for nonminority applicants as well. By this flexible approach, the Law School sufficiently takes into account, in practice as well as in theory, a wide variety of characteristics besides race and ethnicity that contribute to a diverse student body. Justice Kennedy speculates that "race is likely outcome determinative for many members of minority groups" who do not fall within the upper range of LSAT scores and grades. *Post*, at 389 (dissenting opinion). But the same could be said of the Harvard plan discussed approvingly by Justice Powell in *Bakke*, and indeed of any plan that uses race as one of many factors. See 438 U. S., at 316 ("'When the Committee on Admissions reviews the large middle group of applicants who are "admissible" and deemed capable of doing good work in their courses, the race of an applicant may tip the balance in his favor'").

Petitioner and the United States argue that the Law School's plan is not narrowly tailored because race-neutral means exist to obtain the educational benefits of student body diversity that the Law School seeks. We disagree. Narrow tailoring does not require exhaustion of every conceivable race-neutral alternative. Nor does it require a university to choose between maintaining a reputation for excellence or

fulfilling a commitment to provide educational opportunities to members of all racial groups. See *Wygant v. Jackson Bd. of Ed.*, 476 U. S. 267, 280, n. 6 (1986) (alternatives must serve the interest "'about as well'"); *Richmond v. J. A. Croson Co.*, 488 U. S., at 509–510 (plurality opinion) (city had a "whole array of race-neutral" alternatives because changing requirements "would have [had] little detrimental effect on the city's interests"). Narrow tailoring does, however, require serious, good faith consideration of workable race-neutral alternatives that will achieve the diversity the university seeks. See *id.*, at 507 (set-aside plan not narrowly tailored where "there does not appear to have been any consideration of the use of race-neutral means"); *Wygant v. Jackson Bd. of Ed.*, *supra*, at 280, n. 6 (narrow tailoring "require[s] consideration" of "lawful alternative and less restrictive means").

We agree with the Court of Appeals that the Law School sufficiently considered workable race-neutral alternatives. The District Court took the Law School to task for failing to consider race-neutral alternatives such as "using a lottery system" or "decreasing the emphasis for all applicants on undergraduate GPA and LSAT scores." App. to Pet. for Cert. 251a. But these alternatives would require a dramatic sacrifice of diversity, the academic quality of all admitted students, or both.

The Law School's current admissions program considers race as one factor among many, in an effort to assemble a student body that is diverse in ways broader than race. Because a lottery would make that kind of nuanced judgment impossible, it would effectively sacrifice all other educational values, not to mention every other kind of diversity. So too with the suggestion that the Law School simply lower admissions standards for all students, a drastic remedy that would require the Law School to become a much different institution and sacrifice a vital component of its educational mission. The United States advocates "percentage plans," recently adopted by public undergraduate institutions in Texas, Florida, and California, to guarantee admission to all students above a certain class-rank threshold in every high school in the State. Brief for United States as *Amicus Curiae* 14–18. The United States does not, however, explain how such plans could work for graduate and professional schools. Moreover, even assuming such plans are race neutral, they may preclude the university from conducting the individualized assessments necessary to assemble a student body that is not just racially diverse, but diverse along all the qualities valued by the university. We are satisfied that the Law School adequately considered race-neutral alternatives currently capable of producing a critical mass without forcing the Law School to abandon the academic selectivity that is the cornerstone of its educational mission.

We acknowledge that "there are serious problems of justice connected with the idea of preference itself." *Bakke*, 438 U. S., at 298 (opinion of Powell, J.). Narrow tailoring, therefore, requires that a race-conscious admissions program not unduly harm members of any racial group. Even remedial race-based governmental action generally "remains subject to continuing oversight to assure that it will work the least harm possible to other innocent persons competing for the benefit." *Id.*, at 308. To be narrowly tailored, a race-conscious admissions program must not "unduly burden individuals who are not members of the favored racial and ethnic groups." *Metro Broadcasting, Inc. v. FCC*, 497 U. S. 547, 630 (1990) (O'Connor, J., dissenting).

We are satisfied that the Law School's admissions program does not. Because the Law School considers "all pertinent elements of diversity," it can (and does) select nonminority applicants who have greater potential to enhance student body diversity over underrepresented minority applicants. See *Bakke, supra*, at 317 (opinion of Powell, J.). As Justice Powell recognized in *Bakke*, so long as a race-conscious admissions program uses race as a "plus" factor in the context of individualized consideration, a rejected applicant "will not have been foreclosed from all consideration for that seat simply because he was not the right color or had the wrong surname. . . . His qualifications would have been weighed fairly and competitively, and he would have no basis to complain of unequal treatment under the Fourteenth Amendment." 438 U. S., at 318.

We agree that, in the context of its individualized inquiry into the possible diversity contributions of all applicants, the Law School's race-conscious admissions program does not unduly harm nonminority applicants.

We are mindful, however, that "[a] core purpose of the Fourteenth Amendment was to do away with all governmentally imposed discrimination based on race." *Palmore v. Sidoti*, 466 U. S. 429, 432 (1984). Accordingly, race-conscious admissions policies must be limited in time. This requirement reflects that racial classifications, however compelling their goals, are potentially so dangerous that they may be employed no more broadly than the interest demands. Enshrining a permanent justification for racial preferences would offend this fundamental equal protection principle. We see no reason to exempt race-conscious admissions programs from the requirement that all governmental use of race must have a logical end point. The Law School, too, concedes that all "race-conscious programs must have reasonable durational limits." Brief for Respondent Bollinger et al. 32.

In the context of higher education, the durational requirement can be met by sunset provisions in race-conscious admissions policies and periodic reviews to determine whether racial preferences are still necessary to achieve student body diversity. Universities in California, Florida, and Washington State, where racial preferences in admissions are prohibited by state law, are currently engaged in experimenting with a wide variety of alternative approaches. Universities in other States can and should draw on the most promising aspects of these race-neutral alternatives as they develop. Cf. *United States v. Lopez*, 514 U. S. 549, 581 (1995) (Kennedy, J., concurring) ("[T]he States may perform their role as laboratories for experimentation to devise various solutions where the best solution is far from clear").

The requirement that all race-conscious admissions programs have a termination point "assure[s] all citizens that the deviation from the norm of equal treatment of all racial and ethnic groups is a temporary matter, a measure taken in the service of the goal of equality itself." *Richmond v. J. A. Croson Co.*, 488 U. S., at 510 (plurality opinion); see also Nathanson & Bartnik, The Constitutionality of Preferential Treatment for Minority Applicants to Professional Schools, 58 Chicago Bar Rec. 282, 293 (May–June 1977) ("It would be a sad day indeed, were America to become a quota-ridden society, with each identifiable minority assigned proportional representation in every desirable walk of life. But that is not the rationale for programs of preferential treatment; the acid test of their justification will be their efficacy in eliminating the need for any racial or ethnic preferences at all").

We take the Law School at its word that it would "like nothing better than to find a race-neutral admissions formula" and will terminate its race-conscious admissions program as soon as practicable. See Brief for Respondent Bollinger et al. 34; *Bakke, supra*, at 317–318 (opinion of Powell, J.) (presuming good faith of university officials in the absence of a showing to the contrary). It has been 25 years since Justice Powell first approved the use of race to further an interest in student body diversity in the context of public higher education. Since that time, the number of minority applicants with high grades and test scores has indeed increased. See Tr. of Oral Arg. 43. We expect that 25 years from now, the use of racial preferences will no longer be necessary to further the interest approved today.

IV.

In summary, the Equal Protection Clause does not prohibit the Law School's narrowly tailored use of race in admissions decisions to further a compelling interest in obtaining the educational benefits that flow from a diverse student body. Consequently, petitioner's statutory claims based on Title VI and 42 U. S. C. § 1981 also fail. See *Bakke, supra*, at 287 (opinion of Powell, J.) ("Title VI . . . proscribe[s] only those racial classifications that would violate the Equal Protection Clause or the Fifth Amendment"); *General Building Contractors Assn., Inc. v. Pennsylvania*, 458 U. S. 375, 389–391 (1982) (the prohibition against discrimination in § 1981 is coextensive with the Equal Protection Clause). The judgment of the Court of Appeals for the Sixth Circuit, accordingly, is affirmed.

It is so ordered.

Source: *Grutter v. Bollinger*, 539 U.S. 306 (2003).

See also: Affirmative Action; *Berea College v. Kentucky* (1908); College Admissions, Discrimination in. Document: *Regents of the University of California v. Bakke* (1978)

Cobell v. Salazar (2009)

Introduction

Cobell v. Salazar *(2009) is the case regarding the U.S. government's management of over 300,000 individual Native American trust accounts. In 1996, Elouise Cobell along with three other individuals, led a class-action lawsuit to recover millions of dollars of leases and royalties supposed to be held in trust by the Bureau of Indian Affairs and paid out to individual and tribe owners. Under the Dawes Act (1887), her family, like many other Native American families, had been told that the government would lease a portion of their allotment to bring them income. When the Bureau of Indian Affairs was unable to provide Cobell with a financial statement of income earned, Cobell filed the lawsuit that would last 14 years. On December 7, 2009, Cobell accepted a settlement of $1.4 billion dollars. On December 8, 2010, President Obama signed legislation approving funding for the settlement. Excerpted here from the* Cobell v. Salazar *(2010) Class Action Settlement Agreement are the "Background" and "Terms of Agreement" between the two parties.*

Primary Source

IN THE UNITED STATES DISTRICT COURT FOR THE DISTRICT OF COLUMBIA

ELOUISE PEPION COBELL, et al., Plaintiffs, vs. KEN SALAZAR, Secretary of the Interior, et al., Defendants.

Case No. 1:96CV01285-JR

December 7, 2009

US2000 11623208.1

CLASS ACTION SETTLEMENT AGREEMENT

This Class Action Settlement Agreement ("Agreement") is entered into by and between Elouise Pepion Cobell, Penny Cleghorn, Thomas Maulson and James Louis Larose (collectively, the "Named Plaintiffs"), on behalf of themselves and members of the Classes of individual Indians defined in this Agreement (collectively, "Plaintiffs"), on the one hand, and Ken Salazar, Secretary of the Interior, Larry Echohawk,

Assistant Secretary of the Interior—Indian Affairs, and H. Timothy Geithner, Secretary of the Treasury and their successors in office, all in their official capacities (collectively, "Defendants"). Plaintiffs and Defendants are collectively referenced as the "Parties." Subject to Court approval as required by Federal Rule of Civil Procedure ("FRCP") 23, the Parties hereby stipulate and agree that, in consideration of the promises and covenants set forth in this Agreement and upon entry by the Court of a Final Order and Judgment and resolution of any appeals from that Final Order and Judgment, this Action shall be settled and compromised in accordance with the terms of this Agreement. The Parties agree that the Settlement is contingent on the enactment of legislation to authorize or confirm specific aspects of the Settlement as set forth below. If such legislation, which will expressly reference this Agreement, is not enacted on or before the Legislation Enactment Deadline as defined in this Agreement, unless such date is mutually agreed to be extended by the Parties, or is enacted with material changes, the Agreement shall automatically become null and void.

BACKGROUND

1. On June 10, 1996, a class action complaint (the "Complaint") was filed in the United States District Court for the District of Columbia (the "Court") entitled *Elouise Pepion Cobell, et al. v. Bruce Babbitt, Secretary of Interior, et al.*, No. Civ. 96–1285 (RCL) (currently denominated as *Elouise Pepion Cobell v. Ken Salazar, Secretary of Interior, et al.*, 96–1285 [JR]) (this "Action"), seeking to redress alleged breaches of trust by the United States, and its trustee delegates the Secretary of Interior, the Assistant Secretary of Interior-Indian Affairs, and the Secretary of the Treasury, regarding the management of Individual Indian Money ("IIM") Accounts held on behalf of individual Indians.

2. The Complaint sought, among other things, declaratory and injunctive relief construing the trust obligations of the Defendants to members of the Plaintiff class and declaring that Defendants have breached and are in continuing breach of their trust obligations to class members, an order compelling Defendants to perform these legally mandated obligations, and requesting an accounting by

Interior Defendants (as hereinafter defined) of individual Indian trust assets. See *Cobell v. Babbitt*, 52 F.Supp. 2d 11, 19 (D.D.C. 1999) ("Cobell III").

3. On February 4, 1997, the Court granted Plaintiffs' Motion for Class Action Certification pursuant to FRCP 23(b)(1)(A) and (b)(2) "on behalf of a plaintiff class consisting of present and former beneficiaries of IIM Accounts (exclusive of those who prior to the filing of the Complaint herein had filed actions on their own behalf alleging claims included in the Complaint)" (the "February 4, 1997 Class Certification Order"), reserving the jurisdiction to modify the February 4, 1997 Class Certification Order as the interests of justice may require, id. at 2–3.

4. On December 21, 1999, the Court held, among other things, that Defendants were then in breach of certain of their respective trust duties, *Cobell v. Babbitt*, 91 F. Supp. 2d 1, 58 (D.D.C. 1999) ("Cobell V").

5. On February 23, 2001, the United States Court of Appeals for the District of Columbia Circuit (the "Court of Appeals") upheld the Court's determination that Defendants were in breach of their statutory trust duties, *Cobell v. Norton*, 240 F.3d 1081 (D.C. Cir. 2001) ("Cobell VI").

6. Subsequently, the Court made determinations that had the effect of modifying the February 4, 1997 Class Certification Order, determining on January 30, 2008, that the right to an accounting accrued on October 25, 1994, "for all then-living IIM beneficiaries: those who hold or at any point in their lives held IIM Accounts." *Cobell v. Kempthorne*, 532 F. Supp. 2d 37, 98 (D.D.C. 2008) ("Cobell XX").

7. The Court and the Court of Appeals have further clarified those individual Indians entitled to the relief requested in the Complaint in the following respects:

(a) Excluding income derived from individual Indian trust land that was received by an individual Indian beneficiary on a direct pay basis, *Cobell* XX, 532 F. Supp. 2d at 95–96;

(b) Excluding income derived from individual Indian trust land where such funds were managed by tribes, id.;

(c) Excluding IIM Accounts closed prior to October 25, 1994, date of passage of the American Indian Trust Fund Management Reform Act of 1994, Pub. L. No. 103–412, 108 Stat. 4239 codified as amended at 25 U.S.C. § 162a et. seq. (the "Trust Reform Act"), *Cobell v. Salazar*, 573 F.3d 808, 815 (D.C. Cir. 2009) (*Cobell* XXII); and

(d) Excluding heirs to money from closed accounts that were subject to final probate determinations, id.

8. On July 24, 2009, the Court of Appeals reaffirmed that "[t]he district court sitting in equity must do everything it can to ensure that [Interior Defendants] provide [plaintiffs] an equitable accounting," Id. at 813.

9. This Action has continued for over 13 years, there is no end anticipated in the foreseeable future, and the Parties are mindful of the admonition of the Court of Appeals that they work together "to resolve this case expeditiously and fairly," *Cobell v. Kempthorne*, 455 F.3d 317, 336 (D.C. Cir. 2006), and desire to do so.

10. Recognizing that individual Indian trust beneficiaries have potential additional claims arising from Defendants' management of trust funds and trust assets, Defendants have an interest in a broad resolution of past differences in order to establish a productive relationship in the future.

11. The Parties recognize that an integral part of trust reform includes accelerating correction of the fractionated ownership of trust or restricted land, which makes administration of the individual Indian trust more difficult.

12. The Parties also recognize that another part of trust reform includes correcting the problems created by the escheatment of certain individual Indians' ownership of trust or restricted land, which has been held to be unconstitutional (see *Babbitt v. Youpee*, 519 U.S. 234 (1997); *Hodel v. Irving*, 481 U.S. 704 (1987)) and which makes administration of the individual Indian trust difficult.

13. Plaintiffs believe that further actions are necessary to reform the individual Indian trust, but hope that such further reforms are made without the need for additional litigation. Plaintiffs are also hopeful that the Commission which Secretary Salazar is announcing contemporaneously with the execution of this Agreement will result in the further reform which Plaintiffs believe is needed.

14. The Parties have an interest in as complete a resolution as possible for individual Indian trust-related claims and agree that this necessarily includes establishing a sum certain as a balance for each IIM Account as of a date certain.

15. Defendants deny and continue to deny any and all liability and damages to any individual Indian trust beneficiary with respect to the claims or causes of action asserted in the Litigation or the facts found by the Court in this Litigation. Nonetheless, without admitting or conceding any liability or damages whatsoever and without admitting any wrongdoing, and without conceding the appropriateness of class treatment for claims asserted in any future complaint, Defendants have agreed to settle the Litigation (as hereinafter defined) on the terms and conditions set forth in this Agreement, to avoid the burden, expense, and uncertainty of continuing the case.

16. Class Counsel have conducted appropriate investigations and analyzed and evaluated the merits of the claims made, and judgments rendered, against Defendants in the Litigation, the findings, conclusions and holdings of the Court and Court of Appeals in this Litigation, and the impact of this Settlement on Plaintiffs as well as the impact of no settlement, and based upon their analysis and their evaluation of a number of factors, and recognizing the substantial risks of continued litigation, including the possibility that the Litigation, if not settled now, might not result in any recovery, or might result in a recovery that is less favorable than that provided for in this Settlement, and that otherwise a fair judgment would not occur for several years, Class Counsel are satisfied that the terms and conditions of this Settlement are fair, reasonable and adequate and that this Settlement is in the best interests of all Class Members.

17. The Parties desire to settle the Litigation and resolve their differences based on the terms set forth in this Agreement.

TERMS OF AGREEMENT

NOW, THEREFORE, in consideration of this Background, the mutual covenants and promises set forth in this Agreement, as well as the good and valuable consideration provided for in this Agreement, the Parties agree to a full and complete settlement of the Litigation on the following terms.

A. DEFINITIONS

1. Accounting/Trust Administration Fund. "Accounting/Trust Administration Fund" shall mean the $1,412,000,000.00 that Defendants shall pay into a Settlement Account held in the trust department of a Qualified Bank (as hereinafter defined) selected by Plaintiffs and approved by the Court, as well as any interest or investment income earned before distribution. The $1,412,000,000.00 payment represents the maximum total amount that Defendants are required to pay to settle Historical Accounting Claims, Funds Administration Claims, and Land Administration Claims.

2. Amended Complaint. "Amended Complaint" shall mean the complaint amended by Plaintiffs solely as part of this Agreement, and for the sole purpose of settling this Litigation, to be filed with the Court concurrently with, and attached to, this Agreement.

3. Amount Payable for Each Valid Claim. "Amount Payable for Each Valid Claim" shall mean the amount prescribed in section E.3 and E.4 below.

4. Assigned Value. "Assigned Value" shall have the meaning set forth in subsection E(4)(b)(3) below.

5. Claims Administrator. "Claims Administrator" shall mean The Garden City Group, Inc., which shall provide services to the Parties to facilitate administrative matters and distribution of the Amount Payable for Each Valid Claim in accordance with the terms and conditions of this Agreement.

6. Classes. "Classes" shall mean the classes established for purposes of this Agreement: the Historical Accounting Class and the Trust Administration Class (both as hereinafter defined).

7. Class Counsel. "Class Counsel" shall mean Dennis Gingold, Thaddeus Holt and attorneys from Kilpatrick Stockton LLP, including Elliott H. Levitas, Keith Harper, William Dorris, David Smith, William Austin, Adam Charnes and Justin Guilder.

8. Class Members. "Class Members" shall mean members of the Classes.

9. Contact Information. "Contact Information" shall mean the best and most current information the Department of the Interior ("Interior") then has available of a beneficiary's name, social security number, date of birth, and mailing address, and whether Interior's individual Indian trust records reflect that beneficiary to be a minor, non-compos mentis, an individual under legal disability, an adult in need of assistance or whereabouts unknown.

10. Day. "Day" shall mean a calendar day.

11. Defendants. "Defendants" shall mean Ken Salazar, Secretary of the Interior, Larry Echohawk, Assistant Secretary of the Interior—Indian Affairs, and H. Timothy Geithner, Secretary of the Treasury, and their successors in office, all in their official capacities.

12. Fairness Hearing. "Fairness Hearing" shall mean the hearing on the Joint Motion for Judgment and Final Approval referenced in Paragraph D(4) below.

13. Final Approval. "Final Approval" shall mean the occurrence of the following:

   a. Following the Fairness Hearing, the Court has entered Judgment; and

   b. The Judgment has become final. "Final" means the later of:

      (1) The time for rehearing or reconsideration, appellate review, and review by petition for certiorari has

expired, and no motion for rehearing or reconsideration and/or notice of appeal has been filed; or

(2) If rehearing, reconsideration, or appellate review, or review by petition for certiorari is sought, after any and all avenues of rehearing, reconsideration, appellate review, or review by petition for certiorari have been exhausted, and no further rehearing, reconsideration, appellate review, or review by petition for certiorari is permitted, or the time for seeking such review has expired, and the Judgment has not been modified, amended or reversed in any way.

14. Funds Administration Claims. "Funds Administration Claims" shall mean known and unknown claims that have been or could have been asserted through the Record Date for Defendants' alleged breach of trust and mismanagement of individual Indian trust funds, and consist of Defendants' alleged:

a. Failure to collect or credit funds owed under a lease, sale, easement or other transaction, including without limitation, failure to collect or credit all money due, failure to audit royalties and failure to collect interest on late payments;

b. Failure to invest;

c. Underinvestment;

d. Imprudent management and investment;

e. Erroneous or improper distributions or disbursements, including to the wrong person or account;

f. Excessive or improper administrative fees;

g. Deposits into wrong accounts;

h. Misappropriation;

i. Funds withheld unlawfully and in breach of trust;

j. Loss of funds held in failed depository institutions, including interest;

k. Failure as trustee to control or investigate allegations of, and obtain compensation for, theft, embezzlement, misappropriation, fraud, trespass, or other misconduct regarding trust assets;

l. Failure to pay or credit interest, including interest on Indian monies proceeds of labor (IMPL), special deposit accounts, and IIM Accounts;

m. Loss of funds or investment securities, and the income or proceeds earned from such funds or securities;

n. Accounting errors;

o. Failure to deposit and/or disburse funds in a timely fashion; and

p. Claims of like nature and kind arising out of allegations of Defendants' breach of trust and/or mismanagement of individual Indian trust funds through the Record Date, that have been or could have been asserted.

15. Historical Accounting Claims. "Historical Accounting Claims" shall mean common law or statutory claims, including claims arising under the Trust Reform Act, for a historical accounting through the Record Date of any and all IIM Accounts and any asset held in trust or restricted status, including but not limited to Land (as defined herein) and funds held in any account, and which now are, or have been, beneficially owned or held by an individual Indian trust beneficiary who is a member of the Historical Accounting Class. These claims include the historical accounting through the Record Date of all funds collected and held in trust by Defendants and their financial and fiscal agents in open or closed accounts, as well as interest earned on such funds, whether such funds are deposited in IIM Accounts, or in tribal, special deposit, or government administrative or operating accounts.

16. Historical Accounting Class. "Historical Accounting Class" means those individual Indian beneficiaries (exclusive of those who prior to the filing of the Complaint on June 10, 1996 had filed actions on their own behalf stating a claim for a historical accounting) alive on the Record Date and

who had an IIM Account open during any period between October 25, 1994 and the Record Date, which IIM Account had at least one cash transaction credited to it at any time as long as such credits were not later reversed. Beneficiaries deceased as of the Record Date are included in the Historical Accounting Class only if they had an IIM Account that was open as of the Record Date. The estate of any Historical Accounting Class Member who dies after the Record Date but before distribution is in the Historical Accounting Class.

17. IIM Account. "IIM Account" means an IIM account as defined in title 25, Code of Federal Regulations, section 115.002.

18. Interior Defendants. "Interior Defendants" shall mean Ken Salazar, Secretary of the Interior, and Larry Echohawk, Assistant Secretary of the Interior–Indian Affairs, and their successors in office, all in their official capacities.

19. Land. "Land" shall mean land owned by individual Indians and held in trust or restricted status by Interior Defendants, including all resources on, and corresponding subsurface rights, if any, in the land, and water, unless otherwise indicated.

20. Land Consolidation Program. The fractional interest acquisition program authorized in 25 U.S.C. 2201 et seq., including any applicable legislation enacted pursuant to this Agreement.

21. Land Administration Claims. "Land Administration Claims" shall mean known and unknown claims that have been or could have been asserted through the Record Date for Interior Defendants' alleged breach of trust and fiduciary mismanagement of land, oil, natural gas, mineral, timber, grazing, water and other resources and rights (the "resources") situated on, in or under Land and consist of Interior Defendants' alleged:

a. Failure to lease Land, approve leases or otherwise productively use Lands or assets;

b. Failure to obtain fair market value for leases, easements, rights-of-way or sales;

c. Failure to prudently negotiate leases, easements, rights-of-way, sales or other transactions;

d. Failure to impose and collect penalties for late payments;

e. Failure to include or enforce terms requiring that Land be conserved, maintained, or improved;

f. Permitting loss, dissipation, waste, or ruin, including failure to preserve Land whether involving agriculture (including but not limited to failing to control agricultural pests), grazing, harvesting (including but not limited to permitting overly aggressive harvesting), timber lands (including but not limited to failing to plant and cull timber land for maximum yield), and oil, natural gas, mineral resources or other resources (including but not limited to failing to manage oil, natural gas, or mineral resources to maximize total production);

g. Misappropriation;

h. Failure to control, investigate allegations of, or obtain relief in equity and at law for, trespass, theft, misappropriation, fraud or misconduct regarding Land;

i. Failure to correct boundary errors, survey or title record errors, or failure to properly apportion and track allotments; and

j. Claims of like nature and kind arising out of allegations of Interior Defendants' breach of trust and/or mismanagement of Land through the Record Date, that have been or could have been asserted.

22. Legislation Enactment Deadline. "Legislation Enactment Deadline" shall mean December 31, 2009, 11:59 P.M. Eastern time.

23. Litigation. "Litigation" shall mean that which is stated in the Amended Complaint attached to this Agreement.

24. Named Plaintiffs; Class Representatives. "Named Plaintiffs" shall mean and include Elouise Pepion Cobell ("Lead Plaintiff"), Penny Cleghorn, Thomas Maulson, and James

Louis Larose. The Named Plaintiffs are also referred to as the "Class Representatives."

25. Notice Contractor. "Notice Contractor" shall mean a mutually agreeable entity that shall provide services to the Parties needed to provide notice to the Classes.

26. Order Granting Preliminary Approval. "Order Granting Preliminary Approval" shall mean the Order entered by the Court preliminarily approving the terms set forth in this Agreement, including the manner and timing of providing notice to the Classes, the time period for objections and the date, time and location for a Fairness Hearing.

27. Parties. "Parties" shall mean the Named Plaintiffs, members of the Classes, and Defendants.

28. Preliminary Approval. "Preliminary Approval" shall mean that the Court has entered an Order Granting Preliminary Approval.

29. Qualifying Bank; Qualified Bank. "Qualifying Bank" or "Qualified Bank" shall mean a federally insured depository institution that is "well capitalized," as that term is defined in 12 CFR §325.103, and that is subject to regulation and supervision by the Board of Governors of the Federal Reserve System or the U.S. Comptroller of the Currency under 12 CFR §9.18.

30. Record Date. "Record Date" shall mean September 30, 2009, 11:59 P.M. Eastern time.

31. Settlement Account. "Settlement Account" shall mean the trust account(s) established by Class Counsel in a Qualified Bank approved by the Court for the purpose of effectuating the Settlement and into which the Accounting/Trust Administration Fund shall be deposited and from which Stage 1 and Stage 2 Distributions, among other things set forth in this Agreement, shall be paid.

32. Special Master. "Special Master" shall be the person appointed by the Court as provided in paragraph E.1.a.

33. Stage 1; Stage 1 Distribution. "Stage 1" and "Stage 1 Distribution" shall mean the distribution to the Historical Accounting Class as provided in paragraph E(3).

34. Stage 2; Stage 2 Distribution. "Stage 2" and "Stage 2 Distribution" shall mean the distribution to the Trust Administration Class as provided in paragraph E(4).

35. Trust Administration Class. "Trust Administration Class" shall mean those individual Indian beneficiaries (exclusive of persons who filed actions on their own behalf, or a group of individuals who were certified as a class in a class action, stating a Funds Administration Claim or a Land Administration Claim prior to the filing of the Amended Complaint) alive as of the Record Date and who have or had IIM Accounts in the "Electronic Ledger Era" (currently available electronic data in systems of the Department of the Interior dating from approximately 1985 to the present), as well as individual Indians who, as of the Record Date, had a recorded or other demonstrable ownership interest in land held in trust or restricted status, regardless of the existence of an IIM Account and regardless of the proceeds, if any, generated from the Land. The Trust Administration Class does not include beneficiaries deceased as of the Record Date, but does include the estate of any deceased beneficiary whose IIM Accounts or other trust assets had been open in probate as of the Record Date. The estate of any Trust Administration Class Member who dies after the Record Date but before distribution is included in the Trust Administration Class.

36. Trust Land Consolidation Fund. "Trust Land Consolidation Fund" shall mean the $2,000,000,000.00 allocated to Interior Defendants and held in a separate account in Treasury for the purpose of acquiring fractional interests in trust or restricted land and such other purposes as permitted by this Agreement and applicable law.

Source: *Cobell v. Salazar.* 573 F.3d 808, 815 (D.C. Cir. 2009).

See also: Bureau of Indian Affairs; Dawes Act (1887); Indian Claims Commission; Indian Reservations

Arizona Senate Bill 1070 (2010)

Introduction

On April 23, 2010, Arizona governor Jan Brewer signed Senate Bill 1070 into law. The legislation, which allows the police

to detain individuals suspected of being in the country illegally and allows foreign nationals to be charged with a misdemeanor for not carrying proof of residency papers, sparked a wave of controversy as many suggested it would require law enforcement officials to engage in racial profiling. Supporters of the bill disagreed and stated that the bill was essential to stemming the increase of illegal immigration in Arizona. In July 2010, U.S. district judge Susan Bolton placed a temporary injunction against four of the law's provisions: Section 2(B), the portion that deals with police enforcement of immigration laws; Section 3, which criminalizes the failure to carry immigration papers; Section 5(C), which makes it a crime for an undocumented immigrant to apply for or hold jobs; and Section 6, which authorizes warrantless arrests if there were probable cause that a person committed a deportable offense. The injunction was upheld by the Ninth Circuit Court of Appeals, leading Arizona to file an appeal with the U.S. Supreme Court, which agreed to hear the case. On June 25, 2012, the Supreme Court struck down three of the contested provisions but kept in place Section 2(B), perhaps the most controversial aspect of SB 1070. Below is the full text of SB 1070.

Primary Source

Be it enacted by the Legislature of the State of Arizona:

Section 1. Intent

The legislature finds that there is a compelling interest in the cooperative enforcement of federal immigration laws throughout all of Arizona. The legislature declares that the intent of this act is to make attrition through enforcement the public policy of all state and local government agencies in Arizona. The provisions of this act are intended to work together to discourage and deter the unlawful entry and presence of aliens and economic activity by persons unlawfully present in the United States.

Sec. 2. Title 11, chapter 7, Arizona Revised Statutes, is amended by adding article 8, to read:

ARTICLE 8. ENFORCEMENT OF IMMIGRATION LAWS

11-1051. Cooperation and assistance in enforcement of immigration laws; indemnification

A. No official or agency of this state or a county, city, town or other political subdivision of this state may adopt a policy that limits or restricts the enforcement of federal immigration laws to less than the full extent permitted by federal law.

B. For any lawful contact made by a law enforcement official or agency of this state or a county, city, town or other political subdivision of this state where reasonable suspicion exists that the person is an alien who is unlawfully present in the United States, a reasonable attempt shall be made, when practicable, to determine the immigration status of the person. The person's immigration status shall be verified with the federal government pursuant to 8 United States code section 1373(c).

C. If an alien who is unlawfully present in the United States is convicted of a violation of state or local law, on discharge from imprisonment or assessment of any fine that is imposed, the alien shall be transferred immediately to the custody of the United States immigration and customs enforcement or the United States customs and border protection.

D. Notwithstanding any other law, a law enforcement agency may securely transport an alien who is unlawfully present in the United States and who is in the agency's custody to a federal facility in this state or to any other point of transfer into federal custody that is outside the jurisdiction of the law enforcement agency.

E. A law enforcement officer, without a warrant, may arrest a person if the officer has probable cause to believe that the person has committed any public offense that makes the person removable from the United States.

F. Except as provided in federal law, officials or agencies of this state and counties, cities, towns and other political subdivisions of this state may not be prohibited or in any way be restricted from sending, receiving or maintaining information relating to the immigration status of any individual or exchanging that information with any other federal, state or local governmental entity for the following official purposes:

1. Determining eligibility for any public benefit, service or license provided by any federal, state, local or other political subdivision of this state.

2. Verifying any claim of residence or domicile if determination of residence or domicile is required under the laws of this state or a judicial order issued pursuant to a civil or criminal proceeding in this state.

3. Confirming the identity of any person who is detained.

4. If the person is an alien, determining whether the person is in compliance with the federal registration laws prescribed by title II, chapter 7 of the federal immigration and Nationality act.

G. A person may bring an action in superior court to challenge any official or agency of this state or a county, city, town or other political subdivision of this state that adopts or implements a policy that limits or restricts the enforcement of federal immigration laws to less than the full extent permitted by federal law. If there is a judicial finding that an entity has violated this section, the court shall order any of the following:

1. That the person who brought the action recover court costs and attorney fees.

2. That the entity pay a civil penalty of not less than one thousand dollars and not more than five thousand dollars for each day that the policy has remained in effect after the filing of an action pursuant to this subsection.

H. A court shall collect the civil penalty prescribed in subsection G and remit the civil penalty to the department of public safety for deposit in the gang and immigration intelligence team enforcement mission fund established by section 41 1724.

I. A law enforcement officer is indemnified by the law enforcement officer's agency against reasonable costs and expenses, including attorney fees, incurred by the officer in connection with any action, suit or proceeding brought pursuant to this section to which the officer may be a party by reason of the officer being or having been a member of the law enforcement agency, except in relation to matters in which the officer is adjudged to have acted in bad faith.

J. This section shall be implemented in a manner consistent with federal laws regulating immigration, protecting the civil rights of all persons and respecting the privileges and immunities of United States citizens.

Sec. 3. Title 13, chapter 15, Arizona Revised Statutes, is amended by adding section 13-1509, to read:

13-1509. Trespassing by illegal aliens; assessment; exception; classification

A. In addition to any violation of federal law, a person is guilty of trespassing if the person is both:

1. Present on any public or private land in this state.

2. In violation of 8 United States Code section 1304(e) or 1306(a).

B. In the enforcement of this section, the final determination of an alien's immigration status shall be determined by either:

1. A law enforcement officer who is authorized by the federal government to verify or ascertain an alien's immigration status.

2. A law enforcement officer or agency communicating with the United States immigration and customs enforcement or the United States border protection pursuant to 8 United States Code section 1373(c).

C. A person who is sentenced pursuant to this section is not eligible for suspension or commutation of sentence or release on any basis until the sentence imposed is served.

D. In addition to any other penalty prescribed by law, the court shall order the person to pay jail costs and an additional assessment in the following amounts:

1. At least five hundred dollars for a first violation.

2. Twice the amount specified in paragraph 1 of this subsection if the person was previously subject to an assessment pursuant to this subsection.

E. A court shall collect the assessments prescribed in subsection D of this section and remit the assessments to the department of public safety, which shall establish a special subaccount for the monies in the account established for the gang and immigration intelligence team enforcement mission appropriation. Monies in the special subaccount are subject to legislative appropriation for distribution for gang and immigration enforcement and for county jail reimbursement costs relating to illegal immigration.

F. This section does not apply to a person who maintains authorization from the federal government to remain in the United States.

G. A violation of this section is a class 1 misdemeanor, except that a violation of this section is:

1. A class 3 felony if the person violates this section while in possession of any of the following:

(a) A dangerous drug as defined in section 13-3401.

(b) Precursor chemicals that are used in the manufacturing of methamphetamine in violation of section 13-3404.01.

(c) A deadly weapon or a dangerous instrument, as defined in section 13-105.

(d) Property that is used for the purpose of committing an act of terrorism as prescribed in section 13-2308.01.

2. A class 4 felony if the person either:

(a) Is convicted of a second or subsequent violation of this section.

(b) Within sixty months before the violation, has been removed from the United States pursuant to 8 United States Code section 1229a or has accepted a voluntary removal from the United States pursuant to 8 United States Code section 1229c.

Sec. 4. Section 13-2319, Arizona Revised Statutes, is amended to read:

13-2319. Smuggling; classification; definitions

A. It is unlawful for a person to intentionally engage in the smuggling of human beings for profit or commercial purpose.

B. A violation of this section is a class 4 felony.

C. Notwithstanding subsection B of this section, a violation of this section:

1. Is a class 2 felony if the human being who is smuggled is under eighteen years of age and is not accompanied by a family member over eighteen years of age or the offense involved the use of a deadly weapon or dangerous instrument.

2. Is a class 3 felony if the offense involves the use or threatened use of deadly physical force and the person is not eligible for suspension of sentence, probation, pardon or release from confinement on any other basis except pursuant to section 31-233, subsection A or B until the sentence imposed by the court is served, the person is eligible for release pursuant to section 41-1604.07 or the sentence is commuted.

D. Chapter 10 of this title does not apply to a violation of subsection C, paragraph 1 of this section.

E. Notwithstanding any other law, a peace officer may lawfully stop any person who is operating a motor vehicle if the officer has reasonable suspicion to believe the person is in violation of any civil traffic law and this section.

F. For the purposes of this section:

1. "Family member" means the person's parent, grandparent, sibling or any other person who is related to the person by consanguinity or affinity to the second degree.

2. "Procurement of transportation" means any participation in or facilitation of transportation and includes:

(a) Providing services that facilitate transportation including travel arrangement services or money transmission services.

(b) Providing property that facilitates transportation, including a weapon, a vehicle or other means of transportation or false identification, or selling, leasing, renting or otherwise making available a drop house as defined in section 13-2322.

3. "Smuggling of human beings" means the transportation, procurement of transportation or use of property or real property by a person or an entity that knows or has reason to know that the person or persons transported or to be transported are not United States citizens, permanent resident aliens or persons otherwise lawfully in this state or have attempted to enter, entered or remained in the United States in violation of law.

Sec. 5. Title 13, chapter 29, Arizona Revised Statutes, is amended by adding sections 13-2928 and 13-2929, to read:

13-2928. Unlawful stopping to hire and pick up passengers for work; unlawful application, solicitation or employment; classification; definitions

A. It is unlawful for an occupant of a motor vehicle that is stopped on a street, roadway or highway to attempt to hire or hire and pick up passengers for work at a different location if the motor vehicle blocks or impedes the normal movement of traffic.

B. It is unlawful for a person to enter a motor vehicle that is stopped on a street, roadway or highway in order to be hired by an occupant of the motor vehicle and to be transported to work at a different location if the motor vehicle blocks or impedes the normal movement of traffic.

C. It is unlawful for a person who is unlawfully present in the United States and who is an unauthorized alien to knowingly apply for work, solicit work in a public place or perform work as an employee or independent contractor in this state.

D. A violation of this section is a class 1 misdemeanor.

E. For the purposes of this section:

1. "Solicit" means verbal or nonverbal communication by a gesture or a nod that would indicate to a reasonable person that a person is willing to be employed.

2. "Unauthorized alien" means an alien who does not have the legal right or authorization under federal law to work in the United States as described in 8 United States Code section 1324a(h)(3).

13-2929. Unlawful transporting, moving, concealing, harboring or shielding of unlawful aliens; vehicle impoundment; classification

A. It is unlawful for a person who is in violation of a criminal offense to:

1. Transport or move or attempt to transport or move an alien in this state in a means of transportation if the person knows or recklessly disregards the fact that the alien has come to, has entered or remains in the United States in violation of law.

2. Conceal, harbor or shield or attempt to conceal, harbor or shield an alien from detection in any place in this state, including any building or any means of transportation, if the person knows or recklessly disregards the fact that the alien has come to, has entered or remains in the United States in violation of law.

3. Encourage or induce an alien to come to or reside in this state if the person knows or recklessly disregards the fact that such coming to, entering or residing in this state is or will be in violation of law.

B. A means of transportation that is used in the commission of a violation of this section is subject to mandatory vehicle immobilization or impoundment pursuant to section 28-3511.

C. A person who violates this section is guilty of a class 1 misdemeanor and is subject to a fine of at least one thousand dollars, except that a violation of this section that involves ten or more illegal aliens is a class 6 felony and the person is subject to a fine of at least one thousand dollars for each alien who is involved.

Sec. 6. Section 23-212, Arizona Revised Statutes, is amended to read:

23-212. Knowingly employing unauthorized aliens; prohibition; false and frivolous complaints; violation; classification; license suspension and revocation; affirmative defense

A. An employer shall not knowingly employ an unauthorized alien. If, in the case when an employer uses a contract, subcontract or other independent contractor agreement to obtain the labor of an alien in this state, the employer knowingly contracts with an unauthorized alien or with a person who employs or contracts with an unauthorized alien to perform the labor, the employer violates this subsection.

B. The attorney general shall prescribe a complaint form for a person to allege a violation of subsection A of this section. The complainant shall not be required to list the complainant's social security number on the complaint form or to have the complaint form notarized. On receipt of a complaint on a prescribed complaint form that an employer allegedly knowingly employs an unauthorized alien, the attorney general or county attorney shall investigate whether the employer has violated subsection A of this section. If a complaint is received but is not submitted on a prescribed complaint form, the attorney general or county attorney may investigate whether the employer has violated subsection A of this section. This subsection shall not be construed to prohibit the filing of anonymous complaints that are not submitted on a prescribed complaint form. The attorney general or county attorney shall not investigate complaints that are based solely on race, color or national origin. A complaint that is submitted to a county attorney shall be submitted to the county attorney in the county in which the alleged unauthorized alien is or was employed by the employer. The county sheriff or any other local law enforcement agency may assist in investigating a complaint. When investigating a complaint, the attorney general or county attorney shall verify the work authorization of the alleged unauthorized alien with the federal government pursuant to 8 United States Code section 1373(c). A state, county or local official shall not attempt to independently make a final determination on whether an alien is authorized to work in the United States. An alien's immigration status or work authorization status shall be verified with the federal government pursuant to 8 United States Code section 1373(c). A person who knowingly files a false

and frivolous complaint under this subsection is guilty of a class 3 misdemeanor.

C. If, after an investigation, the attorney general or county attorney determines that the complaint is not false and frivolous:

1. The attorney general or county attorney shall notify the United States immigration and customs enforcement of the unauthorized alien.

2. The attorney general or county attorney shall notify the local law enforcement agency of the unauthorized alien.

3. The attorney general shall notify the appropriate county attorney to bring an action pursuant to subsection D of this section if the complaint was originally filed with the attorney general.

D. An action for a violation of subsection A of this section shall be brought against the employer by the county attorney in the county where the unauthorized alien employee is or was employed by the employer. The county attorney shall not bring an action against any employer for any violation of subsection A of this section that occurs before January 1, 2008. A second violation of this section shall be based only on an unauthorized alien who is or was employed by the employer after an action has been brought for a violation of subsection A of this section or section 23-212.01, subsection A.

E. For any action in superior court under this section, the court shall expedite the action, including assigning the hearing at the earliest practicable date.

F. On a finding of a violation of subsection A of this section:

1. For a first violation, as described in paragraph 3 of this subsection, the court:

(a) Shall order the employer to terminate the employment of all unauthorized aliens.

(b) Shall order the employer to be subject to a three year probationary period for the business location where the unauthorized alien performed work. During the probationary period the employer shall file quarterly reports in the form provided in section 23 722.01 with the county attorney of each new employee who is hired by the employer at the business location where the unauthorized alien performed work.

(c) Shall order the employer to file a signed sworn affidavit with the county attorney within three business days after the order is issued. The affidavit shall state that the employer has terminated the employment of all unauthorized aliens in this state and that the employer will not intentionally or knowingly employ an unauthorized alien in this state. The court shall order the appropriate agencies to suspend all licenses subject to this subdivision that are held by the employer if the employer fails to file a signed sworn affidavit with the county attorney within three business days after the order is issued. All licenses that are suspended under this subdivision shall remain suspended until the employer files a signed sworn affidavit with the county attorney. Notwithstanding any other law, on filing of the affidavit the suspended licenses shall be reinstated immediately by the appropriate agencies. For the purposes of this subdivision, the licenses that are subject to suspension under this subdivision are all licenses that are held by the employer specific to the business location where the unauthorized alien performed work. If the employer does not hold a license specific to the business location where the unauthorized alien performed work, but a license is necessary to operate the employer's business in general, the licenses that are subject to suspension under this subdivision are all licenses that are held by the employer at the employer's primary place of business. On receipt of the court's order and notwithstanding any other law, the appropriate agencies shall suspend the licenses according to the court's order. The court shall send a copy of the court's order to the attorney general and the attorney general shall maintain the copy pursuant to subsection G of this section.

(d) May order the appropriate agencies to suspend all licenses described in subdivision (c) of this paragraph that are held by the employer for not to exceed ten business days. The court shall base its decision to suspend under this subdivision on any evidence or information submitted to it during the action for a violation of this subsection and shall consider the following factors, if relevant:

(i) The number of unauthorized aliens employed by the employer.

(ii) Any prior misconduct by the employer.

(iii) The degree of harm resulting from the violation.

(iv) Whether the employer made good faith efforts to comply with any applicable requirements.

(v) The duration of the violation.

(vi) The role of the directors, officers or principals of the employer in the violation.

(vii) Any other factors the court deems appropriate.

2. For a second violation, as described in paragraph 3 of this subsection, the court shall order the appropriate agencies to permanently revoke all licenses that are held by the employer specific to the business location where the unauthorized alien performed work. If the employer does not hold a license specific to the business location where the unauthorized alien performed work, but a license is necessary to operate the employer's business in general, the court shall order the appropriate agencies to permanently revoke all licenses that are held by the employer at the employer's primary place of business. On receipt of the order and notwithstanding any other law, the appropriate agencies shall immediately revoke the licenses.

3. The violation shall be considered:

(a) A first violation by an employer at a business location if the violation did not occur during a probationary period ordered by the court under this subsection or section 23-212.01, subsection F for that employer's business location.

(b) A second violation by an employer at a business location if the violation occurred during a probationary period ordered by the court under this subsection or section 23-212.01, subsection F for that employer's business location.

G. The attorney general shall maintain copies of court orders that are received pursuant to subsection F of this section and shall maintain a database of the employers and business locations that have a first violation of subsection A of this section and make the court orders available on the attorney general's website.

H. On determining whether an employee is an unauthorized alien, the court shall consider only the federal government's determination pursuant to 8 United States Code section 1373(c). The federal government's determination creates a rebuttable presumption of the employee's lawful status. The court may take judicial notice of the federal government's determination and may request the federal government to provide automated or testimonial verification pursuant to 8 United States Code section 1373(c).

I. For the purposes of this section, proof of verifying the employment authorization of an employee through the e-verify program creates a rebuttable presumption that an employer did not knowingly employ an unauthorized alien.

J. For the purposes of this section, an employer that establishes that it has complied in good faith with the requirements of 8 United States Code section 1324a(b) establishes an affirmative defense that the employer did not knowingly employ an unauthorized alien. An employer is considered to have complied with the requirements of 8 United States Code section 1324a(b), notwithstanding an isolated, sporadic or accidental technical or procedural failure to meet the requirements, if there is a good faith attempt to comply with the requirements.

K. It is an affirmative defense to a violation of subsection A of this section that the employer was entrapped. To claim entrapment, the employer must admit by the employer's testimony or other evidence the substantial elements of the violation. An employer who asserts an entrapment defense has the burden of proving the following by clear and convincing evidence:

1. The idea of committing the violation started with law enforcement officers or their agents rather than with the employer.

2. The law enforcement officers or their agents urged and induced the employer to commit the violation.

3. The employer was not predisposed to commit the violation before the law enforcement officers or their agents urged and induced the employer to commit the violation.

L. An employer does not establish entrapment if the employer was predisposed to violate subsection A of this section and the law enforcement officers or their agents merely provided the employer with an opportunity to commit the violation. It is not entrapment for law enforcement officers or their agents merely to use a ruse or to conceal their identity. The conduct of law enforcement officers and their agents may be considered in determining if an employer has proven entrapment.

Sec. 7. Section 23-212.01, Arizona Revised Statutes, is amended to read:

23-212.01. Intentionally employing unauthorized aliens; prohibition; false and frivolous complaints; violation; classification; license suspension and revocation; affirmative defense

A. An employer shall not intentionally employ an unauthorized alien. If, in the case when an employer uses a contract, subcontract or other independent contractor agreement to obtain the labor of an alien in this state, the employer intentionally contracts with an unauthorized alien or with a person who employs or contracts with an unauthorized alien to perform the labor, the employer violates this subsection.

B. The attorney general shall prescribe a complaint form for a person to allege a violation of subsection A of this section. The complainant shall not be required to list the complainant's social security number on the complaint form or to have the complaint form notarized. On receipt of a complaint on a prescribed complaint form that an employer allegedly intentionally employs an unauthorized alien, the attorney general or county attorney shall investigate whether the employer has violated subsection A of this section. If a complaint is received but is not submitted on a prescribed complaint form, the attorney general or county attorney may investigate whether the employer has violated subsection A of this section. This subsection shall not be construed to prohibit the filing of anonymous complaints that are not submitted on a prescribed complaint form. The attorney general or county attorney shall not investigate complaints that are based solely on race, color or national origin. A complaint that is submitted to a county attorney shall be submitted to the county attorney in the county in which the alleged unauthorized alien is or was employed by the employer. The county sheriff or any other local law enforcement agency may assist in investigating a complaint. When investigating a complaint, the attorney general or county attorney shall verify the work authorization of the alleged unauthorized alien with the federal government pursuant to 8 United States Code section 1373(c). A state, county or local official shall not attempt to independently make a final determination on whether an alien is authorized to work in the United States. An alien's immigration status or work authorization status shall be verified with the federal government pursuant to 8 United States Code section 1373(c). A person who knowingly files a false and frivolous complaint under this subsection is guilty of a class 3 misdemeanor.

C. If, after an investigation, the attorney general or county attorney determines that the complaint is not false and frivolous:

1. The attorney general or county attorney shall notify the United States immigration and customs enforcement of the unauthorized alien.

2. The attorney general or county attorney shall notify the local law enforcement agency of the unauthorized alien.

3. The attorney general shall notify the appropriate county attorney to bring an action pursuant to subsection D of this section if the complaint was originally filed with the attorney general.

D. An action for a violation of subsection A of this section shall be brought against the employer by the county attorney in the county where the unauthorized alien employee is or was employed by the employer. The county attorney shall not bring an action against any employer for any violation of subsection A of this section that occurs before January 1, 2008. A second violation of this section shall be based only on an unauthorized alien who is or was employed by the employer after an action has been brought for a violation of subsection A of this section or section 23 212, subsection A.

E. For any action in superior court under this section, the court shall expedite the action, including assigning the hearing at the earliest practicable date.

F. On a finding of a violation of subsection A of this section:

1. For a first violation, as described in paragraph 3 of this subsection, the court shall:

(a) Order the employer to terminate the employment of all unauthorized aliens.

(b) Order the employer to be subject to a five-year probationary period for the business location where the unauthorized alien performed work. During the probationary period the employer shall file quarterly reports in the form provided in section 23-722.01 with the county attorney of each new employee who is hired by the employer at the business location where the unauthorized alien performed work.

(c) Order the appropriate agencies to suspend all licenses described in subdivision (d) of this paragraph that are held by the employer for a minimum of ten days. The court shall base its decision on the length of the suspension under this subdivision on any evidence or information submitted to it during the action for a violation of this subsection and shall consider the following factors, if relevant:

(i) The number of unauthorized aliens employed by the employer.

(ii) Any prior misconduct by the employer.

(iii) The degree of harm resulting from the violation.

(iv) Whether the employer made good faith efforts to comply with any applicable requirements.

(v) The duration of the violation.

(vi) The role of the directors, officers or principals of the employer in the violation.

(vii) Any other factors the court deems appropriate.

(d) Order the employer to file a signed sworn affidavit with the county attorney. The affidavit shall state that the employer has terminated the employment of all unauthorized aliens in this state and that the employer will not intentionally or knowingly employ an unauthorized alien in this state. The court shall order the appropriate agencies to suspend all licenses subject to this subdivision that are held by the employer if the employer fails to file a signed sworn affidavit with the county attorney within three business days after the order is issued. All licenses that are suspended under this subdivision for failing to file a signed sworn affidavit shall remain suspended until the employer files a signed sworn affidavit with the county attorney. For the purposes of this subdivision, the licenses that are subject to suspension under this subdivision are all licenses that are held by the employer specific to the business location where the unauthorized alien performed work. If the employer does not hold a license specific to the business location where the unauthorized alien performed work, but a license is necessary to operate the employer's business in general, the licenses that are subject to suspension under this subdivision are all licenses that are held by the employer at the employer's primary place of business. On receipt of the court's order and notwithstanding any other law, the appropriate agencies shall suspend the licenses according to the court's order. The court shall send a copy of the court's order to the attorney general and the attorney general shall maintain the copy pursuant to subsection G of this section.

2. For a second violation, as described in paragraph 3 of this subsection, the court shall order the appropriate

agencies to permanently revoke all licenses that are held by the employer specific to the business location where the unauthorized alien performed work. If the employer does not hold a license specific to the business location where the unauthorized alien performed work, but a license is necessary to operate the employer's business in general, the court shall order the appropriate agencies to permanently revoke all licenses that are held by the employer at the employer's primary place of business. On receipt of the order and notwithstanding any other law, the appropriate agencies shall immediately revoke the licenses.

3. The violation shall be considered:

(a) A first violation by an employer at a business location if the violation did not occur during a probationary period ordered by the court under this subsection or section 23-212, subsection F for that employer's business location.

(b) A second violation by an employer at a business location if the violation occurred during a probationary period ordered by the court under this subsection or section 23-212, subsection F for that employer's business location.

G. The attorney general shall maintain copies of court orders that are received pursuant to subsection F of this section and shall maintain a database of the employers and business locations that have a first violation of subsection A of this section and make the court orders available on the attorney general's website.

H. On determining whether an employee is an unauthorized alien, the court shall consider only the federal government's determination pursuant to 8 United States Code section 1373(c). The federal government's determination creates a rebuttable presumption of the employee's lawful status. The court may take judicial notice of the federal government's determination and may request the federal government to provide automated or testimonial verification pursuant to 8 United States Code section 1373(c).

I. For the purposes of this section, proof of verifying the employment authorization of an employee through the e-verify program creates a rebuttable presumption that an employer did not intentionally employ an unauthorized alien.

J. For the purposes of this section, an employer that establishes that it has complied in good faith with the requirements of 8 United States Code section 1324a(b) establishes an affirmative defense that the employer did not intentionally employ an unauthorized alien. An employer is considered to have complied with the requirements of 8 United States Code section 1324a(b), notwithstanding an isolated, sporadic or accidental technical or procedural failure to meet the requirements, if there is a good faith attempt to comply with the requirements.

K. It is an affirmative defense to a violation of subsection A of this section that the employer was entrapped. To claim entrapment, the employer must admit by the employer's testimony or other evidence the substantial elements of the violation. An employer who asserts an entrapment defense has the burden of proving the following by clear and convincing evidence:

1. The idea of committing the violation started with law enforcement officers or their agents rather than with the employer.

2. The law enforcement officers or their agents urged and induced the employer to commit the violation.

3. The employer was not predisposed to commit the violation before the law enforcement officers or their agents urged and induced the employer to commit the violation.

L. An employer does not establish entrapment if the employer was predisposed to violate subsection A of this section and the law enforcement officers or their agents merely provided the employer with an opportunity to commit the violation. It is not entrapment for law enforcement officers or their agents merely to use a ruse or to conceal their identity. The conduct of law enforcement officers and their agents may be considered in determining if an employer has proven entrapment.

Sec. 8. Section 23-214, Arizona Revised Statutes, is amended to read:

23-214. Verification of employment eligibility; e-verify program; economic development incentives; list of registered employers

A. After December 31, 2007, every employer, after hiring an employee, shall verify the employment eligibility of the employee through the e-verify program and shall keep a record of the verification for the duration of the employee's employment or at least three years, whichever is longer.

B. In addition to any other requirement for an employer to receive an economic development incentive from a government entity, the employer shall register with and participate in the e-verify program. Before receiving the economic development incentive, the employer shall provide proof to the government entity that the employer is registered with and is participating in the e-verify program. If the government entity determines that the employer is not complying with this subsection, the government entity shall notify the employer by certified mail of the government entity's determination of noncompliance and the employer's right to appeal the determination. On a final determination of noncompliance, the employer shall repay all monies received as an economic development incentive to the government entity within thirty days of the final determination. For the purposes of this subsection:

1. "Economic development incentive" means any grant, loan or performance-based incentive from any government entity that is awarded after September 30, 2008. Economic development incentive does not include any tax provision under title 42 or 43.

2. "Government entity" means this state and any political subdivision of this state that receives and uses tax revenues.

C. Every three months the attorney general shall request from the United States Department of Homeland Security a list of employers from this state that are registered with the e-verify program. On receipt of the list of employers, the attorney general shall make the list available on the attorney general's website.

Sec. 9. Section 28-3511, Arizona Revised Statutes, is amended to read:

28-3511. Removal and immobilization or impoundment of vehicle

A. A peace officer shall cause the removal and either immobilization or impoundment of a vehicle if the peace officer determines that a person is driving the vehicle while any of the following applies:

1. The person's driving privilege is suspended or revoked for any reason.

2. The person has not ever been issued a valid driver license or permit by this state and the person does not produce evidence of ever having a valid driver license or permit issued by another jurisdiction. This paragraph does not apply to the operation of an implement of husbandry.

3. The person is subject to an ignition interlock device requirement pursuant to chapter 4 of this title and the person is operating a vehicle without a functioning certified ignition interlock device. This paragraph does not apply to a person operating an employer's vehicle or the operation of a vehicle due to a substantial emergency as defined in section 28 1464.

4. The person is in violation of a criminal offense and is transporting, moving, concealing, harboring or shielding or attempting to transport, move, conceal, harbor or shield an alien in this state in a vehicle if the person knows or recklessly disregards the fact that the alien has come to, has entered or remains in the United States in violation of law.

B. A peace officer shall cause the removal and impoundment of a vehicle if the peace officer determines that a person is driving the vehicle and if all of the following apply:

1. The person's driving privilege is canceled, suspended or revoked for any reason or the person has not ever been issued a driver license or permit by this state and the person does not produce evidence of ever having a driver license or permit issued by another jurisdiction.

2. The person is not in compliance with the financial responsibility requirements of chapter 9, article 4 of this title.

3. The person is driving a vehicle that is involved in an accident that results in either property damage or injury to or death of another person.

C. Except as provided in subsection D of this section, while a peace officer has control of the vehicle the peace officer shall cause the removal and either immobilization or impoundment of the vehicle if the peace officer has probable cause to arrest the driver of the vehicle for a violation of section 4-244, paragraph 34 or section 28-1382 or 28-1383.

D. A peace officer shall not cause the removal and either the immobilization or impoundment of a vehicle pursuant to subsection C of this section if all of the following apply:

1. The peace officer determines that the vehicle is currently registered and that the driver or the vehicle is in compliance with the financial responsibility requirements of chapter 9, article 4 of this title.

2. The spouse of the driver is with the driver at the time of the arrest.

3. The peace officer has reasonable grounds to believe that the spouse of the driver:

(a) Has a valid driver license.

(b) Is not impaired by intoxicating liquor, any drug, a vapor releasing substance containing a toxic substance or any combination of liquor, drugs or vapor releasing substances.

(c) Does not have any spirituous liquor in the spouse's body if the spouse is under twenty one years of age.

4. The spouse notifies the peace officer that the spouse will drive the vehicle from the place of arrest to the driver's home or other place of safety.

5. The spouse drives the vehicle as prescribed by paragraph 4 of this subsection.

E. Except as otherwise provided in this article, a vehicle that is removed and either immobilized or impounded pursuant to subsection A, B or C of this section shall be immobilized or impounded for thirty days. An insurance company does not have a duty to pay any benefits for charges or fees for immobilization or impoundment.

F. The owner of a vehicle that is removed and either immobilized or impounded pursuant to subsection A, B or C of this section, the spouse of the owner and each person identified on the department's record with an interest in the vehicle shall be provided with an opportunity for an immobilization or post storage hearing pursuant to section 28-3514.

Sec. 10. Title 41, chapter 12, article 2, Arizona Revised Statutes, is amended by adding section 41-1724, to read:

41-1724. Gang and immigration intelligence team enforcement mission fund

The gang and immigration intelligence team enforcement mission fund is established consisting of monies deposited pursuant to section 11-1051 and monies appropriated by the legislature. The department shall administer the fund. Monies in the fund are subject to legislative appropriation and shall be used for gang and immigration enforcement and for county jail reimbursement costs relating to illegal immigration.

Sec. 11. Severability, implementation and construction

A. If a provision of this act or its application to any person or circumstance is held invalid, the invalidity does not affect other provisions or applications of the act that can be given effect without the invalid provision or application, and to this end the provisions of this act are severable.

B. The terms of this act regarding immigration shall be construed to have the meanings given to them under federal immigration law.

C. This act shall be implemented in a manner consistent with federal laws regulating immigration, protecting the civil rights of all persons and respecting the privileges and immunities of United States citizens.

Sec. 12. Short title

This act may be cited as the "Support Our Law Enforcement and Safe Neighborhoods Act".

> **Source:** Arizona Senate Bill 1070. Ariz. Rev. Stat. Ann. § 11-1051 (2010).
>
> **See also:** 287g Delegation of Immigration Authority; Anchor Baby; Anti-Immigrant Sentiment; Immigration Acts; Immigration and Customs Enforcement; National Origins Act of 1924; Operation Wetback; Proposition 187; Unauthorized Immigration; United States Border Patrol

Jan Brewer's Statement on the Federal Lawsuit Challenging Arizona SB 1070 (2010)

Introduction

On July 6, 2010, the U.S. Department of Justice filed a lawsuit against the state of Arizona seeking to halt the enactment of Arizona's controversial new immigration law. That same day, Arizona's governor, Jan Brewer, issued a statement defending her state's right to enforce its own immigration policies. The Arizona legislature, Brewer claims, is not attempting to replace federal authority, but responding to security threats that the federal government has failed to address. Defending Arizona law enforcement officers, Brewer argues that SB 1070 neither encourages racial profiling nor violates the U.S. Constitution. Brewer delivered her statement from Phoenix, Arizona.

Primary Source

Today I was notified that the federal government has filed a lawsuit against the State of Arizona. It is wrong that our own federal government is suing the people of Arizona or helping to enforce federal immigration law. As a direct result of failed and inconsistent federal enforcement, Arizona is under attack from violent Mexican drug and immigrant smuggling cartels. Now, Arizona is under attack in federal court from President Obama and his Department of Justice. Today's filing is nothing more than a massive waste of taxpayer funds. These funds could be better used against the violent Mexican cartels than the people of Arizona.

The truth is the Arizona law is both reasonable and constitutional. It mirrors substantially what has been federal law in the United States for many decades. Arizona's law is designed to complement, not supplant, enforcement of federal immigration laws. Despite the Department of Justice's claims in paragraph 62 of today's lawsuit, Arizona is not trying "to establish its own immigration policy" or "directly regulate the immigration status of aliens." Arizona Revised Statutes §11–1051(E) states that the federal government, along with local law enforcement officers authorized by the federal government, can only determine an alien's immigration status. Subsection (L) of that same section goes on to state that the law "shall be implemented in a manner consistent with federal laws regulating immigration."

The irony is that President Obama's Administration has chosen to sue Arizona for helping to enforce federal immigration law and not sue local governments that have adopted a patchwork of "sanctuary" policies that directly violate federal law. These patchwork local "sanctuary" policies instruct the police not to cooperate with federal immigration officials.

The best thing government can do is to create a stable, predictable environment, governed by an easily understood set of rules or laws. We do not need to make this more complicated than it already is. We must first and foremost create a secure border. Enhanced trade, economic opportunity and freedom will surely follow.

I am pleased that President Obama and the Department of Justice did not pursue the baseless claims of illegal racial profiling in the lawsuit. When signing S.B. 1070, I said, "My signature today represents my steadfast support for enforcing the law—both against illegal immigration AND against racial profiling." Arizona's law expressly prohibits unconstitutional racial profiling. However, words are not enough. For this reason, I ordered the Arizona Peace Officer Standards and Training Board (AZPOST) to develop training on the new law for Arizona's police officers. AZPOST has completed the training course and has published it for the all world to see at www.azpost.state.az.us/SB1070infocenter.htm. AZPOST has done its job professionally and served Arizona well.

I will not stop fighting to protect the citizens of Arizona, and to defend Arizonans in federal court. I have set up a legal defense fund to pay the substantial legal fees that Arizona has been, and will be, forced to incur as a result of all of these lawsuits. Contributions to the Border Security and Immigration Defense Fund can be made at www.keepazsafe.com. My legal team will not hesitate to assert the rights of the State of Arizona in this matter. Arizona will ultimately prevail against the lawsuits—including this latest assault by the Obama Administration. Our laws will be found to be constitutional—because that is exactly what they are.

Governor Jan Brewer, State of Arizona

Source: Statement by Governor Jan Brewer, July 6, 2010. Office of the Governor, State of Arizona. Available at: http://azgovernor.gov.

See also: 287g Delegation of Immigration Authority; Anchor Baby; Anti-Immigrant Sentiment; Arizona Senate Bill 1070 (2010); Immigration Acts; Immigration and Customs Enforcement; National Origins Act of 1924; Operation Wetback; Unauthorized Immigration; United States Border Patrol

About the Editors

Charles A. Gallagher is professor and chair of the Sociology and Criminal Justice Department at La Salle University in Philadelphia, Pennsylvania. His research focuses on social inequality, race relations, and immigration, and he has published over 50 articles, reviews, and books on these topics. His scholarship examines the ways in which the media, state policy, and popular culture construct, shape, and disseminate ideas of race and social mobility. His most recent books include *Being Brown in Dixie: Race, Ethnicity and Latino Immigration in the New South* (with Cameron Lippard, 2011) and *Retheorizing Race and Whiteness in the 21st Century* (with France Winddance Twine, 2012). As a nationally recognized expert on race and social inequality, Professor Gallagher has given over 50 talks on these topics around the country and is a frequent media source, appearing in the press, television, and radio interviews over 80 times. He is currently doing comparative research on whites' attitudes on immigration policy in the United Kingdom and the United States.

Cameron D. Lippard is an assistant professor of sociology at Appalachian State University in Boone, North Carolina. His research focuses on social inequality, race relations, and immigration, and he has published a number of research articles and books focusing on Latino immigrant integration into the American South. His most recent books include *Being Brown in Dixie: Race, Ethnicity and Latino Immigration in the New South* (with Charles Gallagher, 2011) and a research monograph titled *Building Inequality: Race, Ethnicity, and Immigration in the Atlanta Construction Industry*. As a nationally recognized expert on immigration, Professor Lippard has given several talks on the social issues Latino immigrants face while living in new immigrant destinations throughout the United States. His recent focus is on the problems Mexican migrant farm workers face while living in Southern Appalachia.

—

Contributors

R. Randall Adams — LaGrange College

Carol Adams-Means — University of Texas, San Antonio

Daisuke Akiba — Queens College and Graduate Center of CUNY

Leslie M. Alexander — Ohio State University

Nicholas Alexiou — Queens College of CUNY

Renee S. Alston — Georgia State University

Alma Alvarez-Smith — Arizona State University

Rasha Aly — University of Cincinnati

Alex Ambrozic — Memorial University of Newfoundland

Catherine Anyaso — Independent Scholar

Mikaila Mariel Lemonik Arthur — New York University

Stephen E. Atkins — Texas A&M University

Anny Bakalian — Middle East and Middle Eastern American Studies Center

Sandra L. Barnes — Purdue University

Regina Barnett — Indiana University

Jeffrey D. Bass — Quinnipiac University

Mark Bauerlein — Emory University

Michael Beauchamp — Texas A&M University

Stephanie Beard — University of Illinois, Chicago

Virginia R. Beard — Longwood University

James M. Beeby — Indiana University

Valerie Begley — Independent Scholar

Nicholas N. Behm — Elmhurst College

Brian D. Behnken — Iowa State University

Shannon Smith Bennett — Indiana University

Ira Lee Berlet — University of Houston

Ellesia Ann Blaque — Wayne State University

Mehdi Bozorgmehr — Middle East and Middle Eastern American Studies Center

Jazmine Brand — Occidental College

Alfred L. Brophy — University of Alabama

Nikki Brown — University of New Orleans

Thomas Brown — Northeast Lakeview College

Joan C. Browning — Independent Scholar

Reginald Bruster — Independent Scholar

J. Michael Butler — South Georgia College

Dara N. Byrne — John Jay College of Criminal Justice

Cordelia Chávez Candelaria — Arizona State University

Gregory E. Carr — Howard University

Linda M. Carter — Morgan State University

Frank Cha — College of William and Mary

Barbara Chasin — Montclair State University

Dong-Ho Cho — Queens College of CUNY

Tracy Chu	Graduate Center of CUNY	Carmenza Gallo	Queens College of CUNY
Jonathan S. Coit	Eastern Illinois University	Richard A. Garcia	California State University
Ann V. Collins	Washington University	Sheena Kaori Gardner	Mississippi State University
Meghan Conley	University of Tennessee	Gary Gershman	Nova Southeastern University
Aaron Cooley	University of North Carolina, Chapel Hill	Laura Gimeno-Pahissa	Universitat Autònoma de Barcelona
Simon T. Cuthbert-Kerr	University of Scotland, Glasgow	Carol Goodman	Memorial University of Newfoundland
Robin Dasher-Alston	Independent Scholar		
Amanda Davis	University of Florida	Alan Vincent Grigsby	University of Cincinnati
Jane Davis	Iowa State University, Ames	Santiago R. Guerrero-Strachan	University of Valladolid
Olethia Davis	University of Alabama		
Jacob C. Day	Appalachian State University	Kenneth J. Guest	Baruch College of CUNY
Sharlene Sinegal DeCuir	Louisiana State University	Margo Gutierrez	University of Texas
Gerardo Del Guercio	Independent Scholar	John G. Hall	Independent Scholar
Rutledge M. Dennis	George Mason University	John J. Han	Missouri Baptist University
Alan D. DeSantis	University of Kentucky	Skylar Harris	State University of New York
James I. Deutsch	Smithsonian Center for Folklife and Cultural Heritage	Daniel M. Harrison	Lander University
		Sonja V. Harry	Winston-Salem State University
Carol E. Dietrich	DeVry University	James Haskins	University of Florida
Danielle Dirks	Occidental College	Nia Woods Haydel	Georgia State University
Wayne Dowdy	Memphis Public Library and Information Center	Christina S. Haynes	Ohio State University
		Danielle C. Heard	Cornell University
Carla J. DuBose	City University of New York	Max Herman	Rutgers University
Garrett A. Duncan	Washington University	Emily Hess	Case Western Reserve University
Walter R. Echo-Hawk	Independent Scholar		
Shawntel Ensminger	Florida State University	Josiah Heyman	University of Texas, El Paso
Dena J. Epstein	University of Chicago	Samuel Hoff	Delaware State University
Luigi Esposito	Barry University	Arthur Holst	Temple University
Kwame Essien	University of Texas at Austin	Marilyn K. Howard	Columbus State Community College
Amy Essington	Claremont Graduate University	Patrick Huber	Missouri University of Science and Technology
John Eterno	Molley College		
Alex Feerst	Macalester College	Matthew W. Hughey	Mississippi State University
Andrew H. Fisher	College of William and Mary	Tarry Hum	Queens College
Marianne Fisher-Giorlando	Grambling State University	James Ivy	Trinity University, San Antonio
Donald Fixico	Arizona State University		
T. A. Forman	Emory University	Eric R. Jackson	Northern Kentucky University
Janice E. Fowler	Texas Woman's University		
Monroe Friedman	Eastern Michigan University	M. Kelly James	Winthrop University
Julieanna Frost	Siena Heights University	Charles Jaret	Georgia State University
Annie Isabel Fukushima	University of California, Berkeley	Hasan K. Jeffries	Ohio State University
		Bruce Johansen	University of Nebraska

Jessica A. Johnson — Columbus State Community College

Sherita L. Johnson — University of South Mississippi

Jeannette E. Jones — University of Nebraska, Lincoln

Peter Carr Jones — Independent Scholar

Regina V. Jones — Indiana University Northwest

On Kyung Joo — Davison Avenue School

Khyati Joshi — Fairleigh Dickenson University

Gregory Kaliss — University of North Carolina, Chapel Hill

Nicolás Kanellos — University of Houston

Stephen C. Kenny — University of Liverpool

Kwang Chung Kim — Western Illinois University Macomb

Rose Kim — Graduate Center of CUNY

Shin Kim — Chicago State University

Patti Jo King — University of North Dakota

Deeb Paul Kitchen — Florida Gulf Coast University

Gladys L. Knight — Independent Scholar

Karen Kossie-Chernyshev — Texas Southern University

Jeffrey Kraus — Wagner College

Salvatore Labaro — U.S. Census Bureau

Whitney Laster — Vanderbilt University

R. Joyce Zamora Lausch — New Mexico State University

Danielle Lavin-Loucks — Valparaiso University

Jama Lazerow — Wheelock College

Anthony A. Lee — West Los Angeles College

Heon Cheol Lee — University of North Carolina, Asheville

Rebekah Lee — University of London

Talitha L. LeFlouria — Florida Atlantic University

Angela K. Lewis — University of Alabama

Travis Linnemann — Old Dominion University

James W. Loewen — University of Vermont

James W. Love — University of Tennessee

John A. Lupton — Papers of Abraham Lincoln, Springfield, Illinois

Doreen Maller — Independent Scholar

James Maples — University of Tennessee, Martin

Christina Marín — Arizona State University, Tempe

Etsuko Maruoka-Ng — State University of New York

Angie Maxwell — University of Texas, Austin

Louis Mazzari — Bogazici University, Turkey

Denise D. McAdory — University of South Alabama

Jimmy D. McCamey — Fort Valley State University

Barbara McCaskill — University of Georgia

Nancy McCaslin — Independent Scholar

Matt Meier — Santa Clara University

Abraham O. Mendoza — Independent Scholar

Zebulon V. Miletsky — University of Massachusetts, Amherst

Douglas Milford — University of Illinois, Chicago

Mark Edwin Miller — Southern Utah University

Paul T. Miller — Independent Scholar

Adrienne N. Milner — University of Alabama, Birmingham

Dylan A.T. Milner — Independent Scholar

Pyong Gap Min — Queens College and Graduate Center of CUNY

Louis Moore — Grand Valley State University

William A. Morgan — University of Texas

Sheila Bluhm Morley — Calvin College

Ken Muir — Appalachian State University

Komanduri Murty — Fort Valley State University

Emmanuel S. Nelson — State University of New York

Denese M. Neu — Independent Scholar

James Newman — Idaho State University

Romney S. Norwood — Georgia State University

Betty Nyangoni — Trinity University

Sookhee Oh — New School University

James S. Olson — Sam Houston State University

Bobette Otto — Georgia State University

Kathrin A. Parks — Loras College

Suzanne B. Pasztor — Humboldt State University

Barbara A. Patrick — Mississippi State University

Clarissa Peterson — DePauw University

Mika'il A. Petin — George Mason University

Michelle Petrie — University of South Carolina, Aiken

Joyce Pettis	North Carolina State University	Claudia M. Stolz	Urbana University
Francois Pierre-Louis	Queens College	Kaila Adia Story	University of Louisville
Fred L. Pincus	University of Maryland, Baltimore County	Kevin Strait	George Washington University
Brian Piper	College of William and Mary	Hephzibah Strmic-Pawl	College of Charleston
Victoria Pitts	Queens College	Kazuko Suzuki	Texas A&M
Barry M. Pritzker	University of Nebraska	Steve Talbot	Independent Scholar
Michelle A. Purdy	Emory University	Gregory S. Taylor	Chowan College
Sanjeev A. Rao, Jr.	Monmouth University	Jack A. Taylor III	Bowling Green State University
Deirdre Ray	University of Pennsylvania		
Alyssa Ribeiro	University of Pittsburgh	Leanne Taylor	Brock University
Julie Richter	College of William and Mary	Gabriel H. Teninbaum	Suffolk University Law School
Natalie J. Ring	University of Texas, Dallas	Matthew D. Thompson	Old Dominion University
David Ritchey	Collin County Community College	Shatema A. Threadcraft	Yale University
		Ivory Toldson	Southern University
Michael Roberts	San Diego State University	Zoe Trodd	Harvard University
Robin Roger-Dillon	Queens College of CUNY	Aimable Twagilimana	Buffalo State College
F. Arturo Rosales	Arizona State University	Tiffany Vélez	Queens College
Karen E. Rosenblum	George Mason University	Leighton Vila	Virginia Tech University
Jacqueline J. Royster	Georgia Institute of Technology	Jan Voogd	Harvard University
		John A. Wagner	Independent Scholar
Walter Rucker	University of North Carolina, Chapel Hill	Jennifer Jensen Wallach	Georgia College and State University
Paulina X. Ruf	University of Tampa	Katherine Kuehler Walters	Texas A&M University
Fumiko Sakashita	Michigan State University	Thomas J. Ward, Jr.	Rockhurst University
Kijua Sanders-McMurtry	Georgia State University	Frances Ward-Johnson	Elon University
Gabriel Santos	Lynchburg College	Tim Watts	Kansas State University
Carol Schmid	Guilford Technical Community College	Barbara J. Webb	Hunter College and the Graduate Center of CUNY
Mark Schultz	Lewis University	Elizabeth M. Webb	University of Kentucky
Conchita Franco Serri	Santa Clara University	Melissa F. Weiner	Quinnipiac University
Benjamin F. Shearer	Neumann College	Regennia N. Williams	Cleveland State University
Dorsía Smith Silva	University of Puerto Rico	Vernon J. Williams, Jr.	Indiana University
Mary J. Sloat	Garber High School	Jamie J. Wilson	Salem State University
John Matthew Smith	Georgia Institute of Technology	S. Harmon Wilson	Independent Scholar
		Andrew G. Wood	University of Tulsa
Bianca Gonzalez Sobrino	Mississippi State University	Gregory Wood	Frostburg State University
Stephanie Southworth	Clemson University	Donald P. Woolley	Duke University
John H. Stanfield	Indiana University	Jeffrey Yamashita	University of California, Berkeley
Mary Stanton	Independent Scholar		
Barry M. Stentiford	Grambling State University	Philip Yang	Texas Woman's University
Leonard A. Steverson	South Georgia College	Jo York	University of Montana
		Emma Zack	Occidental College

Index

Page locators in **boldface** indicate main entries in the Encyclopedia; (doc.) indicates a document.